TEXT-BOOK

OF THE

HISTORY OF DOCTRINES

BY

REINHOLD SEEBERG

TRANSLATED BY

CHARLES E. HAY

COMPLETE IN TWO VOLUMES

VOL. II

HISTORY OF DOCTRINES IN THE MIDDLE AND
EARLY MODERN AGES

BAKER BOOK HOUSE

Grand Rapids, Michigan

1952

CONTENTS.

BOOK II.

THE PRESERVATION, TRANSFORMATION, AND FURTHER DEVELOPMENT OF DOCTRINE IN THE MIDDLE AGES.

PART I.

HISTORY OF DOCTRINES FROM THE SEVENTH TO THE TENTH CENTURY.

CHAPTER I.

INTRODUCTION. THEOLOGY OF GREGORY THE GREAT.

PAGE

§ 35. *Characteristics of this Period*.............................. 15
§ 36. *Theology of Gregory the Great*........................... 17
   1. Theology, Christology, Councils, Scripture.................. 17
   2. Work of Christ...... 19
   3. Doctrine of Sin and Grace............................... 21
      a. Original Sin... 21
      b. Grace 22
      c. Predestination 23
      d. Repentance 24
      e. Mass, Purgatory 24
   4. The Church.. 25
   5. Relation to Augustine................................... 26

CHAPTER II.

DOCTRINAL CONFLICTS OF THE EARLIER MIDDLE AGES.

§ 37. *Adoptionist Controversy*.............................. 27
   1. Migetius, Elipandus, Felix 27
   2. Alcuin, Decision of the Controversy...................... 28
§ 38. *Eastern Church and Worship of Images. Filioque Controversy*.. 29
§ 39. *Controversy Upon Augustinian Doctrine of Predestination*...... 30
   1. Gottschalk.. 31
   2. Opponents of Gottschalk................................ 31
   3. Leaders of Both Parties................................. 32
   4. Councils at Chiersy, Valence, Toucy...................... 33
§ 40. *Divergent Views Upon Parturition of the Virgin*.............. 33
§ 41. *Controversies Upon the Lord's Supper*...................... 34
   1. Popular Views 34

PAGE

2. Paschasius Radbertus.. 35
3. Critical Estimate... 37
4. Rabanus.. 37
5. Ratramnus... 38
6. Result 39

CHAPTER III.

HIERARCHICAL PRINCIPLE.   HISTORY OF ORDINANCE OF REPENTANCE.

§ 42. *Papacy and Hierarchy*................................... 40
    1. Situation... 40
    2. Problems 40
    3. Donation of Constantine 40
    4. Pseudo-Isidore... 41
§ 43. *Repentance in Earlier Middle Ages*...................... 41
    1. Limitation of Public Repentance 42
    2. Private Repentance....................................... 42
    3. Penitential Praxis and Theory............................ 43
    4. Historical Situation...................................... 46

PART II.

HISTORY OF DOCTRINES IN SCHOLASTIC AGE.

CHAPTER I.

FOUNDATIONS OF HIERARCHICAL AND RELIGIOUS IDEALS AND OF SCHOLASTIC THEOLOGY.

§ 44. *The Church and the World*............................... 49
    1. Cluny 49
    2. Humbert, Gregory VII..................................... 50
    3. Canon Law and the Church 51
§ 45. *Christianity of St. Bernard*............................ 52
§ 46. *History of Theology from Anselm to Peter the Lombard*... 52
    1. Methods of Treatment 54
    2. Beginnings, Lanfranc, Anselm, Abelard, Roscellin........... 55
    3. Abelard's Theological and Philosophical Position, His Followers. 57
    4. Opposition to Abelard, Honorius Augustodunensis, Hugo of St. Victor, Robert Pullus 60
    5. Peter the Lombard, Heads of Doctrine..................... 62
§ 47. *Christology of Abelard and the Lombard. Opposition of Gerhoh.* 64
    1. Christology of Abelard................................... 64
    2. The Lombard, Nihilianism 65
    3. Christology of Gerhoh.................................... 66
§ 48. *Doctrine of Atonement. Anselm and Abelard*............. 60
    1. Anselm's Theory of Satisfaction, Critical Estimate.......... 66

PAGE

2. Abelard's Criticism, His Theory of Atonement 70
3. Bernard *vs.* Abelard.. 72
4. Atonement in the School of Abelard, in Honorius, Hugo, Robert. 73
5. Atonement in the Lombard.............................. 73
§ 49. *Berenger of Tours and Doctrine of Lord's Supper*............ 74
1. Berenger 74
2. Opposition to Berenger 76
3. Development of the Doctrine, Transubstantiation 77
4. Honorius, Hugo, Robert, the Lombard..................... 77
5. Dogmatic Establishment of Transubstantiation............... 78
§ 50. *Definition of Sacraments. Seven Sacraments*................. 79
1. Origin of the Number Seven............................. 79
2. Definition... 80
3. Baptism 80
4. Confirmation 81
5. Lord's Supper... 81
6. Repentance 81
   a. Abelard 81
   b. Hugo 82
   c. Robert Pullus 83
   d. The Lombard 83
7. Extreme Unction.. 84
8. Ordination 84
9. Marriage 85
§ 51. *Conception of the Church*................................. 85
1. Hugo, Robert, John of Salisbury.......................... 85
2. Church, Hierarchy, Relation to State...................... 85

CHAPTER II.

DEVELOPMENT OF CHRISTIAN DOCTRINE DURING SECOND PERIOD OF SCHOLASTICISM.

§ 52. *Aims of the Church. Religious Life. Efforts at Reform*....... 87
1. Innocent III., Boniface VIII............................. 87
2. Francis of Assisi and His Influence 88
3. Popular Practical Christianity 90
4. Preaching, Penitential Praxis 91
5. Heretical Movements, Cathari, Waldenses, Begards 94
§ 53. *History and Characteristics of Theology in the Thirteenth Century.* 96
1. Scholasticism and the Secularization of the Church 96
2. Development of Scholasticism in Thirteenth Century 97
   Alexander of Hales...................................... 98
   Albert the Great.. 99
   Thomas of Aquino, Divisions of the "Summa".............. 99
   Bonaventura 100

                                                                  PAGE
3. Leading Scholastic Ideas 100
    a. Revelation, Scriptures, Symbols, Pope 100
    b. Faith.. 103
    c. Reason *vs.* Faith................................... 104
    d. Universals 104
4. Two Aspects of Scholasticism, Roger Bacon, Lullus, Henry of
    Ghent, Richard of Middleton 105
§ 54. *Doctrine of God and Christology*........................... 106
    1. Advance of Thomas in the Doctrine of God................. 106
    2. The Trinity, Richard of St. Victor, The Lombard, Joachim of
       Floris, Fourth Lateran Council......................... 108
    3. Christology, ... 109
§ 55. *The Work of Christ*....................................... 110
    1. Alexander, Bonaventura 110
    2. Thomas 113
§ 56. *Doctrines of Original State and Sin*....................... 114
    1. Original Righteousness, *Synteresis, Donum superadditum*...... 114
    2. Original Sin 116
§ 57. *Doctrine of Grace and Human Freedom* 118
    1. Man Cannot Deliver Himself 118
    2. *Gratia, creata* and *increata*......................... 118
    3. Grace and Free-will..................................... 119
    4. Justification, Infusion, Forgiveness of Sins, Assurance........ 120
    5. Faith and Works, *Meritum de condigno* and *de congruo*....... 121
    6. Evangelical Councils and Christian Perfection 124
§ 58. *Sacraments and the Church. Dogma of Seven Sacraments*...... 124
    1. Dogmatization by Eugene IV............................. 124
       a. Nature and Number of Sacraments 125
       b. Definition of Sacraments 125
       c. Relation of Sign and Grace........................... 126
       d. Effect, "Character".................................. 127
       e. Ex opere operato..................................... 128
    2. Baptism 129
    3. Confirmation 130
    4. Lord's Supper, Transubstantiation, Concomitance, Accidents,
       Bodily Presence and Local Limitation, Effect, Sacrifice of the
       Mass, Definition of Eugene IV.......................... 131
    5. Repentance 135
       a. Contrition and Attrition, Confession and Absolution,
         Thomas and Duns, Biel............................. 135
       b. Satisfaction... 138
       c. Indulgences... 139
    6. Extreme Unction 140
    7. Ordination 141
    8. Marriage 142

PAGE

9. The Church, In Thomas, Current Definition, *Communio sancto-
    rum*, The Pope 144
10. The Kingdom of God on Earth........................... 146

CHAPTER III.

GRADUAL DISSOLUTION OF SCHOLASTIC THEOLOGY. RELIGIOUS AND
ECCLESIASTICAL CRISIS AT CLOSE OF MIDDLE AGES.

§ 59. *Theology of Duns Scotus and its Significance for the History of
       Doctrines*.. 147
   1. Philosophical Position of Duns............................ 147
   2. Revelation, Symbols, Romish Church, Faith 149
   3. Conception of God, Predestination......................... 150
   4. Sin, Original Sin.. 153
   5. Christology.. 154
   6. Mariology... 155
   7. Redemption, Criticism of Anselm's View.................... 156
   8. Definition of Grace, Habitus, Merit, Justification.......... 158
   9. Sacraments.. 161
  10. Significance of Duns in History of Doctrines................. 162
§ 60. *Criticism of Hierarchical Conception of the Church* 165
   1. Situation of the Curia, Reform Councils, Leo X.............. 165
   2. Marsilius and Occam, Separation of Church and State, Tasks of
      Pope and Clergy, Fallibility of Pope and Infallibility of Scrip-
      tures, Rights of the Laity................................. 167
   3. Theory of Natural Right.................................... 170
§ 61. *Church Life and Religious Agitations at the Close of the Middle
       Ages*... 172
   1. Crisis, Superstition, Expectations......................... 173
   2. Influence of the Church Upon the Masses, Penitential Praxis,
      Attrition, Indulgences, Jubilee Indulgences................. 174
   3. German Mysticism 178
   4. Christian Socialism, Wickliffe............................. 181
§ 62. *Review of History of Theology in the Fourteenth and Fifteenth
       Centuries. Nominalism and Augustinianism* 185
   1. Duns and the Nominalists.................................. 185
      a. Nominalists... 185
      b. Thomists 186
      c. Paduan School... 187
      d. Augustinian Eremites.................................. 187
      e. Return to Augustine, Gerson, Forerunners of the Reformation 188
   2. Nominalist Theory of Knowledge 190
   3. a. Criticism and Skepticism 191
      b. Submission to Doctrine of Scriptures and Church, Theory of
         Inspiration 192

PAGE

4. Faith, *Fides implicita* 195

5. Collapse of the Scholastic System........................... 196

§ 63. *Labors of Later Middle Ages Upon Separate Dogmas and Doctrines* 197

   1. Sin, Human Freedom 197

   2. Atonement, Redemption 198

      a. Aureolus, Baconthorp, Durand, Capreolus.............. 198

      b. Biel.. 198

      c. Practical View of Atonement 200

   3. Sacrament of Repentance, Attrition, Justification, *Meritum de congruo* and *de condigno,* Assurance 201

   4. Lord's Supper... 203

      a. Occam, Durand, D'Ailli, Substance of the Bread......... 203

      b. Bodily Presence, Ubiquity in Occam, Faber Stapulensis 204

      c. Wickliffe's Criticism of Transubstantiation 206

   5. Augustinian Tendency.................................... 207

      a. Bradwardina 207

      b. Wickliffe's Doctrine of Predestination................... 208

      c. Goch, Wesel and Wessel upon Grace.................. 208

   6. Criticism of Sacrament of Repentance and Indulgences by Wickliffe, Wesel and Wessel................................. 209

   7. Conception of the Church in Wickliffe, Wesel and Wessel...... 211

§ 64. *The Renaissance and Humanism in their Significance for the History of Doctrines* 212

   1. Literary Agitation.. 213

   2. Lorenzo Valla, Religious Attitude of Erasmus................ 213

   3. Lack of Reformatory Elements in Erasmus, Colet, Review and Prospect 215

BOOK III.

FURTHER DEVELOPMENT OF DOCTRINE THROUGH THE REFORMATION AND FIXATION OF THE DOCTRINES OF CATHOLICISM.

PART I.

GENESIS OF PROTESTANT DOCTRINE.

CHAPTER I.

THE VIEWS OF LUTHER.

§ 65. *Luther's Place in the History of Doctrines*.................... 221

   1. Luther's Personality....................................... 221

   2. Influence of Sacramental Repentance and of Augustine Upon Luther... 222

PAGE

3. Early and Later Views of Luther Compared.................. 223
4. Luther and Scholasticism................................... 223
5. Evangelical Repentance as Central Point in Luther's Reformatory
    Views... 224
6. Reformatory Work of Luther.............................. 225
§ 66. *Luther's Views Before the Reformation Period*................ 227
  1. External and Internal Word, Law and Gospel 228
  2. Original Sin... 229
  3. Christology and Redemption............................. 229
  4. Grace, Faith 231
  5. Sacrament of Repentance................................ 234
  6. The Church... 234
  7. Old Forms with New Content............................. 235
§ 67. *Criticism of Sacrament of Repentance. Evangelical Repentance.*
    Faith, Sin, Grace, Justification, Atonement................. 235
  1. Theology of the Ninety-five Theses....................... 235
  2.   *a.* Contrition a Fruit of Faith and Love, The Law.......... 237
      b. Confession and Absolution............................ 240
      c. Satisfaction, Advance Upon Previous Theories........... 241
  3.   *a.* Sin and Original Sin................................. 242
      b. Enslaved Will and Predestination...................... 243
      c. Wrath of God, The Devil............................. 245
  4.   *a.* The Law as Natural Right, The Sabbath................ 246
      b. The Gospel 248
      c. The Law 249
      d. The Law and Penitence, Agricola...................... 249
      e. Law and Gospel...................................... 251
  5. Faith... 252
      a. Its Origin, God Revealed in Christ as Loving-Will........ 252
      b. Its Nature—Acceptance, Trust, Faith and Redemptive
          Realities... 254
      c. Faith and Regeneration............................... 256
      d. Feeling, Experience, Assurance........................ 256
  6. Good Works. From Faith, through Christ, in Liberty....... 258
  7. Justification Secured by Faith, Actual and Imputed Righteous-
    ness, Harmony of Luther's Earlier and Later Teachings...... 260
  8. Grace and Gifts... 263
  9. Work of Christ... 265
      a. Satisfaction, Payment, Kingdom of God... 265
      b. Sacrifice, Satisfaction Rendered to the Wrath of God and the
          Law, Release from Dominion of Devil................. 266
      c. Intercession.. 269
      d. Christ the Second Adam, Example, Following of Christ.... 269
      e. Content and Critical Estimate of Luther's Doctrine of the
          Atonement, Relation to Duns......................... 271

PAGE

10. General Summary.. 272

§ 68. *Evangelical Ideal of Life*................................. 273

   1. Significance of Luther's Ideal of the Christian Life............ 273

   2. Christian Perfection 273

   3. Secular Callings.. 274

   4. Content of the Christian Life, The Kingdom of God.......... 275

   5. Luther and Social Problems................................ 278

§ 69. *Word and Sacrament*.................................... 279

   1. The Spirit and the Means of Grace......................... 279

   2. The Word and the Spirit *vs.* the Inner Word of the Fanatics.... 279

   3. Conception of the Sacraments.............................. 282

   4. Baptism, Infant Baptism................................... 283

   5. Luther's Earliest View of the Lord's Supper, Honius and Carlstadt 285

   6. Luther *vs.* Sacrifice of the Mass........................... 289

§ 70. *Reformatory Conception of the Church*...................... 289

   1. Significance of the Leipzig Disputation..................... 289

   2. New Conception of the Church 291

   3. Fundamental Features of the New Conception................ 292

      a. The Communion of Saints, Invisibility of the Church....... 292

      b. The Church and the Means of Grace.................... 293

      c. The Church as Seen................................. 293

      d. The Ecclesiastical Office............................. 293

      e. Nature of the Church................................ 294

      f. Marks of the True Church............................ 294

§ 71. *Luther's Attitude Toward the Traditional Standards of Doctrine, i. e., the Scriptures and the Dogmas of the Church*........... 296

   1. Attitude of Luther Toward the Traditional Standards......... 296

   2. *a.* Sole Authority of the Scriptures........................ 298

      b. Difference as Compared with View of the Later Middle Ages, Christ the Content of Scripture, Biblical Criticism........ 299

      c. Luther's Treatment of the Scriptures.................... 301

   3. Attitude of Luther Toward the Dogma of the Ancient Church.. 302

   4. Attitude of Luther Toward the Trinitarian Dogma............ 304

CHAPTER II.

DOCTRINE OF ZWINGLI. OPPOSITION OF LUTHER AND ZWINGLI UPON THE DOCTRINE OF THE LORD'S SUPPER.

§ 72. *Reformatory Principles of Zwingli*......................... 306

   1. Zwingli's Dependence Upon Luther........................ 307

   2. Authority of the Scriptures................................ 308

   3. Doctrine of Sin.. 309

   4. Work of Christ, Its Objective and Subjective Aspects.......... 309

   5. Faith.. 310

6. The Law of Christ.. 311
7. The Ideal of Life.. 312
8. Predestination, Conception of God...................... 312
9. The Church... 315
10. The Sacraments, Baptism, Infant Baptism................. 316
11. Medieval Limitations of Zwingli......................... 317
§ 73. *Controversy Upon the Lord's Supper*..................... 318
1. Origin of Zwingli's Doctrine, Tactics of the Conflict........... 318
2. Doctrine of Zwingli...................................... 320
3. Luther and the Words of Institution...................... 322
4. Christology of Luther as Related to His Doctrine of the Lord's
   Supper.. 323
5. The Right Hand of God, Mode of Bodily Presence, Relation to
   Occam.. 325
6. Reception and Blessing of the Sacrament.................. 327
7. Marburg Colloquy, Schwabach Articles.................... 330
8. Wittenberg Concord, Bucer, Schwabian Compromise.......... 331

CHAPTER III.
THE NEW DOGMA.

§ 74. *The Augsburg Confession*............................... 332
1. Relations Between the Civil Authorities and Theologians in the
   Establishment of Protestant Doctrine...................... 332
2. Aim of the Augsburg Confession.......................... 334
3. The Trinity, Sin, The Confutators....................... 335
4. Faith, Justification, Doctrine of Justification in the Apology..... 336
5. Good Works, Ideal of Life............................... 339
6. The Church, Ministerial Office.......................... 340
7. The Sacraments, Baptism, The Lord's Supper, Repentance 341
8. Practical Demands....................................... 343
§ 75. *The Earlier Reformed Confessions*....................... 344
Justification, Faith, The Church, The Sacraments.............. 344

PART II.

THE FURTHER DEVELOPMENT AND (PROVISIONAL) COMPLETION OF
PROTESTANT DOCTRINE.

CHAPTER I.

LUTHERAN DOCTRINE TO THE ADOPTION OF THE FORMULA OF CONCORD.

§ 76. *Theology of Melanchthon. Its Significance for the History of
   Doctrines*... 347

PAGE

1. Melanchthon and Calvin.................................... 347
2. First Edition of the *Loci*................................. 348
3. Deviation from Luther in the Theory of Conversion 349
4. Deviation from Luther Upon the Lord's Supper, Article X. in the Variata.. 350
5. Later Revisions of the *Loci*, Attitude Toward the Scriptures, the Ecclesiastical Dogmas, and the Authority of Luther.......... 351
6. Theology and Philosophy.................................... 353
7. The Church, Visible and as Object of Faith, "Pure Doctrine".. 354
8. Justification, The Law and Contrition, The Gospel and the Atonement, Forensic Theory, Faith and Regeneration, Self-consistency of Melanchthon's Theology...................... 358

§ 77. *Theological Controversies in the Lutheran Church from the Death of Luther to the Adoption of the Formula of Concord.*........ 362
1. Significance of Melanchthon for the History of Doctrines....... 363
2. The Interim, Adiaphoristic Controversy...................... 364
3. Majoristic Controversy, Menius, Amsdorf, Flacius............. 364
4. The Antinomistic Controversy, Amsdorf, Poach, Otto.......... 365
5. Controversy Upon the Lord's Supper, Brenz, Crypto-Calvinists, Consecration of Elements............................ 366
6. Synergistic Controversy, Pfeffinger, Strigel, Flacius........... 367
7. The Osiandrian Controversy 369
    a. Osiander's System.................................... 369
    b. His Opponents 373
    c. Stancar.. 374
8. Christological Conflicts.................................... 374
    a. Brenz.. 374
    b. Chemnitz 374
9. Predestinarian Controversy, Aepin Upon Descent into Hell..... 378

§ 78. *The Formula of Concord.*.................................. 378
1. Political Reasons for Harmony, Frankfort Recess, Weimar Confutation, Naumburg Diet, *Corpora Doctrinae* 378
2. Genesis of the Formula of Concord......................... 380
3. Original Sin and Free Will................................. 383
4. Doctrine of Justification................................... 384
    a. Obedience of Christ................................. 384
    b. Imputed Righteousness.............................. 384
    c. Faith and Justification.............................. 384
5. Good Works 385
6. Law and Gospel... 385
7. The Lord's Supper.. 386
8. Christology.. 387
9. Descent into Hell... 388
10. Adiaphora 388
11. Predestination 388

PAGE

12. Factions and Sects 389
13. Critical Estimate of the Formula. 389

CHAPTER II.

COMPLETION OF DOCTRINAL CONSTRUCTION IN THE REFORMED CHURCH.

§ 79. *Theology of Calvin. Its Influence Upon the History of Doctrines.* 390
   1. Theological Type of Bucer, Theology of Bucer, Luther, Bucer,
      and Melanchthon, Bucer and Calvin...................... 390
   2. Calvin as Theologian and Churchman...................... 394
   3. Calvin's Doctrine of the Scriptures and Inspiration........... 395
   4. Conception of God....................................... 396
   5. Sin 398
   6. Atonement and Redemption............................... 399
   7.   *a.* Faith... 401
       b. Repentance 402
       c. Justification...................................... 403
       d. Human Freedom................................... 405
       e. Election 405
   8. The Church and its Organization 408
       a. The Totality of the Predestinated...................... 408
       b. The Visible Church 408
       c. Outward Organization............................... 409
       d. Relation to the State................................ 410
   9. The Sacraments... 411
       a. Definition of a Sacrament........................... 411
       b. Baptism... 412
       c. The Lord's Supper................................. 412
  10. The Significance of Calvin for the History of Doctrines, Medie-
      val Element in His View................................ 414
§ 80. *Triumph of Calvin's Doctrine of the Lord's Supper*............ 417
   1. Bullinger's Revival of Zwingli's Theory..................... 417
   2. The Consensus Tigurinus................................ 417
   3. Reformed Confessions................................... 417
§ 81. *Fundamental Evangelical Principles in Later Reformed Con-*
    fessions.... 418
   1. Reformed Confessions in Harmony with Calvin.............. 418
   2. Atonement, Faith, Repentance............................ 418
   3. The Church, The Glory of God............................ 419
§ 82. *Triumph of the Doctrine of Predestination*.................... 420
   1. Pighius, Consensus Genevensis........................... 420
   2. The Symbols... 421
   3. Remonstrants and Contra-remonstrants, Decrees of Dort....... 421
   4. Place of Predestination in Doctrinal System................. 423
   5. Amyraldus, The Formula Consensus Helvetica 424

PART III.

COMPLETION OF DOCTRINAL CONSTRUCTION IN THE ROMAN CATHOLIC CHURCH.

PAGE

§ 83. *Establishment of Medieval Theology by the Council of Trent*..... 427

  1. Reformation and Counter-reformation...................... 427

  2. Jesuitism.. 429

  3. The Council of Trent..................................... 431

  4. The Scriptures and Tradition.............................. 431

  5. Original Sin, Sin of Adam, Propagation, Relation to Baptism, Concupiscence, Exemption of the Virgin Mary.............. 432

  6. Justification, How Attained, Preserved, Lost, Synergism, Imputation or Infusion, Inherent Righteousness, Prevenient Grace, *Dispositio*, Good Works, Repentance 433

  7. The Sacraments... 438

  8. Baptism 439

  9. Confirmation 439

  10. The Lord's Supper....................................... 439

    a. The Dogma... 439

    b. Withholding of the Cup............................. 440

    c. Sacrifice of the Mass................................ 441

  11. Sacrament of Repentance, Indulgences, Purgatory 442

  12. Extreme Unction.. 445

  13. Ordination... 445

  14. Marriage... 446

  15. Curialism *vs.* Episcopalism, Conception of the Church in the Catechismus Romanus...................................... 446

  16. Significance of the Tridentine Confession for the History of Doctrines 448

§ 84. *Revival of the Augustinian Doctrine of Grace and its Ecclesiastical Rejection*....................................... 449

  1. Decadence of the Augustinian Doctrine of Grace.............. 449

  2. Bajus, The Bull, *Ex omnibus afflictionibus*................. 450

  3. Molina... 451

  4. Jansen, The Bull, *Cum occasione*.......................... 452

  5. Quesnel, The Constitution, *Unigenitus* 454

  6. Immaculate Conception................................... 456

§ 85. *Completion of the Romish Dogma of the Church. The Vatican Council* 456

  1. Episcopalistic Movements, *Declaration du clerge de France*..... 457

  2. Febronius, The Punctation of Ems......................... 457

  3. Synod of Pistoja.. 458

  4. Increased Respect for the Papacy in the Age of the Restoration.. 459

  5. The Vatican Council, *Schema de fide*, Inspiration............. 460

  6. Infallibility of the Pope.................................. 460

  7. Present Significance of Dogma in the Roman Catholic Church... 462

CONCLUSION. Significance of Dogma in Protestantism.............. 464

BOOK II.

THE PRESERVATION, TRANSFORMATION, AND FUR-
THER DEVELOPMENT OF DOCTRINE IN THE
MIDDLE AGES.

PART I.

HISTORY OF DOCTRINES FROM THE SEVENTH TO THE TENTH CENTURY.

CHAPTER I.

INTRODUCTION.   THEOLOGY OF GREGORY THE GREAT.

§ 35. *Characteristics of this Period.*

1. Viewed historically, this period is characterized chiefly by the disintegration of the ancient world. New nations and new governments appear upon the scene. Yet the life of antiquity is perpetuated among the barbarians by the church. Theology becomes the bearer, not of doctrine alone, but of philosophy and culture as well. For this task it was well fitted by the intimate connection of the fixed doctrines of the church with the ancient modes of thought, and by the universal spirit of Augustine. Wisdom belonged to the past. "The first precept of safety is to guard the rule of right faith and to deviate in nowise from the ordinances of the fathers" (Vol. I., p. 387)—such is the motto of the doctrinal history of the period. The only man who indulged in independent speculations, the philosopher Scotus Erigena, was misunderstood by his age. With Augustine, he recognized two sources of knowledge, sound reason (*recta ratio*) and proper authority (*vera auctoritas*). He endeavored from a combination of the two to construct a speculative system. But the speculative-pantheistic tendency prevailed, and the Scriptures were subordinated by means of allegorical exegesis. His speculations had no influence worthy of mention upon the History of Doctrines (cf. CHRISTLIEB, Leben und Lehre des Joh. Scotus Erigena, 1860).

2. The German nations received Christianity from the church in fixed forms and as a fixed formula. For them Christianity became simply dogma, and faith the acceptance of tradition.[1]

---

[1] The only "dogmas," in the full sense of the term, in the Middle Ages as for the preceding period, were those of the Trinity and the two natures of Christ. Cf. *sub.* under Gregory the Great and also, *e. g.*, Agobard, de fid. verit. 3 (Mi. 104, 269), and the Poenitentiale of Theodore of Canterbury (i. v. 6, p. 189, in WASSERSCHLEBEN, Penances): "from a heretic who should not

This, no less than the course of political events, served to confirm the hierarchical idea and the papal power. Rome planted
herself firmly in the new provinces of the Western church (cf.
the Christianizing of the Anglo-Saxons, her relations with the
Franks, Boniface), and, despite many rebuffs, secured power and
maintained it.

3. Upon German territory Christianity was, it is true, conceived and publicly presented in a popular form (vid. the poetry
of Cynewolf, Caedmon, the Heliand, the Crist of Otfrid. Cf.
SEEBERG, Die German. Auffassung d. Christentums in d. frueh-
eren Mittelalter, Ztschr. f. k. Wiss., 1888, p. 91 ff., 148 ff.
HAUCK, KG. Deutschlands, ii. 706 ff.). The spirit of the theologians of the period was influenced by this (vid., *e. g.*, Hauck
ii. 268, 589 ff.); but theology not so much as one should suppose. The development of the practical life of the church produced, indeed, new forms which became influential in shaping
doctrinal conceptions (the church, repentance, the Lord's Supper) and which the church could not ignore in her teaching;
but even here the old formulas were still the sacred material
which lay at the basis of all theological labors.

4. The Greek church knew no Middle Age, for it never got
beyond the range of the ancient problems of Origen, *i. e.*, the
Greek church had no Augustine. The dominant theological authority in the Middle Ages is Augustine. The entire doctrinal
history of the period may be treated as the history of Augustinianism. His ideas controlled the leaders of the church and the
unfolding of all ecclesiastical conceptions and institutions. The
worst features in this development may be traced back to him, as
well as the best. The piety of the age found in his teachings an
unfailing source of inspiration. They were not the Light, but
they testified of the Light. But while Augustine's formulas thus
control the theology of the period, the theologians do not master the
formulas. They accomplished nothing more than the collection and
arrangement of the Sentences of Augustine (ISIDORE of Seville,
† 636 : Sententiarum sive de summo bono, ll. 3. ALCUIN, † 804 :
De fide sanctae trinitatis, ll. 3. RABANUS MAURUS, † 856 : De
clericorum institutione, ll. 3. PASCHASIUS RADBERTUS, † 865 : De
fide, spe et caritate, ll. 3. Cf. Thomasius-Seeberg, DG. II.
13 f.). But even this presentation did not faithfully reproduce
true Augustinianism. It was an Augustinianism misinterpreted
in a Semipelagian spirit and degraded to a popular level. Next
to Augustine, the determining authority is Gregory the Great.

rightly believe the Trinity." To these dogmas the later Middle Ages added
only obedience to the church, the doctrine of the sacraments, and, particularly,
repentance and the doctrine of the Lord's Supper.

The former was understood as interpreted by the latter. The History of Doctrines in the Middle Ages must, therefore, begin with an outline of the theology of Gregory.

5. It follows from the above that we cannot expect to find any real development of dogma in this period. The question in the disputes of the age concerns always the proper understanding or misunderstanding of the traditional formulas, not an actual development of them. Significant as is the period for the History of the Church, it furnishes very little material for the History of Doctrines. As in treating of the history of doctrines throughout the entire Middle Ages, so especially during this period the historian must constantly bear in mind the task immediately before him. He is not to embrace the whole field of theology, but only to portray the movements which prepare the way for and make possible the true doctrinal development of the Reformation period (Council of Trent and Protestant Confessions).[1] The great awakening of piety at the close of this period is to be studied in other connections.

§ 36. *Theology of Gregory the Great.*

The writings of Gregory († A. D. 604) which particularly concern us are the following :

Expositio in l. Iob sive Moralium, ll. 35 ; Homiliae in Ezech., ll. 2 ; Homiliae in evangelia, ll. 2 ; Dialogi, ll. 4 ; Regula pastoralis, ll. 3 ; Collection of letters in 14 volumes. Of the latter, the Liber sacramentorum and the Expositio in l. I regum are critically open to suspicion. *Editions.* The Maurine (Sainthe Marthe), Paris, 1705, in Migne Lat. 75-79. Die Briefe s. Greg. registr. epp. edd. Ewald et Hartmann (Mon. Germ. hist. epist. t. 1, 2). Cf. LAU, Greg. I. d. Gr., 1845. WOLFSGRUBER, Greg. d. Gr., 1890. CLAUSIER, St. Grégoire, Paris, 1886-91. Upon the doctrine of grace, vid. also WIGGERS, Schicksale d. aug. Anthropol., etc., in Ztschr. f. hist. Theol., 1854, p. 7 ff.

1. In theology Gregory is an Augustinian in his formulas, and something of the spirit of the great African is also traceable in his writings. But the ruder elements of the popular theology, which in Augustine are kept in the background, here come again into marked prominence. To this is added a crude superstition and mythological speculations touching angels, demons, etc., as found especially in the " Dialogues." Gregory is consciously orthodox. The Christian faith is for him *fides trinitatis* (mor. xxxiii., c. 10. n. 20 ; in Ezech. l. ii. hom. 4. 11), but includes also the incarnation (ep. l. vii. 15 ; ev. ii. h. 33. 6). The terminology, " trinity of persons " and " one substance " (*substan-*

---

[1] The History of Doctrines in the Middle Ages bears the same relation to that of the Reformation period as does the Ante-nicene to the Post-nicene. Cf. Vol. I., p. 23.

tia), occurs very frequently in his writings (Ez. ii. 4. 7 ; ev. i. 18.
3 ; 19. 7 fin.; mor. xxx. 4. 17).[1] His Christology is just as orthodox : Christ, the *deus homo* (Ez. ii. 1. 4), or the *homo deus*
(mor. xxii. 17. 42), is true God and man : "of one (*unius*) with
the Father and of the same nature" (mor. iii. 14. 26). But the
divine and the human nature, united *inconfuse ac inseparabiliter*,
constitute one person, *unus in utraque natura* (Ez. i. 8. 24 f.).
" For we say that he exists, *of* (*ex*) two natures and *in* (in) two
natures, but we avoid as impious the statement tnat he is to be
considered as composed (*compositum*) of two persons" (ev. ii.
38. 3 ; mor. xviii. 52. 85 ; vid. also mor. i. 18, 26 ; xxiii. 19.
35 ; xxiv. 2. 2 ; xxix. 1. 1 f.; xxxiii. 16. 32 ; ev. ii. 22. 8, etc.).[2]
The Holy Ghost is said to be : "of one substance (*substantia*),
with the Father and the Son" (ev. ii. 30. 3).[3] Gregory knows
himself to be upon these points in harmony with the doctrine of
the church councils. He is orthodox, he holds, who accepts
what *sanctae quatuor universales synodi* accepted, and rejects
what they rejected (ep. vi. 66 ; opp. ii., p. 843). "I confess
that I receive and venerate four councils, just as I receive and
venerate four books of the holy gospel" (ep. i. 25, p. 515;
also iii. 10; v. 51, 54; iv. 38).[4] Thus the authority of the
church is recognized as on a par with that of the Holy Scriptures.
Gregory, indeed, sustained by the strictest theory of inspiration,[5]
sees in the Holy Scriptures the "foundation of divine authority"
(*divinae auctoritatis fundamentum*, mor. xviii. 26. 39). God
through them answers the "open or secret questionings of all
men" (mor. xxiii. 19. 34). They must lie at the foundation of

[1] The divine activity is described, *e. g.*, in Dial. iv. 6: creantem et regen-
tem, implentem et circumplectentem, transcendentem et sustinentem. Mor.
xvi. 37. 45 ; vid. Ez. ii. 5. 10; mor. x. 6. 6.

[2] The birth from a virgin was necessary in order to avoid original sin. Vid.
mor. xi. 52. 70; xviii. 52. 84; xxiv. 1. 3.

[3] Upon the procession of the Spirit, vid. mor. xxx. 4. 17 : "how the
spirit of both proceeds co-eternal from both ;" mor. xxix. 31. 74 : "whose
(*i. e.*, the Son's) spirit is the same spirit who proceeds from the Father." The
symbol attributed to Gregory (opp. ii. 1283): "proceeding from the Father
and the Son." Vid. further in LAU, p. 459 f.

[4] Gregory recognizes also the fifth council, *e.g.*, ep. i. 25, p. 515; ix. 52, p.
966. Cf. Vol. I., p. 276. The authority of the four councils was legally established by Justinian. See Novella 131 : "Therefore we decree that the holy
ecclesiastical rules which have been announced or confirmed by the four holy
councils shall prevail instead of laws. For we accept the doctrines of the
aforesaid councils just as the Holy Scriptures, and the rules just as laws."

[5] Mor. praef. 1. 1, 2 : "Let it be faithfully believed that the Holy Spirit
is the author of the book. He, therefore, wrote these things who dictated the
things to be written." "The writers of sacred eloquence, because, filled
with the Holy Spirit, they are drawn above themselves, become as it were
(something) beyond themselves." The Scriptures are "words of the Holy
Spirit" (Ez. ii. 10. 3).

all preaching ; by their study priests are to be prepared for their
vocation ; the reading of them is most urgently commended to
all.[1] But the force of all this was broken by the introduction of
allegorical exegesis as of fundamental authority (mor. i. 24, 33 ;
xvi. 19. 24).   Thenceforth it became customary to laud the
Holy Scriptures, but also to present as scriptural teaching the
" ecclesiastical " doctrines.

2. In treating of the Work of Christ, Gregory employs the
traditional mode of thought and expression (cf. Vol. I., p.
361 n.).   Christ is the *Redeemer* and *Mediator* of fallen humanity.   " The Lord appeared in the flesh in order that he might
arouse human life by admonishing, stimulate it by furnishing
models (*exempla*), redeem it by dying, and restore it (*repararet*)
by arising from the dead " (mor. xxi. 6. 11).

(*a*) This involves the general conception that Christ surrendered Himself to sufferings and death for us and thereby delivered us from them (Ez. ii. 4. 20 ; i. 9 ; mor. xiii. 43. 48).   To
speak more precisely, this occurs in the following way : God is
angry with the sinner.   Hence there is need of a Mediator, who
as a " mediator of God and man " must *be* God and man—
" through flesh become *redemptor*, . . . *mediator dei et hominis*.[2]
Because he appeared as the only righteous person among men,
and, nevertheless, though without sin (*culpa*), faced the punishment of sin, both persuading man no more to sin and hinder-
ing God from smiting, he furnished an example of innocence
and received the punishment of evil-doing.   By suffering, therefore, he who took away the sin of man by inspiring righteousness and tempered the wrath of the judge by dying, persuaded
both and gave a hand to each, because he afforded man an
example which might be followed and displayed to God deeds
wrought upon himself by which he might be reconciled toward
men " (mor. ix. 38. 61).   The appearing of Christ in our behalf thus appeases the divine wrath.   Upon this conception of
the intercession of Christ Gregory laid great emphasis.   Christ,

[1] Gregory often and energetically advised the reading of the Scriptures, *e. g.*,
mor. vi. 10. 12 ; xvi. 19, 24. Ez. i. 10. 1 ff.; ii. 3. 20 ; ep. ii. 52 ; iv. 31, p.
712 : "The Lord of heaven has for (the good of) thy life transmitted to thee
his epistles." Cf. Vol. I., p. 298 n. Ep. viii. 17 : " But I have inquired
who of you belong to the *collegium* of sacred reading," points to conventicles
for the reading of the Scriptures. The Old and New Testaments differ essentially as presenting the lower (*minora*) and higher (*altiora*) precepts, inasmuch
as the New Testament law addresses itself to the inner disposition. Ez. ii. 4,
5, 9 ; i. 10 ; mor. xviii. 4. 7.
[2] Instead of this exposition of the incarnation we find another : " Because
there was no one among men who could appear before God as a righteous
intercessor, I have made myself a man in order to make propitiation for men."
Mor. xxiv. 3. 6.

as the Righteous One, makes his merit[1] available before the Father. "For to the Only-begotten Son, to plead for man is to demonstrate before the eternal Father that he is himself a man ; and to him, to have asked in behalf of human nature is to have taken upon himself that same nature in the altitude of his divinity" (mor. xxii. 17. 42). The effect of the merit of Christ is, therefore, that God abandons his wrath against sinners.[2]

(b) Another result of Christ's sufferings and death is our deliverance from the power of the devil. Man was in a state of guilt. The devil had a certain claim upon him ("held man, as it were, lawfully "). " This guilt must, therefore, be canceled ; but this cannot be done except through a sacrifice " (sacrificium). But beasts were not sufficient for such a sacrifice ; a man was required, and that a sinless man. Since there was none such, the Son of God became man in order to offer the sacrifice. Since the devil made a mistake in seizing the Innocent One, " he lawfully lost him whom he had, as it were, lawfully held " (mor. xvii. 30. 46 f.). The divinity veiled in humanity was thus the bait which God held out to the devil (mor. xxxiii. 7. 14 ff.).

(c) Of the Mediator it is said: "Who, although he could have striven in our behalf even without dying, nevertheless wished to aid men by dying, since he would certainly have loved us less if he had not taken upon himself our wounds, nor could he have shown us the power of his love if he had not himself borne for a time that which he took from us " (mor. xx. 36. 69). This shows plainly where the emphasis falls in Gregory's theory of the atonement. That Christ was a teacher and an example appears to him the principal feature of his work. He reveals to us the invisible God, instructs us in regard to our sinful state, and teaches us the will of God and his commandments (Ez. ii. 1. 15 f.; ev. ii. 32. 1 ; mor. vii. 2. 2 ; x. 6. 7 ; xvi. 30. 37 ; xxi. 6. 11 ; xxii. 17. 42 ; xxix. 1. 1). To the instruction thus given is

---

[1] Although the expression, "merit of Christ" (meritum), is not found, the conception appears very plainly : " For, interceding for sinners, he shows himself the just man who merited indulgence (indulgentiam mereretur) for others." Mor. xxiv. 2. 4, and ib. 3. 5. " But, because there was no one by whose merits (meritis) the Lord would have been bound to be reconciled with us, the Only-begotten . . . appeared as the only righteous (One), in order that he might intercede for sinners." Cf. ib. xvii. 30. 46. The term, "merit," thereby receives a new application. From ancient times the merita of men had been spoken of, but the term is now transferred to the work of Christ. The Reformation shattered the whole conception as applied to man, but allowed it to stand with reference to the work of Christ.

[2] It may be well here to note that Gregory speaks of the intercession of the saints and martyrs, as well as that of the church with its sacrifices (ep. ix. 52, p. 971 ; mor. xvi. 51. 64 ; xxxv. 8. 13); and also of an intervention (intervenire) of the Holy Ghost (ev. ii. 30. 3).

added the incitement by example. "For the incarnate Lord has displayed in himself everything which he has inspired in us, in order that he might commend by example what he had uttered in precept (mor. i. 13. 17). The life and active work of Christ, as well as his death, are regarded from this point of view (e. g., dial. i. 9; ev. i. 18. 4; 16. 3; ii. 22. 7 f.; 32. 3; 21. 7; mor. xxi. 6. 11; xxviii. 18. 42). The purpose is: "That by present-ing a form for imitation, he might change the life of previous evil-doing" (mor. xxiv. 2. 2).[1] Gregory's theory of redemp-tion follows thus the Western type (Vol. I., pp. 193, 260, 361), since it understands Christ as essentially the historical power of goodness in the world, the teacher and exemplar. The idea of outwitting the devil also appears, it is true, in a terribly realistic form (cf. Vol. I., pp. 295, 361 n.). But it is a fateful phenom-enon that Gregory seeks to combine the objective and subjective aspects of redemption: "Inasmuch as Christ dwelt among us, he both presented before the Father the new humanity and actually renewed humanity by his stimulating influence" (p. 5). All the Middle Age theories of the atonement find their proto-type in Gregory—that of Anselm as well as Abelard's.[2]

3. In his doctrine of Sin and Grace, Gregory reveals himself as an Augustinian, or, at least, a Semi-Augustinian.

(a) The entrance of sin into the world is explained by the weakness of man (mor. iv. 3. 8).[3] The first sin was a free act of the first man (mor. iii. 14. 26). He surrendered his love to God, and hence was compelled to depend upon himself and his own flesh (mor. viii. 10. 19; 6. 8); he became afflicted with spiritual blindness (mor. viii. 30. 49; xi. 43. 59; ix. 33. 50) and spiritual death. "Man the sinner dies in sin, is deprived of righteousness, consumed in punishment" (mor. xii. 6. 9).[4] Through Adam all have become sinners (mor. iv. 27. 53; ep. vii. 14: "We come to this life with merit (cum merito) of our death" (mor. iv. 24. 45). This is effected through the medium of conception. "For conception itself is impurity on account of its

---

[1] Gregory often emphasizes the ideas of example and imitation in treating of the mutual relations among men, e. g., Ez. ii. 3. 20; 10. 18; ev. ii. 31. 4; 38. 15; mor. x. 6. 9. Vid. especially xv. 51. 57, where the sin of children is explained as an imitation of the sin of the parents.

[2] Even the mystic view of Bernard is not foreign to him, e. g., Ez. ii. 1. 16: "Meditating upon his passion with anxious reflection;" mor. xxxi. 52. 104: "Because the hearers are by no means able to understand the secrets of his divinity, they are content to recognize the blood of the crucified Lord."

[3] LAU, p. 376, has sought to find in mor. xii. 15. 19 and ix. 49. 73 the be-ginnings of the donum superadditum; but in this he is in error. Vid. mor. xxiv. 7. 13; viii. 6. 8.

[4] Vid. in mor. xxxi. 45. 87 ff. the seven principal vices: inanis gloria, invidia, ira, tristitia, ventris ingluvies, avaritia, luxuria. Cf. Vol. I., p. 313 n.

carnal delight" (mor. xi. 52. 70 ; xviii. 52. 84). And : "Because
the human race became corrupt (*putruit*) in its first parent as
in its root, it has carried out its barrenness (*ariditatem*) into its
branches" (ep. ix. 52, p. 970 ; cf. mor. xvii. 15. 21). As between Creationism and Traducianism, Gregory, like Augustine
(Vol. I., pp. 344, 377), declines to decide (ep. ix. 52, p. 970).
The consequence of Adam's sin as thus inherited is the damnation of unbaptized children dying in infancy (mor. ix. 21. 32 ;
xv. 51. 57). This has an Augustinian sound,[1] but Gregory cannot make serious practical application of such ideas. For him
sin is still always only weakness and disease. "We are born with
implanted defect of infirmity" (mor. viii. 6. 8). Accordingly,
he describes the human race in its natural state as : "this one
great and sick of very great infirmity—this is the human race
lying languid throughout the whole world" (mor. xviii. 45. 73 ;
cf. xxi. 7. 12). Yet, with all this, freedom (but not goodness)
of the will seems to remain for the natural man (Ez. i. 9. 2) :
"prevenient grace had transformed the free will in him to a good
will." Cf. mor. xxxiii. 21. 39 ; xvi. 25. 30.

(*b*) In the doctrine of grace also we find a similar emaciated
Augustinianism. Gregory emphasizes the fact that without grace
there can be no salvation, no human merits (mor. xxxiii. 21. 38 ;
xviii. 40. 62 ; Ez. i. 10. 45). Only grace as *preveniens* and
subsequens makes us capable of goodness. Grace, therefore,
begins the work : "Celestial piety in advance (*prius*) effects
something in us without our agency (*sine nobis*), so that subsequently it may also effect with us by our free will the good which
we now seek" (mor. xvi. 25. 30). Prevenient grace works in
us the willing of the good ; subsequent grace, that we are able to
do the good (mor. xxii. 9. 20). In the latter, the will now becomes a good will, co-operates. "For the good which we do is
both of God and of ourselves, of God through prevenient grace,
of ourselves through obedient free will" (mor. xxxiii. 31. 40; xxiv.
10. 24 ; xviii. 40. 63). The first thing effected in man by grace
is faith (mor. ii. 46. 71), as an acceptance of the doctrinal
teaching of the church (dial. iv. 1 : "that we should believe
the things which we cannot yet know by experience"). This
beginning is effected through baptism, which works faith and forgives the guilt of antecedent sins, particularly of original sin (Ez.
ii. 10. 7; ev. i. 10. 7; mor. ix. 34. 54; xvi. 51. 57; xviii. 53. 87).
The next step in the process is the imparting of the good will, or
love (*gratia spiritus infusi*, mor. xxx. 6. 22; *munus infusum*, ib.

---

[1] Augustinian, too, is the idea : "Evil is without substance" (Mal. xxvi.
37. 68 ; iii. 9. 15).

1. 5). This is accomplished by the preaching of the word. A sharp discrimination is here observed between the outward, audible, and the inward, divine word (mor. xxix. 24. 49). Through this inward speaking of the word occurs the *inspiratio* or *aspiratio gratiae* (mor. xxx. 1. 4. 5 ; xi. 9. 12 ; xviii. 40. 63) and through it the good will (*bonum velle*), or love, is wrought (mor. xxii. 9. 20 ; Ez. i. 9. 2 ; 7. 16). "For to hear the voice of the Spirit is to mount up by the power of deep inward compunction to love of the invisible Creator" (mor. xxvii. 21. 41). Thus, after faith comes love (Ez. ii. 4. 13). This is thoroughly Augustinian (Vol. I., p. 347 ff.); but how wavering Gregory is upon this point is manifest from such assertions as the following : " For the commandments of the Lord are called justifications (Ps. 19. 92), in which he by correcting justifies us" (Ez. i. 7. 16 ; also ii. 10. 5).[1] According to this, grace would consist in the giving of the commandments ; and such is accordingly the view of Faustus. And it is to be observed that Gregory, in keeping with this, lays great stress upon man's co-operation. Thus place is found for the merit (*meritum*) of man in connection with the idea of reward. If we ourselves co-operate in striving after the good, then : "That which is a gift of the omnipotent God becomes our merit" (Ez. i. 9. 2; ii. 4. 6; mor. xvi. 25. 30; xviii. 40. 63; xxxiii. 21. 40). In the same line is Gregory's assertion that man can do more than is commanded (mor. xv. 18. 20 ; xxvi. 27. 51).

(c) The doctrine of Predestination is retained only in form. The irresistibility of grace appears to be taught (mor. xi. 9. 13 ; cf. Ez. ii. 1. 13), but it is denied in mor. xxx. 1. 5. So, likewise, predestination is taught as a "secret counsel" (mor. xviii. 26. 43) in connection with the "certain and definite number of the elect" (mor. xxv. 8. 20; Ez. ii. 1. 11); but it is, after all, only a result of omniscience : "Whom he calls also elect (Matt. 24. 24), because he perceives that they will persist in faith and good works" (Ez. i. 9. 8; mor. xxv. 8. 19; xviii. 29. 46). The idea is, therefore, that there is a definite number of men whom God appoints to salvation, because he knows in advance that they will accept it. But no one is able to pronounce a certain judgment as to his own election or that of any other person (ev. ii. 38. 14; mor. xxv. 8. 19 ff.; xxiv. 11. 32).[2] Here, too, Gregory wavers, and it is evident that predestination has no important place in his religious convictions.

---

[1] I know of no other reference to *justification* in Gregory's writings.
[2] But *vid.* Ez. ii. 5. 22 : "but one sign of election is the firmness (*soliditas*) of love."

(*d*) Following the course of the Christian life,[1] as depicted by Gregory, we find it interrupted by many sins. God is thereby offended, but man must "abstain even from some things lawful, until by this he may make satisfaction to his Creator" in order that his sin may be forgiven him (ev. ii. 34. 15 ff.). This is repentance. It embraces first of all *compunctio*, or *contritio*, *i. e.*, contrition, mourning, penitence (mor. xxiii. 21. 40; xvi. 29, 36). This is effected either through fear of the merited punishment, or through the flame of love and longing for the heavenly fatherland (Ez. ii. 10. 20 f.; dial. iii. 34; mor. xxiv. 6. 10). Secret sins in the thoughts are washed away by the sinner's tears of penitence and his good works (mor. ix. 55. 83 f.). But in the case of public repentance, there follows a *confession* of sins (mor. viii. 21. 37; xxii. 15. 31; xxxi. 46. 93). When grace has accomplished this, *absolution* is granted: "Whom the omnipotent God visits through the grace of *compunctio*, them the declaration of the pastor absolves" (ev. ii. 26. 6). But the "pastors of the church" also lay a penalty (*poena*) upon those who thus publicly confess their guilt.[2] This is the *satisfactio*[3] which the sinner renders to God by abstaining from that which is otherwise allowable (vid. supra and reg. past. iii. 30; opp. ii. 87). Thus the sinner secures forgiveness from God, who takes the offering or gift (*munus*) for the offense (*culpa*) (dial. iv. 60). We have here essentially the fundamental elements of the Romish sacrament of repentance (cf. Vol. I., pp. 177 f., 195 f., 363 f.). "For there are three things to be considered in every one truly penitent, *i. e.*, the change of the mind, the confession of the mouth, and the punishments of the sin" (*conversio mentis, confessio oris, et vindicta peccati* (in 1 reg. vi. 2. 33).[4]

(*e*) In closest connection with the above stand Gregory's views upon the Sacrifice of the Mass and Purgatory. The whole significance of the Lord's Supper is found in the sacrifice of the mass. He maintains the real presence of the body of Christ (ev. i. 14. 1; 22. 7; also Libr. sacr. post. Theoph. dom. v. praef. opp. iii. 27). But the principal thing is that the appeas-

---

[1] Upon the division of Christian life into *active* and *contemplative*, vid., *e. g.*, mor. vi. 37. 57-61; xxxi. 25. 49; Ez. ii. 2. 2 ff. (=Martha and Mary); reg. past. i. 7. For a portrayal of the ideal of the Christian life, *e. g.*, Ez. i. 10. 9.

[2] The injunction is given: "But let those who preside show themselves to be such that those subject to them may not blush to make known to them even their secret" (sins) (reg. past. ii. 5. opp. ii. 19).

[3] The execution of the punishments (*vindicta*) constitutes the *satisfactio*, as is evident from ep. ix. 52, p. 968 f.

[4] Vid. also the compulsory penitence (*Zwangsbusse*) of clericals, monks, and nuns, *e. g.*, ep. i. 44, p. 537 f.; iv. 9.

ing wafer (*hostia placationis*) be so presented[1] that the sacrifice of Christ for us be repeated : " For as often as we offer to him the *hostia* of the passion,' so often do we renew (*reparamus*) his passion to ourselves for our absolution," and that the church may have in it a means of influencing God in addition to prayer and alms (ev. ii. 27. 7-9 ; dial. iv. 58). There has thereby been given to the church a means of enchantment, which may be of great service, *e. g.*, breaking chains and extending help to the shipwrecked (dial. iv. 57). But it is, above all, an effectual means of bringing help to the souls of the departed. " That for certain light offenses there is to be a *purgatorial fire* before the judgment," is to be believed, according to Matt. 12. 31 ; 1 Cor. 3. 12 ff. (cf. Vol. I., pp. 159, 197 n., 363). Some sins can, accordingly, be forgiven in that world (dial. iv. 39). The sacrifice of the mass is particularly efficacious for this purpose, freeing souls from purgatory (ib. iv. 55).[2]

4. We must yet glance at Gregory's conception of the Church. " The present church is called the kingdom of heaven—for the congregation of the saints is said to be the kingdom of heaven " (ev. ii. 38. 2 ; 32. 6 ; mor. xxxiii. 18. 34). The church is the kingdom, but primarily limited to the *ecclesia justorum, i. e.*, the elect (vid. mor. xxv. 8. 21). The "one, holy universal church" embraces angels and men—men from the time of Abel onward, all believers of the old covenant belonging to it (Ez. i. 8. 28; ii. 3. 17; ev. i. 19. 1).[3] In its concrete form, like its prototype, the ark, it embraces clean and unclean. " In this church, therefore, there can be neither the evil without the good, nor the good without the evil" (ev. ii. 38. 7 f.; Ez. ii. 4. 16 f.). But only in the church are truth and love to be found, only in it salvation

---

[1] Dial. iv. 58 : " Living in himself immortally and incorruptibly, he is for us again immolated in this mystery of sacred oblation. For there his body is taken, his flesh is broken for the salvation of the people, his blood is poured out, not now into the hands of unbelievers, but into the mouths of believers. Hence we consider what is the nature (*qualitas*) of this sacrifice for us, which always repeats (*imitatur*) for our absolution the passion of the Only-begotten. For who of the believing can have a doubt that in the very hour of the immolation the heavens are opened at the voice of the priest, that the choirs of angels are present in that mystery of Jesus Christ, that the lowest things are associated with the highest ? " . . . Also ev. ii. 37. 7. " The host offered with the tears and benignity of the sacred altar pleads in a peculiar way for our absolution, because he who, arising by his own power, now dies no more, through it in his mystery suffers again for us." Then follows the sentence above quoted.

[2] The fourth book of the Dialogue treats exhaustively of conditions in the other world. Vid. especially its conception of the bridge (iv. 36).

[3] Membership in the church is conditioned upon faith in the Trinity, and this the Old Testament believers possessed. Ez. ii. 4. 4, 7, 10 ; 3. 16; mor. xxix. 31. 70.

(mor. xxxv. 8. 13). The holy universal church proclaims that God cannot, except within it, be truly worshiped, asserting that all who are without its bounds will by no means be saved (mor. xiv. v. 5; ep. xi. 46). Only the church's sacrifice avails; only its members are in the valid bond (*compages*) of love; only is its martyrdom meritorious (mor. xxxv. 8. 12; xviii. 26. 40). Separation from the church proves lack of love (mor. xviii. 26. 41 f.). But everything upon which the necessity of the church to salvation depends lies in the hands of the "officers" (rulers, *regentes*, and subjects, *subditi*, mor. xxx. 6. 23; iv. 31. 61; reg. past. ii. 6; in reg. vi. 2. 21). Binding and loosing are prerogatives of the clericals. And "whether the pastor binds justly or unjustly, nevertheless the pastor's declaration (*sententia*) must be revered by the multitude" (ev. ii. 26. 5 f.). They watch over the lives of those under them (*subditi*), lead them to repentance, dispense absolution (mor. xi. 14. 22; xiii. 18. 21; dial. ii. 23), present the sacrifice, etc. For the accomplishment of her work, the church lays claim to the aid of the unchristianized state. "The holy church, because she is not sufficient in her own strength, seeks the assistance of that rhinoceros" (Job 39. 9), *i. e.*, the prince of this world (mor. xxxi. 5. 7).

5. If we compare the Christianity of Gregory with that of Augustine, we reach a remarkable result. Almost everything in Gregory has its roots in the teaching of Augustine, and yet scarcely anything is really Augustinian. That which was un-Augustinian in Augustine becomes the vital element of this Semi-augustinian. The fundamental spirit of Augustine has vanished, and superstition gained supremacy. Everything is coarser, more fixed, and ordinary.[1] The controlling motive is not the peace of the heart which finds rest in God; but the fear of uncertainty, which seeks to attain security through the institutions of the church. "For thus the holy church, in the course of her preaching to the faithful concerning the piety and righteousness of the Redeemer, *mingles hope and fear*, in order that they may neither incautiously trust in his mercy nor in despair fear his righteousness" (mor. xx. 5. 13). There are some rays of light in this dark picture (*e. g.*, the initiative of grace, the emphasis laid upon preaching, incidental remarks touching the nature of the church); but the crude Christianity, which is its characteristic, overshadows them with its sacramental magic, its ghostly miracles, its priestcraft, its superficial conception of sin, and its intoning of merit and reward. And even where Gre-

---

[1] Cf. the opinion of Melanchthon: "Gregory, whom they call the Great, I call the dancer and torch-bearer of the theology now passing away" (Corp. Ref. xi. 16).

gory's teaching was, in itself considered, more correct than that of Augustine, as upon predestination, the better was, as matters then stood, arrayed against the good. Such is the form in which the legacy of Augustine was preserved to the church—even thus a rich inheritance.

CHAPTER II.

DOCTRINAL CONFLICTS OF THE EARLIER MIDDLE AGES.

§ 37. *Adoptionist Controversy.*

SOURCES. The letters of ELIPANDUS, España sagrada v. 524 ff. Migne Lat. 96. Etherii et Beati adv. Elipandum, ll. 2. ALCUINUS adv. Elipandum; adv. Felicem (Opp. ed. Frobenius, 1777, and Migne 100, 101). PAULINUS, ll. 3, c. Felicem, Migne 99. BENEDICT OF ANIANE, Testimoniorum nubecula, Migne 103. AGOBARD, Liber adv. dogma Felicis, Migne 104. Cf. Mansi xii., xiii. GAMS, KG. Spaniens, ii. 2, p. 261 ff. HEFELE, CG. iii., ed. 2, 642 ff. WERNER, Alkuin, 1881, p. 54 ff. MÖLLER, PRE. i., ed. 3, 180 ff. GRÖSSLER, Ueber die Ausrottg. des Adopt. im Reich Karls des Gr., 1879 (Jahresbericht d. Gymn. zu Eisleben). HAUCK, KG. Deutschlands ii., 251 ff. BACH, DG. des MA. i., p. 103 ff. THOMASIUS-SEEBERG, DG. ii., 15 ff. HARNACK, DG. iii. 248 ff.

The great Renaissance of the Carlovingian age was of the profoundest significance for Church History. Its results for the History of Doctrines were comparatively small. So great dependence was placed upon antiquity that no advance was made in dogmatics beyond the interpretation of the Fathers. This is attested by all the controversies of the age, which were essentially disputes about misunderstandings of the accepted teachers of the church.

1. In Spain, a crude attempt was made by a certain MIGETIUS to solve the problem of the Trinity. God, he affirmed, has revealed himself in a three-fold form : as the Father in David, as the Son in Christ, as the Holy Ghost in Paul (Elip. ad Miget. 3. Esp. sagr. v. 526). He was opposed by the aged bishop, ELIPANDUS OF TOLEDO. His Christological theory was championed especially by Bishop FELIX OF URGELLIS. The watchwords, *adoptio, filius adoptivus*, are taken from the Spanish so-called Mozarabic liturgy (*per adoptivi hominis passionem ; adoptivi hominis vestimentum carnis,* etc. Vid. HEFELE, iii. 651, and also HAUCK ii. 257 n.). The theory was that Christ, as the second person of the Trinity, was the " only-begotten of the Father without adoption ; " but that the Son of God assumed, or

adopted, the Son of man, who is thus *adoptivus* and *called God* (Alcuini opp. ii. 568. Esp. sagr. v. 536. Gallandi xiii. 407. Alc. adv. Fel. i. 1). The unity of person is thought to be preserved in this process, inasmuch as, from the time of his conception, the Son of man was taken up into the unity of the person of the Son of God (Alc. l. c. v. 1). He suffered, indeed, only as the adopted (*adoptivus*) man and was buried in his "adopted flesh" only (Elip. iv. 16; Mi. xcvi. 879). The doctrinal type of the Adoptionists is in the line of the Western Christology, which aimed to secure fuller recognition of the humanity of Jesus.[1] They proved the necessity of this upon religious grounds, adducing the resemblance of believers to Christ, their relations to him as members of his body, and his human character (Alc. c. Fel. ii. 4. 14; v. 9; Paulin. iii. 3, 4). Only if an actual man should, with his untainted blood, blot out the deadly handwriting, could we become free from bondage (Elip. ep. 4. 14; Mi. 96. 878. As every man is according to the flesh born from Adam, so everyone obtains the "grace of adoption," who receives it in Christ, the second Adam, born of the virgin (Alc. adv. Fel. ii. 16, also Agob. adv. dogm. Fel. 37). This theory was not really Nestorian, but it was possible to deduce from it consequences which led in that direction. It is scarcely justifiable, therefore, to attribute it to the influence of oriental Nestorians (*e. g.*, GAMS, ii. 2, p. 264 f.). "Adoptionism is to be accounted for by the continued influence of old religious theories, the dependence upon ecclesiastical formulas, and the defective theological culture" (HAUCK, ii., p. 258 n.).

2. This doctrine was vigorously assailed by the Asturians, BEATUS and ETHERIUS; then particularly by the Frankish church. Among its literary opponents the most prominent was ALCUIN. The first charge against the Spaniards was that they are led to teach a double person (*alter et alter*): "Just as the Nestorian impiety divided Christ into two Persons on account of the two natures, . . . so also your untaught temerity divides him into two Sons, one a true and the other an adopted Son" (Alc. adv. Fel. i. 11). Attention was then called to the inconsistency of Adoptionism with the teaching of the Fathers and the church.[2] These attempted refutations display a remarkably defective con-

---

[1] *Assumtio illius hominis; verbum habens hominem*, says Augustine (Vol. I., pp. 260 n., 360. Cf. Hilar. upon Ps. 138. 2. To assume man (*hominem suscipere*) is the standing formula in the Spanish Confession (vid. Hahn, Bibl. d. Symbole, ed. 3, pp. 211, 236, 237, 245 f.). The Synod of Toledo, A. D. 675, says in regard to the Logos—not the Son of man— "He is a son by nature, not by adoption" (vid. Hahn, p. 243, also Hefele, iii. 115).

[2] For special instances, vid. BACH, i. 116 ff.

ception of the real problem at issue. Their authors were content to rest in the simple thought : Christ was God, and as God he has delivered us.[1] Yet they understood that : " In the assumption of the flesh by God, the person, not the nature, of the man perishes" (Alc. adv. Fel. ii. 12). Adoptionism was condemned at Regensburg, A. D. 794 ; at Frankfurt, A. D. 794 ; at Aachen, A. D. 799. Pope Hadrian I. had already rejected it as Nestorianism and blasphemy (Cod. Carol. 99, p. 294. Mansi, xiii. 865 ff.). Under Leo III. it was again condemned by a Roman Council (Mansi, xiii. 1031, probably in A. D. 799). Nothing was gained as a result of the controversy. The opponents of the Adoptionists could not refute them because they were themselves too orthodox to understand them.

§ 38. *Eastern Church and the Worship of Images. Filioque Controversy.*

LIBRI CAROLINI, ed. Heumann, 1731 ; in Migne, 98. 999 ff. ALCUIN, de processione spiritus sancti, Migne, 101, 63 ff. HEFELE, CG. iii., ed. 2, 694 ff., 749 ff. HAUCK, KG., Deutschl. ii. 276 ff., 299 ff.

1. During the controversies concerning images, the popes arrayed themselves on the side of the image-worshipers (Vol. I., p. 304). The Frankish church had assumed the same position. Delegates of Pope Hadrian had taken part in the Council at Nice, A. D. 787, and it had not been thought necessary to take special measures to protect the Frankish church. But Charlemagne took hand in the controversy. The LIBRI CAROLINI contain a keen criticism of the worship of images. God alone, they declare, is to be adored and worshiped (*adorandus et colendus*); the saints are only to be venerated (*venerandi*). Images, on the other hand, are only ornamental objects and reminders. It is, therefore, folly to render them worship. The Council of A. D. 754, which was hostile to image-worship, and the Council of Nice were both pronounced infamous and most incompetent (*ineptissimae*). No attention whatever was given, it is true, to the distinction between veneration ($\pi\rho o\sigma\varkappa\acute{\upsilon}\nu\eta\sigma\iota\varsigma$) and worship ($\lambda\alpha\tau\rho\varepsilon\acute{\iota}\alpha$), the former word having been represented by the term *adoratio* in the Latin translation of the acts of the Council which was forwarded to Charlemagne. Accordingly, the second canon of the Council of Frankfurt, A. D. 794, decided that all *adoratio* and *servitus* are to be withheld from images, and that the Nicene Council is to be condemned (Mansi, xiii. 909).

[1] It is possible that, as HAUCK maintains (ii., pp. 268, 271, 275), the Germanic conception of Christ as the rich God, our God, had something to do with this.

2. The Augustinian theology, as is well known, teaches the procession of the Holy Spirit from the Father and the Son (Vol. I., p. 239 f.). The formula, *a patre filioque procedens*, first meets us, excepting in the Athanasian Creed (Vol. I., p. 241), in Leo I. (ep. 15. 1 : *de utroque processit*, in opposition to Priscillian's Sabellianism, *e. g.*, tract 1); then in the confession of faith of a Council at Toledo (in HAHN, ed. 3, p. 210, probably about A. D. 444); also in the confession of Reccared and the Gothic bishops (A. D. 589, HAHN, p. 232 f.); in Gregory the Great (p. 4); and in A. D. 633, 638, and 675, in confessions of Toledo (HAHN, p. 236, 237, 243). From Spain the term reached the Franks. A council at Gentilly, so early as A. D. 767, appears to have pronounced in its favor (HEFELE, iii. 432). In the Confession of Reccared it already appears inserted in the Constantinopolitan Creed (HEFELE, iii. 48). In this enlarged form, the confession was used under Charlemagne in the Frankish church. Certain Frankish monks were called to account for this at Jerusalem. As Charlemagne had, at an earlier day, instructed his theologians to advocate the *filioque* (Alcuin, de processione spiritu sancto; Mi. 101. Libri Carol. iii. 3., p. 269 ff.), so THÉO-DULF OF ORLEANS now wrote a defense of it (de spiritu sancto; Mi. 105, 239 ff.), and the Council at Aachen, A. D. 809, adopted the doctrine and, most probably, also the term itself. But Pope Leo III. opposed, not indeed the doctrinal position, but the unauthorized enlargement of the symbol (Mansi, xiv. 19 ff.). The latter, however, despite the opposition, maintained its place even at Rome.

§ 39. *Controversy Upon Augustinian Doctrine of Predestination.*

SOURCES. GOTTSCHALK'S († A. D. 868) utterances upon the subject are collected in Migne, 121, 345 ff. Vid. further especially RABANUS, the letters to Noting, Eberard, and Hincmar in Migne, 112. HINCMAR, de praedest. dei et lib. arb., Migne, 125. JOH. SCOTUS ERIGENA, de div. praedest., Migne, 122. FLORUS, sermo de praed., Migne, 119. AMOLO in the Bibl. max. patr. xiv. For Gottschalk, REMIGIUS, de tribus epistolis and Libell. de tenenda immobiliter scripturae veritate, Migne, 121. PRUDEN-TIUS, ep. ad. Hincm., Migne, 115. SERVATUS LUPUS, libell. de tribus quaestionibus, Migne, 119. Ratramnus de praedest., Migne, 121. Mauguin published a collection : Vet. auctor. qui sec. ix. de praed. scrips. opera 1650; cf. HEFELE, CG., iv., ed. 2, 130 ff. BORRASCH, der Mönch Gottsch., 1868. SCHRÖRS, Hincmar, 1884. J. WEISZÄCKER in Jahrbb. f. deutsche Theol., 1859, p. 527 ff. BACH, DG. des MA. i. 220 ff. REUTER, Gesch. d. rel. Aufklärung im MA., 1875, i. 43 ff. THOMASIUS-SEEBERG, DG., ii. 24 ff. HARNACK, DG., iii. 261 ff.

1. Augustine had incidentally spoken of a double predestination (Vol. I., p. 352 n.). ISIDORE OF SEVILLE yet wrote : "Pre-

destination is two-fold, either of the elect to (heavenly) rest, or of the wicked to death'' (Sentent. ii. 6). But in this also the Augustinians of the Carlovingian age understood their master in the same sense as had Gregory the Great (cf. p. 22). Then arose a man who, in a checkered career, had found peace for his soul in the Augustinian doctrine of election (Mi. 121, 362 and 363). The monk, GOTTSCHALK of Orbais, had met with the writings of Augustine, although he did not have the whole Augustine. His thought and emotions centered in the unchangeable God, who, of his own good will, elects men or rejects them. This '' most salutary truth ''was his strength and stay. He paid no attention to the ecclesiastical machinery, the system of good works ('' not by merits, indeed, but by the gift of the Father,'' Mi. 121, 372). '' Just as the immutable God before the foundation of the world through his gratuitous grace immutably predestinated all his elect to eternal life ; so in like manner all the reprobate who will in the day of judgment be condemned on account of their evil deserts has this same immutable God through his righteous judgment immutably predestinated to death justly everlasting '' (in Hincm. de praed. 5). God has not foreordained the evil, but the immutable God has ordained salvation for the one class and them for salvation—a gift of grace (*beneficium gratiae*)—and for others through a decision of justice (*judicium justitiae*), the merited punishment, and them for it (Mi. 121, 350). Each of these is a good act (*bonum*, ib. 358). Hence it is said that God '' has predestinated only good things (*bona*, ib. 349). This cannot be based upon the divine prescience, since God would then be mutable and dependent upon the temporal (Mi. 121, 353). Prescience merely accompanies praedestination ; by it the justice of the latter is attested. With Augustine, Gottschalk regarded the redemptive work of Christ as having reference only to the predestinated (Hincm., de praed. 27, 29, 34, 35, and Mi. 121. 367, 372). That this is genuine Augustinian doctrine cannot be questioned. It became the criterion for the '' Augustinianism '' of the period.[1]

2. Gottschalk's opponents did not understand him. They pressed home upon him, as the '' destroyer of the faith,'' the familiar brutal consequence : '' God makes man sin against his will,'' and is the author of evil, as, *e. g.*, RABANUS, to whose attention the matter was first brought by Noting of Verona. At Mayence, A. D. 848, Gottschalk's doctrine was condemned and he

[1] Even the expression, *trina unitas* (Mi. 121, 364) employed by Gottschalk, which harmonizes with the Augustinian conception, was assailed by Hincmar : *de una et non trina deitate ;* cf. HEFELE, iv. 220 f.

himself delivered for punishment to Hincmar, in whose district
his cloister lay. At Chiersy, A. D. 849, he was terribly
scourged and condemned to life-long imprisonment.

3. But the matter now only assumed wider dimensions. Influential theologians, such as PRUDENTIUS of Troyes, REMIGIUS
of Lyons, RATRAMNUS in Corbie, SERVATUS LUPUS in Ferrières,
defended the theory of a two-fold (*gemina*) predestination as the
Augustinian doctrine, while, on the other hand, RABANUS and
HINCMAR further assailed it.[1] AMOLO and FLORUS MAGISTER
pointed to its disastrous consequences. There was a possibility
of reconciliation between these opponents, for they were con-
tending more or less about words ; but the controversy between
Gottschalk and his adversaries could not be compromised, for
he was an Augustinian and they were Semi-augustinians. Such,
indeed, were also Gottschalk's defenders at heart. Between
them and his opponents the final contention was only in regard
to formulas. The latter would apply the concept of predestination only to the election to life, and base reprobation upon prescience (Hincm., de praed. 16; Mi. 125. 424; Raban., Mi. 112,
155); the former spoke, with Augustine, of a double predestination, but likewise based reprobation upon prescience. But both
agreed that the baptized and believers are predestinated, which
Gottschalk denied. The controlling consideration for the
former—but no less for the latter—was that of the dangerous
consequences for the church involved in the strict theory of predestination. The sacraments would thus be robbed of their
value, becoming a mere form and trifling ; the motive to good
works, *i. e.*, the thought of rewards and punishment, would be
removed, and thus the moral life, as they understood it, would
be destroyed. The terrible bugbear of the predestination sect is
exposed for the execration of the age (Amolo bibl. max. xiv.
333 f. Raban., Mi. 112. 1554, 1562. Hincm., de praed. 2.
15, 18 ff., 24 ff. The 5th Canon of Valence in HEFELE iv. 195 ;
cf. BACH i., 235 ff.). Kurz says : "The spirit of Gregory for
the first time joined issue with the spirit of Augustine, and it
carried the day." The will of man has been wounded by sin.
When grace heals it, it is free to perform good works. Hincmar
asserts, with Gregory, that the good (which we do) is ours and
God's : "God's, through prevenient grace ; ours, through obedient free will" (de praed. 37. 21).

---

[1] Scotus Erigena also, though in his own way, opposed Gottschalk : Sin
and punishment are nonentities, and as such cannot be objects of the divine
will, and hence there is only *one* predestination, *i. e.*, to life. His contemporaries do not seem to have fully understood him, but they suspected his
criticism as an "invention of the devil" (Flor. Mag., Mi. 119, 101).

4. The decisions rendered at the two Councils of Chiersy and Valence, A. D. 853, were in harmony with these views. The four chapters of Chiersy accurately reproduce Hincmar's position. (1) The race became through the fall a *massa perditionis.* "But a good and just God elected from this same mass of perdition according to his prescience those whom he through grace predestinated to life, and predestinated eternal life to them. He foreknew that the others, whom by the judgment of righteousness he left in the mass of perdition, would perish; but he did not predestinate that they should perish, but because he is just he predestinated to them eternal punishment. Hence, they acknowledge but *one* predestination. (2) Grace has made our will (*arbitrium*) free, "by grace set free and by grace healed from the corrupt state." (3) God wishes all men to be saved: "that some perish is the desert (*meritum*) of those who perish." (4) Christ died for all. That his death does not set all free "is the fault of those who are unbelieving, or who do not believe with the faith that works by love." The Augustinian party at Valence, on the other hand, adopted the following statement: "We confess a predestination of the elect to life, and a predestination of the wicked to death; but that, in the election of those who are to be saved, the mercy of God precedes good merit (*meritum bonum*), and in the condemnation of those who will perish, evil merit (*meritum malum*) precedes the righteous judgment of God. But that in predestination God has determined only those things which he himself would do, either from gratuitous mercy or in righteous judgment . . . But that in the wicked he foreknew the wickedness because it comes from them; and did not predestinate it, because it does not come from him." Those are condemned who think that "some are predestinated to evil by divine power, *i. e.*, so that, as it were, they cannot be anything else." The work of Christ is held to apply to all who believe on him.[1] At Toucy, A. D. 860, the controversy was abandoned without any decision having been reached (HEFELE, iv. 217 f.). No decision was needed after Gottschalk was removed from the field.

§ 40. *Divergent Views Upon Parturition of the Virgin Mary.*

SOURCES. RATRAMNUS, de eo quod Chr. ex virg. natus est, Migne, 121. RADBERTUS PASCHASIUS, de partu virginis, Migne, 120. Cf. BACH, DG. i., 152 ff. STEITZ, PRE. xii. 482 f.

Various views were expressed during this period in regard to the

---

[1] These declarations were repeated at Langres, A. D. 859, when they seem to have been confirmed by Nicholas I. Vid. Möller, PRE. v. 327.

partus virginis, which attest the growing disposition toward the worship of Mary. RATRAMNUS taught that the corporeal virginity was, indeed, preserved before, in, and after the birth of Christ ; but that he nevertheless entered the world by way of birth, through a being born (*nasci*), but not through a being brought forth (*erumpi*). RADBERT explained, in reply to the question of certain nuns, that it would be presumptuous to say that Christ was born according to the common law of nature. Such parturition rests under the curse of sin, and the "authority of the church," upon the contrary, teaches through the universal (*ubique ab omnibus*) worship of Mary that she remained free from sin in the womb, and, therefore, entered the world without sin (Mi. 120, p. 1371 f.).[1] Yet this was by no means a universally accepted doctrine. Anselm still spoke of the original sin of the Virgin (cur deus homo ? ii. 16).

§ 41. *Controversies Upon the Lord's Supper.*

SOURCES. Of the writings of RADBERTUS PASCHASIUS, vid. Liber de corpore et sanguine domini (A. D. 831) and his commentary on Matt. xxvi. Mi. 120. RATRAMNUS, de corpore et sanguine domini, Mi. 121. Cf. STEITZ, PRE. xii. 474 ff., 535 ff. RÜCKERT, der abendmalsstreit des MA. in Ztschr. f. wiss. Theol. 1858, p. 22 ff. DIECKHOFF, Ev. Abendmalsl. im Ref. Ztalter, 1851, p. 13 ff. BACH, DG. i., 159 ff. THOMASIUS-SEEBERG, DG. ii., 33 ff. HARNACK, DG. iii., 275 ff. ERNST, d. Lehre d. h. Pasch. R. v. d. Eucharistie, 1896.

1. The Ancient Church produced no dogma of the Lord's Supper. Two methods of presenting the subject are found side by side without any attempt at discrimination. They are commonly spoken of as the *metabolic* and the *symbolic* views (Vol. I., pp. 196, 301, 323). Pope Gelasius I. taught that "the substance or nature of the bread and wine does not cease to exist, although the elements, the Holy Spirit perfecting them, pass over (*transeant*) into a divine substance, as was the case with Christ himself. And certainly the image and likeness (*imago et similitudo*) are honored (*celebrantur*) in the observance (*actione*) of the mysteries " (de duabus naturis in Christo, Thiel. Ep. pontif., p. 541 f.). The theologians of the Carlovingian period, as Augustinians, were fond of emphasizing the symbolic character of the ordinance, presenting it as a memorial and a symbol (vid. RÜCKERT, l. c., pp. 25, 53). On the other hand, as a result of the growing religious materialism, which found in visible miracles the characteristic trait of religion, and of the widening influence of the sacrificial idea, the conception of a transfor-

---

[1] Cf. already Augustine, de nat. et. grat. 36. 42.

mation of the elements became more and more clearly defined. All manner of miraculous occurrences in connection with the celebration were related, as that the Christ-child had been seen at the consecration of the elements in the form of a lamb, and his appearance had led many a doubting Thomas to faith (Germanus in Martène Thes. anecdot. v. 96, 95. Radbert, c. 14. Cf. BACH, p. 166 ff.). And even the theologians in their technical discussions spoke of a " consecrating into (*consecrare in*) the substance of the body and blood of Christ " (Alcuin, ep. 41, 163, 90, in Mi. 100, 203, 423, 289).

2. A decisive step was taken in the first monograph upon the subject which we possess. It was written by a monk of Corbie, PASCHASIUS RADBERTUS. In his book, *De corpore et sanguine domini*, the attempt is made to combine the religious conceptions of the church at large with the theory of Augustine, as follows : (*a*) The omnipotent God does whatever he wishes to do. A miracle of divine omnipotence occurs in the Lord's Supper ; there is a creative act, a *creari* (4. 1 ; 15. 1, upon Matt. 26, Mi. 895). The God who created Jesus in the womb of the Virgin without seminal infusion, " to-day, through the consecration of his sacrament by his invisible power, effects (*operatur*) in the substance of the bread and wine the flesh and blood of Christ " (3. 4). Through this miracle the daily sacrifice for the benefit of the world is made possible (4. 1). The inference is : " so that, immediately after the consecration of Christ, the true body and blood are truly believed (8. 2). The body of Christ is, therefore, really present, and this body is in substance the same body in which Christ was born, suffered, rose from the dead, and which he still possesses in heaven (1. 2 ; 4. 3 ; 21. 9). The question as to the relation existing between the body now really and locally present in heaven (in this following Augustine)[1] and the body present at all places in the Lord's Supper, is not discussed by Radbertus. He speaks of the fruits of the flesh of Christ, and cites in illustration the multiplying of the loaves and increase of the meal, oil, etc., in scriptural miracles (7. 2). " From which wholesome field (*i. e.*, the body of Christ) the living bread of flesh and the drink of blood daily grow abundantly for believers, and are reaped by the faithful " (Ez. 21. 3. 2). According to this, the body is present, and yet there is present only a something effected by the body. To the objection, that as a fact that the bread and wine can be recognized as such by the senses (taste. color, form), Radbertus replies, that

---

[1] Vid. Vol. I., p. 323; also civ. dei xxii. 29. 4 ; in Joh. tr. 50. 4 ; de agone chr. 20. 28 ; serm. ad catech. 4. 11.

the actual eating of body and drinking of blood would be contrary to human custom, and that, just because of the difficulty in question, belief is meritorious (10. 1 ; 13. 1, 2 ; 1. 5 ; 8. 1, 2). The effect of participation consists in a deliverance "from daily faults and slight sins" (19. 3), in the testing and confirming of faith in the presence of the "visible sacrament" (4. 2 ; 1. 5), and in a bodily unification with Christ : "but even our flesh also is through it restored to immortality and incorruption" (19. 1 ; 21. 2). (*b*) Realistic as this sounds, Radbertus yet moves in Augustine's sphere of thought when treating of the reception of the sacrament. He pronounces it a "spiritual thing," which must be understood *in spiritu* (5. 1). Only those who have spiritually apprehended Christ receive the body and blood (8. 3 ; 6. 2). To the unbelieving they are only apparently offered. "Unless through faith and knowledge (*intelligentia*), of what does it taste but of bread and wine to those who eat?" (8. 2). (*c*) This line of thought seems quite out of harmony with the views noted under (*a*) above. Upon the one hand, we receive actually "nothing else" than the body and blood of Christ (20. 3 ; 1. 6 ; 4. 3); on the other hand, it is a spiritual participation of faith. But we have here to do with a "mystery." Hence *figura* and *veritas* must be side by side : "because the sacrament is mysterious (*mysticum*), we cannot deny that it is a figure ; but if it is a figure, we must inquire how it can be verity. For every figure is a figure of another thing and is always referred to that other thing as being the real thing of which it is a figure." In this case there is a *figure*, in so far as we have to do with the sacraments as evident to the senses ; and there is *verity* in so far as through the word of Christ "the body and blood of Christ are made (*efficitur*) from the substance of the bread and wine." This verity, however, only faith apprehends (*interius recte intelligitur aut creditur*). The relationship is like that between the outward appearance of Christ and his divine nature,—or like that between the letter and the word. The visible is present in order that we may through faith attain to the invisible (4. 1, 2). The idea of Radbertus is : In the Lord's Supper there is both a symbol and a reality. The outward visible and sensible forms, which remain despite the transformation, make it a *symbol;* the body of Christ, which is present, is the *verity*. But only he receives the body who believes that it is offered in these symbolic forms. It is, therefore, through (meritorious) faith, or the right understanding of this symbol, that the body is received. Subjectively considered, everything depends upon the merit of faith and the spiritual understanding of the ordinance. The latter may thus be considered the principal thing. We must not overlook, however, the re-enforcement of the idea of faith with that of merit, and the thoroughly un-evangelical conception of faith.

3. This book of Radbertus might have been written, in its principal parts at least, several centuries earlier ; for its leading ideas are those of the ancient church. It does not lead us beyond the obscurity which marked the teaching of the earlier age. And yet it is of the greatest importance. It is the merit of Radbertus, that he preserved the eucharist from being entirely lost in the sacrifice of the mass, that he attached to its reception some sort of personal moral effect.[1] It is true, upon the other hand, that his statement of the problem proved portentous for the development of dogma. Without concerning himself about the historical circumstances connected with the institution of the ordinance or about its religious effects, he understands the words of institution as a legal charter[2] (cf. in Matt., in Mi. 120, 890 f.). But the questions which he raised have never since ceased to agitate the church. We may find much in the doctrine to criticize, but we should not forget that the first attempt to formulate these problems might have proved different, and might easily have been worse.

4. The views of Radbertus met with opposition. Some thought, he reports (in Matt., p. 890 f.), that only the efficacy (*virtus*) of the flesh, and not the flesh—only the *figura*, and not the *veritas*—is present in the sacrament. Against these he maintains his position, appealing to the words of institution and the fact that the forgiveness of sins is (to be found) only in the very blood of Christ. A new turn of thought was given by RABANUS (vid. ep. ad Egilonem, Mi. 112, 1510 ff.). He too maintains that the true body of Christ is daily created by divine power (*potentialiter creatur*, p. 1512) out of the

---

[1] Apart from all other considerations, this is attested by his assigning to the eucharist a place by the side of baptism and the word : "For Christ has left to his church nothing greater in mystery than this and the sacrament of baptism, and also the sacred Scriptures, in all of which the Holy Spirit . . . inwardly works the mysteries of our salvation unto immortality" (I. 4 ; cf. Vol. I., pp. 196 n., 189, 320 f.). Upon the number of the sacraments, vid. 3. 2 : "But the sacraments of Christ in the church are baptism and unction, and also the body and blood of the Lord." Cf. Agobard, De privil. et jur. sacerdotii, 15.

[2] The external conception of the miraculous element in the sacrament should not be overlooked. It is in keeping with the general conception of God, which was, no doubt, largely due to Germanic influences. The doing of wonders is the chief prerogative of God. Creation is, properly speaking, the only form of activity that is worthy of him. Everything connected with religion is miraculous because brought about, or created, by God. God is power.

bread; but he denies the absolute identity of the sacramental
and the historical Christ.   They differ not in nature, but
in the form of their appearance: "Not indeed in nature
(*naturaliter*) but in form (*specialiter*), that body of the Lord
which is daily . . . consecrated from the substance of the
bread and wine for the life of the world, and which is . . .
offered by the priest, is one thing, and the body of Christ which
was born of the Virgin Mary and into which the former is
changed, is in form (*specialiter*) another thing" (p. 1514).
Thus an idea of great importance for the future was injected into
the new dogma.

5. Against the view of Radbertus appeared RATRAMNUS of
Corbie in a publication addressed to Charles the Bold.   He undertakes to answer two questions: Whether the Lord's Supper
contains a mystery which only faith can recognize, and whether
it is the historical body of Christ (5).   (*a*) The bread, he
maintains, remains externally what it is, but, inwardly considered, it is for faith something higher, heavenly and divine, which
is seen, received, eaten, only by the believing soul (9).   There
occurs, indeed, a change into something better (*commutatio in
melius*), but this is to be understood *spiritually* and *figuratively*.
"Under the veil of the corporeal bread and the corporeal wine,
the spiritual body and the spiritual blood of Christ exist."   Outwardly considered, it is bread and wine; for the eye of the spirit,
it is body and blood (16. 21).   "They are figures according to
the visible form; but according to the invisible substance, *i. e.*,
the power of the divine word [the Logos], the true body and
blood of Christ truly exist" (49).   The Lord is spiritually
present through the symbol.   "The Lord is known to be present
in some manner, and that manner is in figure and in image, in
order that the verity may be felt to be the real thing" (84).
This is evidently the view entertained, despite the occasional use
of such terms as *converti, commutari, confici* (13, 15, 28, 30, 42,
43).   (*b*) The second question Ratramnus answers in the negative.   "In appearance (*specie*) it is bread, but in the sacrament
the true body of Christ" (57).   "What appears outwardly is
therefore not the thing itself (*ipsa res*), but an image of the thing
(*imago rei*); but what is felt and known by the mind is the reality
of the thing" (*veritas rei*) (77. 88).   Therefore bread and cup
are memorial signs, likenesses of that which we spiritually receive
(73 ff., 96, 98 ff., 86, 88).   (*c*) What then does the sacrament bestow?   The answer can only be: The invisible bread, the spirit of
Christ, the power of the Logos (22, 26, 44, 64, 83 f.).   Christ,
the Word, is therefore spiritually imparted to us through the mystic
form of the sacrament.   This is the Augustinian view, adapted to

meet the statement of the problem by Radbertus. The religious element which it contains, the spiritual fellowship of Christ, cannot be overlooked. Perhaps Ratramnus would have been able to furnish a more profound and lucid exposition if the problem had not been forced upon him from without and the direction of his thought thus determined for him. The question which he sought to answer was not, how we apprehend Christ in the Lord's Supper, but whether the historical body of Christ constitutes the Lord's Supper.

6. The future belonged to Radbertus, for he had the praxis of the church upon his side. His theory did not, indeed, as a theory secure general adoption ; but the Lord's Supper had become a subject of theological discussion, and the theologians of the age did not get beyond the obscure position of Radbertus. Some already distinctly taught the theory of transubstantiation, as HAIMO of Halberstadt († A. D. 853): " That the substance, *i. e.*, of bread and wine—that is, the nature of the bread and wine—is substantially changed into another substance (*substantialiter convertatur in aliam substantiam*), viz., into flesh and blood " (BACH, i. 213 n.). Others clung to the symbolic view of Ratramnus, *e. g.*, the author of an anonymous tract (BACH, i. 203 ff.): " Thou receivest the sacrament indeed in a similitude, but thou obtainest the grace and efficacy of the real nature " (ib. 205 n. Cf. the " some " who are said to deny the identity of the sacramental and the historical body, in a tract[1] attributed to Gerbert, *De corpore et sanguine domini*, Mi. 139, p. 179). Still others, as the author of the last named tract, called in question the distinction between *veritas* and *figura* (c. 4). Essentially (*naturaliter*) it is the one body of Christ ; in appearance (*specialiter*) we must discriminate it from the latter (5). It is a *figura*, in so far as we see the external bread and wine, but a *verity* when in truth the body and blood are inwardly believed (4). The effect of participation is a quickening of our flesh through the spiritual and bodily substance of Christ for the purpose of its resurrection (9 and 8). It is the position of RABANUS (supra, p. 38) which is here maintained, and it could be easily combined with that of Ratramnus. The discussion did not lead to the final adoption of any form of dogmatic statement.

[1] Upon the question of its authorship, vid. HAUCK, KG. Deutschlands, iii. 302 f.

CHAPTER III.

THE HIERARCHICAL PRINCIPLE.　HISTORY OF THE ORDINANCE OF REPENTANCE.

§ 42. *Papacy and Hierarchy.*

SOURCES. DECRETALES PSEUDOISIDORIANAE ed. Hinschius, 1863 : cf. WASSERSCHLEBEN, PRE. xii. 367 ff. DONATIO CONSTANTINI, especially edited by ZEUMER in d. Festschrift für Gneist., 1888. Cf. FRIEDRICH, die const. Schenkung, 1889, also KRUEGER in Theol. Litztg., 1889, nn. 17, 18. SEEBERG in Theol. Littbl., 1890, n. 3-5.

1. To complete our review of the dogmatic history of the period, we must (1) observe in what particular the hierarchical conception of the Western church was extended and modified, and (2) note the influence exerted upon the Christianity of the world by the church through the ordinance of repentance, whose history we must trace in outline, leaving details to the province of Church History.

2. Charlemagne wielded supreme authority over the Western church, and he recognized the primacy of the pope. These two facts are the roots from which sprung the great conflict between pope and emperor. This relation was not changed essentially in principle, but it was changed in fact, under the immediate followers of Charlemagne. Especially did Pope Nicholas I. (A. D. 858-67) assert in unheard-of fashion the claim of papal power, of dominion over bishops and metropolitans, of authority over princes and the imperial crown. Although his successors did not always maintain his position ; although weak and unworthy popes, devoid of all political influence, sat after him in the chair of Peter ; although powerful emperors enforced their edicts upon the church and made popes prisoners—yet something remained as a permanent gain to the church. The church in general believed in the papal idea, and the popes themselves believed in it. The pope stood, in his sphere as sovereign, on an equality with the emperor. The kingdom of God stands alongside of and above the kingdom of the world. This was not changed when, in A. D. 982, Otto the Great secured the rank of Roman Emperor. Cf. HAUCK, KG. Deutschl. iii. 206 ff., 239 ff.

3. How high-strung were the papal claims is attested by the *Donatio Constantini*, which appeared about A. D. 754. The spiritual emperor is here presented in contrast with the secular emperor, sharing the latter's glory and dominion, and even demanding and receiving service at his hands. To him, as the suc-

cessor of the prince of the apostles, belongs the primacy over the church of the whole world—and secular power as well (c. 11 ff.).

4. But the hierarchial ideals were carried out to their most extreme details in the Pseudo-Isidorian decretals. It will be necessary for us to note scattered utterances occurring in the document and gather a general impression from them taken as a whole. The priestly estate, particularly the bishops, is exalted in unmeasured terms above the laity. No one should venture to prosecute them before the law, for it is the prerogative of Christ alone to pass judgment upon them (Clem. ep. 1. 32 f., p. 40. Anaclet. ep. i. 3, p. 62 f. et pas.). Christ is the head of the church, "but the priests act by legation instead of Christ in the church." And, just as his church is joined to him, so are the churches joined to the bishops, to everyone according to his portion (Evarist. ep. 2. 4, p. 90). The bishops open and close the gates of heaven, and their decision is, therefore, to be accepted even if they be in error (Clem. ep. 1. 39, p. 43). This applies with especial force to the pope, for it is the Lord's will that the church at large shall be governed in doctrine and life by the Romish church (Anacl. ep. 3. 34, p. 84 ; ep. 2. 24, p. 79. Zephyrin. c. 10, p. 133, etc.). Accordingly, no one but God or the bishop of Rome can sit in judgment upon a bishop (Melchiad. ep. 1. 2 f., p. 243 et pas.).[1] For a fuller discussion see THOMAS.-SEEBERG, DG. ii., ed. 2., p. 187 ff. It was thus definitely settled that the popular catholic conception of the church should prevail, and not the higher ideal of Augustine, although the latter was still, as a definition, employed until even a later period. The church is the hierarchy, or the subjects (*subditi*), who obey the prelates (*praelati*). It is the province of the hierarchical state to direct the secular, since its rulers have the truth and the keys of the kingdom of heaven. There remained some elements of truth in these theories also, but the falsehood in them was more potent than the truth.

§ 43. *Repentance in Earlier Middle Ages.*

LITERATURE. WASSERSCHLEBEN, Die Bussordnungen der abendl. Kirche, 1851. REGINO, De synodalibus causis et disciplinis ecclesiasticis, ll. 2. ed. Wasserschleben, 1840. Ps.-AUGUSTIN, de vera et falsa poenitentia, Aug. opp. xvii. 1849 ff.[2] SCHMITZ, Die Bussbuecher u. die Bussdisciplin d. K. 1883. HIL-

---

[1] The fraudulent tendency, afterward so prominent, is manifest in these claims (cf. the removal of the episcopacy from the jurisdiction of civil and metropolitan courts). But the chief gain was to the papacy. Nicholas I. accepted the new theory : "The decretal letters of the Roman pontiff are to be accepted, although they are not joined to (*compaginatae*) the codex of the canons." Mansi Coll. conc. xv. 695.

[2] As to the date of this document, which Gratian and the Lombard

DEFRAND, Unters. über d. germ. Poenitenzbb., 1851. MORINUS, Comment. hist. de disciplina in administr. sacr. poenit. Paris, 1651, and Venet. 1702. STEITZ, Das röm. Bussakr. 1854.   V. Zezschwitz, System d. kirchl. christl. Katechetik i. 485 ff. K. MÜLLER, Der Umschwung in d. Lehre v. d. Busse, wärend d. 12 Jahrh., in den Abhandl. f. Weizsäcker, 1892, p. 289 ff. HAUCK, KG. Deutschlands, i. 212 ff., 252 f., ii. 223 ff., 664 ff. FUNK, in Kirchenlexikon ii. 1561 ff. LOOFS, DG., ed. 3, p. 258 ff. MOELLER, KG. ii. 105 ff., 206 ff.

1. The praxis connected with public repentance in the ancient church had already in the days of Augustine been to some extent abridged.[1] Upon Germanic territory it had been introduced, both in the episcopal courts established by Charlemagne and in a strict (*e. g.*, Regino ii. 1. ff.) ecclesiastical form (Morinus, l. vii. c. 2 ff.). But this public process was distasteful to the Germans. In England it could not be introduced at all (Theodor, Poenitentiale i. 13. 4, p. 197, Wassersch.), and even in the Frankish empire, despite various admonitions, it constantly lost ground (Hauck, ii. 224 f.). It became practically limited by the general adoption of the principle that " the repentance of those whose sins are in public (*in publico*) should be in public (Hraban. de clericor. instit. ii. 30 ; cf. decrees of the Councils of Rheims, Mainz, Chalons, A. D. 813. Hefele, iii. 758, 759, 765 ; De vera et fals. poen. 11. 26). It was accordingly only gross actual sins which were regarded as demanding public repentance.

2. The custom of Private Repentance now arose and soon largely usurped the place of the public ordinance. It was a form of cloister discipline originating in Ireland and England, and introduced into the Frankish empire chiefly through Columba (about A. D. 700), whence it spread to other countries. It was at first not required, but only urgently recommended (Counc. of Chalons, 813, c. 33. Hefele, iii. 765); but as it grew customary, it became also a positive requirement of the church. The penitential books gave directions to the clergy for interrogating the wrongdoer concerning his sins, and determining the appropriate works of satisfaction to be performed by him. The system was certainly not without beneficial results in that age. The sinner was compelled to scrutinize his whole life in search of his sins ; he was induced to look for and to recognize and

already cite as Augustinian, vid. Müller, p. 292 ff.   10. 25 seems to prove that the author was acquainted with the 33d canon of Chalons (A. D. 813). From various indications I would assign it to the end of the ninth or beginning of the tenth century. Its spuriousness was detected already by the critical eye of Busch (Erl. ed., 27. 344. Letters i. 34).

[1] Vid. Vol. I., p. 364 n. Cf. Aug. serm. 82, 7, 10 f.: "Those sins are to be reproved before all which have been committed before all ; those are to be reproved more secretly which have been more secretly committed." For further details, vid. Morin. v. 9.

mourn as sins, not only gross outward offenses, but also the inward evil desire itself (Vinniaus, poen. 2 ff., 17. Columba, poen. 23, 35. Theod. poen. i. 2. 21 f. Halitgar, poen., in Morin. append., p. 8a. Reg. i. 304, p. 147), not only mortal sins, but their ramifications (Poen. Merseb. Wasserschl., p. 387 ff. Regino i. 292, 304, p. 146 f. Corrector Burchardi, c. 181, p. 665).[1] And the advice was given, that not only mortal sins, but every sin by which God is offended, be confessed to the priest (Reg. i. 292). If this involves a deepening of the religious life, it is, on the other hand, closely allied to a lamentable superficiality, as will appear if we examine in detail the practical application of the system.

3. The following outline of the theory, while keeping private repentance primarily in view, is applicable also, with such modifications as are involved in the nature of the case, to the public administration of the ordinance (vid. Morin. vii. 1. 21). (*a*) The benignant God is offended by sin (de ver. et fals. poen. 8. 20; 14. 29). Venial sins are absolved (gelöst) by the use of the Lord's Prayer (Vol. I., p. 364 n.); mortal sins, through the fruits of repentance (*fructus poenitentiae*, de ver. et fals. poen., v. 10). It is necessary now to make satisfaction (*satisfacere*) through suitable repentance (*condignam poententiam*, Reg. ii. 429; i. 303: *condigna satisfactio*). The satisfaction consists in bearing the penalty : "whatever of punishment I may be able to devise, that may suffice for thee" (de ver. et fals. poen. 2. 4). Hence, to do penance is to bear penalty (*poenitere est poenam tenere*, ib. xix. 35).[2] This penalty consists in sorrow (*dolor*) of heart on account of sin, which should continue throughout life (dolorem cum vita finiat, ib. 13. 28); then in the *confessio* before the priest (or even before a layman), which in itself brings a large measure of satisfaction (*multum satisfactionis*, ib. 10. 25); and, finally, in the performance of the appointed works of penance. He who has done, or endured, this is worthy of divine mercy, since he has rendered satisfaction to the divine righteousness (it is necessary (*oportet*) in order that the righteous One may righteously show mercy, ib. 10. 25). Reconciliation, therefore, cannot really occur until after the performance of the works of penance (vid. Vinn. poen. 1. 35. Benedikt Lev. c. i. 116. Hraban. de cler. inst. ii. 30 ; cf. de fals. et ver. poen. 15. 31).

---

[1] Vid., *e. g.*, the confessional formula in Reg. i. 304, p. 147 ; cf. Alcuin, de psalm. usu, pp. 2, 9 ; Mi. 101, p. 498 ff.

[2] In addition to this *vindicative* character, the works of penance have also a *medicinal* value. Vid., *e. g.*, Vinn. 28 : "So that it cures and corrects contraries by contraries." Reg. i. 292, 304, p. 148 : *remedia peccatorum ;* cf. Alcuin, de confess. peccator. 3.

But this rule was not observed.   On the contrary, it became customary to admit penitents before the expiration of the penitential period to the " fellowship of prayer" (*communio orationis*),
and also to full fellowship (*plena communio*) (Theod. poen. i. 12.
4, and many citations in Morin. ix. 16).   It might even be
granted immediately after the *confessio* and the assignment of the
works of penance to be performed (Morin. ix. 17. 7 f.).   In such
cases, however, the subsequent performance of the required penances was taken for granted, for the sinner was not pardoned
through his confession alone (de ver. et fals. poen. 18. 34).   The
motives for this hastening of the process were of a practical
nature, *i. e.*, that the penitent might not be driven to despair or
alienated from the church, etc.   They are, of course, evident
enough in the case of those who secured immediate release from
the penalties imposed by the payment of money.   He who thus
experiences sorrow for sin and confesses the same to the priest
has changed his *mortal* into a *venial* sin (de ver. et fals. poen.
10. 25), and is in consequence no longer subject to the punishments of hell.   But if he do not now bring forth the "fruits of
repentance" in works of penance, he will have to endure the
fires of purgatory (*ignis purgatorius*) (ib. 18, 34).   (*b*) The
sinner applies to the priest ; the latter examines him strictly in
regard to his sins, assigns the atoning works to be performed, and
wishes him forgiveness.   The sinner confesses his sin and begs for
the *intercessio* of the priest, as well as of Mary and the saints
(Alcuin, de psalm. usu, p. 2. 9. Reg. i. 304, p. 147.   Halitgar
in Morin. app., p. 6b.   Corrector Burchardi, 182, p. 666.
Beichtanweisg. Othmars, Wasserschl., p. 437).[1]   The priest
prays to God ("Mayest thou deign to be appeased," *placatus
esse digneris*) and pronounces the absolution : " God Omnipotent be thy helper and protector and grant indulgence for thy
sins, past, present, and future" (Reg. i. 304, p. 148. Corr. Burch.,
182, p. 667. Further particulars in Morin. viii. 8. 1 f., c. 10 f.).
The absolution always bears this deprecatory character, partly in
recognition of the traditional idea that God alone can forgive
sin (August. serm. 99. 9), partly in view of the immediate
situation, inasmuch as the pardon (*purgatio*) of sins could not
really be secured until the works of penance should be actually
performed (*e. g.*, Reg. i. 304 fin.).   (*c*) An important feature
of the system is seen in the *redemption of penances*.   The works

---

[1] The way was prepared for later theories in the thesis: "It is to be
believed . . . that all the alms and prayers and works of righteousness and
mercy of the whole church combine (*succurrant*) . . . to effect conversion.
Therefore, no one can worthily repent (*poenitere*) whom the unity of the
church does not sustain" (de ver. et fals. poen. 12. 27 ; 11. 26).

of penance are chiefly : Fasting (bread and water on Monday,
Wednesday, and Friday), discarding of linen clothing, going
barefoot, pilgrimages (*peregrinatio*), entering a cloister, scourg-
ings (introduced by Dominicus Loricatus, Petrus Damiani,
vid. Morin. vii. 13 f.). It became customary at a very early
period to substitute other good works for the required penances.
These consisted commonly in prayers and alms, as also scourg-
ing, pilgrimages, striking the hands upon a pavement, etc. The
German system of legal composition for crime opened the way
for the adoption of a definite system for such " redemptions."
There were tariffs fixing the character and amount of the works
of substitution. It was considered a special advantage of the
system that the penitential period could be thus shortened. For
example, instead of one day's fasting, fifty psalms might be sung,
or three denarii, or perhaps one, be given to a poor person ;
for one year's fasting there must be twenty-two solidi given in
alms, etc. (Corr. Burch., 187 ff., p. 671 ff.; poen. Merseburg,
41. Canones Hibern., p. 139 f. Beda, poen. 10. 229 f.
Egbert poen. 15 f., p. 246). Worst of all, it was considered
allowable to hire some righteous person to perform these works
(Beda, 8, p. 230. Cummean. poen., p. 463 ; cf. especially
Morin. x. 16 ff.). But the most convenient form of " redemption " was by the payment of money, which had a precedent in
Germanic law ("Wergeld," vid. Schroeder, Lehrb. d. deutsch.
Rechtsgesch., 1889, pp. 75 f., 330 ff., 707).[1] Fixed taxes were
imposed, the payment of which exonerated from liability to penance, *e. g.*: " If anyone is not able to fast and does not know
the psalms, let him give one denarius per day ; and if he has
not the money, let him give as much food as he eats. For one
year upon bread and water let him give twenty-six solidi " (Poen.
Merseberg. 42 ; cf. 148. Columba, 25. Vinn. 35. Poen.
Vindob. 43. Correct. Burch., 2 ff., 50, 190, 195, 198). The
Council of Tribur, A. D. 895, first recognized redemption by
money also for public penances (vid. Hefele, iv. 558). This praxis
was extended through the Crusade movement. The journey to
the holy sepulchre was regarded as the required work of penance (*iter illud pro omni poenitentia reputetur*, Council of Clermont, A. D. 1095, vid. Hefele, v. 222). But not only such as
actually took the journey were credited with the performance of
this penance, but also any person who furnished the necessary
equipment for a crusader.[2] Since great multitudes now received

---

[1] On the other hand, it was, in any case, but a step from penance by almsgiving to redemption of penance by money.

[2] The comments of a contemporary, Leo Cassinensis in his chronicle (iv.
11), are worthy of note. He attributes the First Crusade directly to the " pen-

absolution immediately after confession, this became everywhere the usual praxis (Morin. 10. 20, 22). But inasmuch as, by the fixed rule of the church, the forgiveness of sins depended upon penitence and confession,[1] new problems arose leading to further doctrinal definitions. It was necessary particularly to clearly prove the legality of the works of penance as required after the forgiveness of sins had been already granted, as also the right of the church to substitute money for such works of penance and to insist upon confession to the priest as well as to God. To these problems Scholasticism turned its attention (vid. sub.).

4. Both the best and the worst elements in the Christianity of the Earlier Middle Ages come to view in the history of the ordinance of repentance : on the one hand, the vivid sense of sinfulness (cf. HAUCK, ii. 700 f.; iii. 289), which made the whole life of the believer a perpetual penitence (de ver. et fals. poen. 12. 28),[2] and the confidence reposed in the living God as the only One who is able to help ;[3] on the other, the complete externalizing of religion by the theory of the *opus operatum*. Compared with the ancient penitential praxis, there are here new features of great importance : (*a*) The substitution of private for public penance. (*b*) The extension of the sphere of penitential discipline to a wider range of outward conduct and into the realm of inner experience. (*c*) The consequent representation of man's relation to God as a legal one. (*d*) The introduction of " redemptions " for penalties prescribed. But just at this point the logical sequence of the theory was broken, inasmuch as (*e*) the reconciliation of the sinner was, in course of time, made more and more dependent solely upon penitential sorrow and confession. (*f*) This led to a transformation of the conception of repentance, the forgiveness of sins being associated with a

itents" of the age who were unwilling to forego the carrying of arms (Morin. x. 19. 7).

[1] Thus, for example, in Anselm, Meditat. 4 fin., "to be cleansed (*mundari*) by repentance and confession." But forgiveness is located in the *confessio*, since the latter embraces in itself the intention of the repentant one, *e. g.*, homil. 13 : " They are cleansed in the very confession on account of the repentance which they are about to exercise, . . . they begin to work righteousness, and the working of righteousness is their purification " (*mundatio*).

[2] This conception is frequently met with, as already in Eligius of Noyon : *omnis vita christiani semper in poenitentia et compunctione debet consistere* (in HAUCK, i. 289 n. 1).

[3] In contrast with the unevangelical conception of repentance, it may be well to call attention to the emphasis laid upon faith (*fiducia*) in the penitential praxis, *e. g.*, Otmar of St. Gall in Wasserschl., p. 437 : " swell (*surge*) with faith and true credulity ;" cf. de ver. et fals. poen. 5. 15 ; 7. 18. Sorrow for sin is attributed to a divine inspiration (ib. 17, 33 ; cf. Otmar, l. c., p. 437).

penitent frame of mind and confession, and the works of satisfaction with deliverance from purgatory. It was only after this idea had become prevalent that (*g*) repentance could become a sacrament in the strict sense of the term, for only then was there thought of a special divine gift imparted to the penitent, whereas repentance had hitherto consisted merely in a series of human transactions.

Such was the history of the ordinance of repentance from about A. D. 700 until about A. D. 1100. The History of Doctrines must present it with clearness, as an accurate knowledge of it is essential to a correct understanding of the dogmas formulated in the Reformation period. As the permission of the redemptions gave occasion in that age for a certain evangelizing of the conception of repentance, so, four hundred years later, opposition to them led to an evangelizing of the church.

PART II.

CHAPTER I.

FOUNDATIONS OF HIERARCHICAL AND RELIGIOUS IDEALS AND OF
SCHOLASTIC THEOLOGY.

§ 44. *The Church and the World.*

1. The historical result of the movements and tendencies within
the church from the end of the tenth to the close of the thirteenth
century is found in the reformatory ideas which centered at
Cluny, and which gradually brought the church under their control.   It was an ethical reformation which was sought.   A check
was to be placed upon the secularizing of the cloisters, the rude-
ness and immorality of the clergy, and the anarchy which
marked the social life, especially under the domination of the
robber-nobility.   It was a genuinely reformatory idea—the world
was to adopt the principles of the church, and the church was to
be free from the world.   But both objects were sought in the
spirit, and by the means, of the prevalent type of piety.   The
conception of the " City of God " (*civitas dei*) began to be regarded in a practical way, and the " State " of Charlemagne was
abandoned.   Many measures were employed, such as the revival
of the religious practices of Mysticism, increased severity in
cloister discipline, celibacy of the priesthood, repression of
simony, *i. e.*, investiture by civil authorities, the complete independence of church property.   But the movement was soon
combined with the effort to realize the pseudo-Isidorian ideals
(p. 41), which were interpreted entirely in the interest of the
papal power.   The mystical piety of the ancient Monasticism,
the pseudo-Isidorian writings, and the church property were the
ruling motives in the attempted Reformation.   The church was
actually reformed by it ; but in the line, of course, of the motives
indicated.   It promoted the religious life of the individual, partly
by giving a marked impulse to the worship of saints and relics,
the craving for miracles, superstition, asceticism, pilgrimages,
etc., but also by a real deepening of the religious sensibility.

4   (49)

Cf. SACKUR, Die Cluniacenser in ihrer kirchl. u. allgemeingesch. Wirksamkeit, 2 vols., 1892-94; HAUCK, KG. Deutschl. iii. 445 ff., 459 ff.

2. The movement for reform opened and smoothed the path to the realization of the pseudo-Isidorian ideals by the papacy. This can be studied to advantage in the work of Cardinal Humbert : *Libri tres adv. Simoniacos* (Mi. 143), in which the following line of progress is manifest : Independence of the civil authority on the part of the church, its officials and property (iii. 3, 5, 10), and therefore of the investiture by secular rulers, which is simony (iii. 6, 11 f.); denial of the efficacy of the sacraments when administered by simonists, since simony is heresy and can bring only ruin (ii. 20 ff., 26 ff., 34) ; summons to insurrection against the civil government (iii. 16).[1] The life-work of Gregory VII. aided in the attainment of these ideals. His ideas form the classical expression of the claims of the papacy in the Middle Ages. In the twenty-seven propositions of the *Dictatus* attributed to him, they are presented with precision (cf. especially Ep. ad Herimannum, Registrum viii. 21 ; Jaffé Monum. Gregoriana, Mi. 148 ; also in Mirbt, Quellen zur Gesch. d. Papsttums, 1895, pp. 47-64): The Roman church has never erred and never will err. Only he is catholic who agrees with it. Accordingly, only the Roman bishop is *universalis ;* he has authority over all other bishops, whom he can appoint and remove; his legates outrank all bishops. The other bishops are only his substitutes (registr. i. 12, 60 ; iv. 11), and it is their duty to support him even to the extent of furnishing soldiers when required (reg. vi. 17a; ep. collectae 13 fin.). "To him alone it is permissible to establish new laws according to the need of the time." All the graver matters of dispute in any portion of the church are to be brought before his tribunal (cf. reg. i. 17; iv. 27). "No section [of a law] nor book may be regarded as canonical without his authority."[2] The pope alone decides matters at councils (reg. iii. 10). Only his foot is kissed by the princes. He can remove emperors, but can himself be judged by no one. The canonical ordination gives him sancity : "by the merits of the blessed Peter he is infallibly made holy." He is not only the lord of the church,

---

[1] It is interesting to note the two conceptions of the relation of church and state existing side by side. On the one hand : " That the laity are forbidden to take charge of ecclesiastical affairs just as they conduct secular affairs " (iii. 9 in.); on the other hand : " Just as the soul is higher than the body and instructs it, so the sacerdotal dignity excels and instructs the regal, as, *e. g.*, the celestial the terrestrial. . . . It is the duty of kings to obey ecclesiastics " (iii. 21). This is Augustinian, but Gregory VII. still holds the same position.

[2] In Gratian the inscription of Part I. dist. 19, c. 6 reads : " The decretal letters are counted among the canonical scriptures."

but universal dominion (*universale regimen*) has been committed to him, and he is " prince (*princeps*) over the kingdoms of the world" (reg. ii. 51, 75 ; i. 63). Upon this is based the supremacy of the pope over civil governments and their princes. The latter are to receive their authority in trust from him (reg. viii. 26, 23 ; iv. 28). They stand related to him as the moon to the sun (reg. vii. 25 ; iv. 24). Independent dominion on their part is based on sinful pride. As they are notoriously dependent upon the priests in spiritual things, since they cannot administer (*conficere*) the communion, and do not have the power of the keys, so it is a valid maxim that in secular affairs they are subject to the pope alone. He who can bind and loose in heaven can surely do so on earth (reg. viii. 21). " But if the holy apostolic chair judicially determines spiritual things by the original authority divinely granted to it, why not also secular things ? " (reg. iv. 2). The power of the keys is therefore the magic key which opens up to the pope all authority (cf. iii. 10a ; vii. 14). Gregory indeed allows to the state a relative independence (reg. i. 19 ; vii. 25 ; cf. MIRBT, Stellg. Aug. in der Publicist. des greg. Kirchenstreites, 1888, pp. 91, 94 f., 96), but it presupposes the willingness of the state to serve the church and obey the pope. Thus Gregory had given currency to an ideal of the papacy whose assumptions could not be surpassed. The infallible pope has authority over body and soul, the world and the church, time and eternity. To this extreme was the Augustinian idea of the *civitas dei* carried. He who opposes the pope is a heretic (*e. g.*, Henry IV.; vid. reg. iv. 7, 12 ; viii. 21).[1] All these claims rested, in the last analysis, upon the objective effect of the sacrament of ordination. But the hierarchical idea was carried too far by Gregory (cf. Cyprian, Vol. I., p. 184) when, in his struggle against the marriage of priests and simony, he denied the efficacy of the consecration of schismatics and of the sacraments administered by them (vid. reg. vi. 5b ; v. 14a ; iv. 2 and 11).[2]

3. The reform, as Gregory regarded it, brought the church

---

[1] This is a new conception of heresy. In Irenæus, heresy was the denial of the ecclesiastical, biblical doctrine ; in Cyril, rebellion against the ecclesiastical organization (schism). Now it is opposition to the hierarchy.

[2] Vid. upon these conflicting views during the great conflict the exhaustive discussion of MIRBT, Publicistik in Ztalt. Greg. VII., pp. 378-446. The acceptance of the ecclesiastical or of the sacramental conception, alliance with the reformatory movement or adherence to the hierarchical tradition, determined the position taken in each case as to the efficacy of the simonistic sacraments. " In the later sects which rejected the sacraments administered by unworthy priests was reaped the harvest of the seed which the popes of the eleventh century had helped to sow." MIRBT, p. 445 f. As to Gregory's use of the ban and interdict, vid. ib. pp. 202 ff., 219 ff.

into the most intimate relations with secular life. He exalted
the hierarchical idea as no one before him had done, but at the
expense of reducing the church to the position of a political factor in worldly affairs. "The more completely the religious
spirit of the Middle Ages subdued the world, the more entirely
must the church become the world" (vid. EICKEN, Gesch. u.
Syst. d. mittellalt. Weltanschauung, 1887, p. 741). Well did
Bernard write to Eugene III.: "To evangelize is to pasture ; do
the work of an evangelist, and thou fulfillest the work of a pastor"
(de considerat. iv. 3. 6). Even he acknowledged : "Some are
called to the lot of care ; thou to plenitude of power" (ib. ii. 8.
16), and this *plenitudo potestatis* was the dominion over church
and world. Nowhere is the secularization of the church in this
age more clearly seen than in the impress given to the papal
canon law. The church is to be governed by the laws of the
papal decretals. They have binding authority. Collections of
them are made, and they constitute the law of the church. The
body of laws which had been historically developed was increased
by fraudulent additions. But, in the last resort, above this positive law stood the natural law of reason (vid. supra, Gregory's
argument for the authority of the pope over worldly affairs).[1]
The legal manuals (Gratian's Decretal, etc.) were the controlling authority for the theologians of the day upon the nature and
mission of the church. Since the church had become the world,
it was to be governed by the "divine ecclesiastical law." To
portray the struggles between the papal and the national conceptions of fundamental law, which continued until the Concordat
of Worms (A. D. 1122), is not the province of the History of
Doctrines.

Cf. upon paragraphs 2 and 3, MIRBT, Die Publicistik im Ztalt. Greg. VII.,
1894. MARTENS, Greg. VII., 2 vols., 1894. HAUCK, KG. Deutschl. iii.
752 ff., 844 ff. VON SCHULTE, Gesch. der Quellen d. Kirchenrechts i., 1875.
VON DOELLINGER, Das Pabsttum, 1892, p. 40 ff. MOELLER, KG. ii. 283 ff.
MUELLER, KG. i. 436 ff , 447 ff.

§ 45. *Christianity of St. Bernard.*

But the agitation for reform became the occasion also of an
actual revival and deepening of personal piety. The best
thoughts of Augustine were revitalized. Reverent speculation
(Anselm) drew inspiration from his writings, as well as that mystical absorption in Christ which Bernard of Clairvaux († A. D.
1153) so vividly portrayed to the piously inclined in the Middle

[1] Cyprian already appealed—when it suited his purpose—to the "sound
mind" in opposition to tradition (Vol. I., p. 184).

Ages. To gain a knowledge of the compass of his religious
thought, we must study his homilies upon the Song of Solomon
(Mi. 182). (*a*) The strongest feature of Bernard is the energy
with which he leads the souls of his hearers and readers to immerse
themselves in the contemplation of the humanity of Jesus, particularly his passion. " For what is so efficacious for the curing
of the wounds of conscience, and for the clarifying of the vision
of the mind as sedulous meditation upon the wounds of Christ ? "
(sermo. 62. 7). We should allow the contemplation of his
passion to lie upon our breast like a bundle of myrrh (43. 1 ff.).
Thus God draws near to us in the man Jesus, and his love is revealed to us (61. 4 ; 20. 2 ; 11. 9). (*b*) This love now awakens
a responsive affection in our hearts (20. 7 ; 11. 7). Devout
contemplation of the man Jesus leads us, further, to a blessed
union with his divinity. It is the " outgoing of a pure mind into
God, or a pious descent of God into the soul. Let it receive
him, gliding from heaven, with the deepest emotions and with
the very marrow of the heart" (31. 6). Ecstatic contemplation
is the personal experience (*proprium experimentum*) (3. 1.) of
the soul. It is a blessed and delightful embrace between the
loving soul and its beloved (7. 2 ; 73. 10 ; 75. 1 ; 74. 4.). The
heavens are opened, new ideas flow down from above into the
heart, which, like a fountain, pours forth from within the words
of wisdom. There is the bridegroom present (74. 5 ; 69. 6).
(*c*) But only he can obtain this goal who produces the fruits of
repentance in pious works (3. 2-4 ; 18. 5 f.; 67. 8 ; 11. 2),
who follows Jesus as his teacher, and seeks to follow his example
beneath sufferings and the cross (22. 7 ; 21. 2 ; 61. 7 ; 47. 6 ;
20. 7). He himself gives the needful power to this end : " I
thus receive examples for myself from the man and aid from the
Mighty One" (15. 6). " If I with the name call to mind Jesus the
man, meek and lowly of heart, kind, sober, chaste, merciful, and
conspicuous for everything honorable and holy, and the same as
the omnipotent God, who both restores me by his example and
strengthens me by his aid." (*d*) But Bernard does not himself
attain to a regular and constant life with Christ. The enchant-
ing blessedness of pious contemplation gives place to hours of
poverty, vacuity, and obtuseness of spirit (9. 3 ; 14. 6 ; 32.
2, 4 ; 74. 4). From this Bernard did not draw the inference
of Quietism, but emphasizes the truth that, in addition to the
contemplative life, the active life with the good works of love is
also necessary (58. 3 ; 85. 13 ; cf. de diligendo deo 10):
Martha is the sister of Mary (51. 2). This is all purely a gift of
grace. "Grace restores me to myself, justified freely and thus
liberated from the service of sin " (67. 10 ; cf. RITSCHL, Rechtf.

u. Vers. i. 111 ff.). But Christ has two feet, mercy and judgment. If we were to cling only to the first or the second, the
result would be most injurious security or despair. We should,
therefore, grasp both feet at once (6. 8, 9). (*e*) Bernard here
follows a suggestion found in Augustine : "The humanity of Jesus
is a way to (his) divinity" (vid. Vol. I., p. 361 n.); but when
he, the preacher of Crusades, makes the entire practical knowledge of God dependent upon the contemplation of the good
deeds of the historical Christ, he goes beyond Augustine. For
him—and in this he fixes the type of piety for the Middle Ages—
the whole of Christianity is an *imitation of Christ*. His Christ
is not merely a dogmatic formula, not only the eternal judge of the
world, but the actual historical Christ, the personal revelation of
God, and he led the way in apprehending this Christ in a religious way. But these ideas were interspersed with the demands
of the Areopagite Mysticism. Communion with Christ is at best
attainable only in the ecstatic state. Hence, in the contemplation of the historical Christ, the soul does not after all experience
a revelation of the living and present Lord, and such contemplation is only the bridge by which to reach the ecstatic union.

Cf. NEANDER, D. h. Bern. u. s. Ztalter ed. Deutsch, 1889-90. REUTER,
Ztschr. f. KG., 1877, 36 ff. RITSCHL, Geschichte d. Pietism., p. 46 ff.
SEEBERG-THOMAS., DG. ii. 2, p. 267 ff.

§ 46. *History of Theology from Anselm to Peter the Lombard.*

BULAEUS, hist. universit. Paris, 1655. DENIFLE, die Universitäten d. MA. i.
1885. KAUFMANN, Gesch. d. deutsch. Univ. i. 1888. HAURÉAU, Hist. de
la philosophie scolastique, 2 parts in 3 vols., ed. 2, 1873. NITSCH, Art.
Scholastik, PRE. xiii. REUTER, Gesch. d. rel. Aufklärung im MA., 2 vols.,
1875-77. PRANTL, Gesch. d. Logik im Abendlande, 4 vols., 1855 ff. UEBER-
WEG-HEINZE, Gesch. d. Philos. ii., ed. 7, 1883. RITTER, Gesch. d. Philos.,
vols. vii. and viii., 1844-45. ERDMANN, Gesch. d. Philos. 1, ed. 4, 1896.
STOCKL, Gesch. d. Philos. d. MA., 2 vols., 1864 f. WILLMANN, Gesch. d.
Idealism., vol. ii., 1896, p. 321 ff. LÖWE, der Kampf. z. d. Nominalism. u.
Realism., 1876. SCHWANE, DG. d. mittleren Zeit, 1882. THOMASIUS-
SEEBERG, DG. ii., ed. 2, 55 ff. HARNACK, DG. iii. 512 ff., 419 ff.

1. The term, Scholasticism, is used to designate the theology
of the period from Anselm and Abelard to the Reformation, *i. e.*,
the theology of the Later Middle Ages. Its peculiarity, briefly
stated, consists in the logical and dialectical working over of the
doctrine inherited from the earlier ages. The History of Doctrines cannot attempt to present an exhaustive history of the
genesis and progress of the scholastic method, nor to note in detail all the doctrines espoused by the scholastics, as it would thus
invade the domain of the History of Theology. It is our task
simply to trace the scholastic theology in so far as it was influen-

tial in the creation of new dogmas (the sacraments) or in the modification of the traditional dogma (Augustinianism). The material to be selected must be such as will illustrate the influence exerted by the reformatory and anti-reformatory movements (Councils of Trent and the Vatican) in the moulding of dogmas.

As to the arrangement of the material, the question arises whether we shall present the scholastic doctrines as a whole in the various stages of their development (HARNACK, LOOFS), or trace each separate doctrine in its historical development throughout the entire scholastic period (SCHWANE, THOMASIUS). Much can be said in favor of either method ; but we decide upon the former, although in pursuing it we can scarcely avoid some repetitions, for the reason that the historical development can be thus so much more clearly seen. The method cannot, of course, be carried out to its full extent, as the result would be a history of scholastic theology.

2. The beginnings of Scholasticism were closely associated with the pedantic methods employed in the study of theology in the cloister schools (the schools of Tours and of Bec were of great importance) and in the universities, which began to appear in the early part of the thirteenth century. It received an impulse from the revival of interest in philosophy, and particularly in dialectics, which was enkindled and sustained by the study of Aristotle, as from the middle of the twelfth century onward, and especially since the thirteenth century, theologians became, partly through Arabian literature, better acquainted with all the works of Aristotle. But it was also in no small degree the natural logic of the situation which led to Scholasticism. If the traditional dogma was an inviolable legacy, the spirit of the age could be exercised upon it in no other way than in presenting by dialectic methods the evidence of its harmony with sound reason. This tendency first arrested the attention of the church at large in the controversy of BERENGER († A. D. 1088).[1] He appealed in arguing to the *ratio*, and denounced the senselessness (*vecordia*) of his opponents ; but the latter met him with arguments based likewise upon reason (*e. g.*, LANFRANC). There was an ever-widening circle of disputants who either depended solely upon rational arguments or held that faith should at least find confirmation in the deductions of reason.[2] And although there may have been some theologians who were content to simply ac-

---

[1] As to earlier instances, vid. HAUCK, KG. Deutschl. iii. 331 f., 935, 952 f.

[2] Anselm : cur deus homo ? i. 2 fin. : "They ask the reason because they do not believe, but we because we believe ; yet that which we ask is one and the same thing."

cept the doctrines received by tradition, theirs was not the future
(vid. HAUCK, iii. 956 f., 963 f.).

Two theologians are to be considered as the founders of
Scholasticism, ANSELM of Canterbury († A. D. 1109) and PETER
ABELARD († A. D. 1142).

The contributions of Anselm to the general history of Scholasticism consist in the following particulars : (*a*) He possessed a great
talent for formulation, having the ability to express the traditional
ideas in forms which would arrest the attention of his own age.
His work, *Cur deus homo ?* is, *e. g.*, a masterpiece in this respect,
since Anselm here taught his contemporaries to apprehend the
meaning of redemption under the conceptions of the then prevalent penitential praxis (satisfaction). (*b*) He maintained the
realism of universals. Boëtius had, in the commentary accompanying his translation of the *Isagoge* of Porphyry,[1] left the objective existence of *universalia*, or genera and species, an open
question ; but in the commentary accompanying his translation of
Victorin he pronounced in its favor. The so-called Nominalistic view, according to which the general conceptions are not
realities (*res*), but only sounds (*voces*) and names (*nomina*),
was derived also from a passage in Boëtius, in which the latter
asserts that the reality (*res*) is apprehended by the mind (*intellectus*), and given expression by means of the voice (*vox*).
These problems were discussed at an early period.[2] Anselm
became involved in the controversy through ROSCELLIN of Com-
piegne, who applied the Nominalist theory, that universals are
merely subjective conceptions (breaths—*flatus voci*), to the
Trinity, and thus approached Tritheism (vid. Anselm, ep. ii. 35.
41 ; de fid. trin. 2. 3). This Anselm considered simply foolish-
ness. To him universal conceptions appear as presenting truth
and reality, and the individual species as simply manifestations of
the *genera.* Thought is trustworthy only as it looks to the universal (vid. dial. et verit.). But Anselm did not further develop
these ideas. We have an evidence of his view in the Proslogium
(cf. c. Gannilanum), which presents the ontological proof of the
existence of God, *i. e.*, from the idea of God his real existence is
inferred. The highest can be thought of only as existent ; therefore
God cannot be imagined as non-existent. Existence belongs abso-

---

[1] The passage of Porphyry is as follows : Concerning genera and species I
decline to say, indeed, whether they subsist or are located in the bare intellect alone ; whether they are corporeal or incorporeal substances ; and whether
they are located apart from sensible things or insensible things, and existing in
connection with them.

[2] Vid. PRANTL, Gesch. d. Logik, ii. 118 ff., 41 ff. Barach, Zur Gesch. d.
Nominalism. vor Roscell., 1866 ; also Gunzo v. Novara, Mi. 136. 1294; cf.
HAUCK, iii. 331.

lutely to the highest being (c. Gannil. 3 ff.). (*c*) The object of theological research is faith, of which Anselm has a two-fold conception. He first interjects into subjective faith the idea of a striving after knowledge, which leads to the rule : " The Christian
ought to advance through faith to knowledge, not to come
through knowledge to faith, nor, if he cannot know, recede from
faith. But when he is able to attain to knowledge he rejoices ;
and when unable he reveres that which he is unable to grasp " (ep.
ii. 41). Faith is always the necessary beginning of knowledge.
We must always first of all grasp the object as such. Only then
can an experience (*experientia*) of it be attained, and this then
leads to a knowledge (*intelligere*) of it (de fide trinit. 2). This
is the familiar " faith seeking knowledge : I believe, in order that
I may know " (proslog. 1 ; meditat. 21 ; cur deus homo? 1. 2).
It is a tending toward God (*tendere in deum*, monolog. 75 f.).
Just what Anselm meant by this faith becomes evident when we
consider the other requirement associated with the above, that
the faith of the Catholic church, *i. e.*, the faith of the three
symbols (Apostolic, Constantinopolitan, and Athanasian, vid. ep.
ii. 41), is to be maintained (de fide trinit. 2 in.), and this even
though knowledge (the *intelligere*) in the matter be denied to the
intellect (monolog. 64). This faith, accordingly, which reaches
a higher stage in knowledge, is the acceptance of the teachings
of the church as true, which is at the same time a "tending
toward God," and, just on this account, attains its summit in love
(monolog. 76 f.). This is the Catholic conception. (*d*) With
this conception of faith, it is easy to comprehend how Anselm
could undertake (cur deus homo? i. 1 f., 10, 20, 25 ; ii. 9, 11,
15 ; de fide trinit. 4) to establish the faith of the church (incarnation, existence of God, Trinity) " by reason or necessity," and
could believe that he had " by reason alone made manifest not
only to Jews but even to pagans " (ib. ii. 23) the necessity for
the incarnation. The speculative, rationalistic character of
Scholasticism is here betrayed. The intellectual independence
of the system, the energetic penetration into the nature of
things which we observe, for example, in Duns Scotus, has its
first great representative in Anselm. Cf. REUTER, Gesch. d.
Aufkl. im MA. i. 297 ff. R. SEEBERG, Die Theologie des Duns
Scotus, 1900, pp. 3 ff., 599 ff. Ans. Werke, ed. Gerberon, 1675,
in Mi. 158-59 ; cf. HASSE, A. v. C., 2 vols., 1843-52. RULE,
Life and Times of St. Ans., 2 vols., 1883.

3. Anselm is commonly called the father of Scholasticism, but
if we regard the entire movement, the title of honor belongs
rather more fully to Abelard. This wide-awake, richly endowed,
and keen spirit furnished a wealth of suggestions, both positive

and negative, which continue to exert a marked influence upon the development of Scholasticism, whereas Anselm's views upon particular points, even his discussions of the atonement, seldom find an echo in the subsequent periods. At one time, indeed, in the history of English theology, the spirit of Anselm exerted an important influence. (*a*) When Abelard in his *Sic et Non* (ed. Henke et Lindenkohl, 1851) collected a number of mutually contradictory passages from the Bible and patristic literature, he introduced the method by which Scholastic dialectics sought to reconcile these discrepancies (Sic et Non, prol., p. 1349, Mi.). (*b*) He, too, placed *ratio* beside *fides*. He opposes as well the "pseudo-dialecticians" who think that they can prove everything (theol. christ. iii., p. 1226 f., 1212 f., 1218) as the mere authority-faith, which makes faith rest only in the mouth and not in the heart. "Not because God said anything is it believed, but because it has been proved to be so it is accepted" (introductio ad theol. ii. 3, p. 1050). Faith is the foundation. Faith, particularly the trinitarian faith, is, according to Athanasius, necessary to salvation (ib. i. 4 ff.). Faith is not to be, properly speaking, proved, but only made clear and probable to reason (ib. ii. 2, p. 1040 ; theol. christ. iii., p. 1227). Yet there was in this thinker an independent attitude toward tradition which was foreign to his age. The writings of the fathers are to be read "not with the necessity of believing, but with the liberty of judging." Inquiry is the chief key of knowledge, "for by doubting we come to inquiry, and by inquiring we discover the truth." He halts only when brought face to face with "the excellency of the canonical authority of the Old and New Testaments." Here no error is possible. If it appears so, either the codex or the interpretation must be defective. The opinions of later writers may be erroneous "unless it can be defended either by sure reason (*certa ratione*) or that canonical authority "[1] (Sic et Non, prol. Mi., p. 1347). These principles are not, however, always adhered to. In his expositions of the Trinity, as well as in his theory of the atonement, there is a very prominent rationalistic tendency, as judged by the prevailing view of the age.[2] An illustration of his

---

[1] Cf. Reuter, Aufklär, i. 224 ff., 326 ff. His judgment of Abelard is, however, in keeping with the tendency of the book, one-sided. He has no sympathy with the healthful tone in Abelard's theology, but sees him too largely through the spectacles of Bernard. Vid., on the other hand, DEUTSCH, Pet. Ab., 1883, p. 173 ff.

[2] Vid. Abelard's tract, condemned at Soissons, A. D. 1121, De unitate et trinitate dei, ed. STOLZLE, 1891, and also the Theologia christ. The leading proposition reads : "Thus it is, therefore, that God is three persons, . . . as if we say that the divine *substantia* is powerful, wise, good ; or, rather, that it

intellectual independence is seen in his expositions of the Trinity. He maintains the unity of substance and the personal trinity. He teaches, in full harmony with Augustine, "each one of the three persons is the same substance" (de un. et trin. 32, 36, 76), and he rejects Sabellianism; but he thinks that, although the divine attributes and works belong without division to the entire Godhead, yet in a special and peculiar way (*specialiter et proprie*) power pertains to the Father, wisdom to the Son, goodness to the Spirit. That this attempt to interpret the Trinitarian idea was essentially inferior to the method inherited from Augustine will scarcely be affirmed.[1] (*c*) It is to be remarked, further, that Abelard proposed a new method of dividing systematic theology. In the *Introductio ad theologiam* has been preserved for us only a fragment of his dogmatic scheme. This great work was arranged under the headings: *fides, sacramentum, caritas* (introd. i. init.). Four works have been preserved whose intimate dependence upon Abelard is evident from the adoption of this scheme and from many internal indications: The *Epitome theol. christ.* (first edited by Rheinwald in 1835); the anonymous *Sentences of the Convent Library at St. Florian,* preserved only in manuscript; the *Sentences of Magister Omnebene,* likewise only in manuscript; and the *Sentences of Roland* (afterward Pope Alex. III., ed. GIETL, 1891; cf. DENIFLE, Ab. Sentenzen u. die Bearbeitungen seiner Theol. in Archiv f. Litt. u. KG. d. MA. i., 402 ff., 584 ff., especially 419 ff., 603 ff.). Among the disciples of Abelard was Peter the Lombard, of whom further notice must be taken. Abelard's arrangement of topics preserved in a very marked way for the doctrine of the sacraments the position which that doctrine held in the religious life of the Middle Ages. In correcting the scheme of Augustine's *Enchiridion* by substituting the sacraments for the second heading of the latter, *i. e.,* hope, he proves his dogmatic talent. It is this, too, which, to a great extent has

---

is power itself, wisdom itself, goodness itself" (de unit. et trin., pp. 3, 2, 62).

[1] At the basis of Abelard's theory lies the correct conviction that the interpretations of the Trinity must set forth the three-fold life as *personal,* which is not the case in the analogues of subject and object, appointer and appointed. But Abelard himself falls into the same error when he compares the Trinity with matter and object formed of matter (*materia et materiatum*), and with wax and waxen figure (theol. chr. iv., p. 1288, Mi.); whilst, on the other hand, the declarations that the persons of the Trinity are related to one another as different names for the same object, *e. g., mucro* and *gladius* (de unit. et trin., pp. 51, 6), as attributes to the soul (p. 68), as the three grammatical persons when applied to the same individual (pp. 63, 70), lie very close to the Sabellian theory.

given him such an important influence upon the development of Christian doctrine. (*d*) We must note, finally, the place of Abelard in discussions of the theory of perception. His teacher, WILLIAM OF CHAMPEAUX, had advocated an extreme Realism, maintaining that universals are the true realities, which are present entire and undivided in all individuals, so that the latter do not differ essentially, but their differences are produced simply by the variety of their accidents (Abäl., hist. calamitatum, 2, Mi. 178, 119). Abelard forced his instructor to a modification of this view (vid. Deutsch, p. 103 f., n.). His own utterances upon the question are not entirely clear. On the one hand, general conceptions not only have a subjective existence, but they are called into being as thus subjective by virtue of the nature of things. They are thus objective in so far as begotten of objective things and subjective in so far as existing only in the subject (cf. Glossulae super Porphyr. opp. ed. Cousin ii. 761). Yet, on the other hand, Abelard deduces the species from the genus through the influence of the form, according to the common realistic theory (cf. Prantl, ii. 177 ff.). There are not wanting in his writings, however, utterances which betray a certain mistrust of the conception of universals (vid. Deutsch, p. 106 ff.). His view cannot now be reproduced with certainty, but his limitations of Realism were not lost upon succeeding ages. Works of Abelard, edited by Cousin, 1849-59, in Mi. 178. Cf. Deutsch, Pet. Abälard, 1883.

4. The first half of the twelfth century witnessed a remarkable intellectual activity. On the one hand were those *professores dialecticae*, whose arrogance was so great that, " despising the universal authorities," they thought themselves able to comprehend everything by their little reasonings (*ratiunculis*) (Ab. theol. christ. iii., pp. 1218, 1212 f.); on the other hand, the theology of Abelard and his widespread following (Denifle, Archiv. i. 613 f.). A storm of opposition now arose against the Master. It was charged that the faith of simple believers was ridiculed by him, the mysteries of God emptied of their meaning, the Fathers scorned—that "human genius was usurping all things to itself," that Abelard proclaimed a new "fifth Gospel" (Bernh. de erroribus, Abael. 5. 12; cf. Wilhelm v. St. Thierry in Mi. 180. 249 ff.). Dialectics was declared to be useless and foolish, ridiculous, and even Satanic (JOH. OF SALISBURY, WALTHER OF ST. VICTOR; vid. Bulaeus, hist. univ. Paris. ii. 402, 629 ff. Reuter, l. c., ii. 16 f. Bach, DG. d. MA., ii. 384 ff.). Similarly spoke GERHOH and ARNO of Reichersberg. The former especially charges Nestorianism upon the dialectics of his time (vid. De investigatione Antichristi, ed. Scheibelberger, 1875, and Bach,

ii. 390-722).[1] Abelard was confessedly vanquished by his opponents at Soissons (A. D. 1121) and Sens (A. D. 1141). The agitation led to various attempts to present the "positive theology"
in systematic form. The work of HONORIUS AUGUSTODUNENSIS
(Augsburg or Autun), in which he undertakes to embrace in a
short compass the entire Christian doctrine (vid. Elucidarium
sive dialog. de summa totius christ. theol. in Mi. 172, 1109 ff.)
seems to have appeared even before the outbreak of the controversy, *i. e.*, about A. D. 1120.[2] Then came HUGO OF ST.
VICTOR († 1141) with his great work, *De sacramentis* and the
Summa sententiarum (Mi. 176). The chief content of the Holy
Scriptures consists of the the works of human restoration (*opera
restaurationis humanae*), but for the proper understanding of these
the work of the natural state (*opus conditionis*) must first be presented (de sacr. prolog. 2, 3). From this soteriological point of
view are the doctrines of Christianity presented for the purpose
of promoting a right understanding of the Scriptures. Having
first treated of creation, the fall, original sin, etc. (lib. i. pars
1-7), he comes to *reparatio* (p. 8), and presents the work of redemption in harmony with the ideas of Anselm. The great
Physician has appointed the sacraments as means of healing
(c. 12). These therefore constitute the chief part of the work.
The principal sacraments are baptism and the Lord's Supper
(6, 7). But since the sacraments are *sacramenta fidei*, and
since *fides* belongs to salvation (8), part 10 treats of faith ;
then part 11 of natural law, and part 12 of the written
law. The Second Book begins with a discussion of Christology, followed by a section upon the church, the *ecclesiastici
ordines*, etc. The author then turns to the sacraments, "baptism, confirmation, body and blood, and the minor sacraments
and sacred things" (ii. 9), simony, marriage, vows, vices and
virtues ; then treats of confession and repentance and remission
of sins (ii. 14), and finally of the anointing of the sick and of
eschatology. Hugo professes to be guided throughout only by
the authority of the Scriptures (summ. praef.) Only the faith
that has no experience (*experimentum*), and no reason (*ratio*),

---

[1] Vid. also Rocholl, Rupert of Deutz, 1886, p. 189 ff.
[2] He treats first of God, creation, the devil and the fall ; then of the necessity of satisfaction (here using Anselm, vid. I., 8, 16 f., 21), then of Christ's
life and activity, the mission of the Spirit, the church as the mystical, and the
eucharist as the actual body of Christ. The Second Book treats of sin, predestination (9), the origin of the soul, marriage, ranks, and orders (18), the forgiveness of sin through *confessio* and baptism (20), the prophets and the Holy
Scriptures (27), guardian angels and demons, anointing of the sick (30) and
death. In the Third Book he treats exhaustively of blessedness, perdition,
and purgatory (3). Does i. 2 betray an acquaintance with Abelard ?

is meritorious (ib. i. 11, part 59).[1] However little we may be impressed with the systematic arrangement of this great work, it is very instructive to observe the subordination of the entire structure to the sacramental idea and the disregard of the *ratio*. But already in the Sentences of ROBERT PULLUS († ca. 1150, in Mi. 186), which were accepted by Bernard, the *ratio* asserts its claim along with the *auctoritas* (*e. g.*, i. 12 ; iii. 23), and dialectic investigation begins to appear in the midst of the positive presentation of traditional doctrine. The modern spirit carries the day, but it does so only by making concessions to the ancient spirit.

5. This is most plainly evident in the compendium of a disciple of Abelard, which became the manual of dogmatic study in the Middle Ages.[2] PETER THE LOMBARD († 1160 ; according to some authorities, 1164) in his *Quatuor libri sententiarum* furnished a work which, by virtue of its wealth of materials, its adaptation to the times, and the prudent withholding of the author's own opinions, was admirably fitted to become the basis of further dogmatic labors. The author proposes to set forth faith and the sacraments of the church. He rejects the . . . *garruli ratiocinatores* (i. dist. 4 B) and a " new dogma of their own desiring." He says in the prologue : " We have by the aid of God brought together this volume, in which thou wilt find examples and the doctrine of the greater teachers." His book is, accordingly, a great collection of citations from the Fathers. None the less, however, it is dominated by the *ratio* and the dialectic method. Reason is recognized along with authority (*e. g.*, iv. dist. 4 E ; 15 B). Questions are raised, authorities collected, and a result reached by dialectic treatment ; but in the end the author refrains from a positive solution of the problem in hand (*e. g.*, i. dist. 19 O ; iii. d. 7 N). He crosses swords with Abelard, yet constantly reveals the influence of his method and his teaching. In his positive presentations the Lombard frequently, often in the very terms employed, avails himself of the writings of Hugo of St. Victor and Gratian. Between the Sentences of a

---

[1] The genuineness of the Sentences ascribed to Hugo has been assailed by DENIFLE (vid. Arch. f. Litt. u. KG. d. MA. iii. 634 ff.); but see, on the contrary, GIETL, Die Sentenzen Rol. S. xxxiv. ff. A part of Hugo's Sentences have come down to us as the tract. theologic. of Hildebert of Lavardin (Mi. 171, 1067 ff. Col. 1150 closes with the passage found in Sent. iv. 3, Mi. 176, 121). Cf. HAURÉAU, Les oeuvres de Hug. de St. Vict., 1886, p. 71. As to the spuriousness of the seventh tractate (de coniug.), see GIETL, l. c., S. xl. f.

[2] GERHOH opposed the Lombard, and WALTHER OF ST. VICTOR counted him among the ruinous dialecticians. His orthodoxy was even assailed at Synods (Hefele, CG. v.. ed. 2, 616 ff., 719 f).

certain Master Gendulph and those of the Lombard, there is a manifest relationship. Already in the Middle Ages the Lombard was declared to be the borrower—whether justly or not, cannot be certainly known until the appearance of the work of Gendulph, which is still preserved in manuscript. The Lombard closes the first period of Scholasticism. His dogmatic system is that of the future, *i. e.*, Abelard's method combined with the traditional reverence for authorities.

The Lombard was familiar with the dogmatic works of the Damascene and made use of them.[1] The arrangement of the latter had great influence upon him (Vol. I., p. 285 f.), but he labored also with the Augustinian problems, and treated exhaustively the doctrine of the sacraments. His arrangement, briefly stated, was as follows: Book I. treats of God, his existence, trinity, and attributes; Book II., of the creation, man, sin, liberty, and grace; Book III., of Christology, the work of redemption—and, incidentally, whether Christ had faith and hope as well as love—of the cardinal virtues, the gifts of the Holy Ghost, and the commandments; Book IV., of the seven sacraments and eschatology. If we take a general view of this scheme, its similarity to that of the Damascene will be as evident as its variations from the latter are characteristic. Imperfect as is the plan, defective as its development, and loose its structure, there is yet a decided advance upon the dogmatic system of the Damascene. True, we will seek in vain in either for a real comprehension of the gospel. The Augustinian elements are presented with the Semipelagian interpretation of the Middle Ages. Really, the only feature which challenges our admiration is the consistent development of the doctrine of the sacraments, and here Gratian had already led the way. But it was not only the commendable features of the work, but in even greater degree its faults, that won for it the unique historical position which it came to occupy. It has been printed times without number. The Franciscans have furnished a critical edition in the publication of the works of Bonaventura, vid. vols. i., iv., Quarrachi, 1882 ff. Cf. R. SEEBERG, PRE. xi. 630 ff.; O. BALTZER, Die Sentenzen des Petrus Lombardus (in Bonwetsch-Seeberg, Studien zur Gesch. der Theol. u. der Kirche, viii., 1902. PROTOIS, Pierre Lombard, 1881. Vid. also the

---

[1] It is said of him in i. dist. 19 N: " The greatest among the teachers of the Greeks in the book which he wrote concerning the Trinity, and which Pope Eugene (iii. v. 1145-53) caused to be translated." Another translation is mentioned by Duns Scotus in Sent. iii. dist. 21. quaest. unica, § 4. Then follow citations from the De fide ortho, iii. 6, 4. As to the time of composition of the Sentences, we may accept the years between A. D. 1147 and 1150 (vid. Seeberg, PRE. xi., ed. 3, 631).

Sentences (5 books) of PETRUS PICTAVIENSIS († 1205) in Mi. 211).

The separate doctrines of the period under review must now be examined in so far as they exerted an influence in moulding the forms of doctrinal statement. Such are the following : 1. Christology. 2. Doctrine of the Atonement. 3. Berenger's theory of the Lord's Supper and the fixing of the church's doctrine upon that subject. 4. Doctrine of the Sacraments. 5. Conception of the Church. A few further doctrines will be reserved for treatment in another connection, *i. e.*, Sin, Grace, Liberty, Faith, Works. It is proper for us at this point to call attention to the fact, that the real theological work of the church in the Middle Ages was not performed by the masters of dialectics who followed Thomas Aquinas, but was done in the present period by Anselm, Abelard, Hugo, and the Lombard.

§ 47. *Christology of Abelard and the Lombard.   Opposition of Gerhoh.*

BACH, DG. des Mittelalters, ii. 390 ff.   O. BALTZER, Beiträge zur Geschichte des christologischen Dogmas im 11th and 12th centuries (BONWETSCH-SEEBERG, Studien zur Gesch. der Theol. u. der Kirche, iii. 1, 1898).

1. The Christology of Abelard follows the Western, or Augustinian, type (vid. Vol. I., p. 259 f.). Its fixed premise is : One person in two substances, or natures (*una in duabus substantiis vel naturis persona*). In connection with this, it is maintained with special emphasis, that the immutability of God remains unimpaired. The incarnation does not involve for God the introduction of a new element, "but we indicate a certain new effect of his eternal will" (introd. ad theol. iii. 6, p. 1104 f., Mi.). So also the becoming, in his becoming man, is not to be understood in the strict sense of the word. There is in the incarnation no *mutatio* of the divine nature, and the proposition, God is man, can be understood only in a unliteral sense : *nec homo esse proprie dicendus est* (ib., p. 1107 f., 1106).[1] As to the mode of union of the divine and the human natures in Christ, Abelard reproduced the orthodox formulas, but yet gave a peculiar turn to the thought. Christ is the man assumed by the Word (*assumptus a verbo*); this man now fulfills in all things the will of the divinity dwelling within him. "That this assumed man never sought to do anything because he hoped that it would be agreeable to him-

---

[1] Abelard makes the remark that "transfers of names are often made from the whole to the parts, or from the parts to the whole, *e. g.*, when it is said of the Son of God that he is born (exposit. symb., p. 626, Migne); cf. DEUTSCH, Abelard, p. 302 n.

self, but because he believed that it would be pleasing to God (expos. of Rom. v. 15, p. 963).[1] Thus, at this point also, the keen-witted man indicated a needed modification of the church's teaching by locating the union of the divine and human natures in the sphere of the will or person.[2] Yet he might, not without reason, be charged with Nestorianism.

2. The Lombard, of course, adopts the formulas of the church. The second person of the Godhead assumed the impersonal human nature (sent. iii. dist. 5 C): " he assumed the flesh (*carnem*) and soul (*animam*), but not the person (*personam*), of a man.'' But he was greatly exercised over the question, whether the humanity of Jesus was not, after all, to be conceived of as a *persona*, deciding in the negative, because at the time of the assumption body and soul had not yet been combined into one person (*in unam personam*), (iii. d. 5, A, D, E; d. 10 C). "The intellectual development of Jesus was, accordingly, only apparent,'' not, indeed, in himself, but in others (*in aliis*) (iii. d. 13 B). In treating of the question, whether the Son in the incarnation *became* anything, the Lombard betrays his affiliation with Abelard, since he, though only by silence, indicates his preference for the view, that the Logos merely assumed human nature like a garment in order that he might be visible to human eyes. Thus the Logos-person remains " one and the same unchanged '' (iii. d. 6 F; d. 10). God has become man, because he " has a human nature'' (*est habens hominem*, iii. 7 K). Since, in this case, the human nature is not to be conceived as personal, it was inferred by some that " Christ, according to his human nature, is not a person nor anything'' (iii. 10 A, see also GIETL, p. 179), but not a word can be cited from the Lombard in support of this absurd proposition. The view, which was called Nihilianism, was disapproved by Alexander III., A. D. 1163 and 1179.[3] As a consequence of the sharp discrimination between the divinity

---

[1] This way of regarding the relationship became current in the school of Abelard. Christ is " The Word possessing the man'' and "the man possessing the Word'' (*verbum habens hominem* and *homo habens verbum*), (epitome 24 extra Rol. sent., p. 171 f., 180. Omnebene in Denifle, Archiv. i. 466 f.). Roland here further appeals, and rightly, to Augustine (against Gietl, p. 175 n., vid. Aug. in Joh. tr. 19, 15; cf. Hilarius, de trin. x. 22, Mi. 10, 360, supra, p. 28). The view is clearly stated, Epit. 24, p. 1733, Mi.: " Thus that soul was subject to the Word, so that it could give no motion to the body except as far as the Word inspired.'' Vid. also c. 25, *de volunt. assumpti homin.*

[2] The problem of Christology is to be solved, not in the sphere of nature, nor of attributes, but of the person.

[3] Not condemned. Vid. REUTER, Gesch. Alex. iii., vol. iii. 703 ff. HEFELE, v. 618, 719.

5

and humanity, it was held that divine worship (*latria*) was not to
be rendered to the human nature of Christ, but only servitude
(*dulia*) (iii. d. 7), and that the sufferings of Christ were, as to
substance, limited to his human nature (iii. d. 15 D). This
formally orthodox conception of the subject receives its peculiar
coloring on the one hand from the difficulty of a rational combination of the divine and the human, and on the other hand from
the influence of the Augustinian Christology.

3. But contemporaries felt bound to condemn these views as
Rationalism and Adoptionism. The most elaborate presentation
of the subject in opposition was made by GERHOH of Reichersberg. He follows in the path of Cyril. He starts with the concrete God-man, in whom divinity and humanity are united, in
nature as well as in person.[1] This union is not impossible, since
the finite is capable of comprehending the infinite.[2] Gerhoh
proves the importance of his view by its practical bearing
upon the doctrine of salvation. Since God became man, human
nature has been raised to the right hand of God, and a fire has
entered human nature which destroys sin. The God-man is as
man our way and example, and as God the truth and the life
(*e. g.*, de investig. antichr. ii. 1, p. 190 f.). According to
this view, the Nestorianism of the age is a curse. Christ, the
one God-man, is "to be adored with one adoration" (de glor.
et honore fil. hom. 12. 3, Mi. 194. 1114). Another inference
relates to the presence of Christ in the Lord's Supper. Christ
can at the same moment be in a thousand places at once. "And
whence this unless because the same spiritual body has risen
above all limitation of places and times . . . For neither is
Christ, who, just as he wishes, is everywhere, to be thought of
as corporeally in one place, however beautiful or desirable" (de
invest. ii. 51, p. 299 f. Similarly, ARNO of Reichersberg, vid.
Bach, ii. 685). Thus the balder Western theory was in the early
stages of Scholasticism opposed by the ancient Alexandrian
Christology. See the writings of Gerhoh cited p. 60, and Mi.
194. Cf. BACH, DG. ii. 390 ff.

§ 48. *Doctrine of Atonement. Anselm and Abelard.*

1. In his work, *Cur deus homo ?* Anselm made the first attempt
to present in a harmonious and consistent way the doctrine of

---

[1] The one and the same Christ is "at the same time a divine and a human
person," in proof of which it is naively argued that, as when a person becomes good he is not thereby doubled, so also Christ did not duplicate his
person when his divine person became the human person (de investig.
antichr. ii. 40, p. 278).

[2] The perfectly pure humanity in Christ was, as a white cloud, capable of

the work of redemption (salvation). He seeks to prove upon rational grounds the necessity of the incarnation and redemption, although the omnipotence of God could have stood in no need of these (i. 6). Of any claim of the devil upon man, he knows nothing (i. 7; cf. medit. ii.). In addressing himself to the solution of the problem, he proceeds upon the assumption that man can attain salvation only through the forgiveness of sins (i. 10, extr.). Sin consists in the creature's withholding from God the honor which is his due. "He who does not render to God the honor due, robs God of that which is his and dishonors God, and this is to sin" (i. 11). Man has thus violated the obligation laid upon him as a rational being. The expectation sometimes cherished, that the divine mercy will remit sins, cannot be met, because the non-punishment of sin unatoned for would bring disorder into the kingdom of God, "but it is not proper that God should overlook anything disorderly in his kingdom" (i. 12). But order is preserved by righteousness. "Nothing is less to be tolerated in the order of things than that the creature should withhold the honor due to the Creator— should not render that which he withholds" . . . "God therefore preserves nothing with more just cause than the honor of his majesty." From the necessity of maintaining the order of the divine government and the honor of God is deduced the rule : "It is therefore necessary, either that the honor withheld be rendered, or that punishment follow" (i. 13). By either means the divine honor is vindicated—in the one case, since God thus displays himself as the Lord of the rebellious man (i. 14); in the other, in that the guilty one by a willing satisfaction for his offense re-establishes the violated order. Thus the above-cited rule assumes the form : It is necessary that satisfaction or punishment follow every sin (i. 15). But God has not pursued the way of punishment, or man would have gone to ruin and God would not have accomplished his purpose (ii. 4). God chose the way of satisfaction. Since men are to fill up the number of the angels who fell (i. 16 ff.), God cannot accept them as sinners (i. 19). Satisfaction must however be subject to the rule : "It does not suffice merely to restore that which was withheld ; but, for the contumely inflicted, he ought to restore more than he withheld" (i. 11). But since the most trifling sin, as an improper glance, weighs more than the whole world, a satisfaction must be rendered to God which is more than all things outside of God (i. 20 ; ii. 6). And since man dishonored God by sub-

receiving the divine light, and that light was capable of imparting itself to it. Bach, DG. ii. 425.

mitting to the devil, satisfaction in this case must include the conquest of the devil by man—under more trying circumstances (i. 22 f.; ii. 11). As, on the one hand, the satisfaction required is so great and comprehensive, so, on the other hand, man is absolutely incapable of rendering it, for whatever good he may do he is already under obligation to render to God, and it cannot therefore be taken into consideration as *satisfactio* (i. 20). Satisfaction of the character demanded only God can render. But a man must render it, one who is of the same race, in kindredship with humanity (ii. 8): (Unless there be a satisfaction), " which no one except God can render and no one but man owes: it is necessary that the God-man render it." The God-man must do for the honor of God something which he is not already under obligation to do. This cannot be the obedient fulfilling of the will of God, since this every rational creature is under obligation to render. But the free surrender of his infinitely precious life to death will suffice (ii. 11). The infinite value of this life is more than sufficient as a payment of all the sins of the whole world (ii. 14 fin.; 17). Thus the incarnation and sufferings of the God-man are necessary as a satisfaction rendered to the divine honor. Only incidentally does Anselm indicate a connection of Christ with humanity, speaking (ii. 11 fin.; 19 init.) of the instruction and example which Christ was able and desired to give to men; but the two points of view are not expressly and clearly combined. This oversight explains why Anselm is so lacking in clearness when he attempts to show how the result of the work of Christ inures to the benefit of mankind. The Father cannot suffer the *meritum* of Christ to go unrewarded, or he would be either unjust or impotent. Since he cannot give anything to the Son, who needs nothing, the reward accrues to the advantage of those for whom the Son died. " To whom should he more appropriately attribute the fruit and reward of his death than to those for whose salvation . . . he made himself man and to whom by dying . . . he gave an example of dying for righteousness; for in vain will they be imitators of him if they shall not be participants in his merit?" (ii. 20). " Thus the sins of mankind are remitted " (ib.) In this way the divine justice is preserved as well as mercy (ii. 21). And thus also the doctrine of the Scriptures is proved " by reason alone " (*sola ratione*, ii. 23).

This discussion is of importance as the first attempt to present a connected view of the work of Christ.[1] It is a master-

---

[1] Gregory the Great is to be specially mentioned as a forerunner of Anselm (p. 19). As to Augustine, vid. Vol. I., p. 361 n.

piece, because the author really understands the subject under discussion and makes it intelligible to others. The cross of Christ, which was so often mentioned in pretentious phrases, was here recognized in clearly defined language as a means of salvation. Anselm anticipates the scholastic method, combining logical demonstration with juristic principles. The argument is based upon the (Germanic) legal maxim, which dominates the book : punishment or satisfaction (*poena aut satisfactio*).[1] Of special interest is the attempt of Anselm to deduce the divinity of Christ from his work. Whereas the ancient Greek theology, when speaking of the work of Christ in such connections, had in mind his "deifying" activities, Anselm sought to prove the necessity of his divinity from his sufferings and death. At all events, a proper recognition must be given to the effort of Anselm, not simply to accept the divinity of Christ in a merely external way as a dogma, but to understand it in its inner necessity, and none the less to his tact in bringing the matter home to the hearts of his generation by connecting it with the penitential practices of the day. On the other hand, the serious faults of the treatment of the subject are very apparent : (*a*) Anselm recognizes only a legal relationship between God and man—not, indeed, a personal legal relationship, but that of a subject to his legal ruler. (*b*) Redemption is based in a very one-sided way upon the death

---

[1] Cf. CREMER, Die Wurzeln d. anselm. Satisfactionsbegr., Stud. u. Krit., 1880, 7 ff., and ib. 1893, 316 ff. The attempt is here made to trace the dependence of Anselm's theory upon the fundamental principle of the Germanic legal system, *poena aut satisfactio*, showing that the principle of a substitution for penitential penalties was transferred from the penitential discipline (supra, p.45) to the doctrine of the atonement. Cf. BRUNNER, Deutsche Rechtsgesch. i. 163: "The right of challenge belonged only to the offended party or his blood relative. It depended upon the choice of the relative, whether the offender with his relatives should respond to the challenge (*die Feindschaft tragen*), or render the *compositio* fixed by law." The validity of this association of ideas has indeed been recently called in question from the juristic point of view (vid. Von Möller, Stud. u. Krit., 1899, p. 627 ff.). Möller shows that the Germanic penance through money has itself a primitive character, and that the idea of substitution is not embodied in German jurisprudence. According to this, the parallelism, " *aut poena aut satisfactio*," is not specifically German. Nevertheless, the general conception of the subject may be characterized as Germanic. It is only in the light of this system of procedure that we can understand the inner harmony of the transaction as viewed by Anselm, the emphasis laid upon the divine honor, the princely mildness in the conception of God (ii. 16), the substantial character of the service rendered by Christ (cf. WERGELD), the importance attached to the racial-relationship of Christ to mankind, since only a relative could perform specific works of satisfaction. The introduction of the idea of *meritum* is beset with difficulties (cf. Gregory, p. 20). In other connections also Anselm attributes to the sinner the obligation of rendering satisfaction (*debitum satisfaciendi*); vid. De conceptu virginal. 2.

of Christ, the latter being, under the influence of the juristic conception of the *satisfactio*, regarded as a material contribution.
(*c*) The connection between the active life and the sufferings of
Christ is not made clear.   (*d*) The transfer of the benefits of
the work of Christ to the church is not intelligibly stated.   (*e*)
Above all, the change in the attitude of God toward the sinner
which Anselm maintains cannot be made intelligible from a religious point of view by the means which he employs, etc.

Cf. BAUR, D. chr. Lehre v. d. Versöng., p. 155 ff.   HASSE,
Ans. ii. 485 ff.   CREMER, l. c.   RITSCHL, Rechtfertigung, u.
Versönung. i. ed. 2, 33 ff.   HARNACK, iii. 341 ff., as also the
presentation of the subject by Duns Scot. in Sent. iii. dist. 20
qu. un.

2. If we leave out of the account the theory of redemption
as a ransoming from the devil, which Anselm rightly disowned,
we will find in the theological contributions of the West, in addition to the soteriological construction of Anselm, especially
that conception of the divinity of Christ in which he appears as revealing the love of God, and, by teaching and example,
leading to responsive love and piety.   It was perfectly natural
that this view should soon assert itself in opposition to the theory
of Anselm, as it did in the person of Abelard (vid. RITSCHL, l. c.,
i., ed. 2, 48 ff.   SEEBERG, Die Versönungslehre Ab. u. ihre
Bekämpfgung durch Bernh. in Mitteil. u. Nachr. f. d. ev. K. in
Russl. 1888, 121 ff.; also in Thomas. ii., ed. 2, 124 ff.   MOURIER,
Abél. et la rédemption, thèse Montaub. 1892).   In his commentary upon Romans (under Rom. 3. 22 ff.), Abelard develops his doctrine of the atonement.   He, too, rejects the
theory of a meeting of the claims of the devil.   Redemption has
to do only with the elect, over whom the devil never had any power.
Furthermore, the devil cannot by the wrong perpetrated upon
mankind have gained any right over them.   He can be regarded only a jailer and torturer, to whose power God commits
men.   God could before the death of Christ forgive the sins of
men, as he did in the case of the Virgin Mary.   To what end then
did the Son of God take upon himself the burden of his sufferings ?
If Adam's slight offense required so great an atonement, what
atonement will the slaying of Christ demand?   Shall we think
that God was pleased by the death of his Son, that he on account
of this greater sin forgave the less?   And to whom should the
ransom of the blood of Christ be paid ?   Not to the devil ;
hence, to God.   But is it not improper that the blood of the
innocent should be demanded as a ransom ?   Can God have
pleasure in the death of his Son, so that through it he should
be reconciled to the whole world ? (Mi. 178. 833-36).   There-

fore the opinion of Anselm, that God is reconciled by the death of Christ, is disproved.

Abelard's positive statement of the doctrine is as follows: Through the works of the law no one could have become righteous. But in Christ the love of God was made manifest, in that he assumed our nature, and, as our teacher and example, remained faithful unto death. This love of God admonishes us to an answering love toward God and awakens it in us. By virtue of our faith in the love of God made manifest in Christ, we are united with Christ, as with our neighbor, by an indissoluble bond of love. The love thus awakened in our hearts is the ground of the forgiveness of sins, according to Lk. 7. 47. The phrase in Rom. 3. 25, "for the display of his righteousness," Abelard understands as referring to the righteousness imparted to men, that is, "of the love which justifies us before him" (p. 833). Thus we are redeemed from sin and from fear, since Christ works love in us. "Our redemption, therefore, is that supreme love in us, through the sufferings of Christ, which not only liberates from the servitude of sin, but acquires for us the true liberty of the sons of God, so that we fulfill all things from love rather than from fear of him who has shown to us such grace that, as he himself declares, no greater can be conceived" (pp. 836, 832 f.).[1] Side by side with this line of thought we find another. Under Rom. 5. 12 ff., Abelard declares that Christ, in becoming man, subjected himself to the commandment of love for others. This law he fulfilled "both by instructing us and by praying for us." It is in this way, since his prayers must on account of his righteousness be heard, that Christ "supplements from his merits what was lacking in ours" (p. 865). As instruction is still given by Christ (p. 859), so also his mediation through prayer in behalf of his followers continues (cf. serm. 10, p. 449). We are, therefore, redeemed through Christ, "dying once for us and very frequently praying and diligently instructing us" (p. 861).[2] The view of Abelard is thus evidently: God sent his Son to the sinful human race as a revelation of his love, and as a teacher

---

[1] Cf. 836: But to us it seems that by this means we are justified in the blood of Christ and reconciled to God ; that through this particular favor manifested toward us, that his Son assumed our nature and persisted even until death in instructing us both by word and by example, he has very strongly drawn us to himself through love, so that, inflamed by this great benefaction of divine grace, true love now shrinks not from the endurance of anything whatsoever.

[2] The other passages which claim attention in this connection (serm. 5, p. 419 f.; serm. 12, p. 481 ; serm. 10, p. 452, in Com. to Romans, p. 860) all fall into place naturally in this line of thought, as shown in my comments, l. c., p. 131 ff.

and example.   By this means faith and love are aroused in sinful
men.   This love becomes the ground of the forgiveness of their sins.
On the other hand, the love of Christ leads him to continue to
teach men and to intercede for them before God.   Thus their insufficient merits are completed.   But when Abelard now, in
response to the inquiry, why it was the Son and not the Father
who became man, declares that the Son, or the divine Wisdom
(supra, p. 59), became man, in order to instruct us by word
and example (theol. christ. iv. p. 1278 f.   Cf. serm. 5, p. 423),
it would seem that the former line of thought was the dominating one in his theology (cf. SEEBERG, l. c., p. 136 ff.).   This
theory derives from the treasures preserved in the traditional
theology of the church certain views which serve to counterbalance the one-sidedness of Anselm.   It was in harmony
with the medieval form of piety, since it represented the pious
walk of love as the aim of redemption.   There is lacking,
indeed, as in Anselm, the association of the work of Christ with
the institution of the sacraments.   If the latter were, in the
medieval conception, the vehicles of salvation for the regenerate,
then must they be expressly made intelligible as a product of the
work of salvation.   But as, in Abelard's expositions of the subject, no specific importance attached to the death of Christ, he
fell into the error of one-sidedness in the opposite direction.

3. Abelard's doctrine of the atonement was in turn assailed by
ST. BERNARD (vid. ep. 190, and SEEBERG, l. c., p. 143 ff.).   Abelard, he contended, curtails Christianity, making Christ only a
teacher.   In reality, Christ brings the forgiveness of sins and
justification, and releases from the bonds of the devil (7. 17 ; 8.
20).   Just as little as the example of Adam made us sinners does
the example of Christ suffice for our redemption (8. 22 ; 9. 23).
No place, he holds, is reserved for the blood and the cross of
Christ in the system of Abelard, "who attributes everything
pertaining to salvation to devotion (*devotione*), nothing to regeneration, . . . he locates the glory of redemption, . . . not in
the value of the blood, but in its effects in our walk and conversation " (9. 24).   It is certain, indeed, that the example of the
love of Christ is great and important, "but they have no foundation, and hence no tenable position, if the foundation of redemption be wanting. . . . Therefore neither examples of humility
nor proofs of love are anything without the sacrament of redemption " (9. 25).   Instruction (*institutio*) or restoration (*resti-
tutio*), that is the question (9. 23).   Bernard made practical use,
perhaps to a greater extent than Abelard himself, of the latter's
method, maintaining that we should meditate upon the love of
Christ in order to be incited to a responsive love toward him (in

Cant. serm. 16. 5 ; 43. 1-3). He is our teacher and example (ib. serm. 15. 6 ; 43. 4 ; 22. 7 ; 21. 2 ; 61. 7 ; 47. 6 ; 20. 7 ; 24. 8). But the other aspect of the doctrine is also made prominent. The blood of Christ is the "price of our redemption. Unless he had tenderly loved, his majesty would not have sought me in prison. But to affection he joined wisdom, by which he might ensnare the tyrant, and suffering, by which he might appease the offended God the Father" (vid. 20. 2). Bernard constructed no theory ; but the association of the two conceptions—the love of Christ begets love in response, he is teacher and example ; the blood of Christ redeems us from sin, death, and the devil, and effects the reconciliation of the Father—presents the general view of the subject which prevailed in the Middle Ages.

4. The central thought of Abelard was perpetuated in his followers. Thus, the author of the *Epitome* answers the question, *Cur deus homo ?* with a reference to true love and a good example (chap. 23, p. 1731, Mi.). And the Sentences of St. Florian assert that redemption was wrought "in the person of the Son" in order that, as often as we should recall the love which he has shown for us, we might abstain from sin. We have ourselves, "on account of the wonderful love which he has shown toward us," freed ourselves from our subjection to the devil (*Denifle*, archiv. i. 431). But the other contemporary theologians share the attitude of Bernard, *i. e.*, of Anselm. HONORIUS AUGUSTODUNENSIS repeats the thoughts of Anselm (elucidar. i. 8, 16, 17, 21). Hugo likewise reproduces him. It is necessary to "appease God," and this is accomplished by making good the damage (*damnum restaurare*) and making satisfaction for the insult (*de contemptu satisfacere*). This the God-man does. Even if this method of redemption cannot be shown to be necessary, yet it is the most appropriate, inasmuch as the magnitude of our guilt and of the future glory is thus set forth (de sacr. i. 8. 4, 6, 7, 10 ; ii. 1. 6). ROBERT presents both views. Christ has freed us by his sacrifice rendered to God, not to the devil (sent. iv. 14). This was the most appropriate, though not the only possible, way of effecting redemption (iv. 15). It is an appropriate way, because it makes known to us the magnitude of our sin and of the divine love (iv. 13). The work of redemption is, here too, presented under the aspect of instruction and example (iii. 28).

5. PETER LOMBARD, in his discussion of the problem in the 18th and 19th *Distinctions* of his third book, betrays as well his dependence upon Abelard as his correctness from the ecclesiastical point of view. His starting point is the *merit of Christ*. By his pious life Christ merited for himself glorification and free-

dom from suffering (18 A, B). His death occurred therefore "for thee, not for himself " (18 E). And by it he merited for us admittance to paradise and redemption from sin, punishment, and the devil. " Christ the man was a sufficient and perfect hostage," *i. e.*, for our *reconciliatio* (18 E). According to this, it may be asked *how* this deliverance from the devil, sin, and punishment is effected by his death. To this it is replied, first of all, with Abelard, that the death of Christ reveals to us the love of God. " But so great a pledge of love toward us being displayed, we also are moved and inflamed to love God . . . and through this we are justified, *i. e.*, being released from sins are made righteous. *Therefore the death of Christ justifies us, since through it love is excited in our hearts.*" But this occurs also, according to Paul, through faith in the Crucified. When we are thus freed from sin, we become free also from the devil. But this thought is defaced by the reminiscence from an earlier age, that the cross became a mousetrap and the blood a bait for the devil (19 A). The fundamentally Abelardian tendency of the author is revealed also in the remark (19 F), that we are reconciled to God, who has *always* loved us, by the removal of our sins and hostility toward God. Prominence is also given to the objective aspects of redemption. God became man in order to overcome the devil, because a man or an angel might easily have himself fallen into sin (B). It is further held that Christ delivers us from everlasting punishment by remitting our debt (*relaxando debitum*) (C), and also from temporal punishment, which is remitted in baptism and ameliorated in repentance : " For that penalty could not suffice by which the church binds penitents, unless the penalty of Christ, who absolves for us, co-operates" (D). Thus, according to the Lombard : (*a*) Christ has merited deliverance for us through the *meritum* of his death, since the suffering endured by him works for our deliverance. (*b*) He has overcome, *i. e.*, captured the devil. (*c*) His death has awakened us to love and thereby made us righteous and delivered us. Of especial interest for us is the prominent introduction of the conception of the *merit of Christ* and of his endurance of punishment, and we are particularly impressed by the lack of clearness in the adjustment of the ideas presented in their mutual relations. Thus the idea of redemption did not attain a fixed or complete form in the present period, but the component elements were distinctly wrought out.

§ 49. *Berenger of Tours and Doctrine of Lord's Supper.*

SOURCES. BERENGER († 1088) wrote : Epistola ad Adelmannum and Liber de sacra coena adv. Lanfrancum (ed. A. and F. Vischer, 1834). LANFRANC

(† 1089): De corp. et sang. domini adv. Ber. Tur., in Migne 150. 407 ff.
Cf. Sudendorf, Berangarius Tur., 1850. SCHNITZER, Ber. v. Tours, 1890.
DIECKHOFF, Abendmalslehre im Ref.-zeitalter, i. 44 ff. REUTER, Gesch. der
rel. Aufklärung im MA. i. 91 ff. SCHWABE, Studien zur Gesch. des. 2.
Abendmalsstreites, 1886. BACH, DG. i. 364 ff. THOMAS.-SEEBERG, DG. ii.
43 ff.

1. The doctrine of the Lord's Supper received its scholastic
form as a result of the assaults which a forerunner of Scholasticism directed against the (Radbertian) theory which was at the
time gaining general acceptance in the church. BERENGER
taught as follows : Bread and wine become through consecration the body and blood of Christ, *i. e.*, they become a "sacrament of the body and blood of Christ." Bread and wine signify
(*significant*) the body and blood of Christ ; they are a similitude
(*similitudo*), sign (*signum*), figure (*figura*), pledge (*pignus*).
The reality involved comes not into the hand nor into the mouth,
but into the thought (*in cognitionem*, de s. coena, pp. 431, 223,
ep. ad Adelm.). The elements therefore remain what they were;
but something new is added to them through the consecration,
i. e., the spiritual significance, which is apprehended by the
spirit of the communicant (*e. g.*, p. 125). We appropriate the
sufferings and death of Christ, so that they become inwardly
directive for us (p. 194). According to this conception, only
believers receive Christ's body. In support of his view, Berenger
appeals to the Scriptures (Jn. 6), and to the Fathers, especially
Augustine. He regards the teaching of his opponents as silli-
ness (*vecordia*) ; his own, as the only logical and reasonable
view, required by the proposition : Bread and wine are body and
blood—in which the former remains what it is in order that it
may be the latter (pp. 50, 161). Since the body of Christ
exists in heaven impassible and indivisible, how can the attempt
be made to distribute particles of the flesh in the separate com-
munions in various places (p. 199)? And did not Christ promise to give himself entire to believers, not only parts of himself? Finally, the doctrine of his opponents leads, as he
acutely perceives, to two kinds of flesh (*duae carnes*, p. 200), a
heavenly and a sacramental body (cf. DIECKHOFF, p. 50 ff.). To
estimate Berenger correctly, it is necessary to bear constantly in
mind the theory in opposition to which his views were developed, and to remember also that he had a deeper interest than
his opponents in the religious bearing of the subject. He was
concerned to maintain the idea of personal fellowship with Christ.[1]

[1] A group of the followers of Berenger taught that bread and wine indeed
remain after consecration, but that "the body and blood of the Lord are there
contained, truly but latently (*latenter*), and so that they may be understood in
some such way as though I should say that they are impanated (impanari)"

2. The teaching of Berenger awakened opposition from many quarters. The keenness with which he expounded the Lord's Supper as a *figura*, and the rationalistic method of his argument (REUTER, i. 112, 293. BACH, i. 387 ff.) caused alarm. The "multitude of incompetents" were, as he declares, against him, and even Gregory VII. was unable to protect him. He was condemned at Rome and at Vercelli in A. D. 1050. Although the Papal legate, Hildebrand, at Tours (A. D. 1054), declared himself satisfied with the teaching of Berenger, he was still regarded with suspicion. At Rome, A. D. 1059, he was compelled to assent to a confession which presented transubstantiation in the crassest form: "That bread and wine . . . after consecration are not only a sacrament,[1] but also the true body and blood of our Lord Jesus Christ, and are not only in a sacrament, but in truth handled in the hands of priests, broken and torn by the teeth of the faithful" (HEFELE, iv. 826). Having at a later day again advocated his view in France, where he wrote his treatise, *De sacra coena*,[2] he was, in A. D. 1079, again compelled to recant at Rome.[3] But his views still remained unchanged. "In fact, Berenger was an acute theorizer of the Illumination, but a hero in its defense he was not" (REUTER, i. 126).

3. As a result of these controversies, the Lord's Supper became a favorite topic of theological discussion and the doctrine of Radbert—in a grosser form—the doctrine of the church. LANFRANC, HUGO of Langres (de corp. et sang. christi, c. Berenger, Mi. 142. 1325 ff.). ALGER, of Lüttich (de sacramentis corp. et sang. dom., Mi. 180. 743 ff.). DURAND of Troanne (de corp. et sang. dom., Mi. 149. 1375 ff.), and especially GUITMUND of Aversa (de corp. et sang. chr. veritate in euchar., Mi. 149. 1427 ff.) appeared in behalf of either the old or the new teaching. (Cf. Bach, i. 385 ff.). Guitmund (Mi. 149. 1469 ff.) maintains that there is a change (*mutatio*) in the elements, as is proved by the words of institution, which speak of the body of Christ, not figuratively, but substantively (*substantive*). Thus the church had taught from the earliest times (Lanfr. c. 18), and a whole series of miraculous appearances confirm it (Guitm., p.

(Guitmund, De corp. et sang. chr. i.; Mi. 149, 1430; cf. Alger, De sacr. i. 6; Lombard, sent. iv. dist. ii. D).

[1] Thus the word "sacrament" is no longer regarded as satisfactory; and in reality the Lord's Supper was, according to this theory, not a sacrament in the ancient sense of the term. The conception of the mystery had become quite different.

[2] Written A. D. 1077-78. Vid. Bröcking, Ztschr. f. KG. 1892, p. 177 ff.

[3] Great prominence was here given to the identity of the sacramental body with that born of the virgin and dying on the cross. Vid. Lanfr., De corp. et sang. dom. c. 2.

1479 f.; Durand, Mi. 149. 1418). After the transformation, the properties of the elements (color, odor, taste) remain, in order that participants may not be horrified, and in order that believers may receive the fuller rewards of faith (Lanfr. 18). In every wafer the entire body of Christ—yea, more, the entire Christ—is, by virtue of his omnipotence, present (Guitm. 1434, 1480. Alger, i. 15). Anselm of Canterbury, ep. iv. 107, Mi. 159, 255. Believers and unbelievers alike receive him, the latter not with saving efficacy (*non salubri efficientia*) (Lanfr. 20. Alger i. 20). With reference to the question concerning the relation of the sacramental to the historical body, Lanfranc declares : " Both the same body which was received from the Virgin . . . and yet not the same—the former, so far as relates to essence ; the latter, if thou regardest the appearance (*speciem*) of bread and wine " (Lanfr. 18). Alger endeavored to meet the difficulty thus arising by maintaining that Christ can, by virtue of his omnipotence, be even bodily omnipresent : " In heaven and on earth he can be corporeally present everywhere, in whatsoever way it may please him—contrary to the nature of flesh—always the same and entire " (i. 15, Mi. 785). The term *transubstantio* is first found in Petrus Comester († 1179), in the sermons of Hildebert of Lavardin († 1134), sermo 93, Mi. 171. 776 ;[1] cf. PRE. viii., ed. 3, 69.

4. Even in the early days of Scholasticism the theory of transubstantiation was everywhere advocated. Thus in the school of Abelard,[2] we note especially Roland's Sentences, p. 223 ff.,[3] as also passages from the Florian Sentences and Omnebene, as presented by Gietl (in his edition of Roland, pp. 223, 227, 233, 234), and the Epitome, 29. Also in HONORIUS Augustod. (elucid. i. 28, 30). HUGO is particularly clear : " Through the words of consecration the true substance of the bread and the wine is changed (*convertitur*) into the true body and blood of Christ, the appearance only of bread and wine remaining, substance passing over into substance (*substantia in substantiam transeunte*), (de sacr. ii. 8, 9). Since the body of Christ is not

---

[1] But we find already in GERMANUS PARIS, in Martène Thes. v. 95 : "*transformatur.*" Haimo of Halberstadt, supra, p. 39. HONORIUS Augustod. Eucharistion, c. 3 : "*in substantiam translatum*" (5, 9, Mi. 172. 1252, 1255). STEPHAN Augustodunens. (ca. A. D. 1120), De sacr. altaris c. 16 : "*in corpus meum transsubstantiari*" (Mi. 172. 1293). WILHELM of St. Thierry, De corp. et sang. dom. c. 3.

[2] We have no discussion of the Lord's Supper by Abelard himself, but the harmonious utterances of his followers reproduce his view.

[3] Roland here proceeds already in true scholastic fashion. He, like the other followers of Abelard, discusses the question whether a wafer eaten by a mouse is the body of the Lord (ed. Gietl, p. 234).

omnipresent (cf. ii. 2, 13), he is, therefore, only for the time (*ad tempus*), so long as he will, now present in the Supper as once on earth (ii. 8, 13 ; cf. summ. 6. 2).[1] As ROBERT PUL- LUS (sent. viii. 5), so, too, PETER LOMBARD advocated the trans- formation theory : "It is certain that the true body and blood of Christ are upon the altar ; rather that the whole Christ is there under both the forms, and that the substance of the bread is converted into (his) body, and the substance of the wine into (his) blood" (sent. iv. dist. 10 D). The accidents of the earthly substance remain for the familiar reasons (dist. 11 A E). But as to the manner of the *conversio*, he declines to attempt any further explanation (11 C). He regarded the effect of the sac- rament as consisting in the forgiveness of venial sins and in the perfection of virtue (*perfectio virtutis*, dist. 12 G ; infusion of grace, Hugo, sacr. ii. 8. 7). Finally, he considers the Lord's Supper under the aspect of a *sacrifice*. It is a daily sacrifice : "But he is daily immolated in the sacrament, because in the sac- rament there is a commemoration of that which was once done." The sacrifice is repeated on account of our daily sins. "Christ was both once offered and is daily offered ; but then in one way, now in another" (dist. 12 G). This sacrifice represents that upon the cross only as a picture of the latter (Petr. Pictav. sent. v. 13). Here, as often, theory tardily followed praxis.[2]

5. The doctrine thus elaborated by the theologians was exalted to the position of a fixed dogma by Pope Innocent III. at the Fourth Lateran council (A. D. 1215): "The body and blood are truly contained in the sacrament of the altar under the forms (*speciebus*) of bread and wine, the bread transubstantiated into the body and the wine into the blood by divine power. . . . And this sacrament no one can in any case administer except a priest who has been properly ordained" (Mansi, xxii. 982. Vid. already Can. 6 of the Council of Piacenza, A. D. 1095, HEFELE, v. 216).

---

[1] But side by side with these fruitful ideas stands the barren suggestion that, at the first celebration of the Supper, Christ for a time laid aside his mor- tal nature, and as mortal bore his immortal self in his hands : "In that which gave he was mortal, and in that which was given he was immortal ; and, nevertheless, he who as mortal gave, and he who as immortal was given, were not two but one self" (de sacr. ii. 8, 3).

[2] Other theologians of the twelfth century also treated exhaustively of the Lord's Supper. Vid. BACH, i. 392 ff. Special mention may be made of the theory of RUPERT of Deutz. If Radbert understood the transformation of the elements as a creative act, Rupert conceived it as analogous to the incar- nation. As the divine nature assumed the human without destroying it, "so it does not change nor destroy the substance of the bread and wine according to outward appearance subject to the five senses, when by the same Word he unites the latter in the unity (*in unitatem*) of the same body which hung upon the cross" (in Exod. ii. c. 10, Mi. 167, 617 f.).

The "multitude of incompetents," the logic of the theologians, and the hierarchy combined in the production of this dogma. It was a corruption of the church's best possession (*corruptio optimi*); yet it served at least to preserve one article of religion to the Christian world.

§ 50. *Definition of Sacraments. The Seven Sacraments.*

1. The significance of Scholasticism for the History of Doctrines consists chiefly in the establishment of the Catholic doctrine of the sacraments. The decisive steps in this direction also were taken during the present period. The divine efficiency is located in the sacraments, not in the word. Augustine, as we have seen, had a much more profound conception of the significance of the word. The definition of a sacrament was, to begin with, by no means clear, largely because of uncertainty as to the number to be recognized. Bernard still speaks of many, and enumerates ten (Mi. 183, 271 f.). Hugo of St. Victor recognizes among the sacraments the sign of the cross, the invocation of the Trinity (de sacr. i. 9. 6), and all manner of ecclesiastical symbols and formulas (ib. ii. 9). Roland thus designates the incarnation (p. 157). But in the twelfth century the constant tendency was to give prominence to certain definite sacraments. ROBERT (sent. v. 24) contrasts the unrepeatable (baptism, confirmation) and the repeatable (repentance, the Lord's Supper).[1] HUGO treats in his Summa of: baptism, confirmation, the eucharist, extreme unction, marriage, but also repentance (6. 10 ff.; cf. de sacr. ii. 14), and the power of the keys, which is conferred through ordination (6. 14). This is practically a recognition of the number seven. Here, too, the influence of the school of Abelard was felt. The *Epitome* has: baptism, confirmation, the Lord's Supper, extreme unction, marriage (similarly the sentences of ST. FLORIAN, Denifle, archiv. i. 432); repentance is treated of in the third section of the system under the heading of "love" (c. 35 ff.).[2] ROLAND and OMNEBENE, on the other hand (vid. DENIFLE, l. c., p. 467), have: baptism, confirmation, Lord's Supper, repentance, extreme unction, in connection with which the power of the keys and ordination (Rol., p. 267 f.) are spoken of, and marriage. Since Omnebene appears to have made use of Roland (vid. GIETL, Sent. Rol., p. 54), Hugo and Roland must be regarded as the

---

[1] It is not correct in view simply of the incidental utterance at vii. 14 to regard him as including ordination as a fifth sacrament.

[2] Abelard himself appears to have divided in the same way. Vid. Ethica, c. 23.

first to have placed the number of sacraments at seven. But not until we reach Peter Lombard do we find this number clearly and definitely fixed (sent. iv. 2 A).[1] It was even then still customary to speak of baptism and the Lord's Supper as the chief sacraments, which were said to have flowed from the side of Christ (Lomb. sent. iv. 8 A ; Hugo, de sacr. i. 9. 7 ; ii. 2. 1).

2. The old (Angustinian) definition of a sacrament, as the "sign of a sacred reality" (*sacrae rei signum*) or a "visible sign of invisible grace," was still in vogue (Roland, p. 155 ; epit. i.). But the conception was gradually becoming more precise : "God instituted the remedies of the sacraments against the wounds of original and actual sin" (Lomb. iv. 1 A; Hugo, de sacr. i. 8. 12). They are not merely signs, and were instituted not only for the sake of signifying (*significandi gratia*), but for the sake of sanctifying (*sanctificandi gratia*) (ib. B). Faith and repentance are mentioned as the subjective condition required for a profitable reception (ib. iv. 4 B). But no one so clearly expressed the controlling thought as Hugo : "A sacrament is a corporeal or material element, openly (and) sensibly presented, representing by similitude and signifying by institution, and containing by consecration, some invisible and spiritual grace (de sacr. i. 9. 2). Thus, *e. g.*, it may be said of the water of baptism : "By consecration (*sanctificatione*) it contains spiritual grace" (ib. ii. 6. 2). This fully expresses the sacramental conception which dominates the Middle Ages. The sensuous elements somehow contain grace ; with them grace is infused into the recipients. There are, indeed, differences between the various sacraments : "Some, as baptism, offer a remedy for sin and confer assisting grace ; others, as marriage, are for remedy only ; others, as the eucharist and ordination, strengthen us with grace and virtue" (Lomb. iv. 2 A). As we shall have occasion hereafter to discuss each sacrament separately, we here offer but a few brief comments.

3. BAPTISM accomplishes man's renewal by a putting off of vices (*depositio vitium*), and a contribution of virtues (*collatio virtutum*) (Lombard iv. 3 L). Original sin is remitted, because (1) through the grace of baptism the vice of concupiscence is

---

[1] According to the above, my statement in Thomas. DG. ii., ed. 2, 216, must be modified. It is inaccurate to say that the Lombard was led to enumerate seven sacraments by combining those acknowledged by Hugo and Robert (see note 1, p. 79). It seems chronologically impossible that the Lombard should have been influenced by Roland (vid. Gietl, l. c., p. 16 f.). The Lombard started out with the enumeration customary in the school of Abelard (vid. the Epitome), and, following Hugo, added to these repentance and ordination. But this was a natural result of the theological tendencies of the age.

weakened (*debilitatur*), and (2) guilt (*reatus*) is abolished (*aboletur*) in baptism (ib. ii. 32 B).

4. CONFIRMATION works the bestowal of the Holy Spirit for strengthening (ib. iv. 7 A.; infusion of grace, Hugo, de sacr. ii. 7. 1). "Confirmation is as much worthier than baptism, as it is worthier to be made an athlete than to be cured of disease. . . . Wherefore confirmation is now granted only by a bishop" (Robert, sent. v. 23; Hugo, l. c., ii. 7. 4). Roland, on the other hand, declares that baptism is the worthier in its effect, and that confirmation can be called worthier only because it ought to be administered by a worthier person (p. 213).[1]

5. As to the LORD'S SUPPER, see Section 49, 3, 4.

6. We must examine the discussions of REPENTANCE somewhat more fully, since the theologians of the period attempted to justify upon theoretic grounds the advances made in the statement of this doctrine. Here, too, Abelard and his school exerted a great influence. He taught that (1) True repentance consists in contrition of the heart (*contritio cordis*).[2] Where this exists, God grants the forgiveness of sins (ethica 19). Also the Epitome (35) and Roland (sent., pp. 243, 245). Usually *confessio* will immediately follow contrition (eth. 24; epit. 36; cf. praxis, serm. 8 fin.); it is not, however, a condition required for the forgiveness of sins, but "a large part of satisfaction" (eth. 24). (2) But this forgiveness has reference only to the eternal punishments of sin : "For God, when he pardons sin to the penitent, does not remit all penalty to them, but only the eternal" (eth. 19; epit. 35). The "penalty of satisfaction," on the other hand, was held to release from all *temporal* punishment of sin, either in this life or in purgatory. If these works of repentance are not sufficient,[3] God will complete the punishment "by afflicting with purgatorial punishments either in this or in a future life" (expos. in Rom. 2. 4, p. 840; eth. 25; cf. epit. 37; Roland, p. 248). (3) Roland established the necessity of confession and works of satisfaction as follows : "We offend God by thinking wickedly, and we scandalize the church by acting perversely : and just as we offend both, we owe it to both to render satisfaction—to God through contrition of heart, to the church through confession of the mouth and satisfaction by works, if the nature

---

[1] Vid. also Petr. Pict. sent. v. 9 : "Baptism . . . is more useful . . . confirmation better and worthier and more precious, just as water is more useful than wine, but wine more worthy and excellent."

[2] According to the Epitome, 5, it arises "not from fear of punishment, but from love of righteousness."

[3] Observe the keen remarks of Abelard concerning "some of the priests . . . entrapping those under their care in order that for the oblation of coins they may condone or relax the penalties of the enjoined satisfaction" (eth. 35).

of the time demands" (p. 249). Abelard thus deduced the propriety of works of satisfaction from the necessity of expiating the temporal penalties of sin, and by this means solved a problem raised by the new penitential praxis. But, as he made the remission of the eternal penalty dependent solely upon contrition, he increased the difficulty attaching to another problem of the same praxis, *i. e.*, that absolution seems to be robbed of its chief significance and the office of priest becomes merely to give advice in reference to works of satisfaction for temporal penalties.

(*b*) HUGO of St. Victor, controverting the views of Abelard, becomes, upon the doctrine of repentance as elsewhere, the representative of the hierarchical orthodoxy. For him the *confession* is the chief thing in repentance, as was doubtless the case in the prevalent praxis (cf. supra, p. 46). It presupposes contrition and the willingness to render satisfaction (de sacr. ii. 14. 1 ; summa 6. 10). He who will not make confession is a despiser of God (sacr. ii. 14. 8). But repentance is actually secured only through confession *and* satisfaction : " He confesses his sin to the priest, who imposes upon him a just satisfaction, for he is bound to make satisfaction, not according to his judgment, but according to the judgment of the priest, and *then* the priest releases him from the debt of future damnation " (summ. 6. 11).[1] Absolution accordingly follows confession, but it is granted in view of the satisfaction imposed in connection with the former (see foot-note). Hugo thus theoretically comes to the support of the theory of the older penitential praxis (p. 43 f.). Finally, he vigorously assails the opinion that priestly absolution has only an ecclesiastical and declaratory signification. Against this he argues : The sinner is bound in a two-fold way : "by obduration of the mind and by the debt of future damnation." The former, God removes through the grace which works penitence in us, "so that . . . penitent we merit to be absolved from the debt of damnation " (sacr. ii. 4. 8, p. 565). As the resuscitated Lazarus was by the apostles "loosed " from his graveclothes, so the priests, by means of a power divinely conferred, release the penitent sinner from eternal perdition (ib. p. 565 f.,

---

[1] It is necessary to observe that Hugo is aware that forgiveness depends upon *contritio* and *confessio :* " But there is this remedy, that he repent of his fault in his heart and confess it with his mouth ; which, when he has done, he will then no longer be a debtor of damnation" (sacr. ii. 14. 8, p. 567). The passage above cited does not exclude this view, as the "then" refers only to the imposing of the satisfaction. Cf. somewhat later (p. 149). "The priest releases . . . from the debt of future punishment by absolving through the satisfaction which he imposes."

568, and summ. 6. 11).[1]   In this idea lies the dogmatic significance of Hugo's teaching.

(c) ROBERT PULLUS, on the other hand, locates the essence
of the sacrament in absolution and confession.   "Absolution,
which is, in confession, pronounced above the penitent by the
priest, is a sacrament, since it is the sign of a sacred reality "
(sent. vi. 61).   But the priestly absolution is only the announcement of the forgiveness which God, upon the ground of penitence, imparts to the sinner (ib.; likewise Petr. Pict. sent. iii.
16).   But after absolution it remains necessary to perform the
penitential works (vi. 52).   If the latter be not rendered, they
will be completed by the penalties endured in purgatory (ib. and
vii. 1 ; vi. 59).

(a) The Lombard betrays also here the influence of Abelard.
Repentance embraces the usual three parts (sent. iv. 16 A).   It
is a punishment, and, as such, of a satisfactory nature (poena
satisfacit, iv. 14 A, B, 15 C).   The admission (iv. 17 C),
that forgiveness presupposes only contrition and confession before God, is supplemented by the declaration :   " Confession
ought to be offered first to God and then to the priest, nor if
there be opportunity for this can entrance to paradise be otherwise attained (ib. D), since the latter is a kind of punishment
of sin " (ib. F).   This does not involve any divergence from
Abelard.   Confession is then followed by absolution (dist. 18).
The question, whether God or the priest forgives, is thus decided :
" That God only remits and retains sins, and nevertheless he has
conferred upon the church the power of binding and loosing ;
but he absolves in one way and the church in another " (18 E).[2]
The priests decide whether the sinner " is regarded as released
in the view of the church " (F).   But the priests further bind
and loose by imposing and mitigating the satisfaction, and by
the admission to participation in the sacrament of those who
have been purified by rendering the required satisfaction.   But
since this was, in fact, dependent upon absolution, the Lombard
further interprets his language : It is to be observed that, because they bind some with the satisfaction of repentance, by

---

[1] The practical frame of mind which harmonizes with this theory cannot be
better expressed than by Hugo : " How can I know when my repentance is
sufficient (condigna)? Because thou canst not know this, therefore thou hast need
always to repent. Thou canst make satisfaction ; thou canst not do too much. It
is better to do more than less . . . Nevertheless, in order that the conscience of
the sinner may sometimes find comfort, the mode and measure of external repentance has been appointed, so that when the latter has been completed and
perfected, thou mayest begin to have confidence " (de sacr. ii. 14. 2 fin.).

[2] Here, as often in the Lombard, we have the theology of " Yes and No."
In iv. 18 D the views of Hugo and Abelard are cited.

that very act they show such to be released from their sins, since
penitential satisfaction is not imposed upon anyone except such
as the priest judges to be truly penitent.   But upon any other
they do not impose it, and by that very act they adjudge that
his sin is retained by God (G).   A defective exercise of repentance results in the tortures of purgatory : "And they are
more severely punished than if they had fully completed their
repentance here" (20 B).[1] The Lombard advanced the doctrine
of repentance by assuring to absolution, by virtue of its close connection with confession, a secure place in the sacrament, following in this in the footsteps of Hugo.   The dogmatic contribution of the present period lay in the fact that it began to establish a connection between confession and priestly absolution,
and to argue the necessity of satisfaction in view of the temporal, *i. e.*, purgatorial, punishment of sin.

7. The custom of EXTREME UNCTION, based on Jas. 5. 15,
was in the present period included among the sacraments.   It
serves a double purpose : " for the remission of sins and for the
alleviation of bodily infirmity" (Lomb. iv. 23 B ; Hugo, de sacr.
ii. 15. 3).

8. The origin of the sacrament of ORDINATION has been
traced in Vol. I., p. 319 f.   A new motive was furnished
for the careful statement of the doctrine by the enlargement of
the penitential system and the sacramental conception of grace.
The priest receives through ordination the two keys, *discretio* and
potestas.   " In consecration these two are given to all, *i. e.*, the
office of exercising discretion and the office of exercising power."
Binding and loosing are thereby committed to them (Hugo,
summ. 6. 14 ; cf. Roland, p. 264 ff.; Lomb. sent. iv. 19 A-C).
Yet this is only one aspect of the matter.   Through ordination
is imparted a more abundant grace (*amplior gratia*, Lomb. iv.
24 A), as well as a spiritual power (*spiritualis potestas*) and spiritual
character (*character spiritualis*) (ib. K).   To it those are to be
admitted "who may be able worthily to administer the Lord's sacraments " (ib. B). If this applies to all the seven orders (ostiarii,
lectores, exorcistae, acolythi, subdiaconi, diaconi, presbyteri),
it has yet special reference to the priesthood.   "The word priest
(*sacerdos*) is derived from the Greek and Latin, *i. e.*, *sacrum dans*,
or *sacer dux*.   For just as a king (*rex*) receives his title because he
reigns (*a regendo*), so a priest (*sacerdos*) receives his because he
consecrates (*sacrando*), for he consecrates and sanctifies" (ib. J).
In the conception of this sacrament, as elsewhere, no full and

---

[1] The Council at Aachen, A. D. 836, mentions it among the duties of the
spiritual adviser (Mansi, xiv. 681).   *Item*, at Pavia, A. D. 850 (Hefele, iii.
177).   The custom is first met with among the Gnostics (vid. Vol. I., p. 99).

clear conclusion was attained in the present period, but the controlling thought is clear enough. Ordination imparts the spiritual authority to administer the sacraments, and through them to sanctify the laity (cf. Greg. vii., supra, p. 51).

9. The sacrament of Marriage betrays the juristic origin by the form of statement.

It is clear from the evidence above adduced that the theologians of the twelfth century had already clearly wrought out the materializing of grace through the sacraments. The theologians of the thirteenth century inherited, indeed, a number of unsolved—and insoluble—problems, but also the firmly established fundamental conception which proved the regulating force of medieval Christianity, i. e., Grace is the power efficaciously manifested in the sacraments, whose administration belongs by divine right to the priesthood.

§ 51. *Conception of the Church.*

1. The task of the present chapter would be imperfectly performed if we should fail to note the acceptance by the theologians of the day of the conception of the church which Gregory VII. introduced (supra, p. 50 ff.). The utterances of the Scholastics upon the subject are confessedly meagre. Neither the system of Abelard nor that of the Damascenes gave occasion for its discussion. The conception was a self-evident premise, whose application must be made practically by the canonical laws and theologically in the doctrine of the sacraments. It is, therefore, all the more significant that HUGO of St. Victor and ROBERT PULLUS should have expressed themselves plainly upon the subject. We have also discussions of the relation of church and state in the *Polycraticus* of JOHN of Salisbury († 1180, opp. ed. Giles, 5 vols., 1848. Cf. Gennrich, Die Staats- u. Kirchenlehre d. Joh. v. Sal., 1894).[1]

2. Augustine indicates the starting point in his query : "What is the church except the multitude of the believing, the whole number of Christians?" (*multitudo fidelium, universitas christianorum*). (Hugo, de sacr. ii. 2. 2). But inasmuch as, according to this, believers are simply Christians, this definition by no means brings us "to the true Christian idea of the church" (LIEBNER, Hugo v. St. Victor, p. 446); it only declares that the Christian world constitutes the church.[2] The correct

[1] Vid. also HONORIUS Augustod.: "The highest glory composed of the apostolic and the imperial." Mi. 172.

[2] Interesting is the definition of Alanus ab Insul.: "the church is the congregation of believers confessing Christ and the guardian (*subsidium*) of the sacraments" (de articul. cath. fid. iv. in., Mi. 210. 613).

conception is gained by the division of Christians into rulers and subjects (*praelati et subjecti*) (Hugo, ib. ii. 2. 5 ; cf. Robert, sent. vii. 19 : " prelates governing the church "). This formula, frequently occurring already in the writings of Cyprian (Vol. I., p. 180 ff.), signifies that the right side of the church consists of the clergy and the left side of the laity (Hugo, ii. 2. 3). There are, therefore, two lives or two nationalities, of which one ministers to temporal necessities, and the other administers what pertains to the spiritual life (ib. 3). Each of these nationalities is subject to a ruler, *i. e.*, the king and the pope (ib. 4). The nature of the church is in harmony with this idea, and there are discussions of its *orders, sacraments,* and *precepts.* The gradation of the orders is then treated of. The special privileges of bishops, as compared with priests, are placed upon the ground that otherwise the subjects might take advantage of their superiors and forget the obedience due the latter (ib. ii. 3. 12). The archbishops and the four patriarchs stand above the bishops, and over all is the pope (*papa*), *i. e.*, father of fathers, whom, presiding in place of Peter, the chief of the apostles, every ecclesiastical order is bound to obey, who alone has as prerogatives of his high rank the keys of binding and loosing all things upon earth (ii. 3. 5). No one but God may pass judgment upon him (Johann. Polycr. viii. 23 ; opp. iv. 363). According to the interpretation of the Augustinian conception of the two states which dominates Hugo, it is but a self-evident conclusion that the spiritual power stands far above the secular ; it is the older and has authority to institute the latter and sit in judgment upon it (ii. 2. 4 ; cf. Robert, vii. 7): " This sword, therefore, the prince receives from the hand of the church. . . . The prince is, therefore, a minister of the priesthood, and one who exercises that part of the duties of the priests which seems unworthy of the hands of the priesthood " (Polycr. iv. 3 in.).[1] Yet the state is also to be regarded as a divine institution (Polycr., l. c., iv. 1), but must be subject to spiritual (clerical) direction. Robert expresses the opinion that, according to Matt. 22. 21 : " The priesthood is superior to the kingdom in those things which it administers for God, and the kingdom to the priesthood in those things which pertain to the world " (vii. 7, p. 920 f. Cf. Hugo, ii. 2. 6, 7 ; Gregory VII., supra, p. 50). These utterances furnish a precise outline of the Gregorian conception of the

---

[1] John. says : " Therefore the prince is a minister of the public utility and a servant of equity " (Polycr. iii. 2). The gravest crime is tyranny, which is directed "against the very body of justice." From this is deducted the right of slaying tyrants : " To kill a tyrant is not only allowable, but right and just " (ib. iii. 15 ; viii. 17 in., 18 fin.).

church : (1) The clergy are related to the laity as a government to its subjects. (2) This exalted position of the clergy is explained by their authority to dispense the sacraments. (3) The clergy is a graded organism, whose summit is the pope. (4) The secular power is by divine right subject to the spiritual.

CHAPTER II.

DEVELOPMENT OF CHRISTIAN DOCTRINE DURING THE SECOND PERIOD OF SCHOLASTICISM.

§ 52. *Aims of the Church. Religious Life. Efforts at Reform.*

1. We are now standing upon the summit of the Middle Ages. The cornerstone and foundation of their theological structure were laid in the former period, its scope and tendency determined. The decisive work was not done by the leaders of the thirteenth century, but by their forerunners in the eleventh and twelfth centuries. This is true of the theologians no less than of the ecclesiastics and the reformers of the church's devotional life.

We must first of all trace the development of the hierarchical ideas and the religious ideals, whose introduction was noted in Sections 44 and 45. We recall the firm adherence of the later popes to the principles of Gregory VII. INNOCENT III. claims special attention. He held that " The pope is the vicar (*vicarius*) of Christ, placed midway between God and man, beneath God and beyond man, less than God and greater than man, who judges concerning all and is judged by none (Mi. 217. 658). Thus Aristotle once spoke of the genie as " O, thou to men divine ! " (Pol. iii. 13. 8). Not only the whole church, but the whole world, is subject to the sway of the pope : " James, the brother of the Lord . . . left to Peter not only the whole church, but the whole world, to be governed " (registr. ii. 209). Innocent accordingly sought to adminster the affairs of the church as its sole ruler (cf. the confirmation of bishops, their oath of obedience, their being called to the duty of *solicitudo*, appellation to Rome, the Roman land titles, etc. Vid. the bull of Eger., A. D. 1213, in MG. leg. ii. 224 f.; reg. i. 495, 496), and claimed also supremacy over states. As the moon receives its light from the sun, "so the royal power receives the splendor of its dignity from the pontifical authority" (reg. i. 401, Mi. 217. 1180. Cf. Döllinger, Papsttum, p. 401 f.).[1] These ideas were most abruptly expressed in the bull "Unam Sanctam," issued by BONIFACE VIII., A. D. 1302, whose leading declarations are as follows: "We are compelled by the faith to believe . . . one holy catholic church . . . outside of which there is neither salvation nor the remission of sins. . . . In which there is one Lord, one faith, one baptism. . . . Therefore of this one and only church there is one body and one head, not two bodies, as though it were a monster, viz.: Christ and the vicar of Christ, Peter and the successor of Peter. . . . That in this and in its power are two swords, viz., the spiritual and the temporal. . . . Therefore both are in the power of the church, viz., the spiritual and the material sword ; but the latter to be exercised for the church, the former by the church. The one is in the hand of the priest ; the other in the hands of kings and soldiers, but at the command and permission (*ad nutum et patientiam*) of the priest. But it is fitting that sword be under sword, and that the temporal authority be subject to the spiritual. . . . But that the spiritual power excels both in dignity and nobility any earthly power whatsoever. . . . For, truth being the witness, the spiritual power has (the right) to establish the earthly, and, if it have not been good, to judge it. . . . Whosoever, therefore, resists this power thus ordained of God resists the ordinance of God, unless, like Manichaeus, thou dreamest that there are two principles. . . . Moreover, to every human creature we declare, say, define and pronounce, that to be subject to the Roman pontiff is absolutely necessary to salvation" (*de necessitate salutis*).

2. The writings of St. Bernard exerted a profound influence upon the devout speculation of the following period, but it does not lie within the province of the History of Doctrines to follow them in detail.[2] We must not, however, overlook the protest against the secularization of the church which, at the time when the hierarchy was at the summit of its power, and when even ideas of reform had become merely a means for further secularization, was raised by the Brethren of the Poor Life of Christ. The power of love was revealed in Christ to

---

[1] Innocent maintained that the popes had in the time of Charlemagne transplanted the Greek Empire to Germany, and that in consequence the "right and authority of examining the person elected to be king" belonged to them (de elect. 34, in Mirbt, Urkunden, p. 78).

[2] Vid. the mystical writings of HUGO († 1141) and RICHARD († 1173) of St. Victor; also BONAVENTURA, Itenerarium mentis, as presented in detail in THOMASIUS, DG. ii., ed. 2, 272 ff. Religious mysticism is here systematized and developed into a philosophy. These writings may be described as the beginnings of theological ethics.

FRANCIS OF ASSISI. The poor life of Christ overwhelmed his soul; the imitation of Christ became his ideal. He became the knight of "holy poverty." Poverty set him free from the world. As he, surfeited with the old life, shook off his relations with the world, he soon found something else and more than his ideal had promised—he found himself and individuality. He did not clothe his thoughts in doctrinal statements. The gospel frame of mind was everything to him. The love of Christ kept his tears of joy ever flowing and taught him to perform miracles of love. The whole creation testified to him of the love of God, and all living things demanded of him love. "Everything temporal" was to him "only an image," the image of the soul, which belongs to its God. Thus his life, and with it the whole creation, became a hymn of praise to God, for the service of free love. "Praise and bless the Lord, and render thanks, and serve him with grand humility" (Song of the Sun). "My God and all, who art thou, sweetest Lord, my God; and who am I, an insignificant worm, thy servant? Most Holy Lord, that I might love thee!" (opp. Franc. ed. v. d. Burg, 1849, p. 44). "May the glowing and mellifluous power of thy love absorb, I pray, O Lord, my mind from all things which are under heaven, that I may die from love of thy love, who hast deigned to die from love of my love" (ib. p. 43). Or, as Jacopone sings: "Make me truly to rejoice with—cling to Jesuline; then at length shall I have lived." Francis was made the founder of an order by the church of his age. But he sought and attained more than this. He discovered human individuality and opened to it an immediate intercourse with God. It may, perhaps, be correct to say that he wished to make all men monks; but he did certainly also teach the children of men to become Christians and men. As he found God and love in the Jesus of the gospels, and attained liberation from the world in the following of Jesus, he exerted a powerful stimulus upon his contemporaries. He taught the world the directly individual character and the present blessedness of the religious life, and he led men to look upon the world and mankind simply and without dogmatic spectacles. He glorified poverty and love, and taught men to realize in them the sense of personal *perfection*. His influence can be easily traced in the religious life, as well as in the art and literature, of the following period. This is especially true with reference to the direct and loving appreciation of the human life of Jesus which was manifested in the ensuing age. The one precious pearl of the church's tradition was thus found anew. How exhaustively and how lovingly have not BONAVENTURA (Meditationes vitae Chr. opp. vi.) and LUDOLF of Saxony

(Vita Christi ; vid. also De vita et beneficiis salvatoris Jesu Chr. devotissimae meditationes) portrayed the human life of Jesus : " in order that in all places and deeds thou mayest be in mind, as though thou wast present in body " (Bonav. c. 88 fin.). Into the heart of him who thus regards the life of Jesus there comes a certain " familiarity, confidence and love " for the Lord (ib. proem.). He is, as is constantly emphasized, for us the good example : " Who to this end was sent from heaven to us in order that he might go before us in the path of virtues, and might give to us in his example a law of life and discipline " (Ludolf, prolog.). This is the way " to behold him in spirit " (ib. ii. c. 89). Upon this point cf. SEEBERG, in Ztschr. f. K. Wiss., 1888, p. 163 ff. The lessons taught by St. Francis were, thanks to his monastic order and despite it, not lost upon the Christian world. He was a " pioneer of the reformers."

Cf. HASE, Fr. v. Ass. 1856. SABATIER, Leben d. h. Fr., German translation, 1895. HEGLER, Ztschr. f. Theol. u. K. 1896. K. MÜLLER, Die Anfänge des Minoritenordens, etc., 1885. THODE, Fr. v. Ass. u. die Anfänge der Kunst d. Renaissance in Ital., 1885. EHRLE, in Archiv. f. Litt. u. Kirchengesch. d. MA. iii. 554 ff.

3. The reformatory agitations very naturally exerted a marked influence upon the piety of the laity. This was especially true in regard to the penitential brotherhoods attaching themselves to the third order of St. Francis. But it must be acknowledged, further, that among the great masses of the population an external ecclesiastical religious life was perpetuated. The people believed in God, Christ, the Virgin Mary, and the saints. They believed just " what the church believes."[1] " There is a certain body of the faith to which everyone is bound, and which is sufficient for the simple and, perhaps, for all laymen, *i. e.*, that every adult believe that God is, and that he is a rewarder of all the good. Likewise must all believe the other articles *implicitly*, *i. e.*, that everything which the universal church believes is true." These words of Innocent IV.[2] justly represent the actual state of things.[3] Faith in God consists in the conviction that he guides the for-

---

[1] The "faith" is the Apostles' Creed, *e. g.*, Schönbach, Altdeutsche Predigten i. 41, 46. Its essential content is the Trinity, ib. i. 4 ; ii. 115 ; iii. 114. It includes also the divinity of Christ and the seven sacraments (vid. Altdeutsch. Pred. ed. Wackernagel, p. 77 ff.). Vid. also i. 42 : "I believe all that which I as a Christian man ought to believe." Compare Tertullian's "credidi quod credere debui."

[2] Apparatus quinque libror. decretalium i. 1. Vid. RITSCHL, Fides implicita, 1890, p. 10.

[3] It was the law for inquisitors : They have power to excommunicate laymen disputing publicly or privately concerning the Catholic faith (Bernard. Guid. practica inquisit. iv., p. 207).

tunes of men, rewarding the good and punishing the wicked. Christ by his death overcame the devil (*e. g.*, Schönbach, Altdeutsche Predigten, iii. 76, 174). He became for us an example of virtue, humility, and poverty (*ib.* iii. 7, 238, 252, 40). He is "the heavenly King" (*ib.* iii. 6). By faithful fulfillment of one's duties in the church the favor of God may be secured. Then comes the intercession of the saints, particularly of the Virgin Mary,[1] and the protective influence of relics, and, finally, almsgiving. Life should be spent in constant view of the future world. Every act of the Christian has reference to reward or punishment there.[2] And as he thus stands in constant touch with the other world, so its wonders are constantly injected into the present life.[3] The providence of God, implicit faith, Christ the vanquisher of the devil and the teacher of virtue, ecclesiasticism, alms, saints, relics, and the future world constitute the chief articles of practical Christianity.[4] But in the most culti-vated circles of the age even the utterance attributed to Frederick II. concerning the three deceivers (Moses, Jesus, and Mohammed) found currency (cf. REUTER, Gesch. d. rel. Aufklärung. ii. 276 ff.).

Vid. KNOBLER, Kathol. Leben. im MA., 4 vols., 1887 ff. (after Digby). FÖSTE, Zur Theol. d. Berthold v. Regensburg, Zwickauer Gymnasialpr., 1890. SOMMER, Deutsche Frömmigkeit in 13ten Jahrhundert, 1901. MICHAEL, Kulturzustände des deutschen Volkes während des 13ten Jahrhunderts, 1903.

4. The means by which the church influenced the religious life of the age were chiefly the following : (*a*) *Preaching*, which consisted mainly of admonitions to a moral life, in connection with which doctrine was presented only in general outlines, the liturgy explained, and the history of Christ and of the saints repeated.[5]

[1] Adoration of the virgin was rapidly gaining in popularity. So early as A. D. 1140 an attempt was made at Lyons to introduce a festival of the immaculate conception of Mary, but Bernard expressed himself positively against the idea. Vid. ep. 174. For the position of St. Francis, vid. ep. 11, 12, and p. 40 opp. Konrad of Würzb. in the Gold. Schmiede (especially 210, 282, 488, 632 : Du bist ein êwic fundament—dar ûffe de geloube stât—diu Kristenheit gemûret hat—ir zuoversiht ûf dîne kraft, 1374, 1832, 1992. Altd. Predigten, ii. 79 : "Our Lord is the King and our lady the queen."

[2] Two brothers were expelled from that monastery. Unless these two shall have returned, its condition will never be good. One of these is called Give (*Date*); the other Take (*Dabitur*) (Caesar. Heisterb. dial. iv. 68).

[3] Vid. especially the Dialog. miraculorum of Caesar. v. Heisterbach (ed. Strange, 1851), and Peter Venerabil., De miraculis sui temporis, in Migne 189.

[4] There has, strangely enough, been as yet no systematic presentation of the religious ideas of medieval literature, although SCHÖNBACH has made a beginning : Uber Hartmann v. Aue, 1894.

[5] Cf. LINSENMAYER, Gesch. d. Predigt in Deutschl., 1886, p. 157 ff. Vid. SCHÖNBACH, Altdeutsche Predigten, 3 vols., 1886 ff. Honorius Augustodu-

Then came the *Sacrament of Repentance*. The transformation of the church's teaching upon this point in the twelfth century (supra, p. 45) gave rise to a number of new questions, as: Whether contrition is sufficient in itself, or if it requires also confession before a priest. Gratian still leaves it an open question, whether "sins are remitted upon contrition of the heart, not upon confession of the mouth," or whether "without confession no pardon can be merited" (decret. pars ii.; causa 33; quaest. 3 can. 30, 60, 89). The theologians finally decided for the latter position (vid. sub). Inasmuch as confession before the priest thus became the controlling factor of the sacrament,[1] the indicative form of absolution gradually supplanted the optative.[2] It is, therefore, now the church which, through its representatives, grants "absolution from penalty and guilt." Again, it was asked whether all sins, or only mortal sins, were to be confessed. In general, it was the rule that for a multitude of lighter sins the "general repentance in the church, the Lord's Prayer, fasting, and giving alms to the poor, and, at most, the salutary host of the altar," were sufficient (Hugo, de sacr. ii. 14. 1 ; Lombard. sent. iv. dist. 21 E ; an anomymous tract of the twelfth century, de poenit., Migne 213. 880. Cf. Die taegeliche buoze, Schönb. altd. pred. iii. 34). There was a constantly growing tendency to substitute indulgences for the actual performance of works of satisfaction, and for this purpose various occasions and forms were devised (opposing heretics, jubilee celebrations, the building of churches, feasts of dedication, festivals of Corpus Christi and the Virgin Mary, canonization of saints, brotherhoods, garlands, crucifixes, etc. Vid. WILDT in Kirchenlex. i., ed. 2, 102 ff.).[3] Thus repentance came to be regarded as the chief sacrament: "Where there is repentance (*poenitentia*) there is

---

nens., speculum ecclesiae (Mi. 172). ALANUS, ab Insulis, Summa de arte praedicatoria (Mi. 210). GUIBERT, de Novigent., lib. quo ordine sermo fieri debeat (Mi. 156), col. 26: "But by the grace of God faith now becomes known to the hearts of all, and although it has been necessary very often to inculcate and discuss this anew, yet it is none the less proper to speak even much more frequently of those things which may instruct their morals."

[1] The new view appears with peculiar distinctness in Abelard, Serm. 8 fin., and later, *e. g.*, Schönbach, Altd. Pred. iii. 88.

[2] Honorius still differently, Specul. eccl., Mi. 172. 826. The Synod of Treves, A. D. 1227, already employs the formula : *ego te absolvo* (HEFELE, CG. v. 948). Cf. LEA, Hist. of conf. and indulg., i. 482 ff.

[3] Faith in the virtue of indulgences became a special criterion of orthodoxy. The Council of Constance directed that those suspected of heresy should be asked : "Whether they believe that the Roman pontiffs can grant indulgences on reasonable grounds?" Later, pilgrimages were imposed upon those found guilty of heresy. Vid. Bernard. Guid. practica inquis., ii. 5, 11 ; iii. 1, 8, 13, 45 fin. Meanwhile, the further custom of commutation arose (ib. ii. 11, 22), and for money (ii. 23, 25 ; cf. iii. 45, p. 166 f.).

also indulgence. . . . As often, therefore, as God gives to a man repentance, so often does he give also indulgence '' (Mi. 213. 873). The rule, that for public offenses there must be also public repentance, is still maintained in theory,[1] but, in point of fact, public repentance fell rapidly into disuse. Honorius Augustodunensis already speaks of those performing public penance as ridiculing God (*deum irridentes*, elucidar. ii. 18). In the fourteenth century it had been in many places entirely abandoned. '' In such things, according to the course of the present age, there is seen rather a scandal than edification '' (Durand. sent. iv. dist. 14 qu. 4 a. 3). Innocent III. established the following rule at the Fourth Lateran council (A. D. 1215): '' Let every believer of either sex, after arriving at years of discretion, faithfully confess all his sins alone at least once a year to his own priest, and endeavor with all his strength to observe the penance enjoined upon him, receiving at least at Easter the sacrament of the eucharist. . . . Let the priest be discreet and cautious . . . inquiring diligently as to the circumstances of both the sinner and the sin, from which he may prudently judge what counsel he ought to give to him, and what kind of remedy he ought to impose '' (c. 21, Mansi xxii. 1007). This law was very often emphasized and observed (Councils of Narbonne, A. D. 1227, c. 7; Treves, A. D. 1227, c. 3 and 4; Canterbury, A. D. 1236, c. 18; Toulouse, A. D. 1229, c. 13, where confession three times annually is recommended. Vid. HEFELE, v. 943, 946, 1052, 982).

Cf. GOETZ, Revue internat. de theol., 1894, 300 ff., 431 ff., and Ztschr. f. KG. xv. 321 ff. LEA, A history of auric. conf. and indulgences, 3 vols., London, 1896.

(*c*) The other sacraments must also be mentioned. '' And to them (the priests) the almighty God has committed the seven sacraments in order that they might with these sanctify Christians to the world, as they journey into the world, and as they journey through the world, and as they journey out of the world, with holy baptism, and with holy marriage, and with holy confirmation, and with holy confession and penance, and with the holy body of God, and with holy oil, and with the judgments '' (Berthold of Regensb. ed. Pfeiffer, i. 142). We postpone for the present the further discussion of these, stopping at present

---

[1] *E. g.*, Schönbach, altd. pred. i. 36 : '' A man does penance for his sin in two ways, public and private.'' A discrimination was made between *poenitentia publica* and *poenitentia solemnis*. The latter was appointed only by the bishop, was performed with peculiarly solemn ecclesiastical rights, and could not be repeated (Alex. Hal. summ. iv. quaest. 64 ; membr. 2. Thom. summ. iii. suppl. qu. 28, art. 3. Ricardus de Medievilla in sent. iv. dist. 14, princ. 11, quaest. 1 and 2. Cf. MORIN, de discipl. v. 25. 2 ff. HEFELE, vi. 183, 220, 502).

only to observe how closely the whole course of the Christian life has been bound to the church, *i. e.*, the hierarchy.[1]

5. Finally, brief mention must be made of the heretical movements which assumed such large proportions after the eleventh and twelfth centuries. The controlling aim of Western Christianity was the salvation of souls (*salus animarum*) through the church (Vol. I., p. 192). It was in consistency with this that the church of the Middle Ages expressed its characteristic thought in its theory of the church and the sacraments, especially the sacrament of repentance (penance). The same controlling aim, however, gave impulse also to the heresies and schisms (Novatianism and Donatism) which arose in the Eastern church.[2] Even the great heretical groups of the Middle Ages display their essential characteristics, not in their divergence from the accepted theological views, but in the practical desire to secure liberation from sin and, at least in the conception of their leaders, to reinstate the holy apostolic church. We have to do with the two great branches of medieval heresy—the *Cathari* and the *Waldenses*. The Cathari, indeed, in keeping with their Oriental origin, revived, with various modifications, almost the entire Gnostic system, *i. e.*, Manichaeism (two Gods, Gnostic Christology, Dualism, etc.). But even these agitations culminated practically in the ideas that the Romish church was the whore Babylon, her hierarchs Pharisees, and her sacraments invalid ; whereas the Cathari were the only holy church, with the true and holy hierarchy and effectual sacraments. The " good Christians " and "the true imitators of Christ " are persecuted by the church which is not a church ; but only they can actually release from sin by their baptism and penance (*consolamentum, melioramentum*).[3] Among the Waldenses the doctrinal divergence (denial of purgatory, opposition to the worship of saints and images) was given comparatively little prominence ; but practically these preachers of apostolic poverty rejected finally Rome and its hierarchy (especially the Lombards), opposed their own hierarchy to that of Rome, and offered the true sacrament of repentance to their

---

[1] This is the medieval conception of the relation of the individual believer to the church. Vid. Greg. VII., supra, p. 51, and cf. HAGEN, Minnesinger, iii. 11 a : "Wir waeren doch verirret gar, unt heten wir der pfaffen niht." THOM.-SEEBERG, DG. ii., ed. 2, 214.

[2] The same is true of the Reformation.

[3] Vid., *e. g.*, REINER'S Summa de Catharis, etc. (Martene, Thes. anecd. v.), p. 1764 ff., as well as in the original documents, published by DÖLLINGER (Beiträge zur Sektengesch. d. MA., vol. ii.), *e. g.*, pp. 17, 286, 322, 372 (church); 188, 6, 39, 280, 295 (hierarchy); 197, 280, 198, 371, 115, 294 (sacraments); 280, 313, 323, 326, 370, 373 (repentance) ; and also BERNARD. Guid. practica inq. iii. c. 32, 33 ; iv., p. 222 f.; v. i. 1. 2, 3, 4.

followers.[1] Neither of these parties overstepped the bounds of
medieval Christianity. For them, as in the church at large, Christianity consisted in purification through the sacraments, obedience to the hierarchy, and good works in imitation of Christ.
The church, from her point of view, rightly charged upon them :
" they annulled the sacraments and made void the priesthood."[2]
The immediate result of these agitations, constituting as they
did the most energetic assault upon the church since the days of
Gnosticism, was only a more distinct assertion of the ecclesiastical and sacramental character of Christianity (vid. especially
chapters 1, 3, and 21 of the Fourth Lateran Council, HEFELE,
v. 878 ff., 881 f., 888).   More and more, for faith in God was
substituted the summons to " obey the mandates of the Roman
church."[3]   On the other hand, the " free thinking "[4] heresy of
the BEGARDS, which from the middle of the twelfth century was
propagated in Germany, presents—with its pantheism, its ethical indifferentism, and its essentially anti-ecclesiastical spirit[5]—
a symptom of the growing independence and discontent as
against the church and her institutions.   This is true of the rad-
ical Franciscanism[6] and of the apocalyptic speculations (the
" everlasting gospel "), which from the time of Joachim of
Floris († 1202) agitated and disturbed the church.

Vid. original documents in MÖLLER, KG. ii. 374 f., 383 ; Bernardi Gui-
donis practica inquisitionis haereticae pravitatis ed. Douais, 1886 ; cf. CH.
SCHMIDT, Hist. et doctrines de la secte des Cathares ou Albigeois, 2 vols.,
1849.   DÖLLINGER, Beitr. z. Sektengesch d. MA., 2 vols., 1890.   DIECK-
HOFF, Die Wald. im MA., 1851.   K. MÜLLER, die Wald. u. ihre einzeln.
Gruppen, 1886.   PREGER, Abh. d. bayr. Akad. d. Wiss. xiii., xiv.   PREGER,
Gesch. d. deutschen Mystik, i. 207 ff., 461 ff.   REUTER, Gesch. d. rel.
Aufkl. ii. 240 ff.   JUNDT, hist. du panthéisme populaire, 1875.   DENIFLE,
Das ev. aet. in Arch. f. Litt. u. KG. des MA. i. 49 ff.   EHRLE, Die Spiri-
tualen, iii. 553 ff. ; i. 509 ff. ; ii. 108 ff., 249 ff. ; vi. 1 ff.   HAUPT, Ztschr. f.
KG. vii. 372 ff.

[1] In DÖLLINGER, ii., pp. 7, 287, 252, 306, 97, 288 f., 306, 332, 335
(Romish and Waldensian hierarchy); 256, 115 (sacraments); 288, 304, 332
(repentance).   BERNARD. Guid. pract. inq. iii. 34, 35 ; v. 2, 3, 4, 5, 6.
[2] In addition to the above citations, see the collection of SEEBERG-THOMAS.,
DG. ii., p. 192 f.
[3] This is the ever-recurring formula in the renunciation of heresy. Vid.,
e. g., Bernard. pract. inq. iii. 10 f., 14, 46, p. 168 ; v. 6. 2, 4, 8, 11 ; 8. 7, 10.
[4] " Ein fry Geist " (Döllinger, ii. 386).
[5] Vid., e. g., Döllinger, ii. pp. 384, 390 (impeccabiles), 417, 384, 385 f.,
390 (one with God, pares Christo); 390, 416 (omnia sunt deus.   Omnia
fiunt a deo); 386, 387, 403, 416 (ethics); 398, 416, 398 (Christology, purgatory), etc.
[6] The ideals of Francis are by this party exalted as a " fifth gospel," with the
severest criticism of the church, which has become Babylon.   Vid., e. g.,
Bernard. pract. inq. iii. 39 ; v. 4. 5 ; v. 3. 2, 3 ; 8. 1 ff.   As they very
often combined forces with the Begards, they were also designated by the
latter term.

§ 53. *History and Characteristics of the Theology of the Thirteenth Century.*

See Literature cited under Section 46 ; also ETOLE in Archiv. f. Lit. u· KG. des MA. v. 603 ff. THOMAS.-SEEBERG, Die Theologie des Duns Scotus, 1900, p. 600 ff.

1. The history of the church's intellectual life from the middle of the eleventh to the end of the twelfth century may be depicted in the lives of three men—Pope Gregory VII., St. Bernard, and Abelard. The thirteenth century was likewise characterized by the activities of three great leaders—Pope Innocent III. (§ 52, 1), St. Francis (§ 52, 2), and Thomas of Aquino. The hierarchy had reached the zenith of its power, and maintained its position as against the world and the encroachments of heresy. But at the same time there was quietly inaugurated a process of liberation and refinement of the inner life, and, simultaneously, a fuller and more vigorous development of scientific study than had. been previously known in medieval history. Antiquity was again the teacher. Hitherto only the dialectic writings of Aristotle had been known, but to them were now added his metaphysics, physics, psychology, and ethics.[1] Their study was pursued with eager interest and enthusiasm. Men like Albert the Great and Thomas of Aquino wrote commentaries upon them. There was a larger conception of the universe, and the sphere of thought was refined and more accurately delineated. Aristotle, the "*praecursor Christi in naturalibus*," became the regulating authority and the master of method. The effect of the knowledge of Arabic philosophy was also manifest. The materials and the problems of knowledge were rapidly multiplied. But all knowledge must in the end serve the church. Religion and secular learning are not yet separated. Thus the dogmatic systems continue to grow apace, being presented partly in commentaries upon the Sentences of the Lombard, and partly in independent works (summa theologiae).[2] The ancient dialectic method is still followed, and the wider the range of material becomes, the greater

---

[1] Vid. JOURDAIN, Recherches critiques sur l'âge et l'origine des traductions latines d'Aristotele, 1843. HAURÉAU, hist. de la philosophie scolastique, ii. 1. 124 ff. Upon the culture and learning of the age, vid. V. LILIENCRON, der Inhalt d. allg. Bildung in d. Zeit d. Schol. Munich, 1876. Cf. also PRANTL, in d. Sitzungsberichten d. Münch. Akad., 1867, ii., p. 173 ff. In the Chartularium universit. Paris (ed. Denifle), i., p. 644 ff., may be found a very interesting catalogue of the books which the booksellers of Paris had for sale in A. D. 1286, together with the prices.

[2] The title, "Summa," was employed before the times of the Lombard. Vid. DENIFLE, Gesch. d. Univ. i. 46.

becomes the number of proofs and authorities pro and con, the keener the logical distinctions, and the more complicated the lines of dialectical discussion.   Dogmatics again became, as with the Alexandrines of the second and third centuries, a great system of the philosophy of religion, appropriating for itself all the learning of metaphysics and physics, with all the power of the church and her institutions, and which must never lose from beneath it the basis of the rule of faith and the accredited dogmas of the church.   And yet it was evident that the structure thus reared must fall by its own weight, for during the very period of its construction it was discovered that the elements here joined together were mutually irreconcilable.   The secularized church had a secular theology.   Every church is secularized which strives toward any other goal than the kingdom of God and its gospel ; and every theology is secularized which seeks anything further than a true understanding of the gospel.   And both alike must come to grief—missing the gospel, which they do not seek, and no less the world, which they seek.   This was the sad experience of the medieval church.   Boniface VIII. and Duns Scotus were contemporaries.   The pope, who made the most audacious claims for papal supremacy (vid. § 52, 1),[1] aroused against that theory the opposition which has never since been allayed ; and the theologian who carried the dialectic presentation of the doctrines of the church to the greatest extreme himself fell into error as to the proper relation of faith and philosophy, and gave the final occasion for the severance of the two (vid. sub).

2. Taking a general view of the history of Scholasticism in the Second Period, we observe that nearly all the theologians claiming our attention belong to the Dominican or Franciscan orders.   A few remarks may be necessary to insure a proper understanding of the historical course of events before entering upon the study of the leading theologians of the age.   It is well known that there are sharp lines of contrast between the great leaders (as, *e. g.*, Thomas and Duns).   These find their explanation in the historical development.   All received their inspiration from ARISTOTLE.   But this was in the first instance mainly formal.   In the general conceptions of truth, the predominant influence was chiefly that of Platonic-Augustinian Idealism.   The reality of ideas was acknowledged, and they were regarded from a religious point of view.   From Augustine was borrowed the view of the primacy of the will, in contrast

---

[1] The chief thesis of the bull : *Porro subesse*, etc., is taken from the *Opusc. c. error. Graec.* of Thomas.

7

with the reason. The symbolic conception of the sacraments is also Augustinian. Thus, for example, taught both ALEX-ANDER OF HALES and WILLIAM OF AUVERNE. But Aristotelian-ism gained ground. The reality of ideas began to be questioned. The Greek primacy of the intellect was reässerted. Separate doctrines were more and more subdivided and established upon the basis of Aristotelian dialectics. It appeared to be a "modern" theology which was advanced by ALBERT and THOMAS OF AQUINO. The ecclesiastical authorities at first met these "innovations" with severe censure (STEPHEN, bishop of Paris, ROBERT KILWARDBY and JOHN PECKHAM, archbishops of Canterbury, vid. Chartularium universit. Parisiensis, i. 543 ff., 558 ff., 624 ff.). The Thomistic doctrine is charged with con-tradiction of Augustine. On the other hand, ALEXANDER and BONAVENTURA are lauded (chart. univ. Paris. i. 634). This ac-counts in part for the attempt of the older theology to maintain itself, not hesitating to employ to that end the scientific means furnished by the age, *i. e.*, Aristotelianism. In this attempt Henry of Ghent and Bonaventura were most prominent. But English theology brought important aid to this tendency. The traditions of Anselm were still influential in England. To these was added the stimulus of the important work of ROBERT GROSSETESTE of Lincoln († 1253), who combined the Augus-tinian Realism with a Realism of the empirical philosophy as applied to individuals. Such men as RICHARD of Middle-ton, and, above all, DUNS SCOTUS, as also ROGER BACON, con-tinued to promote this tendency. Thus from various directions the older Platonic-Augustinian theology antagonized the modern Aristotelian dialectic theology, but in such a way as to turn the entire scientific fabric of Aristotle against the Aristotelians.

It may be said that the two tendencies which were once repre-sented by the schools of Tours and Bec, and which then in the first period of Scholasticism found in Abelard and Anselm typical representatives, *i. e.*, the rational-critical and the speculative, have been perpetuated to our own times. Upon one side stood the Aristotelians, and upon the other the Platonizing Augustin-ians. Both parties were, indeed, dependent upon the scientific method of Aristotle ; but the differences which separated them may be rightly traced as above to their source.

We now, having gained a general view of the situation, turn to note the individual theological leaders of the period.

At the head of the list we place ALEXANDER OF HALES (*doctor irrefragabilis*, † 1245). He composed a *Summa universae theo-logiae*. He already betrays the influence of Aristotle. In his great work, the problems and methods of the later Scholasticism distinctly appear, and he exerted a controlling influence upon his successors, particularly in the doctrine of the sacraments. The new spirit is yet more plainly manifest in ALBERT THE GREAT (*doctor universalis,* † 1280). It was he who first employed the system of Aristotle in a comprehensive way in the construction of theology. His discussions upon metaphysics and the theory of knowledge moulded the thought of Thomas. Besides his *Paraphrases* upon Aristotle, special mention must be made of his *Commentary* upon the Sentences of the Lombard, a (not completed) *Summa,* and a *Summa de creaturis* (Opp. 21 vols., ed. Jammy, Lyons, 1651; cf. BACH, Alb. Mag. 1881). In the spirit of Albert, his greater disciple, THOMAS OF AQUINO (*angelus ecclesiae,* † 1274) toiled on. In him, with a comprehensive acquaintance with Aristotle and the ecclesiastical writers (the Areopagite now comes into prominence), were combined complete harmony with the teachings of the church and a genuinely religious spirit, together with pre-eminent dialectic talent. Thomas can scarcely be called a man of genius, but he was as great in systematizing as was Albert in collecting. Among his writings we may mention the *Commentary* on the Sentences of the Lombard, the *Summa totius theologiae,* the *Summa de veritate cath. fidei contra gentiles,* the *Expositio symboli,* and the *Compendium theologiae.*[1] The systematic talent of Thomas is at once manifest in the simple arrangement of the material in his *Summa:* (1) Concerning God. (2) Concerning the approach of the rational creature toward God, or of man. (3) Concerning Christ, who, on account of his being man, is for us the way of approach to God—under which he treats of Christ, redemption, and the sacraments. From God—to God—through Christ: this is the simple foundation thought. The work is confessedly unfinished, closing abruptly at the doctrine of repentance; but it was completed by the disciples of Thomas from his other writings. The scheme of the work is as follows: A question (*quaestio*) is stated, and then divided into a series of articles, each of which is presented in an interrogative form. Then, with the introductory formula, *videtur quod non,* a number of arguments, perhaps from the Bible, the Fathers, or Aristotle, are presented against the question. Then are given, introduced by a *sed contra est,* a number of other arguments on the affirmative

---

[1] They were often edited. Before me lies the Antwerp edition of 1612. I cite the Summa from the edition of Fretté and Maré (Paris, 1882 ff.), and the Compendium according to the edition of Albert, 1896. The literature connected with his name is also almost limitless. Vid. WERNER, d. h. Thom., 3 vols. WAGENMANN, PRE. xvi. 570 ff. PORTMANN, Das Syst. d. Summa d. h. Thom., 1894.

side.   Upon this follows the decision, beginning with *Respondeo dicendum*, and usually answering the question in the affirmative. The supposed counter-arguments are then answered under the captions : *Ad primum, Ad secundum, etc., dicendum.*[1]   We cite an illustration.   In the First Part of the *Summa* the fourth article under the eighth question reads : "Whether to be everywhere is an attribute of God ?   (1) It appears that to be everywhere is not an attribute of God."   Four philosophical arguments are adduced for this position, partly from Aristotle, and then are added two arguments from Augustine.   (2) "But upon the opposite side is what Ambrose says."   (3) Here follows the answer : "I reply : It is to be said, that to be everywhere is, from the beginning and essentially, an attribute of God."   Then we have the establishment of this proposition, and afterward a refutation of the six arguments for the negative : "To the first, second, etc., it is to be said."

With Thomas, the Aristotelian, we here mention his friend, the Franciscan, BONAVENTURA (*doctor seraphicus*, † 1274), who, however, in theology maintained the old Augustinian-Platonic theories.   Bonaventura attached a greater importance to the mystic element in his theology than his predecessors.   It is not to be inferred, however, that he pursued with any the less energy the dogmatic and philosophical problems of his age.   He declared himself, in comparison with Alexander, a "poor and lean compiler" (in sent. ii. declaratio).   Of his writings, we mention his *Commentary* upon the Sentences, his dogmatic *Compendium breviloquium*, and also his *Compendium theol. veritatis*, the *Declaratio terminorum theologiae*, and the mystical *Compendium itinerarium mentis in deum.*[2]

3.   Before scrutinizing the teachings of the age upon separate doctrines, it will be well for us to observe, in the case of Thomas, who was so influential in determining them, the method and aim of scholastic labors.   (*a*) The Object of faith, and therefore also of theology, is supernaturally revealed by God.   The necessity of revelation grows out of the fact that human reason cannot by the power of nature recognize the nature of God, *e. g.*, the Trinity.   But revelation extends also to such matters

---

[1] This is the treatment of material introduced by Abelard. The *conclusio* printed in most editions at the end of the separate articles is not the work of Thomas himself.

[2] His works were often edited : At Rome, 1588 ff.; Lyons, 1668 ; Mayence, 1609; Venice, 1751 ; Paris, 1863 f. The best edition is that of Quaracchi, 1882 ff. HEFELE edited the Breviloquium in 1861 and Vicetia in 1881. It is not to be imagined that Thomas held a monopoly of the theological ideas in the thirteenth century. Bonaventura both as a Mystic and as a Scholastic followed to a large extent an independent course.

as reason might perhaps by itself discover, but only slowly and at a late period (c. gentil. i. 3 ff.; summ. i. qu. 1, art. 1). In this way man becomes absolutely certain in regard to his religious knowledge, since it comes "immediately from God through revelation" (summ. i. q. 1, art. 5). But revelation is contained in the Holy Scriptures. Their real author is God : *auctor sacrae scripturae est deus* (ib. i. q. 1, a. 10). By inspiration God imparted to the prophets definite items of knowledge by the way of transient impression (*impressionis transeuntis*). "Prophecy is a certain knowledge (*quaedam cognitio*) impressed upon the mind of a prophet by divine revelation through some manner of instruction (*per modum cujusdam doctrinae*) (cf. ii. ii. q. 171, a. 2, 6 ; q. 172, a. 3).[1] God has immediately confirmed this by the history of the diffusion of faith, as well as by miracles and signs. And thus he shows the teacher of the truth [to be] invisibly inspired (c. gent. i. 6). It must therefore be said : "The authority of those should be believed to whom revelation has been made" (summ. i. q. 1, a. 8). As the Scriptures must, on the one hand, be believed because of their origin, they are, on the other hand, the only sure and binding authority. "But one uses the authorities of the canonical scripture properly and in arguing from necessity ; the authorities of other teachers of the church in arguing, as it were, from one's own resources, but with probability. For our faith rests upon the revelation given to the apostles and prophets who wrote the canonical books, but not upon revelation, if such there were, given to other teachers" (ib.).[2] Thus did Thomas distinctly proclaim the Holy Scriptures as the revelation of God—as the source and absolute authority of Christian doctrine. Precisely so did Bonaventura also teach : "Authority resides primarily in the Holy Scriptures, which have been wholly established (*condita tota*) through the Holy Spirit for the directing of the catholic faith" (brevil. 5. 7). But revelation is a doctrine.[3] Its necessity is deduced, not from the ex-

---

[1] Vid. Bonaventura in hexaëm serm. 9 (opp. i. 35 f.), *e. g.*, it is proper that faith be confirmed, through the inspired word. Albert, summ. i. tract. 1, qu. 4 ; qu. 5, membr. 2. It will be observed how moderate is the view here taken of inspiration. In the earlier Middle Ages Agobard had rejected the view which so represented the matter as though "the Holy Spirit had not only breathed into them (*inspiraverit*) the sense of the preaching and the modes or arguments of their speeches, but had also himself from without formed in the mouths the corporeal words." Speech is not produced in the prophets as in Balaam's ass (vid. adv. Fredegis. 11, Mi. 104. 166).

[2] Cf. Quodlibeta xii. a. 26 : "The sayings of expositors do not carry with them necessity, that it should be necessary to believe them, but alone the canonical scripture which is in the Old and New Testaments."

[3] The proper object of revelation, *i. e.*, of faith, is the "first truth," or God. Everything else (as the divinity of Christ, the sacraments) is entitled to con-

istence of sin, but from the *debilitas* of the human intellect
(summ. 1 q. 1, a. 5). The lines of thought presented in the
Scriptures must, it was further held, be supplemented. It had
been felt necessary in the church from the beginning, that what
was contained in the Scriptures "diffusedly and in various forms
and in some cases obscurely" should be plainly and briefly stated
in a connected way, *i. e.*, "what should be proposed to all to be
believed." This is furnished in the *symbolum apostolorum*, which
contains the essence of the Christian faith (cf. also Bonav.
breviloq. 5. 7). But since the heretics introduced false doctrines, it became necessary to enlarge and explain this symbol,
which was done by the Nicene Creed, the deliverances of other
councils, and the Fathers.[1] The confession is handed down, "as
it were, by the personality of the entire church which is united
through the faith." A "new edition of the symbol . . .
for the shunning of rising errors" may yet be a necessity. Its
preparation, in such case, is within the province of the pope.
The counsel given in 1 Cor. i. 10 cannot be followed "unless a
question of faith arising concerning the faith should be determined by him who presides over the whole church, so that thus
his opinion may be firmly held by the whole church. And therefore a new edition of the symbol pertains to the sole authority of
the supreme pontiff, just as do all other things which pertain to
the whole church, as the assembling of a general council."
Hence: "by whose authority a council is assembled and his
opinion confirmed" (summ. ii. ii. q. 1, a. 9 and 10 ; cf. q. 11,
a. 2). Accordingly, revelation is handed down to the Christian
world in the symbols and the decrees of councils, and by means
of the papal definitions of the faith. It is of course presumed
that these are in harmony with the authority of Scripture ; but
in reality, side by side with the *auctoritas scripturae*, and above
it, stands the *sola auctoritas summi pontificis*.

sideration "in so far as through these things we are directed toward God, and
we assent to them also on account of the divine truth " (summa ii. ii. q. 1, a. 1).
[1] In the twelve, or as the Scholastics commonly enumerate, the fourteen articles, "are contained those things which are chiefly to be believed (Bonav. in
sent. iii., d. 25, a. 1, q. 1). Three symbols are uniformly acknowledged : the
first is for the teaching of the faith ; the second, for the explanation of the
faith ; the third, for the defense of the faith" (Bonav. compend. theol. verit.
v. 21 ; Centiloq., p. 3, sect. 38. Anselm, ep. ii. 41. Alex. Hales, summ.
iv. q. 37, sect. 9, names four, but enumerates only three : Apostolic, Athanasian, Constantinopolitan, for which Bonaventura names the Nicene. So also
Richard, sent. ii. d. 25, principale 2, q. 1 and 2. Duns, sent. i. d. 26, q. 1,
25. Durand, sent. iii. d. 36, q. 2. Biel, iii. 25, qu. un. Duns, sent. iv. d.
43, q. 1. 11). To the Scripture and the symbols are added the works of the
teachers (*documenta doctorum*), of these, Bonaventura enumerates Dionysius,
Gregory of Nazianzen, Gregory of Nyssa, John of Damascus, Basil, Athan-

(*b*) Since revelation cannot be comprehended by the reason, it follows that it must be acccepted *in faith*. This is necessary, if for no other reason, because otherwise the "merit of faith would be made void" (summ. ii. ii. q. 2, a. 9, 10). Thomas was the first to make a careful analysis of the conception of faith (vid. quaestio disputata de fide, opp. viii. 804 ff., and summ. ii. ii. qu. 1 ff.). He starts with the Augustinian formula : "To believe is to think with assent." The *intellectus possibilis*, or thinking faculty, reaches a conclusion in one of two ways, either that the object impresses itself upon this faculty in an intellectual way as true, or that the faculty is, by the will, inclined to assent.[1] "And thus also are we moved to believe things said, in so far as the reward of eternal life is promised to us if we shall believe, and the will is moved by this reward to assent to those things which are said, although the intellect be not moved by anything intellectual (de fide, art. 1, p. 805 b). That the intellect in this way responds to the impulse of the will is explained by the disposition (*habitus*) of faith divinely infused," *i. e.*, infused into the intellect (a. 4, p. 812 ; cf. Heinrich, quodlib. v. q. 21). Faith is thus incited by the will, but it has its seat in the intellect : "The act of faith consists essentially in cognition, and there is its perfection" (a. 2, p. 809). Faith is therefore an incipient knowledge of divine things, "which are above reason," dependent upon practical motives. It is because of the infirmity of human reason that faith alone is possible in this life. But the goal consists "in perfect knowledge (*cognitione*) of God" (a. 10, p. 820 ; c. gent. iii. 25, 8 ; 26 ; 50, 6 ; iv. 42, 1), and "eternal life will afford perfect knowledge of God" (a. 2, p. 807 b).[2] Upon these principles it can be understood, on the one hand, that faith should be regarded as reaching its consummation in knowledge. and, on the other hand, that faith, since it proceeds from the will, should be held to be meritorious (a. 3), and also that it should receive its moral character (*formatio*) from the will or from love: "faith is formed (*informatur*) by love" (a. 5, p. 813 a ; cf. summ. ii. ii. q. 4, a. 5 and 3 ; q. 2, a. 9). The ordinary layman, indeed, never attains an *explicit* faith (*fides explicita*) embracing all the articles of faith. Of him, it is ever to be said : "He believes *implicitly* the separate articles which

asius, Chrysostom, Hilary, Gregory, Augustine, Ambrose, Jerome (in Hexaëm. vid. 9, p. 36 a).

[1] Faith has to do not with the determination of the "simple natures" (*simplex quidditates*) of things, but with the decision. For we believe the true, and we disbelieve the false (de fide, art. 1).

[2] According to Thomas, the will is subordinate to the intellect, and is spiritual only in so far as it is dependent upon the latter (c. gent. iii. 26. 1).

are contained in the faith of the church."[1]   But Thomas not only
expects of all teachers and spiritual advisers an *explicit faith*, but he
requires the same from the laity also in regard to the Trinity, the
incarnation, death, and resurrection of Christ, and "other
(articles) of this kind, concerning which the church appoints
festivals" (a. 11, p. 822).   This demand is in harmony with
the fundamentally intellectualistic tendency of Thomas.   If final
salvation consists in perfect knowledge, then a certain measure
of knowledge must be attained on earth as a preparation (p.
822 a).   Faith is, therefore, an incipient knowledge of divine
revelation begotten of practical motives of the will.   But the
first subjection of man to God is through faith (summ. ii. ii. q.
16, a. 1).

(*c*) This knowledge is just as little as revelation itself contrary
to reason ; it is above reason (de fid. art. 10 ad 7).   It cannot,
therefore, be the province of theology to prove revelation by
human reason (*ratione humana*).   This would be impossible,
since theology deals with super-reasonable articles of faith,
receiving its principles from God (summ. i. q. 1, a. 5 and 8 ;
cf. q. 32, a. 1).   It can only elucidate somewhat by adducing
those things which the philosophers can also recognize.   The
reasons (*rationes*) of theology are not really "*demonstrative*,
but a kind of persuasions, showing that the things which
presented in the faith are not impossible" (ii. ii. q. 1, a. 5).
They are useful also in refuting opponents (c. gent. i. 9).
But inasmuch as theology operates with the principles of revelation, its knowledge is more certain and more important than
that of all other sciences (i. q. 1, a. 2, 5).   This is essentially
the position of Abelard.   The great scholastics did not possess
the naive confidence of Anselm.[2]

(*d*) This was involved in their relation to the question of
Universals.   Thomas here, in almost the same degree as Albert
before him, follows Aristotle or his Arabian interpreters.   Man
by means of the senses perceives external things separately.
"Nothing is in the intellect which was not in the sense"
(summ. i. q. 85, a. 3 and 7).   There thus arises from the
object a particular form (*forma particularis*).   The active

---

[1] Vid. also Bonav. sent. iii., d. 25, a. 1, q. 3. Upon implicit faith, vid. G.
HOFFMAN, Die Lehre von der fides implicita, 1903.

[2] In the question, whether theology is a *scientia speculativa vel practica*,
Albert adopted the latter view (summ. i. tr. 1, q. 3, memb. 3), Thomas
rather the former (summ. i. q. 1, a. 4).   Thomas argues that theology has to
do not so much with human actions as with the "divine affairs."   There is
here no real contradiction, since this theology, which is no more than
advanced knowledge of the faith, is after all in the conception of Thomas
eminently practical.

intellect (*intellectus agens*) then transforms this in the intellectual faculty (*intellectus possibilis*) into an intelligible species (*species intelligibilis*) (ib. i. q. 79, a. 3 ; q. 85, a. 2). The intellect accordingly nas knowledge of the Universal, but by this it is by no means to be understood that it thereby directly cognizes ideas actually existent. The general conception, which we form for ourselves, is always merely derivative, a *universale post rem*. The universal does not exist as a general idea, but it is in the objects of sense under certain criteria (*universale in re*). Its original type is seen in the ideas of God (*universalia ante rem*), which eternally preëxist in him, as the artist's ideas exist in him before he executes his work. Thus Albert held, and before him Avicenna. Accordingly, the essential nature of things is dependent upon the divine idea, and in so far Plato was right (c. gent. iii. 24). Theoretically, this Aristotelian fully accepted the maxim : " For the present we cannot know (*cognoscere*) God except through material effects " (summ. i. q. 86, a. 2, ad. 1). But as revelation now supplies this defect, the knowledge of this world in its connection of causes and effects becomes a knowledge of God (c. gent. iii. 50). The ideas of God are made manifest in the order of the world.

4. Finally, it may be said that Scholasticism has two aspects. It is orthodoxy, maintaining that the teachings of the church, the declarations of the ecclesiastical canon, the customs and practices of the church, are absolutely and unassailably true. That which actually exists is true, if it be ecclesiastically sanctioned. On the other hand, Scholasticism has a rationalizing tendency. That which is unchurchly is condemned as being unreasonable, and that which is churchly proved to be reasonable, by the intricate methods of dialectics.

Here may be mentioned two great philosophic minds. ROGER BACON († 1294) emphasized the importance of experience and the knowledge derived from it.[1] RAYMUNDUS LULLUS († 1315) demanded, in opposition to the Averroistic illumination,[2] that the positions of the Christian faith be strictly proved : " We propose to prove the articles of faith by necessary reasons." The understanding must follow the faith, and thus they must mount together to the knowledge of the truth, even to the mysteries of revelation.[3] The joyous confidence in the omnipotence of logical demonstration, which marked the early days of Scholasticism, is here revived. But from the theological point of

---

[1] Vid. STÖCKL. ii. 916 ff.
[2] Vid. REUTER, Gesch. d. Aufklärung, ii. 148 ff.
[3] Vid. his Ars magna and cf. NEANDER, Denkwürdigkeiten ii. (1846). STÖCKL. ii. 924 ff.

view, HENRY OF GHENT († 1293) is above all worthy of mention as a sturdy representative of the older theology (he wrote
Quodlibeta, a *Commentary* upon the Sentences, and a *Summa
theologiae*).[1]   In his conception of universals, he varies from
Thomas.   He held that the patterns (*exemplaria*) of things
exist as independent entities in God (quodl. vii. q. 1, 2).   Only
grace can secure for us a view of these (summ. i. q. 2).   He
also maintained an actual existence of matter, which Thomas,
following Aristotle, regarded as a mere potency (quodl. i. q. 10).
Body and soul have not one, but two forms (quodl. iii. q. 15).
Everywhere we find the emphasis laid upon perception and the empirical, as well as upon the religiously-colored Realism of ideas.
In this, as his exaltation of the will above the intellect, Henry betrays his Augustinian character, since the activity of the will is
the dominating and controlling factor in life : "The will out-
ranks the intellect " (quodl. i. q. 14 and 16).   As DUNS SCOTUS
establishes the transition to the last phase of the scholastic
theology, we reserve notice of his position for our next chapter.
We can here but refer also to his contemporary, RICHARD OF
MIDDLETON, who likewise strongly emphasized the significance
of the will in God and in man.   (His commentary on the Sentences was printed, Brixen, 1591.)   For the doctrine of Richard,
vid. SEEBERG, Theologie des Duns Scotus, p. 16 ff.

§ 54.   *Doctrine of God and Christology.*

BAUR, Die Lehre v. d. Dreieinigket u. Menschwerdung, ii. 1842.   J. DE-
LITZSCH, Die Gotteslehre d. Thom. v. Aq., 1870.   RITSCHL, Geschichtl.
Stud. z. chr. Lehre v. Gott, in Jarbb. f. deutsche Theol., 1865, 279 ff. WER-
NER, Thomas, ii. 619 ff.   DORNER, Lehre v. d. Person Christi, ii. 399 ff.   H.
SCHULTZ, Lehre v. d. Gottheit Christi, 1881, p. 153 ff.

1. The doctrine of the Nature of God was not wrought
out by the ancient church, as the entire interest of that age was
absorbed by the Trinitarian problem.   The term " person "[2]
was restricted to the Trinitarian formulae, the divine nature
being described as "substance " or " essense " (*substantia,
essentia*).   And even when this was embellished by the predi-
cates of eternity or of superessentiality, it led no further than to

---

[1] Ed. Venet. 1613. Cf. STÖCKL. ii. 739 ff.   WERNER, Heinr. v. Ghent in
Denkschr. d. Wiener Akad. Phil.-hist. cl., vol. 28, p. 97 ff.   SIEBECK,
Ztschr. f. Philos. u. phil. Krit., vol. 93, p. 200 ff.   For his biography, see
EHRLE in Arch. f. Litt. u. KG. d. MA. i. 366 ff.   For his theology, SEE-
BERG, Theol. des Duns Scotus, p. 605-625.

[2] How persistent are such traditional usages is illustrated in the fact that
Jacobi is the first who speaks of the "personal" God.   Vid. EUCKEN,
Grundbegriffe d. Gegenw, ed. 2, p. 269.

the unfruitful abstractions of the conception of God in Greek
philosophy. Even Augustine defined God as Essence (*essentia*),
and the conception of the Areopagite appeared to be in harmony
with this (Vol. I., p. 290 f.).   This theoretical deficiency was
balanced practically by the doctrine of the divine attributes,
and theoretically by the wealth of personal analogies, in the
Augustinian doctrine of the Trinity, and, still more, by the recognition of God as energetic Will in the Augustinian doctrine of
predestination.   But it was a decided step in advance when
Anselm expressly maintained that God is a thinking Spirit
(monolog. 27. 7 ff.).[1]   Here, too, the teaching of Thomas is
very significant.   He also spoke of God in the Grecian way, as
the supremely Existent (*maxime ens*), the prime Mover (*primum movens*), and gave the maxim : " We cannot consider
concerning God how he is, but rather how he is not " (summa
i. q. 2, a. 3 ; q. 2 init.; compend. 3 ff.).   But in such connections he yet always made it clear that the being of God is *thinking* and *willing* (summ. i. q. 19, a. 1).   Since now God is the
prime Mover, it follows that he is " pure Action (*actus purus*)
and without any admixture of potentiality" (comp. 4, 11 ;
summ. q. 3, a. 1, u. 7 ; 9, a. 1 ; q. 25, a. 1).   Since this absolute
Activity is *thinking* and *willing*, it realizes a goal ; and since God
is goodness, His will is moved only by goodness or—it is *love*
(ib. i. q. 19, a. 2 ; q. 20, a. 1).   The final goal commensurate with
God is He himself.   Everything occurring in the world must
therefore be referred to this goal, since God is the originator of
the world.   From this it is inferred that the fundamental relationship of God to the world is that of love for it.   " When anyone
loves another, he wishes good for him, and so treats him as
he would treat himself, doing good to him as to himself " (ib.
q. 20, a. 1, ad 3).   The thought is clear : God always desires
himself as the final goal.   When he establishes the world, he
desires it from eternity as a means to this end ; in other words,
he is related to it as to himself, *i. e.*, he loves it.   This relation
of God to the world is manifested in that he gives to the world
all things needful and preserves it in its course (this constituting
his *justitia* and *veritas ;* q. 21, a. 1 and 2), and, further, in that
he banishes misery.   This is done when deficiencies are overcome "through the perfection of some good."   This is the
mercy of God (ib. a. 3).   God therefore loves the world, since,
in every action of his bearing upon it, righteousness and mercy
are joined together.   This classical argumentation leads to a
religious conception of God which necessarily includes the idea

---

[1] Cf. the Germanic conception of God in *Cur deus homo?*   Esp. ii. 16.

of a personal loving will. But instead of resting content in this positive conception, Thomas displays the influence of the Greek apprehension of God, *e. g.*, regarding redemption as merely the best adapted means "through which he better and more appropriately attains his end" (ib. iii. q. 1, a. 2). Yet we cannot fail to note in Thomas a positive advance in the doctrine concerning God.

2. This cannot be said in regard to the doctrine of the Trinity. When the Lombard, Alexander, and Thomas cite the spiritual functions of man as furnishing analogies, or when Richard of St. Victor (ll. 6 de trin.) endeavors to find the solution of the problem in love, which requires a "mutual love" and a separateness (*alietas*) of the three persons,[1] they do not overstep the suggestions of Augustine. Only one point calls for our attention here. The Lombard (i. dist. 5) discusses the questions, whether the Father begat the divine *essentia*, or whether the latter begat the Son or himself. He answers them all in the negative. Since the divine essence, or nature, "is common to the three persons and entire in each," the Father would otherwise have begotten himself, *i. e.*, the essence by virtue of which he exists, which is impossible. Furthermore, the divine essence would thus seem to be degraded to a mere relationship of the Godhead. The Lombard decides that the divine essence, which is identical in the hypostases, neither begets nor is begotten ; accordingly, the intertrinitarian life is a relation subsisting between the hypostases. These ideas, which were based upon the Augustinian premise of the strict unity of God, were assailed by JOACHIM OF FLORIS († 1202), who maintained that the discrimination of the divine substance from the persons leads to Sabellianism or Arianism. He himself, like the Cappadocians, proceeds upon the supposition of the three persons, who together constitute one entity (*unum*), one substance (*una substantia*), or one God (*unus deus*), but not simply one individual (*unus*). Collective terms, such as "one herd, one populace," are cited in illustration.[2] The Fourth Lateran Council (A. D. 1215) made the following deliverance : "We believe and confess with Peter Lombard, that there is one certain supreme Entity (*una quaedam summa res*), incomprehensible indeed and ineffable, which truly is the Father, the

---

[1] Cf. MEIER, Die Lehre v. d. Trinit. i. 292 ff. Rich. exclaims : "Behold, how easily reason demonstrates that there must be a plurality of persons in the Godhead ! "

[2] Vid. excerpts from Joachim in the Protocol of Anagni (A. D. 1255), DENIFLE, Archiv. i. 136 ff.; cf. also the citation in Duns Scotus, sent. i. d. 5, q. 1. 3.

Son, and the Holy Spirit, three persons at once, and separately either one of them.   And therefore in God there is a trinity alone, not a quaternity ; because anyone of the three persons is that Entity (*res*), viz., substance, essence, or divine nature, which alone is the source of all things, outside of which nothing can be found.   And that Entity is not begetting nor begotten, nor proceeding ; but is the Father who begets, the Son who is begotten, and the Holy Spirit who proceeds, that there may be distinctions in persons and unity in nature (Hefele, v. 880 f.).   The church of the Middle Ages thus explicitly adopted the Augustinian doctrine concerning God.[1]

3. The Christological discussions of the twelfth century were not renewed in the thirteenth.   The great Scholastics present in their Christology merely a reproduction of the traditional dogma, in which we note however the failure to emphasize that contemplation of the Man Jesus which inspired the devotional ardor of the *Imitatio Christi*.   The fundamental ideas are as follows : The Logos-person, or the divine nature, takes the impersonal human nature into unity with itself.   There is not thus originated *one nature*, but the union is consummated in the person.   "The divine nature . . . united to itself human nature, although not to its very self, but in one person " (Bonav. iii. d. 5, a. 1, q. 1).   "The union was made in the person, not in the nature " (Thom. summ. iii. q. 2, a. 2).[2]   It is the entire human nature which is here involved.   But the result is, after all, not a real combination of the two natures.   The union consists in their common relation to the Logos-person.   The union . . . is a certain relation which may be considered between the divine nature and the human, according to which they meet in the one person of the Son of God.   The *unio* is real, not in the divine, but only in the human nature (ib. q. 2, a. 7).   Accordingly, the incarnation is to be understood only relatively : " But God became man in this, that human nature began to be in the suppositum (ὑπόστασις) of the divine nature, which pre-existed from eternity " (ib. q. 16, a. 6, ad 1).   It is the inherited

---

[1] The Lombard introduces into theology the Cappadocian terminology of the Damascene, and argues in its support (i. d. 19 NO).   But it is important to observe that, even in the sermons of the period, the Augustinian type of the doctrine is preserved.   *E. g.*, SCHÖNBACH, Altd. Pred. ii. 115, 110 ; iii. 115 f. (ein warer got in der heiligen drinüsse.   Der vater und sein wistum und sein minne ist neur ein got).

[2] Thomas accurately defined both terms.   "*Natura* signifies essence (*essentia*), or that which anything is, or the quiddity of a species (ib. q. 2, a. 1); *persona*, the rational, individual substance of a nature (*rationalis naturae individua substantia*) (a. 2, after Boethius); *hypostasis* is the same, with the omission of the term *rationalis*."

defect of this Christology, that while divinity and humanity are placed in opposition abstractly, as infinite and finite, the Christ of the Gospels is only depicted in empty words.[1]   This drift is clearly seen in the discussion by Thomas of the question, whether there is only one being (*esse*) in Christ.   He concludes that, as there is no hypostatic being (*Sein*) in the human nature of Christ, the question is to be answered in the affirmative (ib. q. 17, a. 2).   Finally, the *communicatio idiomatum* is taught, as existing between the concretes, God and man : " They are able to impart to one another the attributes (*idiomata communicare*) of that nature according to which they are spoken of in concrete," as though it should be said : God is man and man is God (Bonav. iii. d. 6, a. 1, q. 1 ; Thom. iii. q. 16, a. 5).   Upon the two wills and two " operations," see Thom. iii. q. 18 and 19.   The present period displayed no independent interest in questions of Christology.[2]   Theologians were content to demonstrate the logical consistency of the traditional teaching of the church.   They learned nothing—nor did they forget anything.[3]

§ 55. *The Work of Christ.*

1. The present period produced nothing new touching the work of Christ.   The attempt was made, as had been done by the Lombard, to combine the objective view, in which the ideas of Anselm were accepted, with Abelard's subjective interpretations. Thus ALEXANDER OF HALES, following Anselm, teaches the necessity of the satisfaction which Christ effects through his "merit" (summ. iii. q. 1, memb. 4 ff.; q. 16, memb. 3 and 4). BONAVENTURA states the doctrine with more precision.   The work of *reparatio* includes (1) That men through Christ, especially through his innocent sufferings, learn to know, love, and imitate God, and (2) that their sins be forgiven them through a worthy (*condignam*) satisfaction.   This makes the incarnation a necessity (breviloq. 4. 1. 9).   " Since a simple creature could not make satisfaction for the whole human race, nor would it be proper that a creature of another race be taken for the purpose, it was necessary that the person of the one

---

[1] How little the problem was understood may be gathered from the fact that Thomas declared that it would have been possible for the Logos to assume two human natures at the same time (ib. q. 3, a. 7).

[2] But note the attempt of Bonaventura in the Breviloq. to find for every Christological proposition a ground in the theory of redemption.

[3] Luther charged upon the Scholastics, that they "make a wall between the Son of God and the Son born of the Virgin Mary " (Erl. ed. 47. 362). This charge cannot be brought against Bernard, but it is true as applied to the scholastic method.

rendering satisfaction be God and man " (sent. iii. d. 20, a. 1, q. 3). The satisfaction is effected through the merit of Christ (*pro nobis mereri et satisfacere*, iii. d. 18, a. 2, q. 2) which he won "not only in action but also in suffering " (*passione*) (ib. a. 1, q. 3. ; cf. brevil. 4. 7). Since in the acting and suffering of Christ there was a " *concursus* of both natures " (brevil. 4. 2), there belongs to the " merit of the God-man—the perfection and plenitude of merit " (ib. 4. 7). " But to make satisfaction is to repay the honor due to God " (4. 9). This was done by the sufferings of Christ as the most appropriate means " for placating God " (iii. d. 20, a. 1, q. 5). Herein is displayed the mercy as well as the righteousness of God (ib. a. 1, q. 2). But with this Anselmian view is combined also the Abelardian idea, that the passion commended itself also as the most appropriate means, because suited to arouse men to a responsive love toward God (ib. a. 1, q. 5). It is to be noted, finally, that Bonaventura, by developing the thought of Christ's relation to the church as the Head to the members, brought into view the connection between the work of redemption and the redeemed, as Anselm was never able to do.[1] Reparation is accomplished, accordingly, by remedying, satisfying, and reconciling (*remediando, satisfaciendo, et reconciliando*, brevil. 4. 2).

2. The noteworthy discussion of the subject by Thomas follows the same line. In Christ as the Redeemer, the human nature comes into prominence ; but to it belongs, in consequence of its union with God, a certain divine efficacy (*virtus*) (summ. iii. q. 48, a. 5, ad 1 ; q. 49, a. 1, ad 1 and 2). This is not incomprehensible, when we remember that the human nature exists only in the divine hypostasis (vid. supra). The work of redemption is thus presented : " Inasmuch as he is also man, it is competent for him to unite men to God by exhibiting the precepts and gifts (of God) to men and by making satisfaction and intercession for men to God " (q. 26, a. 2). In this summary the leading ideas of the discussion are clearly expressed. (*a*) In the human nature of Christ dwells the fullness of all grace (ib. q. 7, a. 1). He is now the Head of the human race, or of the church. From the Head, rank (*ordo*), perfection and virtue overflow upon the members (q. 8, a. 1, 3, 4).[2] On the other hand, the *merit* of the Head inures to the good of the members (q. 48, a. 1 ; q. 49, a. 1) in so far as the latter are willing to belong to the Head. " But the members ought to be con-

[1] But see Bernard, De erroribus Abael., 6, 15 : " Therefore the Head made satisfaction for the members."

[2] Thus even the sacraments, " which have their virtue from the passion of of Christ " (q. 49, a. 1 ad 4).

formed to the Head " (q. 49, a. 3, ad 3). This great conception establishes the proposition, that Christ is the new man, who
is the leaven and principle of the new humanity. (*b*) The
work of redemption is accordingly to be considered primarily
from the point of view, that Christ by his teaching, his acts, and
his sufferings became the teacher and pattern of our race. This
applies to his circumcision (q. 37, a. 1), baptism (q. 39, a. 1),
temptation (q. 4, a. 1, 3), teaching : " By associating with men
. . . he manifested to all his divinity by preaching and performing miracles and by dealing innocently and justly among
men" (q. 40, a. 1, ad 1),[1] and miracles (q. 44, a. 3). It can
neither surprise nor give offense to observe that Thomas applies
this thought even to the passion of Christ : " Through this, man
recognizes how much God loves man, and through this he
is provoked to the loving of God, in which the perfection of
human salvation consists," and " through this he has given to
us an example of obedience, humility, constancy, righteousness,
and other virtues" (q. 46, a. 3 ; q. 47, a. 4, ad 2). The love
(*caritas*) to which we thus attain serves also (according to Lk.
7. 47) to secure the forgiveness of sins (q. 49, a. 1). Even
the resurrection, the ascension, and the session at the right hand
of God serve this end of instruction and suggestion, the last-
named particularly because the exalted Saviour " sends forth
thence divine gifts to men " (q. 53, a. 1 ; q. 55, a. 3 ; q.
57, a. 6). This is the first train of thought : The Head of the
church reveals God to his followers, teaches them, incites them
to good, and bestows his gifts upon them. (*c*) Then comes the
question of satisfaction. The absolute necessity of this Thomas
denies. Since there is no one above God, and he is himself the
" supreme and common Good of the whole universe," he could
even without satisfaction forgive sin (q. 46, a. 2, ad 3). But the
method of satisfaction would most clearly give expression to his
righteousness and mercy, and he therefore chose it (ib. a.
1, ad 3). At this point Thomas parts company with the juristic
conception of Anselm, a departure which is further emphasized
by his view that, on account of the greatness of Christ's love and
the value of his life, " the passion of Christ was not only a sufficient, but also a superabundant satisfaction " (q. 48, a. 2 and 4).
Thus both the necessity and the equivalence of the satisfaction
are surrendered. The satisfaction consists in the passion of
Christ. He bore all sufferings " according to genus " (q. 46,
a. 5), and the greatest possible grief (*dolor maximus*, ib. a. 6).

---

[1] Cf. q. 42, a. 2, an intelligent response to the inquiry why Christ did not
become a writer.

But the passion of Christ is now to be regarded, not from a material, but from a personal and ethical point of view. It was an act of obedience and love : " He suffered out of love and obedience " (q. 47, a. 2), since God " inspired in him the will to suffer for us by infusing love into him" (ib. a. 3). His death was also a sacrifice only in so far as it was an act of free will (q. 47, a. 2, ad 2 ; a. 4, ad 2 ; q. 48, a. 3). If the conception of "merit" forms the basis of man's ethical conduct, according to the theory of the Middle Ages, it is but consistent that Thomas should regard the passion also from this point of view : "Through his passion he *merited* salvation, not only for himself but also for his members " (q. 48, a. 1); for suffering is meritorious "only in proportion as anyone voluntarily endures it " (ib. ad. 1). The expiatory sufferings of Christ are the fundamental basis of our salvation. But that the aim of these is for our justification and the imparting of grace, is not clearly set forth by Thomas. As the stimulating influence of Christ continues in his state of exaltation, "his representation from human nature," in heaven is "a kind of intercession (*interpellatio*) for us" (q. 57, a. 6).

(*d*) The Result of the work of redemption, according to Thomas, embraces the following : (1) The forgiveness of sins, and this through the love begotten in us (vid. under (*a*)), as also through *redemtio* (cf. q. 48, a. 4), since the church is "regarded as one person with its Head" (q. 49, a. 1). This applies not only to original, but also to actual sins (ib. a. 5). (2) The releasing from sin releases also from the devil (a. 2). (3) Releasing from the punishment of sin (a. 3.). (4) The sacrifice of Christ has the effect "that on account of this good found in human nature *God is placated* with respect to every offense of the human race " (a. 4). (5) The opening of the door of heaven on account of the release from sin (a. 5). This genuinely scholastic analysis of the material obstructs a clear perception of the view of Thomas. But we may, in harmony with his spirit, condense the statement of his view as follows : Christ, the Head of the church, is by virtue of this position our Redeemer. (1) Because he reveals God to us, and by love overpowers us and incites us to good, and thereby makes us capable of securing the forgiveness of sins. (2) Because he through his passion reconciles God and renders satisfaction to him, and thereby effects for us salvation and immunity from punishment. (3) Because he by both these achievements delivers us from the power of the devil and opens for us the door of heaven. In this classical presentation of the subject are combined the views of Anselm (in a fragmentary way indeed) and

8

of Abelard.[1]   The result is evidently that forgiveness is accomplished and secured in a two-fold way.   The theory before us is the positive resultant of the discussion concerning the nature of redemption.

§ 56. *Doctrines of the Original State and of Sin.*

Cf. SCHWANE, DG. d. mittl. Zeit, p. 334 ff.

1. The doctrine of the original state stands in most intimate relations with that of sin and with the ethical ideal, and hence requires attention at this point.   It receives its peculiar scholastic form from ALEXANDER OF HALES, whose ideas were perpetuated and modified by Bonaventura, Albert, and Thomas. Its chief peculiarity consists in the strict line of discrimination between the original state of the first man and the additional endowment bestowed upon him by grace (Thom. sent. ii. d. 20, q. 2, a. 3).   (*a*) The inborn, natural ethical state (*habitus*) of man is by some described as original righteousness (*justitia originalis*), by which is meant the harmony of the natural powers and the absence of the concupiscence which now hinders their normal exercise (Bonav. sent. ii. d. 19, a. 3, q. 1. Thom. l. c.).[2] (*b*) To this is added the *donum superadditum*, or

---

[1] This varies from the usual presentation of the case.   The observant reader will be disposed to make an attempt to reduce to one the two chief lines of thought—somewhat perhaps in this way : In becoming man, Christ opened to the human race through his life communion with God, and in his passion attested that the men who should follow him should, despite all the sufferings of the world, remain with God ; and by this means he became the ground of the forgiveness of sins, inasmuch as God looks upon the men who follow him and who have begun in the Christian life in the light of Christ's perfection, and, on the ground of his guarantee, passes upon them a different judgment than he has previously done.   I find some approaches to this in Thomas, *e. g.*, q. 49, a. 3, ad 3 : " That the satisfaction of Christ has effect in us *in so far as we are incorporated in him*," and ib. a. 4 : " That on account of this good found in human nature (*i. e.*, the work of Christ) God is placated . . . *in so far as pertains to those who are united* to the *suffering Christ*."   Not the fact that this good is in Christ, but that it is through him in human nature, serves to reconcile God.   But Thomas did not plainly teach this.

[2] Among the natural ethical powers, especial prominence is given to the *synderesis*, or *synteresis*.   According to Alexander, who first treats the conception exhaustively, the Synteresis is the habitual inclination toward the good which, infallible and inalienable, dwells in man, as well in the reason as in the will (ii. q. 76, m. 1, 2, 3). Similarly, Bonav. ii. d. 39, a. 2, q. 1 ff.; vid. also Heinrich, quodl. i. q. 18.   According to Thomas, this has its seat exclusively in the reason : " A natural *habitus* of first principles of action, which are natural principles of natural law.   Which has an immutable rectitude . . . whose office it is to object to evil and incline to good " (Quaest. disp. de synder. a. 1, 2, opp. viii. 836-838. ; cf. sent. i. q. 79, a. 12, 13, and Alb., De homin. tr. 1, q. 69, a. 1).   But the conscience (*conscientia*) embraces the acts which

added gift of grace. According to some theologians, as, *e. g.*, Henry (Quod. lib. ii. q. ii.; vi. q. ii.) this *donum super-additum* is the first ground of the original righteousness of man. It embraces, in the first instance, the separate "graces gratuitously given," such as the bestowal of the sciences, contemplation, and the immortality of the body. Especially was there given to Adam, as the head of the race, such a measure of knowledge, "that he might always be able to instruct and govern others" (Thom. summ. i. q. 94, a. 3). It was a "knowledge (*scientia*) illuminating the intellect for the recognition of itself and its God and this world" (Bonav. brevil. 2. 11).[1] (*c*) Yet the thing of chief importance is other than this, *i. e.*, the gift of "the grace which makes acceptable" (*gratia gratum faciens*). This *supernaturale complementum* (Alex. ii. q. 96, m. 1. Bonav. in sent. ii. d. 29, a. 1, q. 1) consists essentially in an indwelling of God, or an infused love, adapting the feeling (*caritas habilitans affectum*) to the loving of God (Bonav. ii. d. 29, a. 1, q. 1; brevil. 2. 11). This grace which sanctifies man is a "universal habitus, moulding (*informans*) both the subject and all his powers and works, through which God, dwelling in all his saints, infuses the power of meriting eternal life" (Alb. summ. ii. tr. 16, q. 98, m. 4). This habitus of grace has its seat in the "essence of the soul," not in the separate powers (Thom. i. ii. q. 110, a. 4). According to some, this grace is not imparted to man at the moment of his creation, but at some later point of time; and hence man may and should earn it for himself by a merit of fitness (*meritum congrui*) (Alex. summ. ii. q. 96, m. 1. Bonav. sent. ii. d. 29, a. 2, q. 2. Alb. l. c., tr. 14,

---

in any given instance impel to or restrain from action, or pass judgment upon deeds performed, in either case in accordance with the principles contained in the *Synteresis* (Quaest. de consc. a. 1, ib., p. 840). According to Duns, the Synteresis is the "habitus of principles which is always right," resident in the intellect; whereas the conscience is the "personal (*proprius*) habitus of practical decision." If the former, therefore, contains the principles of ethical conduct, the latter applies these principles in any given case to the conduct (Sent. ii. d. 39, q. 2. 4). The conception of the συντήρησις dates back to Jerome (opp. ed. Vallarsi v. 10) and is further defined by him as *scintilla conscientiae*. NITZSCH (Jarbb. f. prot. Theol. 1879, 500 ff.) makes it appear probable that simply συνείδησις stood originally in the passages in Jerome. E. KLOSTERMANN found manuscript evidence of this (Theol. Littztg. 1896, 637. Cf. APPEL, Die Lehre d. Scholastiker v. d. synt. 1891 and Ztschr. f. KG. xiii. 535 ff. SIEBECK, Gesch. d. Psychol. i. 2, p. 445 ff. SEEBERG, Gewissen u. Gewissensbildung, 1896, p. 69 f.).

[1] This *gratia gratis data* is, according to Thomas, given "in order that another may co-operate in securing justification;" the *gratia gratum faciens*, that through it "man may be united to God." The former is therefore a kind of charismatic endowment. Vid. quaest. de grat. a. 5, p. 988; quodlibeta xii. a. 96, ad 1.

q. 90, m. 1). According to others, it is bestowed upon man together with original righteousness at his creation (Thom. in sent. ii. d. 29, q. 1, a. 2). If the motive of this new doctrine be sought, it is not to be found in the desire to minimize the distance separating the natural state from the state of sin. Such was an incidental result, but not the ground upon which the doctrine was based. The motive lay in a certain Augustinian tendency. An end can be attained only by the exercise of powers commensurate. " But eternal life is an end exceeding the proportion of human nature." There is therefore granted to man the supernatural power (*virtus*) commensurate with that high end. The moral life, however, is conceived under the dominating idea of "merit." And, as acts of merit are to be valid before God, they must be wrought by him (vid. Thom. i. ii. q. 109, a. 5 and 6. Bonav. in sent. iii. d. 29, a. 1, q. 1. Alb. ii. tr. 16, q. 98, m. 4). Therefore, man has need of the impelling power of grace before as well as after the fall (Thom. ib. a. 2).

2. Anselm already reproduces the Augustinian conception of sin as a nonentity (*Nichtsein*). Evil is an "absence of good " (dial. de casu diabol. 11). Original sin he defined as "the lack (*nuditas*) of original righteousness, caused by the disobedience of Adam, through which we are all the children of wrath" (de conceptu virginal. 27). The Lombard saw in original sin a tinder (*fomes*) of sin and an infirmity (*languor*) of nature, its essence consisting in concupiscence (ii. d. 30 F, G). The great Scholastics were the first to discuss the subject with thoroughness, and they agreed substantially in their views. Here, as usual, Alexander marked out the path, and Thomas drew the final formulas. (*a*) Alexander presents original sin under the two aspects of guilt (*culpa*) and penalty (*poena*). In the former aspect, it is a lack (*carentia*) of original righteousness; in the latter, concupiscence (ii. q. 122, m. 2, a. 1). This *carentia* embraces the loss both of grace and of the natural original righteousness, or order of nature, since nature has been sorely wounded by sin. " The natural powers in us and in the first man . . . are weakened and wounded and deteriorated" (Bonav. in sent. ii. d. 24, p. 1, a. 1, q. 2). Accordingly, Thomas defines: " Original sin is materially indeed concupiscence; but formally also a defect (*defectus*) of original righteousness" (i. ii. q. 82, a. 3). (*b*) The possibility of the fall lay in the fact that the creature, "made from nothing and defective, was capable of deficiency in acting according to God " (Bonav. brev. 3. 1); its cause was pride (ib. 3. 9). (*c*) Thomas carefully defines the nature of original sin. It is, as sickness in the body,

a state or condition (*habitus*) attaching itself to the soul in its essence (*essentia*), and hence a *languor naturae*. From this follows both that it is a negation and that it is something positive, *i. e.*, the lack of the original righteousness and the "unregulated disposition of parts of the soul" (i. ii. q. 82, a. 1 ; q. 83, a. 2). The powers of the soul are robbed of their original order and wounded, since "ignorance, malice, infirmity, and concupiscence" now rule in it (ib. q. 85, a. 3). But it is not entirely deprived of "the good of nature," for in that case it would have forfeited reason, and would then be no longer capable of sin (ib. a. 2). Man's natural endowment therefore remains, but it has no more the original inclination toward the good (a. 1). But the latter was, properly speaking, not natural. The conflict of the powers was involved from the beginning in their multiplicity (in sent. ii. d. 32, q. 2, a. 1). (*a*) Finally, the question as to the manner in which the sin of Adam and of parents is transferred to their children is answered, on the one hand, by a reference to the peculiar position of Adam as the head of the race (Alex. ii. q. 122, m. 3, a. 3. Thom. ib. q. 81, a. 1), and, further, by dwelling upon the corruption of carnal conception (Alex. ib. m. 4). Here, however, arises the difficulty, that, as the Scholastics regarded Creationism as the only orthodox theory as to the origin of the soul (Lomb. ii. d. 17 C, H. Bonav. sent. ii. d. 18, a. 2, q. 3. Thom. c. gent. ii. 86. Duns, sent. iv. d. 43, q. 3, 21), the connection between the nature corporeally propagated and the soul infused by an immediate creative act of God is not clear. Bonav. finds a medium in an inclination of the soul toward union with the corrupted flesh (ii. d. 31, a. 2, q. 3). According to Thomas, the propagated bodily nature is impure (i. ii. 81, a. 1 ; c. gent. iv. 50. 4). But the nature is propagated by generation, and the existence of the soul begins only in that act ; therefore the soul also becomes sinful (i. ii. q. 83, a. 1). But this does not make the matter clear. (*e*) The results of sin are sin as an evil, *i. e.*, the disordered nature (*natura inordinata*) and the evil itself—above all, the liability to punishment (*reatus poenae*), or eternal death (ib. q. 87 ; q. 109, a. 7). The punishment of children dying unbaptized is light—they are deprived of the vision of God (*visio dei*, Lomb. ii. 33 E). There is, in their case, not a punishment, but a "defect of nature" (Heinr. quodlib. vi. q. 12). Thus they occupy a median position : "They are without any outward or inward affliction," but "are deprived of the vision of God and of corporeal light" (Bonav. ii. d. 33, a. 3, q. 2. Thom. in sent. ii. d. 33, q. 2, a. 2).

If we now review the course of thought thus developed,

we can find no reason to designate it as un-Augustinian. The Scholastics teach, with Augustine, that through sin man has become subject to ignorance, lust, and death. And that they regard the natural endowments of man as only wounded and distorted, not destroyed, by sin, is also not an un-Augustinian idea. Their Semipelagianism first appears when they attempt to describe the state of the natural man in its relation to the workings of grace. We must therefore suspend judgment until we shall have examined their expositions of grace and human freedom.

§ 57. *Doctrine of Grace and Human Freedom.*

1. " Nevertheless, because human nature has not been totally corrupted by sin, *i. e.*, so as to be deprived of the whole good of nature, but is able even in the natural state of corruption by virtue of its nature to do some particular good thing, as to build houses, to plant vineyards, and other things of such sort, it does not follow that everything good is connatural to it so that it is deficient in nothing—just as a sick man may of himself have some motion, but cannot be perfectly moved with the motion of a whole man unless he be made whole by the aid of medicine " (Thom. i. ii. q. 109, a. 2). By this, every thought of self-redemption is excluded. Salvation must be traced back simply to God, for the attainment of the final goal can be secured only through the Prime Mover—in which aspect God is constantly regarded in Thomas's doctrine of grace : " It is necessary that man be turned (*convertatur*) toward the final goal through a motion of the Prime Mover " (ib. q. 109, a. 6 and 9). If this rule prevailed before the fall, it is thoroughly applied only after the fall (ib. a. 2). This metaphysical rule dominates the doctrine of grace as held by Thomas. Christ is mentioned in this connection only incidentally, as the Head of the church, who was alone in a position to merit the " first grace " for others (q. 114, a. 6 ; cf. Bonav. brevil. 5. 1 init.). Thus grace, and with it everything good in man, is referred to the divine agency, as indeed everything is the result of his agency as the Prime Mover.

2. But what is Grace ? The teachers of this period did not, like Abelard and the Lombard (sent. ii. 27 C, F.; iii. 4 a.) understand grace, or love, as being the Holy Ghost himself (*e. g.*, Thom. in sent. i. d. 17, a. 1). The term grace designates, according to Thomas, on the one hand, the gratuitous motion (*motio*) of God (ib. q. 111, a. 2 ; q. 110, a. 2 ; q. 109, a. 9, ad 2); on the other hand—and this is the vitally important signification—the effect of this divine act (*gratia increata* and

creata). " The motion of the moving God is itself an infusion of grace " (q. 113, a. 8). Grace, it is expressly declared, is not only God's " eternal love " and the " remission of sins " (q. 110, a. 1, ad 1 and 3). It is, in essence, " a certain supernatural thing in man, coming into existence from God " (q. 110, a. 1), an infused condition (*habitus infusus*), which is " in the essence of the soul " (q. 109, a. 9; q. 110, a. 4 ; cf. Bonav. sent. ii. d. 26, a. 1, q. 5). " A certain gift of inward condition (*habituale donum*) is infused into the soul by God " (q. 110, a. 2). It is " supernatural qualities," which are infused into the soul, a " higher nature," which pours forth from God as multifarious force into the " powers of the soul " and renews them (q. 110, a. 2, 3, 4, ad 1 ; cf. Bonav. brevil. 5. 3 : *recreare;* and 5. 4, upon the *ramification of grace*). This is the grace which makes acceptable (*gratia gratum faciens*) as a divine inflowing, which makes man like God and pleasing to him (Bonav. ii. d. 26, a. 1, q. 2). This supernatural, ethical nature inborn in man embraces in itself all virtues, including faith, but above all love, which alone, as Bonaventura says, infuses life into " the whole spiritual machine " (i. d. 14, dub. 6. Thom. q. 3, a. 4, ad 3). Such is the conception of grace—the new nature created by God in the depths of the soul, which makes man capable of good. This idea may find support in Augustine, but it has no footing in the gospel nor in the moral conception of religion. Here, on the contrary, lies—the doctrine of the sacraments being most intimately associated with it—the deepest source of the process by which a mechanical character was impressed upon the religious life of the Middle Ages.

3. Since man is involved in this process, however, the old question of the relation of human freedom to grace again comes to view. Thomas maintains that " conversion," it is true, occurs " through the free will (*liberum arbitrium*), but the free will cannot be converted to (turned toward) God, except when God himself converts it to himself (q. 109, a. 6, ad 11). The will is moved by God. Every supposed preparation for the reception of grace rests upon this " free will moved by God " (ib. a. 7 ; q. 112, a. 2, 3, 4). God himself establishes in us the disposition toward the reception of grace (q. 113, a. 7). The divine causality alone effects moral impulses of the will (q. 111, a. 3). If we regard grace from the point of view of God as its cause, we must speak of *operating grace;* but if we think concretely of the resultant movements of the will, of the consent of man, the term *co-operating grace* will find its place (q. 111, a. 2). Thomas is strictly Augustinian in his ideas ; but, since he assigns the chief place to the infused substantial gift of grace instead of to

the personal divine working, it is necessary—in order not to lose
the personal element entirely—to lay the greater emphasis upon
human freedom, especially in connection with the conception of
merit.   This is seen in Bonaventura, who represents the impartation of grace as having for its end to make men capable of
merit (brevil. 5. 2), which can be attained however only
through the free will (sent. ii. d. 26, a. 1, q. 5).   Under this
practical view of the matter, despite all emphasizing of the
agency of grace, the personal agency of man himself constantly
presses to the front, as will hereafter plainly appear.

4. We now turn to the conception of Justification, which in
the thought of the period embraces the following points : "Four
things are required for the justification of the wicked, *i. e.*,
infusion of grace, a movement of the free will toward God
through faith, a movement of the free will toward sin, and
remission of guilt" (Thom. q. 113, a. 6 ; cf. Bonav. brevil. 5.
3 : "infusion of grace, expulsion of guilt, contrition, and a
movement of free will"). It must be clearly understood, first
of all, what is the object in view in justification. But this is
"a certain transmutation of the human soul" (Thom. q. 113, a.
3, ad 3), or, "the reparation (*reparatio*) of the soul is called
justification" (Bonav. iv. d. 17, p. 1, dub. 1). It is therefore not
justification in the Pauline sense, which is here altogether excluded by the conception of grace ; but the making of man
righteous by virtue of the supernatural power infused. A more
precise analysis yields the following : (*a*) If we start with the
conception of grace as a divine agency, the basis of justification
is the "love with which God loves us" and the "not imputing
sin to man," but this presupposes upon his part the infusion of
grace (q. 113, a. 2, resp. u., ad 2). But it is the other conception of
grace which dominates, *i. e.*, a divine agency "by which man
is made worthy of eternal life" (ib.), and it is in accordance
with this that justification is to be understood. Forgiveness is
therefore the object which is attained through this means.
Thomas has indeed also designated forgiveness as the means of
renewal (*transformation*, q. 113, a. 1), but in this case he evidently uses the former term as expressing the purpose of the divine
will which precedes the entire process (vid. SEEBERG, Duns
Scotus, p. 328, n. 1). (*b*) The chief thing practically is the
infusion of grace. Simultaneously with this, the will is moved to
its acceptance. He so infuses the gift of justifying grace, that
he also, at the same time with this, moves the free will to the
accepting of the gift of grace (ib. a. 3). (*c*) The soul thus incited by grace attains first to faith : "The first conversion to
God occurs through faith." This faith (vid. § 53, 3 *b*) would

be incomplete unless it were given form (*informatus*) by love (ib. a. 4). But faith is necessary to justification, because man must by it be convinced that "God is the justifier of men through the mystery of Christ." (*d*) Since, moreover, "justification is a certain movement (*motus*) by which the human mind is moved by God from the state of sin into the state of righteousness," the will must in justification turn away from sin and toward God (a. 5). (*e*) The end in view is the forgiveness of sins, but in such a way that it is dependent upon the infused grace : "For by the selfsame act God both grants grace and remits guilt" (a. 6, ad 2)—for by far the most important thing is the infusion of grace (a. 7). (*f*) Thomas conceives, too, of this act of justification as occurring in a moment, and not as a continuous process. "The infusion of grace occurs in an instant without progression," and hence also : "the justification of the wicked by God occurs in an instant" (a. 7).[1] Accordingly, the succession noted in the various stages of the process is to be regarded, not as temporal, but as logical. (*g*) An actual certainty of salvation is thus not attainable, since the grace of God lies beyond the sphere of human perception, and hence the possession of grace can only be inferred *conjecturaliter* from good works (q. 112, a. 5). Justification is therefore the making of a sinner righteous. Since sin in him has been in principle destroyed, God regards it as remitted.

5. This view of righteousness makes its aim not a personal intercourse with God, but the making of man capable of performing good works. Hence it is not faith which holds the central place in the religious life, but love and good works. Perfect faith, or the *fides formata*, is bound up with love in one : "An act of faith is perfected and given form (*perficitur ac formatur*) through love" (summ. ii. ii. q. 4, a. 3). But love tests itself in good works, which are good in so far as they are in accordance with the divine commandments. Thus man becomes righteous. "But righteousness consists in conforming one's self to the rules of the law." For this purpose God gave the law, that we might obey it (Bonav. brevil. 5. 9). But, at the same time, there is assured to man by the obligatory law the possibility of meritorious conduct (Bonav. sent. iii. d. 37, a. 1, q. 1). This brings us to the important conception of "merit." As it was the aim of the bestowal of grace upon our first parents in paradise to enable

---

[1] This is established by careful argumentation in the Quaest. disp. de justif. a. 9: Whenever between "the two termini of a change" there is neither a local movement nor a quantitative decrease and increase, "then the transition from one terminus to the other is not (accomplished) in time, but in an instant."

them to perform meritorious deeds, this is likewise the chief object of the grace infused into the sinner. " But grace is properly called an assistance divinely given toward meriting, . . . for it, as the root of meriting, antedates all merits " (Brevil. 5. 2). Grace is, therefore, " the source (*principium*) of a meritorious work " (Thom. i. ii. q. 109, a. 6). The idea of merit is not to be regarded as really applicable between God and man, but only upon the ground of a divine appointment, that God will reward the deeds for the performance of which he has himself given the needed power (ib. q. 114, a. 1). But, since no merit is conceivable without a co-operation of the free will (ib. a. 4), there is, after all, a merit on the part of man. Therefore, all human works originating in the grace of God are merits in the sight of God. By them man merits for himself eternal life and an increase of grace (q. 114, a. 2, 8, 9. Bonav. ii. d. 27, a. 2, q. 3). But he can never, according to Thomas, merit the first grace (*prima gratia*, ib. a. 5); for conduct is at any time meritorious only as proceeding from grace (q. 109, a. 6 ; q. 112, a. 2, ad 1). Discrimination is made between the merit of worthiness (*meritum condigni* or *de condigno*) and the merit of fitness (*meritum congrui* or *de congruo*). The former term describes the conduct in so far as it is purely a product of grace ; the second, in so far as it results from the exercise of free-will. Under the former aspect the conduct is, indeed, worthy of eternal life ; whilst, regarded under the latter, it is to be said of it : " For it seems fitting that to the man acting according to his virtue God should give recompense according to the excellence of his virtue " (q. 114, a. 3. Bonav. ii. d. 27, a. 2, q. 3). But this discrimination is, in reality, a mere abstraction ; concretely, merits exist only in the form of free actions (Thom. a. 4). The Augustinian idealization of the conception of merit (Vol. I., p. 365), which Thomas follows, can scarcely be maintained in practice. This may be strikingly observed in Bonaventura. According to Thomas, as we have seen, a merit before justification is inconceivable, but afterward man may by worthiness (*de condigno*) merit eternal life. According to Bonaventura, a " grace gratuitously given " constitutes the beginning of the process of salvation, forming a connecting link between the " grace which makes acceptable " and the free will (*e. g.*, servile fear, the piety instilled by education, accidental impressions or words).[1] This is, therefore, the influencing of the man through the word, or, as Heinrich says, the calling (*vocatio*) through the external or

---

[1] Bonav. here uses the term in a general way. His specific conception of it is the same as that of Thomas. Vid. p. 115 n. Also, iv. d. 7, a. 1, q. 3, ad 2.

internal word (quodlib. viii. q. 5). So small, in comparison
with the sacrament, is the significance of the word.[1] This
general influence makes man capable of meriting by fitness the
grace which makes acceptable (*gratia gratum faciens*) (ii. dist.
28, a. 2, q. 1; d. 27, a. 2, q. 2). Only after the infusion of the
latter is a merit of worthiness (*condigni*) possible (ii. d. 27, a. 2,
q. 3; brevil. 5. 2); but further grace can be merited only by fitness
(*de congruo*)(ib. q. 2). Without any grace, no merit at all is possible (d. 27, a. 2, q. 1, concl.), but to the attainment of justification
man can, nevertheless, dispose himself by fitness. This, however,
points already toward the later apprehension of the matter, according to which man merits the grace which makes acceptable even
by fitness, in so far as he does what he should do, and, after its
reception, merits salvation by worthiness (Biel, in sent. iv. d. 16,
q. 2, a. 3, dub. 4: " Good works morally performed without love
merit by fitness many spiritual good things ; which is evident,
because they merit the grace of justification." Also, ib. dub. 6 :
" Every act proceeding from love and grace in the pilgrim merits
some grade of essential happiness. . . . He who works, merits
such a reward by worthiness"). There are thus two dominant
elements in the scholastic conception of grace : infused grace and
merit. The Augustinian metaphysics and religion here woven
together with the ancient Western moralism, when strictly interpreted, destroy one another (vid. the *meritum condigni* in
Thomas); in reality, they restrained and thereby supplemented
one another. The idea of merit was made tolerable by the
pious interpretation given to it in the appeal to grace, and into
the conception of grace was introduced through the scheme of
merits the element which it lacked, *i. e.*, that of personal relation to God. We can scarcely avoid the conclusion that this
vulgar conception of merit furnished a kind of corrective of the
scholastic Augustinian conception of grace.[2] Cf. H. SCHULTZ,
d. sittl. Begr. d. Verdienstes, Stud. u. Krit. 1894, 273 ff.

---

[1] The development of the mendicant orders increased the dogmatic significance of the word. In his writing, *De perfectione statuum*, Duns assigns to
the clergy the administration of the sacraments, and to the mendicant friars
the proclamation of the word, exalting the latter far above the former. Vid.
SEEBERG, Duns Scotus, p. 474 ff.

[2] That in such a scheme justification, as connected with faith, could be
brought only formally into consideration (as was the case already with Augustine) is self-evident (*e. g.*, Lomb. iii. d. 23 D: " Through this faith the
wicked is justified, so that then faith itself begins to work through love."
Cf. Robert, sent. iv. 14, and my remarks in Thomasius ii., ed. 2, 179). Instead of being scandalized at this, we should rather note it as an evidence of
religious tact, for to what perversions would not a theory of justification by
faith have led when the latter was regarded as merely an intellectual assent
(*cum assensione cogitare*)?

6. Merit must in the above system logically have for its corre-
late the gaining of eternal life as a reward.   But as Thomas held
it to be possible that one person might by fitness merit eternal
life for another (i. ii. q. 114, a. 6), it was also regarded as possible for a man to earn more merit than is necessary to the attainment of salvation.   The Christian may not only obey all the
commandments of the gospel, but also observe its counsels (*consilia evangelica*).   This occurs when he entirely renounces the
good things of this world, *i. e.*, property, sensual pleasure and
honor, and becomes a monk : "in which three things is
founded the whole religion[1] which professes the state of perfection " (i. ii. q. 108, a. 4.   Bon. brev. 5. 9).   Evangelical perfection, or the ideal Christian life, is thus realized in a monastic
life, or one of similar character (ii. ii. q. 184, a. 2, 5 and 4; cf.
Bonav. apol. pauper. resp. 1, c. 3).   This is the *perfectio supererogationis* (Bon., l. c.), the *justitia superabundans* (brev. 5. 9
fin.).   By this means the treasure of superabundant works is
created (vid. sub.), the multitude of saints placed beside Christ
as *intercessores* and *mediatores* (Thom. iii. suppl. q. 72, a. 2),
and the monastic ideal of life brought within the comprehension
of the common people.

It is, however, only the one side of the medieval ideal of
Christian life which finds explanation in the light of the conception of merit then prevalent.   Starting with the conception of
grace, we discover another ideal, that of a supernatural
"heavenly " life.   If the new disposition (*habitus*) of grace in the
soul is the true life, it is incumbent to root out and destroy the
old soul (heart) with all its powers.   It is by the path of an ascetic "imitation of Christ " that we are to reach the enjoyment
of partnership in his divinity.   The active life (*vita activa*) is
followed by the contemplative (*vita contemplativa*).   To give
vivid expression to this conception was the task of German Mysticism.   We therefore postpone its consideration to the following period.   We desire, however, at this point to direct special
attention to the connection of this ideal of life with the medieval conception of grace.

§ 58. *The Sacraments and the Church.   Fixing of Dogma of
Seven Sacraments.*

Cf. SCHWANE, DG. der mittl. Zt., p. 579 ff.   HAHN, Die Lehre von den
Sacramenten, 1864.   SCHANZ, Die Lehre von den Sacramenten, 1893.

The doctrine of the sacraments received during this period the
form in which it was afterward dogmatically fixed by Pope

---

[1] In the medieval sense, *i. e.*, Monasticism, Order.

Eugene IV. at the Florentine Council of A. D. 1439 (vid. the Bull, Exultate deo, in Mansi xxxi. 1055 ff.; also Mirbt, Quellen z. Gesch. d. Papstt., p. 100 ff.). We shall be compelled, therefore, to follow the development of the doctrine somewhat beyond the limits of our period, citing at once from the definitions of the bull.

1. (*a*) The sacraments constitute the positive product of the work of Christ. Since the salvation of mankind is dependent upon the passion of Christ, and that of the individual upon the sacraments, it is clear "that the sacraments of the new law must have their whole efficacy from the passion of Christ" (Thom. summ. iii. q. 62, a. 5. Alex. summ. th. iv. q. 8, membr. 3, a. 5, § 7. Cf. Biel, sent. iv. dist. 2, q. 1, a. 3). That the number of the sacraments is seven is considered self-evident.[1] The necessity of this is argued in various ways. The Christian life, it is said, is allied in character to the development of the body, and, therefore, needs a sacrament of generation (baptism), one of growth (confirmation), one of nourishment (the eucharist). Then come the healing of daily sins (repentance) and the removal of the remains of sin (unction). From the social nature of men is deduced the necessity for marriage as a means of sanctifying the process of propagation, and for ordination as empowering those who receive it to lead the people (vid. Thom. ib. q. 65, a. 1 ; and, further, in Bon. brev. 6. 3. Cf. Duns, sent. iv. d. 2, q. 1, § 3. Biel, iv. d. 2, q. 1, a. 1). But baptism and the eucharist are the "most powerful sacraments" (Thom. q. 62, a. 5). According to some, they alone were instituted immediately by Christ (Alex. iv. q. 8, membr. 3, a. 2, § 3. Bon. iv. d. 23, a. 1, q. 2), while, at a later period, all the seven were traced back to a direct institution by Christ (*e. g.*, Albert, sent. iv. d. 23, a. 13. Thom. q. 64, a. 2. Duns, iv. d. 2, q. 1, § 4, 5. Biel, iv. d. 2, q. 1, concl. 2).

(*b*) Thomas defines the sacrament as "the sign of a sacred thing, since it is (a means of) sanctifying men" (q. 60, a. 2); Bonaventura, as "sensible signs divinely instituted as medicaments, in which, under cover of things sensible, divine power very mysteriously (*secretius*) acts" (brev. 6. 1; cf. Augustine, doctr. christ. ii. 1). The sensible sign becomes a real sacrament, however, only when it is administered with the *intentio* of producing by it a supramundane effect, or at least "to do what the church does, or, at all events, what Christ has

---

[1] The Third Lateran Council, A. D. 1179, still speaks of burial, the installation of bishops, and "other sacraments," Hefele, v. 713. A Council at London, A. D. 1237, enumerates the seven as the "principal sacraments," Hefele, v. 1056.

appointed" (Bon. sent. iv. d. 6, p. 2, a. 2, q. 1).[1]   The sensible elements (*res sensibiles*) constitute the *materia* of the sacrament ; the words of institution, its *forma ; i. e.*, through the recitation of the words the sacrament is observed (*perficitur*) (Thom. q. 60, a. 7.   Alex. iv. q. 8, m. 3, a. 2).   Accordingly, Eugene IV. defines : "All these sacraments are observed by three things, viz., by the elements as the *materia*, the words as the *forma*, and the person of the minister administering the sacrament with the *intentio* of doing what the church does—of which, if anyone be wanting, the sacrament is not observed."

(*c*) There are therefore together in the sacrament an external sign and grace.   How are these two related ?   Hugo had framed the formula which practically gave direction to the solution of the problem : " The sign contains the grace " (supra, p. 80). This Thomas recognizes as " not unsuitably " expressed (q. 62, a. 3, ad 3).   He is also of the opinion that a causation of grace (*gratiam causare*) may be predicated of the sacrament (ib. a. 1), but he feels too the difficulty.   If grace originated from God, how can it be effected through created objects ?   He sought to overcome the difficulty by discriminating between the *principal* and the *instrumental* cause, the latter (and thus the sacraments) being efficacious as set in motion by the former.   " And in this manner is there spiritual power in the sacraments, in so far as they are appointed by God for (producing) spiritual effect." The words of institution effect a spiritual efficacy (*virtus*) in the external sign, which resides in the latter until this *virtus* has accomplished its end (ib. a. 1 and 4).[2]   But over against this view stands another throughout the whole period of the Middle Ages.   It appears plainly in Bonaventura (also in Richard). We dare not say that the sacraments contain grace.   This dwells only in the human soul.   The sacrament is in itself a symbol, somewhat like a letter with the royal seal.   There exists however a covenant (*pactio*) of God, that he will accompany the use of this sacrament with his own working upon the soul of the recipient.   Thus regarded, it can be positively said of the sacrament only that it, by inciting faith, prepares for the reception of grace ("the motion of faith is excited through the exhibition of the sign").   The infusion of grace results through

---

[1] Duns discusses this point exhaustively.   Report. Paris. iv. d. 6, q. 6. Cf. Biel, iv. d. 6, a. 2, concl. 5.

[2] Cf. Alex. iv. q. 8, m. 3, a. 5, § 1 :   " Power (*virtus*) wonderfully associated with (*collata*) the corporal agent itself."   § 5 : "Consecration (*sanctificatio*) is something coming to the water or oil, and it does not give substantial existence (*esse substantiale*) to the oil or water, but it gives accidental existence" (*esse accidentale*).

a directly creative act of God in the soul, *i. e.* : " By such covenant the Lord has obligated himself to, in some way, give grace to him who receives the sacrament " (Bon. sent. iv. d. 1, p. 1, a. 1, q. 2, 3, 4 ; brev. 6. 1). This view, through its advocacy by Duns Scotus, became the dominant one in the later Middle Ages. Since God alone has power to create, grace can have only an act of God as its direct cause. The sacraments are "sure signs," since the divine covenant with the church makes a *concomitance* of the divine working certain. " The divine will alone is the invisible cause of the effect which the sacrament seals and accompanies. God therefore is the immediate cause of such effect of the sacrament through his assistance to the sacrament, upon which he has arranged always to bestow assistance and confer grace . . . and thus his will alone is the prime and principal invisible cause of this effect " (report. iv. d. 2, q. 1, § 2). We cannot say "that he binds his power to the sacraments " (sent. iv. d. 14, q. 4, 6). Accordingly, the external sign " signifies " that which the accompanying grace inwardly effects in the recipient, as, *e. g.*, in the case of baptism, purification : " But the cleansing of the soul from sin which it certainly signifies, it represents by divine appointment ; from which (it follows that) God, who instituted baptism, assists his sign to the producing of the represented effect " (Biel, iv. d. 1, q. 1, a. 1 ; cf. Durand. iv. d. 1, q. 4, a. 1). This view reminds us distinctly of the Augustinian origin of the definition of a sacrament, being in reality a remnant of Augustinianism in the Franciscan dogmatics : the external sacrament is in and of itself only an image of that which God works in the soul.[1] It was certainly only by artifice that transubstantiation could be maintained under such a definition. Of the two views noted, the church naturally chose the coarser. Eugene IV. writes : " They (the ancient sacraments) did not cause grace . . . but these of ours both *contain* grace and *confer* it upon those worthily receiving them."

(*d*) The sacraments bring to man justifying grace (*gratia justificans*, Thom. q. 62, a. 6). " By sacramental effect I understand the grace making acceptable, which he secures who receives the sacrament not unworthily " (Biel, iv. d. 1, q. 1, a. 2). Thomas here discriminated between the " grace of powers and gifts " and " sacramental grace," inasmuch as the former

---

[1] Thomas had already pointed out the possible consequence of this view : " According to this, the sacraments of the New Testament would be nothing more than signs of grace, although it is held by many authorities of the saints that the sacraments of the New Testament not only signify but cause (*causam*) grace " (iii. q. 62, a. 1).

complete in a general way the nature and powers of the soul, while the separate sacraments produce special effects (q. 62, a. 2 ; q. 89, a. 1 ; vid. also Bonav. iv. d. 1, p. 1, a. 1, q. 6). Later theologians acknowledged the essential identity of all *gratia gratum faciens :* " That there is one and the same grace in kind in all who have grace, whether this be infused through participation in the sacraments, or through merits acquired, or, even without either, gratuitously infused." The difference existing is "only in the mind (*ratione*) and not in reality nor in essence " (Biel, iv. d. 2, q. 1, a. 3, dub. 2 ; vid. already Alex. iv. q. 8, m. 4, a. 2, § 1). But the sacraments impart not only justifying grace. To those which are administered but once is attributed as a " secondary effect " the impartation of spiritual character (*character spiritualis*) which makes man continuously capable of honoring God according to the manner of the Christian religion (Thom. q. 63, a. 1, 2). And, inasmuch as this involves a certain participation in the priesthood of Christ, which is eternal, this " character " attaches to the soul " indelibly " (ib. a. 5). The " character " is therefore the indestructible habitual disposition of the Christian soul—and that " according to the intellectual part—toward those things which are for the promotion of divine worship " (a. 4, 5. Alex. iv. q. 8, m. 3, 4. Bonav. iv. d. 6, p. 1, a. 1, q. 3, 5). Duns located the character in the will (iv. d. 6, q. 11, § 4). But the conception is so lacking in clearness that we are led to infer that Duns (iv. d. 6, q. 9, § 13), as well as Biel, still entertains serious doubts upon the point. Neither reason nor the authorities demand it, and only one passage of Innocent III.[1] can be cited in its favor, and even this Biel thinks can be differently interpreted (Duns, iv. d. 6, q. 9, § 13 f. Biel, iv. d. 6, q. 2, a. 1, concl. 2). But Eugene IV. elevated this point also to the dignity of a dogma of the church : " Among these sacraments there are three which imprint a *character, i. e.,* a certain spiritual mark (*signum*) distinctive from others, indelibly upon the soul. Whence, they are not repeated in the same person."

(*e*) Only one further question concerning the sacraments in general remains to be considered—touching the worthy or unworthy reception of them. It is involved in the conception of the New Testament sacraments, that they are effectual *ex opere operato, i. e.,* through their objective administration. Thus teaches Alexander (iv. q. 8, m. 4, a. 1) and especially Albert (sent. iv. d. 1, a. 1) and all the later writers, *e. g.,* Bonaven-

---

[1] Vid. the passage in Denzinger, Enchiridion symbolor. et definit. n. 341, 342 ; cf. Duns, l. c. : " Therefore solely upon the authority of the church, running up to the present time, it is to be held that character is imprinted."

tura :   "The sacraments of the New Testament justify and confer grace of themselves *ex opere operato*" (iv. d. 1, p. 1, a. 1,
q. 5).   A certain disposition is indeed desired in the recipient,
perhaps faith (Lombard, iv. d. 4, B.   Bonav. iv. d. 1, p. 1, a.
1, q. 2); but the later writers especially confined themselves to
the requirement, that there be no obstacle (*obex*) nor mortal sin.
As an *opus operatum*, the sacrament did not presuppose a good
inner motive (*bonus motus interior*) as necessary to a profitable
reception.   Precisely this was one mark of distinction from the
Old Testament sacraments (Duns, iv. d. 1, q. 6, § 10).   With
this efficacy *ex opere operato* is contrasted that based upon the
personality or action of the participant (*ex opere operante*).
That is to say, if the recipient prepares himself for the reception
of the sacrament, he receives also as a reward, upon the ground
of this merit, a further gracious influence.   " Any sign may be
understood to confer grace in a two-fold way.   This occurs in
one way by the sign itself or the sacrament, or, as some say, by
the deed performed, *ex opere operato*.   Thus by the very fact
that the work (*opus*), *i. e.*, sign or sacrament, is celebrated
(*exhibetur*), grace is conferred unless an obstacle of mortal
sin hinder ; because, besides the celebration (*exhibitio*) of the
sign externally celebrated, a good inner motive is not required
in the recipient by which he may merit grace by worthiness or
fitness, but it suffices that the recipient interpose no obstacle.
. . .   In another way, signs or sacraments are understood to
confer grace by the one performing the work (*ex opere operante*)
and by the way of merit, *i. e.*, that the sacrament externally
celebrated does not suffice for the conferring of grace, but
beyond this is required a good motive, or inner devotion, of the
one receiving the sacrament, according to whose intention grace
is conferred corresponding to the merit of worthiness or fitness,
precisely, and not more, according to the celebration of the
sacrament " (Biel, iv. d. 1, q. 3, a. 1, n. 2).

2. Turning to the separate sacraments, we begin with Baptism.   The material (*materia*) of this sacrament is water, or,
more precisely speaking, washing with water.[1]   The form (*forma*)
consists in the words :   " I baptize thee in the name of the Father,
and of the Son, and of the Holy Ghost."   From the time of Alexander the effects of baptism were more precisely stated than had been
done by the Lombard.   It is said to impart the grace making
acceptable (*gratia gratum faciens*), and this impartation effects
both a capacitating of the soul for the doing of good and the

---

[1] Duns, iv. d. 3, q. 3, § 2 : " The first thing is the visible washing itself, for
this, together with the words as a sign, signifies the first effect of baptism."

forgiveness of guilt and penalty.[1] " He who is baptized is freed from the guilt (liability, *reatus*) of the entire penalty owed by him for his sins " (Thom. summ. iii. q. 69, a. 2), and " through baptism one secures grace and powers " (*virtutes*, ib. a. 4). " From all eternal (penalty) baptism absolves by destroying all sin (*culpa*)" and "grace has a two-fold action, viz., to destroy sin (*peccatum*) and to make apt for good " (Bonav. sent. iv. d. 4, p. 1, a. 1, q. 2 and 3). By it there is effected at the same time a restraint of concupiscence (Lomb. iv. d. 4 F ; ii. d. 32 A. Duns, iv. d. 4, q. 7, § 1). Finally, baptism imparts the spiritual " character," which is to be thought of as an infused disposition (*habitus infusus*). According to this theory, in baptism grace is infused into the sinner, and this grace blots out the sins of the past and weakens the sinful impulses of the recipient. But as these impulses still remain active, there remain also for the baptized the punishments (*poenalitates*) of the present life (Thom. q. 69, a. 3). Both serve for testing and attesting. Precisely the same gifts are granted in infant baptism, any difficulties suggesting themselves in this case being met by the consideration, that baptism confers not separate virtues, but the *habitus virtutum* (Thom. q. 69, a. 6). To secure the benefits of baptism, faith is required in the recipient. In the case of unbelievers (*fictio*), the benefit is secured when they have done penance for their unbelief (Thom. q. 69, a. 10. Bonav. iv. d. 4, p. 1, a. 2, q. 2 f.). In the case of children, an obligation imposed upon the sponsors to see to their instruction in the Christian faith takes the place of the yet lacking confession of faith (Lomb. iv. d. 6 G. Bonav. iv. d. 6, p. 2, a. 3, q. 1).[2] Eugene IV. defines as the effect of the sacrament : " the remission of all original and actual sin, also of every penalty which is due for that sin."

3. There is no advance in the doctrine of later Scholastics upon the sacrament of Confirmation ; for the assertion that it was instituted by Christ (*e. g.*, Albert, iv. d. 7, a. 2), and the attempt to justify the restriction of the right of administering this sacrament to the bishop by all manner of fanciful reasons, do

---

[1] Duns, iv. d. 3, q. 2, § 3 : "God . . . remits the sin of no one except of him to whom he gives grace, for he frees no one from perdition except him whom he ordains to be a son of the kingdom." Also, ib. iv. d. 4, q. 5, § 4 : (God) "is prepared always after the reception of this sign to assist him who has received it for the causing of its effect."

[2] Baptism is preceded by catechisation and exorcism (Lomb. iv. d. 6 H. Thom. iii. q. 71, a. 1, 2). The baptism of the children of non-Christian parents, without or against the will of the latter, was disapproved by Thomas (q. 68, a. 10), approved by Duns (iv. d. 4, q. 9), and declared of doubtful propriety by Biel (iv. d. 4, q. 2, a. 3, dub. 5).

not constitute an advance.   Eugene IV. designates the chrism
as the *material*, and as the *form* of the sacrament, the words : " I
sign thee with the sign of the cross, and confirm thee in the
chrism of salvation in the name of the Father," etc.   The proper
administrator (*ordinarius minister*) is the bishop.   "But the
effect of this sacrament is, that in it is given the Holy Spirit and
strength."

4. "All worship in the church is, as it were, in line (*in
ordine*) toward this sacrament."   These words of Duns (iv. d.
8, q. 1, 3) spoken in reference to the Lord's Supper, express
the practical significance of this sacrament.   The doctrine was
received in completed form from the great Scholastics.   The
only task remaining for the present period was to make the traditional dogma somewhat more acceptable to reason by the arts
of logic, and more conformable to the spiritual tastes of the age.
Here also, Alexander suggested essentially the ideas and problems
which later writers accepted.   The fixed basis of all discussion
was transubstantiation.   When the priest utters the form-giving
words of institution above the *materia*, or elements, the latter
are in their entirety transformed into the entire body of Christ.
"The whole wafer (*hostia*) is actually changed into the whole
body of Christ" (Alex. iv. q. 40, m. 3, a. 5).   This conception may be analyzed as follows :

(*a*) The words of institution, as they are spoken by the priest,
effect the transformation : " Whence also the consecrating power
(*virtus consecrativa*) consists not only in the words themselves, but
also in the power conferred upon the priest at his consecration
and ordination " (Thom. summ. iii. q. 82, a. 1, ad 1).   Thomas
is of the opinion " that in the formal words of this sacrament a
certain power (*virtus*) is created for effecting the conversion of
this sacrament " (q. 78, a. 4).   According to Duns, it is, in
reality, only the divine omnipotence which can effect the change.
But God has appointed the priest as the administrator (Duns, iv.
d. 13, q. 2, 3).   " This is according to gospel law, and not only
according to positive law " (Duns, report. iv. d. 13, q. 2).[1]

---

[1] It is only with great difficulty that a place can be made for transubstantiation in the Scotist view of the sacraments.   The "sensible signs" testify that
the things signified are really "contained under them."   Further : "God
has so established these elements that after their consecration he may assist
them to (the securing of) this presence of Christ" (iv. d. 8, q. 1, 2 ff.).   But
for what purpose then the transubstantiation?   Would it not be in keeping
with the general conception of a sacrament to maintain only an accompanying
of the symbol with an exercise of divine power, either in such a way that a
divine influence be exerted directly upon the soul, or in such a way that Christ
be bodily present without affecting the continued existence of the substance of
the bread?   It was an *adductive* instead of a *productive* transubstantiation, as

(*b*) The transformation occurs in the moment when the words are spoken : " At the end of the utterance of the words the sacrament begins to be " (Duns, iv. d. 8, q. 1, 5). It is a peculiar advantage of this sacrament that it is realized not only in the administration (*in usu*), but already in the consecration of the elements (Thom. q. 78, a. 1).

(*c*) The resultant of the transformation is the presence of the true body and blood of Christ (Thom. q. 75, a. 1), the soul of Christ and his divinity being present, not by way of sacramental power (*ex vi sacramentali*), but by way of real concomitance (*ex reali concomitantia*) (ib. q. 76, a. 1.   Alex. iv. d. 38, m. 5).   On the basis of this, justification was found for the constantly extending custom of withholding the cup from the laity (vid. Thom. q. 80, a. 12.   Alex. iv. q. 32, m. 1, a. 2).

(*d*) The accidents of the substance of the bread and wine still remain, which is, indeed, a new miracle (Alex. iv. q. 40, m. 1, a. 2.   Thom. q. 75, a. 5).[1]   So long as the form (*species*) of the bread and wine is retained, the sacrament continues.   Hence the advocates of this theory did not even shrink from the conclusion, that even if a dog or a mouse should eat the *hostia*, the substance of Christ would remain in it (Abelard.   Thom. q. 8, a. 3, ad. 3.   Cf., as to the course pursued in distributing, HEFELE, CG. vi. 203).

(*e*) The body which Christ gave to his disciples was the immortal glorified body, and of this he himself partook as an example for his disciples.   " And, nevertheless, he who as mortal gave, and as immortal was given, was not himself two, but one " (thus Hugo.   Vid. especially Alex. iv. q. 44, m. 1 and 3.   Thom. q. 81, a. 1 and 3).[2]

Duns Scotus says.   Alexander already suggests the latter theory (" That in this sacrament there is not any transformation, but, upon the utterance of the words, without any transformation, it comes to pass by divine power that the body of Christ is there ").   He suggests as an objection, that this view might lead to a worship of the bread, iv. q. 38, m. 1.   Such was the view also of some followers of Berenger (vid. p. 75 n.   Cf. also Petr. Pictav. sent. v. 12), and Duns (iv. d. 11, q. 3, 3 f.), who presents this explanation as a possible one, and merely says in comment : " Therefore the other way is more suitable than this." But to this theory belongs the future, as we shall see.   Duns continued to maintain transubstantiation only because it was a dogma of the church.   SEE-BERG, Duns Scotus, p. 382 ff.

[1] Although it is said that the substance of the bread and wine do not remain (*non manere*), the term *annihilatio* was avoided, inasmuch as the resultant is the body of Christ.   Vid. Thom. q. 75, a. 2, 3.   Duns, iv. d. 11, q. 4, 14. Biel, iv. d. 11, q. 1, a. 2, dub. 6.   Occam. iv. q. 6, ad dub. 7.

[2] Biel says that Christ gave to his disciples a " body such as he had, *i. e.*, mortal and passible," without feeling the " teeth of those eating it " (iv. d. 9, q. 1, a. 3, dub. 3).   From the other view it would follow, that if the *hostia* of the first celebration had been preserved, Christ would have been, during the

(*f*) But at this point a difficulty emerges whose solution exercised the Scholastics beyond all others : If the body of Christ is, as is confessed, present in heaven at a particular place, how can it be received at the same time in the sacrament at various places ? ALEXANDER'S opinion was that " Christ is circumscriptively, or locally, contained in heaven, but not contained circumscriptively, or locally, under the sacrament " (iv. q. 40, m. 3, a. 7). THOMAS similarly taught " that the body of Christ is in this sacrament in the manner of substance (*per modum substantia*), and not in the manner of quantity (*per modum quantitatis*) " (q. 76, a. 1, ad 3). The Christ who is locally present in heaven is, therefore, not present in a local manner in the sacrament, but only substantially (q. 75, a. 1, ad 3 ; q. 76, a. 4, 5 ; cf. Richard, iv. d. 10, princ. 2, q. 1. Durand, iv. d. 10, q. 10 fin.; vid. also Carthusian. iv. d. 10, q. 1 ff.). Duns rightly rejected this, since a thing without its properties is not conceivable (iv. d. 10, q. 1. 12). Duns himself thinks that God, by virtue of his omnipotence, which is limited only by the logically impossible, can very well cause a body to exist at different places at the same time. We cannot see, he argues, why the relations of a thing to space may not be multiplied (ib. q. 2. 11 ; q. 3. 5). Accordingly, Christ can be at the same time in heaven and at any number of places. The later writers disputed this, for its (realistic) premise is the independent existence of space, while to the Nominalists space is only the object presented as occupying space, upon which theory a spacial existence of Christ in the Lord's Supper is inconceivable. It is rather to be said, that quantity and the property of occupying space are accidental properties of a thing. If the thing be reduced to a point, it yet remains what it was, and, therefore, still possesses the property of occupying space, although it no longer exists in space. It is, therefore, to be said that the body of Christ is present in the Lord's Supper with the property of quantity, but without existing therein as a quantity (vid. especially Occam, tract. de sacr. altar. c. 16 ff. Biel, iv. d. 10, q. 1, a 1 and 2. Cf. fuller discussion at a later point). But these empty speculations, all combined, do not prove the impossible. The body of Christ is local in heaven, and it is in its entirety present in its substance at every celebration of the Lord's Supper. Dogma stands over against dogma, and all the efforts of logic cannot bridge the gulf.

(*g*) Finally, the effect of this sacrament claims attention. In general, it is to be said : " The effect which the passion of Christ

three days after his crucifixion, both dead and alive at once ! (Biel. exposit. canonis miss. lect. 46 L).

has produced in the world, this sacrament produces in man" (Thom. q. 79, a. 1). Regarding it more closely, we may say "that the eucharist was instituted to be a *sacrifice* and to be a *sacrament,* or food" (Biel, exposit. can. miss. lect. 85 D). As the latter, it signifies a strengthening of the spiritual life, the imparting of grace, and the forgiveness of venial sins (Thom., l. c.). The later writers are but logically consistent when, in accordance with their interpretation of the work of Christ, they make this impartation of grace to consist in a reminding of the love of Christ and his pious example, and in the awakening of a responsive affection and inciting to good works. The Supper is a *memoriale divinae passionis.* This view is instructively presented in Biel, exposit. can. miss. lect. 85 B, O, V, X, Y.[1] But, side by side with this effect of the sacrament, stands its sacrificial character. The body of Christ is really offered up: "There is not only a representative (*repraesentativa*), but a real immolation (*immolatio vera*), (Albert, sent. iv. d. 13, a. 23). The sacrifice benefits first of all the participants in the sacrament, but then also others "in so far as it is offered for their salvation," and in so far as they have faith in the sacrament (Thom. q. 79, a. 7, q. 83, a. 1). The sacrifice is also effectual for souls in purgatory.[2] The reality of the sacrifice does not interfere with its being at the same time a representation and reminder of the passion (Biel, l. c., lect. 85 F). But the principal thing is still: "And this sacrifice is of operative effects similar to those which the sacrifice upon the cross itself produced" (Biel, ib. K). This formed the basis of the worst perversions of the practical life of the church (meritoriousness of the mass; private masses; after A. D. 1264, the festival of Corpus Christi). Here also, theology made no advance.

We cite from the definitions of Eugene IV. the following: "For the priest, speaking in the person of Christ, makes (*conficit*)

---

[1] Biel enumerates the following effects: "vivificare, relaxare, inflammare, patientiam dare, nutrire, restaurare, unire, copulare, sanare, conservare, roborare, perducere." Vid. also sermo 46 of Biel's Festival Sermons.

[2] Vid. Biel, sermo 46 R: "It is granted that the fruit of the eucharist is more efficacious as a sacrament, but it is more general as a sacrifice, . . . because as a sacrament it operates only in those who take it, but as a sacrifice it has effect in all those for whom it is offered. But it is offered, not only for those who participate by taking it, but also for all who are standing by, yea, even for the absent, the living and the dead. . . . Although it is granted that sinners are inflamed by partaking (*perceptione*) of the eucharist, but not by the hearing of the mass. . . . Yet even to sinners not contrite nor . . . regarding with displeasure their continuing sins, it is useful to frequently give help (*assistere*) by the office of the mass, and to procure that it be offered for them in order that they may thus merit to be regarded by the Lord with pity, and may be inspired to displeasure in their sins which they yet have."

this sacrament ; for, by virtue of the very words, the substance of the bread is converted into the body of Christ, and the substance of the wine into his blood, yet in such a way that Christ is contained entire under the form of the bread, and entire under the form of the wine, and under any part whatever of the consecrated wafer and consecrated wine, when separated, is the entire Christ.''

5. As the Lord's Supper blots out venial sins, and baptism original sin, so Repentance has been instituted to dispel mortal sins. It is with mortal sins alone that confession and absolution have to do, not with so-called venial sins. A certain displeasure in view of the failing, the repetition of the Lord's Prayer, sprinkling with consecrated water, the blessing of a bishop, are sufficient for the latter, which are not regarded as requiring an infusion of grace (Alex. iv. q. 77, m. 2, a. 5. Bonav. iv. d. 17, p. 3, a. 2. Thom. summ. iii. q. 87, a. 1.; a. 2, ad 2 ; a. 3).[1] Thus the disastrous discrimination between greater and smaller sins,[2] the latter of which were scarcely regarded any longer as actual sins, was justified. This discrimination was necessary, as only by this means could the petition for the forgiveness of sin have any meaning after the sacrament of repentance had been observed.

Turning now to the sacrament of Repentance, we recall the problem which the school of Abelard had left unsolved, *i. e.*, If divine forgiveness follows *contrition*, what need is there of *confession and absolution?* This question was answered, as we shall see, by the Scholastics. In this sacrament also *materia* and *forma* are discriminated. The former consists in acts of the penitent (*actus poenitentis*); the latter, in the words of the priest : I absolve thee (Thom. q. 84, a. 2, 3. Bonav. iv. d. 22, a. 2, q. 2. Biel, iv. d. 14, q. 2, a. 1). The remark, ''that in anything whatsoever perfection is attributed to the form'' (Thom. ib. a. 3), fixes at once in advance the position of Absolution, as constituting the essential element of the sacrament.

(*a*) According to traditional teaching, the first element of the sacrament is *contritio*. To understand the course of development here we must constantly bear in mind that repentance, and particularly its first part, contrition, is already, as an act

[1] According to Duns not even *attritio* is here necessary (iv. d. 17, q. 1, 25).

[2] Thomas (q. 86, a. 4 ; q. 87, a. 2) thus discriminates : '' In mortal sin there are two things, *i. e.*, a turning away (*aversio*) from immutable good, and a turning (*conversio*) toward mutable good ;'' in venial sins, on the contrary, there is present only '' an inordinate turning to mutable good without turning away from God. Eternal punishment, therefore, befits the former, and only temporal punishment the latter.'' Upon this question, see also Biel, iv. d. 17, q. 1, a. 2, concl. 3. Cf. Melanchthon apol., p. 168, 6.

"formed" by love or as a Christian virtue, a product of grace. From this it follows, that contrition in itself merits and effects the full annihilation of guilt and punishment (Thom. suppl. q. 5, a. 2. Cf. Wilhelm v. Paris, de sacr. opp. Nürnberg, 1496, ii. fol. 41 v, 44 v, 46 r). On the other hand, in the sacrament of repentance, *contritio* is represented as an "inclination (*dispositio*) toward the receiving of grace" (Thom. ib. q. 5, a. 1, and iii. q. 89, a. 1, ad 2). But there is no need of any such *dispositio;* in fact, it makes the sacrament entirely unnecessary. Quite forced appears, therefore, the argument of Thomas, that, since no one can know whether he has a degree of sorrow sufficient to secure forgiveness, it is necessary for us to continually avail ourselves of the opportunity of confession and absolution (suppl. q. 5, a. 2, ad 1). And it is no more than an opinion, that the resolution to confess is always combined with contrition (ib.). When we consider, further, that the individual concerned is always one who has fallen into a mortal sin, it is evident that he cannot, without the influence of the sacrament of repentance, even produce contrition in himself. To meet this difficulty a new idea, that of an *attritio,* or purely human inclination toward the reception of grace, is introduced as being sufficient. This furnishes a key for the solution of the above problem, for this half-penitence does not fully merit the forgiveness of sins, and hence room is left for confession and absolution. The word, *attritio,* occurs first in *Alanus of Insulis,*[1] then in Alexander of Hales (iv. q. 74) and *William of Paris* (opp. 11. 45 v), but it is used by them in such a way as to indicate that it was already an accepted term in the language of the schoolmen. Thomas defines it: "Attritio signifies a certain, but not perfect, displeasure concerning sins committed" (suppl. q. 1, a. 2).[2] Its motive is commonly fear: "Servile fear is the source (*principium*) of attrition" (Alex. iv. q. 74, m. 1. Durand, iv. d. 17, q. 1, a. 3).[3] If now anyone has a certain displeasure toward his sin, he is in suitable condi-

---

[1] Vid. Regul. theol. 85 (Migne, 210. 665 C): "is either remitted by attrition . . . although he have not perfectly repented, or dismissed by contrition when he is fully converted from sin."

[2] Upon the two terms, vid. Biel, iv. d. 16, q. 1, a. 1, n. 3.

[3] Cf. Thomas (iii. q. 85, a. 5), who, in answer to the question, "Whether the source of penitence is from fear," replies that the acts of the soul in repentance are the following: "Faith, servile fear, by which one is restrained from sin by fear of punishments, hope, love, filial fear." Accordingly: "It is evident that the act of penitence proceeds from servile fear, as from the first motion of the affection inclining toward it." Cf. also Biel, iv. d. 14, q. 1, a. 3, dub. 6: "In beginners not yet perfect . . . it frequently arises from fear of punishment, which arises from love of self, but in the perfect it arises from the love of God and of righteousness." Durand (vid. supra): "For penitence is conceived in fear."

tion to make confessson. "But if a penitent, prepared as far as in him lies, comes to confession, attrite but not contrite, I say that *confession*, with subjection to the will of the priest and *satisfaction* of the penance enjoined by the priest, is a sign and cause of the blotting out of guilt and penalty" (Alex. iv. q. 60, m. 1, a. 3). Confession is made before the priest, because he only who can consecrate the eucharist has authority over the powers of grace (Thom. suppl. q. 8, a. 1 ; q. 10, a. 1. Alex. q. 76, m. 3, a. 1). Then follows absolution, which brings the divine forgiveness. But it is impossible "that God should remit an offense to anyone without any change of the latter's will" (Thom. q. 86, a. 2). Hence : "There can be no remission of sins except through infusion of grace" (ib. q. 89, a. 1). Absolution, therefore, brings divine forgiveness by effecting at the same time the abolition of the mortal sin by an infusion of grace (cf. supra, p. 120). If the *attrite* person do not now himself interpose an obstacle, he receives grace through confession and absolution (Thom. suppl. q. 18, a. 1).[1] This effects the forgiveness of the liability (*reatus*) to eternal punishment, as well as "something of (*aliquid de*) the temporal punishment." This latter expression, which somewhat modifies the conception of Abelard, is to be attributed to a regard for the "satisfaction," which would otherwise be useless (ib. q. 18, a. 2). Such is the teaching of Thomas.[2] Duns gives a different turn to the doctrine. *Attritio*, according to his view, when it has lasted for a definite time, establishes a merit of fitness (*de congruo*), a claim to the favorable regard of God. The penitent must now make his confession, whereupon grace is infused, or sin is destroyed by the conversion of *attritio* into *contritio*, *i. e.*, since love is imparted, and thereby the *informa attritio* is transformed into the *formirta contritio* (sent. iv. d. 14, q. 2, 14 to 16). The outcome of this is essentially the same as in Thomas, for since absolution infuses grace, it creates love, and by this means transforms the *attritio* into *contritio*. The infusion of grace takes place through absolution. For the *attrite*, the process takes the following course : "For it is sufficient that some displeasure, although imperfect (*informis*), precedes, and then he is capable of sacramental absolution, and through it contrition is awakened" (iv. d. 16, q. 1. 7). And

---

[1] If the confessing person is sufficiently *contrite*, absolution brings an increase of grace.

[2] It became afterward the general scholastic doctrine. Alexander taught differently, *i. e.*, that "absolution from sin (*culpa*) belongs to God alone (iv. q. 80, m. 1), and that the priest can only remit a part of the penalty (m. 2, a. 1), and that temporal and not eternal" (ib. a. 2). Similarly Bonaventura, iv. d. 18, p. 1, a. 2, q. 1.

further : " Thus the priest absolves what he yet binds. For he
absolves from the debt of eternal penalty and binds to the discharge of temporal penalty " (ib.). It may, therefore, be said
that absolution *transforms* eternal into temporal penalty (ib. d.
17, q. 1. 23. Cf. Durand. iv. d. 16, q. 1, a. 3), and thus that
it *forgives* eternal penalty (ib. d. 19, q. 1. 32).[1] We present a
brief summary of the theory of Biel, as a representative of the
later writers : Forgiveness takes place through the destruction of
sin by means of an infusion of grace (iv. d. 14, q. 1, a. 1, n. 2,
4). But for this there is necessary some preparation on the part.
of the sinner. And although this could be done by God without us, yet he requires also something from us " (ib. q. 2, a. 1);
man can and should do " what in him is " (ib. q. 1, a. 2, concl.
2, 3). He should have a detestation of his crime (*detestatio
criminis*) and a displeasure with his sin (*displicentia peccati*)
(ib. concl. 5). Usually, repentance has its beginning in
servile fear ; " for he who fears hell guards against evil things "
(*mala cavet*) (ib. q. 2, a 3, dub. 3). Everything depends upon
the " vow to be contrite " (*votum conterendi*). " Where the
votum conterendi is, there is *contritio.*" To refuse to have detestation for sin is to refuse to acknowledge having sinned (ib. a.
1, n. 2). Thus one finds himself in the state of *attrition*, and
merits grace by his fitness (*de congruo*, d. 16, q. 2, a. 3, dub. 4).
" He has appointed that he will not be lacking to him who does
that which is in him, nor will he withhold grace from him who is
sufficiently inclined to its reception " (d. 14, q. 2, a. 1, opin. 3).
Confession and absolution, then, bring grace, and transform the *attritio* into *contritio.* Despite the variations here in separate points,
the general view is the same. Confession and absolution are
necessary in order that attrition be changed to contrition, and
that sin be blotted out. Thus, the difficulty which cumbered the
theory of Abelard was removed by the introduction of the *attritio.* Although in theory contrition was always spoken of as the
chief thing, in practice it was attrition that carried the day. It
is not easy to say which of the two conceptions was the more
dangerous : the exercise of penitential grief to which was affixed
the reward of forgiveness of sin, or the sorrow for sin which was
to be transformed into complete penitence by the solemnities of
divine worship.

(*b*) After absolution there yet remain temporal penalties for
the sinner. These are met by the satisfaction of works (*satis-*

---

[1] How coolly and rationally, but with what fine-spun theorizing, is not
this process conceived : A certain unrest on account of sin is increased by
solemn confession and absolution to the point of contrition, and thereby sin is
blotted out in a psychological way !

factio operum). Such works, performed for the re-establishment of the divine honor (Thom. suppl. q. 12, a. 3), are, indeed, not an equivalent (*satisfactio aequivalens*), but this does not prevent their being sufficient (a *sufficiens fieri*) before God (ib. q. 13, a. 1). They consist in our denying ourselves something for the honor of God. But we possess goods of soul, of body, and of fortune. The renunciation of these leads to prayer, fasting, and almsgiving respectively. According to Duns, the sinner may decline to accept the temporal penalty (iv. d. 19, § 27 f.).[1] The failure to perform the good works imposed at confession brings, however, suffering during this life and in purgatory.

(*c*) Very important becomes, therefore, the office of Indulgences. They are justified as follows : "It is conceded by all that indulgences have some efficacy, because it would be impious to say that the church did anything in vain" (ib. q. 25, a. 2)! The attempt was made to draw an argument in their favor from the unity of the church. The merits of Christ, as also of the saints, were greater than necessary. Thus arose the spiritual treasury (*thesaurus*) of the church, which consists of these "works of supererogation (*supererogationes*) of the members of Christ," and of the Lord himself (Alex. iv. q. 23, m. 3, a. 1. Albert, iv. d. 20, a. 16). But, since the body of Christ is one, these deeds of some members redound to the benefit of the rest (Thom. suppl. q. 25, a. 2). Inasmuch, further, as the dead who enter purgatory are still upon their journey heavenward, and as they are yet, on account of their sins, before the forum of the church, they also may secure a share in these treasures of grace (vid. especially Biel, expos. can. miss. lect. 57). It is understood, of course, that the church expects in return a work of piety and of profit to the church (*opus pium et utile ecclesiae*) (ib.). Whilst indulgences are granted to the living, however, by the pope "by the way of judiciary authority," they avail for the dead "by the way of supplication" (*per modum suffragii*); "indulgences profit them by the way of supplication, *i. e.*, on account of some work done by another and applied to them by the way of supplication" (ib. L. Cf. Alex. iv. q. 23, a. 2, m. 5. Bonav. iv. d. 20, p. 2, a. 1, q. 5). By indulgences even the entire penalties of purgatory may be averted (Heinr. quodl. viii. q. 19). Authority over indulgences belongs to the pope alone, but he may at will permit the bishops to share it with him

---

[1] Cf. Duns, iv. d. 15, q. 1. 12. Biel, iv. d. 16, q. 2, a. 1. In this connection Biel presents a thorough discussion of a number of important ethical questions, following in this Duns, dist. 15. In general, it may be said, there is at this point a mine of ethical suggestions in the dogmatics of the Middle Ages.

(Thom. suppl. q. 26, a. 1, 3). This is the doctrine taught also by Eugene IV., though not in precisely the same words: "Acts of penitence are, as it were, the material (*materia*) part of the sacrament." Then follows an enumeration of the usual three parts. Of *confession* it is said : "To which it pertains, that the sinner confess entirely to his priest all the sins of which he has recollection." *Satisfaction* "is rendered chiefly through prayer, fasting, and alms." The *form* of the sacrament consists of the words of absolution; its *effect* is absolution from sins. Thus was completed the construction of the sacrament of repentance. The elements composing it remained the same, but they were placed in varying relations to one another. The emphasis was at first laid upon the satisfaction; later, upon the contrition; and then upon the confession, and by this means, in order to impress the necessity of the latter, upon the attrition.[1] But whenever one element is thus emphasized, questions and doubts arise as to the propriety and significance of the others. The Scholastics established the propriety of confession, and thereby provoked a new inquiry, *i. e.:* If absolution brings grace, what is then the need of subsequent works and of indulgences? At this point was aimed the criticism of the closing period of the Middle Ages.

6. The sacrament of Extreme Unction received no additional development in this period. As to its effect, opinion wavered, some attributing to it a removal of venial sins (Bonav. brevil. 6. 11. Duns, report. iv. d. 23, q. 1, 4); others the blotting out of the dregs of sin remaining after the observance of the other sacraments (Albert, sent. iv. d. 23, a. 1. Thom. sent. iv. d. 23, q. 1, a. 2). To this must be added also, when it follows (*quando expedit*), bodily relief or healing. The doctrine of the Scholastics is clearly summarized by Eugene IV.: "The *material* is the oil of the olive, blessed by a bishop." The ointment is applied "to the eyes, the ears, the nose, the mouth, the hands, the feet, the loins." The *form* is: "Through this sacred anointing and his most pious mercy may the Lord pardon (*indulgeat*)[2] to thee whatever through the sight, etc., and likewise in other members," etc. . . . "But the effect is the healing of the soul (*mentis*), and, so far as it succeeds, even of the body itself."

---

[1] Durand directly denies that contrition and satisfaction are constituent parts of the sacrament, maintaining that everything depends upon confession and absolution, and that the sacrament should of right be called the "sacrament of confession" (iv. d. 16, q. 1, and d. 14, q. 1).

[2] Instead of this deprecative form, the indicative form was in use in some churches, Thom. summ. suppl. q. 29, a. 8.

7. The sacrament of Ordination was more accurately defined. Its necessity appears from the need of an order of men who may make application of the *medicamenta* of the sacraments (Bonav. brevil. 6. 12). The *material* is seen in the symbols, or the vessels used in ordination ; while the accompanying words are the *form* (Thom. iii. suppl. q. 34, a. 5. Duns, iv. d. 24, q. 1. 8). Ordination embraces the seven orders (*ordines*), vid. p. 84. Everyone ordained receives thereby the spiritual character (Thom. q. 35, a. 2). In addition, there is granted to him by his ordination the grace making acceptable (*gratia gratum faciens*) in view of the administration of the sacraments entrusted to him (Thom. 35, a. 1).[1] The question here arose whether the episcopacy is an order by itself, or coincides with the presbyterial office. Thomas and Bonaventura declare that, since the eucharist is the highest sacrament, and priest and bishop have the same authority for its administration, the episcopacy is no separate order in the proper sense of that term. Only when the term, *ordo*, is used in a peculiar sense, to indicate a "certain office with respect to certain sacred acts," or as a "distinction of dignities and offices," can the episcopacy—speaking loosely—be described as a special order. Hence : "Beyond the priesthood, there is no degree of rank" (*gradus ordinis*), and : "The episcopate, in so far as it concerns the order of the priesthood, might well be called an order ; but, in so far as it is discriminated from the priesthood, it expresses a certain added dignity, or office, of the bishop" (Bonav. iv. d. 24, p. 2, a. 2, q. 3. Thom. q. 40, a. 5). Duns gives a different turn to the thought. He, too, in view of the high character of the act (*nobilitas actus*) in the administration of the eucharist, regards the priesthood as the highest rank (*supremus gradus*, sent. iv. d. 24, q. 1. 7), but, nevertheless, that order (*ordo*) which has the authority to elevate to this lofty position stands upon a yet higher plane. "But if to simply administer the eucharist (*conficere*) be not the most excellent act in the church, but to be able to appoint anyone to the lofty position which befits such act, then there are not only seven orders, but eight, because the episcopate is then a special grade and order in the church, whose province it is to confer all orders, and, consequently, to establish all in

---

[1] All the orders have a relation nearer or more remote to the eucharist. The priest consecrates ; the deacon is permitted to distribute the blood ; the sub-deacon may bring the material to be consecrated. The others are engaged in preparing for the reception of the sacrament : the acolyte illuminating for worship, the lector bringing the knowledge, the doorkeeper keeping away the unworthy, the exorcist warding off demons (vid. Duns, iv. d. 24, q. 1. 7).

such lofty position'' (report. iv. d. 24, q. 1. 9). This separation of the episcopacy from the ordinary priesthood found advocates in the later Middle Ages.[1] The administration of the sacrament of ordination belongs only to the bishop. Heretics can,
indeed, validly administer this, as the other sacraments,[2] but in
that case it does not bring the *gratia gratum faciens*, on account
of the sin of those who receive the sacraments from them against
the prohibition of the church (Thom. q. 38, a. 2). In this
way it was possible to remain orthodox and yet appropriately
discredit the sacraments administered by heretics. Eugene IV.
designates as the *material* of ordination: '' That through the delivering of which the order is conferred, just as the priesthood is
conferred through the handing of a cup with wine and a plate with
bread,'' etc. . . . The *form* of the priesthood is: '' Receive
authority for the offering of sacrifice in the church for the living
and the dead in the name of the Father,'' etc. . . . The *effect*
is an increase of grace, so that one may be a suitable minister.

8. Marriage consists in the union for life of man and woman
for the purpose of begetting and rearing children. An additional purpose since the fall is the prevention of fornication
(Thom. suppl. q. 48, a. 2). It accordingly embraces a con-
tract (*contractus*) in respect to '' the mutual giving of the bodies
for carnal copulation '' (Duns, iv. d. 30, q. 2. 4; d. 26. 8.
Thom. q. 58, a. 1). To its contraction belongs therefore
mutual consent (*mutuus consensus*) to the latter (Thom. q.
45, a. 1, 2; q. 48, a. 1). The public profession of this
consent constitutes the establishment of marriage (*matrimonium ratum*), and by it is given the right to demand the
conjugal debt (*debitum conjugale*). It is only the actual
copula carnalis which constitutes the *matrimonium consumma-
tum*. Before this consummation, marriage may be annulled by a
previous solemn vow of continence (Thom. q. 53, a. 2) or by
entering an order (q. 61, a. 2). Marriage once consummated
is indissoluble and monogamistic.[3] It is forbidden to the holy
order (*ordo sacer*).[4] Marriage, as a type of the union of Christ

---

[1] *E. g.*, Durand in sent. iv. d. 24, q. 6. 7.

[2] Only penance is excepted (Bonav. iv. d. 25, a. 1, q. 2. Durand, iv. d.
25, q. 1, ad 2), because the validity of absolution always depends upon the
regularity of the priestly jurisdiction, and this is wanting in the case of heretics and schismatics ; as in their administration of all sacraments. Cf. Duns,
report. iv. d. 25, q. 1, 16.

[3] According to Thomas (q. 65, a. 1), polygamy contradicts natural law.
Duns denies this, and considers it possible that after depopulating wars or pes-
tilences polygamy may be revealed by God to the church as allowable (iv. d.
33, q. 1. 6).

[4] Because those established in sacred orders handle the sacred vessels and

with the church, is a sacrament. Its *form* consists of the words of consent, "but not the benediction of the priest, which is sacramental in character " (*quoddam sacramentale*). This sacrament is, therefore, administered by him who uses it (q. 42, a. 1). In the *consensus*, there is an accompanying divine agency which hallows the married life (q. 45, a. 1).[1] Duns expresses himself most accurately, representing as the sacramental effect of marriage the gracious union of souls (*gratiosa conjunctio animarum*, iv. d. 26, § 15, 17). Inasmuch as the two persons desire to belong to each other, God establishes an inner relation between them. As separate effects are mentioned marital fidelity, the repression of lust during the act of copulation, and the turning of its energy toward a useful union (*copula utilis*, Bonav. iv. d. 26, a. 2, q. 2), *i. e.*, the living together of the married pair and their co-operation in the rearing of children (Albert, iv. d. 26, a. 14). To these is to be added what Christian marriage has in in common with the natural ordinance, *i. e.*, that the copulative act, which is in itself unworthy of man, because for the time being depriving him of reason, is in marriage legitimized and excused in view of the blessings which it brings (Thom. q. 49, a. 1). These blessings are progeny and fidelity, to which Christianity adds the sacrament (thus Lombard, iv. d. 31 A, following Augustine, De genesi ad litt. ix. 7. 12). We need not enter upon a discussion of the hindrances of marriage, which were considered at length by the Scholastics.[2] Eugene IV. describes as the *efficient cause* of marriage, the "mutual consent expressed through words concerning the person present." As the *blessings* of marriage, he enumerates : "Children to be received and educated ; fidelity, which each of the married pair ought to observe toward the other," and "the indivisibility of marriage on account of the fact that it signifies the indivisible union of Christ and the church." It is very evident that this last of the sacraments attained but a loose and unfinished form. Neither is there a distinct definition of its material, nor is it clear how or

sacraments, and it is, therefore, becoming (*decens*) that they by continence preserve bodily purity (iv. q. 53, a. 3).

[1] Bonaventura (iv. d. 26, a. 2, q. 3): "Matrimony receives a reason of spirituality and grace when consent is joined with the benediction, where its significance is explained ; and sanctification is obtained through the benediction, and thus in the sacerdotal benediction consists chiefly the spiritual reason." It is remarkable that this idea is not, following the example of the sacrament of penance, crystallized in the formula, that the priestly benediction is the *form*, and the consent of the parties the *material*, of the sacrament. This was done only in sporadic instances during the Middle Ages, though more frequently at a later period. Vid. Kirchenlex. iv., ed. 2, 145 f.

[2] Briefly presented in the Versus memoriales in Bonav. brevil. 6. 13.

whence the consent of the contracting parties has a sacramental character.[1]

9. Such is the Catholic doctrine of the sacraments, as it was afterward adopted substantially unchanged by the Council of Trent. Two elements concurred from the beginning in its construction, the materializing of grace and the hierarchical conception of the church (vid. Augustine). The sacraments infuse grace, but the priests make the sacraments. We have been considering the conception of grace involved, and it remains for us to glance briefly at the conception of the church, where we will find that no advance has been made upon the utterances of Hugo.

(*a*) " The Church is the same thing as the assembly (*congregatio*) of the faithful, and every Christian is, therefore, a member of the church." This definition (Thomas, exposit. symbol. opp. xvii. 69) asserts nothing more than that the Christian community is the church. Thomas employs also, instead of this, the term *communio fidelium* (summ. suppl. q. 23, a. 1).[2] In the church, as in Noah's ark, there is salvation. That is to say, in the "communion of saints" is transmitted, *i. e.*, participation in the sacraments, for this is Thomas's conception of the term.[3]

---

[1] It is true that, for those who express such consent, the creative benediction becomes effective. It may be said, in case they are Christians, that the blessing of the kingdom of Christ is also theirs; but can we think of a display of grace here which would not be identical with that personally experienced? The objection commonly urged by Protestants that, although marriage is acknowledged as a sacrament, virginity is regarded as a higher state, has no force, as a parallel to this is furnished in the case of repentance.

[2] This is the current definition of the church. Vid., *e. g.*, Duns, report. iv. d. 24, q. 1. 5: *universitas fidelium*. In sent. iv. d. 19, § 15: *communio fidelium*. The meaning is peculiarly clear in De perfec. statuum 34. 9: the church is the *congregatio* of all believers, *i. e.*, the Saracens, for example, do not belong to it. Occam. dial. Goldast, monarchia, ii. pp. 402, 503, 471, 481, 498, 788, 799: *congregatio fidelium*, or *communitas fidelium* or *christianorum*, ib. p. 788 ff., 806 f., 810, 814, 923. Marsil. Defensor pac. ii. 2, p. 193; 6, p. 209, in Goldast, monarch. ii. Biel, expos. can. miss. lect. 22 D. Thomas Motter, doctrinale, ii. 9 ff.

[3] The term, *communio sanctorum*, is very differently interpreted : of the *sacraments*, *e. g.*, Abelard (Mi. 178, p. 629), Ivo of Chartres (Mi. 162, 606), Thom. l. c.; of the *saints*, *e. g.*, *Bruno* of Würzburg (Mi. 142, 500), in Schönbach's Altd. Predigten, i. 42 f. 46; of the *angels*, *e. g.*, Alexander (summ. iv. q. 37, § 9); of the *church triumphant* (Gerson, opp. i. 240); of the *saints and the sacraments*, *e. g.*, Bonav. centiloq., p. 3, § 38—worthy of note is the remark of Joslenus of Soissons (Mi. 186, 1488), in which the two are thus combined: "I believe the truth of the sacraments, in which the saints took part, so that I believe what they, too, believed in regard to baptism and the Lord's Supper;" cf. Richard, iii. d. 25, princ. 1, q. 2. Thom. Motter, doctrinale, v. 95 ; of *fellowship of the saints and the spiritual blessings secured by them* (vid. Hasack, Der chr. Glaube d. deutschen Volkes, etc.,

But the sacraments bring us grace. They lead us, further, to the ministers (*ministri*) who have received from the apostles authority for the forgiveness of sins (expos. p. 70). Thus the definition of the church as the congregation of believers fits in exactly with the conception of it as a body politic (*congregatio politica,* Thom. suppl. q. 26, a. 1), consisting of rulers (*rectores*) and subjects (*subditi*).

(*b*) But since the church is an organized state (*politia ordinata*), there is in it a gradation of rulers (Duns, iv. d. 24, § 3). In addition to the lawgivers, there must be some whose office it shall be to adapt the laws to circumstances (Thom. suppl. q. 20, a. 1). All priests are authorized to administer the eucharist, but some sacraments are reserved for the bishop. In regard to the power of the keys, a distinction is made between the key of the order (*clavis ordinis*) and the key of jurisdiction (*jurisdictionis*). The former, which grants forgiveness, belongs to the priesthood. The latter belongs to the bishop alone, and is his power of spiritual dominion, the plenary authority (*potestas plena*) to grant or refuse the sacraments, and also the jurisdiction in the administration of justice (*in foro causarum*). The bishop alone can grant to the priest the right to use the key which belongs to the latter (Thom. sent. iv. d. 18, q. 1, a. 1), in doing which he reserves special cases for his own decision (Thom. suppl. q. 20, a. 2). Hence: "The bishop alone is properly called a prelate (*praelatus*) of the church, and, therefore, he alone has plenary power in the dispensing of the sacraments and jurisdiction in the administration of justice, . . . but others, on account of that which is committed to them by him. But the priests who are set over the people are not simply prelates, but, as it were, assistants" (ib. q. 26, a. 1).

(*c*) But the church is One Body. In harmony with this is the solitary power of the pope (ib. q. 40, a. 6). "The supreme pontiff is the head of the whole church" (Thom. summ. ii. ii. q. 1, a. 10). He possesses "plenitude of power over ecclesiastical affairs" (ib. q. 89, a. 9). He rules in the church as a king in his kingdom, and the other bishops are admitted by him to a share in his care over the church (*in partem sollicitudinis,* Thom. sent. iv. d. 20, q. 1, a. 4). How then is the episcopal related to the papal power? The bishops, too, have by divine right the *plenitudo potestatis* in their own territories, but they have it together with the pope and in subjection to him. Accordingly, the pope has direct jurisdiction (*regimen immediatum*) over all

1868, p. 90); finally, of the *fellowship of the pious of all times and places,* Wessel, opp. p. 809. Erasm. opp. v. 1174.

10

souls, and can assert for himself episcopal rights in every territory. This was of great importance for the mendicant orders
in their preaching and confessionals (Thom. sent. iv. d. 17, q.
3, a. 3. Bonav., Quare fratres minores praedicent? opp. vii.
340 ff. and Explicat. regul. ib. 324 f.). To the pope belongs
law-giving and government in the church. He is to decide what
is correct faith, to publish upon occasion a new symbol of faith,
and to summon general councils (Thom. summ. ii. ii. q. 1, a.
10).[1] He proclaims indulgences (ib. suppl. q. 38, a. 1). He
stands above all princes as the vicar of Christ. If they rebel
against him, he may punish them by removal from office and by
releasing their subjects from the oath of allegiance to them (ib.
ii. ii. q. 67, a. 1 ; q. 12, a. 2 ; sent. iv. d. 44, q. 2). The
church attains its summit in the pope. With Aristotle, it was
held : "But the best government of a multitude is that it be
ruled by one" (c. gentil. iv. 76).

As compared with the leaders of the Gregorian age, the later
writers carried out many ideas to a further extent, and supported
their views by more painstaking argument, but they furnish
scarcely anything essentially new. The Second Council of
Lyons (A. D. 1274) accepted this view of the Romish primacy
(vid. Hefele, vi. 139 f., 141).

10. We stand now at the close of our period. It had inherited an abundance of suggestive thoughts from its predecessor,
which were all accepted and applied. Hence the wealth of
views and ideas in this century. As in the days of Origen and
Augustine, all contradictions seemed blended into a higher harmony. Reason and faith have entered into covenant, ideal and
reality, religion and science, contemplation and speculation, have
joined hands, and the body serves the regnant spirit. More than
this, the world appeared to be at length rendering due obedience
to the kingdom of God. The lord of the church is lord of the
world. Augustine and Aristotle, Anselm and Bernard, Hugo
and Abelard, Gregory VII. and Francis of Assizi—all the results
of their thought and efforts appeared melted into unity in the
writings of Thomas of Aquino. It was then that Otto of Freising wrote: "The kingdom (*civitas*) of Christ appears to have
received already in the present almost all things promised to it
except immortality" (Mon. Germ. scr. xx. 198). And yet,
shortly after the year 1300, premonitions of the coming crisis
began to appear. Of this our next chapter will treat.

---

[1] Upon infallibility, vid., further, quodlib. ix. a. 16 ; contra errores Graecor.
Also Albert, sent. iv. d. 20, a. 17.

CHAPTER III.

THE GRADUAL DISSOLUTION OF THE SCHOLASTIC THEOLOGY.
THE RELIGIOUS AND ECCLESIASTICAL CRISIS AT THE CLOSE
OF THE MIDDLE AGES.

§ 59. *The Theology of Duns Scotus and Its Significance for the
History of Doctrines.*

J. Duns Scoti, opp. ed. Wadding, 13 vols., 1639. Reprinted in the new
Paris edition in Vivès, 1891 ff., 26 vols. We are chiefly interested in the
Commentary upon the Sentences known as the Opus Oxoniense (which we
quote as "sent."), and the abbreviated copy of it in the Reportata Parisiensia
(which we quote as "report."). Cf. Werner, Duns Scotus, 1881. Plezan-
ski, Essai sur la philosophie de Duns Scot., 1887. Seeberg, Die Theologie
des Duns Scotus, 1900, and in PRE. v., ed. 3, 62 ff. Ritter, Gesch. d.
Philos. viii. 354 ff. Prantl, Gesch. d. Logik, iii. 202 f. Erdmann, Gesch.
d. Philos. i., ed. 4, 446 ff. Stöckl, Gesch. d. Philos. d. MA. ii. 778 ff.
Baur, Lehre v. d. Dreieinigkeit, ii. 448 ff., 589 ff., 621 ff., 642 ff., 673 ff.,
690 ff., 727 ff., 759 ff., 823 ff., 861 ff. Ritschl, Rechtf. u. Vers. i. 73 ff
Kahl, Primat des Willens in Aug., Duns Scot., u. Descartes, 1886, p. 76 ff
Siebeck, Die Anfänge der neueren Psychol. in d. Scholast., Ztschr. f. Philos.
u. phil. Krit., vol. 94, p. 161 ff.; 95, p. 245 ff.

1. The history of the dogmatic movements at the close of the
Middle Ages must begin with a study of Duns Scotus († 1308).
For, however true it may be that the masterly skill of this man in
dialectics and his acuteness carried the scholastic method to its
point of highest development, yet it is equally true upon the
other hand—and this must determine his historical position—
that the theological method which he pursued became the controlling influence leading to the dissolution of the scholastic
theories and the crisis in theology.

We must first briefly note the leading positions in the general
conception of the universe entertained by Duns. Upon the
question of Universals he stood upon the basis of a modified
Realism (vid. p. 104). The universal he held to be as well
before as *in* and *after* an object. Everything which exists, exists
also, since everything comes from God, as an eternal original
image in the mind of God (sent. i. d. 35, q. 1, § 12). Here
comes to light an important variation from the view of Thomas,
as Duns lays the emphasis upon the singular, and no longer upon
the universal. The individual being, the *individuitas* or *haeccei-
tas* is, according to his view, the real goal of nature, and is
therefore, as compared with the universal, the higher form of existence (rep. i. d. 36, q. 4. 14). There is an ultimate reality of
being (*ultima realitas entis*) which makes the particular object to

be just what it is. From this results the emphasis laid upon experience as a ground of knowledge (*e. g.*, de anim. q. 15). In
the theory of knowledge, Duns adopts, in a general way, the
prevailing Aristotelian formulas. The intellect apprehends the
intelligible form (*species intelligibilis*) which is presented to it
in the sensible object, and thus begets the conception. He
does not, like Thomas, interject the "intelligible form" between the sensuous perception and the intellect, but it is already
present in the perception and given with it. Hence, upon the
Scotist theory of knowledge, the individual object is as such perceptible (de anim. q. 22. 4). But he very strongly emphasizes
also the spontaneity of the spirit in the act of perception. The
object does not beget the conception in the (passive) spirit, but
the intellect is the organ which apprehends the object and im-
prints the conception. But here the will asserts itself. It impels
to thought, or restrains from it ; it constrains to or prohibits agreement with the conception received (sent. ii. d. 42, q. 4. 5, 10 f.).[1]
Thinking in itself occurs as a necessary and natural process (sent.
i. d. 32, q. 1. 14 ; ii. d. 42, q. 4. 5). It is only through its
connection with the will, which is free, as perception is not, from
the necessity of the causal process, that it receives a personal
and free character. From this originates one of the leading
thoughts of Duns, *i. e.*, the doctrine of the *primacy of the will*. The
entire inner and outer man, with all his thoughts, words, works,
and impulses, is subject to the will. It is the will alone which
makes human conduct good or bad (sent. ii. d. 42, q. 4). The
will, and not the thought, is the organ for the appropriation of the
highest objects and values. Faith does not arise without the consent of the will (iii. d. 25, q. 1. 11). Love is realized in the will,
and blessedness is experienced by it (ii. d. 25, § 13 f., 19 ;
iv. d. 49, quaest. ex latere, § 10 ff.). According to Thomas,
blessedness consists in the intellectual contemplation of the
supreme end, from which contemplation results the joy of the
pacified will (Thom. summ. ii. 1, q. 2-5). According to Duns,
it consists in the apprehension of God, as the present supreme
good, in the voluntary act of love, which brings with it the supreme satisfaction of man's longings. But this joy is only an
accompanying experience, while the real blessedness consists in
the apprehension of God (iv. d. 49, q. 4. 7, 8). The will is
free, for as touching the same object the will has the choice of
a *velle* or a *nolle* (ii. d. 25, § 6). Not in the object therefore
lies the determining ground of the will, nor in the perception,

---

[1] Except when the conception carries its own absolute evidence, Quaest.
subtiliss. in metaphys. 9.

which always but reflects the object, but in the will itself. " Nothing else than the will is the cause of the entire volition in the will " (ii. d. 25, § 22). Only upon the premise of freedom is the possibility of meritorious conduct intelligible (ib.). A strict proof of the freedom of the will, *i. e.*, the existence of a contingent course of action, cannot, indeed, be produced, but it is attested by immediate experience. If anyone were to cast doubt upon contingent conduct and events, he ought to be flogged until he should acknowledge the possibility of not being flogged (i. d. 39, § 13).

This brief summary must here suffice. The interest of Duns centres, not in the universal, but in the singular and in the individual. And in his conception of man, the chief thing is that man himself freely wills. These are ideas which foreshadow a new conception of the universe. The emphasis is laid, not upon ideas nor the perception of them, but as, on the one hand, man himself is nothing more than his individual free will, so the final end, or goal, of the world is to be seen in the concrete separate objects which it contains.

2. What then is the task of Theology? It presupposes revelation. The latter instructs man as to the end which his will should pursue and the means for attaining it (sent. prol. q. 1. 6 ff.). These truths necessary to salvation are presented by the Holy Scriptures. The credibility of the latter is exhaustively proved. The resultant may be stated in two propositions : " That the doctrine of the canon is true," and " that the Sacred Scriptures sufficiently contain the doctrine necessary to the prilgrim " (ib. q. 2. 14). Duns, like Thomas, maintains that this truth is summarized in the Apostles' Creed, or, also, in the three symbols of the ancient catholic church (iii. d. 25, q. 1. 4 ; i. d. 26, § 25 ; iv. d. 43, q. 1. 11). He, however, placed beside the authority of the Scriptures and these symbols, as of equal value, the teaching of " the authentic Fathers " and of the " Romish church " (i. d. 26, § 26). " Nothing is to be held as of the substance of the faith except that which can be expressly derived (*expresse haberi*) from Scripture, or which is expressly declared by the church, or which follows evidently from something plainly contained in Scripture or plainly determined by the church " (iv. d. 11, q. 3. 5). As the church has decided which books belong to the canon, the requirement of subjection to the Scriptures is equivalent to subjection to the church, which "approves and authorizes " the books of Scripture (iii. d. 23, q. 1. 4 ; i. d. 5, q. 1. 8). In the last resort, the Romish church is the only authority. Her utterance decides what is or is not heretical. Even if a doctrine be deprived of all other authority

and all arguments drawn from reason, it must be accepted solely upon the authority of the Romish church (iv. d. 6, q. 9. 14, 16, 17). This is the churchly positivism of the later Scholasticism. The ecclesiastical doctrines are employed as so many legal precepts, and orthodoxy receives a juristic flavor. But, as at a later period, so already in Duns, this positivism is only a counterpoise to an unlimited criticism of the traditional doctrines. He criticizes not only the contemporary theologians, but even Augustine and Aristotle (especially Thomas and Heinrich). In regard to many a traditional dogma, impossibility of proof and aimlessness are openly acknowledged (transubstantiation, habitus), or the possibility of the contrary opinion granted. The decision, however, is always in favor of the Romish doctrine, although under the formal endorsement may lurk many a bold perversion of the sense.

The complex of positive and practical truths[1] of which theology treats is apprehended in faith. Duns acknowledged the possibility of explaining faith in a perfectly natural way, as assent to tradition (*fides acquisita*, vid. iii. d. 23, § 1, 4 ff.). But the "authority of Scripture and the saints" demands the recognition of a supernatural habitus, the *fides infusa* (ib. § 14). This is a habitus infused into the intellect, as the habitus of love is infused into the will. To speak more exactly, it is a *habitus inclinans*, which impels, but does not compel, the intellect to assent. There is thus retained even here some liberty of action for the will (§ 11). This *assensus*, as infused, has a permanence and certainty which does not characterize acquired faith (§ 15 f.). In regard to *implicit* faith, his position agreed with that of Thomas (supra, p. 103).

3. In his discussion of separate doctrines, we will find almost everywhere in Duns suggestions which assumed great importance for later ages. We note first his conception of God. He endeavors from the principles of causality, finality, and eminence to establish the necessity of an Infinite Being, which has its cause or end in nothing else, and which can be outranked by nothing (i. d. 2, q. 2. 10 ff.). But, as in this scheme God is viewed under the aspects of the First Cause (*primum efficiens*) and the Self-acting (*per se agens*), there result a number of valuable

---

[1] Duns strongly emphasized the positive character of theology (sent. prol. q. 2, lateral.). It has an independent sphere, and, as a number of contingent facts are embraced in it, other principles than those of metaphysics (l. c., § 29). He maintains likewise the practical nature of the propositions of theology; for even such doctrines as those of the Trinity or the conception of the Son are of a practical nature, since their aim is to awaken love for the object presented (l. c. § 32).

positive ideas.   First of all, " That the first cause is intelligent
and volitional " (*intelligens et volens*) (§ 20).   This is proved
as follows : There is in the world contingent causality.   Since
now every second cause causes " in so far as it is moved by the
first," the First Cause must also act contingently, *i. e.*, it is free
will (ib.).   "Therefore either nothing happens contingently,
i. e., is evitably caused, or the First Cause thus causes immediately what it would be able also not to cause " (§ 21).   It is
utterly impossible to derive contingency, with Aristotle, from
second causes, for the necessity of the all-embracing activity of
the First Cause would necessitate also the actions of the second
causes (i. d. 39, § 12).   God is, accordingly, to be represented
as free will.   This involves, further, that there can be found no
reason for his willing or not willing, since all willing is absolutely without ground or reason : " And, therefore, there is no
reason (*causa*) why his will willed this, except that his will is
will " (i. d. 8, q. 5. 24).   God, then, wills this or that, because
he wills it.   Good is, therefore, good because God wills it to be
so ; he does not will it because it is good (iii. d. 19, § 7).   All
things, considered in themselves, may be said to be possible to
the omnipotence of the divine will.   This *potentia absoluta* of
God has only one limit, *i. e.*, the logically impossible (iv. d. 10,
q. 2, 5, 11).   God can, therefore, according to his absolute
power, save the already lost Judas ; but he cannot give eternal
blessedness to a stone, nor make undone what has been done.
But by the side of this absolute power stands the ordained power
(*potentia ordinata*) of God, *i. e.*, the manifestations of divine
power upon the ground and within the bounds of laws and ordinances fixed—arbitrarily—by God himself.   God commonly
works according to his ordained power, but it is also conceivable
that he may, upon occasion, by virtue of his absolute power,
vary from the course of the former, or entirely abolish it.   For
example, the rule that no one shall receive glory who has not accepted grace might be abrogated (i. d. 44, § 1-4).   Duns conducts this whole discussion under the heading of the conception
of God as the absolute Being ; but it affords evidence that he
held ideas of God far transcending the limits of such a scheme.
This is proved especially by his important theory, that the sum
total of the relations of God to the world is to be described as
Love.   This idea he develops as follows : God wills, or loves,
himself.   As now all being originates in God, it is subject to
God as its final end, and has, therefore, a share in the love
which God exercises toward himself (iii. d. 32, § 2).   This love
embraces, accordingly, the whole creation, its present and its
future.   But the creation is a composite with a gradation of its

parts according to their relations to the final end. This relationship decides in every separate case the measure of the divine love to be bestowed. This produces the following scheme : (*a*) God loves himself. (*b*) He, therefore, loves that which has immediate relation to himself as its final end, or elect men, *i. e.*, God wills that there shall be men who, with himself, love him, and this loving will is predestination. (*c*) The divine love then directs itself upon the means for the realizing of this predestination, *i. e.*, the ordinances of grace. (*d*) Finally, God, for the sake of the elect, wills the more remote means, *i. e.*, the visible world (l. c., § 6).[1]

The doctrine of the Trinity need not long detain us. Duns, in the traditional way, deduces the Son from the divine thought, and the Spirit from the divine will (i. d. 2, q. 7, 3).

But it is not at this point that the historical significance of Duns' conception of God is to be seen, but in the fact that God is here, more clearly and distinctly than in the writings of Thomas, conceived as a thinking and willing personality, and that love is recognized as the content of the divine activity in the world. But since Duns made the arbitrary will of God the source of all things, faith in the traditional formulas concerning the harmony and order of the universe was shattered. It was, accordingly,

---

[1] Some further remarks upon the views of Duns upon predestination are needful. Although he did not attach much practical importance to the doctrine, he yet applied it theoretically with great zeal. The question, whether a predestinated person can be lost, he answers in the affirmative, since God might have willed the one as well as the other (i. d. 40, § 1, 2). God can, therefore, predestinate any person, or he can fail to predestinate him. Duns answers the objection, that predestination leads to immortality, by asserting that the will of God cannot be limited from without (§ 3). The current conception, that predestination depends upon prescience, he refutes by observing that God always foresees all contingent events in their dependence upon the divine will, and, therefore, the good deeds of men appear as determined by the divine will (i. d. 41, § 10). Besides, this would not apply to children dying in infancy, who are, without any deeds of theirs, either elected or reprobated. Duns himself teaches that predestination has no ground whatever upon man's part ; for the divine will that any creature be saved exists before faith or good works, and hence the latter cannot under any circumstances constitute the ground of the former (ib. § 11). In reprobation, it is true, it appears necessary to grant such a ground in man, the foreseen final sin, since otherwise the justice of the sentence cannot well be conceived (ib.). The difficulties thus remaining were not overlooked by Duns. He suggests, further, that it be supposed that God, while predestinating Peter to glory and then to grace, in regard to Judas, determined nothing at all, but, on the contrary, willed that both belong to the "mass of perdition." Inasmuch as the first-named act of the divine will had relation to Peter, he receives grace and eternal life, while Judas is simply left to perdition (§ 12). The discussion closes with a warning against prying into such matters, and an exhortation that everyone be allowed to hold his own opinion, only so that the divine freedom be guarded against any charge of unrighteousness (§ 13).

no longer eternal ideas and laws, but the positive activity of God, which constituted the material of religious knowledge. On the other hand, a powerful weapon was, by this new conception of God, placed in the hands of the critics of the traditional teachings of the church. If the illogical is to be acknowledged as frequently true, may not the logical also be false? And when once the idea of absolute power has been admitted, may not anything be regarded as conceivable, as possible, or as allowable?

4. The sinlessness of man in paradise was, in and of itself, only potential, since the will as such always involves the possibility of sinning. The actual innocence of the first pair can, therefore, be explained only by their possession of their additional endowment, the *donum superadditum* (ii. d. 23, § 6, 7). There is in man by nature, in consequence of the existence of the sensuous impulses together with the reason and will, an inward rebellion. Only the imparted supernatural habitus of grace is able to subject the lower forces to the higher (ii. d. 29, § 4). If, therefore, concupiscence, or the rebellion of the sensuous nature against the spirit, belongs to the original human nature, original sin cannot possibly consist in concupiscence. Original Sin, on the contrary, is to be described as only a want (*carentia*) of original righteousness (d. 30, q. 2. 3). It has as its material concupiscence, but this gains control and becomes sin only through the loss of the restraining rein (*frenum cohibens*, d. 32, § 7). This view presents the question of the propagation of sin in a new light. Duns opposes the theory of physical inheritance. If sin is in the will, how can the latter make the whole body sick? And if this were the case, why should the seed only, and not the spittle and blood as well, be infected? Or again, how should the inherited physical condition transform the will? (d. 32, § 4 f.). The solution must be reached from another direction. Since the original righteousness was bestowed upon Adam for himself and his posterity, it is a righteousness which they now owe, a *justitia debita*. "By virtue of such a gift, the will of every child of his becomes a debtor" (ib. § 8-12).[1] Conception demands attention in the case only as being that which makes man a child of Adam. Only as descended from Adam, is he a debtor to the righteousness granted to the latter (§ 17). It is evident that the Augustinian theory of original sin is here

[1] It does not harmonize with this, that Duns asserts that our first parents could not have transmitted their righteousness to their posterity (ii. d. 20, q. 1, 3). He maintains, therefore, in this passage that had Adam not fallen, God would by co-operation have regularly imparted grace to the children of the race. This is, however, nothing more than a postulate—to account in some way for the inheritance of sin—in the doctrinal system of Duns.

surrendered in its fundamental principle.   In place of the physical propagation of the original concupiscence, is posited the
ideal obligation of every child of Adam to the supernatural righteousness once granted to Adam.[1]

The teaching of Duns in regard to Actual Sin is in keeping with
this theory of original sin.   The former is a defect in the will.
Instead of loving the supreme good, or God, the will of man
rests content with an earthly end as its supreme good.   He thus
offends also against the divine law revealed to him (d. 37, q. 1,
6 f.).

5. We may, perhaps, venture the opinion that the Christology
of Duns displays a higher appreciation of the human life of
Christ than is manifested by the other great Scholastics.   This
is noticeable especially in his discussions of the impartation of
grace to the soul of Jesus (iii. d. 13, q. 1. 3), and of the knowledge of Jesus (iii. d. 14), in which he maintains that the soul of
Jesus by its union with the Logos possessed at least an inherent (*habituale*) knowledge of all universals, but that it was
subject to the necessity of gaining a progressive knowledge of the
individual and the contingent, so that Lk. ii. 40 is to be understood of a real progress (l. c., q. 2. 16, 20; q. 3. 6 ff.).   It is
granted also that pain could penetrate to the higher part of the
soul of Jesus (ib. q. 15).   Merit likewise is attributed to the
human nature of Christ.   He merited the favor of God, because
he did not yield to his sensuous desires.   He could merit by
fasting, watching, and prayer (iii. d. 18, § 4-6).   But all of this
does not extend to the experiences and visions of the person of
Jesus which occur so abundantly in the devotional literature of
the Middle Ages (supra, p. 89 f.).   This is to be acounted for by
the fact that Duns clings unalterably to the christological scheme
of the ancient church, which he, like the other Scholastics, interprets after the manner of Abelard.   The union is a relation
of subordination (*relatio ordinis*), a relation of dependence of
the human upon the divine nature, a relation which may be compared to that between attribute and substance (iii. d. 1, q. 1. 3).
The divine nature is in no wise limited by its relation to the human.   The latter, in the moment of its genesis, subordinates
itself to the divine nature and receives at once and thereby from

---

[1] Duns abolished the conception of original sin, or substituted for it that of
original debt.   But the substitution, although aiming to maintain the idea of
guilt, or debt, cannot be regarded as satisfactory, for it fails to afford that
which it is the province of the theory of original sin to furnish, *i. e.*, to explain the universality and depth of the conviction of guilt.   If God withdrew
righteousness from Adam, and this could be bestowed upon his descendants
only by a special divine act, it is not easy to see how the sense of guilt can be
traced to the concupiscence originally inhering in human nature.

the latter its personality (ib. § 9 ; d. 2, q. 2. 12). A human personality, or separate existence, of Jesus is in no wise to be maintained (d. 5, q. 2. 4). It has not even an independent existence (*esse*). It has its existence from the divine Logos-person, as my foot exists only by virtue of my existence (d. 6, q. 1. 2 ff.). The proposition : God became man, is not an accurate statement. The becoming was only an experience of the man, not of the Logos. To speak properly, we should say : " the human nature is united personally with the Word " (d. 7, q. 2. 5 ff.). There is a unity of the two natures, which consists in the union, *i. e.*, in the relation of the one to the other (iii. d. 1, q. 2. 10).[1] These conceptions do not indicate an advance in the knowledge of the subject. The doctrine of Duns is certainly orthodox, but it is, in consequence, not clear. Shall it really be thought possible for us to think of that human nature which resists the allurements of sensuality in order to merit the divine favor as absolutely impersonal—as something which, with no existence of its own, has been united as an attribute to the infinite divinity of the Logos? The two currents of medieval Christology—as represented in Abelard and Bernard—here meet, and it is evident that they will not unite—not, at least, in the channel of the traditional formulas. The rational Christology of Abelard discriminated sharply between the finite and the infinite, in order to insure the independence of the finite ; while the pious reflection of Bernard beheld in the human words and deeds of the finite Jesus the revelation of the love of the infinite God. Abelard was mainly concerned for the humanity of Jesus, but he in reality promoted the undue emphasizing of his divinity. Bernard sought the ever-present heavenly Son of God, and he awakened and deepened appreciation for the humanity of Jesus. Abelard's ideas adapted themselves to the traditional formulas, found a place in the dogmatic system of the Middle Ages, and have endured beyond that period. Bernard's ideas were not accepted by the dogmatic system of the Middle Ages, but they influenced the life of the age, and thus frequently made inroads upon the logical consistency of the dogmatic formulas. An illustration of this may be seen in the portraiture by Duns of the man Jesus as acting meritoriously.

6. Duns confessedly owed something of his repute to his championship of the Immaculate Conception of the Virgin

---

[1] During his stay in Hades, Christ was not a man, as, *e. g.*, the Lombard teaches. For in his state of death the various parts of the human nature were not really united with the divinity of Christ, although they may have still existed. Vid. iii. d. 22, § 18 ff. Christ was, hence, in Hades only according to his divinity.

Mary. He casts doubt upon the then current opinion that, since Mary was born of sinful seed, it was necessary for Christ to be her Saviour as well as her Son. The argument drawn from the sinfulness of the seed had no force for Duns. On the other hand, it would appear fitting that Christ should merit salvation for the person most nearly related to him in an absolutely perfect way, *i. e.*, in such a way that she should remain free from original sin.

As God blots out original sin in baptism, so can he also do in the moment of conception. Christ's passion was then accepted in advance by God as the means of her salvation (iii. d. 3, q. 1. 3 f., 9, 14, 17). Mary, therefore, remained entirely untainted by sin. Her descent from Adam does not of itself involve sinfulness. Even if we should hold that the soul originates through generation in the moment of conception, it would not be necessary to regard Mary as sinful, since God could infuse grace into the soul in the very moment when it comes into being (ib. § 17, 20). Measured by the doctrine of Duns upon original sin, the advantage enjoyed by Mary is none too marked. The whole subject in Duns is treated rather as a theological hypothesis, not at all as a doctrine of any special importance.

7. We turn now to the work of Redemption. Duns denies the infinity of the merit of Christ. The merit of Christ is a matter of his human will ; it is the obedience which he rendered (iii. d. 19, § 4 ; iv. d. 2, q. 1. 7). Hence, as the human will of Christ is finite, so is also the merit which he gains through its exercise (iii. d. 19, § 5). This merit of Christ was foreseen by God as the means of human redemption. The divine predestination embraces that merit as the means of realizing its purpose. The passion of Christ was therefore foreordained from eternity by God as the means for the salvation of the predestinated. To it belongs a peculiar value and a special efficacy, not in and of itself, but by virtue of the foreordination of the divine will, which foreordained this means and *will accept it* as effectual (l. c., § 6). The merit of Christ is not of itself good, nor is it of itself a means of salvation, but it is the divine will alone that makes it the one or the other (§ 7). It might, indeed, of itself avail for all men, but it was God's will that its efficiency should be limited to the predestinated (§ 14).

But was the precise form of Christ's sufferings, or any rendering of satisfaction, necessary to man's salvation ? Duns raises this question in a criticism of Anselm's theory. He disputes, first of all, the necessity of a satisfaction, which he holds to have been necessary only because God so willed. But it was not necessary that God should will it, just as the salvation of men is itself not a necessary, but a contingent, act of God (iii. d. 20, § 7). But even granting the necessity of satisfaction, it would still by no means follow that the one rendering it must be God. It is not correct to say that something greater than the whole creation must be offered up to God. Any pious act of Adam would have sufficed to atone for his first sin (ib. § 8). Just as little can the demand that satisfaction must proceed from a man be strictly proved. The value (of the sacrifice) does not lie in the offered object as such, but in the acceptance by the divine will. But it is perfectly conceivable that God might will to accept the deed of an angel, or of a sinless man, as a sufficient atonement. Yea, it would even be conceivable that every sinful man might have rendered satisfaction for himself, if God should, by imparting the primary grace (*gratia prima*), qualify him for meritorious action and accept this as a satisfaction (§ 9). In this criticism it is plainly to be seen that the conception of God entertained by Duns excludes all necessity for the occurrence of the events connected with the passion of Christ. That which came to pass, came to pass according to God's free will ; and entirely different occurrences were in themselves conceivable. That which has actually occurred is, God has willed ; but who will prescribe to him that he has been compelled so to will? This idea is a gain as compared with the rationalistic speculation of Anselm.

Duns gave but a brief positive response to the above question. Christ suffered " for the sake of righteousness." He beheld the sins of the Jews and their perverted adherence to the law. Christ willed " to recall them from that error through his works and discourses." He declared to them the truth, and died for righteousness. To this is to be added, that since he offered his passion in our behalf to the Father, he bound us to himself, and thus to God, with fetters of gratitude. "Therefore he did this chiefly, as I believe, to allure us to his love, and because he wished man to be more securely bound to God" (§ 10). This theory of satisfaction follows most closely the type of Abelard, although Duns declares it possible to make use of Anselm's ideas, if "divine ordination be presupposed" (§ 10). From another passage we may gather how Duns conceived the objective side of the atonement. God will not forgive the sins of the transgressor unless something be offered to him which pleases him more than the sins of mankind displease him. This could only be the obedience of a person more fervently loved by God than mankind would have been loved by him had they not sinned. This was the person of Christ, who in his obedience offered the highest love in enduring death for righteousness' sake (iv. d. 2, q. 1. 7).

For the sake of the obedience and the love of Christ, God bestows grace upon mankind.   There is thus attested in the activity of Christ, as in the divine act of deliverance, the combined action of mercy and righteousness (ib. § 8).

The theory of redemption held by Duns embraces thus two leading thoughts : (1) The pious obedience, or the love, of Jesus is, according to the will of God, acknowledged as meritorious and employed as the means of bestowing grace upon man. (2) This activity of Christ, sealed by his death, has conquered mankind and incited them to love and gratitude.   The obedience and love of Jesus thus became the occasion, on the one hand, for the bestowal of grace by God, and, on the other, for the renewal of mankind.[1]

8. The essential result of the work of Christ is, therefore, that he merited for us the impartation of Grace.   This leads us to examine the conception of grace.   By this term, as *gratia creata* (supra, p. 118 f.), Duns understands the habitus of love, created in man, which inclines the will to meritorious works (ii. d. 27, § 3).   This habitus equips man with a worthiness (*dignitas*), "which consists in a correspondence of merit to reward," by virtue of which man becomes dear to God (§ 4).   Grace is a co-operating

---

[1] Duns himself did not effect a combination of these two lines of thought, having treated the questions involved but briefly.   This may be attempted in various ways.   It may be said, for example, that the love of Christ transformed the character of men, and that this became the ground of God's display of grace toward them.   If we would gain a proper understanding of the view of Duns, we must bear in mind that he conceived the entire work of salvation and grace under the scheme of means and end (supra, p. 152).   In the will of God, priority is given to the glorification and gracious acceptance of the elect above the mission of Christ as the means of effecting grace and of consequent glory.   If we now apply this scheme, further, to the two aspects of the work of Christ in the writings of Duns, the logical priority must be given to the manward aspect, since the object of the work of Christ is to win the elect. From this we might derive the thought : that, in order to be able to awaken love and gratitude in men, Christ used his influence with the Father to secure the bestowal of grace.   But I doubt whether this was the idea of Duns, for he does not by a single word suggest that the granting of grace is the condition upon which alone the love and example of Christ can become effectual.   On the contrary, Christ exerted the latter influence upon the Jews—before grace had been bestowed.   If, on the other hand, we seek to combine the two aspects in the activity of Christ in the way first suggested, thus making the influence exerted upon God dependent upon the result secured in man, we come into direct conflict with the fundamental tenor of the discussion.   It follows that the two conceptions are not to be subordinated the one to the other, but to be co-ordinated—perhaps somewhat as follows : Christ lived among men and prepared them for the grace which he secured from the Father, or, Christ secured grace from the Father for the men whom he by his life won for the Father.   Thus, too, would the relation of Christ and his work to the human race become intelligible.   The important thought, that Christ is the head of the race, which we find in Thomas, is lacking in Duns.

principle (*principium co-operans*) beside the will (ii. d. 7, § 15). Meritorius conduct results therefore from the working together of the will-power and the habitus (i. d. 17, q. 2. 8). Since the will without the habitus can produce an act, but not the habitus without the will, the leading part in this co-operation appears to belong to the will. The habitus simply complements the act (ib. § 9), or it stimulates to its performance (§ 12). The habitus is, therefore, a certain supernatural influence which gives to the will an *inclinatio* to action and secures the performance of the action "with delight, promptly and expeditiously" (ib.). It appears, however, since action without the habitus is perfectly conceivable, that the former has no need of the latter. But then man would act meritoriously by his natural powers alone (*ex solis naturalibus*), which would be a Pelagian doctrine. There must therefore be a supernatural form, which shall imprint its character upon man's actions without limiting his own activity, and thus also his merit! (ib. q. 3. 18, 19).

But it may be urged against the doctrine of the Habitus, that experience does not attest it, since the moral acts referred to may very readily be realized without it (q. 3. 21). Duns silently acknowledges this. But it is not only our separate acts, he holds, which are acceptable to God, but our whole nature, and the ground of this is to be found in the habitus (ib. § 22). Of the habitus it is to be said: "That this habitus, beyond that which is decorous, is a spiritual (power) inclining to determinate actions" (§ 23). The acceptance of an act, on the other hand, as meritorious is entirely a matter of the divine will (iv. d. 22, qu. un. § 9). We may, therefore, discriminate in an act between its substance and its meritorious quality. In the former aspect, the will occupies the place of prominence ; in the latter, the habitus has greater influence, since an act appears more worthy of reward when begotten of love than when begotten of free will (§ 27). The act receives its value in the sight of God—according to divine appointment—from the fact that grace co-operates in its production. The habitus is the rider, the will the steed. As the steed can have value for anyone only in so far as it carries the rider to a definite goal, so the act, produced in the first instance by the will, is made valuable in the sight of God only through its connection with the habitus (§ 28).[1] It can hardly be said that this con-

---

[1] Very interesting are the remarks of Duns, l. c., § 28 : As every intellectual capacity necessarily bears within itself the intelligible object, so must also the moral habituality, to a certain extent, bear in itself the lovable good. When now this habitus incites to activity, the resulting action will be directed toward the good embraced in the habitus. Since the habitus receives its power essentially from the object toward which it is directed, its influence may

ception of the supernatural habitus has been made perfectly plain, still less that its necessity has been clearly demonstrated ! Duns retained the traditional physical conception of grace, but he sublimated it as far as possible. Grace is for him not the *material* of Christian acts, but really only a something which gives to man a new direction, an inclination toward God, and a value in his sight. Duns recognized the fact that there was really no need of the *gratia creata*, and we can easily understand why he was unable to make use of it in his expositions of the moral life. Thus the will remained, after all, as the chief cause of human conduct. But was not Duns, nevertheless, nearer in his views to the proper evangelical conception of the matter than Thomas, or even than Augustine himself?

And what was his conception of Justification ? He discusses it in connection with the sacrament of repentance.[1] We select the doctrine of the *attritio* as our starting-point. This is supposed to establish a merit of fitness (*de congruo*), as a preparation for the achievement of justification. This half-penitence is, therefore, meritorious, and through it man merits justification (iv. d. 14, q. 2. 14, 15 ; cf. d. 19, § 32). But it must be borne in mind that the final cause is not really the human merit as such, but the will of God which has appointed this relationship. Duns discriminates in justification between the infusion of grace and the forgiveness of sins (iv. d. 16, q. 1. 4). The former is an actual change (*mutatio realis*), for before grace is infused it has no existence. The forgiveness of sins, on the contrary, is only an ideal change, since it calls into existence nothing essentially new in man (ib. § 6), and the guilt of man is no real entity, but only the ideal relationship to the desert of punishment (§ 7). Even in God, the forgiveness of sins is no separate act, but God never wills that any man be punished without also willing that—under certain definite conditions—he be no more punished, and he, likewise, never wills that any man be not punished without willing also that, under certain conditions, punishment be meted out to him (ib. § 12). If the forgiveness of sins thus denotes only the ideal and conditional change, that the one liable to punishment (*puniendus*) becomes no longer liable to punishment (*non puniendus*), the infusion of grace is, on the contrary, a real change. It is the factor which really effects justifi-

---

be ascribed essentially to the activity of the said object. But that is merely to say, that the direction of man's activity toward God gives to his conduct its value and character.

[1] This is, therefore, the appropriate connection in which the conception of justification stands. Cf., *e. g.*, Carthusian. iv. d. 17, q. 1, 2. This corresponds with the practical situation of the day.

cation. And, as the infusion of grace is more intimately related
to the object, *i. e.*, to the glorification and gracious acceptance
of man, than is the forgiveness of sins, the former has the priority
in the divine will ; but in the actual execution of that will in
time, the order is reversed, and stands : first, forgiveness of sins,
then infusion of grace (§ 19. Cf. i. d. 17, q. 3. 19 : "that
God naturally remits an offense before he gives grace to him," *i. e.*,
the offender).[1] Here, too, Thomas taught differently (supra, p.
121). Duns denies a causal connection of the two processes,
since neither can be logically deduced from the other (§ 19).

Such is the doctrine of grace according to Duns. By attrition
man secures the merit of fitness. He is thereby prepared for the
reception of justification, or the infusion of grace, particularly in
the sacrament of repentance ; and this enables him to do meritorious works. These are ideas which became controlling forces
in the Scholasticism of the later Middle Ages. But along with
them we note, as also characteristic, the separation of forgiveness of sin and infusion of grace, and the spiritualizing of the
conception of grace. The ideas of Duns served as a support for
the superficial praxis of the church, but, considered in their entire connection, they were nearly always directed against the
Augustinian foundations underlying this praxis. In illustration,
we recall the statement, that there is really no such thing as
"merit" in itself considered, but that God accepts certain definite
acts as merits ; and, on the other hand, the challenge : If everything depends upon the divine acceptance, to what end then the
gradation of merits ?

9. At this point the doctrine of the Sacraments finds its place,
for it is through the latter that grace is infused into man. As we
have already considered them in § 58, we here recall only the chief
principle involved. The sacraments are symbols, which signify the
working of grace, and which, by virtue of a divine covenant, produce in the soul a creative act of God concurrent with their reception. We may describe the sacrament as, to a certain extent,
a cause of grace (*causa gratiae*), inasmuch as it, as it were, compels the accompanying presence of grace (sent. iv. d. 1, q. 5. 12).
The critical ability of Duns is here also displayed (criticism of
the "character"), as well as a certain inclination to differently
interpret and refine the traditional conceptions (repentance and
the Lord's Supper).

---

[1] In this order, Duns follows, as far as I can see, the course of ROBERT
GROSSETESTE in the tractate, De gratia et justificatione hominis (in Brown,
Fascicul. rer. expetendarum et fugiendarum, 1690, append. 282. Cf. Wiclif,
De dominio divin. iii. 5, p. 246 f., ed. Poole). So also WILHELM V. PARIS,
opp. ii. f., 48 v. Cf. also CARTHUSIAN. iv. d. 17, q. 2.

10. It remains for us to characterize the position of Duns in the History of Doctrines. It is hardly saying too much to designate his theology as the key to the dogmatic history of the fourteenth and fifteenth centuries. This is true primarily in a formal sense. The refinement of dialectic art to the point of hair-splitting, the tingling delight in logical proof and disproof, the complicating of linguistic expression—he wrestles with language, and, instead of creating new forms for new ideas, the old forms are split into shreds,—this was learned by latter theologians from Duns. But they also learned from him to apply dialectics ruthlessly and earnestly to even the deepest mysteries of religion. There are no mysteries before which reason must halt. Almost everything is for him open to scrutiny,[1] and the more fully the miraculous can be eliminated the better. "I concede that, even in the things believed, nothing more should be posited without necessity, nor more miracles than necessary" (sent. iv. d. 11, q. 3. 14). All this tended, on the one hand, to hasten the dissolution and downfall of medieval thought ; but it was not only in view of this that it was "timely." It provided for theology, at the proper moment, the forms which assured and directed to it the interest of the age.

As to the material influence of the Scotist dogmatics, its method appears to be only the direct continuation of that of Thomas, i. e., the authorities and reason are to be brought into harmony. But with how much greater enthusiasm and fervency did not Thomas address himself to the task ! For him, dogma and philosophy really coalesced to form one great system of religious philosophy embracing heaven and earth. Thomas yet believed, not only in the absolute truth of the church's dogma, but also in its agreement with scientific knowledge. This second conviction has, in Duns, receded far into the background. Theology and metaphysics are sharply discriminated. It is not the province of theology to construct a universally applicable philosophical system, but a complex structure of practical truths, i. e., truths bearing upon the conduct. Nor is it by any means to be taken for granted that these truths can always be made clear to reason. The criticism of Duns has a keener edge and loftier aim than that of Thomas. In regard to many a leading Romish doctrine he declares, that its suitability for attaining the end in view cannot be proved, and that not much is to be said against the oppo-

---

[1] How much light it casts upon the position and tendency of Duns to observe that he develops his theory of knowledge when treating of the doctrine of angels ; that he presents his psychology under the heading of eschatology ; and that the discussion of the sacrament of repentance gives him opportunity to expound his theory of political economy !

site opinion. Duns is, indeed, particularly fond of throwing out hints of this nature, and yet in the end working out some sort of arguments in support of the proposition in question. But the attentive reader will observe, what is elsewhere openly declared, that the authority of the Romish church is, after all, the decisive consideration. Even the propositions incomprehensible to reason and incapable of proof are true—because Rome teaches them. Duns no longer believes in the agreement of dogma and philosophy ; but he believes in the authority of Rome. Like Thomas, and yet how different ! For, inasmuch as in Thomas these two principles coalesce, his faith in Rome retains a religious character. But since, in Duns, even the incomprehensible and unreasonable becomes truth through the authority of Rome, this authority begins to assume the aspect of positive law. Both the criticism of accepted dogmas and this ecclesiastical positivism exercised a controlling influence upon the theology of the future.

But Duns is not to be counted among the leaders of thought who accomplish only negative results. He wrought also out of the materials of his age positive results for its advancement. And it was this fact that lent such force to his criticisms. His chief contribution of this character was his view of the will as the central function of the spirit, which dominates alike his anthropology and his theology. It is not the world in which man lives, nor the ideas which he derives from it, which explains his conduct and his aspirations—but his will. The will is the innermost faculty in man, the absolutely individual part of his nature. He no longer views with merely theoretic interest the divine panorama of the world's history, but he has himself become a co-operating factor in the shifting scenes. In volition he experiences the highest satisfaction. Man can be understood only by appreciating this will, free in itself and determined by nothing outside of itself. His worth depends upon it. It is the modern man[1] whose features are thus drawn in outline. The estimate of a man according to his own character and deeds, personal responsibility and self-determination,—these are ideas which are involved, at least implicitly, in the psychology of Duns, however imperfect and incomplete the latter may be in particular points. But this theory became even more significant when applied to God. Since God is conceived as the absolutely free Will, many of the categories of the traditional logic are dissolved, and the ground is swept from beneath all the speculations as to what God *must* do, and what must come to pass (cf. the criticism of

---

[1] Vid. also the elaboration of the doctrine of states of the mind by Duns, in SIEBECK, l. c., vol. 95, p. 251 ff.

Anselm). If the absolutely free, and even wanton Will is the ground of all things, then the truth can be learned only by the careful observation of objects and events. This explains the importance attached to the concrete and the empirical, and the appeal to experience, and, at the same time, the unrestrained liberty of thought as over against traditional theories, as well as a certain skepticism, which time and again leads the thoughtful student to rest content with a " probable " or " more probable." This definition of God betokens, however, a really deeper conception of the divine nature. The God of Duns is no longer the "absolute Substance," but a free, living Spirit. He did not venture even here, it is true, to cast aside the ancient formulas, but he conceived the large thought of God as the Loving-Will, the sum total of whose relations to the world is to be regarded from this point of view. Everything occurring in the world, as well as all divine activity, is—in religious reflection—to be viewed from the view-point of predestination. At this point Augustinian predilections exert their influence (cf. also Thomas, supra, p. 107), the Oxford circle from which Duns came being as distinctly Augustinian in temper as they were inclined to empirical investigation.[1] Nevertheless, Duns was no Augustinian. It was upon the basis of the predestination pervading all things and the divine freedom ordering all things that the theory of merit and good works first began to flourish. The ecclesiastical system is not in itself necessary, but it is—and this is more—positively determined upon and ordained by God. Thus the apparently Augustinian premise is transformed into the popular Catholicism of the close of the Middle Ages.

Finally, we can but point to the separate doctrines in which the theology of Duns scored an advance, i. e., a change as compared with the system of Thomas. In nearly all these instances, the later theologians followed in the steps of Duns. We have noted the divergencies in the question of first principles (skepticism and ecclesiastical positivism); the revision of the conception of

---

[1] A history of theology would find it needful at this point to discuss especially the work of the great bishop of Lincoln, ROBERT GROSSETESTE († A. D. 1253), who paved the way for the ideals of the mendicant orders in England and directed toward its goal the awakened scientific impulse (religion in the sense of Augustine, and empiricism in methods). It is to be regretted that we possess as yet neither a comprehensive biography of this great man, nor even an edition of his more important writings. Some material is furnished in BROWN, Fasciculus, etc., appendix, London, 1690. LUARD edited his letters (London, 1861). Vid. his introduction, and LECHLER, Wiclif, i. 177 ff. Also, supra, p. 161 n., and FELTON, Rob. Grosset., 1887. As to his theological position, see SEEBERG, Duns Scot., p. 11 ff. KROPATSCHECK, Das Schriftprincip der luth. Kirche, i. (1904), 359 ff.

God ; the emphasis upon the will in psychology ; the doctrine of the original state and the minimizing, *i. e.*, elimination, of original sin ; the theory of redemption, with the co-ordination of the subjective and objective aspects of the atonement ; the criticism of the Augustinian definition of grace, *i. e.*, the new definition of the habitus ; the significance of the *meritum de congruo ;* the Pelagianism in the order of salvation ; the logical apprehension of the relation between God and man under the scheme of the *meritum ;* the symbolical interpretation of the sacraments, with the severance of sign and substance ; and the criticism of transubstantiation.

Such is the theology of Duns Scotus. It proclaims the approaching downfall of the cosmology of the Middle Ages. Dogma and reason, church and world, threaten to part company. And yet—Thomas looks backward, Duns faces the future.

§ 60. *Criticism of Hierarchical Conception of the Church.*

1. We must here assume the familiarity of the reader with the outward history of the papacy from the days of Benedict XI., the successor of Boniface VIII. The papacy at Avignon reiterated, indeed, with lofty assumption the ancient claims of supremacy. But its dependence upon the course of French politics—the bull *Unam sanctam* was annulled, so far as France was concerned, and Boniface VIII. barely escaped condemnation for infidelity and frivolity— robbed its claims of all force or sacredness.   The great contest against Louis of Bavaria (A. D. 1314-47), despite many humiliations inflicted upon the emperor, set loose a storm of criticism of the papacy, its legality and its claims, which penetrated to its very foundations. The Electoral Union at Rense declared (A. D. 1338) that the electors elect the emperor, and that this election confers upon him the right of government in the empire without any nomination, approbation, or confirmation on the part of the Curia. The papacy, when again transferred to Rome, was rent by the great schism (A. D. 1378).   The moral delinquencies of many members of the hierarchy were well known, but, above all, the avarice of the Romish Curia.   The trade in spiritual offices, the indulgences, the papal taxes, etc., all served but one end, to procure money and much of it.   The unnatural character of the papal dominion made this a necessity ; it was a civil government without the regular sources of revenue. With murmurings against the draining of national resources by the papacy were combined bitter complaints of the immorality and dissipation of the higher as well as the lower clergy.[1] The widespread discontent

---

[1] A striking portraiture of the times is given in the work of NICHOLAS OF

awakened by these abuses led to a constantly growing demand for a reformation of the church, which led to the so-called " Reform Councils " at Pisa, A. D. 1409, at Constance, A. D. 1414-17, and at Basel, 1431-47. The exaltation of the church universal above the papacy was here asserted[1] and utterance given to many pious laments and hopes touching the " necessity of a reformation of the church in head and in members."[2] But there was neither the power nor the courage requisite for a thoroughgoing reformation. And every politic compromise indicated a victory for the old order of things. Thus the popes always grasped again the sceptre, and, despite all the complaints of clergy and laity, the reformation still remained only a pious wish. In the bull, " *Pastor aeternus*," Pope Leo X. announced to the world : " Since also that only the Roman pontiff (in office) for the time being, as having authority over all councils, has the full right and power of summoning, transferring, and dissolving councils, is evident not only from the testimony of the Holy Scriptures, the sayings of the holy fathers, and of the other Roman pontiffs, . . . and the decrees of the holy canons, but even from the very confession of the councils themselves " (Binius, Concil. general. ix. 151). And yet the great spiritual agitation, which disturbed the minds of multitudes for almost two hundred years, was not in vain. The mistrust of Rome and the hierarchy, the critical attitude toward the church and her laws, and, combined with this, the conviction that there is a church of God which is more and better than the hierarchical system of Rome—these ideas were engraven more and more deeply upon the general consciousness. And, just in proportion as the sense of national independence gained in strength and the value of earthly possessions increased, must these critical ideas become more extended in their scope and the unreasonableness of the Romish system

CLEMANGES, De ruina ecclesiae (in VON D. HARDT, Constant. concil. i. 3). He writes, p. 21 : Everywhere they search for. money (*quaestum*); they are greatly concerned about money ; they think money is piety. They do nothing at all unless they believe that, upon their doing it, money may be voted for the increase of their gain. For this they dispute, fight, swear, go to law ; they would bear with much greater equanimity the casting away of ten millions of souls than of ten or twelve solidi. Vid. also the other writings collected in this volume—from D'AILLI, GERSON, etc.; also DIETRICH V. NIEM, De scismate, ll. 3 ed. Erler, 1890.

[1] This council, assembled legitimately in the Holy Spirit, representing the Catholic church, has authority immediately from Christ, to which everyone of whatsoever rank or dignity, even the papal, he may be, is bound to render obedience in those things which pertain to the faith, . . . and to the general reformation of the said church in head and in members (Constanz sess. 5, vid. Mansi, xxvii. 590 ; Basel sess. 2, vid. Mansi, xxix. 21).

[2] Title of a document in HARDT, i. 7, p. 277.

become more evident. Cf. HEFELE, CG. vi. vii. SCHWAB, Gerson, 1858. TSCHACKERT, Peter v. Ailli, 1877. ERLER, Dietrich v. Niem, 1887.

2. The criticism of the hierarchical system in the new period found its fullest expression in the literature which was produced during the conflicts of Louis of Bavaria with the pope. Especially MARSILIUS OF PADUA and WILLIAM OCCAM developed ideas which tapped the very roots of the dominant system (vid. Mars., Defensor pacis. Occam, Octo quaestiones; Compendium errorum papae; Dialogus; Opus XC dierum,—all to be found in GOLDAST, Monarchia ii. Frankf. 1614). The most characteristic feature of these publications is the distinct separation of state and church, politics and religion. As all laws are to be traced back to the people, so the sovereign power lies also with them. They choose their princes and give them their authority; they, therefore, may recall it again and remove the princes from office (Mars. i. 12, p. 169 ff.; 9, p. 168; 18, p. 184 f.). There is no necessity for a papal confirmation of the election, nor for an investiture by the pope, any more than the pope has authority to remove the emperor. The election gives the emperor his power; he stands directly under God (Occ. 8, quaest. 2. 7, 8; 4. 8, 9). As concerns the pope, further, it is held that he is subject to the emperor in all secular affairs, as even Christ allowed himself to be condemned by secular judges, and neither he nor anyone of the apostles ever laid claim to earthly dominion or any kind of coöperative jurisdiction (*jurisdictio coactiva*) whatever, even though the emperor had of his own free-will granted the Donation of Constantine (Mars. ii. 4, p. 195 ff. Occ. 8, quaest. 3. 3, 4; dial., p. 750 f., 785, 959, 956). According to Jerome, the bishops were originally the same as the priests, and it was only at a later day that one of the latter was selected to be, as it were, a superintendent. There can hence be no thought of any such thing as a divine authority of bishops or popes (Mars. ii. 15). The papacy, as such, can by no means be described as an institution absolutely necessary for the church. No more cogent arguments can be adduced for a monarchical than for an aristocratic form of civil government. And even though the monarchy be preferable in civil life, it can scarcely be so in the world-embracing government of the church. Here Christ reigns as the only supreme Head (Occ. dial., p. 818 f.). Thus the question of the papal primacy is treated entirely from the view-point of the natural reason; it has for our author no positively religious aspect. The discussion is regulated by the transfer of the idea of popular sovereignty to the church. The Scriptures, Occam holds, do not teach us that Christ

appointed Peter as the prince of the apostles.   All the apostles received the Spirit in the same way.   Paul does not consider himself subordinate to Peter, and the latter does not preside at the first council.   The injunction to feed the lambs is given to him only as the representative of the other apostles.   Even in Matt. 16, Peter is only " in a certain way " designated as a foundation.   The real and absolutely necessary foundation of the church is Christ.   It is only as an incidental historical foundation that Peter comes into view (dial., p. 846-863. Mars. ii. 22, p. 264).   According to Marsilius, it yet remained to be proved from the Scriptures that Peter was ever at Rome ; and, in any event, Paul was certainly there before him (ii. 16). Accordingly, the papacy is to be regarded as an institution worthy of commendation upon practical considerations, but by no means as one enjoined by religious precept.

The duties of the pope, as of the clergy in general, are purely spiritual.   Christ bestowed upon Peter, as upon the other apostles, the keys of the kingdom of heaven and the power to bind and loose.   They were commissioned to spread the teaching and the moral principles of Jesus, and to baptize believers. But the plenitude of power (*plenitudo potestatis*) consists really in the exercise of the priestly functions of the sacrament of repentance.   But, inasmuch as the forgiveness of sins and the imparting of grace are matters for God alone, the priestly absolution has merely a declarative signification.   Beyond this, the pope—or any other priest—may allow the substitution of a temporal satisfaction for the pains of purgatory.   It seems of doubtful propriety, on the other hand, to allow the clergy to administer the great excommunication.   An unjust excommunication, it is true, does the victim no spiritual harm (" can do no harm for the state of the future world, because God does not always follow the church, *i. e.*, the decision of the priests, when, *e. g.*, they condemn anyone unjustly "); but it is hurtful for the present life through the accompanying disgrace.   It seems, therefore, prudent to commit the duty of casting out from the church to the church itself, or to a council, as suggested in Matt. 18. 17. Finally, to the clergy belongs the power of administering (*conficiendi*) the sacrament of the eucharist (vid. Mars. ii. 6, p. 205-209).   The right of the pope in spiritual things consists, therefore, in the authority to issue precepts and prohibitions in the church as required by the common good (*utilitas communis*). In temporal affairs, he has only the right to proper sustenance : "the right of asking for temporal things for his support and for the execution of his office " (Occ. dial., p. 786).   These sentiments indicate an immense revolution of thought.   The canon law, the jurisdiction of the church, exemption of the church from taxation, and the holdings of the church in property, are all here surrendered, and there remains no intelligible reason why the state should not hold the prebends and the congregations themselves elect and remove their pastors.[1]   The pope ceases to be a dogmatic entity ; he is an administrator of the devotional services of the church, and is bound to the positive instructions of the New Testament.   He is fallible, as are all other men.   He cannot therefore establish any new articles of faith.   His declaration does not make any opinion heretical, but the crucial question in regard to every doctrine is, whether it can be deduced from the Scriptures (Occ. dial., p. 420).   It would be altogether irrational to suspend one's recognition of the truth until a papal declaration could be secured.   Our faith would thus be made subject to the opinion of a man, whereas Paul in the second chapter of 1st Corinthians instructs us not to let our faith rest upon the wisdom of a man, but upon the power of God (compend. error., p. 976).   Here, for the first time, the infallible Scriptures are set over against the fallible pope : " Holy Scripture cannot err " (*errare non potest*); but, "the pope . . . can err " (ib. p. 843).[2]   But if a pope should stubbornly fall into error, *i. e.*, become a heretic, he may, according to both law and reason, be deposed (p. 464 ff., 568 ff.).

God has indeed promised to lead his church into all truth ; but this promise by no means applies to the pope (for popes have become heretics, ib., p. 464, 468 ff., 958, 976, 994), nor to the college of cardinals—not even to the Romish church nor a general council, for in case every member of such a council were to fall into error before his arrival, how should his fallibility be removed by his arrival at a certain locality or place (p. 495 f.)?   It is very possible that God may at certain times so order it that the truth may be preserved among the laity alone :

[1] Vid. especially Mars. ii. 9, 17, 13.

[2] Let it be observed, that it is the same juristic, abstract infallibility which had been ascribed to the pope, which is here transferred to the Scriptures.   It is based upon a strict theory of inspiration, and falls short of the evangelical view of the Scriptures.   But it is yet important to observe that it was practical considerations which determined the attitude of Occam.   His religion drove him to the Scriptures.   But his religion was epitomized in the doctrine of poverty.   When popes and cardinals denied this doctrine, which Occam believed to be found in the Scriptures, it was evident to him that their teaching was erroneous, and he was compelled to assert the authority of the Scriptures against that of the hierarchy.   The same considerations impelled him to free the civil government from the dominion of the hierarchical power.   Thus inner motives led him to the Scriptures.   It would be instructive to compare his experience at this point with that of Luther.   Vid. SEEBERG upon Occam in PRE., ed. 3.

"He is able to give the poor, simple, illiterate, and rustic for the edification of the orthodox church " (p. 498). This dare by no means be limited to the clergy. The clergy have indeed, in the canon law, limited the term *ecclesia* onesidedly to the *clerici*, but the Scriptures understand by it the whole number (*congregatio*) of Christian believers. It may therefore be said that "laymen and women are ecclesiastics (*personae ecclesiasticae*) as truly as the clergy, because they are as truly of the church (*de ecclesia*) as are the clergy " (ib. p. 502). A new conception of the church breathes in these words. The truth surrendered by the hierarchy may be preserved among the women of the church, and if not among them, among the children. The laity have the full rights of membership in the church. Kings and laymen should be admitted even to the councils (p. 603 f., 605 ; cf. Mars. ii. 20). The papal tyranny must not control the church, for the gospel is a law of liberty (p. 776 f.). Plain laymen, guided by the Scriptures, may soar beyond the knowledge of the ecclesiastical authorities. "Let it be granted, that the simple are not legally (*regulariter*) bound to believe anything explicitly except those things which have been by the clergy declared necessary to be believed. Yet the simple, nevertheless, in reading the divine Scriptures with acuteness of reason, in which even the simple are not altogether lacking, observe that something which the pope and cardinals have not declared follows evidently from the divine Scriptures—this they can and ought to in that case believe explicitly, and they are not bound to consult the pope and cardinals, because the sacred Scripture is to be preferred to the pope and cardinals." Further : "The pope and cardinals are not the rule of our faith " (p. 770).

The transformation in the conception of the church which is foreshadowed in this movement consists in the following points : (1) The state is independent of the church. (2) The sphere of the spiritual (clerical) office is not lordship, but doctrine and the administration of the sacraments. (3) The hierarchical organization of the church has become historic, but is not a religious necessity. (4) Not the pope, but Scripture, is the infallible authority in the church. (5) Pope and clergy may err, and are liable to deposition. (6) In secular affairs, the clergy are subject to the secular jurisdiction. (7) The laity are independent members, and the compeers of the clergy, in the church.

3. But these ideas and their critical motive must, in order to be fully understood, be viewed in a wider connection. Very early in the Middle Ages the Old Germanic idea of a purely legal state was so far modified, after the pattern of the church and the

ancient theory of the state, that the state was no longer regarded as existing only by virtue of the law and for its execution, but as having in view the further object of promoting the common weal, and as based upon natural motives.   A compromise of the contradiction between the Germanic idea, that the state exists for the law, and the ancient idea of the subordination of the law to the common weal—both of which ideas existed side by side—was attempted by the combination of the *positive* and the *natural* law.   The statutes of the positive law, it was maintained, whether expressions of the will of the ruler or of that of the sovereign people, have their norm in the law of nature.   Nothing which contravenes the law of nature can be regarded as authoritative.   This primacy of the natural law was, indeed, limited by the condition, that its execution must always be guided by the concrete circumstances in any case.   As the idea of popular sovereignty furnished, on the one hand, the controlling thought in the struggles of the councils against the popes, so, on the other hand, the criterion of the natural law was relentlessly applied in criticism of the positive ordinances of the church.   The ancient juristic ecclesiastical conception of the primacy of natural law,[1] which had hitherto been employed by the church in criticism of secular laws, was now turned against the church herself.   But the application of this weapon was here, no less than in the secular use of it, subject to serious limitation by the positive forms of the church life.   Criticism was applied with a keen relish and carried ruthlessly to its logical conclusions ; but no one thought of abolishing the papacy, the hierarchy, the canonical law, or the accepted dogmas of the church.   Even the boldest agitators sought no more than a correction of the existing system within its own limits.

What is then the content of natural law?[2]   Natural law is the law of reason, and it is the divine law : " Employing the natural dictate (*dictamen*) of reason, this is employing natural law ;" or, " natural reason (*ratio*) is natural law " (Occ. dial., p. 629, 568).   It is, therefore, man's innate ideas of law and order in the world (p. 932).[3]   Now, the same God who implanted these

---

[1] Vid., *e. g.*, Isidor, etymol. v. 4 f.   Gratian, decret., pars I, dist. 5.   Cf. Greg. VII.

[2] I do not enter further upon the differentiation of the *jus naturale, lex dei,* and *commune jus gentium*.   Vid. GIERKE, J. Althusius, p. 273.

[3] The latest offshoot of this theory of infallible moral ideas innate in man is in the modern definition of conscience as the voice of God.   Its origin is to be sought in the idea entertained by the Apologetes—of the Logos-sharing upon man's part.   According to Thomas, natural law is the content of the conscience.   Vid. supra, p. 114 n.   Also SEEBERG, Gewissen u. Gewissensbildung, 1896, pp. 6 ff., 69 f.

ideas in man, has imparted them likewise through inspiration in the Holy Scriptures. The law of God is, therefore, identical with the law of nature (*lex dei et jus naturae*, ib. pp. 772, 778, 783, 786, 934). From this is derived the idea of the absolute authority of the law of reason and nature—and of the Scriptures : " Human laws founded in divine and natural law " (ib. p. 587). " No just positive law can be contrary to natural law " (p. 629). " There can be no law which is repugnant to the higher law or to plain reason." Hence, whatever civil law is repugnant to the divine law, or to plain reason, is no law. In the same way, the words of the canonical or civil law, in any case in which they are repugnant to the divine law, *i. e.*, the Holy Scripture or right reason, are not to be observed " (p. 630). But all of these declarations are but repetitions of definite ideas of the canonical law (vid. Gratian, decret., pars i., dist. 1-9). This was, therefore, the path which led to the establishment of the authority of the Scriptures. Scripture and reason are identical. The Scriptures present not positive revelation, but the universal truth of reason. It is quite evident that in this way the Scriptures should come to be regarded more and more from the view-point of the law. And it is further beyond question, that this entire legal way of apprehending the church and religion could not possibly lead to a spiritual conception of the nature of the church. On the contrary, it was just in this age of reform councils and of conflicts with the Curia that the church came to be almost universally regarded as a polity, based upon juristic principles.

RIEZLER, Die litt. Widersacher d. Päpste, pp. 194 ff., 243 ff.   A. DORNER, Staat u. K. nach Occ. Stud. u. Krit., 1886, p. 672 ff. FRIEDBERG, Die mittelalt. Lebren üb. d. Verhältn. zw. Staat u. K., 1874.   K. MÜLLER, Der Kampf Ludw. d. Bay. mit. d. Curie, 1879 f. GIERKE, J. Althusius u. die Entwicklg. der naturrechtl. Staatstheörien, 1880, p. 77 ff., 123 ff., 264 ff. VON BEZOLD, Hist. Ztschr., vol. 36, p. 330 ff. KROPATSCHECK, Occam und Luther (Beiträge zur Förderung christl. Theol. iv.), 1900.

§ 61. *Sketch of Church Life and Religious Agitations at the Close of the Middle Ages.*

LITERATURE. JANNSEN, Gesch. d. deutsch. Volkes seit Ausg. d. MA. i. 14 A., 1887, and in connection, KAWERAU, Ztschr. f. K. Wiss., 1882, p. 142 ff., 263 ff., 313 ff., 362 ff. MOLL, Die vorref. KG. d. Niederlande, deutsch. Von Zuppke, ii. (1895), pp. 396-406, 554-565, 579-768. MÖLLER, KG. ii., 481 ff., 531 ff. LAMPRECHT, Deutsche Gesch., vol. v. 1, 1894. VON BEZOLD, Gesch. d. deutsch. Ref. (Oncken Allg. Gesch.). GOTHEIN, Polit. u. rel. Volksbewegg. vor. d. Ref., 1878. BERGER, Die Kulturaufgaben d. Ref., 1895. GEFFCKEN, Der Bilderkatechism. d. 15, Jarh., 1855.   Joh. Nider's Formicarius, and in connection, SCHIELER, Mag. J. Nider, 1885, pp. 195-248. HASACK, D. chr. Gl. d. deutsch. Volkes b. Schluss d. MA., 1868. LECHLER, J. v. Wicl. u. d. Vorgesch. d. Ref., 2 vols., 1873. BRATKE,

Luther's 95 Thesen u. ihre dogmenhist. Voraussetzungen, 1884.   Vid. KRO-
PATSCHECK, Das Schriftprincip der luth. Kirche, vol. i. (Mittelalter), 1904.
BRIEGER, Das Wesen des Ablasses vor Ausgang des MA. Leipziger Pro-
gramm, 1897.

1. Every great revolution in the history of religion is preceded
by a crisis period.   Traditional forms and aspirations no longer
satisfy the world.   Some blame the old order of things, and long
for a new order which they know not how to secure.   Others
glorify the old order.   The new requirements of the age, which
even they must recognize, are to be met by the diligent and
thorough use of the old means.   Harsh criticism of the traditional positions and customs and abnormal devotion to them are
here closely associated.   It is still hoped that the stones may be
made bread.   The crisis through which Luther passed in the cloister
had been hovering over the church in the fifteenth century.   The
individuality of the modern man and the deepening of religious
experience crave a personal assurance of faith and inner certainty.   The church offers instead the rule of faith and the
power of the sacraments.   The heart seeks life through the forgiveness of sins ; the church points to confession and absolution.
The consciousness of the independence of the world and its
interests is crushed beneath the ancient claims of the hierarchy ;
the increasing prosperity of the world and the new business en-
terprises are in conflict with the ideal of "poverty."   New
necessities and old methods, with the zealous attempt to draw
from old forms the satisfaction of new requirements—this constituted the crisis.   It was naturally first felt among the cultured
classes ; but it penetrated also the masses.   All the phenomena in
the religious life of this period—the ecclesiastical institutions, the
brotherhoods,[1] the indulgences, the pilgrimages, the increasing
adoration of relics, of Mary and the saints, the spread and exaggerated terrors of the faith in devils and demons,[2] the craze upon the
subject of celibacy,[3] the mysticism, the revolutionary Christian-
social plans, the contempt for the clergy and the monks, are all
closely connected with the crisis.   So loud were the complaints
that eyes were turned to the future in expectation of a new era of
"prophecy" and the "introduction of a new religion."[4]
We must observe (a) the means by which the church at-

[1] Vid. LEA, A hist. of conf. and indulg. iii., 470 ff.   MOLL, KG. ii., 646 ff.
[2] Vid. esp. the bull of Innocent VIII., Summis desiderantes affectibus, the
Malleus maleficarum, and Joh. Nider's Formicarius, lib. v.   Cf. ROSKOFF,
Gesch. d. Teufels, ii. (1869), p. 206 ff., 226 f.
[3] Vid. Examples in SCHIELER, Nider, p. 203 ff.
[4] Vid. Trithemius chronolog. myst. 18 fin.   Cf. SCHNEEGANS, Trithemius,
p. 183 f.

tempted the culture of piety, (*b*) the way of salvation as conceived by the "Friends of God," and (*c*) the scope of the
reformatory ideas of the age.

2. The means by which the church sought to influence the
multitudes remained the same as of old, except that there was—
as required by the demands of the age—an increased zeal in the
use of them.   The duty of preaching is insisted upon with
greater emphasis.   It is required that all members of the church
be acquainted with the Creed, the Lord's Prayer, the Ave
Maria, and the teachings of the church concerning mortal
sins and the sacraments.   Louis of Bavaria, *e. g.*, proved his
orthodoxy by repeating the Lord's Prayer, the greeting of the
angels, and the Apostles' Creed (R. MÜLLER, Der Kampf Lud-
wigs mit der Curie, ii. 75).   This knowledge is to be tested at
the confessional, which thus becomes a religious examination.[1]
The Ten Commandments were frequently here used as the
criterion.[2]   In preaching, the moral element still predominates ;
but with it are combined quite rigid doctrinal discussions,
miraculous narratives, and commendations of indulgences and
the grace accompanying them.   If it cannot be said that the
church shirked the new task assigned her, she certainly discovered no new means to apply in the performance of it.   The
sacraments bring grace, as the power enabling their recipients
to perform meritorious works (HASACK, p. 419, 133, 262 f.).

But Repentance appears as really the chief sacrament.[3]   The
religious unrest of the age and the financial schemes of the Curia

---

[1] *E. g.*, HEFELE, vi. 608, 696, 706, 721, 944.   MOLL, KG. ii. 396 ff., 653 f.
GEFFCKEN, Bilderkatech., p. 24 ff., and suppl., p. 191 f.; Beichtanweisung
aus d. 15 Jarh., ed. Wagner, Ztschr. f. KG. ix. 445, 462.   The "Christian
faith" consists, as before, of the twelve or fourteen articles of the Apostles'
Creed (as to the number, vid. HEFELE, vi. ed. 2, 220 a.); its content is especially the doctrine of the Trinity and Christology, *e. g.*, Gabr. Biel, De festi-
vitat. serm. 21, fol. 214 r, and HASACK, l. c., p. 138 ff.   All are required to
believe "what the holy church commands to believe" (Ztschr. f. KG. ix.
462).   As examples of open heresy, Occam adduces the denial of the unity
and trinity of God and of the birth of Christ from the Virgin (dial., p. 631).
[2] *E. g.*, HASACK, l. c., p. 191 ff., 227 f.   GEFFCKEN, l. c., Ztschr. f. KG.
ix. 445 ff., 462 ff.
[3] The Augustinian, JOHN OF PALTZ, has in his Coelifodina (Lips. 1510)
undertaken to uncover the mine of grace—for the guidance of preachers.   Of
what does he treat ?   First, there is a detailed exposition and application of the
passion history ; then, sins in thought are discussed, and death ; then the sacraments are explained, with all the emphasis upon repentance and indulgences.
In the Supplementum Coelifodinae (Lips. 1516), indulgences are defended at
length and the doctrine of the sacraments again presented.   Vid. also the many
manuals of confession at the close of the Middle Ages, *e. g.*, in HASACK, l. c.
As to the biography of Paltz, vid. KOLDE, Die deutsche Augustinercongrega-
tion, 1879, p. 174 ff.

here joined hands.   The whole religious life of the times finds
its centre in the ordinance of repentance.   Here faith is confessed
and sins are forgiven : here meritorious works are assigned and
men thus *justified;*[1] but here, too, may release from them be
purchased.   The dominant conception of confession and absolution is in thorough conformity with the scholastic theories
(supra, p. 135).   As the logic of the theory led by necessity to
the recognition of attrition as the starting point of repentance
(p. 136), so in praxis the latter came to be regarded as entirely
sufficient.   JOHN OF PALTZ considers the advantage of the new
covenant over the old to consist precisely in the fact, that it
does not require contrition, as does the old, but is content with
attrition, which is then by absolution transformed into contrition, this contrition being the destruction of sin.[2]   To do
this, however, is a matter for the priest (Coelifodina, Cc. 1 v).
" Under the new law, the mode of repenting and of salvation
is easier " (ib. Q. 5 v).   Paltz gives an excellent definition of
attrition.   " And such attrition cannot be better defined in
common   speech   than as ' gallows-penitence '   (*galgenrew*),[3]
because the attrite mourns that he has sinned—on account of the
infernal gallows " (ib. Q. 6 v).   It has for its basis servile fear
and the fear of death, whereas contrition springs from filial fear
and the love of God (ib. Q. 6 r).   Very few get beyond the
former: " About all of our people who confess in Lent do
not have true contrition, nor do they have attrition in the first
grade, because they would then do entirely what they can
to attain true contrition ; but they often have attrition in the
second grade, doing in some measure what they can, and such
are assisted by the priests in the sacramental absolution " (ib.
R. 1 v).   It is therefore sufficient if there be within the heart a
certain discontent with self and fear of hell, begotten by the contemplation of the commandments (supra, p. 174).   This will
be sufficient to secure the forgiveness, *i. e.*, the destruction,
of sin.   There was a recognition of the fact, that in the days of
the first love there had been no need of indulgences : " But now,
love having grown cold in these last times, neither are satisfac-

---

[1] Vid., *e. g.*, in HASACK, p. 137 : " Grace justifies man : whatever infirmity
(Bresten) clings to man, it punishes this, and changes it, and cleanses it with
repentance."

[2] Attrition is transformed into contrition by other means also, *i. e.*, through
extreme unction (coelifod. T. 2 v), the eucharist (Z 6 v), the mass and
preaching (Aa 3 r).   The last-named especially confirms the pyschological
interpretation of this Scotist formula (vid. supra, p. 138).   Cf. also Tetzel's
theses, n. 49 : " attrite and through confession contrite " (Luther, opp. var.
arg. i. 300).

[3] So also Luther, Weim. ed. i. 99.

tions commensurately imposed, nor when moderately imposed are they performed : therefore there is a much more necessary and copious use of indulgences, so that what is lacking through indolence (*acedia*) may be supplemented through the prayers of others (Biel, expos. can. miss. lect. 57, fol. 154 v). It is doubtless true that it was always presupposed, whether expressly so stated or not, that, in order to secure the benefit of the indulgence, the purchaser must have experienced and confessed sorrow for sin : "He who remains in sin, and is neither contrite nor attrite nor has confessed, can by no means secure indulgences (Paltz, Aa 3 r). Just as the sacrament of repentance has respect directly to sin (*culpa*), so the benefit of indulgence has respect to penalty," and that the temporal penalty (ib. X 1 r). This is true even of the so-called jubilee-indulgence, whether so stated in the bull proclaiming the latter or not (ib. Z 6 r). But, on the other hand, attention may be drawn to the formula employed in the proclamation of such indulgences : "I absolve thee from punishment and from guilt" (*a poena et a culpa*). Paltz replies: "But a jubilee is something more than a bare indulgence, because it includes the authority of confessing and absolving, and, with this, the indulgence of remitting penalty, and thus it includes the sacrament of repentance and, with this, indulgence properly so called. . . . Commonly, when the pope gives a jubilee, he gives not a bare indulgence, but he gives also authority of confessing and absolving from all sins, even so far as their guilt. And thus guilt is remitted by reason of the sacrament of repentance which is there introduced ; and penalty, by reason of the indulgence which is there employed" (ib. X 1 r). Paltz, therefore, understands the remission of sin as involved in the authority granted by the jubilee-indulgence to select for one's self a confessor, who shall be authorized to absolve in all cases not reserved to the pope himself (Aa 4 r). Even the latter cases were often included in the authority thus given.[1] The jubilee-indulgence thus indeed embraced in itself the sacrament of repentance. The sacrament must not of necessity be administered by the properly appointed confessor, but sacramental functions may also be discharged by the papal commissary. Thus the papal power intruded upon the province of the pastoral cure of souls, and thus, although the forgiveness of sins

---

[1] *E. g.*, LEA, Hist. of conf. and indulg., iii. 70 n. Cf. HASACK, p. 434 : "Indulgence from penalty and guilt . . . is to be thus understood : Indulgence from penalty is a remitting of the penalty which one ought to suffer for his sin. Indulgence from guilt is complete authority to absolve and release from all sins, even those sins which are to be reserved for the holy Roman chair."

was not itself directly secured by the payment of money, yet the especial administration of the sacraments which carried with it the forgiveness of sins was thus purchased. Under these circumstances, the popular perversions upon the subject may be easily understood. The above formula was in the highest degree open to misunderstanding.[1] Popes expressly rejected it,[2] and theologians pronounced against it. Nevertheless, it was permitted still to play its part of deception and confusion of thought in the church (cf. LEA, hist. of conf. and indulg. iii., p. 57-78. MOLL, ii. 728).[3] Matters were made worse, as the theory of the validity of indulgences for the souls in purgatory (*supra*, p. 139) also found endorsement in praxis.[4] Cf., *e. g.*, Paltz, Cc 1 r, Dd 5 v, etc.[5] The idea that, "as soon as the money rings in the chest, the soul leaps out of purgatory," was only a perfectly intelligible inference.[6]

Such was the course of penitential praxis at the close of the Middle Ages. The frightful danger attending it can be understood only when attrition and indulgences are viewed in their combination, and when the misleading glorification of the latter is considered.[7] A little "gallows-penitence" and the confessional, and then a little money, and the sinner is freed from the fear of hell and purgatory, and even from the performance of works of penance. Money was immediately the means of releasing from purgatory, and mediately of securing the forgiveness of sins.

[1] BRATKE prepared the way for this understanding of the jubilee-indulgences. BRIEGER produced convincing evidence of it (Das Wesen des Ablasses (Leipzig, 1899).

[2] Boniface IX., vid. LEA, l. c., iii. 66 f., the papal plan of reformation at Constance, vid. HEFELE, vii. 341. Benedict XIV., vid. WILDT, Kirchenlex. i. ed. 2, 95.

[3] Cf. already the complaints of Berthold of Regensburg, touching the "penny-preachers." When thou standest up and forgivest one all the sin which he has ever done for a single helbelinc or a few pennies, then he imagines that he has atoned and at once refuses to atone any more. Thou murderer of God and the world and many Christian souls, which thou murderest with thy false comfort, so that he can never be saved (Pred. i. 117). He claims that he has power from the pope, to take from thee all thy sin for a few helbelincs or for a heller (ib. i. 208). The Reformat. Sigismunds, p. 163, edited by Boehm, also speaks of paying dearly for indulgence of sins. Cf. Wessel, De poenit., opp., p. 798 f.

[4] According to LEA, iii. 345 ff., not before Sixtus IV., A. D. 1476. Vid. also BIEL, expos. can. miss. lect. 57 K.

[5] Indulgences may bring even to the lost a mitigation of punishment, PALTZ, Ff. 4 v.

[6] Vid. KAWERAU, Sobald das Geld, etc., 1889, p. 9, 11 f., 17 ff.

[7] A contrite person may, even before confessing, receive an indulgence (Durand, sent. iv. d. 20, q. 4, a. 2. Paltz holds otherwise, Aa 3). How easily may he be deceived as to his condition, or postpone the subsequent confession!

12

But along with this externalizing of religion—which the church herself promoted—were heard also some voices emphasizing the seriousness of repentance and its works.   The whole Christian life is a "doing penance:" "That the whole life of a Christian man is nothing else than a cross" (Hasack, p. 443). But this thought is completed by the additional idea, that we "are obligated to the imitation of the crucified life" of Christ, "since the passion of Christ has not been an entire, but a partial, cause of our salvation" (ib., also p. 477).   The "imitation of Christ" is, therefore, a supplementing of the redeeming work of Christ by effort upon our part !

3.   The so-called German Mysticism, dogmatically considered, furnishes scarcely anything further than a popular rendering of the scholastic, *i. e.*, Thomistic ideas.   But these ideas are applied to the relation of the soul to God.   The practical aspect of the way to God is the controlling one for these writers.   The ideas of the dogmaticians become, under their hands, practical religious truths, which were employed for edification by the widespread circles of the "Friends of God."   The use of the mother tongue deepened the experience and enriched the religious apprehension.   Little as it belongs to the sphere of the History of Doctrines to follow the speculations of the Mystics, it is important, in tracing the transition from the Middle Ages to the Reformation era, to understand the way of salvation as pursued by the pious at the close of the medieval period.   In endeavoring to trace this briefly, we follow chiefly the following :

Master ECKHART († 1327, vid. Pfeiffer, Deutsche Mystiker, ii., 1857. Excerpts from his Latin writings in Denifle, Archiv f. Litt. u. KG. d. MA. ii. 553 ff.), JOHANN TAULER († 1361. Sermons, Basel, 1521), HEINRICH SEUSE (Suso, † 1366, ed. Denifle, MÜNCH., 1880), JOHANN VON RUUSBROEC († 1381. WW. 6 vols., Gent, 1858 ff.), the THEOLOGIA DEUTSCH (ed. Pfeiffer, reprint 3, 1875), the BUCH VON GEISTL. ARMUT (ed. Denifle, 1877), THOMAS A KEMPIS, De imitatione Christi (ed. Hirsche, 1874).

The spiritual life pursues the course : Purification, Illumination, Unification (Theol. D., p. 50).[1]   "A devoted man must be unfashioned from the creature, fashioned with Christ and refashioned in the divine nature" (*entbildet, gebildet, überbildet*, Seuse, p. 248).   He is first a servant, then a friend, and finally a son of God (Ruusbr. vi. 208 ff.).   (*a*) The first step, therefore, is to turn away from the creature and turn toward God. The sacrament and the word of God then exert an influence (Tauler, fol. 65 v); especially repentance and the Lord's Supper are recommended.   These are re-enforced by prayer and the

---

[1] Cf. Dionys. Areop., Hierarch. eccl. 6. 3. 5.

contemplation of the love of God (Eckh., p. 557). Thus man feels himself impelled to a pious and virtuous life, to continuous and earnest self-examination, and penitence. "Purification belongs to the beginning or repenting man, and takes place in three ways, with sorrow and mourning on account of sin, with complete confession, and with perfect penitence" (Theol. D., p. 50). This is the first stage, repentance and its exercises; the struggle for the overcoming of sensuality (*Sinnlichkeit*) is its essential characteristic. (*b*) In the second stage, the *Imitatio Christi* holds the place of prominence. "Thou must break through my suffering human nature, if thou art really to come to my unveiled divine nature" (Seuse, p. 52. Tauler, f. 117 v, 156 r. Theol. D., p. 220).[1] Here the principal thing is thorough-going meditations upon the passion of Christ: "Not with a hasty going over it as one has time and place; but it must be with a fervent love and with a mournful review" (Seuse, p. 396). The life of Seuse testifies with what dramatic vividness and with what barbarous ascetic exercises these meditations were practiced. The aim is sympathy and imitation.[2] But, apart from these, God himself sends sufferings and crosses of various kinds upon man, in order to make him a true follower of Christ. "The swiftest beast that bears you to perfection is suffering" (Eckh., p. 492). "No one so cordially feels the passion of Christ as he to whom it happens to suffer similar things" (Thom. a Kemp. ii. 121). True, there is in these circles a deep conviction that Christ's passion is our "perfect righteousness" (Seuse, p. 393). "And thus has he redeemed us, not with our works but with his works, and with his merits has he made us free and redeemed us" (Ruusbr. iii. 140). "All my comfort and my confidence rests wholly upon thy passion, thine atonement, and thy merits" (Seuse, p. 427 f.).[3] But Seuse writes also: "And yet every man draws to himself only so much of the atonement as he with sympathy makes himself like me," *i. e.*, Christ (Seuse, p. 398).[4] What is this but saying, as this school bluntly puts it, that Christ is only the partial cause of ours alvation? The *Imitatio Christi* (vid. Thom. a K. i. 1. 1; 25. 3; ii. 1. 2) is the religion of these mystics: "Give to me to imitate thee with contempt of the world" (ib. iii. 56. 2). They plunged into asceticism—which

---

[1] Cf. Augustine, serm. 261. 7: "Through the man Christ thou attainest to the God Christ;" also the passages cited in Vol. I., p. 262. Already in Origen, c. Celsus, vi. 68.

[2] Vid. Seuse, p. 52 ff., 321 ff., and SEEBERG, Leben Seuse, p. 28 ff.

[3] Particularly the dying are often urged to pray: "Upon thy mercy and goodness will I die, and not upon my good works" (HASACK, p. 437).

[4] Cf. Thom. in sentent. iii. d. 49, a. 2, 3). Thom. a Kemp. i. 24. 1: satisfactional and purifying sorrow (*dolor satisfactorius et purgativus*).

they regarded as meritorious and entitling to reward (*lonbar*, Seuse, p. 385, 383), but they nevertheless kept alive a love for Jesus and appreciation of his life—as the counterpart to the view which regarded him as a stern celestial judge, before whom Mary and the saints must appear to intercede for us. "As the lodestone draws to it the iron, so does Jesus draw to himself all hearts that are touched by him" (Tauler, f. 43 v). Though all this remains perfectly Catholic, yet these ideas just as truly betoken a "pre-reformation" element.[1] This is the way. Man must return to nothingness (*entwerden*, "unbecome"), for only out of a nothing (*niht*) does God make an it (*iht*), (Eckh., p. 189. Taul. f. 146 v).

(*c*) The goal, finally, is unification with God in the depths of the soul ; and this, too, with God in the inner unity of his nature. "The essence of the soul is united with Nothingness, and the powers of the soul with the works of Nothingness.[2] In this state of absolute passivity God causes his Son to be born in our soul "a hundred thousand times more quickly than the twinkling of an eye" (Tauler, f. 60 r).[3] This state can be experienced in two psychological forms : either in such a way that man in the intellectual process experiences the "vision" (*Schauung*) of the essence of God, or in such a way that "the created will is merged into the eternal Will and therein dissolved and reduced to nothingness, so that the eternal Will alone here wills, acts, and fails to act" (Theol. D., p. 104). The former harmonizes with the Thomistic, the latter with the Scotist theology (RITCHL, Gesch. d. Pietismus, i. 470), although the two forms were not sharply discriminated.[4] The moments of extreme ecstatic exaltation were of brief duration. Lukewarmness and lassitude followed (Seuse, p. 360, 355, 358, 448). The words of the Scriptures —Christ's sweet love-letter, and his presence in the Lord's

---

[1] But it must be ever borne in mind that this conception of the "Following of Christ," which may be traced back to the Apostolic Fathers, is but a mutilated and dislocated presentation of biblical ideas. The following of Jesus means, in the Gospels, that he who attaches himself to Jesus walks with him and finds in him God and the Son of the living God. The result of following him is announced in Matt. 16. 16 and Jn. 6. 67 f.

[2] This is the Areopagite conception of the nature of the Godhead. Cf. my remarks, Thomas. DG. ii., ed. 2, p. 305, A. 2.

[3] Cf. my exposition, Thomas. DG. ii., ed. 2, p. 307 ff.

[4] Cf. my remarks, l. c., p. 310 f. Also Dante, Parad. 28. 109 ff.: "Through vision, therefore, is blessedness attained. Not through love, for this follows only when it has sprung from vision as its source." With Staupitz (ed. Knaake, i. 106), Luther accepted the latter form, vid. Glosses upon Tauler, Weim. ed. ix. 102 : "The whole of salvation is resignation of the will in all things." Also, Thom. a K., iii. 15. 2 ; 56. 1. Goch, dialog. 9. 10 (Walch, Monim. Med. aev. i. 4, p. 129, 132).

Supper—console the pious (ib. 355, 621 f., 450 f. Thom. a Kemp.
iv. 11. 4). They should be always ready to turn aside from the
highest religious transport to prepare a plate of soup for a pauper
(Eckh., p. 553. Taul. f. 128 r, 95 r, 121 r).[1] " He to whom
inwardness becomes outwardness, to him the inwardness becomes
more inward than to him to whom inwardness becomes inwardness " (Seuse, p. 246).

We cannot overlook the medieval mould—ascetism and ecstacy
—in which the controlling ideas here are cast. But, inasmuch as
the entire body of the traditional teaching and culture of the
church is concentrated upon the religious life of the individual
soul, which is to grow by the contemplation of Jesus and by that
intercourse of the soul with him[2] in which blessedness consists,[3]
these men were, nevertheless, "schoolmasters leading to Christ."[4]

LITERATURE. GREITH, Die deutsche Mystik im Predigerorden, 1861.
BÖHRINGER, Die deutschen Mystiker, 1855. PREGER, Gesch. d. deutschen
Mystik, 3 vols., 1874, 1881, 1893 ; cf. DENIFLE, Hist. polit. Blätter, vol. 75,
679 ff., 771 ff., 903 ff., and Archiv f. Litt. u. KG. d. MA. ii. 417 ff. DENIFLE,
Das geistl. Leben, 3 A., 1880.
Upon separate topics : LASSON, M. Eckh., 1868. R. SEEBERG, Ein Kampf
um jenseitiges Leben (Biogr. Seuses), Dorpat, 1889. C. SCHMIDT, J.
Tauler, 1841, and DENIFLE, Taul. Bekehrung, 1879. Upon the Buch v.
geistl. Armut, RITSCHL, Ztschr. f. KG. iv. 337 ff. STRAUCH, Marg. Ebner
u. Heinr. v. Nördl., 1882, and "Offenbarungen d. Adelheid Langmann,"
1875. Upon the Brethren of the Common Life, HIRSCHE, PRE. ii. 678-760.
Particularly SEEBERG in Thomas. DG. ii., ed. 2, 290-315.

4. Not least among the influences leading to the crisis at
the close of the Middle Ages was the change in the conditions
of the business world. (Cf. INAMA-STERNEGG, Deutsche Wirt-
schaftsgesch. iii. 2, 1901.) The traffic in money emphasized
the contrast between the rich and the poor. In the cities
there was an accumulation of capital in the hands of individuals, which proved in the highest degree detrimental to the
general social advancement, as both the nobles and the peasants
realized in sad experience. The Romish canon law was rigidly
enforced, and proved, as always, the ally of the financially
stronger party. The heaviest burden fell, in the last instance,

[1] Cf. Thom. summ. ii. ii. q. 182, a. 1, ad 3.
[2] Thom. a Kemp. ii. 8. 1 : " It is a great art to know how to walk (con-
versari) with Jesus."
[3] Ib. iii. 59. 1 : "Where thou, there heaven," ii. 12. 3 : " Thou hast
found paradise on earth."
[4] Note also the value attached to practical deeds of love. The monastic
idea of forsaking the world is often painfully prominent (e. g., Thom. a K. i.
10. 1 ; 20. 1); but see also the splendid sermons of Tauler upon the earthly
calling (fol. 117 r f., fol. 94 v f.). Cf. UHLHORN, Die christl. Liebestätigkeit, ii. (1884), p. 350 ff.

upon the peasantry. The impoverishment of the latter, the development of the feudal system, and the pressure exerted by the nobles, gave birth to the "social question" of the fifteenth century. As the only social power of the Middle Ages was the church, it was inevitable that these social problems should assume a religious form. The ethics of the medieval church had not risen to the demands of the new economic conditions. The friendly interest with which the most truly religious spirits of the day regarded the suffering peasants did not alleviate their misery. The terrible strain of mind found vent in forecasts and prophecies. Not only the hierarchy, which had become utterly secularized and was ever thirsting for gold, but all the high and mighty of the world as well, were to be destroyed. All secular ordinances and laws were declared null and void, and only the divine law must rule. The pious shall conquer. Wealth will cease to be ; evangelical poverty will become universal, and with it communism will prevail. All are to be equal, made free by "evangelical liberty." God will bring it to pass. The time would soon be ripe, it was thought, to lay hand to the work. This was the *Christian Socialism* of the day, which, in league with "evangelical liberty," pressed on to revolution.[1] Far beyond the circles of those actually engaged in these movements extended the stimulating and disturbing influence of these ideas. What strange contrasts are here blended—ideas as full of contra-

---

[1] Vid. especially "The Vision and Creed of Piers Ploughman" (ed. Wright, Lond., 1856). Die Reformation Sigismunds (ed. Böhm, 1875). Cf. Gesch. des Hans Böheim (BARACK, Arch. d. hist. Vereins f. Unterfranken, xiv. 3, pp. 1-8). The "new" or "divine" order which the Reformation of Sigismund had in view (p. 241, 242, 170) embraces, in addition to all manner of ecclesiastical and social improvements, the demand of "liberty." The latter is deduced, however, from the redemption achieved by Christ: "Christ suffered for us" that he might free us and release us from all bonds, and herein no one is exalted above the other, for we are in the same condition in redemption and liberty, whether noble or peasant, rich or poor, great or small (p. 221, 214, 245, 246f.). In the name of this liberty, feudal serfdom is to be abolished, and woods, pasture, and water (Wald, Weide, Wasser) are to be free to all (p. 222 f.). The imperial and papal codes of law are slumbering, but the "Little Ones" are wakeful (p. 225). This liberty which Christ is said to have brought, constitutes one root of the conception of "evangelical liberty." The other is found in the (evangelical) idea of natural law, *i. e.*, that by nature all are free, and all things common to all (vid. sub). To this must be added the great emphasis laid upon evangelical liberty and the evangelical law in pre-reformation circles (vid. especially Goch, dialog. c. 7, 18, 19). I would thus answer the inquiry raised by Von Nathusius (die christl. soz. Ideen d. Ref.-zeit u. ihre Herkunft, 1897, p. 48 ff.), but, in my judgment, not satisfactorily answered by him, as to the medieval origin of the conception under discussion. As to the eschatological framing of these ideas, vid. WADSTEIN, Die eschat. Ideengruppe, 1896, p. 183 ff., 171 ff. KROPATSCHECK, Das Schriftprincip der luth. Kirche, i. 247 ff.

dictions as was the closing period of the Middle Ages itself! Hatred of the church and love for evangelical law, longing tor more secure possession of property and enthusism for holy poverty, individualistic and socialistic tendencies, practical demands of the present age and lofty apocalyptic expectations (cf. Joachim v. Floris), the gospel and natural law,—here meet.   The result was in keeping with it all—revolution in the name of the gospel.

But even here it was theological ideas which lay in the background, *i. e.*, the evangelical, or natural, law as the criterion for criticism of all existing institutions, and the perfect life to be found in the observance of this law.   But by natural or divine law was understood : "all possession of all things in common, and there is one liberty of all " (Occam, dial., p. 932.   Cf. op. 90, dier. p. 1143).[1]   But above all influential here were the ideas of the great Hussite-Wickliffe movement, or the views of WICKLIFFE († 1384), whom Huss and his adherents interpreted for their countrymen.[2]   Wickliffe's work, *De civili dominio* (i., ed. Poole, 1885), demands attention.[3]   All human rights, it claims, must rest upon divine right.   Accordingly, the unpardoned sinner holds unrightfully what he possesses (i., p. 2 f., 28, 8).   In the sight of God his possessions would belong to the righteous, and he, therefore, steals them (p. 34): "for by the very fact that anyone takes another's goods unjustly, their owner being unwilling or ignorant (of the act), he commits theft or robbery. Since, therefore, every unrighteous man unjustly takes the goods of his body and goods of fortune, which all belong to every righteous person, . . . he in this way seizes or steals whatever goods (he possesses)."   But the righteous are, in Wickliffe's view, the predestinated (vid. sub).   These, accordingly, as the adopted sons of God, have rightful claims to dominion over the whole world : "he has a right to the whole kingdom, . . . therefore everyone thus righteous rules the whole visible world " (p. 47 f.).   They are, therefore, kings, like Christ ; but also bishops, since they must proclaim the holy doctrine.[4]   It is, of

---

[1] Occam borrows this verbally from Isidor, Etymol. v. 4.   Gratian also accepts Communism as guaranteed by natural law, with appeal to Acts iv. 32, Plato and Augustine (Decr. pars i., dist. 8).   Roman law allows, as included in natural rights, only the union of man and wife, the education of children, and the liberty of all.   Vid., *e. g.*, Digest. i. 1.

[2] As to the relation of Huss to Wickliffe, and the controlling influence of the latter upon the Bohemian agitation, vid. LOSERTH, H. u. W., 1884.   The influence of this English theologian upon the continent may, perhaps, be in this respect compared with that of Carlyle in the nineteenth century.

[3] It was widely read in Bohemia.   LOSERTH, pp. 242, 111.

[4] How similar is this to Luther's "Liberty of a Christian Man," and yet how different !

course, not meant by this that the righteous are at once to appropriate to themselves the possessions which others have wrongfully seized. On the contrary, the positive duties of life are contained in the "evangelical law," which term best expresses comprehensively the practical reformatory demands of Wickliffe. The Holy Scriptures, or the "law of Christ" (p. 397), is in and of itself sufficient for the regulation of the entire life of the Christian world (*Ipsa pure per se sufficit regere totum populum christianum*, p. 395).[1] There is really no need of any law beyond the Scriptures for the Christian world (opus evangelic. i., p. 200, ed. Loserth). Civil laws are righteous only in so far as they have the Biblical spirit (civ. dom., p. 400, 139). Only in so far can they claim acknowledgment at the hand of believers (op. ev. i. 367). But the requirements of the evangelical law are met by humility, love, and poverty in the imitation of Jesus : "But humility, love, and poverty are the doctrine of Christ. Therefore, whoever shall not hate those things by imitating Christ as an eagle, knows that he is not of his church" (de eccl., p. 63, ed. Loserth). The life of Christ is the commentary upon his law (trialog., p. 300, ed. Lechler). Ascetic imitation of Christ is, therefore, in the true Franciscan fashion, depicted as the duty of the Christian. "It behooves everyone who is to be saved to follow him either in suffering or in mode of life" (*moribus*) (sermones ii., p. 15, ed. Loserth ; also iii. 491 f.; op. evang. i., p. 105). "We ought to imitate the life of Christ and his apostles as far as we are able" (trialog., p. 456 ; op. ev. i. 469 f.; ii. 140). These are the ideas found in Wickliffe. The predestinated and the pious are the lords of the world, the property of the wicked being robbery and their codes of justice injustice. But, on the other hand, they ought to be imitators of Christ, poor, humble servants of the divine law. These ideas stand side by side. Either of them alone, or both combined, may be capable of arousing a storm of criticism that may shake the world. Either the evangelical law or the rights of nature may be invoked in deadly assault upon all property and law, upon every rank and every ordinance of society.[2] The pious may assert their rights against the ungodly in the name of the gospel. The rights of nature and the imitation of Christ are woven together,

[1] Evangelical law and natural law fall naturally into one, since both are inspired by God, *e. g.*, De civ. domin., p. 1, 22, 37, 28; p. 125 : "Divine created right is divinely inspired right ; human right is right devised by occasion of the sin of humanity."

[2] Wickliffe feels this when he restricts the thought, that civil laws are valid only in so far as they agree with God's law, by the caution : "Therefore the things thus said here are not to be proclaimed too freely to the whole populace" (opp. ev. i. 367).

and the resultant is the holy revolution.   Hussitism first put the ideas into practical execution.

Cf. WIEGAND, De eccl. notione quid Wicl. docuerit, Lips., 1891, p. 58 ff. Von BEZOLD, Zur Gesch. d. Husitentums, 1874 ; ib. Die "armen Leute," Hist. Ztschr., 1879, 1 ff.

§ 62. *Review of History of Theology in the Fourteenth and Fifteenth Centuries.   Nominalism and Augustinianism.*

LITERATURE.   WERNER, Die nachscot. Scholastik, 1883 ; Der Augustinism. in d. Schol. d. spät. MA., 1883 ; Der Endausgang der mittelalt. Schol., 1887. RITTER, Gesch. d. Philos. viii. (1845), p. 547 ff. PRANTL, Gesch. d. Logik, iii. (1867), p. 327 ff.   SIEBECK, Occ. Erk.-lehre, Archiv f. Gesch. d. Philos., 1897, p. 317 ff.   ULLMAN, Reformatoren vor der Ref., 1841-42. RITSCHL, Rechtf. u. Vers. i., ed. 2, 129 ff.   KOLDE, Die deutsche Augustinercongregat. u. Staupitz, 1879. CLEMEN, Joh. Pupper v. Goch, 1896.   KROPATSCHECK, Der Schriftprincip der luth. Kirche, i., 1904.

1. As at the beginning of the twelfth century a keen critical mind furnished the occasion, both positively and negatively, for the great theological agitation of the twelfth and thirteenth centuries, so again, at the beginning of the fourteenth century, a critical thinker directed theological ideas into new paths.   The former movement conducted to the culminating point of Scholasticism ; the latter, to its fall.   Thus far we may find a parallel between Abelard and Duns Scotus.   The method of Duns controls his opponents as well as his adherents.   Nothing is too lofty nor too sacred, too firmly settled nor too well attested, to be called in question.   This method, which stands in intimate relation with the conception of God as the absolute, unregulated Will, became the lever for the critical unsettling of dogma, employed particularly and in a far-reaching way by the so-called Nominalists.   The Lombard brought the materials together ; Thomas framed definitions ; Duns built up and demolished arguments ; Occam advocated the positively valid, though not without robbing it of the nimbus of rationality.

(*a*) Although Duns was not yet a Nominalist, the way was prepared for the transition to Nominalism by his emphasizing of the singular and the individual (p. 147).   The work was completed by his greatest pupil, WILLIAM OF OCCAM († ca. 1350).

Vid. esp. super quatuor libr. sent. and Centilogium theologic., Lyon, 1495. Quodlibeta, Strassburg, 1491. De sacr. altaris, Strassburg, 1491. Summ. totius logicae, Bologna, 1498. Major summ. log., Venet. 1508. Exposit. aurea super totam artem veterem, Bol. 1496. The writings upon church polity, vid. supra, p. 167. In these and the following citations of literature, I have been guided by no bibliographical interest (for which see Werner), but merely cite the editions which I have used.

Following Abelard, Thomas and Duns, Occam is the fourth

typical figure among the Scholastics.   An intellectual acumen
that moved with ease amid the finest subtleties of thought,
a devotion to abstraction and rational criticism of the strictest
type, are his striking characteristics.   He is keenly interested in
politics; but in politics, as in theology, he is a fanatical champion
of logic.   One looks to him in vain for warmth of feeling or
devotional language.   His logic is keen, but its edge is turned
when it meets the authority of the Romish church.   The reader
cannot escape a painful impression, when the talented author
apologizes for his bold conclusions as harmless intellectual exercises, or quotes a large number of opinions without stating clearly
which of them accords with his own judgment (octo quaest., p.
391, 398 ; dial., p. 504, 546, 771 ; de sacr. alt. c. 6, fin.)!
His Nominalistic theory of knowledge (vid. sub) as well as
his critical skepticism (upon both, vid. sub, 2 and 3) spread
rapidly in all directions (esp. ADAM GODDAM, ROBERT HOLKOT,
JOH. BURIDAN, MARSILIUS OF INGHEN, PETER D'AILLI. Quaestiones super libr. sent., Strassburg, 1490).   But it is scarcely
correct to consider his theological standpoint as merely a consequence of his Nominalism.[1]   His critical radicalism is rather to
be explained as, on the one hand, a direct application of the
Scotist method ; and this method led him, on the other hand, to
the position of external ecclesiastical positivism.   The last
important representative of this tendency was GABRIEL BIEL
(† 1495, vid. Collectorium sive epitoma in Sentent. ll. iv. Tüb.,
1501, with the Expositio canonis missae, Basel, 1510.   Cf. also
Sermones de tempore u. de festivitatibus, Hagenau, 1515.   Cf.
LINSENMANN, Theol. Quartalschrift, 1865, 195 ff., 449 ff.,
601 ff. WERNER, Endausgang, p. 262 ff.).   At the same time,
however, pure Scotism still found adherents (e. g., VORILLON
and FRANZ LYCHETUS, who wrote a commentary upon the Opus
Oxoniense).

(b) Parallel with the Nominalist tendency, was still preserved
a line of Thomist theologians (e. g., HERVAEUS NATALIS, † 1323 ;
cf. Seeberg, PRE. vii., ed. 3, 771 ff. PETRUS DE PALUDE,
† 1342); but even such Dominicans as DURANDUS DE ST.
PORTIANO († 1334, vid. in iv. libros mag. sentent., Paris, 1508
et pas.) departed from the doctrine of the great teacher of their
order.   The most energetic defender of Thomism against the
Scotist theology was the General of the Thomists, JOH. CAP-
REOLUS († 1444. Defensionum theologiae divi doctoris Thomae,
ll. iv., Venet. 1483. Cf. Werner, D. h. Thom. v. Aq. iii. 151

---

[1] E. g., BAUR, Dreieinigkeit ii. 872 f. Thomas, ii., ed. 2, 92 f. WAGEN-
MANN, PRE. x., ed. 2, 691.

ff.). DIONYSIUS RICKEL (Carthusianus) († 1471, vid. in sent. Venet. 1584) deserves mention in this connection, as he attached himself in essential points to Thomas, although giving, in his eclectic fashion, an excellent summary of the theories of the various scholastic teachers (cf. Werner, Endausgang, p. 134 ff., 206 ff.). The commentaries written by THOMAS SEL VIO (Cajetan) upon the *Summa* of Thomas and by Sylvester Ferrariensis upon the *Summa contra gentiles* (cf. Werner, l. c., p. 305 ff.) extend into the Reformation period.

(*c*) Side by side with these two tendencies, we note a third, which sought to combine certain mystical notions with Averroistic ideas.[1] Its prominent representatives are PETRUS AUREOLUS († ca. 1345, Sentence-comm. and Quodlibet, Rome, 1596), JOH. V. BACONTHORP († 1346, Quaest. in iv. libros sent. and Quodlibet, Cremona, 1618), and JOH. DE JANDUNO (ca. 1320). The last-named especially maintained that the Averroistic ideas of the eternal world and of the one intellect common to all men are rationally necessary truths, *i. e.*, he did not adopt the Thomistic interpretation of Aristotle, but held that of Averroes as the more correct because it made a fundamental distinction between theology and secular philosophy. But, since the Christian conception of salvation can be maintained intact only on the basis of the faith of the church, it was necessary to cling to the ecclesiastical dogmas (Werner, Nachscot. Theol., p. 5 f.). This tendency, with its extreme Realism, was dominant in the theological school of Padua (*e. g.*, URBAN of Bologna, † 1403; PAUL of Venice, † 1429; AUGUSTIN NIPHUS of Suessa, † ca. 1550, etc. Vid. Werner, Endausgang, p. 142 ff.). This view, which prevailed in northern Italy, and outlasted Nominalism by about a hundred years, requires no further notice in the History of Doctrines.

(*d*) Neither can the school of Augustinian Eremites be compared in importance or completeness of thought with the two tendencies first named. At their head stood AEGIDIUS OF COLONNA (also called Romanus, † 1316. The best edition of his Comm. upon the first three books of the Sentences, Cordova, 1707, Kirchenlex. iii. 669). Among his adherents were JACOB CAPOCCI, † 1308; GERHARD OF SIENA, PROSPER OF REGGIO, ALBERT OF PADUA, SIMON BARINGUNDUS, THOMAS OF STRASSBURG († 1357, vid. ll. iv. in mag. sentent., Strassburg, 1490 and passim). But despite the aim of this school to maintain Augustinianism, their theory of sin and grace is by no means

---

[1] Cf. RENAN, Averroès et l'Averroïsme, 3 A. 1866; and briefly, ERDMANN, Gesch. d. Philos. i., ed. 4, 339 ff.

that of Augustine (vid. Werner, Der Augustinismus, p. 171 ff., 181 ff.). The resolution adopted A. D. 1287, to make the theology of Aegidius the doctrine of the order (vid. Ossinger, Bibl. Augustiniana, 1786, p. 237), had comparatively slight effect. Gregory of Rimini († 1358, Lectura in l. i. and ii. Sent., Paris, 1482) advocated variant views, accepting Nominalism, on the one hand, and then demanding strict adherence to Augustinianism, which he held is to be freed from the wrappings of Peripateticism. He was therefore honored with the title, *Doctor Authenticus.* He strongly insisted that man was created in a state of grace, and that concupiscence is the material of original sin. Sin is transmitted through the sensuous concupiscence of the generating act.[1] That in other points the popular theology of the Augustinians before the Reformation did not overstep the bounds of the common Catholicism, may be seen, *e. g.*, in the Coelifodina of Johann of Paltz (supra, p. 175).

(*e*) The tendency which crops out in men like Gregory had from the middle of the fourteenth century been influencing the minds of many theologians, *i. e.*, the desire for a return to the genuine Augustine, or to the simple teaching of the ancient church. In A. D. 1400 Joh. Gerson wrote : " A reformation seems to be necessary in the faculty of theology. . . . First, that useless doctrines without fruit or solidity may not be so commonly discussed, since through these the doctrines necessary to salvation and useful are deserted. . . . Second, that those who are (not) scholars are misled through these (teachings), because they think that those persons are chiefly to be regarded as scholars who give themselves to such things, despising the Bible and the doctors. . . . Through these teachings, theologians are ridiculed by the other faculties : for they are, on this account, called Phantastics, and are said to know nothing concerning solid truth and morals and books. . . . Through these (teachings) the church and the faith are edified neither internally nor externally."[2] A remedy is to be found by lecturing not only, as was customary, upon the first book of the Sentences, but upon the last three, and lectures should be presented in a simple way, and with practical reference to the religious and moral conditions of the age (Gers. opp. ed. Dupin

----

[1] Both Aegidius and Gregory taught the maculate conception of Mary. *Thomas of Strassburg* championed the immaculate conception. Werner, p. 176 f.

[2] In the later commentaries upon the Sentences (already in Hervaeus, and especially since Occam), the metaphysical questions of the First Book really claim the first place in importance and in the space devoted to them. Theology is lost in metaphysics or canonical casuistry.

i. 122 ff.). The faults here noted are manifest in the scholastic literature of the age. When criticism found itself limited by the dogmas of the church, it became empty and fruitless. And a theology which created a thousand difficulties and suggested a thousand possibilities, only to return at last to the formulas so laboriously criticized, became, together with its advocates, ridiculous. Demand was made for a practical and churchly theology, and gradually the beginnings of such a theology began to appear. Side by side with the commentaries upon the Sentences, we find treatises and brochures upon popular theology, expositions of the Creed, directions for confessing, " patterns of virtue," etc.[1] A simple outline of dogmatics is presented, *e. g.*, in the *Compendium theologiae* found among the works of Gerson.[2] If works of this character led back to the simple forms of the earlier theology, there was at the same time a return to Augustine. Many influences contributed to this movement. Against the rising tide of Pelagianism, THOMAS OF BRADWARDINA († 1349) lifted the standard of Augustinian doctrine, not however without first refining it into a system of Determinism (vid. De causa dei c. Pelagium et de virtute causarum, London, 1618. Cf. R. Seeberg, PRE. iii., ed. 3, 350 ff.). In the mind of Wickliffe the conception of the Supreme will of God was associated inseparably with that of predestination, and thus became a critical weapon against the church and the clergy. His chief opponent, THOMAS NETTER († 1431. Doctrinale antiquitatum fid. cath.), endeavored to expound the Catholic doctrine from the Scriptures as in opposition to the views of Wickliffe, and with an avoidance of the scholastic forms. He thus helped to prepare the way for the final statement of the church's doctrine in the Confession of Trent (vid. SEEBERG, PRE. xiii., ed. 3, 749 ff.). The more profound piety of the Mystics produced a certain congeniality in temper and thought with Augustine. And wherever the deeper religious needs came into collision with the externalized church, they found in him both religious nutriment and

---

[1] The libraries furnish a mass of such material in manuscript. These documents are partly in refutation of the charges ventilated at the Reform Councils. But cf. in connection with them the mystical tractates, which also present outlines of popular theology. Wickliffe as a theologian followed strictly the scholastic method ; but, as he always contrived to give to his monographs a practical and reformatory bearing, even he strengthened the union of theology and the church.

[2] This book first expounds the Creed ; then the Decalogue. It then treats of the seven sacraments, of the three theological and the four cardinal virtues, of the seven gifts of the Spirit, of the eight Beatitudes, of the various sins— and, finally, the definitions of pyschology are discussed, with constant reference to sin. As to the question of its authorship, see SCHWAB, Gerson, p. 780.

weapons for the conflict.   This is true of all the men who are
commonly spoken of as the Forerunners of the Reformation,
such as JOH. PUPPER OF GOCH († after 1475), JOH. RUCHRATH
OF WESEL († 1481), JOH. WESSEL († 1489).   But Augustine
could give to no one more than he possessed himself ; and hence
these men, in the decisive question concerning grace and justification, still held to the Catholic conception of infused grace
(vid. sub).   They had no more real grasp than the later
Scholastics upon the principle of the sole authority of Scripture
in matters of faith.   It follows, that the term "Forerunners of
the Reformation" is a misleading one[1] (vid. Ritschl, Rechtf. u.
Vers. i., ed. 2, 129 ff.).

This hasty review is sufficient to reveal the activity and
versatility of the intellectual life of the fourteenth and fifteenth
centuries.[2]   But the progressive impulse in this play of forces
came practically from the Nominalistic and Augustinian circles,
and to them we must now turn our attention.

2. We first view the positions of Nominalism, as presented in
Occam (cf. SEEBERG, PRE. xiv., ed. 3).   Man's knowledge
has to do with propositions, not with things.   Nature produces
only the individual object (sent. i. d. 2, q. 4 X).   The Universal
does not objectively exist, but only in the subjective understanding (ib. q. 8 E).   In order that knowledge may come into
existence, there is needed only the intellect (*intellectus*) and the
thing perceived (*res cognita*); the mediating intelligible forms (*species sensibiles et intelligibiles*) are superfluous (contrary to Duns,
supra, p. 147), "because in vain is that accomplished through
more stages, which can be accomplished through fewer "[3] (sent.
ii. q. 15 O).   Objects beget in us a sensuous impression.   From
this, the intellect is able to beget in the mind a picture (*fictum*),
a copy (*simulacra, idola, phantasmata, imagines*), of the actual
object (ib. q. 17 S, i. d. 13, q. 1 J), which is of course only a
representatively (*objectively*), and not a really (*subjectively*)
existent copy (ii. q. 15 SS).   "The intellect, seeing anything
outside of the soul, constructs a corresponding thing in the

---

[1] This is notably true of SAVONAROLA († 1498), who was in theology
a Thomist, and whose reformatory labors pursued strictly the line of the
medieval conception of the relations of church and state, and the ascetic ideal
of Christian life.

[2] Regarded separately, with almost every name mentioned in the above
review is associated a wealth of historical questions of biographical, literary,
dogmatic, and philosophic interest.   Protestant theology will find it increasingly necessary to devote far more attention and industry to this field of investigation than has been customary.

[3] A favorite principle with Occam, as it had been with Duns, derived
originally from Aristotle.

mind " (ib. i. q. 8 E).   This copy corresponds exactly with
the object copied.   Over against these results of first intention
(*termini primae intentionis*) originating directly from the actual
individual object, stand the results of second intention (*termini
secundaeintentiones*), which are naturally (*naturalitur*) constructed
by the thought from the former.[1]   These are the abstract conceptions, which assert something as common to the separate
objects, *i. e.*, the Universals (ib. ii. q. 25 O).   There is no
objective existence corresponding to them.   They are simply a
result of the inability of the human mind to apprehend a single
object without at the same time thinking of it as having a general
character.   For example, when one sees a white object, or
several white objects, he is compelled to think of the abstract
property of whiteness—or, we cannot look upon a thing as having bulk, or as related to other things, or as continuing to exist,
without thinking of quantity, or relation, or duration.   It is easy
to see from this why knowledge, or science, should be concerned
only with conceptions and definitions, not with real objects.
But according to Occam, conceptions of both the classes named
are truly real entities (*vere entia realia*), *i. e.*, as " qualities subjectively existing in the mind " (quodlib. iv. 19 ; v. 13), and
they correspond to existing reality.   It is utterly unjust to
accuse Occam of robbing concepts of their content and seeing in them only figments of the imagination.   He writes :
" The universal is not such a figment, to which nothing similar
in the subjective[2] being corresponds, as if it were only imagined
to be in the objective being (sent. ii. q. 8 H).   Intoning, as
he does so strongly, the activity of the soul in the act of perception, and shattering so completely the illusive dreams of
Realism, Occam is the real originator of the modern theory of
knowledge.

3. This more precise theory as to the nature of perceptions
was enlisted in the service of the critical assaults upon the traditional dogmatics.   (*a*) Dogma, it was held, cannot be scientifi-
cally proved.   With equal right entirely other views might then
be advocated.   In his *Centilogium*, Occam presents a number of
examples : If God assumes any other nature than his own, the
propositions : " God is an ass, God is a stone," are also possible (concl. 7).   If the Son became the son of Mary, so might

---

[1] Here belong also intelligible processes, such as acts of the thought or will,
desire, sorrow, etc., which man experiences within himself and which can
become the direct objects of thought, *i. e.*, which furnish an *intentio prima*,
or a directly-formed conception (sent. i. prol. q. 1 HH).

[2] *Subjective*—substantively, or objectively : *objective*—imaginatively.   The
meaning of the terms is now just the reverse.

also the Father (8) or the Holy Ghost (9). From the doctrine of the *communicatio idiomatum* might be drawn such propositions as, "God is the foot of Christ," or, "the foot is the hand " (13). The Trinity is undemonstrable, and can be known only through infused faith (*fides infusa*) (55). Differences of ethical merit cannot lead to corresponding differences of reward, since the latter is infinite (92). In a similar way, transubstantiation is criticized ; the proofs for the unity of God surrendered (Biel, sent. i. d. 2, q. 10); it is declared probable that God created the world in eternity (ib. ii. d. 1, q. 3 A); or taught that God could have forgiven sin without the repentance of the sinner (Occ. sent. iv. q. 8 M); or, that God might have just as well have commanded as prohibited hatred against himself, theft, murder, etc. (sent. ii. q. 19). (*b*) But it by no means follows that the dogmas of the church are to be surrendered, nor their acceptance made a matter of indifference. On the contrary, it is declared : "This is my faith, since it is the Catholic faith ; for whatever the Roman church believes, this alone and not anything else do I believe, either explicty or implicitly" (Occ. de sacr. alt. 1. 16; quodlib. iv. 35). The authority of the church's doctrine is supported by that of the Scriptures. But this is done—theoretically at least—in a different way from that adopted by Thomas or Duns (supra, p. 101 f., 149). Only those truths are Catholic which the Holy Scriptures teach : "Therefore the Christian is not by the necessity of salvation bound to believe ; nor is he to believe what is neither contained in the Bible, nor can be inferred by necessary and manifest consequence alone from the things contained in the Bible " (Occ. dial., p. 411, 769 f., Goldast). "An assertion of the canonical Scripture is of greater authority than an assertion of the Christian church " (D'Ailli in Tschackert, Petr. v. Ailli, append., p. 10). But these doctrines are true because inspired by God, whether as natural and innate in all men, or as revealed for recording in Scripture. The pope or the church can by their declarations alter absolutely nothing in these truths (Occ. ib., p. 419). "Human authority is by no means to be relied upon in those things which pertain to the faith, because our faith is above the human intellect " (p. 432). The truths of the faith are binding simply on account of their conformity to the Scriptures (Biel, sent. iii. d. 25, q. un. dub. 3 ; d. 24, q. un. dub. 3). The credibility of the Scriptures is acknowledged "because there it has been written and asserted by suggestion (*instinctu*) of the Holy Spirit (Occ., p. 822, 834). God immediately infused the knowledge here contained into the minds of the Biblical writers as the most perfect certainty or evidence (Biel, iii. d. 24, q. un. concl.

7).[1] Should anyone, therefore, call the Scriptures in question he would have to be regarded as a heretic : " Whoever says that any part of the New or of the Old Testament asserts anything false, or is not to be received by Catholics, is to be regarded as heretical and stubborn " (Occ. ib., p. 449). D'Ailli, indeed, placed the authority of the New Testament above that of the Old, and could even ascribe to some of the writings of the New Testament an "authority greater" than that of others (Tschackert, append., p. 9); but this had no practical significance. As, now, "all things to be believed are contained in the canonical Scriptures," there can be no quantitative enlargement of the body of truth. The three ancient symbols merely summarize the biblical ideas, or explain them as against the heresies which have arisen (Biel, iii. d. 25, q. un., a. 1 ; a. 3, dub. 2. Durand. iii. d. 26, q. 2, a. 2). " It is evident that the church, or the pope, by ordaining or making a new symbol, . . . does not make new Catholic truths or articles, but declares anew that certain truths have been and are Catholic " (Biel, ib. a. 3, dub. 3 fin.; cf. expos. can. miss. lect. 41 L). But, plainly as the principle of the exclusive authority of the Scriptures is here theoretically expressed, our authors did not undertake to make practical application of it. The teachings of the Scriptures and of the church are unconsciously placed upon the same level (*e. g.*, Occ. l. c., p. 434, 459, 475 ; sent. i. d. 2, q. 1 F).[2] Occam, *e. g.*, declares that he will hold to transubstantiation on account of the authority of the Romish church, although he knows of another view which explains everything better and is not contrary to the Bible, which does not expressly teach transubstantiation (quodlib. iv. 35 ; de sacr. alt. 3). He would not support the usual theory of original sin, unless there were " authorities of the saints " in its favor (sent. ii. d. 26 U). It appears to be safer to submit to ancient authority.[3] " To the apostolic sanctions

---

[1] Biel says (sermon. de temp. fol. 157 r): " But the canonical Scriptures of both Testaments are believed to have been written, the Holy Spirit dictating and inspiring." Paul is the " celestial secretary " (D'Ailli, sermones, Strassb. 1490, form Y 5 v). Durand. sent. prol. q. 1 L : " We assent to them (the articles of faith) alone or chiefly upon the authority of the Scriptures, which we believe to be inspired by God." D'Ailli : " All the canonical Scriptures have been revealed by the same infallible author," *i. e.*, God (Tschackert, Petr. v. Ailli, append., p. 9). Vid. also Duns, sent. iv. d. 14, q. 3. 5. Wickliffe, de civil. dom. i. p. 418, 439 : " Scripture divinely inspired." Other citations may be found in Holzhey, Die Inspirat. d. h. Schr., 1895, pp. 94-119.

[2] Occam (de sacr. alt. 3) even says : " This (transubstantiation) is believed to have been divinely revealed to the holy fathers."

[3] Ritschl's comments upon Occam (Fides implicita, 1890, p. 28 ff.) are unreliable, as he was unacquainted with the thorough discussion of the questions

and decrees which are not certainly contrary to the divine and
natural law of Holy Scripture, although there should be some doubt
of this, assent and obedience are to be rendered'' (Biel, serm.
de temp. fol. 157 r).[1]   It is remarkable that the same men who
apply reason so sharply in criticism of the dogmas of the church
and subordinate them to the sole authority of the Scriptures, are
yet always ready in any given instance to submit to the ''Romish ''
doctrine.   But we should not on this account wonder at their
studied irony, nor doubt either their honesty or their courage.
If I understand the matter rightly, this wavering stands in intimate connection with the juristic conception of the church.
Just as in civil life the law of nature holds primacy and yet finds
application only in a form adapted to the precepts of positive
law (supra, p. 171 f.), so it is also in the church.   Here, the accepted dogma, or the Roman doctrine, is the positive law ; the
Scriptures (and reason) correspond to the law of nature (supra,
p. 171 f.).[2] The application of the latter criterion produces a rad-
ical criticism of dogma and church ; but this criticism is shattered—very much as in the political world—upon actual concrete
conditions—upon the positive legal status of the Romish church.
Neither in church nor in state has the criticism based on the law
of nature abolished the existing positive law, although logical
consistency might require that it should do so.   But, since all attempt to prove the teachings of the church to be conformed to
reason has been abandoned upon principle, ecclesiastical positivism asserts itself in the naked form : I believe what the Romish
church believes !   This position could, of course, not be permanently maintained.   The longer criticism pursued its way, the
more intolerable became the positivism of the church, and the
longer the latter held sway in the church, the more improper
must the bold criticisms appear.[3]

at issue in Occam's writings upon church polity.   On p. 30, the *Dialog.* is referred to as ''not printed,'' but see G. HOFFMANN, Die Lehre der fides implicita, 1903, p. 153 ff.

[1] Such a man as D'Ailli could, upon occasion, write of the books of the
Bible : '' We thus receive the canonical or divine Scriptures on account of the
authority of the Catholic church, which so receives and approves them ''
(Tschackert, append., p. 11).

[2] It is, of course, not implied that the entire contents of the Scriptures fall
under the heading of the law of nature ; but, regarded as a whole, they claim
the same primacy over the positive ecclesiastical principles devised by man, as
the law of nature given to man by God holds over positive human laws.

[3] These theologians, on the one hand, identified the law of reason with the
teachings of the Scriptures, and, on the other, regarded the latter as in conformity with the teachings of the church.   Both ideas are equally perverted,
and both errors combined in preventing them from seriously applying their view
of the authority of the Bible.   Hence, they never established the authority of

4. The truths of Scripture are apprehended in Faith. (*a*) "Faith is a certain adherent (*adhaesiva*) and firm knowledge (*notitia*) of truth pertaining to religion, received through revelation" (Biel, iii. d. 23, q. 2, a. 1 D). In its essential nature, faith is intellectual assent (*assensus*): "To believe is an act of the intellect assenting to the truth, proceeding from a command of the will" (ib. C). But revelation embraces only to a small extent truths which are necessary, or evident to reason; the majority of its teachings are contingent truths, for which it would be impossible to present a scientific demonstration (Occ., sent. prol. q. 1 N; q. 7; quodlib. ii. 3. Biel, iii. d. 25, q. un., a. 1, n. 3), or which may even directly contradict reason. "Whoever is a Catholic and believing Christian can easily believe anything to which he could by no means by his natural powers assent." Here God comes to his aid: "God, out of his grace, infuses into him a *habitus*, through the medium of which (*quo mediante*) he is able to assent to any article of faith whatsoever" (Occ., centilog. 60). This is the *fides infusa*, without which no act of faith would be possible.[1] It is a "quality (*qualitas*) produced by God in the soul," which inclines the understanding to the act of faith." This habitus is infused in baptism (Biel, iii. d. 23, q. 2, a. 1 G. Occ., quodlib. iii. 7). But, in order that acts of faith may be actually performed, there is always further needed an acquired faith (*fides acquisita*). No child can come to faith, despite the faith infused into it, unless it secure also, through instruction or the reading of the Bible, the concrete faith directed upon particular, separate truths (Occ., sent. iii. q. 8 LM). (*b*) However untenable the conception of the "infused faith" may be, yet our Dogmaticians, in employing it, are guided by a certain presentiment of a real truth. It was their great aim to gain a special sphere for the religious life. The pious reader of the Bible, Biel explains, enlarges not so much his knowledge as his faith, since he is through the infused faith inwardly bound to the authority of Scripture (iii. d. 24, q. un., a. 2, concl. 5). But again, in so far as the material furnished by revelation for faith is not accessible to reason as such, theology is not in the usual sense of the term a science (Occ., sent. prol. q. 1. Biel, sent. prol. q. 7). (*c*) Occam thus defines the *fides implicita* : "To believe implicitly

the Scriptures upon any secure basis. It was not establishing it to take from the pope his infallible authority and transfer it to the Bible! But this is the basis of Occam's regard for the Bible. Vid. supra, p. 169, n. 2.

[1] But Occam in Quodlib., iii. 7, has introduced this conception as required neither by reason nor by experience . . . nor by inference but solely by authority. Cf. Duns, supra, p. 150.

is to firmly assent to some Universal from which many things follow, and not to pertinaciously cling to anything contrary to it" (dial., p. 434). Faith in the doctrine of the Scriptures is thus also included in the category of implicit faith. It is the idea, already familiar to us (supra, p. 103), that we accept everything taught by the Scriptures, i. e., by the church, as taught by these authorities : "Everything contained in the canonical Scriptures is true" (Biel, iii. d. 25, q. 1, a. 1, n. 2 ; expos. can. miss. lect. 12 B : "I believe as the church believes "). The technical formulas of the doctrine of the Trinity and of Christology fall, for the laity, under the "implicit faith "[1] (ib. a. 2, concl. 5), as well as the facts of biblical history, which cannot be experienced (ib. a. 1, n. 2). Even if a layman, in thus obeying his prelate, should believe what is false, "such a one would not only not sin, but he would even, by thus believing what is false, merit" (words of Innocent III. in Biel, l. c., a. 1, n. 2). But every believer must unconditionally possess *explicit* faith in Christ as the Redeemer (ib. a. 2, concl. 3 ; further, concl. 5). It is therefore the specific Catholic conception of faith which here again meets us. Faith is knowledge, (*notitia*) and assent (*assensus*) in regard to the biblical revelation. Faith is the same in all persons ; but some believe explicitly, others implicitly (ib. concl. 4).

5. Such are the principles of Nominalistic Scholasticism. Within the old forms a new ferment is stirring ; but the new wine has not yet burst the old bottles. The Scriptures are the sole authority in the church. It is felt that they constitute a canon of criticism ; but yet no dogma is overthrown, nor is any *right* of the hierarchy molested. Reason calls in question the bold systems of the past. Theologians surrender the systems, but allow the definitions to stand. Or, they doubt the separate doctrines, but believe the whole. Skepticism forms a league with the positivism of the church—doubt with implicit faith—and they counterbalance each other. There is an undefined sense of a really positive theology within reach ; but what is actually cultivated is a fruitless criticism, a "negative theology." But, amidst all the murkiness of thought, two ideas are never lost sight of, i. e., the authority of the Scriptures as over against the church and her dogmas, and the feeling that the Christian religion is no ordinary human system of religious philosophy, but a special, positive, and clearly marked whole— the historical revelation given by God, which only faith can

---

[2] But Occam claimed also for himself the right of cherishing *implicit* faith in the doctrine of transubstantiation (!) (De sacr. alt. 1, supra, p. 192). Cf. also account in Moll, KG. d. Niederl. ii. 562.

apprehend.   The league between the gospel and speculative thought, which held sway in the church from the days of Origen, was glorified by the Scholastics also ; but it was finally shattered, too, at their hands.   Duns and the Nominalists proved it untenable.   It is this service chiefly which establishes their position among the forces preparing the way for the coming Reformation. It would be a serious error to criticize their separate teachings and ignore the chief service rendered by them.

The separate doctrines are here of interest to us only because of their significance in the historical development.   In the closing period of Scholasticism, as we have already treated of the sacraments in § 58, and of repentance in particular in § 61, 2, we shall need to examine only the views held upon sin, redemption, grace, and the appropriation of salvation, together with the modifications in the doctrine of the Lord's Supper. We have, likewise, no occasion to attempt a presentation of the Augustinian tendency in all its details ;[1] and shall therefore confine ourselves to a few remarks touching the doctrine of grace and to criticism of the conception of the church and of the theory of indulgences.

§ 63.   *Labors of the Later Middle Ages Upon Separate Dogmas and Doctrines.*

1. As the conception of God held by Duns regulated the theistic speculations of the Nominalists, so in nearly all doctrines they attached themselves more or less closely to the *Doctor Subtilis*.   This is evident in their views of Sin and Liberty. The rebellion of the sensuous nature against the spirit is natural. The *donum superadditum* removed it, and in consequence merits became possible (Biel, ii. d. 30, q. 1, a. 1-3).   Original sin "consists in a privation of the original righteousness owed" (Biel, ib. q. 2, a. 2, concl. 3.   Occ., sent. ii. q. 26 U ; cf. Durand, ii. d. 30, q. 3).   Yet an infection of children through the generating act is also maintained (Biel, ib. q. 2, a. 1, concl. 1.   Duns differs, *supra*, p. 153).   But, despite sin, the natural freedom of the will remains perfectly intact.   " The integrity of his natural will, *i. e.*, its freedom, is not corrupted by sin ; for that is really the will itself, and not separable from it" (Biel, ii. d. 30, q. 1, a. 3, dub. 4).   " Through mortal sin nothing is corrupted nor destroyed in the soul" (Occ., sent. iv. q. 8 and 9 D).   That these assertions are irreconcilable with the Augus-

---

[1] Of how little interest for the History of Doctrines such a discussion would be may be seen in CLEMEN'S work upon Goch.

tinian doctrine of original sin is very evident.[1]   Vid. also Biel,
De festivit. serm. 33.

2. The doctrine of the Atonement and Redemption is treated
entirely in the spirit of Thomas and Duns.   The subjective aspect is the more prominent, but the objective is not wanting.
The relation of the two to one another remains, as heretofore,
without clear definition.

(a) AUREOLUS, BACONTHORP, DURANDUS, and CAPREOLUS follow in the tracks of Thomas.   The merit of Christ is of infinite
value, and is capable of affecting atonement for all (Aur. iii. d.
20, q. 1, a. 1.   Bac. iii. d. 32, a. 1.   Capr. iii. d. 18, a. 3.
Dur. iii. d. 19, q. 1, a. 2: "The passion of Christ was a sufficient
and superabundant satisfaction for the sin of the whole human
race. . . . Christ, by suffering out of love and obedience,
offered to God something more acceptable than the recompens-
ing of the sin of the whole human race required "").   Anselm's
idea of the necessity of satisfaction is rejected (Aur. l. c., q. 2.
Dur. d. 20, q. 1).   But redemption through the passion of
Christ is, nevertheless, the most suitable way, since man is in this
way assured of the magnitude of the divine love and incited to
a responsive affection, and receives also the example of Christ to
stimulate him to the practice of every virtue (Dur. ib.).   The
redemption wrought by Christ is realized only in the case of
those "who are joined to him as members to the Head," or
"through real imitation, i. e., when we suffer after the similitude
of Christ" (Dur. d. 19, q. 1, a. 2).[2]

(b) GABRIEL BIEL, on the other hand, follows Duns more closely.
Christ, from the time of his conception onward, by his obedience
merited for us grace and glory : " for he was in the very moment
of his conception a man perfect in every grace and virtue and
meritorious work " (iii. d. 18, a. 2, concl. 2).   This merit becomes efficacious through the *acceptio divina* (d. 19, a. 2, concl.
1), but only for the predestinated : "Only for the predestinated
did he merit final grace and glory," for "no one finally obtains
salvation unless he was predestinated from eternity."   Here also
Biel follows Duns (supra, p. 152).[3]   Salvation rests upon the divine

---

[1] As to the views of this period upon the immaculate conception of Mary,
see Esp. Occam, quodlib. iii. 9. 10, and cf. WERNER, Nachscot. Scholast.,
p. 347.

[2] Wicliffe argues the necessity of a satisfaction upon the ground that man
must perform an act of humility, which, in contrast with Adam's presumption,
shall lower him beneath himself (trialog., p. 215 f., ed. Lechler).

[3] The idea of predestination occurs very frequently in his writings.   The
eucharistic sacrifice brings "remission of sin ; not, indeed, to all, but to the
predestinated" (Biel, sermon. defestiv. fol. 279 r).   The church is the "multitude of the predestinated " (expos. can. miss. lect. 22 E.; vid. also sent. d.

predestination, and the passion of Christ is only a means for its realization : " If Christ had not suffered, the elect would never-theless have been saved, because before the passion of Christ God foresaw that the elect would be saved " (ib. concl. 4). By the side of this conclusion stands the other, that, although the pas-sion of Christ primarily (*principaliter*) secures salvation for us, yet our own working (*operatio*) coöperates. For, when anyone becomes a recipient of grace, he needs, upon his part, a certain disposition of the will, such as *attritio ;* and this implies a merit of fitness (*de congruo*). In the case of the baptized child, a sub-stitute for this is found in the merit of the sponsors. The per-son thus equipped with grace performs works having merit of worthiness (*de condigno*), and these become a ground for the in-crease of grace. It is concluded therefore : " That, granting that the passion of Christ is the principal merit on account of which are conferred grace, the opening of the kingdom and glory, yet it is never the sole and entire meritorious cause. This is evident, because with the merit of Christ always concurs some work, such as the merit of fitness or of worthiness of the one re-ceiving the grace or glory " (concl. 5). Thus the merit of Christ finds its necessary complement in our merit. This final conclu-sion is here—not illogically—derived from the idea of merit ; but it is essentially an outgrowth of the Thomistic idea, that we became partakers of the results of the work of Christ only in so far as we are in life conformed to his image (supra, p. 178 f., 179 f., n. 4).[1] This merit of the obedience of Christ, as thus more sharply defined, God accepts as a satisfaction for the sins of all who believe on Christ (d. 20, a. 3, dub. 1). This course of divine dealing cannot; of course, be described as necessary (ib. a. 2, concl. 1); and Anselm is thus refuted with the weapons of Duns (ib. a. 1).[2] On the other hand, the plan of salvation may be shown to be most admirably adapted to the end in view, since it binds us to God and stimulates us to love him

---

27, a. 3, dub. 4). WERNER (Endausgang, p. 285) interprets the above-cited passage from the Sentences as teaching "the universal efficacy of Christ's redemptive act for all the descendants of Adam."

[1] This relationship between Biel and Thomas is, with justice, maintained by an ascetic document dating from the beginning of the sixteenth century, which reproduces the thoughts of Biel (in HASACK, p. 477), where we find also the declaration (p. 443): " Since the passion of Christ was not an entire, but a partial, cause of our salvation." In general, this formula represents ad-mirably the religious conception of the day. But we find, on the contrary, in Duns, iii. d. 19, § 8 : " Christ, as the entire cause (*totalis causa*), merited for us the opening of the gates of paradise."

[2] Yet Biel, like Duns (supra, p. 157), is not indisposed to accept the argu-ments as valid, " divine ordination being presupposed " (q. 20, a. 1, n. 1 B).

in return (ib. a. 3, dub. 2), and also because God chose this plan and no other (ib. a. 2, concl. 2).

(*c*) It is not correct to say that "the fundamental ideas of Anselm's theory were nevertheless generally accepted" (THOMASIUS, Christi Person u. Werk, ii., ed. 3, 165). Anselm's theory is accepted by no one. On the contrary, we constantly meet the fundamental ideas of Abelard, almost always indeed combined with the older thought of the merit of Christ which avails before God as the ground of divine grace. This combination appears also in the popular treatises of the day, particularly in the mystical literature.[1] The passion of Christ is here treated in the spirit, and often in the very language, of Bernard. Its purpose is to reveal to us God's love and incite us to responsive love and imitation.[2] On the other hand, salvation and eternal blessedness are with the greatest earnestness made dependent upon the objective merit of Christ and the satisfaction rendered by him, the contemplation of which is especially commended to the dying.[3] It is a favorite thought (Anselm, supra, p. 70) that in the redemptive work of God justice and mercy concur (*e. g.*, Biel, sermon. de festiv. fol. 225 v). Exceedingly instructive is a sermon by Biel (De circumcis. domini). Here Anselm's doctrine is first presented in bold outlines, and from it deduced the concurrence of the justice and mercy of God (l. c., fol. 197 v). But this work of Christ has for its purpose the efficacy of the sacraments: "The sacraments . . . by which man is directly disposed to the reception of grace, which is the health and life of the soul ; for these he merited efficacy by the shedding of his blood " (fol. 198 r). "Christ, as true God and man, instituted the sacraments, primarily (*principaliter*) according to his divine nature, meritoriously according to his human nature" (ib.). This medicine gives grace, " by which they are able to merit eternal blessedness " (199 v). But even this institution of the sacraments is a work of the grace which grants the means of salvation

---

[1] The numerous sermons and meditations upon the Passion in the Incunabula-literature of before and after A. D. 1500 are especially instructive. Space forbids the citation of these separately. See both views also in WESSEL, De causis incarnat. 6 (opp. p. 424 f.), and GOCH, vid. Clemen, Goch, p. 131 ff.).

[2] *E. g.*, WESSEL, De caus. incarn. 1, p. 414 : " Nothing is so effectual for turning the minds of men to good as pious exercise in the life and passion of the Lord." G. Biel, passionis dominic. serm. (Hagenau, 1515), form A 3 ; expos. can. miss. lect. 85 XY.

[3] Cf. supra, p. 179, n. 3. Upon Christ as atoning sacrifice, *e. g.*, in WESSEL, De caus. incarn. 19, p. 455 ; de magnitud. passion. 39, p. 539 ; 40, p. 541 ; 44, p. 549. Cf. in HASACK, p. 155 f., 143 : " Thou wilt to-day interpose between thy wrath and my transgression the most dear and acceptable sacrifice, Christ." Vid. also MOLL, KG. d. Niederl. ii. 657 f.

to its enemy, as well as of the justice which rewards in accordance with the work of Christ, *i. e.*, through the institution of the sacraments (sent. iv. d. 2, q. 1, a. 3, dub. 1 ; cf. Duns, iv. d. 2, q. 2. 8).   The so-called objective aspect of salvation may, accordingly, be reduced to the proposition, that Christ has secured for us the medicine of the sacraments (cf. Duns Scotus).

3. It has already been remarked (p. 174), that the religious life is moulded under the influence of the sacrament of repentance.   It is accordingly under this heading that the development of personal piety is treated.[1]   The problem is the conversion of the sinner.   (*a*) It is for the sinner—as is repeated until it becomes wearisome—to do what in him lies (*quod in se est*), and God will then not suffer grace to be lacking (*e. g.*, Biel, sent. ii. d. 27, q. un.).   The sinner acts from himself up to the point of attrition.   But, according to Paltz, even this is to be traced back to the influence of a grace gratuitously given (suppl. R 2 r; 4 r).   " Nevertheless, if we do what is in us, so that we have attrition, he changes for us that attrition into contrition—sometimes of his own motion (*per se*) before the reception of the sacraments, sometimes in the reception of the sacraments, which is more certain " (ib.).   The sacraments, and even divine worship before their reception, effect this transformation (see citation, p. 175), in connection with which man receives simultaneously the peculiar grace (*gratia gratum faciens*) infused by the sacraments.   By contrition mortal sin in him is destroyed, and by the sacrament the power of doing good is infused.   (*b*) This is the Justification of the sinner.   The ultimate disposition being fixed by an act of the free will, grace, which is the form of justification, is immediately infused by God (Durand, iv. d. 17, q. 1, a. 3).   There is need of faith in connection with this process only in so far as the disposition to accept the grace which is the prerequisite of the process, *i. e.*, faith, is necessary.   " Therefore for the reception of justification in the adult there is required a motion of the free will, according to which it consents to grace.   And, because the first motion through which he consents to grace is a motion of faith, therefore that motion itself is a motion of faith.   Thus Romans, chapter 5, justifies through faith " (Paltz, R 2 r).   Justification may, like generation, be understood in two senses : as the gradual movement toward righteousness, or as a change without movement (*mutatio sine motu*).   In the former sense, it occurs gradually (*successive*); in the other, " justification is effected in

---

[1] Cf., in addition to Biel's Book of Sentences, also JOH. OF PALTZ, who, in the supplement of his *Coelifodina*, treats of conversion and justification in connection with a discussion of the sacrament of repentance.

an instant " (ib. R 5 r). When the sinner thus becomes righteous through the infusion of grace, he receives at the same time
the forgiveness of sins.[1] (*c*) But the infusion of grace is also the
basis of meritorious works,[2] which are accordingly imposed in the
confessional. By this means the entire process is brought under
the view-point of merit (supra, p. 122). The dominant terminology is derived from Duns (p. 160). The general definition
is : " A meritorious act is an act called forth (*elicitus*) by free
will, accepted for the repaying of some recompense (*ad retri-
buendum aliquod praemium*), (Biel, ii. d. 27, a. 1, n. 2 ; cf. iii.
d. 18, q. un.). The initiatory steps, which man is able to take
in his own strength, *e. g.*, the *attritio*, produce the merit of
fitness (*de congruo*). " The soul is able, by the removal of an
obstacle and by a good movement toward God elicited by free
will, to merit the first grace by fitness," since it is just for God to
reward this merit by imparting grace (ib. concl. 4 ; cf. iv. d.
14, q. 1, a. 2, concl. 5 : *meritum de congruo ad justificationem ;*
d. 16, q. 2, a. 3, prop. 4 ; Durand, i. d. 17, q. 2, a. 2). But
through the infusion of grace the works become merits of
worthiness. " A merit of worthiness (*condigni* or *de condigno*)
is an act elicited by free will for a recompense (praemium) of
someone according to a debt to be repaid to justice." An
" equality " and " proportion of merit to reward " is here required
(ib. ii. d. 27, a. 1, n. 3).[3] By means of these merits, man
secures for himself both an increase of grace and eternal glory
(vid. also Paltz, coelifod. Bb 3 r and suppl. R 4 r).[4] (*d*) The
possibility of being sure of the possession of grace was denied by
Biel, though asserted by Duns (ii. d. 27, a. 3, dub. 5). The
unworldly ideal of life, and the dualism between the religious and
the secular life, were perpetuated (cf. the Mystic literature).
But here also, the views of the church were in conflict with
modern advancement and its ideals.[5]

---

[1] Some follow Thomas (p. 120), and conceive of it as the logical consequent
of the infusion of grace, *e. g.*, Paltz, R 5 r : " Grace is infused before guilt is
remitted, because through grace the guilt is remitted ; " Biel, iv. d. 14, q. 1, a.
2, concl. 5. Others, with Duns, reverse the process (p. 161), *e. g.*, Occ.,
iv. q. 8 and 9 L : " Yet in fact and as a rule, the expulsion of guilt is
previous to the infusion of grace." Vid. also supra, p. 161, n.

[2] Cf. HASACK, p. 133 : " It (grace) moves the free will to do well and to
think well, to live well and to work well, and it gives power for all praiseworthy undertakings. . . . Grace makes all work meritorious. . . . But
grace is given, that man may with (the assistance of) grace perform all things
appointed."

[3] Yet Durand asserts, that, in the strictest sense, man can secure this merit
with men only, and not with God (i. d. 17, q. 2, a. 2).

[4] Cf. HASACK, p. 262 f.

[5] Yet such a man as Biel had a certain comprehension of the economic con-

Our review makes it very evident that in the theology of the Schoolmen only the sacramental and Pelagian tendencies made progress.   The free will and the sacraments are the two forces which mould the Christian life.

4. In regard to the Lord's Supper, mention must be made of a theory which found many adherents.[1] (a) It is the view mentioned already, and not without sympathy, by Duns, *i. e.*, that, even after the creation of the body of Christ, the substance of the bread is retained, and not merely the accidents (supra, p. 131 n.).   Occam calls attention to the fact, that the Scriptures do not contain the theory of transubstantiation (de sacr. alt. 3), and he plainly intimates that the view, that the substance of the bread and wine remain, is "very reasonable:" "Neither is the contrary to this contained in the canonical Bible, nor does it any more include any contradiction, that the body of Christ coëxists with the substance of the bread, than (that it coëxists with) its accidents, nor is it repugnant to reason" (quodl. iv. 35 ; cf. centilog. 39 C).   Nevertheless, out of regard for the Roman church, he will continue to hold transubstantiation (sacr. alt. 1, 5).   But the entire tenor of his discussion (vid. sub) testifies that he is not serious in his submission.[2]   DURAND also acknowledges the possibility of the retention of the earthly sub-

---

ditions of the age, and when treating of repentance made excellent comments upon it, *e. g.*, against the communism based on the law of nature (iv. d. 15, q. 2, a. 1, n. 1), upon war (ib. q. 4), upon the method of taxation (ib. q. 5, a. 2, concl. 3), upon the wild-game abuses (ib. concl. 5), upon trading and prices (ib. q. 10, a. 1, n. 2), upon the question of coinage and interest (ib. q. 9, 11), etc. Cf. also ROSCHER, Gesch. der Nationaloekonomik, p. 22 ff.

[1] The high regard for the mass continues (vid. supra, p. 134). Cf. Luther, Weim., ed. vi. 375 : "That they made of it a sort of magic ! Some have masses held, that they may become rich and that it may go well with them in their business ; some, because they think that if they hear mass in the morning, they are safe for the day from all distress and danger ; some for their sickness; some for things even more foolish and even sinful,—and yet find priests so stupid as to take money and do their will.   And, further, they have now made one mass better than the others, and esteem one as useful for this purpose, another for that. . . . Here everyone keeps silent and (they) let the people go on for the sake of the accursed, shameful penny."   In connection with the idea that the Lord's Supper blots out venial sins, stands the view that, as Christ atoned for original sin, so the eucharistic sacrifice atones for daily sins, *e. g.*, Pseudo-Thomas, Opusc. 58, c. 1 (opp, ii. 42). Cf. Confes. Augsb. 24.

[2] A contemporary of Duns, the Dominican JOHN OF PARIS (ca. 1300), declared in favor of the retention of the substance of the bread, which however combines with the body of Christ to form one "subsistence," so that there are indeed two corporeities (*Corporeitäten*), but only one body. Vid. his work: Determinatio de modo existendi Corpus Christi in sacr. alt. alio quam sit ille quem tenet eccl., ed. Alix, London, 1686. Cf. Kirchenlex. vi., ed. 2, 621 f. ARGENTRE, Collectio indiciorum, i. 264 ff.

stances (iv. d. 11, q. 1, a. 3) ; likewise BIEL (expos. can. miss. lect., 41 J); THOMAS OF STRASSB. (iv. d. 11, p. 1, a. 2 ; cf. also Dionys. Carthus. iv. d. 11, q. 1), and JOH. v. WESEL (vid. ULLMANN, Reform. vor d. Ref. i. 330, 390). D'AILLI zealously supports this view, " because it is altogether possible that the substance of the bread coëxists with the substance of the body. This mode is possible ; it is repugnant to neither reason nor the authority of the Bible ; it is far easier to be understood and more reasonable " (in sent. iv. q. 6 E).[1] WESSEL also holds to both the presence of the body of Christ (de eucharist. c. 8, 16 ; opp. 1614, p. 673, 688 f.), and the con- tinued existence of the bread, " which truly vivifies and refines alone by signifying (*significatione*) and by pious commemo- ration " (c. 13, p. 683). The chief thing is that Christ " desired to be corporally near (*cominus*) to those longing for him " (c. 23, p. 695 ; 24, p. 697), and that spirit and life are thereby brought to us (c. 8, 9, 10). (*b*) For the completion of this theory, we must bear in mind the conception then held of the presence of Christ's body in the Supper (cf. supra, p. 116). We follow here chiefly Occam. According to the Nominalistic view, quantity has no independent existence, but it is the " how much " of a thing ; it is not separate from the substance or the qualities of an object (sacr. alt., form B 2 r and c. 17). The quantity of a thing may be increased or diminished, as by compression or by exten- sion, without the thing becoming thereby a different thing. Ac- cordingly, a thing may become, like a mathematical point, with- out quantity, without thereby changing its substance (ib. c. 37 ; sent. iv. q. 4 H ; cf. Biel, Sent. iv. d. 10, a. 1, n. 2). In this way the body of Christ exists in the Lord's Supper : The body of Christ is not quantitatively (*quantum*) in the sacrament of the altar (sacr. alt., form B 6 r and c. 31, 41). The bodily pres- ence of a thing may be of two kinds : " To be *circumscriptively* in a place is for anything to be in a place, a part of which is in a part of the place and the whole of it in the whole place ; but to be *definitively* in a place is when a whole thing is in a whole place and not beyond it, and the whole of it is in every part of that place " (quodl. i. 4).[2] Examples of the latter are seen in the angels and in the human soul, which are present entire in every part of the space which they occupy as well as in the entire space. Thus also the whole Christ is present in the *hostia*, just as he is equally in all its parts (sacr. alt. c. 6). If now the body of Christ exists at the same time with the bread in

---

[1] To this Luther appealed in his De captiv. Babyl., Weim. ed. vi., 508.
[2] Biel added the further category, *repletive* (sent. i. d. 37, q. un. a. 1).

the *hostia*, two questions arise : (1) How the same body can be present at the same time in different places, and (2) How its parts can coëxist in one place.   The former is answered by a reference to the simultaneous presence of the soul in all parts of the body.   In reply to the second question, it is to be said, that the body of Christ is not in the Supper quantitatively, and therefore we are not to think of a correspondence between separate parts of the space with parts of the body.   There is hence no necessity to inquire whether the body present is the glorified or the natural body (sent. iv. q. 4 J K O).   While the body of Christ is at one place in heaven in extended form and quantitatively, it is also present everywhere as a whole in the host (cf. Biel, iv. d. 10, a. 2, concl. 2, and expos. can. miss. lect. 43).[1]   But this presence is not confined to the host : " The body of Christ is present to everyone, is present to himself immediately, and consequently that form of bread, *i. e.*, the host, has nothing to do with (*nihil facit*) the presence of the body " (Occ., ib. N).   Thus regarded, it may be said that the body of Christ can be everywhere (*ubique*) just as God is everywhere (centiloq. 25, 28).[2]   This way of apprehending the matter, which had an influence on Luther, suggests the following comments : (1) The abstract logical method of considering the subject, and the references to the institution of the Supper, and even to the act of worship involved, are not clear.   (2) The eucharistic body of Christ stands in boldest contrast with his actual body— it is a certain omnipresent Something.   (3) As Occam weaves in the problem, How two bodies can be at one place, he betrays the fact that transubstantiation is not in his mind.   (4) Transubstantiation maintained its place in the canons of the church, but the theology of the closing era of the Middle Ages took no delight in it.[3]   Cf. RETTBERG, Occ. und Luther, Stud. u. Krit. 1839, 69 ff.

---

[1] Vid. also Durand, iv. d. 11, q. 1, a. 1, 2.

[2] Cf. also (concl. 23), the view that a stone fallen from heaven might cleave through the body of Christ without dividing it or meeting with any opposition in its course.

[3] We must not overlook at this point the teaching of FABER STAPULENSIS, † 1536 (cf. GRAF, Ztschr. f. hist. Theol. 1852, 3 ff., 165 ff.), since the attempt has been made to trace to him Luther's doctrine of the Lord's Supper (Hospinian, Calixtus).   At the first Supper Christ was present both sensibly and also concealed, sacramentally and impassibly, beneath the outward signs. The result was a union (*unitio*) between him and the participants, which brought to the latter immortality (Comm. upon the Fourth Gospel, Basel, 1523, fol. 115).   Thus he is again present at every subsequent celebration of the Supper.   "For, always remaining in heaven, he, existing everywhere, descends *immobilely* into every believer, whom he vivifies and nourishes." He gives immortality and life (ib. fol. 318 f.).   But in this his presence is a

(*c*) In this connection we must recall the very bold and cut-ting criticism which was during the Middle Ages directed against the doctrine of transubstantiation. It originated with Wickliffe (vid. his work of A. D. 1382-83, De eucharistia, ed. Loserth, 1892 ; cf. Fasciculus zizaniorum, Mag. Joh. Wiclif, ed. Shirley, 1858, p. 115 f.) and was spread by Huss (vid. De corpore Christi) and the Hussites (cf. LOSERTH, in the introduction to De euchar., p. xliv ff.). Transubstantiation is to Wickliffe's mind worse than heathenism : "They believe worse than the pagans, that that consecrated host is their God " (p. 13 f.). It is a new doctrine, against which the Scriptures and reason pro-test (p. 71). It has against it the testimony of the eyes (p. 57), and involves in all manner of contradictions. Will God then destroy a portion of the entire substance of the body (p. 129), or will he cause the body to grow at every celebration of the ordinance? (p. 193). According to Wickliffe's own view, we must dis-criminate sharply between the *sign*, or *sacrament*, and the *body* (p. 18, 38, 112 ; trial., p. 248). The words of institution are to be understood *tropice*, or *figurative*. Their effect is that they to the bare natural existence (*nudum esse naturale*) of the bread add a superadded sacramental character (*superadditum esse sacramentale*) (p. 153, 35, 83, 291). The bread signifies the body of Christ, upon which we should spiritually direct our attention and remembrance. "That change does not destroy the nature of the bread, nor alter the nature of the body . . . but it effects the presence of the body of Christ and destroys the pre-eminence of the bread, so that the whole attention of the worshiper is concentrated upon the body of Christ " (p. 100). "Not that the bread is destroyed, but that it *signifies* the body of the Lord there present in the sacrament " (p. 101, 121). But this presence of Christ is a spiritual one, mediated through the symbol : "That the body of Christ is there virtually and in the sign—not the body of Christ as it is in heaven, but the vicarious sign of it " (p. 303, 271, 83 f.). Then, as to the eating : " We do not tear the body of Christ with the teeth, but

bodily one : " Who is divinely everywhere, and also *corporeally wherever he will*" (ib. fol. 402 v). But only the believing recipient obtains this blessed presence (fol. 318 r). Faber here lays special emphasis upon the *personal* presence of Christ (*praesentia salvatoris*). The punishments inflicted upon unworthy participants are educational (according to 1 Cor. ii. 29, ff.). Vid. Epp. div. Pauli, Paris, 1512, fol. 97 v. This important composition is distinguished by its independence of tradition. Faber pays no attention to the Scholastic problems. He sought to draw directly from the sources, and insists upon the personal and bodily presence of Christ, without concerning himself about the how. This does indeed remind us of Luther's original position, but without any evidence of historical connection between the two.

we receive it spiritually " (p. 13). It is eaten, not corporeally, but spiritually, by the believer, since his mind is fed from the memory of the body of Christ (p. 308, 17). This is the doctrine of the Scriptures, which the teachers of the first thousand years—when Satan was bound (Rev. 20. 2)—also advocated (p. 286). It commends itself particularly by its simplicity, as the yoke of the New Testament law is always light (p. 119). This is essentially a reproduction of Augustine, with his view polemically developed and directed against the Catholic doctrine.

5. We are thus already brought into contact with the labors of the Augustinian school upon the doctrines of the church. First of all, we note the resuscitation of the Augustinian doctrine of grace. The latter embraces predestination, which now becomes its leading thought. If predestination was with Augustine an auxiliary line of thought, it now becomes the first principle. With him it was anthropologically developed ; here, in a strictly theological way. The conception is further undesignedly combined with the Scotist conception of God : the absolute Lord of the world rules absolutely as he will, and hence the inexplicable predestination.

(*a*) BRADWARDINA was especially severe in his arraignment of the age upon the charge of Pelagianism. Free will, man's own strength, merit—is everything, and thus predestination is earned (vid. de causa dei,[1] i. 31, p. 602, ed. Savil.). Thus, he maintains, do his contemporaries teach. On the contrary, he has learned by experience that not merit, but grace alone, saves us (i. 35). Everything which exists and happens is made and brought to pass by God (i. 3, 32 ; ii. 29 f.). Divine foresight (*providentia*) is in reality fore-determination of the divine will (*praevolentia voluntatis*) (i. 27, p. 261). All that happens rests upon the immutable "antecedent necessity" of the divine determination (i. 25). No one can pray better than by saying : Thy will be done. This being the case, all merits fall to the ground (i. 39). Here predestination finds its place. It is "a pre-ordination of the divine will concerning a rational creature ;" and there is a two-fold (*gemina*) predestination (i. 45). All the gifts of grace are grounded upon it : "The effects of predestination are the conferring of grace in the present, justification from sin, good merits, final perseverance " (ib., p. 422). Grace is a "habitus of the soul gratuitously infused by God " (i. 23). The determinism into which this theory leads (*e. g.*, iii. 27,

---

[1] The very numerous manuscripts in which this work has been preserved, even upon the continent, attest its wide distribution.

p. 704)[1] Bradwardina rejects, maintaining free-will (ii. 1, 2 ;
iii. 1). Cf. SEEBERG, PRE. iii., ed. 3, 350 ff.

(b) WICKLIFFE also exalts predestination to the central place
in his theology.   God alone is the cause that some are predestinated and others only foreknown (*praesciti*).   "God
necessitates individual active creatures to whatever action he
desires (*ad quemlibet actum suum*), and thus some are predestinated, *i. e.*, ordained to glory after labor, and some are foreknown, *i. e.*, ordained to everlasting punishment after a miserable life" (trialog., p. 122).   But human freedom is not thereby
excluded : "But God cannot determine that I shall merit
or demerit, unless I also determine" (de dom. div., p. 149).
The predestinating grace is the deepest ground for the bestowal
of grace upon the sinner.   Grace is both, as *gratia increata*, the
"divine volition, by which God determines to do good to a
creature," and, as *gratia creata*, the infused "good quality, by
which the creature is formally acceptable to God" (ib., p.
236 f.).   But this quality is the condition of the "*acceptatio*, by
which God accepts a man" (trial., p. 152 f.; de dom. div.,
p. 238).   Since this divine acceptance is taken into the account,
the personal nature of grace comes to some extent into view.
But it is the imparting of grace which first capacitates man for
meritorious conduct (dom. div., p. 241).   Since God " pre-
veniently (*praeveniendo*) incites and necessitates to meriting
. . . the freedom of the will being preserved," it follows, that
every creature merit is, as such, only a merit of fitness (ib.,
p. 226 f., 242, 249).   It is evident that the Catholic conception of grace underlies also the theory of Wickliffe, but the
gratia increata, or the free loving will of God, receives at
his hands through predestination and acceptance an actual
importance which does not attach to it in the popular teaching.
It is the old conception, but there is yet in it an element which
points the way to a new apprehension of the subject.   The
divine loving will is the chief thing, and the infused quality is
only a means for its realization.   Should it be inconceivable that
other means might also be found for the accomplishment of the
divine purpose ?

(c) The Catholic doctrine of grace was not repudiated even
by the more popularistic theologians of this school, such as GOCH.
He combats the Pelagianism of his day, and maintains the necessity of grace for salvation, since faith and love are supernatural
acts, which man cannot render without the aid (*auxilium*) of
grace (dialog. c. 5, Walch, monimenta med. aev. i. 4, p. 91,

---

[1] Cf. Wickliffe's critique, De dominio div. i. 136 f., 148 ft.

94-97). The *infusio gratiae* consists in this : that God begets in us "a supernatural faculty (*facultas*) for doing supernatural acts" (c. 14, p. 162). The acts thus performed are meritorious (c. 19, p. 192 f.). The *fides formata* makes the soul acceptable to God (c. 4, p. 86). According to WESEL, the forgiveness of sins is the infusion of the *gratia gratum faciens* (adv. indulg. 18, in Walch, monim. med. aev. ii. 1, p. 126). Likewise WESSEL : "Concerning justification it is evident enough, because that sins be taken away is nothing else than to have justifying love, which he who does not have remains in sin. In order, therefore, that he may take away sin, it is necessary to infuse righteousness" (de magnitud. passionis, c. 7, opp. Groning, 1614, p. 466). God accepts the sinner on account of faith, faith being regarded as including love : "And since faith is the source of love, therefore it is also accepted on account of its offspring" (c. 45, p. 550). That is, God will bestow upon the believer the righteousness secured through the satisfaction rendered by Christ (ib. p. 551). "Therefore neither our faith . . . nor the sacrifice of Christ, but the determination of God accepting the sacrifice of Christ, and through Christ accepting the sacrifices of Christians, is our righteousness" (c. 44, p. 549). These are all medieval ideas. As long as they are not abandoned, all the admirable attempts to overthrow the monastic ideal which are found, *e. g.*, in Goch, and the idea of evangelical liberty (which grace does not destroy, but completes) which is not to be resigned in favor of any vow, as though without the latter there can be no "perfection of Christian life" (dial. c. 7, p. 109 ff.; 11, p. 144 ; 12, p. 155 ; 9, p. 125 ff.)—are but a beating of the air. The same must be said of the emphasis laid upon the rights of property : "The proprietorship of law may consist with the highest evangelical perfection ; the proprietorship of love is simply inadmissible and forbidden to all Christians through the precept of love (c. 22, p. 234). But in these thoughts there breathes the atmosphere of a new era. The Holy Scriptures, which in these circles, as in the church in general, are recognized as the highest authority (vid. esp. Goch, Epistola apologetica, in Walch, monim. med. aev. ii. 1, p. 4 ff., 10, 11) begin to be employed as a critical standard, by which not only the laws of the state (p. 183 f.), but the ordinances and ideals of the church as well, are measured.

6. This leads us a step further, to the criticism of the Sacrament of Repentance and Indulgences. "There are two principal sacraments, in which the church is being ruined, viz., the sacrament of the eucharist and the sacrament of repentance" (Wickliffe, De euch. et poenit., in Loserth's edition of De

14

eccl., p. 329). Wickliffe denies the necessity of the sacramental confession, which does not harmonize with the "liberty of the law of the Lord" (ib., p. 331 ff., 341). He combats indulgences most vigorously as a scandalous traffic and blasphemous presumption of the pope (ib., p. 340 ; trialog. iv. 32, p. 357 ff. Cf. Huss, Quaestio disputata . . . de indulgentiis, opp. Norimb. 1558, i. 174 ff.). WESEL teaches that God alone forgives the eternal penalties of sin, which he does by the infusion of grace. To the priest belongs only a sacramental ministration (*ministerium*). There exists a " covenant established with priests " (adv. indulg. 23, 26, 27, 28 ; in Walch, monim. med. aev. ii. 1). Since now God himself imposes temporal penalties for sin in this life, it is clear that indulgences have no ground to rest upon. They would do away with purgatory altogether (ib. 47). The pope can remit only the penalties which men have imposed (34). The doctrine of indulgences has the Scriptures arrayed against it ; they are only " pious frauds upon believers " (50). WESSEL is still more severe. Under his hand, the whole sacrament of repentance falls to pieces. The pope can only outwardly separate any person from the church ; and when he does so, his action has no direct significance for the inner life (de sacr. poenit., opp. p. 772 f., 776, 781). This sacrament has really nothing to do with the matter. God grants the spirit of love, and with it contrition. This is already a work of infused grace : " The contrite (is) righteous before the sacrament " (p. 790).[1] " Repentance, if it be a sacrament, does not need contrition " (ib.). Similarly, it is God alone who forgives sin ; the priest has no judicial power in administering absolution (p. 794 f.). Should God, who remits the eternal penalties, not forgive also the temporal (p. 798)? And if he does not do so, he is but exercising the educational discipline of a father (ib.). Thus the satisfaction to be rendered by good works also falls to the ground. Grace gives peace. What is the benefit of the dismissal "in peace " and the assurance of the forgiveness of sins, if the sinner still remains subject to the severest penalties (p. 800)? It is not a question of a contrite body, but of a contrite heart (p. 801). Satisfaction, strictly interpreted, ends in a blasphemy ; for Christ did his work completely. We receive forgiveness from grace alone, and do not have to contribute anything by works of satisfaction (p. 802).[2] Indulgences can accordingly be understood only as remitting ecclesiastical

---

[1] Cf. my remarks, supra, p. 135 f.

[2] Vid., on the other hand, the view discussed, supra, p. 199.

penalties (p. 781).[1]   The whole theory is overthrown ; but the
infused grace still remains.

7. Finally, we must notice the conception of the Church,
especially in WICKLIFFE (De eccl., ed. Loserth) and HUSS (De
eccl., opp. i. Norimb. 1558).   (*a*) In harmony with the idea
of predestination, the church is here defined as the *congregatio
omnium predestinatorum*, whether the latter belong to the past,
the present, or the future—whether they be men or angels,
or even Jews and heathen (Wickliffe, p. 2 f., 5, 70, 409. Huss,
fol. 196 v, 201 r).   The foreknown (*praesciti*) do not belong
to the church as thus conceived.   They are not *of* the church,
although they are empirically *in* the church : they no more
belong to the church than filth and foul humors belong to the
body (Huss, fol. 199 v).   Whether anyone really belongs to the
church, *i. e.*, is predestinated, can only be judged with probability from his life (Wickliffe, trial., p. 325. Huss, fol.
198 v).   In the sense of the assembly of the predestinated, the
church is an object of faith, since it may be thus brought under
the category of Heb. 11. 1 (Wickliffe, eccl., p. 409. Huss,
fol. 204 v, 206 v).   In proportion as Wickliffe's opposition to
the accepted doctrines spread, this conception of the church,
combined with the emphasizing of the exclusive authority of the
"law of Christ," became the critical canon.   The pope errs,
when he has the Scriptures against him (eccl., p. 563 f.).   So
far from being the head of the church, it is even open to
question whether he is a member of the church (p. 464.)
Therefore, no man's salvation can depend upon him (p. 33);
and his excommunication can exclude no one from the true
church (p. 72).   (*b*) WESEL and WESSEL base their criticism
upon other grounds.   Wesel declares that the hierarchical order
of the church is "derived from paganism and forbidden by the
word of Christ" (adv. indulg. 42).   In the church universal
the *church of Christ* exists as a part ; and only the latter is holy
and spotless (ib. 52 f.).   According to Wessel, the spiritual
authority rests upon a compact (de potest. ecclesiastica, opp.,
p. 752).   But Christians, as rational beings, must criticize their
leaders, and not blindly follow them (p. 753).   The latter are
"not therefore to be heard simply on account of their pastoral
authority" (p. 755).   "A currupt prelate desires the obedience
of his subjects, in order that he may rule them at will"
(p. 757).   False teachers are not to be followed (p. 762 f.).
If the prelates violate the compact, not observing the law

---

[1] Vid. also the discussion of the sacrament of repentance in MARSILIUS,
Defensor pacis, ii. 6, p. 205 f. Goldast.

as it applies to them, then is the other party, *i. e.*, the subjects, free from every obligation. Such prelates must be deposed. If they are still tolerated, it is only as abandoned
women are tolerated in the cities for fear of other evils (p. 765 f.).
It is not the clerical office which establishes the unity of
the church, but its one Head, the one divine truth,[1] and the faith
and love of its members (767, de poenit., p. 778-781). In
this communion the spirit of love is infused (cf. supra, p. 209).
This is the " *communio sanctorum :* " All saints have fellowship
(*communicant*) in true, essential unity : as many as cling to
Christ with one faith, one love ; under whatsoever prelates they
live ; however the latter may ambitiously contend or dissent or
err, even though they be heretics ; in whatever localities in
space ; separated by whatever intervals of years ; and this is
that *communio*, of which we speak in the Creed : I believe in the
communion of saints " (de comm. sanct., p. 809). From this
spiritual communion no declaration of the church can sever (de
poenit., p. 782). The criticism of these men does not extend
any further than that of Marsilius and Occam (p. 167); but it
attests the wide distribution of the critical temper. It was aided
by the fact that the church was coming to be regarded ever more
clearly and positively as a spiritual body. The *communio sanctorum*, the *congregatio predestinatorum*,—such is its essential
character. The place for its discussion is under the Creed, not
under canon law. The forms of the latter are either to be
repudiated, or are of temporary value, in the course of historical
development. Cf. SEEBERG, Begr. d. Kirche, i. 65-77. GOTT-
SCHICK, Ztschr. f. KG. viii. 357 ff. BUDDENSIEG, Joh. Wiclif,
1885, p. 157 ff. WIEGAND, Quid de eccl. notione Wicl.
docuerit ? 1891, p. 11 ff., 92 ff.

§ 64. *The Renaissance and Humanism in Their Significance for
the History of Doctrines.*

LITERATURE. J. BURCKHARDT, Die Kultur der Renaiss. in Ital. 4. A.,
1885. GEIGER, Renaiss. u. Humanism., 1882. VOIGT, Die Wiederbele-
bung des klass. Altertums, 2 vols., 2 A, 1880 f. VAHLEN, Lorenzo Valla,
1870. GEIGER, Reuchlin, 1871. VON BEZOLD, K. Celtis in Hist. Ztschr.,
1883, 1 ff., 193 ff. DREWS, Pirkheimer's Stellung z. Ref., 1887. STICHART,
Erasmus, seine Stellung z. Kirche, etc., 1870. SEEBOHM, The Oxford Reformers, ed. 2, 1869. LEZIUS, Zur Char. d. rel. Standpunktes d. Erasm.,
1895. KAMPSCHULTE, Die Univ. Erfurt in ihrem Verh. z. Humanism. u. z.
Ref., 2 vols., 1858. MAURENBRECHER, Gesch. d. Kath. Ref. i. 119 ff., 349 ff.

---

[1] " For we believe in God—not in the Catholic church, not in a Latin council,
not in the pope," p. 779. " Since therefore it is not obligatory to believe
man, neither will it be obligatory to believe the pope," p. 780.

Dilthey, Archiv. f. Gesch. d. Philos., 1891, 604 ff.; 1892, 337 ff. K. Müller, KG. ii. 167 ff. p. 228 A. Z. 1 v.

1. The spiritual unrest of the fourteenth and fifteenth centuries constituted the starting-point for a revolution in the whole conception of the universe and in the civilization of the world. The latter was accomplished beneath the banner of Individualism. The circle of interest extended beyond the limits of the church and her dogmas. The individual emerges. A man is something more than a member of the ecclesiastical or civil corporation, for he is himself a separate something. The world is looked upon with other eyes—it is not lying in wickedness. Nature and history, man in himself and in his association with his fellows, the state and society at large—are seen in a new light. New criteria are applied : the independence of the spiritual and political spheres, individual character, personal responsibility and honor. In proportion as this spirit was propagated must ensue alienation from the existing order and criticism of it ; or, at least, the best men had neither time nor inclination to pursue that which was officially regarded as the best. The reformation of St. Francis, the spread of the Mystic type of piety, the criticism indulged in by Duns and the Nominalists, the revived interest in literature and art (Dante, Petrarch, Boccaccio), and the political and social conditions, combined to create a new spiritual atmosphere. But the most powerful factor in this combination was antiquity. The treasures of the ancient world were brought to light and comprehended. In cultivated circles, especially in Italy, antiquity assumed the leadership and, for not a few, took the place of the church. Its treasures were studied with an indescribable enthusiasm.[1] The ancient world appeared to furnish the ideal of life and culture.

2. Such a profound movement could not but prove highly significant for the History of Doctrines. This is true in a general way, in consequence of the enlarging of the intellectual horizon, the increased study of languages, the introduction of the historic method, and of historico-philological criticism—the evidence adduced by Lorenzo Valla of the spurious character of the Areopagite, the non-apostolic[2] composition of the Creed, and the forging of the *Donatio Constantini*, suggesting what might be expected from the last-named source. To these influences must be added especially the new method of discussion modeled after the ancient patterns. The method of questions, with the *pro*

[1] Cf. the account of the body of a young girl of ancient Rome found in 1485 : " She was beautiful beyond all that can be said or written."
[2] Cf. Thieme, Aus d. Gesch. d. apostolicums, 1893, p. 4 ff.

and *contra*, followed by the "resolutions," yields to the simple presentation required by " reason and sound sense." The technical Latin of the Middle Ages makes way for the toilfully-won language of the classic authors, *i. e.*, the Latin is becoming a dead language. The Italians, for the most part, avoided theology ; but Humanistic circles in England (Colet, † 1519, and Thomas More, † 1535) and Germany (especially Reuchlin, † 1522, and Erasmus, † 1536) showed a different disposition. The traditional theology of the Scholastics at least was rejected, although some thoughtful minds still recognized its value: " Scotus and his like are useful for study (*ad rerum cognitionem*), but useless for speech " (*dicendum*) (Erasm., ratio concionandi. ii. opp. Ludg. Bat. 1704, v. 857). The *scholastica dogmata* are not articles of faith (Erasm., ratio verae theol., opp. v. 90). The Scriptures and the Church Fathers are the true authorities. " We may therefore philosophize upon the sacred writings in so far as our industry leads us to the conclusions which Paul has recorded. But those who have not fixed for themselves this limit, but choose this profession in order that they may bring forth any kind of paradoxes or novelties by which they may win the admiration of the populace, who are always ready to admire insipid things, are vanity-mongers (*mataeologi*), not theologians. . . . Now into the sacred assemblies themselves this ostentation has penetrated. . . . I see the simple multitude panting and hanging eagerly upon the lips of the orator, expecting food for their souls, desiring to learn how they may return better to their homes, and there some theologaster . . . ventilates some frigid and perplexing question from Scotus or Occam " (ib. v. 135 f.). " I had rather be a pious theologian with Chrysostom than an invincible one with Scotus " (ib. 137). " Scotus seems to have given these men such great confidence that, without having even read the sacred writings, they yet think themselves unlimited theologians" (enchiridion, 2, opp. v. 8). Erasmus, therefore, published not only the New Testament in Greek (A. D. 1516), but also the works of Jerome, Cyprian,[1] Hilary, Irenæus, Ambrose, Augustine, Chrysostom, and Origen. It was the aim to liberate theology from dogmatics, and introduce a practical, ethical—undogmatic—Christianity. We cannot fail to note here a certain flavor of Augustinian piety, however unwilling the leaders of the movement were to reproduce the entire Augustine. At this point the efforts of the theologians of a practical turn, whether Augustinians or Mystics, and those of the pious Humanists

---

[1] Cf. LEZIUS, Der Verf. d. pseudocypr. Traktates de duplici martyrio, Neue Jarbb. f. deutsche Theol., 1894.

coalesced. In this sense, Humanism possesses a "pre-reformatory" character. But, earnestly as the Humanists desired to reform the church, they yet shrunk with terror from the Reformation and the "tumult" it occasioned. Erasmus frequently thus expressed himself as the movement assumed a serious form. The tragedy of his life is thus explained. He was prevented by internal and external motives from pressing forward as the new and great agitation surged about him, and he could not retreat.[1] It was his fate, like Moses, to die in the land of Moab.[2]

3. Consequently, no positively influential ideas emanated from Humanistic circles. Despite all their criticism of the church and its doctrines, despite their exaltation of worldly delights— which too often, especially in Italy, led to brutal egotism and sordid self-indulgence—the old religious ideas maintained their sway, and in times of distress, in life or in death, the heart turned to them for comfort. This was seen in the case of the leaders of the movement themselves. "Lived like heathens and died like Christians—was applicable to very many of the representatives of the new classical culture" (Bezold, l. c., p. 212). We may study the same phenomenon in Erasmus. There was very much of the "modern man" about him, but yet he remained, in his unmarried and unsettled life, a monk of the higher order. And even his religious ideas, particularly in the pre-reformation period, do not rise beyond the religious conceptions of the Middle Ages. It is, to state it briefly, the piety of the *Imitatio Christi* which he commends. "Let this be thy . . . rule : set Christ before thee as the sole centre (*scopus*) of thy whole life, to whom alone thou mayest bring all thy studies, all thine efforts, all thy leisure and thy business. But I think Christ to be not an empty word, but nothing else than love, simplicity, patience, purity, in short, everything which he taught. . . . To Christ tends everyone who is lifted to virtue alone " (enchir. 4, p. 25). But the History of Doctrines has no occasion to attempt a portrayal of the theology of Erasmus,[3] nor that of his friend, COLET, who so

---

[1] Cf. esp. the attractive sketch of LEZIUS, Zur Char. . . . d. Erasm., p. 46 ff.

[2] Vid. Luther's opinion of him in Köstlin, Luther, i., ed. 4, 688 f.

[3] Upon particular points Erasmus furnishes much that is of importance; *e. g.*, his remark as to the gradations of authority in the books of the New Testament (opp. v. 92, 1049); the Bible written under dictation of the Holy Spirit (v. 274); his criticism of the *homousios* (v. 1090) and of the sacrament of repentance (ib. 167, 944, 1046); his legal conception of Sabbath observance (v. 1190 f.); his symbolic view of the Lord's Supper (iii. 521 f., 892 ff., 1028, 1891 ; v. 1019); his definition of faith as *fiduciam, collocare in deo* (v. 105, 777, 798, 1079, 1147, 1166 et passim). We do not yet possess a detailed presentation of his views. Vid. STICHART, and esp. LEZIUS.

earnestly sought to understand the writings of St. Paul.[1] The
fundamental ideas are always the same. Christ came down from
heaven in order to teach us to despise the world and its possessions, and practice peace, love, and harmony, and to confirm
this teaching by his example. " For his life is a doctrine excel-
ling all human (doctrine)'' (*Beatus Rhenanus* upon Zwingli,
opp. vii. 58). But to this is to be added faith in the *evangelical
doctrine*, which is laid down in the Scriptures, the Apostles'
Creed, and the Fathers (Erasm. v. 8, 1162, 162 ; i. 653).

Such is the dogmatic history of the Middle Ages. At the
first glance it may be thought that doctrinal development was
carried backward by more than a thousand years. The declarations of Scripture, the Apostles' Creed, the Fathers, and the
dogmas of the ancient church, appear to be all that remain in the
shiftings of history. There were extended circles in which this
was felt to be the case. But history never simply turns backward. Other forces were in the field, and they, too, were alive,
and have perpetuated their vitality to the present day. There
was a complicated play of forces ; even the ancient and despised
was still a force to be reckoned with. We must differentiate
three groups in the closing period of the Middle Ages, which
were capable of various combinations. (1) The Popular Catholicism, the official ecclesiasticism. It does not scorn the
help of the " Moderns " (*i. e.*, Nominalists), but it begins to
rely upon the "old theology " of the thirteenth century. (2)
The "negative," critical theology of the Nominalists. They
preserved their claim to recognition by their theory of the *fides
implicita*. (3) The Mystic, Augustinian, and Humanistic tendencies. To them the future seemed assured, for they sought
to serve the cause of reform and progress. Which of these ten-

---

[1] His Opuscula theologica, ed. Lupton, London, 1876, lies before me.
Particularly in his commentary upon Romans, his effort to be Pauline is noticeable. He strongly emphasizes the *justitia fidei sola* (p. 209). " By this
sole faith of Christ one enters the kingdom of heaven ; believers are righteous ;
the faith of Christ is righteousness" (p. 230), and this gratuitously :
" through grace men believe, and through grace believers are justified " (p.
251). The divine will alone is the ground of justification (p. 254). But
faith is to be more precisely defined as : " The faith of Christ with imitation
and representation of him " (p. 241, 272), or " Justifying faith imports in its
signification imitation of Christ and co-operation with him " (p. 248). In harmony with this must be understood the declaration : "By this (*i. e.*, faith) believers are justified, so that they may do well in love. . . . Believers, if they
imitate Christ Jesus, God will crown this righteousness" (p. 261 f.; cf. p. 186:
"made righteous (*facti justi*) by God, that we may live righteously "). Colet
thus taught essentially as did Thomas (supra, p. 120). God infuses grace
into the sinner, which produces: first, faith, and then love and good works.
Further than this, he, like Erasmus, did not attach himself to any particular
scholastic theory.

dencies—and with what combinations and concessions—would have gained the victory, if no new element had been introduced? It will not be without profit to reflect upon the problem. The future did actually produce the humanistic Nominalism of the Socinians, the Augustinianism of the Jansenists, the Thomism of the Moderns. But a fourth spiritual power appeared amid the play of forces—the Gospel, or the Reformation. This introduced a new element. Old problems were pushed aside, and the questions pressing for solution assumed a different form.

BOOK III.

FURTHER DEVELOPMENT OF DOCTRINE THROUGH THE REFORMATION AND FIXATION OF THE DOCTRINES OF CATHOLICISM.

PART I.

GENESIS OF PROTESTANT DOCTRINE.

CHAPTER I.

THE VIEWS OF LUTHER.

§ 65. *Luther's Place in the History of Doctrines.*

LITERATURE. The works of Luther are cited in the following pages from the Weimar edition (= W) and from the first issue of the Erlangen edition (German Works = E); de W. = De Wette, Luther's Briefe, 6 vols., 1825 ff.; opp. ex. = Opera Exegetica and var. arg. = Varii Argumenti—both of the Erlangen edition ; Gal. = the large Commentary upon Galatians in the same edition. Cf. KÖSTLIN, M. Luther, 2 vols., 5th edition by Kawerau, 1903. KOLDE, M. L., 2 vols., 1883 ff. KÖSTLIN, Luther's Theologie, 2 vols., 1863, 2d ed., 1901. TH. HARNACK, Luther's Theologie, 1862-86, 2d issue, 1901. LOMMATSCH, Luther's Lehre v. eth. rel. Standp. aus, 1879. LUTHARDT, Die Ethik Luther's, 2d edition, 1875. PLITT, Einleitung in d. Augustana, i., 1868. MÖLLER-KAWERAU, KG. iii., 1894. RITSCHL, Rechtf. u. Vers. i. 141 ff. THOMASIUS, DG. ii., ed. 2, 330 ff. LOOFS, DG., ed. 3, 345 ff. HARNACK, DG. iii., ed. 3, 726 ff.; cf. KÜBEL, Neue kirchl. Ztschr., 1891, 13 ff. HERING, Die Mystik Luther's im Zusammenhang s. Theol., 1879. LIPSIUS, Luther's Lehre v. d. Busse, 1892. THIEME, Die sittl. Triebkraft des Glaubens, 1895. SCHÄFER, L. als Kirchenhistoriker, 1897.

1. In the crisis periods of history there is commonly no lack of vigorous thought and great possibilities. There were now many possibilities in view. But which of these, if achieved, could have solved the problems of the great crisis now threatening the doctrinal structure of the church, as well as the moral and social life of the world? Altogether, they did not extend in scope beyond the horizon of medieval piety. But in the midst of the sultry calm and dark forebodings of those days appeared a man who had something practical to propose in the face of all the vague possibilities. He trod like a giant through his age, tramping to earth what a thousand years had held in veneration; but everywhere new life blossomed in his footsteps. It was the wonder-worker of modern times, MARTIN LUTHER (b. A. D. 1483). He was a genius without parallel, and yet his was a "simple soul." He possessed the wonderful faculty of realizing in the clear depths of his own experience all the emotions and needs of his age. "Yet he possessed" also, "in his

religious genius, a unique and peculiar energy which carried his contemporaries along, at least for some distance, in his path as by a power beyond and higher than their own.   He was born to deal with men and govern them '' (DILTHEY, Archiv f. Gesch. d. Philos. v. 356 f.).   His power lay in his faith, which he discovered amid the stress of dark and terrifying spiritual struggles. The firm assurance of evangelical faith which he had himself won, he proclaimed to his age with the amazing vividness which only personal experience can give, with the force and versatility of a true religious genius, and with the holy passion of a prophet. Looking back upon his life, he himself declares : '' God led me on like a horse whose eyes have been blind-folded that he may not see those who are rushing toward him,'' and ''that a good work should seldom be undertaken or accomplished through wisdom or foresight—everything must be accomplished in the midst of error or ignorance '' (E. 57, 31 f.).   Men listened to him.   He led them back from scholastic speculations to the firm ground of historical revelation, from dogma. to faith.   The Reformation, so longed talked of, here became a reality, and in a way which no one had anticipated.   And only gradually has the Christian world learned to understand clearly its controlling principles, to draw the inevitable conclusions and estimate it correctly from a critical point of view, casting aside the peculiar and sometimes incongruous wrappings that have partly concealed its true character.   It would be idle to wish that the great age of the Reformers might itself have wrought out to a logical conclusion all that was involved in the new principles.

2. It is very significant, that the peculiar religious experiences of Luther in the cloister fall within the sphere of the sacrament of repentance and the overvaluation of the monastic life.   The controlling element in the penitential praxis was not for him attrition, but contrition.[1]   Luther sought to force himself to contrition by meditating upon his sins.   He was thus led to '' bungling work and doll-sins '' indeed ; but he also discovered, as the chief source of trouble, sin in the sense of sinfulness.   As his own contrition never reached the required depth, so, on the other hand, absolution—the formula for which makes forgiveness dependent upon the ''contrition of the heart, the good works which thou hast done from love of Christ '' (KÖSTLIN, M. Luth. i. 5, 64)—brought him no certainty of the forgiveness of his sins.   The—genuinely Catholic—suggestion, that it was his

---

[1] In theory, contrition alone was generally spoken of, but in practice attrition alone was usually thought of, as the '' beginning of penitence '' (E. 25, 130).   But this lightening of the burden permitted by the dogmatics of the age, Luther would not allow to himself.

duty to believe the forgiveness of sins, pointed him in a new direction. He learned that not separate acts, but love to righteousness and to God, constitute the criterion of true repentance (Staupitz). From this time onward, Luther fell more and more under the influence of Augustine and Mysticism. It is perhaps the greatest work of Augustine, that he prepared the way in following which this, his greatest son, found Paul. Gradually Luther is led in his inmost experience into the very heart of scriptural ideas, and such terms as *grace* and *righteousness* receive a new meaning.

3. There meets us, hence, in the very first connected utterances of Luther (§ 66), an entirely new apprehension of religious truth. The differences between the " first form " and the later forms of Luther's theology are commonly very much exaggerated. If we consider the technical terminology, there is indeed a manifest difference ; but if we have in view the actual content and logical results of his ideas, we can scarcely reach any other conclusion than that Luther had before A. D. 1517 already grasped the conceptions and attained the points of view which gave character to his life-work. This can be traced, as will be done in the following pages, in the peculiar construction of nearly all the theological definitions of the later Luther. But it is most important of all to observe that he, at the very beginning of his career, makes practical application of his new idea of faith ; for the leverage of Luther's reformatory principle lies, not in justification, nor in a new theory of grace, but in the conviction that faith is the *form* of true religion. "He who believes, has" (*e. g.*, E. 27, 180). But this central conviction dominates his very first writings, and it is instructive to observe what a transforming influence it exerted upon the theological views there presented (vid. sub). It will be advisable, nevertheless, to present separately the first utterances of his new thoughts, as their historical relations can thus be more clearly seen.

4. Luther, it is well known, had pursued a thorough course of Scholastic study, making himself familiar particularly with the Lombard, Occam, D'Ailli, and Biel. This schooling is often apparent in the earlier period (*e. g.*, W. 1. 367 ff.). But the influence of these studies was a permanent one. He had imbibed the outline and organization of the theological ideas of Scholasticism, and they remained as the points of connection in his theological thinking. In the most of his definitions, the form of construction can be understood only if we bear this fact in mind.[1]   Yet

---

[1] Luther was accurately acquainted with the separate Scholastic writers, as may be seen from his writings during the indulgence controversy—*e. g.*, his opinion of Duns, W. 2. 403, and of Occam, 6. 183.   E. 24. 347 : "Occam,

Luther was confessedly a passionate opponent of Scholasticism, as well as of Aristotle. "Thomas wrote many heretical things, and is the cause of the dominance of Aristotle, the devastator of pious doctrine" (W. 8. 127). But the motive which impelled him in this opposition was different from that which inspired the hounding of the Scholastics by the Humanists. His criticism was not directed primarily against the formal defects of the system. He regards the teachings of Biel as good, except upon the topics of grace, love, hope, faith, and virtue (De W. 1. 34); at a later date, he speaks approvingly of the Lombard, with the exception that what he has said of faith and justification is "too thin and weak" (E. 25. 258).[1] This is the ground of Luther's opposition : "That carnalizer of consciences, *theologistria*," with its doctrines of free-will, merit, righteousness, and works, directs to a false way of salvation, which leads only to doubt and despair : "I lost Christ there ; now I have found him in Paul" (W. 2. 401, 414, 503, 447). It destroys the gospel (W. 2. 416, 465) and opposes "sacred theology" (ib. 416). It mixes Scripture and philosophy (E. 63. 162).[2] "Scholastic theology is nothing else than ignorance of the truth and scandal placed side by side with Scripture" (W. 8. 127).[3] Many have assailed the formalism of Scholasticism ; Luther attacked its substance, and he overthrew it.

5. Luther's decisive religious experiences were gained in connection with the sacrament of repentance, under the stress of a false conception of repentance for which he struggled to find a substitute. This was the starting-point from which his fundamental religious ideas were developed. The latter may, therefore, be comprehended under the conception of *Evangelical Repentance, constituting a Substitute for the observance of the Sacrament of Repentance.* This is the point of view from which the work of Luther must be considered in the History of Doctrines.

my dear Master ;" Scotus and Occam are "the best two." He himself counts himself among the *Moderni*, or Nominalists, W. 9. 9 ; cf. 1. 226 and op. var. arg. 5. 137 : *sum Occanicae factionis.* As to his studies, see Glosses upon the Lombard, W. 9. 28 ff. ; and in the Mystics, upon Tauler, ib. 97 ff.

[1] W. 1. 391 : "Not that I entirely condemn them (the Scholastics), for they have done their part." Cf. especially the remarkable contrasting of the problems of the Scholastic and the Evangelical theology, E. 24. 372 ff.

[2] " . . . Origen, who soured and spoiled the Scriptures by philosophy and reason, as with us the universities have hitherto done."

[3] With this agrees Luther's opinion of Aristotle : " the constructor of words, the deluder of minds" (W. i. 612). In addition to his Moralism, he charges upon him, that his God does not act mightily in the government of the world, but "governs the world blinkingly, as a woman rocks her child in the dark" (E. 10. 321 ; 7. 239 ; W. 6. 457 f.). Vid. NITZSCH, Luth. and Arist., Kiel, 1893.

All his ideas in regard to penitence and faith, faith and works, sin and grace, law and gospel, together with his new ideal of life, constitute a complex of religious conceptions which were developed under the pressure of and in opposition to the sacrament of repentance.[1] This brings his work, however, into the very centre of the current of religious development in the West. The controlling thought in the latter is always the salvation of souls (*salus animarum*) (Vol. I., p. 192 f., 199). Repentance, forgiveness, new life were, hence, the inspiration of all conflicts and schisms from the days of Calixtus to the Fanatics of the Reformation era. One ideal runs through all these movements : the congregation of *saints*. The great church thought of the holiness of her ordinances, the *opus operatum*. To this her critics had nothing to oppose, in the last analysis, but human works, the *opera operantis*—not holiness and righteousness. In the conception of the righteousness of faith, Luther found the solution of the problem. Everything comes to the sinner from God ; but it becomes his only when it begets in him a powerful, glowing, vital experience. Yet the heart does not place its confidence in this experience in so far as it is its own ; but only in so far as it comes from God. This is now both entirely objective and entirely subjective. It is broad enough to embrace all that was right in the position of the church as against the schismatics, and all that was right in the contentions of the latter against the church.[2]

6. We cannot here attempt a review of the reformatory work of Luther. A few observations must suffice. The question of the authority of the church forced itself upon his attention already in the indulgence controversy.[3] The Leipzig Disputation (A. D. 1519) brings Luther to the conviction that the pope and

---

[1] Melanchthon recognizes this in Corp. Ref., xi. 728 : Luther makes evident the true and necessary doctrine ; for that there was densest darkness upon the doctrine of repentance is manifest. Discussing these things, he shows what is true repentance. Cf. v. 568 ; vi. 90 f.; i. 350 ff.; viii. 311.

[2] Regarded from the viewpoint of the medieval church, the Reformation may be considered as the last of the schisms in the Western church. But it must, in that case, be freely acknowledged that it is profoundly and entirely different from all schismatic movements.

[3] Vid., besides, the 95 Theses : Disputat. pro declarat. virtutis indulgent.; Ein sermon v. ablass u. gnade, 1517 ; Asterisci ; Sermo de poenit. Eine freiheit des sermons päpstl. ablass u. gnaden belangend ; Resolutiones disputationum de indulg. virtute ; sermo de virtute excommunicat. (these in W. 1). Eine kurze unterweisung, wie man beichten soll, 1518. Unterricht auf. etl. artikel ; sermo de duplici justitia ; Ein sermon vom sakr. d. busse, 1519 (W. 2). Confitendi ratio, 1520 (W. 3). Cf. esp. for this period the Disputat. c. scholast. theol., 1517. The Heidelberg Theses, 1517 (W. 1), the small commentary upon Galatians, 1519 (W. 2). Responsio ad libr. Ambros. Catharini, 1519 (opp. v. a. 5).

15

councils may err, and that the Scriptures are the only authorized authority in the church.[1] The outward barriers which had hitherto restrained Luther's spirit are thereby broken down. The eyes of men of culture and of all friends of reform are now turned upon him. He is recognized as a prophet. His cause is no longer a theological tournament; it is the cause of the people. Thus, stimulated and sustained by the longings and hopes of his people, he enters the greatest year of his life, 1520. With wonderful energy he wields the sword and plies the trowel. The old theory of the sacraments is demolished; there is a new conception of the church; the new ideal of Christian life appears; good works are understood in the evangelical sense; and the program of practical reformation is clearly indicated.[2] Then follows the fiery trial at Worms, the test of sincerity at the Wartburg and in face of the fanaticism[3] at Wittenberg. Political circumstances then open the way for the development of evangelical church life[4] and the spread of the gospel. But to this period of development belong also separations (1524-25). The powerful movement for reform had quickened into new life the other reformatory tendencies of the age, and it seemed as though they might be combined in one current with it. Humanists, Mystics, and social reformers stretch out their hands to Luther. And he recognizes the " other spirit " in them and repels them.[5] It is among the greatest acts of his life. He thereby lost his unparalleled popularity. He, whom nothing had hitherto been able to withstand, was now compelled to realize the inexorable limitations which beset all human efforts. To this was added the alarming revela-

---

[1] Ad dialog. Silv. Prierat. de potest. papae, 1518 (W. 1). Acta Augustana, 1518. Disputat. et excusat. adv. criminationes Ioh. Eck. Resolut. Lutheriana super proposit. sua XIII.; the proceedings of the Disputation at Leipzig (W. 2).

[2] Von den guten Werken; vom Papstt. z. Rom wider den hochberümten Romanisten z. Lpz.; Ein sermon v. N. T. d. i. von der h. Messe; an den christl. Adel deutscher Nation von des christl. Standes Besserung; De captivit. babyl.; Wider die Bulle des Endchristes (W. 6). Also Von der Freiheit eines Christenmenschen (E. 27 and op. v. a.), all in 1520. In 1519: Ein sermon v. d. hochw. Sakr. der Taufe; Ein sermon v. d. hochw. Sakr. des h. hochw. Leichnams Christi (W. 2). Vid. also Themata de votis; Vom Misbrauch der Messe; De votis monasticis, 1521 (W. 8); An die Herren deutschen Ordens, 1523 E. 29).

[3] Vid. the Eight Sermons, 1523 (E. 28).

[4] E. g., Ordnung eines gemeinen Kastens; Von d. Ordnung des Gottesdienstes, Taufbüchlein, 1523. Deutsche Messe, 1526 (E. 22). Traubüchlein (E. 23); the two catechisms, 1529, etc.

[5] De servo arbitrio, 1525 (op. v. a. 7); Wider d. himml. Propheten, 1524-25 (E. 29). Ermanung zum Frieden; Wider d. mörderischen u. räuberischen Rotten der Bauern; Ein Sendbrief v. dem harten Büchlein wider die Bauern, 1525 (E. 24).

tions of the church visitations. From this time forward a certain austerity of temper is noticeable in the Reformer. Severe utterances touching the "coarse, common man" and "the full and foolish Germans" now belong to his constant repertoire.[1] There is a lowering also of his ecclesiastical ideals.[2] But he remains true to himself and the gospel, even against Zwingli.[3] The evangelical views are now summarized in the Augsburg Confession.

The most wonderful thing in Luther was that his opponents could never confuse him nor force any concessions from him. On the contrary, every obstacle which he met but served to open up new treasures from the deep mine of his fundamental religious idea; as, in opposition to the Fanatics, he defined more accurately the significance of the means of grace, and against Erasmus maintained salvation by grace alone.

We have thus indicated the points of view from which the reformatory ideas of Luther will be presented in the following pages. One of the most important tasks of the History of Doctrines is thus set before us. For whether we regard Luther as the destroyer of the foundations of the old dogma, or as the originator of new dogmas, it is evident that either opinion can be sustained only by a thoroughgoing study of his teachings. Above all is it the duty of those who extend the scope of the History of Doctrines into the age of Protestantism to furnish a complete portraiture of Luther. It is astonishing to find in some Protestant works upon the subject lengthy discussions of Augustine, Thomas, etc., but only a short sketch of Luther.[4] This is out of all due proportion, whether we regard the matter from the standpoint of medieval doctrinal development or in the light of the Protestant Confessions.

§ 66. *Doctrinal Views of Luther Before the Period of His Reformatory Activity.*

LITERATURE. Expositions of the Psalms, with work upon the Penitential Psalms, lectures upon Judges, sermons and tracts to A. D. 1517 in Weimar edition, vols. i., iii., iv. Cf. DIECKHOFF, L. Lehre in ihrer ersten Gestalt, 1887.

[1] Cf., *e. g.*, E. 24. 305, 309; 22. 255, 181, 194; 4. 405; also the complaints of the great change of sentiment, 14. 225 f., 233; 47. 14 f., 210 ff.; 48. 375.
[2] Cf. KOLDE, Ztschr. f. Kirchengesch. xiii. 552 ff.
[3] Wider die himml. Propheten u. Bildern u. Sakr. 1524-25 (E. 29); letter to the Strassburgers, 1524 (De W. 2. 574 ff.); Vorwort z. Syngramma suevicum, 1526 (E. 65. 180 ff.); sermon v. Sakr., 1526 (E. 29); Das diese Worte, Das ist mein Leib; noch feste stehen, 1527; Bekenntnis v. Abendmal Christi, 1528 (E. 30); Kurzes Bekenntnis v. h. Sakr. 1545 (E. 32).
[4] A praiseworthy exception is found in the Leitfaden of LOOFS.

1. The high regard for the Scriptures, which is already so evident in Luther, is scarcely more pronounced than was usual in the writers of the later Middle Ages (*e. g.*, W. 3. 517; 4. 531; 1. 52). But a new path was opened by his conception of Christ as the real content of the Scriptures (1. 219). Highly significant, too, was his view of the difference between the Law and the Gospel. The external word of the preacher reaches only the ear of the hearer; "but God speaks (*sonat*) and teaches inwardly to the heart" (3. 124, 514). Human speech effects nothing "without the co-operation and inward infusion (Ps. 38. 2) of God." There is an "inward whispering: Thy sins are forgiven thee" (1. 175, 190, 201).[1] This is the Augustinian view. (Vol I., p. 321). The word falls into the two categories of law and gospel. These terms are often synonymous with the Old and the New Testament, *e. g.:* "The law teaches the knowledge of self; but the gospel, or the New Testament, teaches the knowl- of God" (4. 565, 567). In this sense, the law is the rude vesti- bule to the gospel (3. 249). It conceals the New Testament ideas (4. 251, 305), such as evangelical grace and the righteous- ness of faith (3. 560). It is unable to give to anyone a good will, or love (4. 250). But, since it can call forth only outward works, it makes men in the end hypocrites (4. 566). It makes men sinners, but the gospel comforts and saves them (4. 566). But Luther finds law also in the New Testament, since the latter teaches the spiritual understanding (*intelligentia*) of the law: "But this understanding of the law spiritually much rather slays, because it makes the law impossible to fulfill, and thereby makes man despairing of his own strength and humiliated" (1. 105). This is, however, a foreign, and not the peculiar, office of the gospel (1. 113; 4. 87.) Its own mission is to comfort and lift up all who have been smitten and humbled by the law. "Therefore, as much as the gospel has caused grief by interpreting the law, so much and more does it cause rejoicing by proclaiming grace" (1. 105, 106, 108, 113). The gospel humiliates, not only by its interpretation of the law, but also by manifesting the works and the glory of God and thereby revealing the sin and shame of man (1. 111 f.). Finally, the gospel imposes a cross and chastisement upon man, since it subjugates the old man (4. 253; 3. 462). The gospel may therefore be called a compound (*mixtum*): "because the gospel imposes cross and life, peace and war, good and evil, poverty and riches. And this is most truly a salutary mixture so

---

[1] It is the word of the gospel, vocal or written, *i. e.*, the Holy Scriptures (3. 404).

long as this life lasts " (3. 516). If it is therefore the chief office
of the gospel to proclaim grace and consolation, it yet deepens
also the understanding of the law and humiliates and chastens
the sinner.[1] We shall treat the doctrinal points resulting from
this general view in the order : sin, freedom of the will, Christ,
grace, faith, righteousness.

2. Luther did not suffer while in the cloister from outbreaks
of any particular sin. He was oppressed by the sense of sinfulness, or Original Sin. He recalls attention to it : "No one is
longer solicitous for the mortification of the tinder (*fomes*) and
the root-sin, but they are concerned only for the cutting off
(*amputandis*) of actual sins by contrition, confession, and satisfaction " (1. 67). But original sin (*peccatum originale*,[2] *Erb-
sund*, 1. 197) is the concupiscence filling the whole man (1.
126, 225), which is the root of all *peccata actualia*. "It is an
abiding sin in this present time " (1. 168, 86), "a very corruption (*corruptio*) of nature " (1. 121), since the memory, the
understanding, and the will are weakened by it (3. 453). This
is the old man, "which absolutely does not love God, nor
fervently hunger and thirst (for him), but thinks to find full
satisfaction for mind and spirit in created things " (1. 146). It
has a horror, not a fear, of God ; "but horror is the seed-bed
of hate " (1. 39).[3] The "nature and essence " of man is,
from his birth, an evil tree and a child of wrath (1. 188).[4] Just
as little, therefore, as the will is free to do good (1. 148, 224),
is man able to prepare himself in worthiness (*de condigno*)
or in fitness (*de congruo*) for the reception of grace (1. 147,
148, 70).

3. In Christology, certain definite fundamental conceptions of
Luther are already quite prominent. The doctrine of the two
natures of Christ (3. 467) is, for example, presented in its
practical religious aspect. We recognize the divinity of Christ,

---

[1] Cf. the frequently recurring declarations, that man must become nothing,
must be judged and crucified, before God can work in him, *e. g.:* 1. 183 f., 112,
113, 119, 227, 186, 189, 201 f., 214 ; 3. 513, 288 f., 291, 466 ; 4. 376 f., 412.
Vid. also the view of the Mystics, supra, p. 180.

[2] Definition, 4. 690; cf. 9. 73, 75.

[3] Luther retains the Scholastic idea of the Synteresis (supra, p. 114 f.) :
"Therefore, just as the synteresis of the understanding (*rationis*) is also conformed to the wisdom of God, although the entire understanding may be
totally non-conformed to it, so the synteresis of the will is conformed to the
will of God " (1. 36, 558 ; 3. 238).

[4] The wrath of God is attributed to the creature, without having a real existence in God : "God does not, properly speaking, afflict by approaching, but
by departing and leaving in the hand of creatures." This is the biblical
idea, that God is angry when he forsakes. Luther's conceptions at this time
harmonize with Creationism (4. 342).

since we attribute all our blessings to him and expect salvation wholly from him, as well as render him obedience : "To confess that Christ is God is to restore and refer to him all good things received from him, . . . to hope for all good things from him, and to put our trust in no creature" (1. 123, 140). His divinity is "a gracious will to pity and help" (1. 203). "That he pities, proves him to be God and distinguishes him from others, who cannot pity (*misereri*) since they are themselves objects of pity (*miseri*). Therefore he who pities and is good, is God" (4. 248.) But Christ concealed his divinity in his humanity, so that it remained in the Father (*divinitatem suam abscondi ab eis in patre,* 3. 502 f., 124). He put away from him his power : "He banished (*subtraxit*) all his power by which he would have been able to resist them (his enemies) and in every way subjected himself to infirmity" (3. 121). Thus, even his divine works were concealed in the humiliation of his passion (3. 547).[1] Thus God came to us. "Since God pitied us, he also adapted himself to our infirmity, so that he came to us as a man, concealing his divinity and thereby removing all terror" (4. 647; 1. 201). There is, therefore, no knowledge of God, save only in the humanity of Jesus. "All ascent to the knowledge of God is perilous except that which is made through the humility of Christ, because this is Jacob's ladder. . . . Wherefore he who, of himself, makes haste to know God, is hastening to the abyss of despair. . . . In other works God is recognized according to the greatness of his power, wisdom, and justice, and there his works appear to be exceedingly terrible ; but here is seen his most gentle pity and love, so that thus his works of power and wisdom may be contemplated with confidence" (4. 647, 648). God has come to us in Jesus, as the Temple of God (1. 203), through the incarnation. In him alone is God to be known (202).

This is the great revelation of God to us : his love and righteousness are revealed in Christ (1. 140). This, to speak precisely, embraces two ideas : Christ dwells in us (4. 328, 3, 8), as a "counsel of example," and, through his sacraments, an "aid of grace" (1. 77). In the former aspect, his zeal for our salvation inspires our zeal for the same.[2] He still lives in his followers, and incites them to all good. The kingdom in which Christ reigns is the church (4. 85). "And thus

---

[1] It harmonizes with the emphasis thus laid upon the humanity of Jesus that Luther even held it permissible to speak of him as exercising faith (4. 267).

[2] This idea appears to be related to that of Biel, that Christ is only the partial cause of our salvation (4. 596, 645).

it truly comes to pass, that the life of Christ does not lie quiet
in his believing follower, because it has never lain quiet, but
always lives and acts. . . . We do not live, speak and act, but
Christ lives, acts and speaks in us ; because what we do and say
is accomplished by his acting within us and impelling us"
(4. 646). No law is able to transform the will and make it
good ; but the life of Christ effects this, moving our will to
imitation (4. 646 ; 1. 121). The Christ in us is not idle, but
most active (1. 140). But it is only one aspect of the work of
Christ that is thus described. The same Christ has also fulfilled
the law for us, endured for us the wrath of God and death, and
overcome the devil (1. 35, 59 ; 4. 609). He is our righteousness (1. 171, 140 ; 3. 174), and his merits are imputed to us
by God (1. 140). "Thou, Lord Jesus, art my righteousness,
but I am thy sin ; thou hast assumed mine and given thine to
me ; thou hast assumed what thou wast not. . . . Therefore
not except in him, by sincere despair of thyself and thy works,
canst thou find peace" (De W., 1. 17). Christ's blood cleanses
us (1. 189, 121). He is the hen, under whose wings we find
rest and peace (1. 31, 35, 117). "Now henceforth our God
is no more the exactor of righteousness and the judge, but he is
through his pity a saving (power) within us" (4. 609). He
does not simply causally work our righteousness, "for that is
dead, yea it is never given, unless Christ himself is also present"
(1. 219).

These are the permanent, fundamental features of Luther's
Christology and Soteriology. The historical Jesus is the revelation of God. In the love of Christ his divinity is revealed ; but
the power of the latter he conceals. The Christian experiences
Christ as a present and active reality in his life. Christ hereby
becomes an active force within him, both as the law and pattern
of goodness setting him free to do good and making him capable
of doing it, and as the righteousness transferred from him to us.
Christ's fellowship with us brings us both a new life and the forgiveness of sins ; it makes us good both in the real and in the
ideal sense of the word. This leads us to consider the conception of grace and the subjective forms of the blessings it
confers.

4. According to the traditional dogmatics, the activity of
grace is two-fold, embracing the infusion of new powers and the
forgiveness of sins. This must be borne in mind if we would
understand Luther correctly. When guilt has been removed,
sickness must be replaced by health (3. 453 ; i. 65, 68, 43, 84 :
justificante et imputante). The infusion of grace is not a momentary act, so that at once all grace is given and all sin blotted

out.   That idea leads to despair, as Luther had learned in his own experience (1. 43).   "The *infusio* is an interior illumination of the mind and inflammation of the will . . . this is necessary for the extirpation of concupiscence, until it shall be perfectly extirpated " (1. 66).   It brings the " good-will directed straight toward God, seeking God alone " (1. 191), and it infuses love (1. 115; 4. 250).   As Christ was conceived by the Holy Ghost, so every Christian is through love born anew and justified by the Holy Ghost (3. 468).   It purifies us :   " But that purification (*purgatio*) is a work of God and an infusion of grace, a justification without us " (*sine nobis*, 1. 118).   It washes and purifies us continually (1. 186, 189).   The essential factor in the righteousness infused by grace is *faith*.   " Faith is righteousness" (1. 118, 84).   It is from God, who gives the true, fundamentally good righteousness, which is the faith of Christ (1. 213).   To pray for faith is the same as to pray for life or righteousness (4. 325).   When God, therefore, graciously " begets and creates " the new man, *i. e.*, works righteousness in him (1. 215 ; 3. 154) through the Holy Spirit (1. 218), this righteousness consists not so much in works, as in hope, love, and especially faith (1. 84).   So little does this appear to depend upon the inward state, that Luther traces it to a divine covenant : " Faith and grace, by which we are to-day justified, would not of themselves justify us unless a covenant of God caused them to do so " (3. 289),[1] *i. e.*, that he who believes and is baptized shall be saved (Mk. 16. 16).

This presentation of the subject runs entirely within the lines of medieval theology.   But Luther's new definition of faith leads us further.   What is faith, and how does it originate ?   We recall the fact that the accepted dogmatic scheme found place for an *acquired faith* in addition to the *infused faith*, and that the later Scholasticism laid special stress upon the former (supra, p. 150, 195).[2]   " When thou hearest that he suffered for thee, and believest, there springs up already confidence toward him and tender love, and thus perishes all love of (other) things as useless, and there arises a passionate regard for Christ alone as the

---

[1] This is a Scotist idea.   Thus Luther occasionally declares of every human preparation for receiving grace, that the latter is given, not through such preparation, but by virtue of a divine covenant (4. 329).

[2] The Scotist criticism prepared the way for this (p. 150, 159 f.).   We can understand the advance of Luther from the position held by Duns, although Luther rejected the self-acquired faith as a work of man himself in favor of the infused faith (vid. § 67, 5)!   And, similarly, the new conception of grace may be explained by the fact that the *gratia creata* first recedes behind the *gratia increata* (p. 118 f.), and then makes way for the latter.   It follows that the imputed grace crowds the infused from the field.   Here, too, Duns performed some preparatory work (p. 160).

One Thing necessary, and there remains to thee nothing save Jesus only, he alone enough and sufficient for thee, so that despairing of all things thou hast this Only One, in whom thou hopest for all things, and, therefore, lovest him above all things. But Jesus is the one true and only God whom when thou hast, thou hast no strange God " (1. 399 f.). This is a faith wrought by God, but yet inwardly acquired and experienced —a faith alive and practical, the experience (*experimentum*) of despairing of self in order to allow one's self to be led by God alone (1. 88).[1] This faith, as it springs from the contemplation and experiencing of Christ, "consists more in taking from God than in giving, more in longing than in having, more in becoming than in being pious " (1. 212). But since the Christian recognizes that all his blessings come from God, he gains confidence in him (1. 74 ff.). "His whole life is a trusting, depending, waiting, hoping, in God " (1. 210). "And hence faith takes away from us ourselves and the things that are ours, referring all things to God with praise and gratitude " (1. 123). Faith is a "possession of things hoped for " (4. 271). This faith is, therefore, upon the one hand, the entreating, struggling faith of Augustine (Vol. I., p. 347); but it is, on the other hand, something more, *i. e.*, the apprehending of God in Christ and trust in God. Its essential content is Christ (1. 219); what is his, becomes ours ; there is between us and him a *perfectum matrimonium* (1. 104). This leads to the *new conception of grace*. The actions resulting from the infused love find a filling out of their imperfection in the fullness of Christ, " because the fullness of Christ is accepted instead of it, until it is also made perfect " (1. 115): not only thus, however, but in the comprehensive sense, that without any regard to any beginnings of subjective righteousness, the righteousness of Christ alone is our righteousness : "That the Father in his mercy imputes to us the righteousness of his Son " (1. 140). Thus sin is no more imputed to us, but forgiven (1. 86). Lust remains in us. "It is here, but God in grace does not impute it to us " (1. 168). "For to such an one he does not impute sin, because he imputes righteousness to him " (3. 175). But this righteousness is mine only in so far as I accept it. "For his mercy is my righteousness. . . . For what is mercy, if I do not accept it ? . . . But my righteousness signifies that I am accepted by the One showing mercy " (3. 43). But this comes to pass through faith.

This is Luther's Soteriology in its first form. Two lines of

---

[1] This does not conflict with the fact that outward perception and recognition of this faith are still excluded (he does not see nor experience it, 1. 102).

thought pervade it.   God infuses grace, *i. e.*, faith and love ;
he makes us righteous.   But since faith is regarded as a confidence in the revelation of God inwardly acquired, it may also be
said, that faith lays hold on Christ and thereby also upon the
righteousness, or forgiveness of sins, which exists in him and is
imputed to us.   The *gratia infusa* is here supplanted by the
Christ living and acting within us.   It is no longer the sacraments—Luther very seldom mentions them in this connection—
but the word concerning Christ which produces the result.   But
this Christ is " most active " within us (1. 140) ; and, although
the righteousness of faith is not given to us on account of our
works, yet it is given to enable us to perform works (*ad opera*,
1. 119).   It may be said : " For righteousness is from God,
since, when we are righteous, it is because God justifies and imputes " (1. 84).

5. The religious processes above traced are actualized in experience in connection with the observance of the Sacrament of Repentance.   Let us glance at Luther's view of that sacrament.
Contrition springs from meditation upon the blessings conferred
by God and upon our ingratitude as revealed by our sins : " All
these things reflected upon and compared with our own sins wonderfully stir up hatred and detestation of ourselves, but love and
praise of God."   But this penitence arises from love to God and
to righteousness (1. 99 ; cf. supra, 136 n. 3, 175).   " This contrition must be so brought about (*paranda*) that it may proceed,
not so much from hatred as from love " (1. 446).   But neither
the completeness of this contrition nor confession following it
imparts the certainty of forgiveness, which comes to us only
through *faith :* " Simply believe the word which the priest utters
in absolution, that the absolution may be based upon neither his
merit nor thine own " (1. 131).   The true satisfaction is that
required in Lk. 3. 8 : it is a " service of the whole Christian
life."   Where private confession and satisfaction are taught in
the Bible, Luther does not know (1. 98).   Through them we
cannot secure any righteousness, but only through faith (1. 102).
He regards indulgences with suspicion.   If no one can be sure
of the contrition of another person, it is mere trifling to maintain that a soul escapes from purgatory through indulgences ; for
if the individual concerned had not true contrition, the indulgence would not secure his pardon (1. 66).   Moreover, the
grace imparted impels us to perseverance in the self-mortifica-
tions of repentance, so that the true Christian does not desire
any indulgence (1. 68).

6. It is to be observed, finally, that upon other points
Luther is during this period very conservative.   The worship

of Mary and the saints,[1] the seven sacraments, transubstantiation, the mass, and the infallibility of the church are still maintained.   He has no idea of assailing them (vid. Köstlin, L. Theol. i. 221 ff., Engl. transl. i. 200 f.); but it may be observed that the elements of his later conception of the church may be found already in his writings.   The church is the City of God.   "It is built, not by human teachings or works, but by the word and grace of God alone" (1. 202 ; 4. 400). It is the summary of the works of God, or the new creation (3. 154).[2]   But since the church is thus the work of God, or of his word, its essence is invisible and perceptible only by faith : "Because the church is a labor and construction (*opera et factura*) of Christ, it does not outwardly appear to be anything, but its whole structure is internal, invisible before God; and thus they are known, not to the carnal eyes, but to the spiritual in the mind and in faith " (4. 81 ; 3. 154, 367).

7. Everywhere, beneath the old forms the new life was swelling.   Let us once more recall the leading features of the latter : The recognition of man's moral oondage ; the new apprehension of the humanity of Jesus as the absolute revelation of God ; the conception of faith as a laying hold upon Christ, together with trust in God ; the thought of Christ working in us ; the idea of the righteousness of Christ and the forgiveness of sins graciously attributed to us.   It is a new understanding of religion which finds expression in these views, however all the elements of the past—the ancient dogmas, the Augustinian apprehension of sin and grace, the criticism of the scholastic and pre-reformation eras, the mystic attempts to mount from the man Jesus to God, with their doctrine of the indwelling of Christ—may have prepared the way before it.

§ 67. *Criticism of the Sacrament of Repentance and Exposition of Evangelical Repentance.   Faith, Sin, Grace, Justification, Atonement.*

1. "The right way and the proper manner, than which no other is to be found, is the most worthy, gracious, holy sacrament of repentance " (W. 2. 715).   "But I, a poor brother, have kindled a new fire, and have bitten a great hole in the pope's pocket, by attacking confession " (W. 8. 340).   The central point in Luther's work lay in the abolition of the sacrament of re-

---

[1] *E. g.*, 4. 694 : " And thus the divine Virgin holds the medium between Christ and other men," with reference to her conception.

[2] The *communio sanctorum et bonorum* (4. 401) is to be interpreted in the neuter gender.

pentance and the substitution for it of the new conception of faith
and justification. This must also be our starting-point. In the 95
Theses (A.D. 1517) we find the traditional view of the sacrament
of repentance, as well as some echo of the criticism of the preceding period and of Luther's own evangelical views. (*a*) Luther
does not here assail indulgences as such. They are to be highly
esteemed (Th. 69, 38, 7, 71), and he proposes to combat only
the abuses connected with them (72). The pardoning power of
the pope can extend only to the canonical penalties imposed by
himself, and not to every penalty (5, 20, 21, 34). As regards
the dead, they are valid only in the way of supplication (26).
The forgiveness of sins has in his view only a declarative force
(38, 76, 6). The *thesaurus* of the church is not to be found in
the merits of Christ and of the saints, as these are effectual without the pope (58); but "the keys of the church bestowed through
the merit of Christ" constitute it. (*b*) But this is not in
the present day the character of indulgences. The indulgence-
preachers are in many ways responsible for the abuses, as if souls
were freed from purgatory as soon as the money rattles in
the chest (27, 28, 86), and as though the certainty of salvation
may be purchased (52, 30-32). Good works appear to be no
longer necessary. It might be asked why the pope does not
employ his power to empty purgatory (82, 84), and why
he does not spend his own money to build St. Peter's (86).
The church is being exposed to ridicule (90). (*c*) Our Lord
and Master Jesus Christ, by saying : Repent, intended that the
whole life of believers should be repentance (1). This is not
said, of course, with reference to the sacramental acts, but to the
mortifications of the flesh and the hatred of self (2-4). In this
sense, the penalty (*poena*) of sin remains as long as we live on
earth (4). But if this self-mortification is a duty, then the true
penitent will prefer the penalties, *i. e.*, the works of love,
to indulgences (40, 41, 43, 44). But he cannot by these means
gain a consciousness of forgiveness. "Every truly contrite
Christian has plenary remission of penalty and guilt due him,
even without letters of pardon (36); and he has this through his
participation in Christ and the treasurers of the church (37).
The hierarchy cannot pardon the least sin as to its guilt (76);
there belongs to it only the declaration of that which God does
(38). Therefore, God alone forgives the guilt of sin ; but the
penitent exercises himself in good works. Indulgences are not
necessary. They are indeed dangerous, in so far as they may by
outward means make the sinner feel secure, and in so far as they
give to him something which is altogether uncertain. If scarcely
anyone is certain of his *contritio*, how much less of the attain-

ment of *plenaria remissio?* (30-32). He who has not money in superabundance need pay out nothing for indulgences (46).

Such are the Theses. They are less energetic than many criticisms of earlier date (supra, p. 210). But yet—carried to their logical conclusions—they leave very little remaining of the sacrament of repentance. The contrite sinner secures forgiveness —it is taught with Augustine—to what end does he then need confession and absolution? Works are moral exercises : then indulgences, and works of satisfaction as well, have no ground to stand upon. As indicated in the first Thesis, the repentance which fills the whole life occupies for Luther the central place, and no longer the sacrament of repentance.[1] Cf. DIECKHOFF, Der Ablass-streit, 1886. BRATKE, L.'s 95 Thesen, 1884. BRIE-GER, Das Wesen d. Ablasses . . . mit Rücksicht auf L.'s Thesen (Lpz. Progr. 1897).

2. Luther's utterances in the following years develop these ideas in both their positive and their negative aspects. The essence of repentance consists in *Contritio*. (*a*) But true contrition is secured by the contemplation of righteousness, which begets in us love for the good, and, through this, sorrow for our sins (W. 1. 319). "But this contrition is to be produced in such a way that it may proceed, not so much from hatred as from love. But it proceeds from love, . . . if a man reflects with himself upon the benefits of God conferred upon him throughout his whole life. . . . All these things, reflected upon and compared with our own sins, wonderfully stir up hatred and detestation of ourselves, but love and praise of God " (W. 1. 466). The opposite course is most vigorously rejected. He who determines to attain sorrow for sin simply by the contemplation of it, becomes a hypocrite, and is sorry only from fear of punishment. He really gets no further than attrition (ib. 319, also W. 2. 160 f., 421, 363, 368 ; 6. 160, 610. Cf. E. 31. 182, 183 ; 18. 6).[2] An actual penitent frame of mind can thus, according to Luther, be induced only upon the basis of positive love for the good,

---

[1] In this consists the historical significance of the first Thesis : all depends, not upon the sacramental acts, but upon the penitent disposition of the heart. This introduction follows the example of the medieval discussions of the subject, which open with a presentation of the virtue of repentance. Particularly in Duns, the sacramental acts are really only means for promoting repentance as a self-mortification dominating the whole Christian life. Vid. my discussion of Duns' doctrine of repentance in Abhandl. f. Alex. v. Oettingen, p. 172 ff.

[2] The last two passages prove that Luther in writings of the years 1530 and 1537 could advocate exactly the same views as in his tract, *De poenitentia*, of the year 1518. But it is of the greatest importance, that he here denies entirely the possibility of begetting contrition before the reception of grace. His own conflicts in the cloister therefore fall under the head of attrition.

which measures its own conduct by the good, and not by the presentation of duties and penalties.   But it is important to scrutinize the theological connection of this thought.   It was clearly
expressed by Luther at the Leipzig disputation (1519): All the
Scholastics, he maintains, agree with him, "since they all agree
that contrition ought to be produced (*fieri*) in love, . . . that
contrition is produced, love impelling and enjoining" (W. 2.
263, 364, 371, 422).[1]   This is, in fact, correct, for contrition is
an act " formed " by love (p. 135).[2]   But it must be said at the
same time : (1) That this love presupposes faith— for such is the
traditional relation—and (2) That Luther is not here thinking
primarily of the empirical beginning of conversion. It is not to be
denied, however, that Luther, during the years of the indulgence
controversy, not infrequently made even the initial penitence of
the Christian life dependent upon faith and love : "The great
thing is a heart contrite from nothing else than faith ardently regarding the divine promise and threatening, which, beholding
the immutable truth of God, alarms, terrifies, and thus makes
contrite the conscience—again exalts and consoles and keeps it
contrite, so that the truth of the threatening is the cause of the
contrition, and the truth of the promise the cause of the consolation if it is believed, and by this faith man merits the forgiveness of sins" (W. 6. 545 ; 1. 542, 364).   Thus faith produces
contrition and maintains it.   Not fear, but the gentle goodness
of God allures the sinner to repentance (W. 2. 362, 363, 370).
In the moment when we hear that Christ suffered for us, faith
and love arise (W. 1. 399).   Contemplation of the sufferings of
Christ transforms man, and in them we recognize the magnitude
of our sin (W. 1. 137): "This contemplating essentially transforms man and, very nearly like baptism, regenerates him " (ib.
139).   " This faith justifies thee, will make Christ to dwell, live,
and reign in thee " (ib. 458).   Thus as we contemplate the
goodness of God in Christ, true contrition appears, while at the
same time man is preserved from despair."   "When true contrition is about to arise from the goodness and benefits of God,
especially from the wounds of Christ, so that man first comes to
(a sense of) his ingratitude from the contemplation of the divine
goodness, and from that to hatred of himself and love of the

---

[1] Eck acknowledged that this is the higher position, but that it is one
which, on account of frailty, cannot be attained (W. 2. 361). Luther was
brought to his view through Staupitz, De W. 1. 116.

[2] If, then, grace produces this condition, Luther has a right to say : " It is,
therefore, expressly Pelagian heresy to say that repentance begins before love
of righteousness ; but love of righteousness is from God, and not from nature "
(W. 2. 421, 362).

goodness of God, then tears flow, and he will heartily hate himself, but without despair, since he will hate his sin, not on account of its penalty, but on account of his view of the goodness
of God which, being beheld, preserves him that he may not despair, and may hate himself ardently, even with delight" (1.
576).[1] Thus God crushes the sinner's heart by showing him
favor.[2] But in that perturbation (*conturbatione*) begins salvation (540).   But "the grace of contrition is given to no one,
but at the same time the merits of Christ are given to him"
(612). This great unrest is the beginning of grace (595).
Contrition lasts—as *habitualis poenitentia*—through the whole
life (322, 652), being experienced daily (W. 2. 160, 408, 409 f.
E. 29. 357). Repentance in this sense can certainly not be
identified with the temporal acts of the sacrament of repentance
(W. 1. 531; 8. 109). "Because this is at length to exercise
living and true repentance, to separate the heart from vices for
God's sake, and to keep it separated and to separate it the more.
But thou who dost practice only that sacramental repentance and
initial repentance before the eyes of men, whose fervor and tumult
cannot last without a miracle, thou hast devised an impossibility"
(1. 649 f.).   The meaning is here, that love of the good springs
up simultaneously with faith in the heart.   The divine benefits,
together with the good now ardently desired, beget in us shame
and grief on account of the sins yet clinging to us.   To this is
now added the law, which, as the standard of the good, "co-
operates in giving a knowledge of sin, but in no way effects penitence."   "I concede that the law, the recounting of sins, the
contemplation of penalties, can terrify the sinner; but they never
make him penitent" (W. 2. 362).   The Commentary on Galatians already lays very great stress upon this influence of the law.
It is said to teach man to know his weakness and his wrong, to
show us the good.   It can, indeed, never awaken in us a desire
for the good, but only increase the desire for evil (2. 526 f.);
but it even in this way drives us to Christ (528).[3]   This is the

---

[1] The endurance of the pains of hell (W. 1. 557. Cf. E. 12. 387; De W. 2.
125) is thus excluded as an abnormal experience; cf. Gottschick, Ztschr. f.
Theol. u. K., 1891, 255 ff.

[2] Ib. "But then (at the infusion of grace) the man is so ignorant of his
justification that he thinks himself to be very near to damnation, and does not
think this to be an infusion of grace, but an infusion of wrath."

[3] Hence the law makes no one pious, but teaches only the outward piety of
hypocrisy, W. 6. 353 f. W. 2. 720 suggests a further use of the law: "But the
hard-hearted, who do not yet desire comfort of the conscience, and who have
not experienced the same torture, to them the sacrament (of repentance) is of
no benefit. They must first be made tender and timid, that they may also long
for and seek this comfort of the sacrament." The method of threatening must
thus, after all, be employed in dealing with such as are still impenitent.

true childlike fear of God, even though something of servile fear (*timor servilis*) may yet ever cleave to it throughout life on earth (W. 1. 321 f.). "Love being possessed, man is at the same time moved to the fear of God, and thus repentance begins from fear in love" (W. 2. 364, 369, 396). There thus arises an exultant hatred of sin (1. 543), faith meanwhile restraining from despair (632). Thus repentance, both as a state of life and as the beginning of life, is a fruit of faith and love, however much the law may contribute to its production.

This repentance now begets in the heart a positive desire to perform good works. The man is willing to bear the penalties (W. 1. 597); impelled by the Spirit and the Christ dwelling within, he brings forth fruits of repentance (1. 532, 649, 364; 2. 424).[1] (b) Luther at an early period recognized the impossibility of confessing all mortal sins (W. 1. 322; 2. 60; 6. 162, 545). The thought then soon occurred to him, that we are really under obligation to confess our sins only to God (W. 6. 158 f.), and that the confession required by the church is only a human ordinance (8. 152 f.). Hence we can confess to whomsoever we will; we are even free to omit confession to man altogether, if we but confess to God (8. 161, 182, 175, 181. E. 28. 248, 308; 29. 353; 10. 401; 23. 86 f.). From this position Luther never wavered, although he always warmly commended voluntary private confession (8. 168, 173, 176, 178; 6. 546. E. 23. 26 f.; 28. 249, 250, 308).[2] Absolution is to be received in faith. In so far as we, in receiving it, believe the divine promise, it is effectual (W. 1. 595). "Thy sins are forgiven, if thou believest them forgiven" (ib. 631, 542). It is faith in the institution of absolution by Christ which is here meant (W. 2. 14, 59). Everything depends upon this faith: "It depends not upon the priest, not on thy doing, but entirely upon thy faith; as much as thou believest, so much thou hast" (2. 719, 715). Luther still, indeed, at first understands this in the Catholic way: Grace and faith are infused (1. 364), and forgiveness results from the infusion: "Remission of guilt occurs through the infusion of grace before the remission of the priest" (1. 541).[3] But the essential thing is, after all, only that

---

[1] In view of this connection, Luther laments that works no longer, as of old, precede absolution, since the sincerity of the contrition would thus be tested, W. 1. 551, 661.

[2] In A. D. 1519 he demands that, together with the "testing" of the penitence, faith be also tested (W. 2. 720; cf. the severe arraignment of the confessional manuals, 6. 163, and E. 15. 469 f.; 22. 3), and similarly in 1526 (E. 29. 358; cf. 11. 185. Conf. Aug. 24. 6: "But none are admitted unless they have previously been examined").

[3] Cf. W. 1. 542: Remission effects (*operatur*) the grace of God; 543:

the word be believed ; and to this end there is no need of the ecclesiastical machinery.

(*c*) Satisfaction cannot be shown to be commanded by God (W. 1. 324, 383 ; 6. 610). The same is to be said of Indulgences (1. 384 ff.).[1] The *thesaurus indulgentiarum* is rejected (2. 161). Luther for a time adheres to the idea of Purgatory, despite some suspicions (1. 555, 563 ; 2. 161, 423, 323 f., 332, 324 f.; 2. 70 ; 6. 17, 370), but at a later period recognizes it as an invention (*e. g.*, 11. 362). Of the penalties of " satisfaction " there yet remain only moral works and readiness to bear the cross. " God changes eternal into temporal penalty, viz., that of cross-bearing " (W. 2. 161).

Luther appears to have preserved almost the entire structure of the sacrament of repentance. But this is only in appearance. Every separate part of it is recast and the structure as a whole demolished. Into the place of attrition, or contrition, has come that repentance which has not to do "piece-meal" with some particular works, but extends " over the whole person with all its life and conduct" (E. 11. 282), and which springs, not from slavish fear, but from love. Instead of the sacramental confession, it is required : " This confession is now so highly necessary, that it should not be omitted for a moment, but should be precisely the whole life of a Christian " (E. 11. 154). Accordingly, every sermon becomes an absolution (11. 267). But by the side of repentance stands *Faith*. This element is now woven into the penitential process by Luther.[2] Satisfaction was replaced by the good works which spring from faith. The sacrament of repentance as a whole is therefore disintegrated. It is only "invented folly " (E. 9. 299 ; 279 f.; smalc. art. iii., 3. 313 ff.). Into its place comes the moral and religious state of evangelical repentance, consisting of penitence, faith, and good works (E. 10. 401),[3] and embracing justification and the forgiveness of sins. Luther began with criticism of the sacra-

---

" Remission of sin and donation of grace, to justify and to heal ; " 428 : "God showing mercy and infusing."

[1] Luther often (W. 1. 587 f.) declared, according to the popular understanding of the matter, "that they sold indulgences for the divine grace which forgives sin" (E. 24. 337 ; 26. 18). Theologically, he thus expresses himself : " In all indulgence bulls he (the pope) promises forgiveness of the sins of all who have mourned (*bereuet*) and confessed (*gebeichtet*)" (E. 28. 175 ; 31. 141), who have "mourned and confessed and give money " (25. 132). Eck well expresses the doctrine as understood by the masses (W. 2. 352 f., 359).

[2] A partial anticipation of this is seen in the testing of faith at the confessional toward the close of the Middle Ages. Supra, p. 174.

[3] Only penitence and faith are commonly spoken of as elements of repentance (*e. g.*, E. 6. 340 ; 3. 76 f.; 11. 293, 296 ; 17. 125 ; 19. 64 ; 23. 39), but it is clear that works fall under the same heading.

16

ment of repentance, and he substituted for it evangelical repentance.   Of a change in his views concerning the initial penitence,
we shall speak in another connection.

We have thus outlined the views of Luther at this period upon
the topics of repentance, faith, works, and the pardon of sin.
We have yet to trace his teachings concerning sin, the relation
of law and gospel, and the work of Christ.

3. In regard to Sin and the moral Bondage of the Will, he maintained the same positions which he had taken in the earliest period
(supra, p. 229).   (*a*) Before the fall, Adam was inclined only
to good (E. 15. 46).   Since the fall, he and all his descendants
are subject to sin.   The human race is a *massa perditionis* (W.
1. 427 ; 2. 526.   E. 28. 206).   Every individual of the race is
full of sins (W. 1. 427), his nature full of lust (W. 2. 412 f.).
Human works may appear outwardly beautiful, and yet be mortal
sins (W. 1. 353).   Every sin is a mortal sin (W. 2. 416, 419).
"And there is therefore included briefly and barely in this
word, Sin, what one lives and does without and outside of faith
in Christ" (E. 12. 111).   Sin constitutes a kingdom of the
devil (W. 2. 96).   Especial emphasis is laid by Luther upon
original sin.[1]   He proposes to defend Augustine's conception of
it against the Pelagianism of Rome (W. 1. 272, 649.   E. 11.
281).   The Scholastics of all schools, with the single exception
of Gregory of Rimini (supra, p. 188), were Pelagians (W. 2.
295 f., 303, 394 f., 308).[2]   The danger of that tendency lies
in the fact that it leads to work righteousness (E. 14. 245 ; 30.
365).   This opposition forms the central nerve in Luther's
presentation of the subject.   Through the act of generation,
which is performed in evil lust, sin passes from parents to their
children.   It is inherited sin, or nature-sin (E. 19. 15), as being
the real chief sin (10. 305 ; 15. 49).   As the formative
material in father and mother is corrupt, it remains so in the
children (E. 11. 246 ; 19. 15.   W. 2. 167).   From Adam
down, the nature and essence of man is corrupt (E. 10. 304 ;
46. 67).   Human nature is "an evilly disposed nature" (E. 7.
289), a "corrupted nature" (E. 9. 234 ; 15. 187 ; 20. 155),
a flesh poisoned by sin (15. 47 ; 20. 157, 297), in which evil
lust reigns (15. 48 ; 18. 73).   In his doctrine of the "old
man," Luther however strongly emphasizes the spiritual, moral

---

[1] The Scotist definition : Want of original righteousness (E. 15. 46) does
not influence his conception.   The contrast to original sin is the *wirkliche
Sünde* (E. 10. 306), which is simply a translation of *peccatum actuale*.   Vid.
also W. 9. 73, 74 f., 78.

[2] But Pelagianism is the "chief heresy," E. 19, 184.   Upon Gregory, see
STANGE, Neue kirchliche Ztschr., 1900, 574 ff.; 1902, 721 ff.

side of sin.   Its essence consists in "blindness and wickedness"
(9. 288), "the despising of God, inborn inward impurity of
heart, the disobeying of God's will" (12. 111), "unbelief, the
despising of God, disobedience" (9. 15), but, above all, in
unbelief, as the "real chief sin" (12. 110 ; 50. 57 ; 63. 16)
and "cause of all sin and crime" (13. 158 ; 47. 54).   "The
chief righteousness is faith ; again, the chief wickedness is
unbelief" (12. 178).[1]   It is just the distinguishing feature of
the "natural man," that he has not the Spirit.   Strongly
as Luther emphasizes the natural depravity of man, he just as
positively recognizes also the ability of the natural man.   "The
natural light" sustains the striving after good, without indeed
knowing the good (10. 182 ; 35. 68).   It may protect against
the lusts, but not against lust (14. 151).   In secular affairs, in
law and order, reason judges very correctly (12. 90 f., 109),[2]
although in spiritual matters it appears as the "devil's strumpet"
(29. 241).

  (*b*) The consequence of natural depravity is the Bondage of the
Will.   Free-will is for the non-Christian only a word (W. 1. 354.
E. 29. 353).[3]   His will is free only to do evil, but not to repent
(W. 1. 359 ; 2. 362, 702. E. 7. 239, 302).   But it is maintained, on the other hand, that no compulsion to either good or
evil is exerted upon the will (W. 1. 365 ; 2. 370).   The significance which the absolute bondage of the sinner holds in
Luther's circle of thought from the beginning explains his bitter
assault upon the *De libero arbitrio* of Erasmus.   Luther's work,
De servo arbitrio (1525, opp. var. arg. 7), reveals a fundamental difference from the Semipelagianism of the cultured circles of
his day.[4]   This is not saying, however, that his theoretical system was an expression of his fundamental religious position.   To

[1] E. 9. 313 gives a classification of sins : If we gather all sins upon
one heap, they fall into two classes, which are the devil's own work, namely,
lies and murder.
  [2] The term Conscience (*Gewissen*) is very often used by Luther in the
general sense of the moral consciousness.   As to its nature, see W. 8. 606 :
"For conscience is not a power (*virtus*) of working, but a *power of judging*,
which judges concerning works.   Its proper work is to accuse or excuse, to
make either guilty or acquitted, fearful or secure.   Wherefore its office is not
to do, but to dictate *concerning things done and to be done*, which make either
guilty or saved, in the sight of God."   Similarly in E. 47. 23, 59 ; 18. 58, 22 :
"If we sin greatly, our conscience gnaws us, leaves us no rest ; my heart
passes the judgment : I shall be punished for this."   The medieval conception
is reproduced in E. 29. 156 : "The *natural law*, written upon every man's
heart."   Cf. supra, p. 171.
  [3] But see W. 6. 27 : "wounded in (his) free will."
  [4] But Erasmus' statement of the question : "Either free will or physical
unfreedom" had an undue influence upon Luther.

the theory of man as free and determining his own destiny he opposes the almighty, all-working will of God. He, not man himself, effects salvation. But this thought is enlarged to a metaphysical determinism: "That God works all things in all things."[1] Hence everything that happens, happens by absolute necessity. This thought is, however, combined with the Scotist idea of the absolute independence of God's will and appointments: "Because he wills, therefore what happens must be right" (p. 260). God is also working in the wicked, but it is their fault that they do evil. It is as when a carpenter cuts badly with a sharp hatchet (p. 255 f.). Everything is the work of God, even the fall of Cain, although Luther does not enter upon the question of the genesis of evil in the world. From this follows, as a logical consequence, the absolute double *predestination* and the subjugation of the free will: "With this thunderbolt he hurls down and crushes the free will to its foundations" (*penitus*, p. 132). What we so name is in reality only the particular form of man's activity, which requires a peculiar divine energy operating upon him. The will is not coerced, but acts according to its own inclination and desire ; but it attains to the doing of good only through the divine action upon it. Man is passive in his relation to God ; God alone has a free will (p. 158). Man is, as Luther, adopting an old metaphor, says, like a steed. He wills what God or the devil wills, just in so far as he is guided by God or the devil (157). But why God converts some and leaves others to destruction we do not know. That is a matter of his secret will, in regard to which we dare ask no questions. It is for us to be guided by his revealed will. In this way Luther attained the end which he had in view, *i. e.*, he proved that free will was inconceivable, and that grace was the sole agency in conversion. This was the essential thing for Luther. The Scotist and Deterministic[2] ideas were only means for reaching this end. We can understand, therefore, why he did not employ them more frequently, but, on the contrary, with all his emphasizing of the moral bondage of the natural man, appealed constantly to God's earnest will, revealed in the word, to save all men (E. 54. 22 ; 55. 162 ; opp. lat. 2. 170). Christ

[1] Cf., *e.g.*, E. 11. 110: "All created things are masks and disguises of God, which he chooses to permit to work with him and help him do all manner of things;" or 35. 252, according to which praying and working "are merely a pure sham-battle." But, on the other hand, we find the queries : "Who can coerce the will of a man ?" (E. 24. 310). "Who can control his heart ?" (ib. 311).

[2] This is the conception of predestination found in Bradwardina and Wickliffe. Luther appears to derive it directly from Augustine. See also LOOFS, DG. 376 n.

bore the sins of *all* men ; if all believed, all—and not alone the predestinated—would be saved (46. 107 f.).   The method of the *De servo arbitrio* presents therefore nothing more than theoretical lines of thought employed as auxiliary to the main purpose. But, as is well known, Luther always maintained the correctness of the conclusions here drawn; vid. Comm. in Gen.   Cf. LUTHARDT, Lehre v. freien Willen, p. 91 ff.   LÜTKENS, L. Praedest.-lehre, Dorpat, 1858.   KATTENBUSCH, L.'s Lehre v. unfr. Willen, Gött., 1875.

(*c*) Luther's views concerning the Wrath of God must be considered in this connection.   Upon the sinner is visited the wrath of God, which " condemns (him) in advance to death, that we must be eternally *separated* from God " (14. 117).   " God cannot deny his nature, *i. e.*, he is not able not to hate sin and sinners, . . . otherwise he would be unjust and would love sin " (Gal. 1. 338).   This relationship to God we have inherited from Adam (46. 67).   But, since God punishes sin, it is clear that sin is our fault : " For since there is wrath here, there must also be guilt, which merits such wrath " (E. 14. 117 ; 19. 213 ; 8. 177). " The word sin embraces the eternal wrath of God and the whole kingdom of Satan " (Gal. 1. 54).   " Death is the eternal penalty of God's wrath " (E. 20. 161).   To feel one's self *forsaken of God* is to experience the wrath of God (39. 44, 46).   Even children dying unbaptized are lost (W. 6. 26).   The sinner, when he is "separated " from God regards "him alone as a stern judge " (17. 37).   The unbeliever remains under wrath (46. 29; 47. 25, 31).   The Christian, on the other hand, recognizes God as *nothing but love*.   He is no longer to think of him as a wrathful judge (47. 21 f., 342).   " For God alone is the Man who ceases not to do only good to the world " (E. 19. 364 f., 377, 366).   If the Christian has now learned to know that *his nature is nothing but love*, he knows then " that, so far as we are concerned, even his works of wrath must be nothing but love," since they serve for the subjugation of our foes and to our " testing " (47. 21).   " There is, therefore, with God no wrath nor disfavor, and his heart and thoughts are nothing but pure love, as may be seen in all his works before our very eyes " (E. 19. 369, 370).   Thus, whoever is " separated " from God experiences his wrath ; the Christian knows him as " nothing but love."[1]

---

[1] The believing Christian cannot and dare not by any means represent God to himself as angered and placated (*iratum et placatum*), as the sacrifice of the mass requires (W. 8. 441).   Cf. 47. 342 : " For he who thinks of God and believes that he is a wrathful God, will also find him such ; for as one holds, believes, and imagines concerning God, so is he also, and one finds him also so, namely, a wrathful God."

He who considers the death of Christ recognizes "how im-
measurably great and terrible is the wrath of God against sin,
and again how unutterable, yea, how unsearchable, is the mercy
and grace of God toward us condemned men" (E. 3. 100).[1]

4. In his understanding of the relation between the Law and
the Gospel, Luther also continued within the lines originally
drawn by him (supra, p. 228). No one attains salvation,
except as the law performs its work upon him before the gospel.
Law and gospel are the word of God, but each in a peculiar
sense (E. 19. 235).   Not to have recognized this difference, is
the greatest fault of the Romish theology. Luther never wearied
of urging this distinction in ever-new applications.   "This
difference between the law and the gospel is the highest art in
Christianity, which each and everyone who boasts or accepts the
name of Christian should know and understand " (E. 19. 235).

(a) The Law is a divine requirement, rule, and mirror.   It
tells what man ought to do and has not done.   " It reveals what
man is, what he has been, and what he shall again become "
(E. 14. 151).   What it says to the heart is confirmed by
the conscience (14. 153).   But what is here to be understood
by the "Law?"   The Mosaic law, in so far as it "made
particular laws and ordinances," i. e., was a positive system of
laws, is only a "Jewish-Saxony code."   But in so far as it
coincides with inborn *natural right*, it is a permanent requirement
valid for all times, which has received a peculiarly excellent expression in the Mosaic law.   " Where now the law of Moses and
the law of nature are one thing, there the law remains and is not
outwardly abolished, only spiritually through faith. . . .   Therefore image-making and Sabbath and everything which Moses

---

[1] Luther shared the vivid faith in devils and demons which characterized
the close of the Middle Ages.   But it must not be overlooked that he represented the central processes of the religious life without making any essential
use of these views.   Large sections of his sermons may be searched in vain
for any reference to the devil.   His conceptions here also were more spiritual
than those of the Middle Ages.   He added, so to speak, a hellish majesty
to the devil, and the comic aspects of the popular belief disappear entirely.
Touching the work of the devil, he says: " When impurity abounds, the
devil fills the arteries and bones as full of such evil lust as man permits "
(E. 17. 3).   "A Christian must know this, that he is sitting in the midst of
devils, and that the devil is nearer to him than his coat or shirt, yea, nearer
than his own skin, that he is round about us, and that we are always at dag-
ger's points with him" (17. 178, 180 ff.   See also 11. 269 ff.).   The devils
are very shrewd (17. 182, 195).   They exist in great numbers (17. 191):
" How many devils do you suppose were there . . . at the Diet of Augsburg?
Every bishop had brought with him so many devils—as many as a dog has
fleas on it about St. John's Day " (ib. 210).   Upon the fall of the devil, see
46. 3 f.; upon angels and the protection rendered by them, 17. 177 ff., 182 f.,
189, 202, 216, 219; 10. 151.

appointed more than and beyond the natural law, since it has no natural law, is free, void, and done away with " (E. 29. 156 f.; 46. 84, 87; 47. 25). God's law, or love, is natural law (E. 20. 125; 22. 104, 202). These written laws are to be included under the category of the reason, since they have flowed from it as from a fountain of law (E. 20. 106).[1] As Luther shared the medieval conception of an inherited natural law (supra, p. 171 f.), he therefore recognized the " Law " only in so far as it agreed with the latter. In connection with it, he thought of other means of convincing us of our sins. From this point of view, the sufferings of Christ became also a preaching of the law (E. 13. 116 f.; 11. 147). The entire law, however, including the decalogue, together with the laws of the church (Gal. 1. 181. W. 2. 527), does not give life, but slays (W. 2. 468; 6. 353). It has not the power to move or renew man inwardly, but remains an inflexible, tormenting requirement (46. 75). Thus it calls forth the hatred of the sinner against itself (W. 2. 498, 532). The works which he performs without being inwardly conquered by the good, merely upon the requirement of the law, are done from fear of punishment (W. 2. 532), and are in the last analysis therefore hypocritical (2. 513; 6. 354). A "servile spirit" arises in man's heart (E. 7. 247). The law makes him really worse (W. 2. 525, 527), however far outward integrity may be secured by it (E. 7. 283, 284). The righteousness of works which it produces is no righteousness at all : " That righteousness of works is most truly nothing else than to love sin, to hate righteousness, to detest God with his law, and to adore the greatest wickedness" (Gal. 2. 103). Since the law thus presses upon man and he cannot inwardly and actually meet its demands, there seizes him, on the one hand, a terror at the thought of God and desire to escape from him (E. 9. 179); he becomes an enemy of God, without being able to escape from him (E. 18. 73). But, on the other hand, a great longing fills his heart to be free from this pressure. This impels him toward Christ and the gospel (W. 2. 528, 532. E.

[1] This passage is very instructive in showing Luther's conception of the Old Testament law. It is indeed a divine revelation ; but it is universally valid only in so far as in harmony with the moral ideas inborn in man. We may here detect a remnant of the natural theology of the Middle Ages. The conclusions which might be drawn from this position—denial of the total depravity of the natural man, the superfluity of the preaching of the law—Luther did not realize. From this point of view we may understand also his interpretation of the Third Commandment and his naturalistic and rationalizing way of regarding the observance of Sunday. See esp. the Larger Catechism, Symbol. Bücher (Müller), p. 401 f. In his works as early as 1518 : W. 1. 436 f. Cf. G. HILLNER, L. Stellung in d. Sonntagsfrage in Mitteil. u. Nachr. f. die ev. K. in Russl., 1888, Sept.-Oct.

7. 289). It awakens displeasure with himself, the resolution to
amend the life (6. 390, 339), and a thirst for the grace of God
(E. 7. 251).

(b) Preachers should begin with this preaching of the law, and
never cease (E. 10. 123 f.); for the world surely needs it (10.
283 ; 48. 210). The knowledge of sin must first be preached;
the consciences of men must be terrified by the divine wrath ;
the sinner must feel that he, with his sinful lust, belongs to
the devil and is lost (E. 14. 15). Only then, after he recognizes his sin, can Christ and grace begin their work (E. 11. 328 ;
13. 295; 51. 270). Only after the preaching of the law has
had its effect, follows the consolation of the gospel, according
to Lk. 24. 47 (E. 29. 139 f.; 11. 327 f.; 27. 124. Gal. 1.
186 f.; 2. 115). Then should be preached, along with repentance, the forgiveness of sins (3. 354). "That is all a preaching of the law, however or whenever it is done, which preaches
of our sins and God's wrath. Again, the gospel is such a preaching, which shows and gives nothing else than grace and forgiveness in Christ. . . . Yea, where is there a more earnest and
terrible announcement and preaching of God's wrath against sin
than the sufferings and death of Christ ? . . . But so long as all
this preaches God's wrath and terrifies man, it is not yet the real
preaching of the gospel nor of Christ, but a preaching of Moses and
the law against the impenitent" (E. 13. 116). "The law is that
which displays what we must do ; the gospel, where we are to
get the power to do it. . . . The law reveals the sickness ;
the gospel gives the medicine " (14. 14 ; cf. 19. 239 f.; 48.
200). "The law has its goal, i. e., how far it is to go and what
it is to accomplish, namely, to terrify the impenitent with God's
disfavor and wrath and (to lead up) to Christ " (19. 236). He
who rests under the law, is without grace and without the Holy
Spirit (12. 112). If he is not to fall into despair, the gospel
must soon come to his aid (E. 12. 372). With the gospel
comes the Spirit ; Moses must now withdraw, and the law
is robbed of its power (12. 251 ; 9. 251 ; 19. 246). The
gospel proclaims the goodness of God and the forgiveness of sins
(7. 156, 327 ; 10. 89). With it, the Spirit enters and quickens
the man inwardly, bringing with him Christ, who reigns in us.
By this means faith, desire and love for the good, and a new
pious life are produced in man (9. 240, 278 ; 13. 234, 265 ;
51. 302). The gospel effects the new birth (12. 323). The
law inwardly transforms no one ; it is only the Holy Ghost who
does this (52. 296).[1] But the new man needs no law. "Just as

---

[1] The Holy Spirit does not therefore come through the preaching of the law,

three and seven—not ought to be, but are ten, nor is any law or rule to be sought for making them ten . . . so a righteous man—not ought to, but does live well, nor does he need a law which may teach him to live well" (W. 2. 596.   E. 22. 66 f.). The Christian has nothing to do with the law (E. 13. 35, 37, 39).   "It is therefore the highest art and wisdom of Christians not to know the law" (Gal. 1. 16).   Christ has abolished it (W. 6. 354).   Neither the Mosaic law nor the law of nature can longer require anything, since there is no longer need of any requirement.

(c) The law is designed, therefore, to awaken the repentance which is involved in conversion.   To this end it is to be preached.   But it is to be preached also for the maintenance of order among the rude and coarse populace, and to be taught to children (E. 13. 51 ; 19. 246).   The influence of the civil law lies in the same direction.   The same fundamental principle finds expression in all codes of laws.   Finally, even converted Christians, being yet flesh, have need of admonition and the presentation to them of the divine will (13. 118).   "Thus must Moses without Christ do his work, that it may drive those who are not Christians, or, in other words, the old man.   For he does not thereby make Christians pious; but this indeed he does, he shows them what their calling is, which they according to the Spirit willingly observe—not that the flesh either will or can so readily follow that they do not on its account still need to be put on their guard and admonished" (13. 41).

(d) We cannot fail to observe the difference between this view of the subject and that presented above (under 2 a).   In the large Commentary upon Galatians (A. D. 1535), Luther writes: "But man, being humiliated through the law and brought to the knowledge of himself, *then he is made truly peni-tent*, for true penitence begins from fear and the judgment of God" (Gal. 1. 193).   But in his publication, *Von den Schlüsseln* (A. D. 1530), we meet again the other position :

but comes afterward, since it is only through the gospel that he acts : "Now the Holy Ghost is not the law, nor the reverse.   Where the law is, there the Holy Ghost is not. . . .   The law is not intended to and cannot make pious, but the Holy Ghost makes pious before God" (E. 52. 297 ; 47. 359).   Parallel with this way of apprehending the process, we find another, which traces penitence directly to the *preaching of Christ*, which awakens terror before the wrath of God and the purpose of amendment.   "But such penitence man cannot himself awaken ; it is the *work of the Holy Ghost* which he begins in us through the word of God, which first reveals sin and at the same time announces the penalty of sins, eternal death."   Here penitence is represented as awakened by the Holy Spirit, whereas faith does not appear to come until afterward (E. 6. 339 f., 389 f., 356).   See also 63. 127 : "The wrath of God is revealed through the gospel" (A. D. 1522).

"In order that repentance also may be begun from desire and love" (E. 31. 183). And in a sermon of A. D. 1537, he declares: "Hypocrisy indeed comes from the law, but true repentance follows only from the name of Jesus Christ" (18. 6). One thing is here clear. In the first passage, "repentance" designates the transitory penitence of the yet unconverted, wrought by the law.[1] In the other two passages, it is the evangelical repentance, springing from faith and love, and filling the whole life. Apart, however, from this difference in the use of the term, two things are historically certain. (1) Luther, from the beginning to the end of his activity, urged the preaching of the law, since it is its office to humiliate, awaken an initial penitence, and point to Christ. (2) He also, from the beginning to the end of his activity as a reformer, urged a repentance which, springing from faith and love through the agency of the gospel and of the Holy Ghost, indicates a conflict with evil filling the whole Christian life.[2] And we note also (3) as an episode in the controversy concerning confession, the view that the religious process in the Christian's heart begins with faith and love, and that only as a result of these does repentance ensue. If I am correct, the last-named view is to be attributed to the effort to retain in the life of the believer only a complete penitence and to avoid everything analogous to the traditional *attrition* (supra, p. 237). But as early as A. D. 1524, upon the occasion of a controversy upon the question, whether the law must of necessity precede the gospel, he maintained, with appeal to Lk. 24. 47, that law and gospel are to be preached, since the latter comforts only those who have through the former learned to know their sin. The law is also to be used for the outward disciplining of the rude and ungodly (E. 53. 250).[3] Cf. KAWERAU in Beitr. z. Ref.-gesch., dedicated to Köstlin, p. 61 ff. Melanchthon's utterances in the "Unterricht an d. Visitatoren," 1528, follow the same line. Through the preaching of the law, the people are to be stirred up to penitence and fear. "For along with this it is

---

[1] This is still the dominant use of the term in the praxis of the church. Using it in this sense, how could we understand Luther's first Thesis? Cf. E. 6. 151: "Ceasing from evil, regret, and sorrow for it—he calls repenting (*Busse thun*); believing on Christ he calls being converted to God (zu Gott sich bekehren)," and 27. 194: "Penitence (*die Reu*) flows from the commandments, faith through the promise of God."

[2] The law here comes under consideration only as a directive and confirming agency.

[3] Under these circumstances Luther could write: "And, in fine, it is more necessary to preach and urge the law of God than the gospel, because there are many wicked who must be restrained through the compulsion of the law, but the pious who understand the gospel are few and known to God" (53. 249).

useful to preach of faith.'' The law is to be proclaimed also in order to incite the justified to good works (C. R. xxvi. 51 ff.). It cannot be said that this is a change from Luther's position. Yet so early as A. D. 1527 Melanchthon was violently assailed for holding this opinion by Joh. Agricola, who deduced penitence from love of righteousness. Luther succeeded in allaying this conflict (cf. Kawerau in Stud. u Krit., 1880, p. 24 ff.), but ten years later Agricola renewed his assault, maintaining that repentance should be taught as produced, not by the law, but by the gospel. There is no need whatever, he held, for the preaching of the law. ''The decalogue belongs to the hall of justice, not the pulpit.'' Man is overpowered by the kindness of God, and thereupon renounces his former life and shrinks from incurring the displeasure of his heavenly Father (Luth. opp. var. arg. iv. 420 ff. Förstemann, Neues Urkundenbuch, i. 304. Kawerau in Beitr. z. Ref.-Gesch., etc., p. 65 ff.). Luther opposes him in the six disputations against the Antinomians, arguing anew in defense of the position which he later, as is well known, maintained. The right to appeal to the earlier Luther can be only to a limited extent granted to Agricola, for Luther had always attributed an influence of some kind to the law, and, in view of the practical demands of the years 1527-28, it was an extreme of folly to speak as did Agricola.

(e) Law and gospel represent for Luther two opposing conceptions of the universe. The natural man's view of God and the world is always legalistic (e. g., 46. 87 ; 48. 148). The gospel opposes this ; the mercy of Christ lays hold upon man's heart and transforms him. He allows Christ to lay hold of him, and he lays hold of Christ. This is the source of all good in him. But only he will allow himself to be transformed by Christ who has—according to the appointment of God and under his guidance (the law)—seriously struggled with the legalistic view of the world and has, in his own sin, experienced its insufficiency.[1]

---

[1] But the problem is not thus solved. It is not evident how the law (which is from God, but does not exert the specific divine energy of the Holy Ghost, p. 248 n.) produces contrition. How can the good control us, before we have been inwardly laid hold of by it and have recognized it as good? Luther silently assumes such a recognition, presupposes it upon the basis of the ''law of nature,'' or even of a certain general faith in Christianity, but yet discriminates between the application of the law to the *justificandi* and to the ''wild'' and ''rude.'' But is there not thus presupposed a certain initial faith before the working of the law? However distinctly this may differ from the specific saving faith—Agricola in his first controversy spoke of a faith in the threatenings of the law (*fides minarum*), see Kawerau, Stud. u Krit., 1880, 43—which, as Luther shows, cannot arise before there is a full consciousness of guilt, yet it just as distinctly differs from it as being its beginning.

"How is it possible to preach about the forgiveness of sins, where sin is not first present?" (32. 73, 70). In history, the revelation of law preceded the revelation of grace : "This occurs to-day individually and spiritually in every Christian in whom is found a season of law and a season of grace following in turn" (Gal. 2. 109).

Cf. TH. HARNACK, L. Theol. i. 479 ff. HERRMANN, Die Busse des ev. Christen, Ztschr. f. Theol. u. K., 1891, p. 28 ff. LIPSIUS, L. Lehre v. d. Busse, 1892. GALLEY, Die Busslehre Luther's (Beiträge zur Förderung christl. Theol. iv. 2, 1900).

5. The definition of the gospel leads us to consider Luther's conception of faith. (*a*) Christian faith has, in his view, for its object simply the peculiar, positive revelations of God in the words and works of Christ. Christ says : "Come to me, I will refresh (*tränken*) you, *i. e.*, in me and through me you shall find the word and doctrine, which will comfort and strengthen your heart" (E. 48. 199 ; 13. 55, 172 ; 14. 1). Only in the man Jesus is God actually to be found ; here he wishes therefore to be sought, found, and called upon (E. 10. 181 ; 7. 68 ; 41. 385 ; 47. 179, 296, 344, 348 ff.; 48. 334 ; 49. 92, 183 f.; 49. 83 f.; 50. 197). Christ is the "true epistle," "the golden book" in which the gracious will of God is revealed (W. 8. 274 f., 276. E. 10. 187 ; 12. 381). God is "hidden in the despised man, Christ" (W. 8. 381). Just in the Crucified do we discover the

Such a "part of faith" (*Stück des Glaubens*) Luther himself recognizes in the disciples before the resurrection (12. 171). But in positing this legal penitence before true repentance, Luther really establishes a pendant to attrition. It was the same considerations which led him to the acknowledgment of such a legal penitence, and the Scholastics to their theory of attrition (p. 135 f.). It is also with him, in the last analysis, a doing by man of "what is in him" (W. 4. 261), although there remains the immense difference, that he did not allow to this initial penitence in any sense a *meritorious* character! It may, perhaps, be said, that Luther, both in his pre-reformatory period and again in his later years, regarded his experiences beneath the pressure of "the law" in the cloister as normal, and only during that episode felt them to be simply the result of erroneous views. But even thus, there still remains the vast difference between his position and that of his opponents, that the law and the actual gospel are to be proclaimed together ; and also his contention, that "repentance" is not a sacramental act, but the very substance of the moral development of the Christian. I remark, finally, that both the lines of thought thus traceable in Luther are borrowed from the representations of the law in the New Testament. It is abolished and powerless, as the rule of conduct which is to make righteous (Paul : Rom. 6. 14 ; 10. 4); and it remains, as the expression of the divine will (Jesus : Matt. 5. 17). But with the latter thought as a point of departure, and in view of the positive confirmation of the law in the discourses of Jesus, might not Luther have secured some more important place in his theory for the authority of the Old Testament law?

loving-will of God.   From the kind heart of Jesus[1] we mount
up to the heart of God (W. 2. 140 f., 84; 1. 362, 614.   E. 9.
17 f., 247; 12. 297, 381).   Christ should, therefore, not be
preached as "a history and narrative from chronicles," but in
such a way as to tell us "why Christ came, how we are to use
and enjoy him, what he has brought and given to me" (27.
187).   This is the right way to find God, and not the opposite
course of beginning to speculate from the basis of the divine
majesty and government of the world (E. 19. 50 f.; 20. 132,
138).   In Christ we may gain a conception of God as he is, so
"that we do not place instead of him in our hearts a horrible
bugaboo or scarecrow, but long for him rightly, as he wishes to
be and has represented himself" (E. 16. 206).   If we do not hold
to the revelation given us, we will picture him to ourselves "as
the painters paint the devil, with long horns and horrible fiery
eyes" (ib. 203. 208).   In Christ we have the good gathered
up as into one word (W. '1. 341), and in him we have the very
nature of God.   That nature is "merciful will, kind will" (E. 7.
68, 72, 74, 76; 12. 230, 246, 260, 311, 325, 373; 11. 96;
14. 193); "nothing but love" (14. 49); "divine nature is
nothing else than pure benevolence" (*eitel Wohlthätigkeit*, 7.
159);[2] "an eternal power and divine energy" (3. 302; 10.
188).   Christ is free, since he is the deliverer (21. 99).

In these ideas are manifest two steps in advance, *i. e.*, the
Christian religion, and hence also theology, is understood as a
positive entity (in contrast with all innate religion of reason or
nature); and the nature of God, which is to be apprehended by
faith, is defined as an eternal and almighty loving-will.   By either
of these conceptions the religious character of Christianity is
assured.[3]

[1] Cf. his combating of the popular belief, which looked upon Christ as a
"tyrant " and "judge" (*e. g.*, E. 13. 49; 15. 485; 16. 144; 19. 222; 20.
151; 47. 23.)

[2] In all these explanations, the divinity of Christ is assumed by Luther as a
fixed premise (vid. sub), but his ideas carry him also beyond the ancient
Greek doctrines of the Logos.   In opposition to the view that the "Word of
God . . . is a light which shines naturally and has always shone in the reason
of men, even of the heathen," he says : "These are all still human, Platonic,
and philosophical ideas, which lead us out of Christ into ourselves.   The
Evangelist, on the other hand, desires to lead us out of ourselves into Christ ;
for he does not desire to deal with nor speak of the divine, almighty, eternal
Word of God except as in the flesh and blood which walked upon the earth.
He does not wish to scatter us out among the creatures which were created by
him, that we may there run after him, seek him, and speculate about him as
do the Platonists ; but he wishes to recall us from those high-flying and widely-
wandering thoughts of Christ " (E. 10. 181).

[3] In both, however, Luther follows impulses which passed from Duns into
the life of the later Middle Ages (cf. supra, p. 164, 150 n.).

(*b*) When God thus through the gospel, which is always accompanied by an influence of the Spirit, reveals to men his love in Christ, faith arises (W. 2. 140.   E. 7. 164, 76, 109 ; 28. 417). The love of God overpowers our hearts.   "Thus God has nothing but the best, and this he shares with us, nourishes us, supports us, waits upon us through his Son.   Thus our heart is converted to follow Christ" (W. 1. 275).   "But when thou hearest that he suffered for thee, and believest, there arises already confidence toward him and tender love " (ib. 399 ; 6. 216. E. 47. 341, 346).   The first thing that is to be said of this faith is therefore, that is a *taking* and a *receiving*.   "But that such bestowed righteousness should be in us . . . this comes to pass alone through faith, for it must always be received and accepted by us.   Now it cannot be grasped by us otherwise than with the heart" (E. 12. 118).   Faith lays hold upon the benefits of God (W. 8. 35 ; E. 12. 118), the works of Christ (E. 14. 286 ; 10. 101 : "Therefore, in order that thy faith may remain pure, do nothing but hold still ; let it receive good, accept the work of Christ, and let Christ exert his love upon it "), atonement and salvation, with all gifts from above (7. 178, 227, 272, 304).   It is God, therefore, who begets faith in man when the latter accepts the divine revelation.   With this, as Luther said at an earlier period, God infuses faith into men.   But this does not mean that a *quality* is thereby imparted to them, as the Scholastics taught, but that the heart is penetrated by the word of God, and the dominion of Christ is inwardly experienced : "The heart is imbued with the same truth of the word and through the word is convinced of the truth" (W. 6. 94).[1]   Christ is in the soul by faith as king ; the will as servant (W. 1. 283).   Faith is therefore a having (W. 1. 595.   E. 12. 169 ; 27. 180).   God, accordingly, through the revelation in Christ, leads us to accept that revelation.   If now the content of the revelation be the unchanging purpose of God to save us, the acceptance of it must take the psychological forms of obedience, confidence, or trust.[2]

---

[1] Luther most vigorously rejects the *fides acquisita* of the Scholastics (supra, p. 150, 195 f.), for this is supposed to be secured by man's own efforts, whereas it is in fact only through a divine influence that we can attain faith.   He therefore advocates the *fides infusa*—this it is which justifies (W. 2. 566, 146 ; 6. 85, 89, 95 ; 8. 323).   No one can apprehend an article of faith "without grace and the giving of God" (E. 18. 111).   This leads us back to Occam (supra, p. 150).   If the medieval conception of grace be abandoned, no importance then attaches to the figure of an "infusing."   Despite of it, in fact, it may be said that it is the *fides acquisita*, which constitutes a prelude to Luther's psychological conception of faith, rather than the idea of an "infused faith."
[2] This remark finds confirmation in the fact that Luther at an earlier period discriminated between *fides* and *fiducia*, by the former designating the accept-

"If faith be genuine, it is a certain sure confidence of the heart and firm assent, by which Christ is apprehended" (Gal. 1. 191). Faith is "confidence in God's mercy" (W. 6. 209.   E. 7. 66 ; 11. 50, 116 ; 14. 41 ; 18. 46), the assurance that God, and he alone, will make it well with us (E. 22. 15, 16, 135).   Faith is therefore not a theoretical belief of certain things (E. 7. 242),[1] but it is the practical confidence, that we are ourselves through the work of Christ in favor with God (12. 97, 149, 164, 174, 333 ; 13. 203 ; 27. 187), and that we and our works will be pleasing in his sight (W. 6. 206, 209).   In the light of this, we can understand the declaration : "Faith is never concerned with things past, but always with future things" (W. 8. 323).

But this confidence in the grace of God is based upon the contemplation of a historical revelation : and it is in particular historical facts that the latter has been given.   Hence, this confidence with regard to the future embraces also the conviction of the reality and potency of definite facts of the past.   "It is not enough to believe that Christ has come, but also that he has come as St. Paul here relates, namely, that he was sent from God and is God's Son ; likewise, that he is true man ; likewise, that his mother is a virgin ; likewise, that he alone fulfilled the law ; likewise, that he did this not for himself, but for our good and grace" (E. 7. 261; 23. 18).[2]   Rome, on the contrary, knows only the outward *fides historica*[3] (47. 12 ff.)   "To believe the resurrection of Christ is nothing else than to believe that we have a reconciler before God" (12. 171 ; 20. 141).   The same inner relationship of ideas prevails also in the exposition of the Apostles' Creed in the catechism.   The connection of thought is therefore as follows : The revelation of God in Christ influences us to its own acceptance, which occurs when we place our trust in the love of God as recognized by us and are convinced of the reality of the historical events in which God was revealed to us.[4]

---

ance as true, and by the latter the personal application to one's self (W. 1. 593 ; 2. 458).

[1] It is no contradiction of this statement, that Luther upon occasion says : "Faith means properly the holding to be true . . . what the gospel says about Christ and all the articles of faith" (E. 12. 204 f.) ; for the context shows that even here we are to think of a practical religious insight.

[2] To make a universal application of this idea lay far from the thought of Luther and from the needs of the age.   The birth of Christ from a virgin he supported from the necessity that the Saviour should be sinless, which would not be tenable if he had been sexually generated (*e. g.*, E. 7. 263 ; 10. 131, 306 ; 11. 246 ; 14. 161 ; 15. 52 ; 20. 155 ; 29. 49, 52).   Even though this argument be not convincing, it is instructive to observe the attempt of Luther to find a religious basis for the doctrine.

[3] Cf. his strictures upon "milk-faith" (E. 46. 219).

[4] Faith originates in the reason, but extends also to the will : "For wher-

(*c*) This saving faith, or the trust awakened in us through the revelation of Christ, is, further, the beginning of an absolutely new state of life.   Faith is no natural human work, but something new which God effects in man, the directing of the life toward God.   With faith comes the new birth of the man. " Now the divine birth is nothing else than faith " (E. 10. 206 ; 11. 311).   Faith "renews man " (13. 236).   It is "a living, real thing, makes man entirely new, transforms his disposition, and converts him wholly.   It goes down to the foundations and there occurs a renewing of the whole man " (ib. 267).   It is in harmony with this, that the principle of the new birth, or the Holy Ghost, becomes with faith, according to Luther, effectual in man to his regeneration and renewal (8. 223, 308, 307 ; 7. 240 ; 12. 112 ; 11. 314 ; 14. 149).   The usual representation is that the Holy Ghost through the gospel effects regeneration and renewal, whose first and essential element is faith (W. 1. 632. E. 4. 184 ; 8. 223 ; 7. 171 ; 10. 206 ; 12. 324, 404 ; 24. 325 ; 46. 269 f., 275 ; 61. 125 ; 63. 124).   But, inasmuch as the renewal effected by the Spirit does not develop into activity until after the entrance of faith, it may also be said that the effectual workings of the Spirit follow faith (W. 6. 206, 356).   At all events, the first activity which the gospel begets in man is faith.   And he who believes has begun an entirely new life. " Your faith is not a dream and fancy, but it is life and deed " (W. 8. 385.   E. 24. 325).   It is a life with Christ and from Christ, for he lives and reigns in us (W. 1. 455, 458 ; 8. 608). "Out of a dry block" God makes "a new flourishing tree" (E. 7. 170).   Thus the believer, since his life takes the new direction toward God, is a new man, who now endeavors to love God and be obedient to him (W. 8. 357, 363.   E. 12. 90 ; 10. 289 f., 184 ; 12. 324).

(*d*) Having seen that faith is a work of God, and that its essential nature is trust, as the beginning of a new state of life, there yet remain to be noted, according to Luther, some accompanying phenomena.   First of all, we may observe that faith is intimately associated with a Feeling and Experience of divine grace.   Luther says indeed : " Feeling is against faith, faith against feeling ;" but his meaning here is only that faith

---

ever reason goes, there the will follows after ; wherever the will goes, there follow love and desire " (E. 10. 207 ; 11. 200 ; 22. 135 ; cf. W. 1. 66 ; vid. the polemics against Eck's assertion : " The will is in the soul as a king in his kingdom") (W. 1. 283).   According to this, Luther does not accept the Scotist idea of the primacy of the will.   With regard to the relationship of the reason and the will in faith he thus agrees to a certain extent with Thomas (supra, p. 103), Duns (p. 150), Biel (p. 195) ; but he places a higher estimate upon the share of the will in faith than any of the medieval theologians.

reaches out beyond "what we can apprehend by reason and the senses." It has, according to Heb. 11. 1, nothing whatever to do with "the things which are seen" (E. 11. 198; 12. 165, 89, 341; 14. 55, 62, 231; 46. 276. W. 1. 541). "But when feeling and thinking fail, then comes another light, another feeling" (E. 11. 200). The believer feels directly that he has a gracious God (W. 8. 106). He has and feels Christ and the workings of grace in his heart (E. 9. 278 f.; 7. 170; 48. 333). He feels that Christ has power, and "is man enough for the devil" (E. 20. 148). He feels the Holy Ghost, as well as sin, within him (8. 311; 49. 179). The immediate inner observation of these things effects an experience, not uncertain opinions (*persuasiones*, 50. 28 f.). "For a Christian life consists entirely in the exercise and experience of those things which we daily hear and read from the word of God" (9. 95). The Christian experiences the care of God (W. 6. 125). The "experience of faith" "feels" the presence of Christ (E. 29. 334 f.). In order that the faith that is in us may be steadfast, experience must enter. "Although I should preach of God for a hundred years, that he is so kind, sweet, and merciful, and helps men—and have yet not tasted this by experience, it yet all amounts to nothing, and no one thereby learns to trust God aright" (E. 13. 155). Creation and redemption are not realities for us, "if we do not also experience and feel them to be so" (E. 23. 249). Without such personal experience, Christ is not our Saviour (E. 18. 7 f., 45 f., 47). Only where this feeling and this experience are present, do we become "sure of (our) faith" (E. 14. 220. W. 2. 458), "sure of salvation"[1] (E. 7. 275), and only there is the truth of the gospel and of the doctrine confirmed (E. 12. 362, 386; 13. 118; 23. 250, 267). The immediate (direct) feeling and the abiding experience of the living object of faith are therefore the final evidence of its reality (E. 13. 183 ff.). Only thus is an inner certainty possible, according to Luther; not through trust in one's own works, which are always uncertain (E. 58. 375 f.). This experience is not of itself identical with the act of faith. The feeling may at times be wanting, so that faith must depend solely upon the word (E. 12. 309; 18. 47; 14. 45: "before we experience or feel it." W. 2. 117); but, as a rule, it accompanies every act of faith, as indeed the entire Christian life. "And there comes to him unsought and undesired the feeling and experience, precisely in and through such thinking (*vormuthen*) or believing (W. 8.

---

[1] Luther, on the other hand, most vigorously denounced the false "security" of the impenitent, e. g., W. 2.·737. E. 18. 8; 9. 185, 187.

357, 379).[1] And if thou dost not experience it, then hast thou
not faith, but the word hangs upon thine ears and floats upon
thy tongue like foam upon the water '' (E. 13. 184 ; 28. 298).

The believer experiences a light and joyful heart (W. 2. 714).
With faith is intimately associated the feeling of present blessedness.   '' Thou must have heaven and be already saved before
thou doest good works.''   The Christian life is a waiting for the
blessedness which we already have (E. 7. 165 ff.; 11. 3, 196 ;
12. 329, 331 ; 14. 120 ; 16. 116, 138 ; 47. 367 ; 48. 24 f.;
46. 26).   The Christian therefore leads a life of peace, joy, and
liberty (E. 11. 321 ; 7. 272).   He has a '' courageous, bold,
and unterrified heart'' (W. 6. 275 ; 1. 273. E. 63. 125).   In
all affairs of his outward life also he consoles himself with the
thought of the providence of God (W. 8. 215 f. E. 9. 138 ;
10. 241, 244 ; 12. 332 ; 13. 175, 252 ; 47. 183).[2]   Faith impels to prayer ; yea, it is itself prayer (14. 47).   It makes us
thankful (9. 49) and capable of decision in spiritual things (12.
90), etc.

6. But the most important phenomena resulting from faith are
Good Works.   Christ dwells in the believer and moves him
to imitate the works which he himself has done (W. 1. 364,
649).   '' But he lives in us, not speculatively, but really, most
intimately, and efficaciously (Gal. 2. 134).   Further, if faith is
the new attitude of man toward God, it in consequence works
in him as a '' leaven '' (W. 8. 106); it is the beginning of the
pious life from which proceed all good works.   The works which
the believer performs are hence, in so far as they proceed
directly from faith, sinless and good[3] (E. 12. 160 ; 7. 229 ;
10. 4).   Faith (the Spirit) gives power to fulfill the law
(12. 113; 9. 259), and that willingly and with delight (7.
290, 296 ; 10. 88).   The good is written upon the heart as a
law of the Spirit, as a '' living will and an experimental life ''
(W. 2. 499).   The energy of faith finds expression in good
works.[4]   '' For, as faith brings to thee blessedness and eternal

---

[1] There are elements here—and they are intimately connected with Luther's
conception of faith—which present him in the light of a pioneer of the views
which have been prevalent among us since the days of Schleiermacher.   The
method of detecting the agent in the effect is very common in Luther, e. g.:
Where faith is, there also grace and the Holy Ghost (E. 7. 164; 12. 99,
267 f.); where works, there faith (13. 228).

[2] Luther can even say, that faith makes man a god, since all things are
now possible to him (E. 10. 311 ; 11. 52).

[3] With this, indeed, we meet concurrently the thought, that imputed righteousness also makes the works good.

[4] So far as faith is exercised by ourselves, it may also be considered as
a '' work ''—yea, it is the '' chief work '' (W. 6. 204, 206, 210).

life, so does it also bring with it good works and is unrestrained. For just as a living man cannot refrain, but must exert himself, eat and drink and find something to do, and as it is not possible that such works should fail to appear as long as he lives, and as he does not need to be commended and driven to do such works, but, if he is only alive, does them—so nothing more is needed in order that we may do good works than that it be said : ' Only believe,' and thou wilt do everything of thyself'' (E. 12. 16 f., 399; 47. 20). The Holy Spirit brings it to pass '' that the commandment of God now begins also to live in the heart of man, for he now comes to have desire and love for it, and begins to fulfill it, and thus eternal life begins on earth'' (9. 248). It is a pleasure for the believer to serve God ; for this reason he does good, not for the sake of laying up '' merits '' for himself (W. 6. 207). The heaven within us, which faith has brought us, does these works ''·without any seeking after merit '' (E. 7. 165). Gratitude prompts us to fulfill the will of God and to practice upon our brethren in turn the love which we experience (E. 27. 189 ff.). In such connections, Luther not infrequently maintains that works attest the presence of faith (E. 13. 66, 228, 237 f., 266. Gal. 2. 165). This does not, of course, mean that the works make the man pious. The contrary is true—the man must first be good, then will good works follow, as only the good tree is able to bring good fruits (W. 2. 71, 492. E. 7. 249; 27. 191 ff.). The doctrine of Christ is not ''about doing and not doing, but about becoming ; so that it may be said : not new work done, but first become new ; not lived otherwise, but born otherwise'' (E. 12. 399). Only those works therefore are good which are done by him who has through faith become a good man. But whether these works come from faith or from the Holy Spirit, it is clear that they have nothing to do with the law. They are done in the ''liberty of faith '' (e. g., W. 2. 425, 479, 485, 560, 497 ; 8. 372, 594 f. E. 7. 268, 270; 29. 140 f.). But since these works are effected in the heart of man by the Spirit, they naturally are in harmony with the works of actual morality as enjoined by the law (W. 6. 204, 225).[1] Thus the Christian performs, indeed, the works of the law, but with free delight in them, and not because they have been commanded. To summarize : The Holy Spirit works faith as the beginning of regeneration. By this means man becomes actually good Faith

---

[1] Cf. Müller, Symbol. Books, 444 : That outside of the Ten Commandments no work nor thing can be good and pleasing to God, let it be as great and precious as it may in the eyes of the world.

becomes the beginning of a new and pious life.　Cf. THIEME,
Die sittl. Triebkraft des Glaubens, 1895.[1]

7. Only now are we in position to examine Luther's doctrine of
Justification.　Here, too, the ground originally taken by him was
maintained (p. 231 f.).　But we must bear constantly in mind that
the theological tradition of the age discriminated in the process of
justification between the infusion of grace and the forgiveness of
sins, the former being a real and the latter an ideal change in the
sinner (p. 120 f., 160 f., 201 f.).　Luther, in harmony with
this conception, regards the matter—viewed in the first aspect—
as follows: The faith which God awakens in man effects a real
inward righteousness (*justitia interior, intus justificatur peccator.*
W. 1. 118, 632 ; 6. 98).　Faith is the inward righteousness
which heals the malady of the soul of man and makes him righteous (*rechtfertig*) (W. 8. 106, 111; 2. 13, 14, 424.　E. 22. 138,
248 ; 12. 89; 13. 238), for Christ and the Holy Spirit dwell in
their power in the heart of the believer (W. 2. 458, 490, 749.
Gal. 1. 245).　Thereby man is made really righteous (E. 12.
89.　W. 8. 605).　This righteousness is, however, by its very
nature subject to a process of development, which is never completed in this life.　" Everyone who believes in Christ is righteous, not yet fully in reality, but in hope.　For he has begun to
be justified and healed. . . .　But meanwhile, while he is being
justified and healed, what remains of sin in the flesh is not imputed to him for the sake of Christ, who, although he is without
any sin, has now become one with his follower and intercedes for
him with the Father (W. 2. 495).

Here appears, it will be observed, a new line of thought.
While the process of making righteousness is being carried forward, the sins yet cleaving to him who believes on Christ are *not
imputed* to him.　The sins of him who is undergoing the process
of justification are forgiven, on the one hand, because he is beginning to be righteous—which is God's doing—and, on the other
hand, because he is living in fellowship with Christ.　" Thus,
because through faith righteousness and the fulfilling of the law
have been begun, therefore for the sake of Christ in whom they
believe, what remains of sin and of the law yet unfulfilled is not
imputed.　For faith itself, where it has been born, has this as
its office, to purge the remains of sin from the flesh " (ib. 497).

---

[1] The superficial charge brought against Lutheranism by its opponents of all
ages and all parties, that in Luther's circuit of thought good works and
morality are not sufficiently provided for, is utterly refuted in THIEME'S work.
It may be said, on the contrary, that in no other of the Reformers does the
moral principle penetrate so deeply and directly to the very centre of the religious life.

" Sin remains there, but, because it has begun to be driven out
(*expurgari*), it is not imputed to him who is driving it out "
(ib. 414).   In precise harmony with these utterances of A. D.
1519, it is said in 1522, that, although there are still many sins
in us, " Yet grace does so much, that we are accounted altogether
and fully righteous before God . . . takes us completely under
its protection for the sake of Christ, our advocate and mediator,
and on account of the fact that (its) gifts have been begun in us "
(E. 63. 124).[1]   The idea is :   Inasmuch as sin has been in principle shattered in the believer, and God looks upon him in Christ,
sin is forgiven and not imputed.   The Smalcald Articles (A. D.
1537) follow the same line of thought :   " That we, through faith,
secure another and new heart, and God, for Christ, our mediator's
sake, will and does consider us as entirely righteous and holy.
Although sin in the flesh is not yet entirely banished nor dead,
yet he will not impute nor recognize it.   And upon such faith,
renewal, and forgiveness of sin then follow good works.   And
what in these is yet sinful or defective, just for Christ's sake
shall not be reckoned as sin or defect, but the man shall both in
person and in his works be called and be entirely righteous and
holy, out of pure grace and mercy shed abroad and poured out
upon us in Christ " (E. 25. 142.   Cf. 11. 171 ; 46. 260).
The only difference observable in this exposition is that the declaration of man's righteousness by God is no longer based expressly upon the beginning of righteousness within man *and* the
work of Christ, but only upon the latter.   But the difference is
only apparent, and Luther is right when he claims to have thus
taught " hitherto and always " (ib.) ; for in the very first years of
his reformatory activity he finds the ground of our comfort and
confidence only in the mercy of God (A. D. 1519, W. 2. 100).[2]
Christ is our righteousness, since he, as the bridegroom to the
bride, gives what he has to us and bears our sin (W. 2. 146.
De W. 1.17.   E. 27. 182 f.).   Thus he teaches also at later
periods.   In so far as we hide ourselves in Christ, who has made
full atonement for our sin, and like chickens seek protection under
the wings of this hen, we are righteous before God.   " For our

---

[1] Cf. W. 8. 92 (A. D. 1521) : Because they believe, and are living under
the kingdom of mercy, and sin in them is condemned and assiduously morti-
fied, therefore it is not imputed to them.   Also ib. 109, 111.   E. 8. 255 ;
9. 310; 7. 226 ; 12. 97, 100, 103; 13. 239, 267 ; 14. 17.

[2] Cf. W. 6. 133 (A. D. 1520) : "We rest, I say, in the righteousness of
Christ, by which he is righteous, because we cling to this, through which he is
acceptable to God and intercedes as our advocate for us and makes himself
entirely ours . . . as impossible as it is therefore that Christ in his righteousness should not be acceptable, so impossible is it that we by our faith, by
which we cling to his righteousness, should not be acceptable."

faith and all that we may have from God is not sufficient, yea it
is not genuine, unless it seeks refuge under the wings of this hen
and believes firmly that not we but Christ can render and has
rendered satisfaction for us to the righteousness of God, and that
grace and salvation are granted to us, not for the sake of our
faith, but for Christ's sake'' (E. 7. 178; 3. 424; 10. 226; 15.
381, 485; 28. 417; 46. 71.   W. 8. 111 f.).   If we look upon
the faith which we have, it is only a beginning of righteousness
(Gal. 2. 312 ; cf. E. 16. 256) ; but if we look upon Christ, who
is embraced by this faith as a precious stone in a ring, it may be
said : '' God regards him as righteous'' (Gal. 1. 195, 322, 339).
The true, abiding righteousness is wrought in us by the gracious
forgiveness of sins guaranteed us through the work of Christ and
through his ''return to the Father'' (E. 25. 76; 50. 60 f.; 7.
299.   Opp. ex. 19. 43.   Opp. var. arg. 5. 438).   ''Sin is indeed
still present, but it is forgiven'' (E. 5. 251).   It is another's (*eine
fremde*) righteousness which is transferred to us (E. 14. 12.
Opp. ex. 5. 269) : '' That we may become righteous and delivered from sin through forgiveness of sins'' (E. 5. 247).   And yet
it remains true, in Luther's mind, that abiding righteousness before God belongs to him alone in whom actual righteousness has
through faith begun to exist,[1] not indeed because this faith as a
human activity constitutes the subjective beginning of actual
righteousness, and thus embraces in itself also love (per contra,
Gal. 1. 137), but because it, as a work of the Christ *most actively
working in us*, and by virtue of the power of Christ, furnishes
the guarantee for the continuance of the process of advancing
actual righteousness.   Not for the sake of man's faith, but because Christ, the Redeemer, constitutes the substance and power
of this faith, does God, through the forgiveness of sins, pronounce the believer righteous.   '' Therefore it is not our righteousness, but Christ's righteousness—yea, this righteousness is
Christ himself, and yet becomes my righteousness if I believe''
(E. 3. 435; 50. 61.   Opp. ex. 18. 189 f.).

[1] Very instructive is his development of the parallel between the influences
flowing from Adam and from Christ (E. 13. 120) : '' As sin has been inherited
by us from Adam, and has now become our own, so must also Christ's righteousness and life become our own, in such a way that the same power of righteousness and life may work in us, just as though they had also been inherited
by us from him.   For there is in him not a merely personal, but an actual and
powerful righteousness and life—yea, a fountain which gushes and flows forth
into all who become partakers of himself, just as from Adam sin and death have
flowed into man's whole nature.   And it is therefore now declared that men
become righteous and alive from sin and death, not from themselves or through
themselves, but through the alien righteousness and life of this Lord Christ,
namely, when he touches them with his hand and imparts to them through the
word his work and power to blot out sin and death, and they believe the same.''

Whoever will be at pains to compare with this the utterances of Luther at the beginning of his career must confess that he has steadfastly kept within the lines which he then marked out : (1) Christ, or the Holy Spirit, works faith.   In the believer (the regenerated) Christ is efficaciously present, together with the Holy Spirit, through and in his faith.   Man is thereby renewed (*verneuert*), made "actually" righteous.   "Justification is, in fact, a certain regeneration into newness (of life) " (Jen. 1. 540 v).   (2) But this fermentative energy of faith is a progressive and not seldom interrupted process.   The sinner can hence find secure comfort only through the fact that God, by virtue of the union between Christ and the believer effected and made effectual in faith, imputes to him the righteousness which Christ has secured for him, *i. e.*, forgives him his sins.   This is the "personal" righteousness which avails for the whole man and makes him, despite his sins, acceptable to God.   In this are firmly rooted the consolation of the believing conscience and the assurance of salvation.[1]

If we now review these delineations of the process involved in the justification of the sinner, it must, it appears to me, be evident to all that the deepest motives of the Pauline and Johannine cycles of thought find expression in them ; but, none the less, that they are moulded formally upon the pattern of the medieval idea of justification.   But, in place of the infused grace of the earlier theology, is now the Christ working effectually in us.   And the powerless forgiveness of sins, which was in one way or another merely a pendant to the *gratia infusa*, is replaced by the energizing consciousness, inseparably connected with the contemplation of the life and work of Jesus,[2] that his redemptive work means for us the forgiveness of our sins.[3]

8. This leads us to Luther's conception of Grace.   It must be

---

[1] Cf. Opp. ex. 19. 48 (A. D. 1532) : " These are the *two parts of justification.*   The former is the grace revealed through Christ, that through Christ we have a God appeased, so that sin is no longer able to accuse us, but the confidence of conscience in the mercy of God is reduced to certainty.   The latter is the bestowal of the Spirit with his gifts, who illuminates against the pollutions of the spirit and the flesh."   So also, E. 12. 285.   It is no more than a dividing of this second element of righteousness, when Luther in other connections discriminates between an "inward " and an "outward " righteousness, describing the former as " righteousness in the heart " and the latter as the "fruit, result, and proof" of the former.   *E. g.*, E. 13. 238, 269.   W. 2. 146.

[2] Here, as in connection with the above remarks upon the " workings" of Christ, must be borne in mind, what Luther has said (see supra, pp. 230 f., 252 f.) touching the contemplation of Christ and the continued activity of the exalted Saviour.

[3] If this doctrine of justification shall appear " unlutheran " to any, they must explain to their own satisfaction the fact that it comes from Luther !

said here, first of all, that Luther never wearied of assailing every form of work-righteousness and all claims to human merit. This is a leading point in his reformatory ideas. As he who now performs good works does not aim thereby to gain merits, since God is, in the last instance, the original source of the works (E. 7. 165. Cf. above under 6),[1] so also by the conception of the forgiveness of sins all meriting or atoning is excluded (E. 15. 385; 9. 257 f.; 24. 98; 46. 106). By his own merit can no one become righteous or be saved (46. 69; 43. 362); nor can anyone even act meritoriously before the reception of grace (43. 360). "When we are speaking of that which concerns the Christian life . . . how we may become pious before God and secure forgiveness of sin and eternal life, then *all our merit is absolutely excluded* (*rein abgeschnitten*) and we should not hear nor know anything of it" (E. 43. 359. Gal. 1. 185 f., 193 f.). Thus is this idea, which had since the days of Tertullian exerted its fateful influence in the Western church, finally ejected from the Christian conception of religion.[2] But this was made possible by the new understanding of grace ; for so long as the conception of the latter as a substantial endowment prevailed, the legalistic view of the relation between God and man, together with the associated notions of merit, constituted a counter-weight to it, preserving the personal element in the relation of man to God.

The dominant idea in the medieval doctrine of grace is the *gratia creata*, as a quality created in man (*e. g.*, Biel, p. 195). Against this idea Luther's criticism is directed. "I accept grace here properly as meaning the *favor of God*, not a quality of the soul as our more recent writers have taught" (W. 8. 106, 92 f. E. 7. 170). God's favor, his merciful will, as it is revealed and proclaimed by Christ, is grace (W. 6. 209. E. 7. 128 f.; 10. 90, cf. 50. 61 ; 46. 69). Hence it follows that God—just because he is love—forgives sin. The effect of this grace is not a quality "attached" to the soul, but forgiveness and salvation (E. 5. 246 f.). From the grace of God thus understood must be discriminated the gift bestowed upon its recipient. "Grace and gift differ in this, that grace properly means the favor, or regard, which he in himself cherishes toward us, by which he is disposed to pour upon us Christ and the Spirit with his gifts" (E. 63. 123 ; 12. 285). This is by no means to be understood as equivalent to the gifts of the *gratia creata ;* for

---

[1] We may therefore understand also the declaration, that works are unsuited, yea, even offensive, and a hindrance to justification. (E. 10. 161.)

[2] Upon the popular use of the idea—drawn from the Scriptures—see E. 43. 364 ff.

grace in the sense of gift is most clearly discriminated from the
"quality" of the old theory. "It is a very great, strong,
powerful, and active thing—this grace of God. It does not lie,
as the dream-preachers falsely teach, in the souls of men and
sleep and allow itself to be carried by them as a painted board
carries its color. Nay, not so! It carries, it leads, it drives,
it begets, it transforms, it works all things in man, and makes
itself felt and experienced." This is the grace which "transforms and renews" man (E. 7. 170 f., 30. 368).[1] It is the
same thing to which Luther applies the term, Gift. The two
elements in the definition are therefore related as follows : (1)
Grace expresses the favor, or the loving-will, of God, as revealed
in his not imputing sin. (2) The word "grace," or "gift,"
designates the peculiar workings of this loving-will within the
heart of man. With these two aspects of grace naturally correspond the two meanings of the term, Justification (p. 263). The
old conception of grace, as wrought out by Augustine (Vol. I.,
p. 350 f.) is here overthrown. From the time of Duns, the irre-
sistibly-working natural power of grace had been but a respect-
able phrase (see note, i. e., on this page). The Augustinianism
of the closing Middle Ages (supra, p. 207) then sought to repris-
tinate Augustine's doctrine of grace. Luther replaced and surpassed it with the idea of the personal loving-will of God, which
is omnipresently and omnipotently accomplishing its work in the
hearts of men. It is in this only that we discover the deepest religious motives underlying Luther's *De servo arbitrio* (p. 244 f.).
Luther's God is the Almighty Loving-Will—almighty power,
present in all that exists and shall exist (30. 58), almighty
energy also in the outworking of love.[2] The grace of this God
is a working force, not a quiescent quality in the soul.

9. Faith in the grace of God embraces the conviction that the
forgiveness of sins is granted "not for nothing, nor *without
satisfaction of his righteousness* (justice). For there can be no
room for mercy and grace to work upon us and in us . . . satisfaction must first be rendered most completely to righteousness,

---

[1] The "Sophists," Thomas and Scotus, say of it, "that it adorns and helps
to produce the works" (ib.); cf. supra, p. 158, 119.   Luther rejected the
gratia infusa, as an empty notion. At this point the criticisms of Duns prepared the way, as the *gratia infusa* was for him little more than a phrase
(p. 159 f.). Luther rejected the "infused grace" not because it attributed
too much to God, but because it attributed *too little* to him.

[2] But Luther never, when unfolding his religious ideas, especially in his
sermons, permitted these principles to lead him to determinism or predestination. For him there exists between God and man a personal and ethical
relation. It must not be forgotten, that the power of love of which he thinks
is, in the last analysis, the spiritual power of the person of Christ.

Matt. 5. 18." (E. 7. 175). This compels us here to consider the "Work of Christ."[1] (*a*) It is Luther's firm conviction that justification does not rest upon an arbitrary imputation by God, as the passion of Christ would otherwise have been unnecessary (E. 7. 298). In this, he takes up arms against the Scotist theory of an arbitrary divine will.[2] "But if the wrath of God is to be taken from me and I am to obtain grace and forgiveness, then must it be merited (*abverdienet*) from him by someone; for God cannot be favorable nor gracious toward sins, nor remove penalty and wrath, unless payment be made and satisfaction rendered for them" (11. 290; 9. 381 f. W. 2. 137). But Christ, in obedience to the Father, serving our race in love, has offered this satisfaction or payment to God through his life and death (E. 8. 177; 15. 57 f. W. 1. 270; 2. 146). The purpose which inspired him in so doing was to obtain for himself the human race as a kingdom and to become their Lord (W. 2. 97. E. 22. 66). All his acts and his endurance were subordinated to this purpose, to become the Lord, that is, "a helpful power to his subjects." His government is forgiveness of sins, peace and righteousness (E. 20. 146 f.; 48. 265 f.; 50. 61). He rules through the gospel of the forgiveness of sins (E. 14. 251; 7. 55; 8. 229; 40. 88). "For we should regard Christ's kingdom as a great and beautiful dome or roof, everywhere stretched out above us, which covers us and protects us from the wrath of God; yea, as a great wide heaven where nothing but grace and forgiveness shine and fill the world and all things, so that all sins are in comparison scarcely as a spark to the great wide ocean" (14. 181 f.). But, as his reign brings to men the forgiveness of sins, so does it bring also the fullness of all virtue, faith, love, purity, happiness, and obedient service. "This flows over upon the Christian world from its Lord, who is a head and beginning of all grace and virtue" (W. 6. 13 f.). The purpose of the work of Christ is therefore the establishment of the kingdom of God, *i. e.*, he becomes Lord, in that he forgives sins and inspires to a new life.

(*b*) The Acts and Sufferings of Christ are subordinate to this purpose.[3] Luther presented the so-called objective aspect

---

[1] Luther uses this term, E. 7. 109; 14. 115. Upon the atonement as a reconciliation of love and righteousness, cf. supra, p. 67, 112, 156 f., 200. Vol. I., p. 295, 361.

[2] But he does not, like Anselm, postulate the necessity of the atonement upon general grounds, but deduces it as an inference from the actual fact of the passion of Christ. On the contrary, see the Scotist ideas, supra, p. 151 : "God is not pious because he does this work, but the work is right, good, holy, and well done, because he himself does it" (E. 35. 168).

[3] Let it be observed, further, that Christ here appears everywhere as the

of the atonement with energy and with variety of form.   The sinful race was under the wrath of God, under debt to him, fallen under the power of the devil, under obligation to the law, subject to penalties for the transgression of the law, or to eternal death (E. 15. 57).   But Christ has entered the race, and in such a way that he bore for us the lot which had become ours through sin : " But now has he stepped into our place and for our sakes suffered law, sin, and death to fall upon him " (51. 272).   He pays and makes good for our debt, so that we are released from it (6. 371 f.).   He is sacrifice and payment for the sin of the world (12. 246, 118 ; 18. 49 ; 2. 249 ; 3. 100 ; 47. 46 ; 48. 97 ; 50. 246).   Christ " as himself guilty " has " stepped into the place of our sinful nature, heaped upon himself and vanquished all the wrath of God which we had merited " (7. 302 ; 11. 290).   He was compelled " to feel in his tender, innocent heart the wrath and judgment of God against sin, to taste for us eternal death and perdition, and, in short, to suffer everything which a condemned sinner has deserved and must eternally suffer " (39. 48).[1]   But all this he endured, " that the wrath of God might be placated, in order that we might stand in grace and have forgiveness " (W. 8. 442. E. 10. 418 ; 11. 290 ; 12. 283 ; 311 ; 14. 119 ; 20. 161).   He likewise fulfilled in our stead and for our benefit the law, which affected only sinners, and endured the penalties prescribed for its violation (E. 15. 260 f.; 1. 310 ff.; 14. 154 f.; 161).   He thereby " rendered satisfaction to the law " (15. 17 ; 11. 314), i. e., the law has, since he has satisfied its demands, no right and no further claim to men (15. 57 f., 262).[2]   He also robs the devil of his " right and

---

God-man.   His divinity is recognized in his works, e. g., from his mediatorial activity (E. 18. 225 ; 16. 211); or from the infinite nature of the atonement and his appeasing of the wrath of God (11. 290; 49. 139; 46. 366; 45. 315 f.; 46. 46); or from his exercising of the sovereignty of God in the world (10. 345 ; 40. 50. Opp. ex. 23. 308; 18. 85); or from his power to save (47. 6, 198); or from the fact that we can believe only on God (47. 44).

[1] Luther can, of course, not mean to say that Christ was eternally dead and accursed, for the latter could not be the case, if for no other reason, because the former was not true.   He means that Christ endured, as all other consequences of sin, also an abandonment by God which corresponded with that awaiting the lost.   See W. 2. 260: " was forsaken by God, as one who is eternally accursed."   Cf. 20. 161 ; 46. 191.

[2] That is, since the law laid hold upon Christ, the sinless One, Christ robbed it of its power over the race.   It is made powerless.   This is explained in a thoroughly mythological way (cf. the outwitting of death and the devil, 45. 318; 46. 370); e. g., E. 15. 261 ; 18. 176 f.   But in the last citation above appears the expression, "to satisfy the law."   In order to understand this, we must clearly keep in mind the fact that the relation established by the law between man and God is to be regarded as one, not of private, but of public obligation.   This is of the very highest importance, for it reveals the

power " over men, because he "slew Christ without any guilt "
(49. 250; 33. 107).

Christ therefore became a sacrifice for our debt ; he endured
the wrath of God, took upon himself the works and penalties of
the law, suffered the assaults of the devil and of death.   All this
carries us back to the will of God, who would not forgive before
satisfaction had been rendered to his justice.   "God, nevertheless (*i. e.*, despite his mercy) required that satisfaction be made
for sin, and that his honor and law be recompensed."   His
mercy sent forth Christ, "who merited it for us and in our
stead" (15. 385. Cf. 12. 266).   The death of Christ was the
payment, or satisfaction, for our sins (19. 74, 211 f.; 11. 290 ;
28. 240).   Thus God requires also that positive satisfaction be
rendered to his law, which is accomplished by Christ's perfect
meeting of its demands.   What he did in this respect is as
though we had ourselves done it (7. 177 f.; 11. 314 ; 1. 312).
Luther's idea is thus: The ordinance of the law, established by
God for the sinful race of men, has been with its penalties abolished by Christ, in that he fulfilled the law and endured its
penalties—and that in such a way that the sufferings of Christ
prevent the execution of the penalties of the law, while his active
fulfillment of the law's requirements deprives the whole ordinance
of the law of its force.   Thus Christ passed through the whole
course of human existence from conception to the state of the
dead, and thereby "consecrated and hallowed it " (20. 156 ff.,
150).   "In him and through him " we become free from death
and all misfortune (ib. 172).   He who holds to him in faith is
for his sake free as well from the works as from the penalties of
the law.   Christ bestows upon us his piety and his sufferings
(12. 230).[1] His obedience, innocence, and holiness are our consolation (1. 311; 7. 178. W. 1. 593).

entirely different meanings attached by Luther and Anselm to the " satisfaction " rendered by Christ. In Anselm, the satisfaction is brought to God personally, as to an offended private man ; according to Luther, it consists in the
fulfilling of the divinely given system of laws by our representative, Christ.
Since satisfaction is rendered to this moral order of the world and it is thus
recognized and actually honored, the wrath of God is appeased, and the law
made powerless. There is thus presented a really ethical view, capable of the
most profound interpretation, in contrast with the objectionable anthropo-
morphism of Anselm. Here again Duns prepared the way for Luther. Sent.
iv. d. 14, q. 1, 7.

[1] For ethical purposes, Luther stripped the conception of " Satisfaction " of
its validity, as he had already (supra, p. 264) done with that of merit (11. 296,
280 : " Therefore let this word, Satisfaction, henceforth be nothing and dead in
our churches and our theology, be committed to the judges and to the schools
of the jurists, where it belongs and whence the papists derived it ; " vid. Tertul.,
Vol. I., p. 133). Yet in the doctrine of Redemption both conceptions play

(*c*) Christ has, according to the will of the Father, appeased wrath, satisfied the law, and effected the forgiveness of sins. Grace is now maintained through his continuous intercession in heaven.   We need no sacrifice, since his blood atones eternally (E. 8. 154; 9. 236; 28. 240) and he "without ceasing offers before God" (W. 6. 369; cf. 1. 703.   E. 7. 109; 12. 118; 47. 23).

These thoughts are for Luther of great practical importance. Since sin at all times yet clings to the believer, he experiences also the divine wrath directed against him.   To counteract this, he lays hold of the thought that Christ intercedes for him before the Father.   He who now by faith is united to Christ becomes certain that, for the sake of Christ's intercession, God forgives him his sin (Gal. 1. 338 f.), for that intercession silences the demands of the law upon us, since he has fulfilled it; and he frees us from sin, death, and the devil, since he has vanquished them.   But this avails for us only in so far as we "creep beneath his mantle and wings," *i. e.*, believe (E. 14. 154 ff., 159, 156; 48. 275).   Since Christ intercedes for us, and his work is well pleasing to the Father, we are sure of being in favor with God (E. 15. 237 ff.).   "But we are very certain that Christ is pleasing to God. . . .   In so far, therefore, as Christ is pleasing and we cling to him, in so far we also are pleasing to God . . . and although sin clings in the flesh . . . nevertheless grace is more abundant and more powerful than sin. . . . Wherefore sin is not able to terrify us nor make us doubtful concerning the grace of God in us.   For Christ, the most mighty giant, has borne the law, condemned sin, abolished death and all evils.   So long as he is at the right hand of God interceding for us, we cannot on account of ourselves doubt concerning the grace of God" (Gal. 2. 164 f.).

(*d*) But Christ is not only our representative before God; he also represents God among us.   This comes to pass in that he reveals to us the love of God and thereby awakens in us faith and love.   According to this, a further element must be included in the Work of Christ.   Christ not only secures the revelation of the grace of God, but he also imparts it to us.   "It was necessary for him to appear before God for us and be our veil, shield, and hen, beneath whom we have forgiveness of sin and salvation from the wrath of God and from hell.   And *not only this*, but he in addition gives the Holy Spirit, that we may also follow him

a leading rôle in Luther—and until the present day!   (Upon the term merit, see also E. 7. 179, 194, 195; 15. 385; 28. 417.   W. 1. 309, 428, etc.) But this is with Luther no inconsistency, for both conceptions fall within the lines of the relation between man and God as fixed by the law.

and here begin to quench and crucify sin'' (E. 14. 161 f.). As the intercession of Christ applies both to his earthly life and to his present existence, so also does his revealing agency. Christ once on earth revealed God, and he now does so again, in that his word is preached, the Spirit sent by him, and thereby a new life begotten within us (*e. g.*, 14. 155).[1] He is the ground of the forgiveness of sins, and is at the same time the source of faith and of personal righteousness (Opp. ex. 18. 189. E. 14. 119 f., supra, p. 260 ff.). "Therefore has God given us, in the first place, a man who should make complete satisfaction for us to the divine justice. In the second place, he through the same Man pours out grace and rich blessing.'' This occurs through regeneration (7. 177). "This is grace upon grace, that we are pleasing also to the Father for the sake of the Lord Christ, and that we also through Christ receive the Holy Ghost and become righteous'' (46.68). From Christ, as the Second Adam and head of the new race, streams into us new life and righteousness, for he dwells and reigns in us (E. 13. 225 f. W. 2. 531, 502, 529). It is only a varied application of this thought, when it is said that the love of Christ begets a responsive love in our hearts (W. 2. 523 ; 6. 117. E. 12. 258 f., 312), or when he is represented as our pattern, or, in the earlier writings, as a "divine legislator'' (W. 1. 533).[2] But in the discussions of Christ as our pattern, we observe a connection between this subjective aspect of redemption and its objective side. To regard Christ merely as an example is papistic and fanatical error (E. 8. 235 f., 248 ; 9. 244 f.; 15. 388 ; 29. 278).[3] "Imitation does not make sons, but sonship makes imitators'' (W. 2. 518. E. 29. 211). We must first accept Christ in faith "as a sacrifice and portion'' and thereby become blessed and righteous, and only then follows "the example and imitation'' (E. 7. 303 f.; 8. 3).[4]

[1] Luther thus ascribes to Christ a representative agency toward men similar to that which he exercises in behalf of men before God. But it must be remembered that the revelation of Christ through the Holy Spirit, being limited to the Word, cannot go essentially beyond the historical revelation made during his earthly life. E. 12. 300, and cf. § 69, 2.

[2] Luther afterward expressly rejects this term, *e. g.*, E. 7. 298 ; 47. 302.

[3] How striking is this remark in view of the history of the *Imitatio Christi*, *e. g.*, supra, p. 178, 179.

[4] Luther often speaks of the *Following of Christ* in the sense of the imitation of him as our pattern, *e. g.*, W. 1. 338, 364, 320, 613, 697 ; 2. 138, 141, 147 f., 151, 501, 747 ; 6. 275 ; 8. 367, 420. E. 29. 11 ; 8. 157, 234, 247, 251 ; 9. 51 ; 11. 52, 171 ; 14. 46 ; 15. 175, 425, 462 ; 17. 41. Only seldom, so far as I can recall, did he designate the "Following'' in the original sense (supra, p. 180, n. 1, cf. E.. 48. 276) expressly as faith (W. 1. 275); but this idea lies at the foundation of his entire conception of the faith obtained in the contemplation of the historical Christ.

(*e*) Reviewing now the work of Christ as thus portrayed, it is evident that, as in the medieval presentations of the subject, the features of that work having relation to man are to be discriminated from those relating to God. Christ reconciled the Father, and he revealed God to us. In the first aspect of his work, all the conceptions of the traditional teaching are preserved, *i. e.*, satisfaction, merit, sacrifice, deliverance from sin, death, hell, devil, etc.[1] Yet it is important to observe that there is here, after all, a certain modification of the thought. Luther's fundamental idea of the subject is as follows: On account of sin, God has placed the race under the law, with its demands and penalties. The relation of man to God is accordingly not to be apprehended in the light of private obligation (law), but in that of public law (supra, p. 267, n. 2). The legal ordinances thus expressing the will of God have not been observed, but their penalties could be borne only by those who were guilty of their violation. To this divine ordinance Christ rendered satisfaction in our stead through his fulfillment of the law and through the endurance of its penalties. Thereby it became possible for God to abrogate the legal ordinance, since his love has now been revealed to men in Christ, renewing them and filling them with the consciousness that they now enjoy his favor (grace).

It is very clear from this that, in Luther's conception, the reconciliation of the Father by Christ precedes the bestowal of grace as its basis. But it is equally true, that there is lacking here, as distinctly as in Thomas or Duns (p. 114 n. 1, 141 n.), any clear explanation of the inner relationship of the two ideas. This could be secured only by showing the reconciliation of the Father to be a necessary means for securing the end in view, *i. e.*, the bestowal of grace. But this Luther never attempts to do. Since the nature of God is love, the revelation of his righteousness (justice) does not abrogate his mercy. The mission of Christ is to be traced back to the divine compassion. But in what connection does the selection of the particular form of Christ's work stand with the end in view? Why does not love directly abolish the ancient ordinance? To this Luther responds: Because God willed that satisfaction must first be rendered to the latter. The mercy of God sends Christ to bring to us the forgiveness of sins, but God wills that it shall first be earned, or merited (*abverdient*), from him through the satisfaction to be rendered by Christ (15. 385 ; 12. 266; 7. 299 f.).[2] It is therefore

---

[1] The "Sermon von der Betrachtung des heil. Leidens Christi," A. D. 1519, W. 2. 136 ff., is peculiarly instructive as displaying the variety of aspects under which Luther could present the sufferings of Christ.

[2] The last of these citations summarizes Luther's view in a classical form:

the will of God—and nothing more can be said—that the bestowal of grace, or the introduction of a new ordinance, shall
follow only upon the ground of the allaying of his wrath through
the satisfaction of the old ordinance.[1] The connection existing
between this two-fold character of the work of Christ and the
duplex nature which we have traced in grace, justification, faith
and sin, is self-evident.

Cf. HELD, De opere Jesu Chr. salutari (Gött., 1860). VON HOFFMAN,
Schutzschriften, ii. 23 ff. TH. HARNACK, L. Theol. 288 ff. GOTTSCHICK,
Propter Christum, Ztschr. f. Theol. u. K., 1897, p. 352 ff.; 1898, 406 ff.

10. The entire Christian life is a repentance. But contrition
is no longer a fruitless self-torture, for it stands in league with
faith. And works are no more attempts to render satisfaction,
for God performs them through faith. This repentance is to fill
the entire life. It takes the place of the discipline once exacted
through the sacrament of repentance. Luther's central ideas
can be understood, as we have shown, only when regarded from
this point of view.

Our study of the new conception of moral works leads us, further, to consider Luther's ideal of life ; and the examination of
his conception of the work of Christ leads to the doctrine of the
Word and Sacraments, and also to that of the Church.

" Although now purely out of grace our sin is non-imputed to us by God, yet
he would nevertheless not do this, unless satisfaction should first be fully and
superfluously rendered to his law and his justice. It was required that such.
gracious imputation should first be purchased and secured for us from his justice.   Therefore, since this was impossible for us, he appointed One for us in
our stead, who should take upon himself all the punishment which we had
merited, and fulfill for us the law, and thus avert from us God's judgment and
reconcile his wrath."   It will be observed how strictly the discussion is here
held to the ideas of law, with its fulfillment and penalties.   The firm relationship here established marks a step in advance which is intimately connected
with Luther's general doctrinal position.   The idea of " superfluous " satisfaction is derived from the Thomistic theology (p. 112, 198).

[1] The influence of Scotist ideas is here unmistakable.   That Christ reconciled the Father was simply because God willed that he should do so.   Only
in this sense could Luther speak of a necessity, and a " must " in connection
with'the atonement (see previous note), just as in Duns and Biel.   But in
other aspects also, if I am correct, Luther's way of regarding the matter is formally parallel with the conceptions of Duns and Biel (vid. supra, p. 157,
200), since in them also the purpose to effectually bestow grace upon men
(through the institution and agency of the sacraments) was associated with the
arbitrarily ordained condition of a previous reconciliation of God through the
merit of Christ.   This historical parallel will explain the peculiar lack of connection between the two aspects of the work of Christ.   To speak of an " absolute necessity " of the atonement as maintained by Luther (Th. Harnack, L.'s
Theol. ii. 304 ff.) is therefore in my opinion misleading.   A solution of the
problem thus stated it is the province of Dogmatics to seek with the most careful study of the Scriptural ideas involved.   The History of Doctrines can only
state the fact, that it is not to be found in the writings of Luther.

§ 68. *The Evangelical Ideal of Life.*

LITERATURE. Cf. RITSCHL, Gesch. d. Pietismus, i. (A. D. 1880), 36 ff. LUTHARDT, Gesch. d. chr. Ethik, ii. (1893), 25 ff. UHLHORN, Die chr. Liebestätigkeit, iii. (1890), 3. ff. EGER, Die Anschauungen Luther's von Beruf., Giessen, 1900. SEEBERG, Luther's Stellung zu den sittlichen und sozialen Nöten seiner Zeit., Leipzig, 1902.

1. The crisis at the close of the Middle Ages was occasioned, not only by the dissolution and practical insufficiency of the "dogma" of the church, but by the conflict between practical life and the church's ideal of what life should be (cf. supra, p. 173, 181 f.). The Reformation achieved by Luther was, accordingly, not a reconstruction of doctrine, but the vigorous enforcement of a new ideal of life. Ritschl has rendered good service in emphasizing this. For the medieval Christian, faith was subjection to the canon law of the church. Sin was located chiefly in the sensual impulses of nature. The natural was essentially evil. Hence, the natural order of human life in the state was the direct contrast to the kingdom of God, or the church. At this point the ideas of Luther entered a mighty protest. He drew the conclusion from the entire previous course of development ; or, more properly speaking, he substituted vigorous Christian ideas for the negations and skepticism, the longings and anticipations of the past. The fourteenth and fifteenth centuries had, it is true, prepared the way for him. But in his spirit criticism became assertion, the unchurchly and secular became churchly and biblical. His criticism did not end in the helpless pusillanimity of Occam, nor in the worldly frivolity or secret qualms of conscience which marked so many of the Humanists. He recognized the right of every man to gain for himself religious conviction, without constraint, and pointed to Christ as the way to its attainment. He taught that, since God created man, his natural impulses and ordinances are in accordance with the will of God. No one need be ashamed of them.[1] He recognized the lawfulness of the natural life and of the civil organism, beholding in them ordinances of God which are not sinful. The natural forms of existing things are not essentially evil, but according to God's will, however men, as Luther never forgets, may continually pollute them.

2. From this point of view we may understand his demolition of the medieval ideals both in the sphere of individual life and

---

[1] *E. g.*, E. 10. 440: Dear lad, be not ashamed that you long for a maid, and the maid longs for a lad. Only let it lead to marriage and not to wantonness, and it is then no disgrace to you, just as little as eating and drinking are a disgrace. Cf. 29. 39 ; 28. 199, but also E. 22. 205.

18

in that of the state. The ethics of the desensualizing theory beheld the "state of perfection" in the life of the *religiosi, i. e.*, the monks (p. 124). Luther saw therein only a self-chosen and, in the deepest sense, ungodly sanctity (E. 28. 231). This is not Christian perfection (W. 8. 328. E. 9. 287; 7. 321; 8. 13; 12. 227). Good works, as they are performed either in accordance with the so-called "evangelical counsels" (*consilia evangelica*), which come from the devil (W. 8. 585. E. 22. 65), or in pursuance of the sacrament of repentance (W. 6. 207, 208, 209, 210 f., 212; 8. 366, 378. E. 7. 245; 10. 234, 273; 13. 208, 217 f.), are not good works pleasing to God; for they neither result from the free inner impulse of the heart, nor do they benefit anyone. "It is most shamefully repugnant and contrary, not only to the word of God, faith, Christian liberty, and the precepts of God, but to thee thyself" (W. 8. 639, 605, 616. E. 10. 425; 29. 39). The marks of really good works (p. 259) are wanting in these, *i. e.*, the impulse from within, or freedom; the divine commandment; and usefulness. It is better to rear one's children well than to make pilgrimages or build churches (W. 2. 169 f.). And since these works are unnatural, the pursuit of them bears bitter fruit, as may be seen in all those who have taken the (monastic) vows; for example, in the "unchaste chastity" of the monks (E. 29. 17, 327; 10. 426). This is one objection which Luther constantly presents against the Romish ideal of life: its works are unnatural and purely legalistic. And just because they are so, they are regarded as "meritorious," which forms his second ground of objection to them. But, as these works are rejected, there remains no place for the "saints." Whatever in them was good, was wrought by God (W. 1. 420). They have had no power to render satisfaction even for themselves (ib. 606). There are no superfluous (*überlängliche*) works (*opera supererogationis*, E. 14. 35).

3. In the sphere of civil life, also, the rightfulness of the natural order is to be recognized as in accordance with the will of God. "The secular law and sword" exist in accordance with the divine ordinance (E. 22. 63, 76), for they are necessary for the world (73). Hence the Christian may with a good conscience hold a civil office (73, 80), provided he can thus benefit his neighbor (78).[1] This is especially true of the "Christian prince." "Service" is his calling (94 ff.). But, essentially,

---

[1] This is true even of war: "What else is war than a punishing of wrong and evil? Why does anyone go to war, except because he desires to have peace and obedience?" (23. 249. Cf. 16. 195). From this we may understand Luther's attitude toward the "thieving and murderous peasants."

the civil government has to do only with the outward conduct of
men (87), whereas Christ reigns only in the hearts of men by his
Spirit (E. 22. 70). In the duty resting upon the government
is included a solicitude for culture and education (schools), as
well as for social conditions. But "the secular government has
laws which do not extend further than over body and property
and what is outward in the world. For over the souls of men
God cannot and will not allow anyone but himself alone to rule.
Therefore in matters which have to do with the salvation of
souls, nothing but God's word must be taught or accepted (22.
82, 83, 86; 45. 115). Thus the boundary line of the civil
authority and the rights of liberty of conscience are preserved.[1]
(Cf. LEZIUS, Gleichheit u. Ungleichheit, in Greifswalder Studien,
1895, p. 287 ff. WARD, Darstellung . . . der Ansichten
Luther's vom Staat u. seinen wirtschaftlichen Aufgaben, 1898.)

4. The State of Perfection (*status perfectionis*) is to be (possessed) of a living faith, a despiser of death, of life, of glory,
and of the whole world, a servant of all in fervent love (W. 8.
584). Faith and love (or works) are the content of the
Christian life. "Now faith and love are the whole life of a
Christian man. . . . *Faith receives, love gives* " (W. 8. 355,
362, 366, 385 f. E. 7. 159, 161; 8. 40, 71, 75; 9. 280 f.,
137; 10. 20; 46. 254). "Thus faith remains the doer and
love remains the deed" (E. 8. 63). "Faith brings man to
God; love brings God to men. Through faith man allows God to
do him good; through love God does good to men (E. 14. 40).
But all this is not to be required by compulsion or law. The
Christian life is a life of freedom, since the good is wrought in
the heart by God and is done with delight. Hence no commandments have validity here. This is "evangelical," or
"Christian liberty," or "the liberty of faith."[2] The law is
valid only for the outward man (vid. supra, 3), where it is necessary, particularly for the rude "Lord Omnes" (E. 24. 140 f.).
These ideas are grandly developed in the tract, *Von der Freiheit
eines Christenmenschen*. Through faith the Christian becomes a
free lord of all things. In faith he lays hold upon the man

---

[1] But Luther places the law of nature (cf., p. 171) above the "written law
or the counsels of the jurists:" "The highest law and master of all laws
remains the reason" (E. 22. 95, 257). "Such free judgment does love pronounce, and natural law, of which all reason is full" (ib. 104).

[2] *E. g.*, W. 1. 530, 647, 675; 2. 486; 8. 327, 330, 334. E. 10. 425;
12. 363 f.; 29. 188 f., etc. The pope and the fanatics, according to Luther,
destroy this liberty; the former by commandments, the latter by prohibitions
(29. 189). Against Carlstadt he formulated the practical canon, "that
everything should be free which God does not in clear language forbid in the
New Testament" (29. 188).

Christ, and the righteousness of the bridegroom becomes a property also of the bride, the soul (E. 27. 183). Again, the soul through faith is filled with all goodness (181), so that it needs no law nor commandment. Hereby the Christian is made free. Since he does good with inward heartfelt delight, because the word of Christ dwells in his soul, he does not require the demands of the law. Is God now his in faith, there is thereby given to him the certainty that all things must work together for his good (185), as he has now, on the other hand, to appear before God in intercession for others. Thus the Christian is a king and a priest. "Through his kingship, he has power over all things; through his priesthood, he has power over God" (186). But the Christian must also "govern his own body and associate with his fellow-men." This requires a disciplining and exercising of the body, that it may become obedient and conformable to the inner man.[1] But faith is an inward appreciation of the benefits of God, and hence begets the inner impulse to do what will please God, *i. e.*, to serve one's neighbor. "There thus flow from faith, love and desire toward God; and from love, a free, willing, joyous life of service of one's neighbor" (196). These are the true good works, as they flow forth freely from the heart and bring good to others. "For whatever work is not designed to serve another . . . is not a good Christian work" (198). Thus the Christian is through faith a free lord, and through love a ministering servant.

These remained controlling principles with Luther. Faith is the acceptance (*Hinnahme*) of God and his benefits. These so overpower our hearts that—and also through the Holy Spirit (E. 19. 376)—there follows a self-surrender (*Hingabe*) to God, as a "great fervent love" to him (E. 14. 4). But this love leads us with inward desire to subject ourselves to the will of God (E. 7. 161). And thus out of love to God arises love to our neighbor (W. 8. 386. E. 14. 34, 46; 28. 207; 9. 284). Love is accordingly defined as the will to do good : "Love is nothing but simply to do good and to be useful to all men, friends and foes" (W. 8. 362). "But to love is from the heart to wish good to another" (W. 2. 604).[2] Thus all love is *service*, and the Christian's whole life is a service for God and his brethren (W. 2. 148; 8. 360 f., 367). We know that we were created

---

[1] These ideas produce a complete transformation as to the province of ascetic exercises. These are not a self-mortification nor a meritorious work, but the disciplining and exercise of the natural powers, which they thus make fit agencies for the accomplishment of good in the Christian sense. See R. SEEBERG, Askese, PRE. ii., ed. 3, 138 f.

[2] With this definition compare p. 107.

for the sake of others (E. 8. 263), and that we are instruments
in the hand of Christ (12. 365). But such service can be rendered only by really good works, such as we may learn from the
Ten Commandments, and not by the self-chosen Romish works
(E. 9. 287 ; 10. 411 f.; 11. 318; 13. 159). These are the
works which belong to the natural course of life, in which we
should manifest toward our fellow-men "love, humility, patience,
gentleness" (E. 9. 287, 289 f.). This we should do, furthermore, each in his own particular calling : "serve God in his
calling and thank him that he uses him also in his position in life
as an instrument" (9. 290). The moral equality of all callings,
even the lowest, is continually assumed (e. g., E. 7. 228 ; 10.
233 ff.; 8. 259 f.; 16. 137 ; 17. 258 ; 18. 85 ; 19. 337, 352 f.;
30. 367 ; 48. 273). To serve God in the forms of the natural
life and calling by the humble service of love toward the brethren
—such is the appointed task of the Christian's life. But the
power for such service springs from faith, or from God.

But this is also the path to a realization of the Kingdom of
God. This term has in Luther a two-fold significance. On the
one hand, it indicates the dominion which Christ exercises in
begetting faith and life through the word and granting the forgiveness of sins (E. 14. 181 f., cf. supra, p. 266; 21. 115 ; 14.
238 f., 240, 251 ; 18. 234 ; 39. 34 f.; 15. 21 f.; 12. 2 f.; 51.
181 ; 34. 26 : "Christ's kingdom must on earth rule in our
hearts"). On the other hand, it signifies the sphere in which
this dominion is exercised, or mankind, in so far as they place all
that they do or can do at the service of God (W. 2. 97 ; 22.
166). Hence, all virtues in their fullness are combined in this
kingdom : "The kingdom of God is nothing else than to be
pious, orderly, pure, kind, gentle, benevolent and full of all
virtue and graces ; also, that God have his being within us and
that he alone be, live, and reign in us. This we should first of
all and most earnestly desire" (W. 2. 98). Since Christ exercises his dominion upon us, we become and grow to be members
of his kingdom.[1]

This is what is meant by true evangelical perfection in the
sense of Luther. But it is not to be thought of as a completed
attainment, but as a continual striving. This is true of faith,
which maintains itself amid all manner of assaults, so that it be-

---

[1] The term "kingdom" in Luther, as in the New Testament, very often
(e. g., E. 4. 356 ; 23. 311 ; 18. 233 ; 15. 21 ; 29. 295) signifies "dominion."
He always, as do the Scriptures, thinks of it as in close association with its
Ruler (e. g., 2. 95). It is the result of the work of Christ in the world. In
this sense, it is a purely religious conception ; but, since men strive with all their
power for its realization, it is also the supreme ethical ideal.

comes " tried and experienced faith " (W. 8. 378. E. 14. 52).
The same is to be said also of the entire scope of the inner life :
" It is and remains upon earth only a beginning and increasing,
which will be completed in yonder world " (E. 27. 188). This
ideal of life eradicates the ancient disposition, imbibed from
Hellenism, to flee from the world. It makes possible a life of
active interest in the duties of the natural life and secular vocation, yet in perfect consistency with the most profound religious
experience.

5. The recognition of the validity and independence of the
natural life awakened in Luther the desire to see civil and social
affairs regulated by the principles properly underlying them.
The dispute between the peasants and the nobility had to do, it
appeared to him, with purely secular affairs (E. 24. 283, 277 f.).
The gospel neither advocates communism (ib. 291), nor does it
abolish feudal service (281). The peasants may be never so
clearly in the right, yet let them not press their legal claims in
the Christian name (273). " In the name of the gospel " they
act against the gospel (275). The social question of the age
was accordingly in his view not an ecclesiastical, but a natural
and civil one.[1] But it by no means follows that the church has
nothing to do with this question and its solution. How little
such an idea would harmonize with Luther's meaning[2] is evident
from his broad program of reform, as seen in his Address to the
Nobility, and in his energetic discussion of social problems,
as in his "*Zinskauf*" and "*Kaufhandlung und Wucher.*" But
as the Address is dedicated, not to the church, but to the nobility,
so for himself Luther declined to assume responsibility for the
solution of the technical questions involved.[3] The church calls
attention to the abuses, demands that they be corrected, and
gives her counsel and encouragement to that end ;[4] but to the
state, *i. e.*, to the social organization, belongs the execution of
the task. This is, briefly stated, Luther's attitude upon such
questions.

[1] The peasants claimed to be "a Christian mob or union," "Christian
brothers" (24. 265, 290), and on that ground claim for themselves "divine
right" (265) and "evangelical liberty" (270). These terms had for them the
genuine medieval significance, supra, p. 171, 182.

[2] We must here let the " whole Luther" be heard, which will at least not
be "unlutheran."

[3] *E. g.*, W. 6. 6 : "But it is no part of my work to announce whether five,
four, or six per cent. is to be paid. I leave it to the decision of the laws, so
that where the ground is so good and rich, six per cent. may be taken."

[4] DILTHEY, Arch. f. Gesch. d. Philos. v. 366, rightly says : In the name
of the new Christian spirit, Luther demands a reorganization of German society
in its secular and ecclesiastical ordinances.

Cf. Schmoller, Zur. Gesch. d. nat.-ök. Ansichten in d. Ref.-zeit, in Ztschr. f. d. ges. Staatswiss, 1860, 461 ff. Erhardt, Die nat.-ök. Ansichten d. Ref., in Stud. u. Krit., 1880, 672 ff. Also, Braasch, L. Stellung z. Sozialism., 1897. W. Köhler, Die Quellen z. L. Schrift an den Adel., 1895. Seeberg, Luther's Stellung z. u. den sittlichen u. sozialen Nöten s. Zeit., 1902.

§ 69. *Word and Sacrament.*

1. In the religious processes depicted in § 67, a personal influence is exerted by God upon the human heart. It is in keeping with a true conception of the nature of man in its sensuous and social features, that Luther does not conceive of such influence as mystical and direct.[1] In order to win the hearts of men, God makes use of elements of this world and its history ; of Christ and the word which testifies of him ; as also of the sacraments instituted by him. Only through Word and Sacrament[2] does the Spirit, operating upon the heart (*intus operans*), come to us (W. 1. 632 ; 2. 112. E. 29. 208 ; 9. 210 ; 11. 223).[3] Through these are mediated the great chief miracles, which Christ performs upon the soul, and which are far greater than the bodily miracles which he wrought (E. 16. 190 ; cf. 58. 95 ; 59. 3). This view was confirmed and deepened, particularly in the conflict with the "fanatics."

2. But before the outbreak of the fanatical movement, Luther's doctrine was firmly established in its essential features. In the word alone does God work in the hearts of men : "The word alone is the vehicle of grace." Therefore man should hear the word and meditate upon what he has heard (W. 2. 509, 95, 112, 453 ; 1. 698). Only in this form can we apprehend Christ : "He is of no benefit to thee and thou canst not know anything about him, unless *God put him into words*, that thou mayst hear and thus learn to know him" (W. 2. 213). Luther discriminates here, however, between the "inward" and the "outward" word. Yet the two are closely associated : "But when the outward goes rightly, the inward does not fail to appear ; for God never suffers his word to go forth without (bringing) fruit. He is with it, and himself teaches inwardly

---

[1] The mystical way in which Augustine rings the changes upon the theme : "God and the soul," is not characteristic of Luther. His praise is given to faith : "For the two belong together, faith and God" (Müller, Symb. Book, 386, 388. E. 49. 20). But this faith is wrought by the Word, and its content is the God revealed in Christ.

[2] See the association of the two in Augustine, Vol. I., p. 320 f.

[3] Word and sacrament, according to Luther, differ in the fact, that the former is addressed to the church at large, the latter specifically to the individual (E. 29. 345 ; 11. 157 f.).

what he gives outwardly through the priest " (ib. 112). The
words of the priest are, accordingly, accompanied with an inner
working of God upon the heart.

From the beginning of the third decade of the sixteenth
century, there was an energetic effort in both Germany and
Switzerland to carry forward and complete the evangelical
reformation by exalting mystic and ascetic ideals.   The pro-
moters of the movement were representatives of the mystical
piety of the closing Middle Ages, with which they not infrequently combined apocalyptic visions or socialistic principles.
The " Imitation of Christ " with a " sensible tasting of his sufferings," the " divesting self of material things," the " becoming naked and barren of all created things," the " righteousness
of dying to the world," "the righteousness of the Spirit,"
the " inward call," the " heavenly voice," the " inner word," the
" tedium," and the " reformation " of the Christian world into
a " congregation of saints,"—such are the watchwords of this
party.   But, above all, they held that no importance attached
to an external ecclesiasticism, or to the outward word and sacraments.   The " Spirit " does everything, and has no need of
infant baptism or the " bodily " word.[1]   This agitation has importance for the History of Doctrines, because it gave occasion
(Zwickau prophets, Carlstadt, Münzer) to Luther to verify and
deepen his doctrine touching the word.

In opposition to the idea of a direct operation of the Spirit,
Luther maintains: " Since now God has sent forth his holy
gospel, he deals with us in two ways: first, outwardly, and
secondly, inwardly.   He deals with us outwardly through the
spoken word of the gospel and through bodily signs, such as
baptism and sacrament.   Inwardly, he deals with us through the
Holy Spirit and faith, together with other gifts; but all this in

---

[1] Luther describes these religious theories very thoroughly in his publication, *Wider die himmlischen Propheten, e. g.*, 29. 138, 146, 152, 173, 177,
180, 168, 160, 278, 285, 295, 177, 209 f.   Cf. H. LÜDEMANN, Reformation
and Taüfertum, Bern, 1896. . . . The "inner word" may be thought of as
accompanying the outer word (thus Augustine, and at first Luther).   It may
also be conceived as a direct speaking of God to the soul, which was the idea
of the Fanatics (*e. g.*, DENK, Stud. u. Krit., 1851, 177, 184, cf. 131.   SEB.
FRANCK, in Hegler, Geist u. Schrift in S. F., 1892, p. 83 ff.).   It may be
understood therefore as the innate intuition of reason, or as the Conscience :
"The conscience, which is the Godhead and Christ himself, who now dwells
in our hearts, understands and decides what is evil and what is good " (TH.
THAMER, vid. Neander, Thamer, 1842, p. 27, 24 f., 26 f., 28, 29, 38 f.,
cf. 47).   It is interesting to observe that Seb. Franck regards the idea of communism as a part of man's inherited moral endowment (HEGLER, p. 92).   Cf.
supra, p. 183.   Upon the entire question, vid. R. GRUTZMACHER, Wort und
Geist, 1902.

the manner and order, that the *outward part shall and must precede, and the inward come afterward and through the outward*, so that he has *determined* to give the inward part to no man except through the outward part" (E. 29. 208; 47. 391; 49. 86). "In the same word comes the Spirit and gives faith where and to whom he will" (29. 212). From this time, Luther never ceased to lay emphasis upon this point. Where the word is, there are Christ and the Spirit (9. 275, 229, 236; 11. 35; 14. 326; 47. 57, 198, 221 f.). The Spirit himself "speaks to the heart" and "impresses" the word upon the heart of the hearers. He "touches and moves the heart" (9. 232, 274; 13. 184, 286; 8. 308; 11. 206; 28. 298: 47. 353 f.).

The relation of the outward word to the divine operation accompanying it is explained by Luther in various ways. The Spirit enlightens "with and through the word" (14. 188). The power of God is "with it and under it" (11. 131). Of the Spirit it is to be said, that he is given "through the word and with the word external and preceding" (Smalc. Art., Müller, 321), and that he "comes with and through the word, and goes no further than so far as the word goes" (12. 300). The Holy Spirit therefore teaches nothing else and nothing more than what the words "which pass out of the mouth of Christ from one mouth to another" contain (ib.). He does not enlarge the sphere of revelation, but he with divine power adapts the revelation made to the individual and his needs. Luther discriminates therefore the purely human operation of the word from the resultant operation of the Holy Spirit "in," "with and through," "with and under" the word,[1] but in such a way that the latter occurs absolutely only through the former.[2]

---

[1] E. 18. 38 : "Along with this preaching office, God is present, and through the spoken word touches to-day this heart, to-morrow that heart. All preachers are nothing more than the hand which points out the way, which does no more than stand still and allow (us) to follow or not to follow the right path. . . . They are not the persons whose duty it is to make anyone pious. God alone does that."

[2] These formulas display an interesting parallel to those upon the Lord's Supper. Viewed in detail, the matter is not perfectly clear. Luther began with Augustinian differentiation of the outward and the inward word, but he modified it by positing a fixed connection between the two. For this the Scotist theory of the sacraments appears to have originally furnished the suggestion. God has "determined" (29. 208) that wherever the word goes, a divine influence shall accompany it. Vid. also 45. 215 f.: "No one can rightly *understand God according to the Word of God* unless he receives it [*i. e.*, this ability] immediately from the Holy Spirit. But no one can have it from the Holy Spirit, unless he experiences it, tries it, and feels it (*er erfahr es, vorsuchs una empfinds denn*); and in this experience the Holy Spirit teaches as in his own school, outside of which nothing is taught but appearances, words, and idle prattle."

Medieval theology constructed the doctrine of the sacraments. Luther was the first to frame a doctrine of the Word of God.[1] Of the Bible, we shall speak in another connection.[2] Cf. R. Grutzmacher, Wort und Geist, 1902, 9. 8 ff.

3. As to the general conception of the nature of the sacraments, it is to be observed, that Luther started with the Scotist idea, that the sacraments are efficacious signs (*efficacia signa*) of grace (W. 1. 595). But this is modified by placing them in the most intimate association with faith. Their effectual operation depends upon faith (ib.). They are " signs which help and incite to faith . . . without which faith, they are of no benefit " (W. 2. 686, 693). " And it depends altogether upon faith, which alone brings it to pass that the sacraments effect what they signify" (2. 715; 6. 24). The sacraments are symbols which awaken faith, and thus promise grace to all, but confer it only upon believers (6. 86). The sacrament is a sign : " That is, it is external, and yet has and signifies something spiritual, in order that we may through the external be drawn to the spiritual " (6. 359). In this, Luther has fallen back upon the Augustinian conception. The sacrament is a symbolic transaction, which brings to the believer that which it outwardly signifies. This idea meets us also later, but with the modifications, that the sacrament gives something also to the unbeliever, and that great stress is laid upon the fact that there is a real influence exerted. But, in and of itself, it is, even at later periods, spoken of as an "outward sign," as a "seal or signet ring " (E. 12. 178 f.; 16. 48, 50, 52). In the tract, *De captivitate Babylonica* (A. D. 1520), Luther sharply criticises the Romish doctrine of the sacraments. Of four of the seven sacraments, he asserts that the Scriptures know nothing at all. There remain only three (baptism, the Lord's Supper, and repentance), although, strictly speaking, even repentance dare not be described as a sacrament (W. 6. 549, 572).[3] It therefore gradually became customary—repentance having now entirely lost its sacramental

---

[1] The " Word of God " is for Luther primarily the oral proclamation, since through this God operates upon the heart. But this operation occurs only when such proclamation is in content a presentation of the biblical revelation ; *E. g.*, W. 1. 391. E. 9. 230; 36. 197 ; 46. 240; 65. 170; 3. 347.

[2] Due attention should be given at this point to the ideas formulated at about this time ; that the reformation is to be effected not by violent means, but through the proclamation of the word (E. 28. 217 f., 219, 221, 227 f., 308, 310); that outward customs may be retained (28. 237); and that in such matters the rabble (Pofel) is not to have the deciding voice (29. 160, 162 f., 166 f., 206, 226).

[3] In A. D. 1519, he already calls them the two chief (*furnemliche*) sacraments, W. 2. 754.

character—to count only two sacraments (E. 28. 418 ; 29. 208 ; 12. 179).

But the general definition is here of little importance. As, from the time of Duns, the theory of the Lord's Supper did not fit into the general definition of a sacrament, but was carried along independently (supra, p. 131 n.), so was it likewise with Luther, particularly in the case of the Lord's Supper, but also noticeably in the case of baptism. We must therefore treat directly of the two sacraments in turn.

4. Luther presents a connected view of his theory of baptism in the *Sermon von dem heiligen, hochwürdigen Sakrament der Taufe* (A. D. 1519). The sign is to be distinguished from the signification (*Bedeutung*) of baptism. The latter consists in (1) The duty of dying to sin ; for by baptism a sentence of death is pronounced upon the natural man : "Therefore drown thyself in the name of God." Thus a blessed dying begins with baptism (W. 2. 728). (2) The "spiritual birth." This, like the "increase of grace and righteousness," "begins in baptism, but continues also until death" (ib.)—on the ground that God through baptism contracts a covenant with man, from which result both regeneration and the forgiveness of sins, so that both are continuous : "and begins from that hour to renew thee, pours into thee his grace and Holy Spirit, who begins to crucify the nature and sin" (730). Sin yet remains in man (728) ; but, since God considers it as in principle shattered, he does not thereafter impute it to the sinner : "will not look upon it nor condemn thee for it, is satisfied in regard to it, and is pleased that thou art thyself continually desiring and attempting to slay it" (731). In this fact, that God has "bound" himself no longer to impute sin to the baptized, lies the peculiar consolation of baptism (732, 733). It is here evident that the theory of baptism harmonizes precisely with the original view of justification through the word : regeneration and, in connection with it, the forgiveness of sins (cf. p. 260 f.).

This remained essentially the view of Luther, except that, at a later period, just as in the case of justification, forgiveness is no longer so closely associated with the—divinely wrought—renewal. In baptism, the triune God is present ; the Holy Spirit being particularly operative (E. 19. 76). The word and will of God make it what it is, so that it is not merely a "sign" (Large Catechism, Müller, Symb. Bb. 495, 487 f., 489. "Baptism is united with and confirmed by the divine word and appointment)."[1] It thus secures an "admission to all divine blessings" (E. 22. 165. W. 2. 746).

---

[1] But, on the other hand, baptism is still "nothing more than an outward

This involves two things. (*a*) The Holy Spirit through baptism effects regeneration. It is "a spiritually-rich water, in which the Holy Spirit is, and in which he works; yea, the entire holy Trinity is present, and the man who is baptized is then called regenerated" (E. 46. 266; 16. 69, 74; 29. 341).[1] Thus the heart is washed clean (8. 226), the whole nature transformed (7. 169), the Spirit granted (Cat. 493), grace "infused" (12. 387. W. 2. 168). But since baptism is an act but once performed, it assures of the continuous readiness of God to renew the sinner : "Therefore baptism also remains always, and thou canst not be so far nor so deeply fallen from it but that thou couldst and shouldst again hold fast to it" (E. 16. 99). With this continual renewal, proceeding from God, are given also the impulse and the obligation to constantly renew ourselves. The slaying of the old Adam and the arising of the new man is the duty of the baptized, "so that Christian life is nothing else than a kind of daily baptism" (Cat. 495, 496, 498. E. 16. 103). In baptism is involved the duty of making the whole Christian life a repentance (Cat. 496 f.).[2]

This is one aspect of baptism. But, despite the renewal thus effected, our life remains sinful, and original sin is still operative.

(*b*) The second blessing which the baptismal covenant carries with it is the certainty that God is ever ready to *forgive us our sins*. "They are all forgiven through grace, but not yet all healed through the gift" (W. 8. 107, 57, 88, 93; 2. 160, 415. E. 15. 50; 16. 141). God has in baptism embraced us and laid us upon his bosom (E. 13. 38); all sins are now and shall be forgiven us. Hence, the sinner should ever anew "creep to (his) baptism" (E. 16. 119. Cat. 492). This sign has been given us by God, to assure us that he will through Christ be gracious to us (E. 12. 163, 205), and that we are really admitted to a place beneath his sway and "incorporated" into his kingdom (12. 212). This means, in the sense of Luther, nothing else than that we, by virtue of our fellowship with Christ, al-

sign, that is to admonish us of the divine promise. If we can have it, it is well. . . . But if anyone could not have it, or if it were denied to him, he is nevertheless not lost, if he only believes the gospel. . . . Therefore he who has the sign, which we call sacrament, and not faith, has a bare seal attached to a letter without any writing in it " (E. 12. 179).

[1] "At an earlier period the Scotist foundation underlying the conception of the sacrament was more evident : That the priest pours upon the child, signifies the holy, divine, and eternal grace which is together with this (*do neben*) poured into the soul" (W. 2. 168).

[2] "Thus *resipiscentia*, or repentance, is nothing else than a sort of retracing of the steps and return to baptism, so that that is again sought and practiced which was indeed before begun and yet through negligence intermitted" (Cat. 497).

ways experience the forgiveness of sins and renewal to a better life.

In Luther's view, baptism has thus a double blessing, or effect. God enters into a covenant relationship with the baptized, which signifies : (1) That the Holy Spirit is always present and operative for his renewal.[1] (2) That he always finds God ready to forgive him his sins for Christ's sake. Baptism therefore brings : "namely, victory over death and the devil, remission of sins, the grace of God, Christ with his works, and the Holy Spirit with all his gifts" (Cat. 491). But, since only the believer is capable of enjoying such experiences, it is to be believed that God in some way endows infants brought for baptism with faith, on account of the believing presentation of them and the prayer offered in their behalf by their sponsors (*e. g.*, De W. 2. 126, 202. W. 6. 538. E. 28. 416; 11. 62 ff.; 26. 255 ff. Cat. 494).[2]

These are the leading principles of Luther's doctrine of baptism. We meet in them precisely the same ideas already found in the discussions of grace and justification. In a certain sense, his doctrine of baptism is therefore a complement to his doctrine of the grace operative in the word. Baptism both begets a disposition to yield to the influences exerted by the word, and it accompanies and individualizes those influences.

5. Luther's doctrine of the Lord's Supper, in the form which it assumed through the conflict with Zwingli, will require attention hereafter. We have now to do with his view of the sacrament before the outbreak of the controversy. We take as a starting-point the tract : *Ein Sermon von der hochw. Sacrament des Leichnams Christi u. von den Bruderschaften* (A. D. 1519). The "meaning or work" of the sacrament is here said to be "*com-*

---

[1] Of the highest importance upon this point is the remark, E. 12. 215 f.: "Where the word goes and is heard and baptism is desired, there it is commanded to administer baptism to both old and young. For where the word as the chief part goes right, there everything else goes right also ; where the word or teaching is not right, there is the other also in vain, for neither faith nor Christ is there."

[2] Luther accordingly does not think here of a "vicarious faith" of the sponsors. "The faith of the sponsors and the church implores and obtains for them personal faith, in which they are baptized and believe for themselves" (11. 63). The lack of reason in the child does not, to Luther's mind, make against the possibility, that they may have faith, as it is just reason "which chiefly resists faith and the word of God" (11. 65 f.). But is such faith in any way psychologically conceivable? See KÖSTLIN, L. Theol. ii., ed. 2, 237 ff., where my view is inaccurately stated. With respect to infants dying unbaptized, Luther afterward said that they are "without doubt admitted to grace by him" (God) on account of the intercession of parents and sponsors (E. 3. 166 ; 23. 340).

munio.'' It establishes a fellowship with Christ and all saints in heaven and on earth, so that all blessings, sufferings, and sins become common to all. Accordingly, the communicant may console himself with the merit of Christ, and his representation of and intercession for the saints above and the church on earth (W. 2. 743, 744): "That we here lay aside from us all misery and distress upon the church (*gemeyn*), and particularly upon Christ'' (745). But we are ourselves also obligated by this *communio* to render to others the service which we here enjoy: "Thou must . . . learn, as this sacrament is a sacrament of love, and as love and help have come to thee, to show love and help in return to Christ in his needy followers. For here must thou grieve for all the dishonor of Christ in his holy word, all the misery of the church, all unjust sufferings of the innocent . . . here must thou protect, act, and pray, and if thou canst do no more, have pity. . . . Behold, thus thou bearest them all, and thus do they all bear thee again, and all things are common—good and evil'' (745, 747). The fellowship thus effected by the Lord's Supper is symbolized in the bread and wine, composed of many grains and separate grapes, and in the fact that we eat and drink the bread and wine and thus transform them within our bodies that they become one thing with us. It is taught, further, that this sign is a "perfect" one, viz.: "his true natural flesh *in the bread*,'' since "the bread is changed (*verwandelt*) into his true natural body, and the wine into his natural true blood'' (749). In reply to the question, "where the bread remains, when it is changed into the body of Christ,'' Luther warns against "subtlety.'' "It is enough that thou knowest that it is a divine sign, in which Christ's flesh and blood are truly present—how and where, commit to him'' (750).[1]

But Luther's interest centres in this bodily presence of Christ only in view of the conviction that "Christ has given his body, in order that the meaning of the sacrament, *i. e.*, fellowship and the interchange of love, might be practiced, and he esteems less highly his own natural body than his spiritual body,'' *i. e.*, the fellowship of his saints. Hence the communicant should fix his mind more upon the spiritual body of Christ than upon the natural body, for the latter without the former would be of no benefit (751). The presence of the body of Christ in the Lord's Supper is therefore designed to remind us that he surrendered this body in order that a fellowship of love might be established. We shall meet this idea again.

[1] Literally, transubstantiation is here retained (cf. W. 8. 435), but really Luther is only concerned to hold fast the idea that the body is "in" the bread.

The presence of the body of Christ in the Lord's Supper was thus the fixed belief of Luther from the first. Its denial he regarded as a Hussite heresy (W. 6. 80). But from A. D. 1520, he expressly rejected transubstantiation. It is a Thomistic fiction, that only the accidents of the bread and wine are preserved, but not the substance. It is refuted by eyesight. Luther now, appealing to D'Ailli (supra, p. 204), adopts the view prevalent in theology since Duns and Occam (p. 131 n., 203), that the substance of the bread remains, and with it the body of Christ is at the same time given (W. 6. 508. E. 28. 366 ff.).[1] Bread and wine are signs, "under which is truly Christ's flesh and blood" (W. 6. 365, cf. *sub pane et vino*, W. 8. 440 ; *im Brot*, E. 29. 336). The significance of this presence of the body of Christ consists in the fact, that it is "a powerful and most noble seal and sign" (W. 6. 359. E. 28. 412 ; 29. 350 ; 22. 40): That is, the presence of the body of Christ attests and confirms the grace of God, for it was this body which was offered up to obtain grace for us. "In order that this divine promise might be for us the most certain of all and might render our faith most secure, he appended the most faithful and most precious pledge and seal of all, viz., the very price of the promise itself, his own body and blood with the bread and wine, by which he has merited that the blessings of the promise be given to us, which he paid also in order that we might receive the promise" (W. 8. 440 ; 6. 230, 358. E. 22. 40 ; 29. 350). Luther's meaning is : The body of Christ, as it is symbolized by the bread and really present in it, is by its presence the clearest evidence of the grace of God toward us. It does not occur to him to doubt the bodily presence,[2] but its significance consists alone in deepening the impression of the word. This is the important thing, and the believer may even do without the sacrament (W. 6. 355 f., 362, 363. E. 22. 39 f.). As the sacrament can be received with benefit only by him who believes in the atonement and intercession of Christ (E. 28. 240), its blessing consists in the fact, that we therein "remember" Christ and are thereby "strengthened in faith" and "made ardent in love" (W. 6. 358 ; 8. 437. E. 22. 40 ; 28. 240). This strengthening of faith, together with the gift of the body of Christ will-

---

[1] His condemnation of transubstantiation is here a mild one, provided that doctrine be not made an article of faith (W. 6. 508). "No great importance attaches to this error, if only the body and blood of Christ are left, together with the word." (A. D. 1523. E. 28. 402.)

[2] The idea of a purely symbolical interpretation occurred to him indeed : "because I saw well that I could thereby have given the pope the greatest thump." De W. 2. 577.

ingly given to death for our sins, assures us of the forgiveness of sins (E. 29. 347 f.). Nothing is here made to depend upon the *eating* of the body. The consciousness of the bodily presence[1] of the Lord increases within us faith in (the offered) grace, and thus produces the assurance of the forgiveness of sins. On the other hand, the fellowship into which he here enters with us is for us the most powerful incentive to serve him and our brethren in love (E. 29. 351). "You have two fruits of the holy sacrament: one is, that it makes us brethren and fellow-heirs of the Lord Christ, so that from him and us one loaf results; the other, that we also become common and one with all other believers . . . and are also one loaf" (E. 11. 186. Vid. also W. 19. 96, 99).

This is Luther's original doctrine of the Lord's Supper.[2] The most profound impulses of his religious consciousness contributed to its formulation, *i. e.*, the Christ in us, who becomes ours only by virtue of the apprehension of his historical character, and the summing up of all the results of his activity in the forgiveness of sins, faith, and love.

It was not until A. D. 1522 that Luther was confronted with a new problem. He learned from certain Bohemian Brethren, that they regarded the bread and wine as bare symbols (cf. Wickliffe, supra, p. 206). At the same time, HONIUS of Holland laid before him by letter the interpretation of the *Est* in the words of institution, as equivalent to *significat*. Then appeared CARLSTADT with his strange idea, that the "This" of the words of institution relates to the body of Christ, while the "Take" and the "Eat in remembrance of me" refer to the bread. These suggestions opened up new questions for Luther. The relation of the body to the elements, and the exegesis of the words of institution, claim the chief attention. From this time forward, he calls for a simple adherence to the words of Scripture (E. 28. 412 f.; 29. 329, 321, 216, 331); when the Bible says "is," we dare not interpret it as meaning "signifies" (28. 393, 396, 398). But the bodily omnipresence of the Lord is not to be disputed, as he does not travel up and down between heaven and earth (29. 289, 293 f.).

Luther, as we have seen, never denied the real presence of the body of Christ in the Lord's Supper. But as the question of the

---

[1] E. 11. 187: "If I believe that his body and blood are mine, then I have the Lord Christ entire, and everything that he is able to accomplish." According to this and the above, a *personal* presence and fellowship of Christ is also to be maintained. On the other hand, Luther rejected (28. 412) speculation upon the concomitance of the divine nature (supra, p. 132), and discriminated between the presence of the body and that "of the entire Christ, *i. e.*, of his kingdom (lordship)" (29. 295).

[2] What practical applications may be made of these ideas!

"How" of that presence now comes to the front, he is led to ascribe to it a greater and independent significance. Whereas the body was originally only a means of realizing the sacramental gift, it afterward comes to be regarded as being the gift itself, as we shall have further occasion to observe.

6. We note, finally, that, from A. D. 1520, Luther expressed himself clearly and positively in favor of the reception of the Lord's Supper in both elements (W. 6. 502 ff., 78 f.   E. 28. 296; 11. 161) and against the sacrifice of the mass.   The Scriptures do not teach the latter (W. 8. 421).[1]   Neither would it be possible for us to bring a sacrifice (W. 6. 367), nor is it necessary for us to appease God (W. 8. 441 f.).   He denounced the abuses which have made of the mass simply a magical jugglery (W. 6. 375, supra, p. 203, n. 1). We should offer to God nothing but prayer, thanksgiving, and praise (6. 368), together with the faith "that Christ in heaven is our priest, offers himself for us without ceasing, presents and makes acceptable us, our prayers and our praises" (6. 369 f.).

§ 70. *The Reformatory Conception of the Church.*

LITERATURE.   KÖSTLIN, L.'s Lehre v. d. Kirche, 1853, and L.'s Theol., i. 248 ff., Engl. Tr. i. 289 ff.   KOLDE, L.'s Stellung z. Concil. u. Kirche, 1876. SEEBERG, Begriff d. Kirche, i. 85 ff.   GOTTSCHICK, Ztschr. f. KG. viii. 543 ff. SOHM, Kirchenrecht, i. 460 ff.

1. The chief elements of Luther's conception of the Church may also be traced in his writings of the pre-reformation period (p. 235 f.) ;[2] but they were made powerless by his bondage to the canonical ideas upon the subject.   The pope, as such, is still regarded as an authority (W. 1. 582, 670, 683 ; 2. 30), and he yet looks to councils for new articles of faith (W. 1. 582 ff., 681 ; 2 36 f).   This wavering and confusing attitude terminated with the controversy with Eck and the Leipzig Disputation (A. D. 1519).   Luther had asserted that the primacy of the Romish church over all others had not been exercised in the days of Gregory I., at least not over the Greek church (W. 2. 161), and that, according to the Fathers, the pope was only a *co-episcopus*

[1] See the interesting discussion of the origin of the mass, W. 6. 365 f.

[2] GOTTSCHICK has rightly, in opposition to Ritschl, myself, and others, proved Luther's independence of Huss.   At the time of the Leipzig Disputation, Luther was not acquainted with Huss's book upon the Church (E. 24. 22, cf. ENDERS, L.'s Briefe, ii. 196) and he had only a slight knowledge of his sermons, gained while at Erfurt (E. 65. 81).   Since the formula, *congregatio praedestinatorum*, does not affect Luther's conception of the church, we cannot think of the acts of the Council of Constance as the source of his views upon that topic.   His conception of the church is based upon Augustine and the current medieval definition, *communio fidelium* (supra, p. 144, n. 2).

with the other bishops (2. 20, 229). At this point the controversy began. Luther maintained his position (2. 185). Peter does not, according to the Scriptures, stand above the other apostles (ib. 235 f.). The Council of Nice did not attribute primacy to the Roman bishop (238, 265, 397, 672). The duty of obedience to the pope is not called in question, but it is like that which is due to any government, even that of the Turk (186). The papacy is based, not upon divine, but only upon human right; for such passages as Matt. 16. 18 f. have nothing to do with the pope (187, 189 ff., 194). The papal decretals, upon which the claims of the papacy are based, are mere human laws (201). On the other hand, it is the divine law, according to 2 Pet. 2. 13, that the pope, together with all his subordinates, should be subject to the emperor (220 f.). As Peter exercised no secular authority, the ecclesiastical jurisdiction is not of divine right (223). And Luther finally comes to doubt whether, after all, "any other head of the whole church has been appointed upon earth except Christ" (239). Luther now, at Leipzig and elsewhere, defends the proposition, that Huss was right in calling the church the general assembly of the predestinated (*predestinatorum universitas*). But as this definition was condemned at Constance, Luther found himself driven to the further assertion: "*Nor can a Christian believer be forced beyond the sacred Scriptures, which are properly the divine law*, unless some new and proved revelation should be added; for we are forbidden by divine law to believe except what is proved either through the divine Scriptures or through manifest revelation" (W. 2. 279). A principle of immense scope is thus established, that in all questions affecting doctrine the Scriptures are, as the divine law, the only decisive authority. This idea is not new. It lay at the basis of the medieval criticisms of the papacy (supra, p. 169, 172), and Luther himself had made use of it at an early period.[1] But the establishing of it as a fundamental principle and the energetic concrete application of it were new. The new canon is directed against the councils in general, especially the venerated Council of Constance, and against the pope as well (W. 2. 283 ff., 313, 404, 314, 397). "A council cannot make divine right out of that which is not by nature divine right" (308). To establish the Romish papacy by divine right is a "new dogma," which is not binding. The church needs no head (313 f.). The hierarchical system is not biblical, nor of divine right (379, 433 f.). The canon law begins to totter (423).

---

[1] Cf. UNDRITZ, Neue kirchl. Ztschr., 1897, 579 ff. As the idea was widely current in the later Middle Ages, no importance attaches to its use by Carlstadt, A. D. 1518 (KOLDE, L.'s Stellung z. Concil., p 34).

The great significance of the Leipżig Disputation and the conflicts which preceded and followed it lies in the fact, that Luther
was thus led to break fundamentally and permanently with the
Romish conception of the church and the authorities upon which
it depended (canons, pope, councils, ecclesiastical authority). In
place of the latter, was now acknowledged the *sole authority of the
Holy Scriptures*. The way was thus open to carry out and
apply the ideas of reform, the old barriers being broken down.
Criticism presses forward with rapid pace against Rome (*e. g.*,
W. 6. 287 ff., 290 ff. E. 31. 257, 310), the pope as anti-
christ (De W. 1. 239.   W. 6. 289, 331, 598, 603; 8.
470, 183; 9. 701 ff. E. 28. 224; 17. 25, etc.), the councils (W. 6. 79, 138, 258; 8. 150.   E. 22. 143 f.), and
the tradition of the Fathers (E. 31. 205; 11. 10 ff.; 12. 138;
14. 330).

2. But we turn to view the new conception of the Church,
as Luther first develops it in detail in the tract, *Von dem
Papsttum zu Rom* (A. D. 1520). The church is "an assemblage (*vorsamlunge*) of all Christian believers on earth"
(W. 6. 292), and, furthermore, "an assemblage of hearts in one
faith," or "a community (*gemein*) of saints" (293). Since
this assemblage is represented as a spiritual fellowship, the
principle of its unity is not to be seen in an accidental historical body, such as Rome or the papacy, but in Christ
(294 f.), for it is he who so operates upon the members of the
community (*Gemeinde*) that they are thereby united into one community. As the Head, he infuses his "disposition, temper,
and will" into the community (298). The church is therefore the spiritual association of those who believe on Christ,
established and sustained by him. But by the word "church"
is also understood the organized association of those who believe on Christ, "an outward thing with outward actions,"
and the order of the clergy (296). This "outward bodily
church" (*Christenheit*) and the "inner spiritual church"
(Christenheit) are to be carefully discriminated, but not separated. They are related to one another as body and soul in
man (297). It is, of course, of chief importance that we belong to the spiritual church, but this membership stands in
close connection with membership in the external church. At
this point appears the new element in Luther's theory. By
the introduction of the word and sacraments, he prevented the
dissolution of the conception of the church as held by Augustine and the reformers of pre-reformation days. The word
and sacraments, as externally and sensibly set forth, call
into existence the inner spiritual church. "For where baptism

and the gospel are, there let no one doubt that there are also saints, even though it should be only children in their cradles" (301). The church is therefore, in one aspect, an external, visible association. But this is not "the true (*rechte*) church which is believed." Since, however, the word and sacraments are here operative, faith concludes that here in the external association may be found a community of saints. Thus the church is an object of faith, and not visible, "for what is believed is not bodily nor visible" (300, 301).

3. In this simple combination, the way is pointed out for the solution of the problem of the nature of the church. Luther held without wavering to these principles, not indeed without adapting them to the practical needs of his time. Two things here demanded his attention, *i. e.*, the establishment of an evangelical church order, and defense against the theories of the Anabaptists. If the former task compelled him to a fundamental discussion of the form to be assumed by the external church, in order that it may be an appropriate agency for the production of the *communio sanctorum*, the conflict with Anabaptism emphasized the necessity of such an ecclesiastical system (supra, p. 280 f.). In opposition to Rome, he asserted : Only the word and the sacraments are necessary to the existence of the church ; and against the Anabaptists : Without the word and sacraments no church ! We must note a few features brought into prominence in the further development of the doctrine concerning the church.

(*a*) The spiritual nature of the church is maintained without abridgment of any kind. The church is the *communio sanctorum* (W. 6. 606, 131. Op. ex. 15. 357), for these words are "nothing else than a gloss, or interpretation, by which someone wished to indicate what the Christian church is" (Large Cat. 457). It is the "assembly (*Versammlung*) of all believers" (W. 8. 163), the "holy Christian nation" (E. 25. 355), the regenerated (46. 258). It is holy, because the Holy Spirit reigns in it (W. 8. 163). Those who belong to it are all priests in the spiritual sense (ib. 247 f., 251 f., 254, 382, 415, 417, 470). Thus considered, the church is the "new creation of God" (W. 6. 130), the product and sphere of the redemptive work of Christ (E. 46. 154); or it is the "kingdom of God," in which Christ reigns through the Spirit and faith (E. 29. 3;[1] cf. p. 277).

[1] Upon the relationship of the kingdom and the church, see E. 5. 231 : "Such kingdom of heaven begins on earth below and is called by another name, the Christian church, here on earth, within which God reigns through his word and his Spirit." The church is therefore the kingdom of God in its temporal, historical course of development.

The church in this sense is an object of faith, and may therefore, upon the basis of the definition, Heb. 11. 1, be described as *spiritual* and *invisible* (see citations, supra, p. 235, and also Op. var. arg. 5. 295. W. 6. 300; 8. 419, cf. the exposition of the kingdom of Christ as "invisible." E. 12. 96, 127; 17. 236, cf. 63. 168; 19. 26).[1] (*b*) The agency of Christ which incorporates individuals into the church is, however, bound to the chosen means, the word and sacraments; for through them God gathers the community, and they bring the Spirit (E. 9. 124; 12. 406; 22. 142; 49. 220; 50. 75 ff., 48. 68, 346). Hence the peculiar character of the act of faith by which the existence of the church is recognized. Wherever the means of grace are, there faith assumes the presence of a—perhaps very small—community of saints (25. 358, 360; 22. 142). (*c*) By this course of reasoning the necessity for an outward ecclesiastical association is maintained. The church must, further, always exist as an empirical historical entity. Thus considered, it is "the number or multitude of the baptized and believing who belong to a priest or bishop, whether in a city, or in a whole land, or in the whole world" (E. 31. 123). It is evident, also, that membership in the church is necessary to salvation, "for outside of the Christian church is no truth, no Christ, no salvation" (E. 10. 162, 444; 12. 414; 22. 20; 9. 292; 48. 218 f.). (*d*) All this may be said of the church, because the word and sacraments are absolutely essential to its existence. It follows, also, that all the members of the church are called to bear a part in the proclamation of the word, and that the congregation should do all in its power for its own edification (*e. g.*, E. 12. 222, 278). But since the congregation can no longer expect charismatically-endowed preachers, and since the preaching of the word dare not be discontinued, provision must be made for an office to administer the word and sacraments, without allowing this office to interfere with the duty of every individual to bear testimony to the truth (E. 17. 250; 22. 146 ff.). The "keys," *i. e.*, teaching and preaching (15. 395), belong really to all Christians (W. 8. 173), but the public official exercise of this duty, as is

---

[1] Already in the middle of the third decade of the century, the Evangelical party in Franconia assert against the Romanists: "This church is *spiritual* and *invisible*, not that we do not see the persons, but that no one knows which really belong to the Christian church" (in ENGELHARDT, Ehrengedächtnis der Ref. in Franken, p. 97, 123). This is no longer the original method of establishing the point. Luther meant to indicate by the term, *invisible*, only that the nature of the church is spiritual, and hence invisible and an object of faith; and did not apply it as discriminating among the members of the visible church. Cf. Wickliffe and Huss, supra, p. 211). The term was, as appears from the above, first used by Luther, and afterward by Zwingli.

strongly emphasized in opposition to the Anabaptist propaganda, should be restricted to officials regularly called (E. 31. 218, 214 ff.; 48. 298 f.). The object of every divine service is the preaching of the word (22. 153, 155, 235). Whatever is essentially an affair of the congregation is to be actually administered by an office, viz., the preaching of the word, with the administration of the sacraments and the care of souls (E. 22. 113; 31. 315). "Therefore upon whomsoever the office of preaching is laid, upon him is laid the highest office in the church" (E. 22. 151; 9. 220; 19. 205). The office of the pastor can therefore not be outranked by a higher ecclesiastical office, as that of a bishop (28. 181; 47. 16) and the hierarchy; for, according to the analogy of Christ's rulership, no outward government dare be exercised in the church, such as that of the pope, but only "to rule souls through the word of God." There is no ecclesiastical government which has authority to impose laws without the permission and will of the congregation, "but their reigning is nothing else than to use the word of God, and thereby guide Christians and vanquish heresy" (E. 22. 6, 93 f.; 46. 183 ff. Thus the relationship of the word and the Spirit requires an ecclesiastical office.[1]

(e) But since the church must, according to this definition, always be an external association, it is evident that there must belong to it empirically a great number of inchoate, imperfect, and even hypocritical members, who can have no share in its spiritual exercises (E. 9. 303; 14. 211; 16. 247; 2. 53, 61 f.; 25. 363; 65. 66. Gal. 3. 151 f.). Regarded empirically, therefore, the church is like a field in which tares are growing among the wheat.[2] (f) This must be borne in mind when speaking of the evangelical church of the New Testament. If the question be raised, which of the two churches, the Romish and the Evangelical, is the "true" (rechte) one, the answer cannot be given on the basis of their comparative morality. But, since the object of the outward organization of the church is to bring Christ to men through the word, therefore it can lay claim to the title, "true church," just in proportion as its preaching of the word is in harmony with this purpose, i. e., is truly evangelical.[3] The mark of the true church is, accordingly, that in

---

[1] The purely secular character which every form of church government has and must have, in Luther's view, is evident from the above, cf. SOHM, 517 ff.

[2] This affects the conception of the character of public worship, and explains Luther's reference to sinful assemblies of more mature Christians in his *Deutsche Messe*, W. 19, 73, 75, 112.

[3] Cf. E. 26. 42; 31. 389: I have, thank God, reformed more with my gospel than they could perhaps have done with five councils.

it the gospel is purely preached (E. 31. 366), that it has the
"teaching, faith, and confession of Christ" (12. 245, 249;
48. 224 ff.; 49. 230; 50. 10 ff.).   This can be known from the
agreement of its doctrine with the "word of Christ" (12.
289): "That the true church holds with me to God's word"
(28. 279; 9. 230).   Our doctrine is "the Scriptures and the
clear word of God" (13. 219, 223).   The "pure doctrine"
is therefore of the highest importance, since every corruption of
it must immediately influence the life (15. 358; 16. 101; 26.
35 f.).   Hence, the church dare not tolerate false teachers (E.
26. 37 f.).   As, therefore, the inner unity of the church is
established through Christ as its head, so its external unity is
secured through the pure doctrine of the gospel.[1]   "Therefore
this unity of the church is not said to be, and is not, the having and
holding of any one form of outward government, law, or ordinance, and church customs, as the pope and his crowd profess
and wish to have all excluded from the church who will not in
this be obedient to him. . . .   It is called one holy catholic or
Christian church, because there is here one pure and uncorrupted
doctrine of the gospel and outward confession of the same" (9.
293).   Where this old, true doctrine[2] has free course, i. e.,
where the Apostles' Creed is confessed, there the conditions are
present for the existence of the *communio sanctorum,* and hence
there is the true church.[3]   There has been a change in the

---

[1] We dare not here, if we would not lose the spirit of Luther, overlook the
practical aim of the "doctrine."   Even the theoretical construction of the
doctrinal system is, to his mind, subordinate to the great aim of interpreting
and appropriating the gospel. (*E. g.,* W. 2. 469.)   This is attested by his
according to all Christians the right to pass judgment upon the doctrine and
preaching of the church (22. 145; 12. 367; 13. 182 ff.; 46. 232 f.; 47.
354).   But this assumes an inner experience secured through the hearing of
the gospel, which may be used as a criterion.   "If thou knowest God, then
hast thou already the level, measure, and yard-stick, by which thou canst judge
all the doctrine of the Fathers. . . .   Who teaches you this?   Thy faith in
thy heart, which believes only this (13. 185).   Thou must thyself decide.   It
means for thee thy neck—it means thy life.   Therefore God must say to thee
in thy heart, 'This is God's word;' otherwise it is undecided" (ib. 183).
There was, accordingly, in Luther's mind no thought of a doctrinal hierarchy.
[2] The papal teachings are a "new" doctrine (*e. g.,* E. 17. 142, cf. 51.
103, where "Scripture and experience" are represented as "two touch-stones
of the true doctrine").   The Evangelical party have the "old doctrine" and
are therefore "the old, true church."   "For whoever thinks alike and holds
alike with the old church, he belongs to the old church" (E. 26. 14).
[3] Although Luther declares the Romish church to be a "devil's church,"
because it confesses "untrue articles," he yet holds that in it the Lord
through baptism and the word "nevertheless retains the young children . . .
and some adults, but very few, who have turned to Christ again at their
death" (E. 26. 28, 281; 4. 59 ff.).   Strictly speaking, the false church has
no right to the property of the church (26. 39, 59).

meaning of this term.   Once it signified the "true church, which
is believed" (W. 6. 301); it is now the church of pure doctrine
(E. 12. 245, 249; 26. 43; 28. 379; 48. 359 f.).   Once it
was a purely religious, now it is an empirical conception.[1]   The
doctrinaire tendency which may attach itself to the watchword,
"pure doctrine" (*reine Lehre*), is entirely foreign to Luther.
The doctrine of the church embraces the gospel, and the latter is
a power which lays hold upon the entire life, begetting faith,
love, and works, and binding Christians together in inward and
outward fellowship.[2]

§ 71. *Luther's Attitude Toward the Traditional Standards of
Doctrine, viz., the Scriptures and the Dogmas of the Church.*

LITERATURE.   ROMBERG, L.'s Lehre v. d. heil. Schrift, Wittenberg, 1868.
THIMME, L.'s Stellung z. heil. Schrift, Neue kirchl. Ztschr., 1896, 644 ff.
KATTENBUSCH, L.'s Stellung zu den ökumen. Symbolen, Giessen, 1883.   II.
PREUSS, Die Entwicklung des Schriftprincips bei L. bis zur leipziger Disput.,
1901.   SCHEEL, Luther's Stellung zur heil. Schrift, 1902.   W. WALTHER, Das
Erbe der Reform. i., 1903.   THIEME, Luther's Testament wider Rom, 1900.

1. In the preceding paragraphs we have traced the leading
features of Luther's teaching in so far as it has affected the History of Doctrines.   It may be said that here all is new.   Luther
knew how to present the Gospel in all its heights and depths as
no man had done since the days of Paul and John.   We may
best understand how he was led to this profound knowledge of
the truth by noting, first of all, his new conception of Faith—
not the intellectual acceptance of a dogma, nor the theoretical
conviction of the correctness of a formula, but the heartfelt experience of the omnipotence of love revealed to us in Christ.
This experience makes of me a new man, and inspires me with
the powers and impulses of another world.   But this experience
involves also the assurance that I enjoy the favor of God, although sinful impulses are yet felt within.   There now springs up a
new life, which is full of true evangelical repentance.   The dominion of the sacrament of repentance is abolished by true repentance; the works once demanded by the former being replaced
by the works of my earthly calling and the introduction of a new
ideal of the Christian life.   But even more than this may be truly

---

[1] It is scarcely necessary to guard here against the misunderstanding of this
change as involving a limitation of the religious character of the church.   The
church of the pure doctrine has value or significance only in so far as it is a
means for the establishment of the *communio sanctorum*.

[2] I still maintain the positions taken in my *Kirchenbegriff, 1. 88*, as to the
social-ethical tendency of Luther's conception of the church, despite the criticisms of K. MÜLLER (Symbolik, p. 326 f.).

said.   As Luther interprets Christianity, with all its facts and
doctrines, from the view-point of faith, all his utterances have
the direct impress of religious experience.[1]   What he sought to
tell of all things was, what influence they might have upon the
believing heart and how the latter might secure such influence.
In this way he fell upon simpler, yet at the same time more profound, formulas than many of those which tradition had handed
down.   He held to Augustine's doctrine of original sin, or, to
speak more accurately, restored it ; but for him the essence of
sin lay no longer in sensuous desire, but in unbelief.   He often
reproduced the theological and Christological formulas of the
ancient church ; but the God of his experience was not the infinite
" Subsistence " (Vol. I., p. 340 n.), but the omnipotent Loving-
will.   He spoke of grace and its gift to us, even of " infused
grace ; " but he meant by it not a " quality glued in," but the
efficient power of love which transforms our hearts.

The re-discovered gospel bore within itself the hidden impulse
for the construction of new theological formulas, and with lavish
hand, and almost recklessly, Luther dashed them from his pen.
But the reformation of the theology which he effected was not
directed by any thought of a complete revision of the traditional
dogmatic system.   It was Luther's aim to obtain a secure and
permanent place for the newly-won conceptions touching the religious life (faith, justification, grace, works, the enslaved will, the
gospel, the law).[2]   He never wearies of seeking to impress them
upon his hearers and readers.[3]   Under the guidance of this cen-

---

[1] Cf. 58. 398 f.: " There is only one article and rule in theology ; he who
does not know and have this is no theologian, viz., true faith, or trust in Christ.
All the other articles continually flow into this one and out again, and the
others are nothing without this."   Similarly in Gal. i. 3.

[2] From this fact, as exemplified particularly in Luther's writings and the
Epistle to the Romans, it may be understood that Melanchthon should have
failed to treat of the Trinity and Christology in his first edition of the Loci.

[3] There may be found in Luther a very great variety of propositions, each
of which is declared to be the "chief article," or "the sum of the gospel."
In reality, they all amount in the end to the same thing.   I cite a few groups :
Justification and the forgiveness of sins, e. g., E. 31. 250: "The word of
grace and forgiveness of sins, and that we become righteous and are saved
alone through Christ without merit : for this is the chief article, out of which
all our doctrine has flowed, which was held and confessed at Augsburg before
the emperor, as it is based upon the Scriptures."   Cf. Müller, Symb. Bb., 300.
De W. 4. 151.   E. 8. 184, 236; 11. 157; 14. 188.   *Repentance and forgiveness*, 11, 279.   *Grace, forgiveness, liberty*, 13. 30; 40. 324.   *Christ,
the God-man, who delivers us*, 13. 49, 56, 204; 15. 155; 16. 254; 9. 213;
10. 346 ; 12. 246 f.; 18. 24; 19. 390; 47. 45, 58; 48. 98.   But not our free
will, 10. 218; 14. 33.   *Grace and love*, 14. 73; 22. 233; 25. 76.   Gal. 1.
322.   *Faith and baptism*, 12. 204.   *Faith and works*, 16. 140.   *The Trinity*,
9. 1, especially the contents of the Creed, 28. 413 f., 346 f.; 13. 221 f.; 49. 5,
and the symbolical writings.

tral idea, he moulded anew all doctrines that came within his range. Whatever stood in its way, he rejected, as, *e. g.*, the medieval Semi-pelagianism and doctrine of grace, the whole theory of the sacraments, the hierarchical system, work-right-eousness, and the doctrine of merits. And just as readily did the fanatical notions of an immediate operation of the Spirit fall beneath the weight of the reformatory principle. Other doctrines, on the contrary, which did not collide with his religious principle, he conserved. If he had been entrusted with the construction of the doctrines of the Trinity or of Christology, he would certainly have framed formulas different from those of Nice or Chalcedon. This does not imply connivance, nor calculation of consequences[1] — not even a lack of logical consistency. With a genuine historic sense, he allowed the formulas in question to stand, for the sake of the important truths imbedded in them. Here arises for us a new question : What was Luther's attitude toward dogma?

2. Before attempting an answer to this query, we must have a clear understanding upon another point. We have seen that Luther, impelled by his central reformatory principle, was led by an inner necessity to abandon the theories of the medieval church and replace them with new doctrinal statements. Faith, with its independent assurance, its " feeling " and " experience " (p. 257. E. 13. 185, 183, supra, p. 295, n. 1, 2.), here became at once the critical and the constructive norm. (*a*) But, in the decisive hour at Worms, Luther appealed not only to his religious experience, but also to the authority of the *Holy Scriptures*. In this he established a further canon for the reformation of doctrine. He habitually appealed to it—very naturally—in controversy with his opponents, and was controlled by it in his own religious life.[2] Its importance became clear to him at the Leipzig Disputation (p. 289 f.). Only the "divine law " (*das göttliche Recht*), or the Scriptures, dare rule in the church : " What is asserted without the Scriptures or proved revelation may be held as an opinion, but is not necessary to be believed " (W. 6. 508 ; 2. 297, 279, 309, 315). No water dare be mingled with this wine (W. 8. 141 f.; 143 f.) ; no lantern held up against this sunlight (ib. 235). The word of God, not the

---

[1] For the legal status of the Reformation, the retention of the Trinitarian and Christological formulas was of the highest importance.

[2] E. 28. 350 : " Now I handled the abomination (indulgences) at first almost tenderly and gently and handsomely, and would very gladly have allowed the papacy to stand and have helped it be something ; *but the Scriptures* I was determined to have uncorrupted, pure and certain : I did not yet know that it (the papacy) was contrary to the Scriptures, but only considered it to be *without Scripture*, as other worldly government set up by men."

teachings of men—Christ, not philosophy, must rule the people of God (ib. 144, 146, 149, 345. E. 9. 232 ; 11. 7 ; 28. 298). The servants of Christ must teach only his word (E. 7. 82). The word itself is to be taught ; it is not to be bound by the interpretation of it, as does Rome (W. 2. 339. E. 11. 31), nor be robbed of its meaning by neglect of the context (W. 2. 361, 425 ; 8. 348). This principle became the more firmly established for Luther in proportion as the necessity of an authoritative norm became apparent among his own following. He thus withstood Iconoclasts and Fanatics, and upon this basis constructed the new evangelical organization of the church. It was henceforth a maxim: "Thou must plant thyself upon a clear, transparent, strong statement of the Scriptures, whereby thou canst then hold thy ground" (E. 28. 223). From this may be understood his insistence upon the *est* in the formula of the Lord's Supper. But there is nothing essentially evangelical as yet in all this reverence for the Scriptures, for it had been quite common in the Middle Ages (supra, p. 101, 149, 192 ff.). The strict view of inspiration which Luther sometimes expresses ("the writing of the Holy Spirit," "the Spirit's own writing." Op. ex. 7. 313; 1. 4. E. 27. 244 ; 11. 248 ; 45. 301 ; 52. 321, 333)[1] was also current in the later Middle Ages (p. 193 n.). But for Luther the Scriptures were something more than the "divine right," or law inspired by God, as Occam and Biel regarded them.

(*b*) This is proved by a number of considerations which point to another conception of the Scriptures. (1) At the close of the Middle Ages the natural law (*naturrecht*) innate in the reason was represented as equivalent to the divine law (*göttliches Recht*) of the Scriptures (supra, p. 171 f., 192 f., 184 n). Since Luther denies this (E. 11. 30 ; 19. 266),[2] revelation is not for him equivalent to the general dictates of reason, but has positive and peculiar content. (2) This content is Christ and the revelation given through him. "If I know what I believe, then I know what stands in the Scriptures, because the Scriptures contain nothing more than Christ and Christian faith" (W. 8. 236). The Holy Spirit, operative in the New Testament authors, merely carried out what Christ said : "As the evangelist John

[1] See many more instances in ROHNERT, Die Inspirat. d. h. Schr., 1889, p. 144 ff.

[2] This is not contradicted by the fact that Luther would at first accept only "what the holy father proves with Scripture or with reason" (E. 27. 21), nor his readiness at Worms to be convinced "by proofs of Scripture or by clear reasons" (KÖSTLIN, L.'s Leben, i. 452). Luther here means citations from Scriptures or evident inferences from such citations. Cf. Occam, supra, p. 192.

wrote many more things than Christ said just at this time, but yet always keeps to this one purpose, to most thoroughly present the article concerning the person, office, and kingdom of Christ, of which Christ also himself speaks'' (E. 12. 135 f., 138, 141). Thus is for Luther the specific content of all Holy Scriptures defined. That which is valuable in them, and which determines their character, is their relation to Christ. "This is also the proper touch-stone for the criticism of all books, if we observe whether they treat of Christ or not, since *all Scripture testifies of Christ* (Rom. 3. 21), and St. Paul will know nothing but Christ (1 Cor. 2. 2). That which does not teach Christ is not apostolic, even though St. Peter or St. Paul should teach it. On the other hand, whatever preaches Christ would be apostolic, even if Judas, Hannas, Pilate, and Herod should do it'' (E. 63. 157). (3) In this connection, Luther's critical opinions concerning the Scriptures are very significant. Thus, he asserts that the text of the prophecies has often fallen into confusion; the discourses were presumably not committed to writing until afterward, and then by redactors (63. 57, 74; 62. 123). The prophets were often in error (*fehlten*), when they prophesied of worldly events (*von weltlichen Läuften*) (E. 8. 23). The books of the Kings are more trustworthy than the Chronicles (62. 132). By whom Genesis was composed, is a matter of indifference (57. 35). It would be better if the book of Esther were not in the canon (op. ex. 7. 195. E. 62. 131). The composition of Ecclesiastes by Solomon is doubted (E. 62. 128). The reports of the synoptic gospels are not of uniform value (30. 314, 331; 14. 319). The Epistle of Jude is derived from the Second Epistle of Peter (63. 158). The Epistle of Hebrews errs, in denying a second repentance (ib. 155), "and is apparently composed of many parts.'' James wrote "a right strawy epistle . . . for it has certainly no evangelical character about it'' (ib. 115), *i. e.*, "he teaches nothing'' about Christ, and connects righteousness with works (156 f.). He even says: "James talks wildly'' (*delirat*) (op. ex. 4. 328. W. 2. 425). Luther did not originally regard the Apocalypse as a prophetic or apostolic book, "because Christ is neither taught nor known in it'' (63. 169 f.). He remained in doubt as to its authorship (159).[1] Great emphasis was laid by him upon the testimony borne to the various books by the ancient church.[2] On this ground, Hebrews, James,

---

[1] Luther attaches very little value to prophecies touching outward events, but places the Apocalypse in this respect upon a level with Joachim of Floris and the Lichtenberg prophet! (E. 8. 22).

[2] Already, A. D. 1519, at Leipzig, he rejected Macc. II. as not canonical (W. 2. 325, 329, 339). As to the Apocrypha in general, see 63. 91 ff.

Jude, and the Apocalypse are distinguished in the Prefaces of A. D. 1522 from the "real certain chief books" (63. 154). But the inner canon is for him yet more important. The Gospel of John and Paul's epistles, especially Romans and First Peter, are "the real kernel and marrow among all the books. . . . For in these thou findest not much description of the work and miracles of Christ; but thou findest here portrayed in the most masterly way how faith in Christ overcomes sin, death, and hell and gives life, righteousness, and salvation—which is the real character of the gospel" (63. 144 f.; 51. 327). In consistency with this view of the Scriptures, historical oversights and errors in the sacred writings disturbed Luther but little (*e. g.*, E. 14. 319; 46. 174; 50. 308 f.; 62. 132. Walch, Luth. WW. xiv., 1208, 1293 f.).[1] They did not affect the real grounds of his confidence.[2] (4) It is again in perfect consistency with the above, that Luther's acknowledgment of the authority of the Scriptures is not based upon their official recognition by the church,[3] but upon the *experience* of their truth : "Everyone must believe only because it is God's Word and because he is satisfied in his heart (*inwendig befinde*) that it is truth (E. 28. 340 ; 47. 356), *i. e.*, a reality and not a mere 'idea'" (48. 29).

(*c*) The principles thus avowed indicate a conception of the character of the Holy Scriptures entirely different from that underlying the medieval formulas employed by Luther as cited in paragraph (*a*) above. We must not be too ready therefore to regard such declarations as the hasty utterances of superabundant enthusiasm, and magnanimously absolve the Reformer from responsibility for them. This is forbidden, not only by the fact that they occur for the most part in carefully composed passages, such as the prefaces to his publications, but especially by the important consideration that they stand in very intimate connection with his reformatory conception of faith. There thus results an entirely new conception of the authority and inspiration of the Scriptures. Their specific content, in both the Old and the New

---

[1] It is thus seen that Luther employed "criticism" in the widest variety of forms. Almost all the criteria employed at the present day were applied by him in his own way.

[2] In the sense of Occam or Biel, Luther's position is simply *heretical*, since the Christian is under obligation to accept all the books of the Bible and believe everything found in them (supra, p. 192). It is very remarkable that the opponents of Luther did not make more capital out of his bold utterances in this direction. It is true, indeed, that similar views were held by such men as Erasmus and Cajetan (cf. KUNZE, Glaubensregel, heil. Schrift u. Taufbekenntniss, 1899, p. 516 ff.).

[3] D'Ailli still taught differently, supra, p. 191, n. 1.

Testaments, is Christ, with his office and kingdom. It is this content in which faith is interested, and which faith verifies by inner experience. This is therefore the important thing in the Scriptures. It must accordingly be the impelling motive in the special divine agency which gave the Scriptures their peculiar character. In other words, the testimony of the Holy Spirit in the Scriptures is the testimony to the great facts of salvation and redemption. This is the purpose of their inspiration, and in proportion as they fulfill it do they substantiate their claim to be regarded as an authority in matters of religion.[1] This makes them the criterion and touch-stone, by which all the teaching of the church must be attested as evangelical truth (e. g., E. 9. 207, 372; 12. 289; 13. 208; 15. 144; 18. 22; 48. 69, 92; 46. 231, 240). This places the above-cited passages touching the authority of the Scriptures in a new light. The Scriptures were for Luther an absolute authority. But although he could in controversy employ them as "divine law" in contrast with "ecclesiastical law," yet they were an actual authority for him only as the primitive and original testimony to Christ and his salvation. This determines their nature and their form.[2]

But, when thus regarded, the Scriptures dare not be co-ordinated with justifying faith as the second principle of Protestantism. The controlling principle is faith; and, since only the believer can understand the Scriptures, and they exist only to minister to faith, they are subordinate to it. This view produced a new and profounder conception of the authority of the Scriptures. The ancient problems: wherein the authority of the Scriptures really consists, how is it to be proved, and what its relation to that of other writings—were fundamentally solved by Luther, since he recognized this authority as based upon religious grounds —a statement which is not invalidated by the fact that Luther did not always in praxis adhere strictly to his own principle.

3. We are now in position to understand Luther's attitude toward the Dogmas of the Ancient Church. We have seen that

---

[1] Cf. the remarkably characteristic declaration, E. 11. 248: "Thus I would take Moses, the Psalter, Isaiah, and also the same Spirit, and make just as good a New Testament as the apostles wrote; but since we do not have the Spirit so fully and powerfully, we must learn from them and drink out of their well."

[2] The doctrine of the Scriptures in the dogmatic system of the present day must be framed with due regard to the principles of Luther as above deduced, although the latter were not reduced by the Reformer himself to a complete doctrinal form. How, for instance, could a verbal inspiration be sustained in view of Luther's derogatory remarks upon particular passages in the canonical books, his recognition of redactors, who have collected the materials of many of the books, and his acknowledgment of errors?

he rejected as unbiblical the medieval doctrine of the sacraments, and denied the infallibility of the pope and the councils. But what was his attitude toward the ancient dogmas? (cf. esp. his tract, *Von den Conciliis und Kirchen*, 1539, the three Symbols of 1538, and the other symbolical writings). It is very clear, in the first place, that Luther acknowledged and frequently reproduced the Nicene doctrine of the Trinity and the Chalcedonian Christology. Also, that he treated the symbols of the ancient church with great respect, especially the Apostles' Creed, which, he declared, contains all the principal articles of faith (28. 413 f., 346 f.; 9. 29 ff.; 13. 221 f.; 20. 297 f.).[1] But this is not to be understood as implying that he believes these symbols or councils as such, and thus subjects himself to an earthly authority. His liberty in this respect is manifest from his criticism of the ancient terminology. "That if my soul loathes the word, *homousion*, and I am unwilling to use it, I am not a heretic ; for who will compel me to use it, provided I hold the thing which is defined from the Scriptures by the council " (W. 8. 117 f.).[2] He objected to the word "*Trinity*" (E. 6. 230), declaring that it "sounds cold," and was "discovered and invented" by men (E. 12. 378); although he afterward admitted that the form of expression is not important, as "original sin," for example, is not found in the Scriptures (E. 25. 291 f.; 28. 382 ; 29. 183 f.). And in his tract, *Von den Conciliis*, etc., he "with masterly historical criticism"[3] denies all binding authority to the ancient councils. The highest council was that of the apostles, and it enjoined refraining from blood, an injunction which no one now observes. "If we want to be guided by councils, we must recognize this one above all others ; if we do not, then we need not recognize any of the other councils, and *are therefore free from all councils*" (25. 240). Just as little are all the decrees of Nice observed (244, 251 f.). And no council has set forth "the whole Christian doctrine " (261). The decrees of councils are not on their own account true, but because they repeat the old truth, as given to the apostles by the Holy Spirit (266 f., 295, 328, 331). Councils likewise have "no power to form new articles of faith, but should indeed smother and condemn new articles, in accord-

---

[1] E. 20. 155 : " I have a little book which is called the CREDO. . . . This is my Bible, which has stood so long and still stands unshaken, to this I hold fast, to this I was baptized, upon this I live and die." E. 9. 29 : "Thus this Symbol has been excellently and briefly composed out of the books of the holy prophets and apostles for children and plain Christians, so that it is fitly called the Apostles' creed, or faith."

[2] Eck, on the other hand, at Leipzig highly lauded the ecclesiastical definition of the homousia. W. 2. 335. Erasmus already criticises it. Opp. v. 1090.

[3] E. g., his investigations concerning Nestorius, 25. 304 ff.

ance with the Holy Scripture and the ancient faith." Thus, at Nice, Constantinople, Ephesus, and Chalcedon, the "new articles" of Arius, Macedonius, Nestorius, and Eutyches were rejected (333, 345). Luther's idea is, that the dogmas are true only in so far as they agree with the Scriptures; they have no authority in themselves. But the truth of the Scriptures is inwardly attested. Hence it may be said, in harmony with Luther's idea, that the Holy Spirit begets in us an experience of the truth of the doctrine (of the Creed) (E. 23, 249, 267; 20. 148); for in no other way can we be led to faith than by being practically and inwardly convinced of that which has been taught (20. 141, 136, 144 f.; 22. 15 f.).[1] The doctrine of the two natures in Christ is in itself of no interest to the Christian; it is only from the work of Christ that he learns to understand it (35. 208).

We have thus before us the criteria and rules which Luther applied in the criticism of religious utterances of all kinds. A thing is true, if it is attested by faith, by his own experience, and by the Scriptures. The outward and legalistic testing of religious views by the standard of the ancient dogmas has been abolished; the ancient canon of VINCENT OF LERIUS shattered. But, beyond this, the legalistic use of the Scriptures is itself upon principle abandoned. Luther's attitude toward the Bible was thus very different from that of Occam. The problems which in every age arise in this field of study, in consequence of advancing historical knowledge, may all be adjusted to the principles of Luther and thus find their solution. That his praxis was not always consistent or worthy of imitation can be here merely suggested.

4. In conclusion, we may at least touch upon a further question: Was not Luther's peculiar apprehension of religious truth limited or restrained by the recognition and acceptance of the Trinitarian and Christological dogmas? The reader of his discussions of the knowledge of God in Christ (supra, p. 252 f.) receives at first the impression that the Father was revealed in the words and works of Jesus, and that a separate divinity of the Son is therefore not in the author's mind. But, on the other hand, Luther emphasizes most vigorously the idea that the divinity of the Son is revealed in his own life. He is true God and true

---

[1] Hence the papists have, in Luther's opinion, the whole second article of the Creed only "with the mouth"—"in the heart they deny it," since they hold that "man is not so utterly lost," and credit him with "free will" (E. 20. 142; 46. 87; 63. 154). It is evident that everything is made to depend, not upon the acceptance of the traditional formula, but upon a practical experience, upon the basis of which alone can the formula be really comprehended. Critical objections to any one of the facts asserted in the Creed had never fallen under Luther's observation.

man, two natures and one person (E. 7. 185 f., 196). His
human life, with its deprivations, sufferings, and temptations, is
depicted in the most animated and vivid way (E. 13. 307; 10.
131 f., 299 ff.) This man was entirely under the guidance of
the divine nature. It was "personally present" in him (7.
185). His human nature does not see and feel everything, but
what the divine nature permits it to feel and know—hence Jesus
does not know when the day of judgment shall be (ib.). Thus
it becomes, since the Spirit more and more profoundly and constantly controls it, the " instrument and dwelling place of the
divine nature " (10. 300). Yet, in his passion and death, the
divine nature " lay entirely hidden and quiet within him, and
did not assert itself nor shine forth " (3. 302; 39. 47 f.,
supra, § 66, 3), as, upon the other hand, Jesus restrained his
omnipotence and, as it were, concealed it (37. 33; 39. 55;
40. 49). The intimate conjoining of the divine and human
natures, as the emphasis laid upon the reality and genuineness of
the human life of Jesus, is by no means a product of the sacramental controversy, but is closely connected with the most profound tendencies of Luther's thought : in the words and works
of Jesus, God is revealed. But, in the first line of thought, it
seemed necessary to think of the Father ; in the latter, only
directly of the Son (cf. 8. 156 ff.; 40. 109).[1] The difficulty
cannot be overcome by assuming a Modalistic conception of the
Trinity,[2] for Luther reproduces the orthodox doctrine in its
regular form (e. g., Smalc. Art., Müller, 299 ; 9. 2 ff. 22,
32, 116, 231 ; 10. 166, 171 f.; 12. 378 ff.; 16. 79, 108 f.;
18. 23 ; 30. 363 f.; 45. 294 f.; 308 f.).[3] It is true, that even in
so doing he manifested a Western feeling. The term "Trinity"
(*Dreifaltigkeit*, three-foldness) does not please him, because

---

[1] Upon the Christology of Luther, cf. TH. HARNACK, L.'s Theol. ii.
126 ff. THOMASIUS, DG. ii., ed. 2, 573 ff. H. SCHULTZ, Gotth. Christi,
182 ff. LEZIUS, Die Anbetung Jesu neben d. Vater, Dorpat, 1892.

[2] Cf. LOOFS, DG. 358. A. HARNACK, DG. iii., ed. 3, 752 f. This position
is not justified, but it is true that Luther had a strong consciousness of the one
personal God.

[3] Cf. 28. 136 : God is "not only one person ; " but, on the other hand, see
30. 227, 217. Christ is "one undivided person with God ; " cf. also the remark, 7. 189 : " The Holy Spirit is easily believed," " if a man is brought
so far as to regard two persons as One God." The Holy Spirit is a separate
person (49. 149); his divine nature is recognized in his working (49. 391);
in word and sacrament he works (49. 220 ; 50. 75, etc.) faith and everything
good in man. He is a comfort against the Evil Spirit in the world (49. 382).
The place in which he is revealed is the church : " Learn . . . how and where
thou shouldst seek the Spirit : not up above the clouds . . . but here on
earth below is he, just as the church is on earth . . . so that we may draw
him into the office and government of the church, the word and sacrament"
(49. 223 f.).

20

God is "the supreme Unity." Simply *Dreiheit* (threeness)
"sounds entirely too ironical." The comparison with three
angels or men will not do, for there are not "three Gods."
"There is indeed in the Godhead *ein Gedrittes* (a tripartate
reality) but this same *Gedrittes* consists of persons of the One
only Godhead (6. 230).[1] Luther was therefore not a Monarch-
ian. But he had a vigorous consciousness of the absolute unity
of God, and this enabled him to see in each trinitarian person
the entire Godhead. God is therefore fully revealed through
Christ (30. 62 ; 45. 295; 47. 180 ; 49. 93), just as through the
Holy Spirit, with his sway in the hearts of men (16. 214).
Father and Son are "one nature, one will," "one heart and
will" (47. 305 f.; 49. 144). Where one part is, "there is
certainly the entire Godhead" (50. 94). There is therefore no
contradiction between the expressions referred to and Luther's
consciousness of the Trinity—all the less since Luther did not conceive the nature of the Godhead as "Subsistence," but as omnipotent Loving-will. He was able to combine this idea in his
own mind with the traditional content of the doctrine concerning God. The theoretical problems which arise in this connection never presented themselves to his mind.[2]

CHAPTER II.

DOCTRINE OF ZWINGLI. OPPOSITION OF LUTHER AND ZWINGLI UPON THE DOCTRINE OF THE LORD'S SUPPER.

§ 72. *The Reformatory Principles of Zwingli.*

SOURCES. Zwingli's Works, edited by Schuler and Schulthess, 8 vols.,
1828 ff. Among the writings of Z., the following are the most important for
our purpose : Von klarheit und gewüsse des worts gottes, 1522; Uslegen und

---

[1] Cf. Augustine : *deus ter*, not *dii tres*. Vol. I., p. 240.

[2] If the divine nature is to be conceived as Loving-will, how must we then
represent to our thought the trinitarian life of the Godhead, particularly the
divinity of Christ? The divinity of Christ consists chiefly in this, "that the
Father has just the will which I have" (47. 306, 308, 315). "This will of
the Father thou canst not miss, if thou keepest thyself to the man Christ, but
meetest him in this man" (ib. 318; 48. 142). Luther represents to himself
the trinitarian life as a conversation in God (45. 300 ff.; 50. 82). These are
problems which Luther has left to Protestant dogmatic theology. DILTHEY
also recognizes that Luther's faith does not touch "the material of the ancient
Christian dogma"—Arch. f. Gesch. d. Philos. v. 358 ff.

grund der schlussreden, 1523; Ynleitung, 1525; Von göttl. und menschl. gerechtigkeit, 1523 (vol. i.). Archeteles, 1522; De vera et falsa relig., 1525 (vol. iii.). De provident., 1530; fidei ratio, 1530; fid. exposit., 1531 (vol. iv.). Cf. MÖRIKOFER, Huldr. Zw., 2 vols., 1867-9. R. STÄHELIN, Huldr. Zw., 2 vols., 1895-7, cf. PRE. xvii. 584 ff. HUNDESHAGEN, Beiträge zur Kirchenverfassungsgesch., etc., i. 1864, 136 ff. MÖLLER-KAWERAU, KG. iii. 44 ff. ZELLER, Das theol. Syst. Zw., 1853. SIGWART, U. Zw., 1855. SPÖRRI, Zwinglistudien, 1866. A. BAUR, Zw. Theol., 2 vols., 1885-9. USTERI, Initia Zwinglii, Stud. u. Krit., 1885, 607 ff., 1886, 95 ff. RITSCHL, Rechtf. u. Vers. i. 165 ff. SEEBERG, Zur Charakteristik der ref. Grundgedanken Zw. in Mitteilgn. u. Nachr., etc., 1889, 1 ff., and Thomasius, DG. ii., ed. 2, 395 ff. LOOFS, DG., ed. 3, 381 ff. NAGEL, Zw. Stellung z. Schrift, 1896.

1. At the close of A. D. 1506, while Luther was seeking "a gracious God" in the cloister, ULRICH ZWINGLI (b. A. D. 1484), became pastor at Glarus. His pastorate was a stormy and eventful one. When Luther in 1517 began the great conflict, Zwingli was at "Einsiedeln in the Dark Forest," searching in the Scriptures for the true "philosophy of Christ." The former stepped forth from the loneliness of inner struggles into the great conflict of the church; the latter had learned to know men and human life before devoting himself in solitude to his studies. Luther was impelled by the religious needs of his own heart, the personal experience of faith making him a reformer. Zwingli followed the counsel of Erasmus and the humanistic tendency of the age, in turning to the "very purest sources." His point of departure was different from that of Luther, *i. e.*, the humanistic, critical temper of the age, as differentiated from the church and its teachings—a return to the sources, or the conviction that only the doctrine of the Bible is the truth. These were ideas which Erasmus advocated, and which the majority of the cultured classes applauded. It was under these circumstances that Zwingli began his study of the Scriptures. The scope of his reformatory activity was in consequence, from the first, wider than that of Luther, and he was more conscious of a definite purpose. The idea of a reformation, which only gradually dawned upon Luther, was the controlling motive with Zwingli from the beginning. From A. D. 1519 he labored in Zurich, preaching the Scriptures, taking up one book after another. Reformatory ideas, in the proper sense of the term, were at first foreign to him (USTERI, Stud. u. Krit., 1886, 122 ff.). As the religious lever of his work as a reformer was undoubtedly found in the idea of justification through Christ and by faith, it is natural to inquire from what source he derived this idea; and there can be no doubt that he derived it, as well as his fundamental reformatory views, from Luther. This is manifest, not only in view of his known acquaintance with the writings of Luther (USTERI, l. c., 141 ff.), but as well from the form of his doctrinal

writings, as they are found in his "Schlussreden" and "Usle-gung."[1] Zwingli started with the Erasmian ideas of a reforma-tion. This led him to the Scriptures; but it was Luther's range of ideas that continually guided him in their interpretation. At the central point of his apprehension of religious truth, Zwingli is dependent upon Luther. But, as the more comprehensive aims of the school from which he sprung fitted him, on the one hand, for more varied application and a more speedy realization of the reformatory ideas; so, on the other hand, he retained some ele-ments which were not up to the evangelical standard, and which betray their origin from the medieval conceptions of the humanistic party.[2] This explains his agreement with Luther in the central doctrines, as well as the divergence of their theological and ecclesiastical views.

2. In endeavoring to depict the reformatory ideas of Zwingli, we must begin with the emphasis laid by him upon the Authority of the Holy Scriptures. Here the will of God is revealed to us (i. 54. 207), and here the Holy Spirit teaches us "all that we should know of God" (176). All doctrine is to be based upon the inspired word (i. 81. 177; iii. 51. 359). The proclama-tion of the latter and obedience to it are the essential tasks of the Reformation (i. 36. 38; iii. 70). This was the point of departure which regulated all his thinking: "Is it proper to conform to (*obtemperare*) divine things or human?" (iii. 67). This went, indeed, beyond the attitude of the medieval reformers toward the Scriptures; for with Zwingli they were more than a book of external laws. His obedience to them was a result of inner religious experience (i. 79). But he never attained in

---

[1] Zwingli's dependence upon Luther may without hesitation be asserted as a settled historical fact. USTERI, l. c., and STÄHELIN, Zw. i. 164 ff., 175 f., furnish the material to substantiate this, although their own judgment upon it is limited to a "perhaps." We can understand their hesitancy from the fact that Zwingli himself denies all such dependence (i. 253 ff.; iii. 489, 543; vii. 144; ii. 2. 20 ff.). But we can understand also the sad self-deception to which he has here fallen a victim. The study of the Scriptures was and remained for him the source of his doctrinal views; and he found Luther's ideas in the Scriptures—after he had learned them from Luther. It is some-what similar to this, when he disputes Luther's claim to having brought forth the Scriptures from their obscurity by pointing to Erasmus and Reuchlin (ii. 2. 21). Cf. also KAWERAU (Möller, KG. iii. 46).

[2] In Luther, the general demands for reformation, in so far as he joined in them, were thoroughly subordinated to the religious principle; for it was not those demands which had awakened his energy and directed his course. With Zwingli, they occupied an independent position side by side with the religious principle; or, rather, the latter stood related to them as means to an end. Those who embraced the Erasmian conception of reform, unless they gained also the religious experience of Luther, found what they sought in Zwingli rather than in Luther. Of this, history furnishes many illustrations.

his relation to them the lofty religious freedom of Luther.[1] Zwingli holds the humanistic view, that the Scriptures are the original source of primitive Christianity ; yet he also applies the medieval, juristic conception, that they constitute the divine law which is to regulate public life.

3. In order to understand Zwingli's conception of Justification, we must familiarize ourselves with his doctrine of Sin. Adam was created free, but died through his sin, and with him the whole human race. " There he and all his race in him died as dead as stone " (1. 183, 196). Sin, as original sin, is " the infirmity and defect (*Bresten und Mangel*) of shattered nature." In this invalided nature, the flesh is more powerful than the spirit. From this disease of original sin grow individual sins like branches from a tree (i. 190, 264, 60 ; iii. 203). "Sin, then, is when, the law of the Creator being neglected, man prefers to follow himself rather than the banners of his leader and Lord " (iii. 169). Sin is disobedience toward God. The sinner cannot obey the law of God (1. 184 f.), because his nature has been "shattered" (*zerbrochen*). But original sin in itself is only "a defect which one derives from birth without his own fault " (ii. 1. 287; i. 309 ; iii. 203 f.). The longing for eternal life is likewise innate (1. 59, 58), since the "natural law," or an internal illuminating and drawing agency of the Spirit of God, still remains to all men, even the heathen : "although I think that few of them have understood it " (i. 326, 360 f.). Accordingly, all truth in the natural man is inspired by God (iv. 36, 93, 95 ; iii. 156). But, however this may be, for practical purposes we must regard sin as a shattering force which excludes all possibility of self-deliverance.

4. Christ is the Deliverer. In the work of deliverance (salvation), the divine Mercy finds exercise, and at the same time satisfaction is rendered to the divine Justice (i. 186 ; iii. 180 ; iv. 475). (*a*) Christ has by his innocent sufferings made payment to the divine justice (1. 186, 387 ; ii. 2. 7 ; iii. 194, 187, 198, 498). He suffered for us, bought us, reconciled us with God (*ut iratus placetur*, iii. 181), became a sacrifice for us, and delivered us (1. 76, 179, 233 f., 236 ; iii. 189, 197, 209, 194). There is therefore no need of the sacrifice of the mass (i. 237), nor of other mediators, such as the saints (i. 268 ff.). His payment of the debt covers not only original sin, but all sins (i. 264; ii. 198 ; supra, p. 203, n. 1). He, the Innocent and Just, fulfilled the law for us (i. 213, 263, 309). The latter he

---

[1] Zwingli holds the Humanistic view, that the Scriptures are the original source of primitive Christianity ; yet he also applies the medieval, juristic conception, that they constitute the divine law which is to regulate public life.

did as God, since his will was the divine will ; the former, as a
pure man, who could render a spotless sacrifice (i. 264). By
thus effecting our deliverance, God "by this example of justice
removed from us our languor and torpor and displayed himself
to us as he was—just, good, and merciful" (iii. 180).[1] (*b*) This
last idea leads further. Christ is also by his works the
Revealer of God. He has made known to us the will
of God (i. 179). This, strictly speaking, carries beyond
the mere fact of deliverance : "is come not alone to deliver
us, but also to teach true love of God and works which God
requires of us" (180). He thus becomes our leader (195) and
pattern (313), whom we should follow (iii. 194, 211). Thus
the agency of Christ is two-fold : "For Christ everywhere in-
culcates these two things, viz.: redemption through him, and
that those who have been redeemed by him ought now to live
according to his example" (iii. 324). (*c*) Christ's redemptive
act now becomes ours through his relation to us as our Head,
and in the way appointed, *i. e.*, through our believing in him.
"But Christ is righteous and our Head, and we are his members ; therefore we the members come to God through the
righteousness of the Head" (i. 310), and : "If we believe upon
the Lord Christ Jesus, that he is our propitiation, etc., then is
he our entire perfection before God, our salvation, our payment
and atonement" (i. 186). He who believes on Christ is counted
by God as righteous (iii. 164) and has the forgiveness of sins
(i. 296, 393 ; iii. 230); so far, that is, as he follows Christ.
"Whence also his righteousness is our righteousness, if only we
walk, not according to the flesh, but according to the Spirit"
(iii. 209 f.). These are clear and thoroughly evangelical ideas.
Christ has endured for us the penalty of unrighteousness and performed the works of righteousness. Because we believe on him
and hold to him, God for his sake regards us as righteous.

5. Here arises the further question : How about Faith and its
origin ? The revelation of the love of God in Christ overcomes
us : "So that . . . at length the great humility of his mind
and his deeds of mercy . . . compel us to hold him in love and
to anticipate all good things from him" (i. 186, 311 ; iii. 205).
Faith is thus confidence in the grace of God. "For faith is
that by which we rest immovably, firmly, and undistractedly
upon the mercy of God" (iii. 231). But it is not to be understood in the sense of the *fides acquisita* (iii. 174. Cf. Luther, supra,
p. 254, n. 1), but it is wrought by the Spirit of God (iii. 223).

---

[1] But Zwingli adds : "or, that we may not presume to say too little about
his counsels, because it thus pleased him." Cf. Luther, supra, p. 271.

The Spirit makes man's spirit (*Gemüth*) "to understand his word" (i. 389) and gives man's spirit to understand that the word "comes from God" (1. 81). As one reads the Scriptures, comes the consciousness: "I have experienced that" (79). Hence, because the Spirit of God incites, we understand and comprehend the teachings of the Scriptures as the word of God. Thereby we are overpowered with a sense of satisfaction and inward health: "For Christian faith is something which is felt in the soul of believers, as health in the body" (iii. 198). To state the matter briefly in the sense of Zwingli, we may say : The Holy Spirit so moves man, that he feels the Scriptures to be the truth, and thereby attains confidence in the grace of God. This is faith. The Scriptures, as doctrine, have thus for him a significance different from that which they have for Luther, whose faith arose directly from the experience of the efficacious working of Christ (supra, p. 252 f.).

6. The movement begun in us by the Holy Spirit continues in such a way that good works follow faith (i. 278, 311). Since God thus works in us, we are his "fellow-workmen," *i. e.*, "tools in his hand" (406). Although the "infirmity" (*Bresten*) still clings to us and we sin in many ways, yet God continually "moves" us again, so that we return to him. And thus our very sin compels us to take refuge anew in God (i. 191 f.). Since now the Spirit of God works in believers that which is good, they no longer really need the law, "for the Spirit is above the law ; and where it is, there one no longer needs the law" (1. 212, 214).[1] The example of Christ takes the place of the law. "Therefore there is need of no law, for *Christ is his law;* upon him alone he looks, yea, Christ guides and leads him alone, so that he needs no other leader, for Christ is the end of the law" (1. 213). As the example of Christ here replaces the old law as an outward rule of conduct, it may also be said that all who are born of God obey his word (111. 178). In this sense, the law remains, and is even a part of the gospel. "The gospel thus understood, namely as the will of God revealed to men and required of them, contains in itself . . . commandment, prohibition, precept, and obedience ; so that all commandment and prohibition of God must remain in force forever" (i. 209 ff., 308).[2] The believer is to fulfill his commandments, except the tinsel-work of the ceremonial law (i.

---

[1] Cf. also the freedom from the law of Sabbath-observance, which recalls Luther's position, i. 317.

[2] Cf. also in i. 308, 554, the complaint concerning those who speak insolently (*unbescheidenlich*) of the law, representing that it makes us despair and hate God (referring to Luther).

311, 586), *i. e.*, the commandments, in so far as they coïncide
with the "law of nature" (i. 359, 361). The law is therefore
the permanent moral rule of conduct (i. 359, 325 ; iv. 102). But
it can be fulfilled only as God works in us the necessary power.
"The believer does it not of his own power, but God works in
him the love, the counsel, and the work, as much as he does"
(i. 311). But when we, warmed by the fire of love within us,
fulfill the law, we do it freely, not under compulsion (111. 205).
Herein is a further modification as compared with Luther—
Zwingli does not realize that "the law" is the expression
of an entirely different conception of life, and he unconsciously makes the gospel a "new law" (1. 311). God
impels us, but he impels us to the fulfilling of his commandments. Luther laid more stress upon the negative than upon
the positive character of the law ; Zwingli, on the contrary, put
the chief emphasis upon the latter.

7. In seeking to discover Zwingli's Ideal of the Christian
Life, we shall find especially instructive his tract entitled : *Quo
pacto ingenui adolescentes formandi sint* (iv. 149 ff.). Faith here
stands first. Christ is our attorney, surety, and advocate ; he has
opened for us the way to the Father. He who believes on him,
to him are his sins forgiven. But faith is also the principle of a
life of ceaseless striving after the good: "Only believers
experience how Christ gives them no ease and how cheerfully
and joyfully they address themselves to his business" (p. 152).
Among the means of preserving the spirit in this exalted state,
the study of the word stands first, but the example of Christ is
also particularly mentioned. As Christ gave himself for us, so
should we also not live unto ourselves, but seek to become all
things to all (155 f.). At the same time, we should be always
humble as was Christ. "He will therefore be perfect (*absolutus*)
who resolves to emulate Christ alone" (157). A life in the
assurance of faith and in the steadfastness of love in the imitation
of Christ—this is the ideal. The Christianity of Zwingli is
thoroughly practical. "It is the duty of a Christian man, not
to talk magnificently about doctrines, but to be always doing
great and difficult things with God" (158). Only when life is
conducted in obedience to God and his word, in true doctrine
and right living, is justice done to the glory of God (*e. g.*, i.
237, 322, 392, 398. Cf. iii. 165, 132, 48 f.).[1]

8. These are the fundamental reformatory principles of Zwingli.
Their essential agreement with Luther's ideas must be evident to
all. With these fundamental ideas were, however, combined a

[1] Cf. also the discourse of Schmidt of Küssnacht, i. 536 f.

number of subordinate convictions which help to explain the
new form assumed by his teaching in opposition to the medieval
views.   In opposition to the Romish doctrine of *merit* and works,
he developed his theory of predestination.   God is " an eternally
existent Working and Knowing " (i. 276) ; " the eternal
Power of all good, and an unchangeable Working " (277) ; and
"the first moving Cause " (278).   Yea, he is, properly speaking, Causality itself, since all second causes are only figuratively
speaking causes (iv. 96).   God rules in the world, as the soul
in the body.   Nothing can transpire which is contrary to his
will (iii. 283).   Everything which occurs may be traced back
to his power.   The believer recognizes that his works are really
works of God, and that he " is only an instrument and tool by
which God works " (1. 276).   This is divine providence.
" Providence is the perpetual and immutable government and
administration of the affairs of the universe " (iv. 84).   This
leads to the denial of all accidental occurrences as well as of all
free actions (iv. 93).   Everything, even evil, is based upon the
will of God (iv. 112 ff.).   This determinism involves the doctrine of *Predestination* (iii. 283) : " He elects one, to be fitted
for his work and use ; another, he does not desire " (i. 276).   " So
that thus election is attributed only to those who are to be saved ;
but those who are to be lost are not said to be elected, although
the divine will has determined also concerning them, but for the
repelling, rejecting, and repudiating of them, by which they
may become examples of justice " (iv. 115).   It is in accordance with the sole agency of God, that when some are saved and
others lost, the fate of both is ascribed to the divine will.   Everything depends upon the eternal election of God.   Only in the
elect is faith wrought ; it follows election, and is a sign of its
presence (iv. 121 ; vi. 1. 215, 340 ; vi. 2. 106, 105, 155).   He
who believes is elect.   But even the elect who die before attaining faith will be saved.   " For it is election which saves (*beatos
facit*)" (iv. 122, 123).   Only in a figurative sense can faith be
traced to the preaching of the word.   God uses the latter only
as an instrument: " He implants faith, as with an instrument,
but his own hand being also very near.   This inward drawing
is (the work) of the Spirit directly operating " (iv. 125).
Election alone saves ; it works everything good in man.
Only upon the ground of fixed election can man be sure
of salvation (iv. 140).   One thing is clear—and this was what
concerned Zwingli—that this doctrine excludes all insistence
upon works and merits.   " By the providence of God therefore
are abolished at once both free will and merit, for since it determines all these things, what are our parts, that we should be able

to think anything done by ourselves? But since all works are from him, how shall we merit anything?" (iii. 283; iv. 116; i. 275 f., 278). The Synergism of the Middle Ages is thus shattered by the doctrine of the sole agency of grace. Zwingli in this entered upon the path pursued by Luther in his *De servo arbitrio.* But there is still an essential difference between the two. While Luther never allowed his speculative determinism to effect his Soteriology, it assumed great importance in Zwingli's religious thought. He constantly recurs to it. While Luther once broaches the idea, Zwingli lays a constantly-increasing stress upon it, particularly in the controversy with Anabaptism. His ideas were doubtless moulded by Thomas of Aquino and the Stoic conception of God.[1] In fact, the parallel to Thomas' doctrine of grace is very striking. As the latter, for example, reduces grace finally to the idea of the Prime Mover (p. 118), so also does Zwingli (vid. supra). Whereas Luther conceived of God as Almighty Love revealed in Christ, Zwingli did not make this positive limitation of the earlier conception. God is to be known before Christ : "The knowledge of God by its very nature precedes the knowledge of Christ" (iii. 180).[2] It is certainly a perversion to describe the determinism of Zwingli as the "fundamental principle" of his theology, since his doctrine of justification had other sources and motives. But neither is it correct to regard it as a passing episode. It is a foreign, but permanent, intrusion—otherwise than in the case of Luther—into the warp and woof of his religious thought.[3] This foreign element robs

---

[1] IV. 139 : "To be of the universe is therefore to be of God ; " cf. 90: "What he (Pliny) calls nature, we call God." Seneca, p. 95, 93, the doctrine of ideas : "These patterns of all things God has within himself." He studied Thomas, iv. 113. And shall we see no connection between the division of his material in the *Comm. de ver. et fals. religione* (God, to whom religion tends, and man, who by religion tends to God) and the arrangement in the *Summa* of Thomas? (cf. supra, p. 98).

[2] The whole passage—which combats a fundamental thought of Luther's—reads : "That therefore our rivals shall here say, that we have hitherto discoursed of piety in such a way as to have made no mention of salvation through Christ and of grace, they caw in vain : first, because whatever we have said concerning the fellowship of the soul and God has been thus said also of Christ just as of God (for Christ is God and man) ; second, because the knowledge of God by its very nature precedes the knowledge of Christ."

[3] I cannot therefore agree with K. MÜLLER (Symbolik, 450), when he pronounces it just as improper to bring the charge of a metaphysical determinism against Zwingli as against Luther. He has failed to take account of the *increasing* significance of the theory for Zwingli. Cf. also DILTHEY'S opinion as to the "pantheism" of Zwingli (Archiv. f. Gesch. d. Philos. v. 370). The close-drawn lines of the whole document, *De providentia dei*, attest both the humanistic and philosophical trend of Zwingli and the lingering influence of Thomistic metaphysics upon him.

man indeed of the freedom of the will, but it also inspires his will—as an instrument of the almighty divine agency—to the most strenuous activity. "A long list of stern, heroic spirits down to Cromwell stands beneath the influence of this attitude of will (DILTHEY, Arch. f. Gesch. d. Philos. v. 369).

9. Another consequent of Zwingli's reformatory views is seen in his conception of the Church. The hierarchical view disappears entirely. Christ alone is the foundation of the church. All disciples, "all believers and teachers," receive the keys, *i. e.*, the authority to preach the gospel (i. 386, 387 f., iii. 215, 221). The prelates are not the church, but it is "the entire congregation of all those who are founded and built up in one faith upon the Lord Jesus Christ." With this congregation at large is contrasted the individual congregation, or *kilchhöre* (i. 197 ff., 656; iii. 125 ff.). The church, as the communion of saints, that is, of all believers (iii. 131), is not visible, since its members are scattered throughout the whole world (i. 201). It is composed of believers, who place their confidence in Christ alone, and obey, not human ordinances, but the authority of the divine word (i. 201 f.). That is the true church, which never errs, which clings to the word of God, and follows only the shepherds who bring that word (iii. 129). These simple conceptions were afterward modified by the introduction of the idea of predestination. The invisible church now becomes the totality of the elect and believing of all ages (vi. 1. 337, 447). Whereas, in the earlier writings of Zwingli, the conceptions of the true church universal and the *communio sanctorum* are not kept distinctly separate, this is now done. The separate congregations, or *Kilchhören*, form in combination the universal *ecclesia sensibilis*, or *visibilis* (iii. 574, 576 ff., 580, 586; vi. 432; viii. 380), in which the *ecclesia spiritualis invisibilis*, or *electa* is contained (iv. 8 f., 58). The source of the latter's existence is to be found solely in predestination. Therefore may children, even though baptism effects no real change in them, be fully qualified members of the church. It was, in part, the effort to maintain his theory of baptism against the Anabaptists and yet preserve the membership of children in the church, which led to this application of predestination to the conception of the church (cf. GOTT-SCHICK, Ztschr. f. KG. viii. 604 ff.). But the church thus falls asunder into two unconnected parts: the elect of all ages and places, including noble heathen whom we shall meet in heaven—[1] in short, all whom the Spirit shall have transformed by the exer-

---

[1] *E. g.*, Hercules, Theseus, Socrates, Aristides, Antigonus, Numa, Camillus, the Catos and Scipios, iv. 65; vi. 1. 242; 2. 69; viii. 179; vii. 550.

tion of his omnipotence—and the historical fellowship of believers in Christ.   There exists no necessary connection between the two, for "a conductor (*dux*) or vehicle of the Spirit is not necessary" (iv. 10).   See SEEBERG, Begr. d. Kirche, i. 78 ff.

10. This brings us to the conception of the Sacraments. Zwingli here adopts the Augustinian, purely symbolical view, which was also advocated by Erasmus.   The sacraments are nothing more than "a sure sign, or seal" (1. 239).   They, on the one hand, remind the believer in a symbolic form of salvation and its blessings, and are, on the other hand, a means by which he testifies his membership in the church of Christ.   There resides in them no kind of purifying or sanctifying power ; they are simply signs in the sense indicated (iii. 229, 231 ; iv. 117). We dare not attribute to the symbols the "things which belong to the divine power alone " (iv. 119).   Only two signs of this kind were instituted by Christ ; the other five sacraments are to be abolished as not being commanded by him.[1]   Baptism also falls under this symbolical point of view.   Through it we engage ourselves to Christ (is " either a candidate or a soldier of Christ "), and we receive a symbol, " that we are to conform our life to the rule of Christ" (iii. 231, 643).   It is an "initiative sign," an engagement, as when a member of a confederacy wears a white cross as a badge of his membership (ii. 1. 242, 249). If Zwingli himself at first entertained doubts as to the propriety of infant baptism (ii. 1. 245 ; vii. 365), he distinctly advocated it after the Anabaptists began to make it a prominent object of their assaults (A. D. 1525.   See esp. Von Tauf, Von Wiedertauf, and Von Kindertauf).   But while Luther in these conflicts was led to value more highly the historical and positive ordinances, Zwingli thought that he could best sweep away the foundations of the Anabaptist party by making baptism a bare symbol, and, particularly, by insisting upon it as an obligatory symbol.   By the greater stress laid upon predestination and the purely external character of baptism, it appeared that the great importance attached to baptism by the opposing party might be best shown to be unjustifiable ; while by insisting upon the obligatory character of the ordinance its administration to children was made to appear necessary.   It was in combating the Anabaptists that the speculative and philosophical element became more promi-

---

[1] See criticisms in the "*Uslegen*," etc.: confirmation, 1. 240 f.; unction, 241 ; against confession to men (*lyselbicht*), with slight criticisms of Luther, 393 f., 400, cf. iii. 543, 562 ; ii. 2. 22 ; confession to be made only to Christ, 396 f.; the priest is only to be asked for advice, 394 ; works of penance, 397 ; indulgences, 398 ff.; purgatory, 402 ff.   Against the priestly character of the clergy—the priesthood an "office," not a rank, 414 f.

nent in Zwingli's teaching. His determinism, having served him as a weapon against the Romish work-righteousness, was turned also against the mystical dreams of a visible congregation of saints. Upon Zwingli's doctrine of the Lord's Supper, see § 73. Cf. STÄHELIN, i. 484 ff. USTERI, Darstellung d. Tauflehre Zw., in Stud. u. Krit., 1882, 205 ff.

11. Zwingli proclaimed the truth of the gospel, and drew the doctrinal inferences which seemed involved in it. The source upon which he depended was primarily the Holy Scriptures. But he felt himself also in full accord with the doctrine of God and the Christology found in the ancient symbols (i. 57 ; iv. 3 ff.). He presented no original ideas in these connections. He conceived of God as the all-working Power, and at the same time accepted the orthodox formulas, without attempting to harmonize the two conceptions. His Christology has the Nestorian tendency of the Scholastics (see below). His interpretation of original sin harmonizes with that of the later Middle Ages. His theory of the sacraments follows the symbolic view not infrequently held in the Middle Ages. He mingles philosophical theories with his presentations of the gospel, lacking Luther's sense of the positive character of revelation—Duns and the Nominalists having here prepared the way. Thus Christianity became a kind of philosophy deduced from the Bible. In view of these characteristics of his teaching, it may be said that the undeniable difference between Zwingli and Luther—despite their common understanding of the gospel—is to be explained by the fact, that Zwingli received his impulse originally from the Erasmian illuministic tendency, and that, in consequence, the medieval ideas continued to exert a greater influence upon him than upon Luther.

As in the particulars already noted, so also in his practical operations in the church, Zwingli betrays his dependence upon the medieval ideals. But the theocratic ideal which he pursued allows to neither church nor state its proper position. On the one hand, the secular government conducts the discipline of the church in such a way that the doctrine of the latter becomes directly the law of the state ; while, on the other hand, the secular government is absolutely subject to the authority of the Scriptures, its laws and ordinances being valid only in so far as they are scriptural. If the government acts in a way contrary to the Scriptures, it is to be abrogated. The subjection of the church to the state is only apparent, for the laws of the state are, after all, valid only in so far as they conform to the law of the church, or the Bible. This is a genuinely medieval idea.[1] The carrying out of his re-

---

[1] Supra (p. 172, 183 f.). Cf. Zw. i. 524 : "My lords should also prescribe no law otherwise than out of the holy undeceptive Scripture of God. If they

formatory work embraced both a new system of doctrine and a new order of social and practical life, which must be enforced by the agency of the state. Christianity is an affair of the state, but the state is the organ of the church. Like Savonarola, Zwingli sought to reform his city according to the divine law of the Bible, with the help of the secular power. It was also in accord with the example of Savonarola, that Zwingli's political ambition was not satisfied with the direction of his native city, but associated his direct reformatory labors with political combinations of the widest and most daring character (cf. LENZ, Zw. u. Landgraf Philipp, in Ztschr. f. KG. iii. 28 ff., 220 ff., 429 ff.). Thus, in every sphere of his doctrinal and practical activity, we are impressed with the medieval and humanistic limitations of Zwingli, and that, too, in such forms as to emphasize the contrast between his ideas and those of Luther.[1]

§ 73. *The Controversy Upon the Lord's Supper.*

LITERATURE. DIECKHOFF, Die ev. Abendmalsl. im Ref.-ztalter, i. 1854. THOMASIUS-SEEBERG, DG., ii. 522 ff., 571 ff. BAUR, Zw's Theol. ii. 292 ff. STÄHELIN, Zwingli, ii. 213 ff. KÖSTLIN, Luther, ii., ed. 4, 66 ff. W. WALTHER, Reformirte Taktik im Sakr.-streit der Ref., in Neue kirchl. Ztschr., 1896, 794 ff., 917 ff. KAWERAU (Möller, KG. iii.), 74 ff. KÜBEL, PRE. xvi., ed. 2, 121 ff. JÄGER, Luthers relig. Interesse an der Lehre von der Realpräsenz, 1900.

1. The difference in the views of Zwingli and Luther found expression in the controversy upon the Lord's Supper. But Zwingli had already, before the outbreak of the controversy, developed his view of the Lord's Supper to a certain degree of maturity. The theory of transubstantiation he had from the beginning regarded with suspicion (WW. vii. 391). He received the impulse to the construction of a positive theory, as he reported to Melanchthon, from Erasmus (C. R. iv. 970). The purely symbolical view was in harmony, as well with the critical humanistic school of thought, to which he originally belonged, as with his general conception of the sacraments and the separation of the immediate divine operations from all earthly media,

should become negligent at this point and recognize anything else, as I hope (they may) not, I would none the less stiffly preach against them with the word of God." See also "Schlussreden," 42: "But should they (the government) become untrustworthy and act beyond the rule of Christ, may they be deposed by God." Zwingli here has in mind by no means simply the form of the republican constitution. On the basis of his conception of popular sovereignty, it is his view that "the mass of the people," or the "greater part," are authorized to "cast out" ungodly kings (see Vol. I., p. 318).

[1] I do not, of course, forget that Luther also had medieval limitations.

to which he advanced.   It therefore fits logically into the frame-work of his theological ideas, although it cannot be regarded as a criterion of his fundamental reformatory principles.   For as, one the one hand, he derived his ideas upon the subject from a foreign source, so also in the illuminated circles of the day the symbolical theory was in the very air.   His ideas were brought to a definite conclusion only in consequence of the correspondence of Honius with Luther (p. 288), in which the former interpreted the *est* as equivalent to *significat*.[1]   The publication of Zwingli upon the subject seems not to have become known until the latter part of A. D. 1523 (LOOFS, DG. 387 n.).   Thenceforth he is clear in his mind.   Basing his argument upon Jn. 6 ("the flesh profiteth nothing"), he, in harmony with Augustine and the older Scholastics (Vol. I., p. 323 ; supra, p. 133 f.), con-ceives of the existence of the body of Christ in heaven as local, and accordingly rejects the presence of the body in the Lord's Supper, being thus, of course, compelled to interpret the words of institution in a purely symbolical way.   He was from the first conscious of the deviation of his ideas from those of Luther, which explains in part the zealous assertions of his (supposed) independence of the Saxon reformer (supra, p. 308).   If he at first, indeed, represented this difference as a merely formal one, though emphasizing the idea of a repeated memorial (Wieder-gedächtniss, i. 257), yet he very soon resolved to assail the theory of Luther, and from the year 1525 built up a carefully planned and vigorous propaganda for the purpose of winning the Southern Germans to his view, at first through the fictitious letter to Alberus (iii. 591 ff.).[2]   Like-minded friends rallied around him with advice and aid (Oecolampadius,[3] Bucer, Capito), and means of doubtful character were employed (the corruptions in Bugenhagen's commentary upon the Psalms, and the notes in the translation of Luther's Church Postils).   There was a feel-ing of strong confidence that Luther's view could be explained

---

[1] The formula, *significat*, has a point of attachment in the general sacra-mental theory of the later Middle Ages (supra, p. 127).   What was relatively new was really only the application of the formula to the Lord's Supper, which held an exceptional position in relation to the medieval sacramental theory.   But see already Wickliffe, supra, p. 206.

[2] The following among Zwingli's writings have a bearing at this point : the Comm. de ver et fals. relig., 1525 (iii. 239 ff.); Subsidium sive coronis de eucharist, 1525 (iii. 326 ff.); Ad Io. Bugenhagen, 1525 (iii. 604 ff.); Un-derrichtung vom Nachtmal, 1526 (ii. 1. 426 ff.); Amica exegesis, 1527 (iii. 459 ff.); fründlich verglimpfung, 1527 (ii. 2. 1 ff.); Dass dise worte Christi . . . ewiglich den alten einigen sinn haben werdend, 1527 (ii. 2. 16 ff.); Uiber Luther's buch bekenntniss genannt, 1527 (ii. 2. 94 ff.).

[3] Oecolampadius entered the controversy with his tract, De genuina ver-borum Christi . . . expositione liber, 1525.

away as simply the product of hypocrisy and timidity (*e. g.*, vii. 390 f.). Zwingli and his friends were impatient in their desire to measure swords with Luther and undermine his authority, and counseled against the use of prudent or pious tactics in dealing with him. (See proofs adduced in WALTHER, l. c., p. 815 ff., 916 ff.)[1] And they actually succeeded in stirring up a serious agitation against Luther's doctrine in Southern Germany, although their efforts met with some determined opposition upon that territory (Osiander, Brenz, the Syngramma, Pirckheimer).[2] These facts must be kept in view if we would understand the severity of Luther when he finally broke his silence and entered the fray.[3]

2. Zwingli's theory is a simple one. Bread and wine are signs of the body and blood offered up in sacrifice for us. These signs signify the body and blood thus offered, and thus remind us of the redemptive act (*e. g.*, iii. 599). The *est* of the words of institution is therefore equivalent to *significat* (ii. 2. 41 ff., 61 ; iii. 257, 336, 553, 606). Only faith can apprehend and appropriate salvation ; but faith has to do only with spiritual entities. Hence the eating of the body of Christ can signify only the believing appropriation of the salvation secured for us by the sacrifice of that body. Christ is present in the Supper only " by the contemplation of faith " (*contemplatione fidei*), but not " in essence and really " (*per essentiam et realiter*). Faith in Christ

---

[1] Bucer writes very characteristically to Zwingli : " O Flesh ! O Satan ! what work hast thou made for us ! It shall be destroyed by us for the promotion of the glory of God, and we shall see this arrogance vanish " (Zw. opp. vii. 521). Luther expresses his opinion of the conflict from the moral point of view with unsurpassable clearness (E. 30. 266): "My free, open, simple snapping at the devil is to my notion much better than their poisonous, plotting assassination, which they practice against the upright under the pretense of peace and love." As to the method of his opponents, see also 30, 24, 38, 61, 98, 139, 148 ff., 160, 205. It is more important to set forth clearly the spirit of these opponents and the historic basis of it, than to shudder at the thought of Luther's coarseness in dealing with them.

[2] See Bilibaldi Pirckheimeri de vera Christi carne et vero ejus sanguine ad Io. Oecolamp. respons. Norimb. 1526, and B. Pirckh. de vera Chr., etc., respons. secunda, Norimb. 1527. The argumentation of these documents touches the positions of Luther at many points (*e. g.*, the clearness of the words of institution—see the first response, form B, 7 r, E 4, and in the conclusion, upon the definition of a *tropus*, E 5 v ; against the *significat*, F. 2 r and the two resp. F. 8 r); even in the conception of the ubiquity : "And it would not indeed be impossible with God . . . that one body, most highly clarified, should be in many places " (1st resp. F. 5 v). But STÄHELIN (Zw. ii. 269 f.) is in error when he represents Pirckheimer as having " first " introduced the idea of the ubiquity into the controversy, as Luther had already done so in 1525 (E. 29. 288 f., 294). Pirckheimer had read Luther (*e. g.*, resp. 1 F. 3 v, 6 v ; H. 1 r, 2).

[3] See Luther's writings during the controversy. Cf. supra, p. 227, n. 3.

is really the eating of his body. "The body of Christ is then eaten, when his death (*caesum*) for us is believed" (iii. 243 f., 595, 331; iv. 53, 118). If we would take the eating of the body of Christ seriously, we would come into conflict, on the one hand, with the maxim, that the flesh profiteth nothing (Jn. 6. 63 f.; ii. 2. 85 ff., 184 ff.); and, on the other hand, collide with the limitation of Christ's body to locality (ii. 2. 81 ; iii. 332, 338, 512). Moreover, at the time of the institution of the Lord's Supper, the blood of Christ had not yet been shed (iii. 333 f.).

The Christology of Zwingli is at this point called into service. While Luther interprets the traditional dogma from the viewpoint of personal unity, Zwingli always premises the abstract difference of the two natures. God "assumed human nature" —the incarnation signifies nothing more than this (ii. 2. 69 f.). As in the history of Christ's earthly life his two natures are to be carefully discriminated (so that, for example, he according to his human nature does not know the day of his second coming, yet according to his divine nature knows all things, iii. 537 f.; ii. 2. 67), so also his divine nature fills heaven and earth, while at the same time his human nature is limited to a particular place in heaven (for, as created, it is " not infinite ") and is a type of our resurrection (ii. 2. 71, 72, 81 : "willst also never be able to maintain that the human nature of Jesus Christ is in more than one place "). If now in the Scriptures that is ascribed to the one nature which belongs to the other, or attributes of the one nature are attributed to the entire person, this is to be explained through the figure of speech known as *Alloeosis*, or "interchange," *i. e.*, it is a rhetorical " exchange by which, when speaking of the one nature of Christ, we use the terms belonging to the other " (iii. 525 ; ii. 2. 68 f.). Thus, if it is said of Christ that he is at the right hand of God, this, strictly interpreted, applies only to his divine nature (ii. 2. 71). Zwingli's ideas as to the divine and human natures of Christ and his personal unity are here orthodox (*e. g.*, ii. 2. 66 ff., 82 ; ii. 1. 449). But for the great thought in Luther's theology—that even the human words and works of Christ are a revelation of God—he has no comprehension.[1] His Christology remains absolutely upon the plane of the medieval conception. The divine and human natures are assigned to the opposite categories of finite and infinite nature. The consequences of this

---

[1] STÄHELIN is not entirely correct, when he (Zw. ii. 175) describes, as the reformatory factor, in Zwingli as in Luther, " the overwhelming impression of the vision of Christ upon the sensibilities of the soul burdened by sin." Cf. supra, p. 314, but also p. 310.

position came to light in the controversy upon the Lord's Supper.

The Lord's Supper is thus, according to Zwingli, on the one hand, a memorial celebration designed to remind us of the redemption wrought by the death of Christ; and, on the other hand, a profession of adherence to Christ in the presence of the congregation, and thus the assuming of an obligation to lead a Christian life (iii. 601).[1]

3. We found, as the result of our study of Luther's doctrine of the Lord's Supper (supra, p. 288), that he from the beginning taught the presence of the body of Christ in the Supper, and in such a way that the body, as a seal of the forgiveness of sins wrought by it and by the word appropriated by faith, strengthens and confirms the communicant in his faith. The theories of Carlstadt, who misinterpreted the τοῦτο ; of Zwingli, who interpreted the *est* as meaning *significat;* of Oecolampadius, who explained the σῶμα as a sign of the body,—all fell beyond the lines of his thought. It was just at this time, moreover, that Luther became thoroughly convinced of the indissoluble connection between the empirical word and the exertion of the Spirit's agency. Here appeared to be another attempt, similar to that of the Anabaptists, to tear the two asunder (E. 30. 136, 353). Finally, he felt the new theory to be unspiritual and unchurchly, and he was convinced that it was unscriptural as well. The words of the institution appeared to him simple and plain. What need for interpretations of such plain terms as bread, wine, body, blood, eat, drink, is (29. 329, 331 ; 30. 33 ff., 154, 293, 355)? And as the words point to reality, this is confirmed by the circumstance that the traditional preservation of them is in all the sources in the same simple form (30. 311), and by the consideration that symbols are characteristic of the Old Testament, not of the New (ib. 338). Accordingly, he inferred that we truly eat the body of Christ in the Lord's Supper (29. 338; 30. 30, 103). " But how this occurs, or how he is in the bread, we do not know, and are not to know. We should believe the word of God, and not dictate ways and means to him " (30. 30). The

---

[1] Zwingli thus summarizes the errors of Luther: (1) That the body of Christ, naturally eaten in this sacrament, confirms faith. (2) That the body of Christ, naturally eaten, forgives sins. (3) That the body of Christ is naturally brought in the vehicle of the words spoken. (4) "That when I offer the body of Christ to be naturally eaten, I bring the gospel very near to him to whom I offer this, and to whom I give the body and blood " (iii. 561). Also, ii. 2. 93 : "That the flesh of Christ is an entirely spiritual flesh ; that the body of Christ is, like the divine nature, omnipresent, . . . that the body of Christ, bodily eaten, preserves our body for the resurrection, . . . gives and increases faith."

exegetical difficulties of the words of institution never troubled Luther, and he denied the application of Jn. 6 to the Lord's Supper (30. 79 ff.). Nor did the manner of the union of the body and bread disturb him. There was another problem, however, which awakened his most profound concern. His opponents asserted the impossibility of the bodily presence at many places. If Luther meant to maintain his position, it was, therefore, incumbent upon him to prove that the ubiquity of the body of Christ was conceivable (30. 49, 56, 58, 70, 201, 206, 282).

4. In order to follow the arguments employed by Luther in support of this position, we must bear two things constantly in mind. In the first place, for Luther, as a scholastically trained theologian, the problem was not an uncongenial one ;[1] and, in the second place, his Christology furnished the materials to be used in its solution. He had from the beginning thought of the two natures of Christ as so united that the man Jesus was, in all his words and works, the expression and organ of his divine nature. He knew no God except the One revealed in the man Jesus. God " is present and substantial " (*gegenwärtig* und *wesenlich*) in all created things, but he " dwells" in Christ bodily, so that one person is man and God (30. 63). When these ideas are considered in the light of the formula of the doctrine of the two natures, the inference is, that the two natures are " one single person " (30. 63, 206 f., 211, 222), in absolutely inseparable union, so that where the one is the other must also be (211 f.). There subsists between the two a relation like that between body and soul (204); and the flesh of Christ is, therefore, being permeated by God, " nothing but spirit, nothing but holiness, nothing but purity " (231). It is " a divine flesh, a spirit-flesh." " It is in God and God in it " (30. 125 ; 48. 26, 58). God has become completely man, so that all human attributes, such as suffering and dying, have also become his (25. 310, 312, 314). " Out of the infinite God has been made a finite and definable man " (47. 182). The *communicatio idiomatum* is thus taken in its full meaning (25. 309). All the activity and suffering of the man is also the activity and suffering of God (30. 62, 67 ; 46. 332 f). " Whatsoever I behold in Christ is at the same time both human and divine " (47. 361 f.). " Wherever thou canst say, Here is God, there must thou also say, Therefore Christ the man is also here. And if thou shouldst point out a place where God was and not the man,

---

[1] Supra, p. 133, 204. Luther had the feeling of superiority of a dogmatically (scholastically) trained theologian as compared with Zwingli. The latter was for him "a self-grown doctor; they generally turn out so " (30. 267).

then would the person be already divided, since I might then say with truth, Here is God, who is not man, and never yet became man. But nothing of that God for me ! . . . Nay, friend, wherever thou placest God for me, there must thou also place for me the human nature. They cannot be separated and divided from each other. There has come to be One person " (30. 211).[1] The divine nature gives its peculiarity (attributes) to the human nature, and the human nature also in return its peculiarity to the divine nature (30. 204 ; 47. 177). It is no more wonderful that God dies, than that he became man (25. 312). Hence Luther could see in the *Alloeosis* only " the devil's mask " (30. 203, 205, 225), for this separation of the works of the two natures no longer permits us to see in the human nature the full revelation of God. It misleads us, after the fashion of the Scholastics, to take refuge in the divine nature and cling to this, looking away from the man Jesus (47. 361 f.). It robs the atoning work of Christ of its specific divine value (25. 312 f.; 30. 203; 18. 225). It is, therefore, by no means a product of polemical necessity which we behold in Luther's Christology, as developed in the controversy with Zwingli. It is the same Christology which he had advocated from the beginning. And this doctrine marks an advance in the development of the traditional Christology—effected by evolution from within. The divine nature no longer swallows up the human nature, but the latter is the organ and bearer of the former. It is precisely the unqualified preservation of the human nature which makes Jesus capable of really becoming the God revealed among us. Luther's most profound ideas concerning the knowledge of God and faith may be understood in the light of these principles (supra, p. 252 f.). But historical fidelity requires the recognition of the fact, that Luther in the controversy upon the Lord's Supper extended his Christology by including an inference not previously drawn. The practical identity of the divine and human natures in the earthly life of Jesus is deliberately transferred to the state of exaltation. If the words and deeds of Jesus on earth were the words and deeds of God, then are the works of the Lord in heaven also the works of the man Jesus. And this means that the man Jesus is at the same time the omnipotent and omnipresent Lord of the world. If he is present in the Lord's Supper, he is there also the man Jesus ; and since he arose from the dead bodily, his body is also present in the sacrament. Thus the theory of the Ubiquity is,

---

[1] Luther does not yet employ the term, Person, in the modern sense. It corresponds precisely with the ancient " Hypostasis," *e. g.*, 30. 204 : " Because body and soul is one person." Luther elsewhere speaks of Christ as "one person " with God (30. 216, 227).

in Luther's understanding of it, only a logical inference from his Christology.[1]

5. Luther opens the discussion with a definition of the term : the Right Hand of God. This cannot be conceived of as a "golden chair" beside the Father (30. 56 f.). We must here recall Luther's conception of God as the "omnipotent Power." If now God is the all-permeating and all-moving Will, then his Right Hand is simply everywhere. If God is "substantial and present at all places," in "the smallest leaf upon the trees," in "the most inward" and "most outward" things (58),[2] then his Right Hand is also "everywhere in all things" (64). Accordingly, Christ is also omnipresent, and that, too, in his body, *i. e.*, he reigns and has power over all things. "If he is to have power and reign, he must certainly also be there present and substantial" (65). This must, of course, be applicable in a general sense, even apart from all thought of the Lord's Supper.[3] The body of Christ is in every stone, in fire and water. But we can really find and apprehend him only where he has in his word directed us to seek him (29. 338). "But he is then present for thee when he adds his word, and thereby binds himself, and says : Here shalt thou find me." He is omnipresent, but in his divine mode of presence incomprehensible : "He has now also become incomprehensible, and thou wilt not seize upon him, although he is in thy bread, unless it be that he may bind himself to thee and assign thee to a particular table by a word, and point out to thee the very bread by his word" (30. 69 f.). As the divine nature, so also is Christ in his body near to all, "and it is only a question of his revealing himself" (30. 67); but this takes place in the words of institution, which instruct us to seek and find in a particular loaf him who is essentially present in

---

[1] A peculiarity of Luther's Christology is the lack of a sharp discrimination between the states of humiliation and exaltation. This may be understood, when we remember that his practical religious mode of apprehension saw in the man Jesus the full and real revelation of God. If we recall his definition of the divinity of Christ as the omnipotent Loving-will (p. 253), the question arises : How, in the light of this, shall all the Ubiquity be conceived in harmony with Luther? We might, perhaps, reply : The omnipotent Redeeming-will, which became one with the man Jesus, is present with the man Jesus in the Lord's Supper, in order by this presence to assure us of the reality of redemption. But Luther did not draw these inferences.

[2] "Therefore must he be himself present in every creature in its most inward and most outward (parts), around and about, through and through, beneath and above, before and behind, so that nothing can be more truly nor profoundly present in all creatures than God himself with his power."

[3] Even the earthly body of Christ was "present everywhere," 30. 67 ; upon the glorification of his body Luther lays but little stress, 30. 98 ff.; cf. Occam, supra, p. 205.

every loaf. The presence of the glorified body is to be conceived of in the same manner as the divine presence in the world
in general. God is not " such an outspread, long, broad, thick,
high, deep Being," filling the world as straw fills a sack (ib.
221); as though God were such a great outspread Object, reaching through and out beyond every created thing " (213, 216).
We are not, therefore, to think of any local, sensible presence.
There are, says Luther, "three ways of being in a place : *locally*
or *circumscriptively*, *definitively*, and *repletively* (207). The first
indicates a purely spacial relation, as of wine in a cask. Anything
is *definitively*, or " incomprehensibly," at a place when it does
not correspond with the portions of space in the latter ; as an
angel may be in a whole house, in one room, or even in a nutshell (208). The mode of presence is *repletive*, or supernatural,
" when anything is at the same time in its entirety at all places and
fills all places, and is yet measured and contained by no place "
(209).[1] This repletive existence is now attributed also to the body
of Christ (211). All things are " as related to the body of
Christ, present and penetrable " (210, 216). His body was
present *circumscriptively* during his earthly life, " since it took
and gave space according to its size " (216). The *definitive* form
of presence is to be attributed to the body which passed out of
the closed grave and through the locked doors, and to the body
present in the bread (216). As the soul is present at the same
time in the whole body just as in every separate part ; as vision
or sound reaches over great distances ; as sound passes through
air, water, boards, and walls, and enters many ears at once, in
such a way are we to conceive also of Christ's presence in the
Lord's Supper (29. 333 f.; 30. 216, 218 f.). We are, hence,
to represent to ourselves the presence of Christ in the sense in
which God as the Omnipotent Will dwells in all things, or in
which the soul permeates the body, and not in the " crude, fat,
and thick ideas " of the circumscriptive mode of existence (215).
The word " in " is not to be understood in the sense in which
"straw is in a sack and bread in a basket " (223). Not in this
external, local way is Christ's body in the Lord's Supper, but in
some such way as color and light are in the eye (66. 189 f.).
A " sacramental unity" (*Einigkeit*) exists between the body
and the bread (297, 300). But the body, which is here spoken
of, is the veritable body of Christ which was born of the Virgin
(89).

If we compare with this Occam's doctrine of Ubiquity, p.

---

[1] This classification is of scholastic origin. The first two modes are derived from Occam (supra, p. 204). The three-fold classification (adding the
repletive mode) was taken from Biel (Sent. i. d. 37 qu.).

204 f.),[1] it is clear that Luther was influenced by Occam. Both the classification of the modes of spacial existence, and the super-spacial existence of the body of Christ in the Lord's Supper and in all existing things, point unmistakably to that source. But a profound difference is here traceable. While Occam, in addition to this bodily presence everywhere, thinks of the real body of Christ as in one place in heaven ; for Luther the body of Christ is, by virtue of the *communicatio idiomatum*, absolutely omnipresent. Occam appends to the current medieval doctrine a speculative inference, postulating a certain Something which may figure as the body of Christ in the Lord's Supper. Luther defends the religious idea, that, just as we apprehend Christ only in the positive forms of his human life, so he is present in the Holy Supper also as the man Jesus with the human nature (including his body) by which he effects our salvation. What he is most earnestly striving for will be evident if we compare his original conception of the Lord's Supper : "The same Christ who has secured for us grace and the forgiveness of sins is present in the Lord's Supper in order to assure us of his redeeming act."[2] Here lies the nerve of his opposition to Zwingli and Oecolampadius. The sacrament is not "a sign of a future or absent thing ; " but a "form of the thing present and yet invisible." Under the visible form of bread and wine are "his invisible body and blood present" (105). The important thing, for which he contends, is that Christ, and Christ the historical Redeemer, is himself present, and that we are not merely to think of him as present by an effort of our imagination. The scholastic material by which he seeks to establish this position is regarded as means to the end in view.[3]

6. With this view harmonize also the utterances of Luther concerning the Reception and Fruits of the Sacrament. We do really eat and chew the body of Christ, and the pope was therefore justified in requiring this confession from Berenger (supra, p. 76). But the bread is the body, as the dove is the Holy Spirit ; for "no one sees, grasps, eats, or chews the body of Christ, as we visibly see and chew other flesh. For whatever we do to the bread is well and properly applied to the body of Christ, on account of the sacramental unity" (297, cf. 57. 75 f.). The bread is therefore really eaten, but with it at the same time the

---

[1] See already Alger, supra, p. 77, and Gerhoh, p. 66.

[2] Cf. 29. 348 ; 48. 23 ; 30. 85, 134, 137 : "What is the difference now ? Yea, how is it any better for them to eat flesh and bone with the soul, than that we should eat it with the mouth ? "

[3] Luther himself wished these explanations to be regarded only as possibilities, which do not exclude other explanations, 30. 200, 202, 210, 217.

spiritual body of Christ; bread and body are at the same time and together present (300). There results "a substantial (*natürlich*) unification of the body of Christ with us, and not alone a spiritual, subsisting in the mind and will" (202). But despite this *manducatio oralis*, our reception of this gift must be spiritual, *i. e.*, the heart must believe the presence of Christ in the bread, which the word proclaims (90 f., 93, 185).[1] Only faith apprehends life and salvation in the present body of the Lord (130). This is the spiritual eating, which must accompany the bodily eating (86, 185). The body of Christ is therefore present in the Lord's Supper, but only the believer understands and grasps this and has in consequence the blessing which the body brings: "That which is given therein and therewith, the body cannot grasp nor take to itself; but this is done by the faith of the heart which discerns this treasure and desires it" (Large Cat., Müller, p. 504).[2]

From this we may understand Luther's view of the Benefit of the Sacrament. The body of Jesus, whose presence in the bread faith apprehends, strengthens faith (135) and gives to it the assurance of the forgiveness of sins (136). The presence of the body and blood of Christ brings us the salvation which he has secured by means of this body and blood. The new testament is here and brings us "the forgiveness of sins, the Spirit, grace, life, and all blessedness" (338). Thus the word, combined with the Redeemer offered by it and bodily present in the sacrament, effects a strengthening of faith, the sense of forgiveness, life, and salvation.[3] To this spiritual effect produced by the

[1] But unbelievers also receive the body (*manducatio infidelium*), although to their own hurt, 29. 346; 30. 369, 86, 343). Cat. 509. But those who do not at all believe the words of institution, such as the Fanatics, receive nothing but bread and wine (30. 132. Cat. 504).

[2] The presence of the body and blood, as Luther always maintained, involves the personal presence of Christ, by virtue of the personal unity (29. 295; 30. 130 ff.). On the other hand, the idea that the older German linguistic usage, in which *Leib* (body) is equivalent to "person" (*e. g.*, in Luther, 45. 13 f.: "In the German language we do not call a dead man a 'body,' but a living man who has body and soul"), influenced Luther's conception of the "body" of Christ, is, so far as I can see, without any foundation.

[3] 30. 338 f.: "The words are the first thing, for without the words the cup and bread would be nothing. Further, without the bread and cup, there would be no body and blood of Christ. Without the body and blood of Christ, there would be no new testament. Without the new testament, there would be no forgiveness of sins. Without forgiveness of sins, there would be no life and salvation. Thus the words, in the first place, embrace the bread and the cup (to constitute) the sacrament. The bread and cup embrace the body and blood of Christ. The body and blood of Christ embrace the new testament. The new testament embraces the forgiveness of sins. The forgiveness of sins embraces eternal life and salvation. Behold, all this do the words of the Lord's Supper offer and give to us, and we grasp it by faith."

Lord's Supper is added further, in harmony with the representations of the ancient church (Irenæus, ib. 116 ff.), an effect upon the body of the recipient. The body of Christ is a pledge which gives to our body the assurance that it shall, by virtue of the "eternal food" thus received by us, also live forever (72). This "spiritual food" transforms the poor "moth-sack," so "that it also becomes spiritual, that is, eternally alive and blessed " (101 f. 132, 135). But this second train of thought, which was of course particularly adapted for use against Zwingli, had but a secondary importance for Luther. He could omit it altogether in his exposition of the subject on the Large Cate-chism,[1] where the whole benefit of the sacrament is made to consist in the strengthening of faith, or in the consciousness of the forgiveness of sins, and that, too, in a way thoroughly in keeping with Luther's original conceptions, viz.: The word proclaims forgiveness; the Christ present confirms and seals it, as it is he himself who secured it for us. "Therefore we come to the sacrament in order that we may there receive such a treasure, through which and in which we obtain remission of sins. Wherefore this? Because the words are here and give these things to us. If therefore I am commanded by Christ to eat and drink, in order that he may be mine and may confer a benefit upon me, it is, as it were, a certain pledge and surety, or rather the very thing itself which he has presented and pledged for my sins, death, and all evils" (Müller, 502).[2] In view of this resultant, the divergence of Luther's later from his earlier view of the Lord's Supper must not be overestimated. The bodily presence of the Saviour in the bread and wine for the sealing of the words of institution, for the strengthening of faith, and for giving assurance of the forgiveness of sins, was beyond question his leading thought. The only addition made to this was the adoption of certain definite ideas as to the mode of presence of the heavenly body, to which he was led by the course of controversy upon the subject. These were, in the first instance, only auxiliary ideas, but they gradually assumed the character of permanent elements in the dogma of the Lord's Supper.[3]

[1] Or at least set it in new relations, p. 509: The sacrament is "nothing but a wholesome and comforting medicine, which may help thee and give thee life in both body and soul. For where the soul is restored, there help is given also to the body."

[2] Cf. the discussions as to "worthy" and "unworthy" communicants (504 ff.). Faith, together with the sense of unworthiness, makes worthy (504, 509 f.). "Therefore we call those alone unworthy who do not feel their faults nor are willing to be (regarded as) sinners" (510), i. e., "who are insolent and wild," 508. Under no conditions dare we think of the sacrament as "though it were a poison, in which we should eat death" (509).

[3] Luther from this time most vigorously rejected the position of those who

7. The Colloquy at Marburg could not, under the circumstances, lead to harmony, although Zwingli, impelled by political considerations ("*Burgrecht*")[1] made as large concessions as possible to the Lutherans. Agreement was indeed reached upon fourteen articles of faith, modeled upon formulas drawn by Luther (Trinity, Christ, original sin, faith, justification, word, baptism, works, civil government). In regard to the Lord's Supper, there was agreement in the demand for "both forms according to the institution of Christ," in the condemnation of the mass, and in the assertion that "the spiritual partaking of this body and blood " is "especially necessary for every Christian." But there remained the difference that they "have at this time not agreed whether the true body and blood of Christ are bodily in the bread and wine " (art. 15). Luther, although he had not hesitated to express to the Strassburgers his conviction that they had "another spirit," yet hoped for a "good-natured friendly harmony, that they may in a friendly spirit seek among us for that which they lack " (E. 36. 322). Zwingli wrote : " Luther, impudent and contumacious, was vanquished . . . although he meanwhile declared that he was unconquered " (opp. viii. 370). Upon the return journey to Wittenberg, the Saxon theologians drew up the Schwabach Articles, which assert of the Lord's Supper : " That in the bread and wine the true body and blood of Christ are truly present, according to the word of Christ" (art. 10). This doctrine belongs with others to the faith of the true church : " Such church is nothing else than believers in Christ, who believe and teach the above-named articles and parts " (art. 12). And they really reproduced the doctrine of the Lutherans. The fault lay, not in this exaltation to the position of a "dogma," but in the fact that a peculiar theological method of establishing the doctrine very soon began to be included in the " pure doctrine " itself.

Cf. KOLDE, Luther, ii. 308 ff., and Der Tag v. Schleiz, in Abh. f. Köstl., 1896, p. 94 ff. STÄHELIN, Zwingli, ii. 395 ff. The text of the Marburg and Schwabach Articles in KOLDE, Die Augsb. Conf., 1896, p. 119 ff., 123 ff.

held that there is here no article of faith, and we should therefore not quarrel about it, but each one should be allowed here to believe as he wishes (32. 406 ; 30. 43). This is the opinion of some laymen, such as Henry of Kronberg : " My understanding is not competent to reach an opinion " (see BOGLER, H. v. Kr., Schriften des Vereins f. Ref.-gesch., 57, p. 14). See also Luther's opinion upon Schwenkfeld's doctrine of the Lord's Supper, 30. 285 ff., 305, 354 ; 32. 397, 404 ff. Also KADELBACH, Ausfürl. Gesch. K. v. Sch., 1860, p. 104 ff.

[1] Considerations of the same character—the possibility of reconciling the Emperor—influenced the opposition of Melanchthon, whom the Strassburgers regarded as their real and most dangerous opponent.

8. Nor did the *Wittenberg Concord* (A. D. 1536) produce an actual and permanent agreement.   From the time of the Diet of Augsburg, Bucer labored unweariedly to bring about an agreement between the Saxons and the theologians of Southern Germany.   His formula was : "That the true body and the true blood of Jesus Christ are truly present in the Lord's Supper and are offered with the words of the Lord and the sacrament." [1] Both Luther and Melanchthon hoped that an understanding might be reached upon this basis.[2]   But Luther did not change his own opinion.   Although he was willing to refrain from laying special stress upon the assertion, that the body of Christ is present also for the unbelieving, yet the formula finally adopted expresses his view : "that with the bread and wine are truly and substantially present, offered, and received (*vere et substantialiter adesse, exhiberi et sumi*) the body and blood of Christ." Just on this account the Wittenberg Concord failed to attain the desired result.   Cf. KOLDE, PRE. xvii., ed. 2, 222 ff.   BAUM, Capito u. Butzer, 1860, p. 498 ff.

[1] As in general, so in the doctrine of the Lord's Supper, Bucer found his point of departure in Luther (see the summary of his preaching, Strassburg, 1523), form g 3 v.   During the sacramental controversy, he was on Zwingli's side.   His view at this time is given in Ennarrationum in evang. Matthaei, l. ii. (Argentorati, 1527), p. 329 ff.: As food strengthens the body, so the recollection of the deliverance and forgiveness of sins wrought by Christ strengthens faith.   Thus the body is truly eaten, p. 329 r.   To this end Christ instituted the Supper, p. 330 r.   The transition to his later position was made possible by the strongly emphasized assertion, that we at least with our spirit eat the body of Christ (p. 330 v, 336 v, 333 v), and through the misinterpretation of Luther's doctrine : "They contend that the body of Christ is really . . . transported into the bread by the word, *i. e.*, that the body of Christ is really present in the bread " (p. 331 r, 338 r).   But influential, above all, were political considerations and the feeling that " what ought to be for us the symbol of the warmest love, some evilly disposed men have made the occasion of the most violent hatred and of the separation of brethren and of the rending of churches" (l. c., p. 329 v).

[2] Cf. the formula of compromise agreed upon at about this time between Blaurer and Schnepf for Wittenberg : " That the body and blood of Christ are truly, *i. e.*, substantially and essentially (*substanzlich und wesentlich*), but not quantitatively, nor qualitatively, nor locally, present and offered."

CHAPTER III.

THE NEW DOGMA.

§ 74. *The Augsburg Confession.*

LITERATURE. PLITT, Einleitung in d. Augustana, vol. ii. 1868. PLITT, Die Apol. d. August., 1873. ZÖCKLER, Die Augsb. Conf., 1870. KOLDE, Die Augsb. Conf., 1896 (together with the Marburg, Schwabach, and Torgau Articles, the Confutation, and the Augustana variata). TSCHACKERT, Die unänderte Augsb. Konf. nach den besten Handschriften, 1901. FICKER, Die Confut. d. Augsb. Bek. in ihrer ersten Gestalt, 1891. KNAAKE, Luther's Anteil an der Augsb. Conf., 1863. VIRCK, Melanchthons polit. Stellung auf d. Reichstag zu Augsb. 1530, Ztschr. f. KG. ix. 67 ff., 293 ff. THOMASIUS-SEEBERG, DG. ii., ed. 2, 364 ff. LOOFS, DG. 397 ff. MÖLLER-KAWERAU, KG. iii. 94 ff. J. W. RICHARD, Luther and the Augsburg Confession, in the Lutheran Quarterly, 1899 and 1900. .

☞ In the references in this section, a. indicates an article in the Augsburg Confession; p. refers to a page in Müller's Symbolische Bücher; the second figure following, to a paragraph upon the same page. The excellent English translation in JACOBS, Book of Concord, may be used, as Müller's paging is there carried in the margin.

1. The adherents of the Lutheran doctrine gave confessional expression to their religious convictions at Augsburg in 1530. It was not their aim to establish a "new dogma," but they on the contrary desired only, as they professed adherence to the ecumenical symbols, to furnish the proof that they really held the genuine old Catholic faith. But the doctrine which they presented in the Confession became nevertheless the fixed dogma of the new church. It formed originally the charter of the Smalcald League, and gradually became the recognized standard of pure doctrine for the universities as well as for the congregations (as proved in Möller-Kawerau, iii. 98 f.). The same may be said of the Apology. But it was the Religious Peace of Augsburg, A. D. 1555, which first officially and plainly designated the Augsburg Confession as the standard, by which new associations in the church were to be tested in order to secure recognition from the empire. While we must leave to Symbolics the more precise treatment of this subject, it is necessary for us to consider the question, in what forms the new doctrine attained recognition as the official teaching of the church. The dogmas of the ancient church received a canonical character from the fact that they were the decrees of general councils which were "accepted" by the church at large. These decrees were recognized and given legal force by the state, or by an ecclesiastical authority—the Roman bishop—recognized by the state. The former was the case with the dogmas of the Greek church; the

latter, with the decrees promulgated during the Pelagian and Semipelagian controversies. The council did not itself possess binding authority ; for when the acceptance, *i. e.*, the civil recognition, was withdrawn because another council had adopted new and contrary decrees, the decrees of the former were annulled. This is plainly illustrated in the conflicts within the Greek church. The medieval conception of the church changed the formal basis of accepted dogma and led to the establishment of the rule, that the decrees of ecumenical councils, or the doctrine of the Romish church, or the formal proclamation of a pope, received *eo ipso* dogmatic authority in the church. Dogma became simply the formal statement made by official teachers of the church. But the authority which these were supposed to possess was shattered in its very foundations by the Reformation. The congregations were looked to for the reformation of doctrine and life, as to them belonged the right of passing judgment upon doctrine (supra, p. 295 n.). Practically, however, the princes were regarded as the agency possessing the necessary power for the carrying out of reform. Luther had voiced this sentiment in his "Address to the Nobility," and this led to the unique fiction of "emergency bishops" (*Notbischöfe*). The princes were utilized for these ecclesiastical purposes, not as being the bearers of the specific civil authority, but as representatives of "Christianity," *i. e.*, of the congregation at large, and particularly as "prominent" (*praecipua*) members of it (thus expressed first by Melanchthon, Schmalk. Art., Müller, p. 339, 54. C. R. iii. 244). When the new church fellowship had taken tangible shape through the carrying out of the ideas of the Reformation by the secular authorities, the princes and magistrates were at once recognized as its official representatives. Negotiations were entered into with them, and they became the public defenders of the new doctrine. The theologians formulated the latter, but they attained a legal character only when adopted by the secular government ; and this applies to their inner contents as well as to the outward form. This principle was first openly recognized in the decree of the Diet of Spires in 1526, although indeed the real force of the latter was only the postponement of an imperial decision. It then became the guiding principle for the organization of the new church, and received the legal sanction of the empire through the Religious Peace of Augsburg. The teachings of the Evangelical church— in Reformed as well as in Lutheran districts—thus became the fixed doctrine of the church, or dogma, when the doctrinal statements formulated by the theologians were "accepted" by the secular government in the name of the church. There was in this a certain analogy with the genesis of the dogmas of the ancient church. As a result, the dogmas of the church were no longer, as in the Middle Ages, the creation of merely ecclesiastical, *i. e.*, hierarchical procedure. Nor does there lie behind them the mystical authority of general councils. They are propositions which the theologians hold to be biblical, and to which the church at large, *i. e.*, the state, gives assent. But it is not, as in Greek Christianity, the civil authority as such which expresses this assent, but the state as the representative of the church at large. The latter idea is a genuinely medieval one. The state is not yet recognized as the organism of secular jurisprudence nor sharply discriminated from the church. From this combination resulted all the weaknesses of territorialism. But the latter were associated with the concrete application of the theory, and not with the principle itself. The principle is expressed in the simple axiom : The doctrine of the church, or dogma, is biblical truth, discovered by theologians, but recognized and accepted by the Christian congregation as such. This was Luther's meaning when he clearly and distinctly granted to the congregation the right to pass judgment upon doctrine.[1]   Cf. as to the bearings upon ecclesiastical jurisprudence, SOHM, Kirchenrecht, i. 322 ff., 330 ff., 560 ff., 658 f.

2. The Augsburg Confession was composed by Melanchthon, but it reproduces, though as a "gentle-stepper" (*Leisetreterin*), the thought of Luther.[2] The "timidity" and "philosophy" of Melanchthon, and his attempts to moderate and compromise, do not belong to the History of Doctrines. But it is important to bear in mind the circumstances under which the Augsburg Confession was prepared. It was the Emperor's chief desire to discover whether the Protestant doctrine was in harmony with the twelve articles of the Christian faith (KAWERAU, Agricola, p. 100. C. R. ii. 179). Eck had in 404 theses charged almost all heresies upon the Protestants. These considerations required of the Reformers a distinct emphasizing of their agreement with the doctrine of the ancient church and a clear rejection of all heresies. It appeared to be important, likewise, to avoid all fellowship with Zwingli, whose political aims made him an object of suspicion (C. R. ii. 25 ; i. 1099, 1106). In all these particulars Melanchthon's personal inclinations were in accord with the

---

[1] This does not exclude a recognition of the fact, that Luther always maintained his demand for the general recognition of a harmonious pure doctrine, *e. g.*, 32. 406.

[2] Melanchthon had before him, when composing the Augsburg Confession. on the dogmatic side the Schwabach Articles, and on the practical reformatory side the so-called Torgau Articles. Upon the latter, see BRIEGER in the Kirchen-geschichtl. Studien f. Reuter, 1888.

demands of ecclesiastical policy. But all this was only the outward framework for the real task, *i. e.*, to present the fundamental ideas of the evangelical party, and to show clearly that they demolish the monastic ideal of life and the external legality of the Romish church, but that they have no connection with the revolutionary tendencies of the Anabaptists. The Confession, therefore, undertakes to present the evangelical doctrine as the genuine ancient doctrine, which is supported by the Scriptures as well as by the better Fathers, *e. g.* (p. 91 f., 29). " Only those things are recited," it is said in the Epilogue, " which seemed to be necessary to be said, in order that it might be known that nothing is received among us in doctrine and ceremonies contrary to the Scriptures or to the Catholic church ; because it is manifest that we have been most diligently on our guard lest any new and impious doctrines should creep into our churches." Not all evangelical convictions found expression under such a rule (*e. g.*, C. R. ii. 184, 182 f. Luther, Briefe, De W. iv. 110, 52); but, on the other hand, nothing was asserted which had not been included in the faith of the evangelical party.

3. Articles I.-III. reproduce the results of the dogmatic labors of the ancient church : " One divine essence . . . three persons of the same essence and power" (a. 1). Original sin consists in the inheritance of sin : " Without the fear of God, without trust in him, and with concupiscence." This marks the connection of Luther's thought with that of Augustine (cf. Apol., p. 79. 7 ff.; 81. 23). The main practical point of the doctrine is seen in the condemnation of the idea, that a " man may by the powers of his own reason be justified before God " (a. 2 ; cf. a. 20. 9, 10 ; p. 88. 9 f.). In respect to the power of " working (*efficienda*) the righteousness of God," man, without the influence of the word or of the Spirit, is not free, although he has " some power to work a civil righteousness and to choose the things subject to reason " (a. 18 and p. 219. 73). Sin is concentrated in a historical kingdom of the Evil One. " The history of the world shows how great is the power of the devil." Hence, " it will not be possible to recognize the benefits of Christ unless we understand our evils" (p. 86. 50). This is the religious point of view from which sin is regarded. Of Christ it is said : " two natures, . . . inseparably joined together in unity of person." The object of his work was, " that he might reconcile the Father to us and might be a sacrifice, not only for original guilt, but also for all actual sins of men."[1] The result

---

[1] Also, a. 24. 21, where the blotting out of daily sins is represented as wrought by the sacrifice of the mass. Cf. Zöckler upon this passage, and supra, p. 203, n. 1; also Zwingli, opp. iii. 198.

of his resurrection and ascension is his dominion over his followers and their sanctification through the Holy Spirit (a. 3 ; cf. p.
94. 40). Further, " Christ does not cease to be Mediator, after
we have been renewed." He remains such, " in order that for
his sake we may have a reconciled God, even though we are unworthy." For his sake, who is always interceding for us before
the Father, we have the forgiveness of sins (p. 116 f., 42, 44).

These are the initial principles, which the new church held in
common with the old. Yet they are not absolutely identical.
The Confutators were, from their point of view, right in object-
ing to the " born without the fear of God, without trust in him,"
as a definition of original sin (Ficker, p. 8). They quote
Luther's remark in regard to the *homousios,* and call attention to
the fact, that the trinitarian formulas as such are not found in the
Scriptures (ib. p. 4 f.). The deliberate hostility of the critics
should not blind us to the fact, that a difference in point of view
is here revealed.

4. Article V. marks the transition to the evangelical principle :
"Through the word and sacraments, as through instruments, is
given the Holy Spirit, who worketh faith where and when it
pleaseth God in those who hear the gospel, namely, that God,
not for our merits' sake but for Christ's sake, justifieth[1] those who
believe that they are for Christ's sake received into favor." The
word and the sacraments are the means through which the Spirit
begets faith. But faith " doth not only signify a knowledge
of the history," . . " which believeth not only the history,
but also the effect of the history, namely, this article, the remission of sins " (a. 20. 23 ; p. 96. 51). " But this is to believe,
to trust in the merits of Christ, that for his sake God wisheth to
be reconciled to us " (p. 99. 69); " to *desire and accept* the
offered promise of remission of sins and justification " (p. 95.
48 ; p. 94 f., 44 ff.; 139. 183). This is evangelical saving faith,
as the trusting acceptance of the grace of forgiveness which has
been revealed through the work of Christ. In this light may be
understood the central thought of Justification : " That men
cannot be justified before God by their own powers, merits, or
works ; but they are justified freely (*gratis*) for Christ's sake
through faith, when they believe that they are received into favor,
and that their sins are forgiven for the sake of Christ, who hath by
his death made satisfaction for our sins. This faith doth God impute for righteousness before him " (a. 4 ; cf. 24. 28 ; p. 123.
93; 105. 97). Here the whole Romish system is excluded :

---

[1] The German translation of the *Editio princeps* is important : " Are accounted righteous before God for Christ's sake." Cf. KOLDE. Augsb. Conf.,
p. 28.

"they teach only that men treat with God through works and merits" (p. 97. 60). The relationship between God and man is not to be thought of in accordance with the scheme of merits : "as though Christ had come for the purpose of delivering certain laws, through which we might merit the remission of sins" (p. 89. 15). But neither is it as though the "knowledge of the history concerning Christ," together with the infusion of a "habitus inclining us the more readily to love God," would suffice (p. 89. 15, 17). In all of this human merit still remains. Nor does the distinction drawn between the merits of fitness (*congrui*) and of worthiness (*condigni*) help matters ; for if God must of necessity reward the *meritum congrui* by the bestowal of grace, it is in reality a *meritum condigni* (p. 90. 19).[1] Only faith justifies. It does this, however, not as being in itself a worthy work, nor as being the beginning and source of good works, but solely because it apprehends the grace revealed and promised in Christ, and applies and appropriates this to itself (p. 96. 56 ; 102. 84, 86 ; 100. 77 ; 113. 27 ; 115. 40 ; 99. 71). Man therefore becomes righteous through an "*imputation of another's righteousness.*" This is Christ's righteousness.[2] But since faith is the only appropriate organ for the apprehension of this righteousness, it is our righteousness. "Faith is righteousness in us imputatively, *i. e.*, it is that by which we are made accepted before God on account of the imputation and ordination of God" (p. 139. 186).[3] The leading elements in the conception of justification are here brought into conjunction. The law terrifies the heart with the wrath of God ;[4] the gospel awakens in it trust in Christ, or the assurance that God for Christ's sake forgives us our sins and regards us as righteous (p. 101. 79 ff.).

Faith is thus represented as the reception of the grace revealed in Christ, and justification as the forensic declaration that the person involved is righteous. But faith is also at the same time the beginning of a new life. "This faith, encouraging and consoling in these fears, receives the remission of sins, justifies and quickens ; for this consolation is a new and spiritual life." The Holy Spirit, who works faith through the word, works in and with faith a new life (p. 98, 63 ff., p. 177, 60). Only it

---

[1] These terms are here used in the sense attached to them from the time of Duns Scotus. Cf. supra, p. 161, 202.

[2] And Christ alone, not " partly our works," p. 130. Cf. Biel, supra, p. 199).

[3] Cf. p. 99. 69 : " For how will Christ be Mediator if we do not believe (*sentimus*) that for his sake we are accounted righteous ? " p. 99. 62 : " this forgiveness, reconciliation, and righteousness are received through faith."

[4] The same influence is also ascribed to the gospel, p. 98. 62.

must be borne in mind that justification in the above sense does
not depend upon faith in so far as the latter is considered as the
beginning of a new life. But faith is also the beginning of the
regeneration of man, or of the process of making him actually
righteous.   Inasmuch as faith sets free from the sense of guilt,
the heart becomes animated, peace and joy enter, and also
eternal life "which begins here in this life" (p. 105. 100).[1]
The Holy Spirit has begotten faith, and faith brings with it the
Spirit, thereby renewing the man (p. 108. 115).   Hence we
might more appropriately designate faith than love as the grace
making acceptable (*gratia gratum faciens*, p. 108. 116).   But,
as faith is a new life, it also produces "new movements and
works in man" (p. 130. 129).   The Apology itself summarizes
its view of justification as follows :   "Thus far we have shown with
sufficient fullness and from testimonies of Scripture, that by faith
alone we obtain the remission of sins for Christ's sake, and that by
faith alone we are justified, *i. e.*, from unrighteous men are made
rightous, or regenerated" (p. 108. 117). Therefore, faith, which
is begotten by the Holy Ghost, is (1) the organ for the apprehension of grace, and (2) the beginning of a new life.   In the
former sense, it receives the imputed righteousness of Christ ; in
the latter, it is the beginning of ethical rightness in character and
conduct. But the former is the fundamental element (p. 100. 75).
From it, *i. e.*, from the sense of the forgiveness of sin, the Apology
psychologically deduces the inward renewal ; for he who has become sure of the forgiveness of his sins, becomes at heart free and
joyful (supra).[2] This portraiture of justification and sanctification in the Apology corresponds exactly with the conceptions of
Luther, except that he laid still more stress upon the actual
righteousness wrought by faith (supra, p. 260 ff.).[3] Upon the
doctrine of justification in the Apology, compare the treatment

---

[1] Upon the idea of eternal life as begun by faith on earth, see also p. 215.
54 ; 287. 10 ; 110. 111 ; 216. 58 ; 146. 231.
[2] Melanchthon, p. 101. 79, assails the Scotist separation of forgiveness and
infusion (Duns, iv. d. 16, q. 2. 6, cf. supra, p. 160).
[3] The terminology of p. 100. 72 ff. presents difficulties : "And because to
be justified means from unrighteous men to be made righteous, or to be regenerated, it signifies also to be pronounced or accounted righteous, for the Scriptures speak in both ways."   That is, the general sense of *justificari* includes
"also" the particular form of justification indicated by the term *justum
pronuntiari*.   Upon the basis of this is constructed the following syllogism :
1. Since the chief thing in justification is forgiveness, we may say : "To obtain
remission of sins is to be justified, Ps. 32. 1.   2. By faith alone, and not on
account of love or works, we obtain remission of sins, although love follows
faith. 3. Therefore, by faith alone we are justified," and that in the sense that
"from unrighteous men we are made righteous, or regenerated" (p. 100.
75-78). The conclusiveness of this deduction may be doubted.

of the subject by Loofs, Stud. u. Krit., 1884, 613 ff. Eich-
horn, ib. 1887, 415 ff. Frank, Neue kirchl. Ztschr., 1892,
846 ff. Stange, ib., 1899, 169 ff.

5. Faith is followed by Good Works as its fruits. "For
good works are to be done on account of God's command ; likewise, for the exercise of faith ; likewise, on account of confession
and giving of thanks" (p. 120. 68, a. 6. 1 f.). They spring from
the Holy Ghost, or from regeneration and justification (a. 20.
29, p. 109. 4)[1]—both the "spiritual movements" and the
"external good works" (p. 110. 15). But works are in no
way the ground of justification (a. 20. 9, 27). Good works are
accordingly such as spring from the agency of the Holy Spirit
and the impulse of faith, and as are performed according to the
will of God (a. 20. 27); and hence, such as are in accord with
the commandments of God, and not with the self-made ideals of
the Catholic church (a. 27. 57). By virtue of their origin in
the inward man, these works are performed in Christian liberty
(a. 28. 51). These four criteria determine the character of
good works in the evangelical sense. Accordingly, all civil and
secular occupations are, contrary to the view of the Anabaptists,
good works (a. 16; a. 26. 10). Marriage likewise assumes a
new dignity (a. 23). On the other hand, the works of monastic
observances and of an external ecclesiasticism are not good
works (a. 26. 8 ff.). It follows, further, that ascetic exercises
are not in themselves good works, but are undertaken for the
purpose of preparing ourselves to do good works: "Not in
order that through this discipline he might merit remission of
sins, but in order that he might have a body apt and fit
for spiritual things and for doing his duty according to his
calling" (a. 26. 38). Finally, this conception of good works
gives birth to a new Ideal of Life. In contrast with the perfection of the monastic vows, evangelical perfection embraces
the Christian life in its religious central impulse, and, as well, in
its discharge of the duties connected with the secular calling.
"Christian perfection is to reverently fear God, and again to conceive great faith and confidence that we have a reconciled God;
to ask and certainly look for aid from God in doing all things in
connection with our calling ; and meanwhile outwardly to diligently perform good works and attend to our vocation" (a. 27.
49, cf. p. 216. 61 f.; 281. 48 ff.). But this perfection exists
only in the form of earnest effort: "For they ought to strive
after perfection as long as this life endures, and always grow in

[1] It is only upon the ground of the personal experience of the divine mercy
that God becomes for us an object of affection (*objectum amabile*), p. 110. 8.

the fear of God, in faith, in love toward their neighbor and the like spiritual gifts '' (p. 279. 37).

6. Articles VII. and VIII. present the evangelical conception of the church. There will always be a holy church. '' But the church is the congregation of the saints, in which the gospel is rightly taught and the sacraments rightly administered '' (a. 7). Since the word and the sacraments constitute the church, it may be said : '' And unto the true unity of the church it is sufficient to agree concerning the doctrine of the gospel and the administration of the sacraments,'' but it is not necessary that ceremonies and traditions be everywhere the same (ib., cf. Torgau Art., i.). This church, which holds the pure doctrine and *in which* the preaching is in harmony with this doctrine, cannot possibly, as is the common belief, be the church as an object of faith, or as the so-called '' invisible church.'' Melanchthon, on the contrary, in the note to Article XII. of the Schwabach Articles (supra, p. 294 f.; cf. Luther's conception of the '' true, *rechten*, church,'' supra, p. 294), expresses the opinion, that there has always been and always will be a true church, *i. e.*, men who hold essentially the pure evangelical doctrine (cf. C. R. xii. 481 f., 483, 433), and that this church requires for its continued existence only the word and the sacraments. Since in this congregation assembled around the word there will always be a '' fellowship of faith and of the Holy Spirit in the hearts '' of men (p. 152 f., 5, 8), it is called *congregatio sanctorum;*[1] but since it exists in an empirical earthly form, there are always '' many hypocrites and wicked men mingled in it '' (a. 8, p. 157. 28). These ideas are in the end practically the same as Luther had expressed. But the definition of the church is constructed by Melanchthon from a somewhat different point of departure from that of Luther. Luther started with the idea, that the presence of the word guarantees to faith the existence of believing Christians, or the (invisible) church. The differences in the proclamation of the word led him afterward to discriminate between the true and the false (visible) church. Melanchthon begins with the idea, that there has always been and always will be a true (visible) church, but shows, further, that it can never exist without a commixture of wicked men and hypocrites. In the church, which is in its essential nature the *congregatio sanctorum*, there are found a kingdom of Christ and a kingdom of the devil ; but only members of the former are really members of the church (p. 154 f., 16 ff.).[2] There has

[1] For the '' saints,'' and they only, are properly the church.

[2] This different point of departure explains also the later construction of Melanchthon's definition of the church (vid. sub). He always starts

always been, Melanchthon means to say, a congregation (of professing Christians), which possessed the gospel, as did the association of evangelical believers existing at that time. In this congregation—not outwardly corresponding with it in dimensions—is the kingdom of Christ, *i. e.*, the church as an article of faith. The marks which prove the existence of the former, and therefore enable us to infer the existence of the latter, are the " pure doctrine of the gospel[1] and an administration of the sacraments in harmony with the gospel of Christ " (p. 152. 5).

From this definition of the church were drawn a number of inferences. (1) That the bishops do not have the right " to ordain anything contrary to the gospel " (a. 28. 34). (2) That the peculiar power and authority of the church is the preaching of the gospel, and therefore : " The preaching office is the highest office in the church " (p. 213 ; p. 215. 54 ; a. 28. 5, 8, 10). (3) That all other ordinances in the church are of purely human origin and must prove their legitimacy by the gospel (a. 26. 28). (4) That the church has no right to claim or exercise any kind of secular authority (a. 28. 2 ff.). The " power of the sword " (*potestas gladii*) must not be confused with the ecclesiastical power (*potestas ecclesiastica*), which includes only the " power of the keys," or the " commandment of God to preach the gospel, remit and retain sins, and administer the sacraments " (a. 28. 2-5, 10 f.). Hence the gospel cannot come in conflict with civil and social ordinances, but, on the contrary, confirms them (p. 215. 56 f.).

7. This brings us to the evangelical doctrine of the Sacraments, which is treated in Articles IX.-XIII. Of Baptism it is taught, that it is necessary to salvation, and that through it " the grace of God is offered ; " that children also, who are to be baptized, are received into the favor of God " (a. 9). Sin is forgiven, not annihilated (p. 83. 36). Of the Lord's Supper, it is said : " That the body and blood of Christ are truly present

with the visible church. The (later) heading of Art. vii., *De Ecclesia*, should rather have been *De perpetuitate ecclesiae*. Cf. Apol., p. 153. 7, 9. C. R. xii. 524, 432, 482 ; xxv. 688, and my comments in Neue kirch. Ztschr., 1897, 143 f., n.

[1] This expression points beyond question (cf. a. 28. 70 and *doctrina fidei*, p. 101. 81) to the specific evangelical conception of salvation and grace ; for this was, in Melanchthon's view, all that was lacking in wide circles of the ancient church ; but it does not exclude—on the contrary includes—the acceptance of the ancient dogmas (cf. C. R. xxiii. 600). To the marks of the true church belongs also beyond question, according to Melanchthon, as the following words attest, the Lutheran conception of the sacraments. It was Luther's main argument in support of his doctrine of the Lord's Supper, that it was " in harmony with the gospel of Christ."

and distributed in the Lord's Supper (a. 10); that they are "truly and substantially" present, and "we speak of the presence of the living Christ" (p. 164. 57).[1] Melanchthon *intended* to reproduce in the language of the Augsburg Confession the doctrine of Luther (C. R. ii. 142). The Confutators interpreted Article X. in the sense of transubstantiation (Ficker, p. 40),[2] and Melanchthon, so far from contradicting them, even introduced into the Apology a citation containing the expression "changed (*mutari*) into flesh" (p. 164. 55).[3] Private absolution is recognized, but not in the sense that the preceding confession is an "enumeration of all faults" (a. 11 ; also a. 25). Repentance is open to everyone who turns from his sins, and the church must grant him absolution. Repentance consists of two parts. One is *contrition*, or terrors stricken into the conscience through the knowledge of sin ; the other is *faith*, which is conceived by the gospel, or absolution. . . . Then ought to follow good works, which are fruits of repentance (a. 12). These two, or three (p. 171. 28 ; cf. supra, p. 241, n. 3), parts therefore constitute evangelical repentance. Here again it is very evident that the general evangelical conception of salvation furnishes the direct contrast to the theory of the sacrament of repentance, and presents a substitute for it ; for the ideas we have just cited simply summarize what has been already presented in the discussion of faith, justification, and works. This is still more distinctly brought to light in the extended discussions of the Apology. The law and the gospel are the substance of the Scriptures (p. 175. 53). The law, as also the gospel (according to Lk. 24. 47), first exercises its office of rebuke upon man and begets contrition. "We say that contrition is the true terrors of conscience, which feels that God is angry with sin, and grieves that it has sinned. And this contrition thus occurs when sins are censured from the word of God, because this is the sum of the

---

[1] This language is chosen in view of the charge of the Confutators, that by Luther's view there is present in the bread "a body alone, without the accompaniment of soul and blood," and that thus he "offers a dead body of Christ," Ficker, p. 41.

[2] As did also later Catholic writers (*e. g.*, HEPPE, Gesch. d. Prot. iv. 371 f. This interpretation of the German text : "That . . . body and blood . . . are present under the form (*Gestalt*) of the bread and wine," is not an impossible one, since the form (*species*) of the bread, according to the Catholic theory, remains despite the transubstantiation.

[3] Strictly speaking, Melanchthon cites Vulgarius (Theophylact) only to prove that the Greeks also teach the presence of the body of Christ. He by no means thereby commits himself to their *mutari*, and did not, therefore, "drag in" this term (as LOOFS asserts, DG. 399). But we dare not deny a fatal diplomacy in the choice of the citation. Upon the entire question, see CALINICH, Ztschr. f. wiss. Theol., 1873, 541 ff.

preaching of the gospel, viz., to convict of sin and to offer remission of sins and righteousness for Christ's sake, . . . and that, as regenerate men, we should do good works" (p. 171. 29).[1] But, since the preaching of the gospel accompanies that of the law, contrition is followed by "special faith : this faith follows terrors in such a way as to overcome them and render the conscience pacified. To this faith we ascribe that it justifies and regenerates, since it frees from terrors and brings forth in the heart peace, joy, and a new life" (p. 177. 60). Hence the gospel, or absolution, as the better Scholastics also recognized (supra, p. 137), constitutes the real substance of the sacrament of repentance (p. 173. 41). The proclamation of the gospel is, therefore, the real power of the keys (a. 25. 3 f.).

As the Confession places Article XIII., on the use of the Sacraments, after the discussion of baptism, the Lord's Supper and repentance, it is evident that it recognizes three sacraments (cf. Apol., p. 202. 4).[2] The general conception of the sacraments is not merely that they are marks of profession (as in Zwingli), "but rather that they are signs and testimonies of the will of God toward us, for the purpose of awakening and confirming faith in those who use them" (a. 13. 1). They are "rites" (*Riten*) instituted by God, which, in connection with the word (of institution), move the heart, since they reach us through the eye as does the word through the ear. "Wherefore the effect of both is the same" (p. 202. 5). Now, as God has affixed definite promises to these rites, faith is necessary as the prerequisite for their proper reception (a. 13. 2 ; p. 204, 19 ff.). The sacraments are, therefore, to be evangelically defined as signs, through the observance of which God gives that which the words employed in their institution promise. As their substantial result is the strengthening of faith, so faith is also the prerequisite for their profitable reception. The Apology rejects the Scholastic doctrine, that they bestow grace by virtue of the mere administration of them (*ex opere operato*, p. 204. 18).[3] The religious character of the sacramental acts is here in an admirable way preserved.

8. The remaining articles of the Confession, especially those directed against the prevailing abuses, have already been referred to as far as they have important bearing upon the History of

---

[1] The question, when contrition springs from love and when from fear, is waived aside as profitless scholastic disputation, p. 171. 29.

[2] But the Smalcald Articles enumerate two sacraments, p. 485. 1.

[3] The corresponding words of the Augsburg Confession (a. 13. 3) were not in the original document, as the Confutators (Ficker, p. 48) do not mention them.

Doctrines. We mention here only the articles upon the saints, who are not to be regarded as mediators in addition to Christ, nor to be worshiped (a. 21. Upon Mary, see p. 227); upon the marriage of priests (a. 23), the prohibition of which is contrary to the law of nature (p. 236 f.); upon the mass (a. 24); upon confession (a. 25); upon discrimination of meats (a. 26); upon monastic vows (a. 27); upon episcopal authority (a. 26); and of Christ's return to judgment (a. 17).

Reviewing the entire document, it may be said that the Augsburg Confession affords a clear, compact, and thorough presentation of the views of Luther in their fundamental features.

§ 75. *The Earlier Reformed Confessions.*

LITERATURE. NIEMEYER, Collectio confessionum in ecclesiis reformatis publicatarum, 1840. K. MÜLLER, Die Bekenntnisschriften der reformirten Kirche, 1903. THOMASIUS-SEEBERG, ii., ed. 2, 417 ff. K. MÜLLER, Symbolik, 398 ff.

1. The original documents which here demand our attention (Tetrapolitana, 1530. Basileensis prior, 1534. Helvetica prior, 1536) are only in a general way in accord with the views of Zwingli. The influence of Bucer's irenic efforts is already traceable in them (vid. sub).

2. It must be distinctly noted, first of all, that these confessions also give clear expression to the doctrine of justification by faith alone. This is " the highest and most prominent chief article . . . that we are preserved and saved alone through the simple mercy of God and through the merit of Christ. . . . Such high and great benefits of divine grace and the true sanctifying of the Spirit of God we receive not from our merits and powers, but through faith, which is a pure gift and bestowal of God " (Helv. 12. Tetr. 3. Bas. 83).[1] The sole authority of the Scriptures is also maintained. Only that is to be preached which is found in them, or deduced from them (Tetr. 1. Helv. 1).

The fundamental reformatory principle excludes the meritorious character of works and justification by means of them (Bas. 83). But as faith is, in one aspect, the receptive organ by which all the gracious gifts of God are appropriated, it is also, in another aspect, the fundamental principle of a new moral life. " This faith is a sure, firm, yea, an undoubted foundation and apprehension of all things which we hope for from God, who

---

[1] These figures indicate articles of the confessions, except in the case of the Basileensis, where they refer to the marginal numbers in Niemeyer.

causes love, and hence all virtues, to grow from it. . . This faith, which does not rely upon its own work, although it performs innumerable good works, but upon the mercy of God, is the real true service, by means of which we please God '' (Helv. 13).

The spiritual nature of the Church is here also plainly asserted (Helv. 14. Bas. 81. Tetr. 15). In the doctrine of the sacraments, there is a general agreement with Zwingli. The sacraments serve " for the begetting of faith and brotherly love " (Bas. 81) ; but yet they are—according to the Helvetica—not only symbols (*symbola*), but they " consist of signs and at the same time realities " (*signis simul et rebus*). Thus in baptism, water is the sign, and regeneration and adoption the reality ; in the Lord's Supper, bread and wine constitute the sign, while the reality is " the imparting (*communicatio*) of the body of the Lord, the procuring of salvation, and the remission of sins." This is however upon the condition, that an inner reception by the heart accompanies that of the outward symbols (21. 16). The chief attention is naturally given to the Lord's Supper. Christ is the food of believing souls. Our souls are through faith refreshed by his flesh and blood (Bas. 81 f.). Christ left his body to his disciples as food for the soul (Tetr. 18). The difference from Luther's view here remains evident, however carefully it is kept in the background. A carnal presence (*carnalis praesentia*) is expressly denied. The Supper brings a commemoration of the Crucified One, and thus refreshes our hearts (Helv. 23). Zwingli could certainly have subscribed these statements in detail ; but we can nevertheless discern here, as elsewhere in the Confessions, a certain modification of his ideas. There is here an effort to associate the spiritual influence as closely as possible with the bodily reception of the sacraments.[1]

---

[1] This softening down of Zwingli's ideas is manifest also in the theory of original sin (Bas. 80. Helv. 8). Predestination is not discussed, but the characteristic separation of the divine influence from the earthly means remains as the fixed premise to the doctrine of the means of grace.

PART II.

THE FURTHER DEVELOPMENT AND (PROVISIONAL) COMPLETION OF PROTESTANT DOCTRINE.

CHAPTER I.

LUTHERAN DOCTRINE TO THE ADOPTION OF THE FORMULA OF CONCORD.

§ 76. *Theology of Melanchthon and its Significance for the History of Doctrine.*

LITERATURE. SCHMIDT, Ph. Mel., 1860. HARTFELDER, Mel. als Präceptor Germ. (= Mon. paed. vii.), 1889. HERRLINGER, Die Theol. Mel., 1870. TRÖLTSCH, Vernunft u. Offenb. bei J. Gerh. u. Mel., 1890. RITSCHL, Die Entstehung d. luth. Kirche, Ztschr. f. KG. i. 51 ff.; ii. 366 ff. LOOFS, DG., ed. 3, 408 ff. SEEBERG, Mel. Stellung in d. Gesch. d. Dogmas, Neue kirchl. Ztschr., 1897, 126 ff.[1] HAUSSLEITER, Aus d. Schule Mel. (Greifswalder Festschr.), 1897. SELL, Mel. u. die deutsche Ref. bis 1531 (Schriften des Vereins für Ref.-Gesch., 56), etc. DILTHEY, in Archiv. f. Gesch. d. Philos. vi. 226 ff., 347 ff.

1. In the first period of Protestant doctrinal history, we have familiarized ourselves with the genesis of the Lutheran and Reformed Doctrines. We studied first of all the religious ideas of Luther in their peculiar character and force, and sought to understand them in the light of the circumstances attending their development. We then followed the course of Zwingli, and the influence of his teachings.

The second period is marked by the development and provisional[2] completion of doctrinal construction in the Protestant church. If in the first period ideas were produced and new ideals created, the second period addressed itself to the task of constructing forms and formulas for their permanent embodiment. The former was an essentially religious, this an essentially

---

[1] A part of this article is reproduced in the present section.

[2] The completion of dogmatic statement thus attained is described as merely "provisional," partly upon general historical principles, for we can of course not tell in advance to what modifications, additions, and omissions the Protestant doctrines may yet be subjected in the church. But the word has also a special significance, as guarding against the error of regarding the present forms of statement as final, which would be an unauthorized dogmatic opinion.

theological era. Melanchthon and Calvin are the leaders in the toil of the second period. The historical transition from the first to the second stage of development may be easily understood. Luther had restored the gospel to the church ; but his religious instinct preserved him from the attempt to simply reproduce the thought of the apostolic age, ignoring the entire historical development which intervened. Upon the contrary, many ideas and elements derived from the past became coëfficients in the shaping of his religious views.[1] This was at first quite unavoidable in the sphere of external historical forms. Continuity of life demands points of attachment to the forms of the past. But as, in this case, a great literary and scientific revolution preceded the religious movement, the direct dependence of Protestant theology upon the scholastic materials of the preceding epoch was less marked than might otherwise have been expected.

2. It was Melanchthon who, on Lutheran territory, rendered the important service of providing a system of doctrine for the youthful Protestant church. His universal culture, which fitted him, by the publication of many text-books, to become the instructor of his age in the spheres of general philosophy and philology, his delicate sense, so averse to all extremes and disturbances, and his wonderful talent for formulating, fitted him to become the *Praeceptor Germaniae* also in the sphere of theology. As early as A. D. 1521 appeared the first draft of his *Loci* (ed. Plitt-Kolde, 1890). There is here presented in brief and compact form an excellent epitome of Luther's views touching the plan of salvation. The Scriptures alone, it is held, furnish the "form of Christianity" (*forma christianismi*) ; they alone establish articles of faith (p. 59, 139). The doctrines immediately connected with Soteriology are presented, but no attention is devoted to the doctrine of the Trinity or to Christology.[2] Sharp protest is entered against the injection of philosophical speculations into religion.[3] A fuller description of the work would be apart from our present purpose (see my review in Neue kirchl.

---

[1] In this sense the entire period from the time of Augustine may be described as pre-reformatory. We can in the light of this understand also the simple retention of the dogmas of the ancient church.

[2] Melanchthon accepts the Nicene doctrine (p. 139 f.), but he thought that a "compendium of Christian doctrine" might be given — following the example of the Epistle to the Romans—without detailed theories in regard to God and Christ (p. 64, 61) ; cf. C. R. I. 305 : "for I condemn metaphysical theories, because I think it a great peril to subject celestial mysteries to the methods of our reason."

[3] See his fine remark, p. 37 : "For just as in these modern times of the church we have embraced Aristotle instead of Christ, so, immediately after the beginning of the church, Christian doctrine was weakened through Platonic philosophy."

Ztschr., 1897, 129 ff.), although we shall have occasion to examine the later theological views of Melanchthon. His aim is
here very distinctly to present the teachings of Luther. But we
notice a characteristic materializing and leveling down of the
ideas of Luther, while upon certain points the author knowingly
advocates positions differing from his. Both these tendencies
became most highly significant in their influence upon the devel-
ment of doctrine, although the former is to be regarded as the
more important in its results. We begin with the deliberate doctrinal divergences.

3. There were two doctrines upon which Melanchthon consciously differed from Luther, viz., free will and the Lord's
Supper. That he wavered from his original deterministic position is perhaps to be attributed to the influence of the polemical
writings of Erasmus against Luther (cf., *e. g.*, C. R. i. 688).
As early as 1527, in his exposition of the Epistle to the Colos-
sians, he recognizes human freedom in the sphere of the outward
life, although no one can fear and love God except he be impelled by the Holy Spirit (cf. LUTHARDT, Die Lehre vom fr.
Willen, p. 162 ff.). Similarly, in the *Unterricht der Visitatoren*, xxvi. 78. In the Augsburg Confession, he purposely
avoids questions concerning predestination (ii. 547). And upon
the occasion of a disputation at Wittenberg in 1534, he pointed
out that neither religion nor morality could be harmonized with
the Stoic doctrine of the necessity of all events (x. 70 f., 785 ff.).
Already in the *Loci* of 1535, Melanchthon attributed to the
human will an active, although small, part in producing conversion. He there recognizes three causes of conversion : the word,
the Holy Spirit, and the human will. He explains, further, that
the will either determines to accept or determines not to accept
the grace of God (xxi. 376 f., 332). He expresses himself most
plainly upon this point in the third revision of the *Loci* (A. D.
1543). His inner motive is opposition to the Stoic ἀνάγχη. Man
yet retains freedom as a power of applying himself to grace (*facultas applicandi se ad gratiam*) (xxi. 652, 659 f.). Accordingly,
in conversion God stirs the heart through the word read or heard,
and the heart then, by virtue of a certain freedom yet left to it,
decides for or against God. "God anticipates (*antevertit*) us,
calls, moves, aids ; but we must see to it that we do not resist "
(658).[1]

[1] In order to rightly judge this view of Melanchthon's, we must bear in
mind (1) That he holds strictly to the doctrine of original sin, and therefore
excludes every form of salvation by man's own efforts (xx. 1. 669), and (2)
That he sought, in opposition to the doctrine of predestination, which he understood as magical, morally untenable, and deterministic, to retain the personal

4. In a similar way, Melanchthon gradually lost confidence in Luther's doctrine of the Lord's Supper. He at first shared the symbolic conception of Augustine, as advocated by Erasmus. He then fully adopted the view of Luther (*e. g.*, C. R. i. 760, 823, 830, 1109 f.). Zwingli's theory appeared to him at this time and afterward as profane (ib. i. 1067, 1077). In Marburg, he assisted Luther in making a collection of citations from the Fathers in confirmation of the latter's position. With his growing respect for the consensus of the ancient church, he was very profoundly impressed by the dialogue of Oecolampadius, which produced evidence that, in a closer study of the Church Fathers, the symbolical view might also be found in their writings. He confessed this to Luther (ii. 217); yet he still clung to the Lutheran conception (ii. 212, 222 f., 226; i. 1109 f.). This is also the position taken in the tenth article of the Augsburg Confession (ii. 142). The formula of Bucer (supra, p. 331), appeared to him to prepare the way for a union of the divergent parties (ii. 498 f.). But he still distinctly maintains the bodily presence of Christ (ii. 311, 315, 787, 801). He was able, indeed, to accept the formula which Luther now framed, *i. e.*, that the body of Christ is "crushed with the teeth" (E. 55. 75 f.), only as "the spokesman of another's opinion" (*nuntius alienae sententiae*, ii. 822). But, in view of the testimonies of the ancient church, he could find no rest. "I affirm the true presence of Christ in the Supper. I am not willing to be the author nor defender of a new doctrine in the church" (ii. 824; cf. xxi. 479; ix. 785). At heart, he inclined more and more to the view of the theologians of Southern Germany (ii. 824, 837, 841 f.; iii. 292). Melanchthon always held to the presence of the Lord in the Supper, but he became less and less satisfied with Luther's conception of that presence. At a later period, he never wearied—at least in his private correspondence—of inveighing against bread-worship (ἀρτολατρεία), as against the "Stoic necessity" (*e. g.*, viii. 362, 791, 660). He fell back whenever possible upon the thought, that there is in the Lord's Supper a "communion of the body and blood of Christ." He denied the bodily ubiquity of Christ (vii. 780, 884; viii. 385; ix. 387, 962, 963), and emphasized in contrast the spiritual presence of Christ: "The Son of God lives and reigns, and wishes to be present in the sacrament instituted for this purpose, and joins us as members to himself" (xv. 1112).[1] In this sense is the tenth article of the Augustana

and moral element in conversion. But he did not succeed in the solution of the problem.

[1] Cf. iii. 514 (A. D. 1538): "Not to depart very far from the ancients, I have affirmed a sacramental presence in the celebration (*in usu*) and have said

Variata (A. D. 1540) also to be understood : " Concerning the Lord's Supper they teach, that with the bread and wine the body and blood of Christ are truly offered to those eating in the Lord's Supper.[1] The " damnant " is here also wanting. Cf. HERR-LINGER, Theol. Mel., p. 124 ff.

5. The *Loci* of Melanchthon, after the second revision, fell more and more into the track of the traditional doctrinal statements. Refraining from the attempt to trace the development of his theological views, we present a general summary of them based upon the third redaction of the *Loci*. The pedagogical character of the work has become increasingly prominent as it has been popularized in the manner so characteristic of the author.[2] The simplicity of form and the desire to secure practical usefulness exclude the discussion of the more profound problems and extended logical proof of the positions taken.[3] Although, even in the last revision of the *Loci*, Melanchthon followed no methodical plan beyond the enumeration of the separate doctrines, yet the study of his later writings makes it manifest that the Reformer had at least grouped his theological ideas around certain definite fundamental principles. These were (1) the combination of ideas involved in justification and the new conception of repentance, and (2) the conception of the church (cf. xxviii. 371 f.). These ideas constantly recur. They lay nearer to his heart than all else. To make them plain to all, and to impress them upon all hearts, appeared to him his chief duty. They may be designated as the two focal points in the theology of Melanchthon.

We take as our starting-point the question as to the Sources and Standards of Christian truth, which Melanchthon of course answers by pointing to the Holy Scriptures. Therefore let us regard it as a great blessing of God, that he has given and pre-

---

that with these elements *Christ is truly present and efficacious. This surely is enough.* Nor have I added such an inclusion or conjunction by which the body would be joined to the bread. . . . Sacraments are pledges that something else is present with the things received."

[1] The formula of Bucer and the Wittenberg Concord (supra, p. 331) here exerted a controlling influence, but the possibility of an interpretation favoring transubstantiation is excluded. But it is significant that the *vere et substantialiter adesse* of the Wittenberg formula is omitted. Luther himself originally intended to express himself in a way similar to this in the Smalcald Articles : " That under bread and wine the true body and blood are present," etc., but wrote instead : " The bread and wine in the Lord's Supper are the true body and blood of Christ." (See KOLDE, Stud. u. Krit., 1893, p. 159.) However true it may be that the formula of the Augustana Variata may be interpreted in a Lutheran sense, it is equally true that it was in reality designed to favor the divergent conception of Melanchthon.

[2] " With every new issue, paper and tradition exerted greater influence " (DILTHEY, l. c., vi. 230).

[3] Cf. the remark of Erasmus, C. R. iii. 87.

served to the church a certain book, and binds the church to it.
That company of people alone is the church, which embraces this
book, hears it, teaches it, and retains its true sense in the worship of God and in the regulating of conduct (xxi. 801).[1] As no
parallels can be found in the writings of Melanchthon to the free
utterances often made by Luther in regard to the letter of the
Scriptures (supra, p. 300 f.), so also his conception of the authority of the Scriptures receives a different coloring from his endorsement of their teachings as being the same as embraced the
three ancient symbols of the church (xii. 399, 568, 608; v.
582).[2] Their doctrine he approves as being genuinely Catholic.
"This is a Catholic association (*coetus*), which embraces the
common consensus of prophetic and apostolic doctrine, together
with the belief (*sententia*), of the true church.   Thus in our Confession we profess to embrace the whole doctrine of the word of
God, to which the church bears testimony, and that in the sense
which the symbols show" (xxiv. 398; xxi. 349).[3] He condemns whatever varies from the *symbola accepta* (iii. 826, 985;
ix. 366).   He will not extend his hand to any "new dogma"
(i. 823, 901, 1048), nor alter anything in the ecclesiastical
formulas, for "often a change of words begets also new beliefs"
(xxiv. 427).   This high valuation of the ancient symbols is very
different indeed from the attitude of Luther toward them. Whilst
Luther most clearly declares that they have value for him only because, and in so far as, they agree with the Scriptures (supra, p.
304), Melanchthon makes no express limitation of this kind in
his endorsement of them.   Thus again, the ideas of Luther
are contracted and materialized.   To the symbols of the ancient
church was added, as we have seen, the Augustana.   But this is
not sufficiently explicit.[4]   The genuine, true doctrine is that of
Luther.   Melanchthon was the first to understand the relation of
Luther to the historical development of the world, and he ex-

---

[1] Cf., *e. g.*, xxiv. 718 ; xii. 479, 646 f., 649, 698 ; xxiii. 603 ; xi. 42 ; v.
580 : "has revealed in certain testimonies, and given a particular doctrine and
word."   Here are the germs of the later theory of inspiration.

[2] Osiander assailed the subscription of the three ancient symbols and the
Augsburg Confession under oath, which was customary at Wittenberg (xii.
6, 7).   Upon the daily devotional use of the Apostles' Creed, see xxv. 449 ;
xxiv. 394, 581.

[3] Cf.: "With true faith I embrace the whole doctrine handed down in the
books of the prophets and apostles, and comprehended in the Apostolic, Nicene, and Athanasian symbols" (Thesis of A. D. 1551, in HAUSSLEITER, l. c.,
p. 95).

[4] III. 286, 298, 1000, 827, 929 : "Confessio u. Apologia," v. 581 ; ix.
386 ; viii. 284 ; xxxiii. p. xxxviii. names, besides the three ancient symbols,
"Catechismus u. Bekenntnis Lutheri u. Confessio," ix. 319, 366, 618,
213 f.   Also Smalcald Articles.

pressed it with classical lucidity. He counts him among the mighty heroes of the church and her faith: Isaiah, John the Baptist, Paul, Augustine, and Luther. "Luther brought to light the true and necessary doctrine" (xi. 728 ; cf. vi. 57, 72, 73, 92 ; vii. 398 ; xi. 272). We must hold fast to the pure doctrine, namely, the *confessio Lutheri* (xi. 272 f.; viii. 49).[1] It is the doctrine of the Church and of the University of Wittenberg (xi. 327, 600 ; xxi. 602 ; iii. 1106). But the truth of the church's doctrine is attested also by the experience (*experientia*) of the pious (xxi. 420 ; xii. 426 ; cf. Luther, supra, p. 256 ff.).

6. This, therefore, is the truth : The teachings of the Bible, as understood and summarized by the ancient doctrinal standards, Luther and the Wittenberg theology. To the understanding and presentation of this truth all other sciences minister as "handmaids" of theology (xi. 394), not only by pedagogically sharpening the intellect for the apprehension of Scriptural truth, but also by furnishing the necessary preliminary scientific knowledge. Without scientific education, the theologian could produce only unconnected and confused statements, which would beget innumerable errors and a "cyclopian" monster (xi. 280). Hence the church needs, not only grammar and dialectics, but also physics and philosophy. "Not only for the sake of method . . . is philosophy necessary, but also many things must be taken (*assumenda*) by the theologian from physics." Thus the theologian derives his physiological, psychological, and logical definitions from the sphere of the arts and sciences (*orbis artium*) (ib. 281, 934). It is, in other words, the popularized philosophy of Aristotle, which theology requires as a prerequisite and support. To this naturally-acquired knowledge it adds that derived from the Scriptures. The light of reason (*lumen naturale*, xii. 514, 577, 648) furnishes every man with a number of innate moral and religious ideas. It plays as important a rôle in Melanchthon's line of thought as the "law of nature" in the later Middle Ages. In the application of this principle, he follows largely the example of Cicero. There is a natural religion, a natural morality, and a natural law. Although sin may have beclouded this light, it yet remains as an endowment of human nature. It cannot be denied that a dangerous tendency is thus inaugurated. Theology appears to be the product of a combination of the cosmology of the ancient world and the "articles of faith" derived from the Scriptures.[2] Cf. DILTHEY,

---

[1] The co-ordination of "Gottes Wort und Luther's Lehr" is perfectly in accord with Melanchthon's feeling. See already Anton Otto, C. R. viii. 460 : "the faith (*sententia*) of Luther, that is, of Christ."

[2] This combination reminds us of Thomas (supra, p. 100 f.), but DILTHEY

Archiv., etc., vi. 236 ff. TRÖLTSCH, l. c. HARTFELDER, Mel.,
p. 161 f., 181 f., 240.

7. In this last period of Melanchthon's labors, he emphasizes
with great energy the idea, that those who confess the correct faith
are the true church—thus following Luther also in the conception
of the Church (p. 294 f.). He recognizes the altered conditions—
there being now an evangelical church organization, having as
its distinguishing mark the possession of the true doctrine—in
most clearly from this time onward designating the visible assembly of the called (*coetus vocatorum*) as the church. "The
visible church is the assembly of those embracing the gospel of
Christ and rightly using the sacraments, in which God through
the ministry of the gospel is efficacious and regenerates many to
eternal life, in which assembly, nevertheless, are many unregen-
erated, but assenting to the true doctrine" (xxi. 826, and constantly. See Neue kirchl. Ztschr., 1897, 154, n. 1). This definition and the connection of thought in which it is found very
clearly reveal the general conception of Melanchthon. The true
church under any circumstances exists only where the true doctrine is found. Thus Zacharias, Anna, Elizabeth, the shepherds,
etc., since they did not accept the official teaching of their age,
but remained steadfast in the true doctrine, constituted the true
church in that age. God provides that there shall always be
some servants of his word, like Zacharias, as faithful representatives of this true doctrine. Only in this true church, in which
are gathered the really called, may believers and the elect be
found,[1] as only there is the church, in which God is known, confessed and worshiped, as "he has revealed himself" (xxi. 834).[2]
In the Middle Ages the church existed only where the doctrines
of an Augustine and Bernard, a Tauler and Wessel, were taught
(xxi. 837; xxiv. 309; xxv. 862 f.). They only, according to the
Scriptures, are churches, "which hold the pure doctrine and are
in harmony with it" (*in ea consentiunt*, xi. 273). Only in
this church are to be found the forgiveness of sins and justifica-

---

(p. 238) very properly points out the difference—that Melanchthon does not,
like Thomas, unite faith and philosophy in the construction of a system of metaphysics, but only makes the natural consciousness his point of departure.
Nevertheless, this Melanchthonian combination led historically to the orthodoxy of the seventeenth, as well as to the illumination of the eighteenth century.

[1] This is the "church of the elect," xxi. 913; xii. 678: the "church of
the regenerate;" xii. 589, 431; xxiii., p. xxxv.: the "eternal church;" xi.
760: the "elect" alone in this "army of the called;" xii. 567. On the other
hand, the term, true church (*ecclesia vera*), is used to designate the church
which holds the true doctrine; but only in this are the "true members of the
church," *i. e.*, the "saints"—see xxiii. 599.

[2] Cf. xi. 273; xii. 567; ix. 557; xxv. 220 f., 325, 640; xxiii. 597 f.

tion (xi. 400). But those who, like the Romish church, do not hold the central principle of the true doctrine, but persecute the real church, do not belong to the true church.[1] Yet Melanchthon also maintains the conception of the church as an *object of faith*, since it is only by faith that we can be assured that there is really in this visibly assembly (*coetus*) a number of elect persons (xii. 368 f.; xxiv. 365, 368, 400, 405; xxv. 148 f., 221, 677; viii. 284). The marks which attest the existence of the "true visible church," and at the same time assure to faith the presence of a "church of the regenerate" within the former, are therefore the true evangelical doctrine and the proper administration of the sacraments—to which Melanchthon afterward habitually added—reverence (*reverentia*), or obedience, to the ministry (*obedientia ministerii*).[2]

Such is the church. In it the divine purpose is being accomplished in the world. It is the realization of the aim of the work of Christ.[3] But this it is, because in it alone the truth of God is apprehended by men and becomes effectual through them. To maintain this doctrine in its simplicity and purity is the task of theology, as well as of every branch of science. This end is to be served by universities, princes, and states (xi. 272, 326 f.; iii. 198; viii. 401; vii. 666. HARTFELDER, p. 437). It may be said that the maintenance and spread of "pure doctrine" is the great motive which inspired Melanchthon's life-work, as a Reformer of the church and of the universities, as a theologian, philologian, and teacher.[4] This involved again, as compared with Luther, a narrowing of the horizon, resulting not merely from the great importance attached to the "pure doctrine," but from the fact that the life-giving energy of the church was attributed

[1] XII. 526, 628; xxiii.; p. xxxvii.; xxiv. 781, 855: "There is the church where are the fountains of Israel. . . . The Turks are not the church, neither are the Papists."

[2] XII. 599, 433, 602, 655; xxiv. 367, 401, 502; xxv. 129, 685, etc. The peculiar importance attached to the clerical office (see also xxv. 692) marks one of the materializing features of Melanchthon's later writings. The church, he holds, is neither a tyranny nor a democracy, but an honorable aristocracy (*honesta aristocratia*), xii. 367, 496; cf. also ii. 274, 284, 334, 376; iii. 942.

[3] XXI. 345; xxiv. 307; xii. 520: "To this end he established the human race, that there might be a church obeying God and worshiping him," 566; xiii. 199; xxiii. 198; xii. 339, 539, 616, 634, etc.

[4] This explains his severity toward heretics (*e. g.*, Servetus), ii. 18; iii. 197 f., 199, 241 f.; viii. 520 ff.; iv. 739; xii. 696; xxiv. 375, 501. On the other hand, we may thus also understand his fatal attitude toward the Interim, vii. 382 f., 322 f., and toward Calvin and his party; for, aside from the deviations which had separated himself as well from Luther, he believed himself to be in doctrinal accord with Calvin—and everything to his mind depended upon doctrine.

directly to the latter. It cannot be denied that in these views of Melanchthon are to be found the germs of the errors of the orthodoxy of the seventeenth century.[1] Melanchthon even defined faith, as, in the first instance, an "assent," with which intellectual act, the voluntary act of trust is necessarily associated (xxi. 790). But this is only a passing remark, trust still remaining for him the first and controlling element of faith. " This consolation is trust, by which the will acquiesces in the promise of mercy granted for the sake of the Mediator. But trust in the mercy embraces also a knowledge of the history, because it looks upon Christ, whom it is necessary to know as the eternal Son, crucified, arisen, etc., for us. And the history must be brought into relation with the promise, or effect, which is presented in the article: 'I believe in the forgiveness of sins' " (ib. p. 743 ; vi. 910). None of these passages must, of course, be interpreted as making the salvation of the individual dependent upon the possession of the pure doctrine. " Although the true church . . . preserves the articles of faith, nevertheless that true church may itself hold the articles of faith with obscurity on account of erroneous conceptions of them." If very much in the teaching even of the Fathers is overlooked, if they have only held fast to the fundamental truth, how much more must be forgiven weakness and errors found among the laity (ib. p. 837 f.; cf. xii. 433 f.; xxiii. 599, 601, 207). The important matter is only that the proper foundation be laid in the acceptance of the chief doctrine. He does not regard all separate doctrinal statements as of equal importance, but expressly recognizes a gradation of doctrines. " But this faith embraces all the articles of the Creed, and refers the others to this one: 'I believe in the forgiveness of sins' " (xii. 406, 540; xxi. 422). There are chief articles, which are important above everything else. The chief article is that concerning the blessings of Christ, or justification.[2] In this lies the whole practical comfort of the Christian religion, and it is in their relationship to it that all the

---

[1] This remark is not a novel one. See G. ARNOLD, Kirchen u. Ketzerhistorie, ii. Bk. 16, c. 9, 4 ff. ZIEROLD, Einleitung zur Kirchenhistorie (Leipzig u. Stargard, 1700), i. 387 ff., 384; recently RITSCHL, Die Entstehung der luth. Kirche, in Ztschr. f. Kirchengesch. i.

[2] Cf., *e. g.*, xxiii. 600, 280; v. 582 (original sin, grace, faith, works, sacraments); vi. 116; vii. 117 f., 532, 433; xxv. 863. Cf. also similar lists in Luther (supra, p. 297, n. 3). But note also, in a disputation held under Melanchthon, the remark in reference to the Athanasian Creed : " When they say, ' This is the Catholic faith ' (*fides*), they do not mean this trust (*fiducia*). But nevertheless the principal good work and destruction of the kingdom of Satan is to think rightly (*recte sentire*) concerning God, to confess God," etc. (in Haussleiter, p. 51).

other doctrines receive their position and significance.   It may, perhaps, be correctly said, that Melanchthon in this really means to say no more than that spiritual life can be aroused and flourish only when the gospel is actually preached.   But it would be an error, in view of such a remark concerning Melanchthon's personal sentiment in the matter, to minimize the historical results traceable to the form in which he expressed that sentiment. And it will scarcely suffice to interpret him as holding merely that the church has in the pure doctrine a substantial means for the effectual proclamation of the gospel.   This was certainly essentially what Melanchthon meant.[1]   But he *said* more than this.   Only they are members of the church who preserve " the doctrine uncorrupted," *i. e.*, the foundation, namely, *all* the articles of faith and the teachings of the decalogue.[2]   And it is just in the uncompromising one-sidedness of this position that its power and significance lie.   It was in the sphere of doctrine, as including the ideal of practical life, that the issue had been joined with Rome.   Under the circumstances of the age, it could have occurred in no other sphere.   The " pure doctrine " was the only legal title to existence held by the youthful evangelical church.   This was a controlling factor in her political fortunes ; it opened the nations to the new church.   Hence the duty of proclaiming the pure doctrine must be constantly impressed upon her preachers,[3] for the age was full of echoes of the scholastic teachings and superstitions of the past.   There was still a strong tendency to disputations upon doctrine and its forms, and it was needful to decline many a hand outstretched to the Reformers with proffers of assistance or of sworn alliance.   The practical conditions of the

---

[1] See the fundamental definition, supra, p. 354; "those embracing the gospel " and the "true doctrine."   We may, perhaps, say, that when Melanchthon speaks of the evangelical doctrine, he thinks primarily of saving truth in the narrower sense of the term (cf. xxiii. 600).   As in his first edition of the Loci, the Trinity and Christology were regarded rather as matters for reverent contemplation than for teaching, so it is known that shortly before his death he still hoped to gain clear ideas in regard to these objects of faith only in a higher world.

[2] XII. 433 : "It is necessary that those who receive the uncorrupted doctrine of the gospel . . . retain the foundation, all the articles of faith, and the doctrine of the decalogue."   The text of the C. R. places the " and," not after faith, but as follows : *et omnes articulos fidei doctrinam decalogi*, which can hardly be correct, as it is said in almost immediate connection : " By the term *consensus in fundamento* is required agreement in the articles of faith and in the decalogue."

[3] Cf. the catalogue of doctrines in the " Examen ordinandorum," and the remark : "that they upon opportunity present these questions in an orderly way in their sermons, so that the people may among themselves reflect and meditate upon a clear and fundamental outline of the Christian doctrine which is necessary . . . to (lead them to) conversion and to faith," xxiii., p. xl.

age gave birth to the formula of Melanchthon, and it in turn
reacted upon the age. We may to-day recognize its one-sidedness without calling in question its historical justification. It
undoubtedly fixed upon the Lutheran church for a long time to
follow something of the character of a school; but it was also
the legal title upon which that church based, maintained,
and justified its existence. Cf. SEEBERG, Begriff d. Kirche, i.
104 ff.

8. The Church of the Pure Doctrine—this is the one focal point
in the intellectual horizon of the later Melanchthon. The other
is Justification, or—which is the same thing (supra, p. 235 ff.)—
the substitute for the sacrament of repentance. It appears at first
but an illustration of the lack of strict systematic order in Melanchthon, that the terms discussed under the heading of repentance, such as faith, works, justification, etc., have all been already
exhaustively treated in an earlier portion of the Loci. But it
is also an evidence that these religious processes are not to his
mind limited to the praxis of confession, but that the latter praxis
merely includes also these processes.[1]

Melanchthon's starting-point is the Law. The law is the immutable wisdom of God, a rule for discrimination between good
and evil. It teaches men that there is a God, and what is his
character, that he has placed all men beneath this rule of life and
will punish all who do not live in accordance with it (xii. 614,
658 f.; xxi. 421, 685, 741, 885). Since now all men are from
their birth guilty and subject to condemnation, the law brings
primarily to all men judgment and condemnation; it leads us to
recognize that we are under the wrath of God (xxi. 692 f.; xxv.
777). But since even the regenerate still commit sin, the law
awakens in them also a sense of the wrath of God. To this are
to be added reflections upon the misery of life in this world,
future punishments, and the necessity for the atoning death of
Christ (xxi. 876, 883 f.). The result of this—faithfully pros-
ecuted—preaching of the law is *contrition*. The latter, however,
would but drive man to despair, if preaching of the law were not
at once accompanied with the proclamation of the gospel. The
gospel, as the announcement of the forgiveness of sins, teaches us
to know Christ and the blessings which he bestows (xii. 605).[2]

[1] We cannot fail to note here a formal approach to the Romish model, especially when we remember the importance again attaching to the confessional
in the latter half of the century. Cf. Von ZEZSCHWITZ, Katechetik, i. 570:
"Thereby (*i. e.*, through the combination of private confession and examination upon doctrinal points) the Lutheran Church substantially reädopted the
pedagogical system of the Middle Ages in a purified form. Cf. also RITSCHL,
Gesch. d. Pietismus, ii. 201 f., 539 f.

[2] Parallel with this narrower definition of the Gospel, Melanchthon recog-

At this point the doctrine of the Atonement is considered. If we are to speak of mercy to the sinner who is alarmed at thought of the divine justice, so there must be some means of accounting for this change of the divine attitude toward him. This require-ment Melanchthon meets by substantially reproducing the satis-faction theory of Anselm, to whom he expressly refers, thus ex-hibiting both the divine and the human natures of Christ in their connection with human salvation. In this alone lies the significance of Christ's redeeming work : "Christ has a ministry of teaching, but this is not his principal office. He was sent chiefly to be the victim for the human race, to be their Redeemer, to free us from the curse of the law.''[1] The tempering of justice with mercy was brought about by Christ's bearing the punishment for us, or bringing a sacrifice and an "equivalent price," and thereby satisfying the justice of God. As such service could be rendered only by a man, so, on the other hand, only God could offer a "price equivalent" for the "infinite wickedness" of the race (xxiv. 78 f., 569, 579; xxv. 171, 776; xii. 577 593, 446 f.; 616, 424, 428; xxi. 733, 743, 904). The obedience of Christ was the price rendered for us (xii. 424, 607; xxiii. 451).[2] Christ is now standing before the Father and interceding (*inter-pellirt*) for us, for the whole church, as for everyone who prays to him. "We are righteous on account of Christ, his righteous-ness which he discharged in doing and bearing being imputed to us" (xxiv. 216). His "merit" and "intercession" are the foundation of the Christian faith (xii. 426). The effect of this redeeming work is the forgiveness of sins and the imputa-tion of the righteousness of Christ, the impartation of the Holy Spirit of love and righteousness and of the new eternal life (xxiv. 80. 216, 654 f., 656, 748, 775, 798, 873, 864, 875; xxiii. 452; xv. 895).[3]

Faith lays hold upon the consolation which the gospel pro-

---

nizes also a broader conception, according to which it is "the preaching of repentance and the promise" (following Lk. 24. 47); xii. 589, 640; xxi. 732 f.

[1] XXV. 171 f.; xxiv. 78: "The final cause of the incarnation of the Son is that he may be a victim, the placator of the wrath of God." But in xxiv. 694, the object of the sending of Christ is said to have been the gathering, preservation, and sanctification of the church. In xv. 133, teaching and atone-ment are co-ordinated.

[2] According to xxiv. 242; xxv. 175, the fulfilling of the law by Christ had also a vicarious significance.

[3] "Eternal life," as Melanchthon often insists, begins in the present life, xxiv. 625: "The beginning of eternal life is in this life, *i. e.*, by faith to know this eternal God who has sent his Son, and it is to know him to be reconciled through the Son, and to call upon him, to ask and expect consolation in all tribulations. This faith and consolation in genuine griefs is a taste of eternal life."

claims, *i. e.*, it appropriates justification, or the forgiveness of sins. But with justification there is at the same time given the Holy Spirit, who begets a new life. Thus upon *contritio* and *fides* follows *justificatio*, and together with the latter is effected *regeneratio*, or *renovatio* (xxi. 427 f.). "And when God remits sins, he at the same time gives to us the Holy Spirit, who begins new powers (*virtutes*) in the pious" (742). Justification is conceived strictly as a forensic act, and hence clearly discriminated from renewal. *Justificatio* is a "forensic term," and indicates the "remission of sins" and "reconciliation or personal acceptance" (*acceptatio personae*, 742). In this consists the essential work of grace. "Let this therefore be the definition of grace. Grace is the remission of sins, or mercy promised for Christ's sake, or gratuitous acceptance, which the gift of the Holy Spirit necessarily accompanies." Even here, in the doctrine of justification, Melanchthon's conception varies from Luther's form of presentation. According to Luther, the Spirit works faith through the word. Faith is both the principle of a new life and the organ for apprehending the forgiveness of sins. To justification belongs the begetting of faith and the new life, as well as the forgiveness of sins (supra, p. 260 f.). This was also the position taken by Melanchthon in the Augsburg Confession and the Apology (supra, p. 336). *Now* faith seems to arise before the bestowal of the Spirit and before regeneration.[1] Faith apprehends the purely forensic decree of justification. And because this occurs, the Spirit is also granted to the individual for his regeneration. The inseparable connection which is in Luther always maintained between regeneration, justification, and sanctification is thus broken. These are the ideas which underlie the thoroughgoing revision of the Articles IV. and V. in the Variata Edition of the Augsburg Confession.[2] Whether the complete separation (*"reinliche Scheidung"*) of justification and sanctification is to be regarded as a step in advance or not, can only be decided by dogmatical and exegetical study. We here merely call attention to the fact, that Melanchthon, under this new grouping of the conception referred to, was

---

[1] There is here a peculiar lack of clearness in Melanchthon, since faith is for him on the one hand a product of the Holy Spirit working through the word (xii. 607, 426 f.), and yet, on the other hand, is supposed to precede the bestowal of the Spirit. Faith is accordingly a prerequisite of justification and begotten by the Holy Spirit, and yet, according to the recognized formula, the Holy Spirit is imparted only as a consequence of justification, *e. g.*, xxi. 742, 421, 427. Cf. HERRLINGER, p. 54.

[2] If the Augsburg Confession is to be interpreted in accordance with the Apology, then the prevalent formula of the Lutheran doctrine of justification finds its symbolical support in the Variata !

not able to make the ethical motive power of faith as manifest as in
Luther's theory. Faith is now for him essentially nothing more
than the organ, by which the forgiveness of sins is apprehended.
It is not, indeed, merely a historical knowledge, but the repose
of the will in the proffered gracious acceptance—confidence in
the grace of God. From this practical experience (faith as confidence, *fiducia*, applying this benefit to ourselves) of the effects
of the history and the doctrine, may be understood the intellectual conviction of both the history and the doctrine (xxi. 422,
743, 746, 785, 886 ; xii. 431). "Faith signifies to *assent* to
the promise of God (which is in the *intellect*), and with this assent
is necessarily connected *confidence* (which is in the will), willing
and accepting the promised reconciliation and acquiescing in the
Mediator set forth" (xxi. 790).[1] Since the sinner now desires
above everything else the forgiveness of sins, justification takes
place (xxi. 742). But, as the impartation of the Spirit renews
the man, reconciliation must necessarily be followed by good
works and a righteousness of a good conscience. Upon a detailed examination of the nature of good works as represented by
Melanchthon we need not enter. They are necessary, since
without them faith would be lost (for it is not compatible with
sinful thoughts or deeds), and, further, since they have been
commanded by God and are in keeping with the dignity of the
Christian calling (xxi. 429, 762, 775 ff.). They are works
which are really good on account of the faith which prompts
them, and which may also be spoken of as "meritorious," but
not in the sense that they merit the forgiveness of sins. They,
however, merit other spiritual and material blessings (xii. 448,
454).

It will be observed that we have here a combination in a fixed
order of all the elements which are of prime importance, in the
view of Melanchthon, for the development of the religious life.
But it is just as evident also that this entire general theory finds
its closest parallel in the Reformer's doctrine of repentance.
Contrition, faith, and new obedience are for him the constituent
elements of *poenitentia*,[2] to which he adds confession and
absolution.[3] There can be nothing suspicious in this, unless re-

[1] XXI. 759 enumerates : *notitia, assensus, fiducia ;* but the last two terms
are used as equivalents (see also HAUSSLEITER, p. 22) : "Faith is to assent to
every word of God given to us and in this promise of the gospel, and it is confidence acquiescing in the Mediator."

[2] XXI. 877 ; xxv. 62 ; xxiv. 426. Melanchthon at first enumerated only
contritio and *fides.* C. A. 12 ; Apol. 12, 28 ff.; xii. 506 f., 510 ; Erl. 23. 39.

[3] From the contrition which precedes faith must be discriminated the *contritio cum fide*, which awakens, not like the former a servile, but a filial fear
(*timor*), and which has a purer sorrow for sin (*purior dolor*). It does not

pentance and justification were again limited to the confessional, and the first Thesis of Luther thereby discredited. Of itself, it is ground for neither criticism nor surprise that the doctrine whose definition started the whole reformatory movement should furnish the frame-work for the systematic construction of the entire compass of religious truth won by the Reformation.

It would be an error to infer from Melanchthon's method of arranging his doctrinal views in separate "*Loci*," that he has transmitted his religious ideas in a confused and unconnected form. On the contrary, he summarized all the results of his religious study under two headings : the Church and Justification by Grace. The former of these is most intimately associated with the conception of "pure doctrine," and the latter with that of the law and the gospel. This double complex of ideas presents, in the theology of Melanchthon, a substitute both for the conception of the church which dominated the ecclesiastical life and for the sacrament of repentance which regulated the practical piety of the Middle Ages. This furnishing of new guiding principles for both ecclesiastical and individual religious life is a matter of such immense historical significance as to abundantly atone for any defect in his method of presentation. In formulating his definition of the empirical church, he fixed a goal, toward which not only all the gracious dealings of God were seen to tend, but toward which, as well, all human effort might be directed. As no one might hope for salvation outside of this church, all the moral and scientific energies of the age were pressed into the service of this supreme aim. This conception impressed a uniquely ecclesiastical character upon the intellectual and practical life of more than two centuries. But the conception of the "pure doctrine" was the boundary-line within which the self-consciousness of this church was developed and confirmed. Although modern theologians may deem the limits thus affixed too narrow—there were historical reasons for allowing them no wider scope—it cannot be denied that the consciousness of having in possession the pure doctrine became one of the most powerful coëfficients in the expansion and preservation of the church thus endowed.

§ 77. *The Theological Controversies in the Lutheran Church from the Death of Luther to the Adoption of the Formula of Concord.*

LITERATURE. SCHLÜSSELBURG, Haereticorum catalogus, 13 parts, 1597 ff.

flee from God, but seeks him and his forgiveness with the acknowledgment of its sin (xxi. 886 f.).

WALCH, Einleitung in d. Religionsstreitigkeiten innerh. u. ausserh. d. Luth. Kirche, 10 parts, 1730 ff.   PLANCK, Gesch. d. prot. Lehrbegriffes, 6 vols., 1781 ff. (1-3 in ed. 2, 1791 ff.).   HEPPE, Gesch. des deutschen Protestant- ism. 1555-81, 4 vols., 1852 ff.   FRANK, Theol. der CF., 4 vols., 1858 ff. THOMASIUS-SEEBERG, DG. ii., ed. 2, 425 ff.   LOOFS, DG., 438 ff., 422 ff.

1. The significance of Melanchthon for the History of Doc- trines may, in accordance with the foregoing review, be sum- marized in three particulars : (1) He gave permanent form to the ideas of Luther, thus laying the foundation for the theology of the following period and determining the direction of its progress.   Luther created a new church ; Melanchthon estab- lished a theology in harmony with it.   (2) He laid down the lines within which the spiritual life of the ensuing centuries was to be developed, obtaining a secure position for secular learning and the natural sciences by setting them in an auxiliary relation to the church of the " pure doctrine."   Thus the maintaining and the proclamation of the pure doctrine became more and more the essential and constituent function of the church.   Doctrine threatened to swallow up life.[1]   (3) He advocated a number of theological doctrines of his own, at variance more or less with those of Luther.   Although he proceeded cautiously in this direction during Luther's life-time, it is important to observe that the latter allowed these divergences of his associate to pass unchallenged.   They assume importance, although supported by very many of Melanchthon's disciples, only in view of the strict definition of " pure doctrine " and of the authority of Luther, which had been, by the efforts of Melanchthon himself, carried to the highest point and stamped as dogmatic.   The practical application of these principles and views led to the lamentable doctrinal controversies in the period from the death of Luther to that of Melanchthon.   Both the unfortunate waver- ing of Melanchthon in connection with the Interim—when the doctrine appeared to him to be sufficiently guarded—and the bitter assaults made upon him by the so-called Gnesio-Luth- erans for his lack of firmness upon that occasion and for his doctrinal divergences find explanation in the one-sided character of his later conceptions of the church and of doctrine.[2]

The great prophetic age of Protestantism was followed by a didactic age.   We can understand the necessity for the tran-

[1] But it is unfair to ascribe this onesidedness entirely to the influence of Melanchthon (Arnold, Ritschl, and others), for (1) The same thoughts are found not seldom in the writings of Luther, and (2) Melanchthon only gave expression to a tendency which dominated the period and characterized its particular stage of cultural development.

[2] With the above compare also my article, Die Stellung Mel. in d. Gesch. der Kirche u. der Wiss., ed. 2, Erlang., 1897.

sition ; but it proved a retrogression similar to that from the days of the old prophets of Israel to the great Synagogue ! We must glance briefly at the leading controversies of the period.

2. THE INTERIM AND THE ADIAPHORISTIC CONTROVERSY. Melanchthon and the Wittenberg theologians announced themselves prepared (see BIECK, Das dreifache Interim, Leipz., 1721, p. 361 ff.) to accept the so-called Leipzig Interim, A. D. 1547. In this document, justification was modified and made to signify "that man is renewed by the Holy Spirit, and can fulfill righteousness with his works (*Gerechtigkeit mit dem werk vollbringen kann*), and that God will for his Son's sake accept in believers this weak beginning of obedience in this miserable frail nature" (BIECK, 372).[1] In addition to this, the episcopal jurisdiction was restored, and almost all the Romish ceremonies were to be again introduced (p. 377 f., 380 ff.). It is not surprising that on every hand a most bitter conflict was precipitated. Melanchthon by his course on this occasion forfeited the confidence of wide circles of his former friends. The controversy is known as the *Adiaphoristic*, because the chief question at issue was, whether it is morally permissible to yield in unessential external matters, provided the chief matter, *i. e.*, pure doctrine, be conserved. To this the Wittenbergers answered in the affirmative. Their opponents (esp. FLACIUS, vid. PREGER, Flac. i. 142 ff.) applied the principle : "Nothing is indifferent ($\dot{a}\delta\iota\dot{a}\varphi o\rho o\nu$) in a matter of confession and abuse (*in casu confessionis et scandali*)."

3. THE MAJORISTIC CONTROVERSY. Luther was accustomed, upon occasion, to employ the paradox, that good works are a hindrance to justification (supra, p. 264, n. 1). Melanchthon, on the contrary, declared them to be necessary. (*a*) George Major (A. D. 1552), following the latter suggestion, maintained that good works are necessary to salvation, since no one is saved by wicked works and no one without good works. He then further explains, that they are necessary for retaining salvation (*ad retinendam salutem*). JUSTUS MENIUS, after A. D. 1554 (vid. Thomasius, ii. 473 ff.), held a similar view. These ideas were by no means meant to be understood in a Catholic sense, but were simply designed to establish the profound connection between faith and a new life, and were therefore genuinely Lutheran in their tendency. But AMSDORF and FLACIUS raised a vigorous opposition. The former declared, that anyone who would defend the statement that good works are necessary to salvation was a "Pelagian, a Mameluke, and denier of Christ"

---

[1] Free will is treated in harmony with Melanchthon's views (p. 362 f.). It is asserted that "God does not deal with man as with a log, but draws him in such a way that his own will also co-operates."

(SCHLÜSSELBURG, Catal. vii. 210). The latter argued, that, if faith alone justifies and saves, this cannot be said in any sense of works (Wider den Evangelisten des h. Chorrocks, 1553, form C.). And in the same way the preservation of the state of grace can be based only upon faith. In the whole course of the Christian life, faith must maintain its dominant position and dare not share the latter with good works (vid. Schlüsselb. vii. 162 ff., 534 ff., 572 ff.). This criticism did not indeed apply to the tendency of Major and Menius. Melanchthon wished to rest in the proposition : "New obedience is necessary," and advised that the qualifying words, "to salvation," on account of the possibility of interpreting them as involving the idea of merit, be used only in connection with faith (C. R. ix. 498 f., 405 ff., 474 ; viii. 410 ff.). (b) But the opposing party now went further. They asserted that the gift of the Holy Spirit is only "an appendage, consequence, and supplement of grace" (Synod at Eisenach, A. D. 1556, in Flacius, De voce et re fidei, p. 199) or, "Renewal is an entirely separate thing from justification" (Flac., De justif., 182). This position was really only a logical inference from the Melanchthonian conception of the doctrine of justification (supra, p. 360). But while Melanchthon himself had, in his theory of the ethical necessity of good works, a certain corrective for the severance of justification and renewal, Amsdorf pressed on to the bold assertion, that "good works are injurious to salvation," and in other declarations threatened to carry out the idea of freedom from the law to the extreme statement : "God does not care for works" (cf. C. R. viii. 411). But not only Melanchthon and his school opposed these excesses in doctrinal statement ("in the divine order man owes obedience," C. R. ix. 370, 474 ; cf. den Endlichen Bericht vnd Erklerung der Theologen beider Vniversiteten Leipzig u. Wittemberg, 1570), but Gnesio-Lutherans also recognized the necessity of the new obedience as proceeding from the inward impulses of the new heart (vid. Schlüsselb. vii. 572 ff., 603, 615, 617 ff.).

4. THE ANTINOMISTIC CONTROVERSY is most intimately connected with the foregoing. At the Synod at Eisenach, Amsdorf had proposed the thesis : " Good works are, even in the forum of the law and in the abstract (de idea), not necessary to salvation (SALIG, Gesch. d. Augsb. Conf. iii. 56 f.). In endorsing this, ANDREAS POACH maintained, that it is the office of the law only to accuse and condemn, and that the gospel alone leads to the doing of good : "After grace has been obtained and remission of sins and salvation accepted, we cease to do evil and begin to obey God" (SALIG, iii. 58 f. Schlüsselb. iv. 265 ff.,

338 ff., 342, 344). ANTON OTTO advanced to crass Antinomianism, affirming that there is no "third use of the law;" that
the new obedience belongs not to the kingdom of Christ, but to
the world, as to Moses and the supremacy of the pope; that the
Christian is "above all obedience." We should pray God that
we may remain steadfast to our end in faith without any works
(cf. PLANCK, v. 1. 62 f.). It was the old ideas of Agricola
which were thus continually reäppearing, although Luther had
refused to countenance them (supra, p. 251).

5. THE EUCHARISTIC CONTROVERSY. Calvin's doctrine of the
Lord's Supper (vid. sub) was enabled for some time to prosecute a silent propaganda in Germany, as Melanchthon and his
followers maintained a friendly attitude toward it. In A. D.
1552, JOACHIM WESTPHAL, the Hamburg pastor, raised his voice
against it. He pointed out that Calvin's view of the Lord's
Supper was not that held by Luther. Immediately there was
great excitement. Wild conflicts were waged in Bremen (Hardenberg and Timann), in Heidelberg (Tilmann, Hesshusen, and
Klebitz), in the Palatinate (cf. SCHMID, Der Kampf d. luth.
Kirche um Luther's Lehre v. Abendmal, 1868, p. 151-225).
Under the leadership of BRENZ, the church of Würtemburg
(Synod at Stuttgart, 1559) pronounced in favor of the Lutheran
doctrine. Melanchthon anxiously avoided a public deliverance.[1]
He died in 1560. The Wittenbergers, at the request of their
Electors, temporized, condemning Zwingli and defending themselves against "Flacian innovations." The atmosphere was clarified by the " Exegesis perspicua et ferme integra de sacra coena,"
1574, written by JOH. CUREUS in Glogau (ed. Scheffer, Marburg,
1853). In this document the doctrine of the ubiquity of the
body was controverted, with keen polemic against the Lutheran
conception of the communicatio idiomatum.[2] Christ is present
for believers only according to his divine nature and personally.
"The substance of this Supper is communion (κοινωνία) with
Christ. As now this ingrafting (insertio) cannot be effected, as
we have often declared, without faith, so the sacraments have
been instituted for believers, and not for the ungodly" (p. 24 f.).
The book thus summarizes the author's view: "Believers are,

[1] "I beg of you," he wrote to Hardenberg, "dissimulate much (multa dissimules)" (C. R. viii. 736; cf. ix. 15 ff., 960: "To answer is not diffi-cult, but dangerous." Against Brenz, ib. 1034 f.).
[2] This, it was held, destroys the true corporeality of Christ and is Euty-chian (e. g., p. 41). "The body of Christ is, as it were, abducted from us; therefore no part of his substance (substantiae) is infused into us" (p. 11). "We think, indeed, of no magical nor physical binding of Christ to the word or sacraments, but we say that he is, according to his covenant, most freely efficacious in believers through the word and sacraments" (p. 10).

in the use of the bread and wine, made by faith true and living members of the body of Christ, who is present and efficacious through these symbols, as through a ceremonial agency (*ministe-rium*), inflaming and renovating our hearts by his Holy Spirit. But unbelievers are not made participants or communicants (κοινωνόι), but are guilty of the body of Christ on account of their contempt " (p. 26). This document became the occasion for a severe condemnation of the Saxon *Crypto-Calvinism,*and the express rejection of Calvin's doctrine of the Lord's Supper. Melanchthon's doctrine was pronounced in harmony with that of Luther, but the doctrine of the ubiquity was disapproved (Torgau, A. D. 1574).[1] Cf. HEPPE, Gesch. d. deutschen Prot. ii. 431 ff.

6. THE SYNERGISTIC CONTROVERSY. (*a*) PFEFFINGER in Leipzig had in A. D. 1555, following Melanchthon (supra, p. 349), taught in his *Quaestiones de libertate voluntatis humanae*, that man is in conversion not " purely passive," as a statue, but must also do his part. The ability to give *assensio* must in him be called into exercise for the actualizing of conversion. Against this AMS-DORF and FLACIUS protested. Two startling events then surprised the church. VICTORIN STRIGEL, at the very seat of Gnesio-Lutheranism, suddenly announced himself as a Synergist (A. D. 1559), and FLACIUS, the fanatical champion of the pure doctrine, in combating him, fell into the grossest of all heresies. In A. D. 1560, a disputation was held at Weimar between Strigel and Flacius (see Disput. de originali peccato et lib. arb. inter M. Flac. Ill. et Vict. Strigel, 1562. Also, SALIG, Gesch. d. Augsb. Conf. iii. 587 ff.). (*b*) Strigel taught : No man can be converted to God by his own power without the Holy Spirit. But neither can conversion occur by magic nor by compulsion. God takes into consideration, among other things, the nature of man, as a creature endowed with a will. The natural difference existing between a free agent (*liberum agens*) and a natural agent (*naturaliter agens*) (Disput., p. 22, 210) is the ground of a special divine agency adapted to the peculiar character of man. " The will cannot be coerced, . . . if the will could be coerced it would not be will, but rather non-will " (*voluntas*, p. 82, 25, 73, 176). Sin has not abolished and de-

---

[1] We may mention also the superstitious conception of the *consecration* taught by JOH. SALIGER and FREDELAND in Lübeck and carried by the former to Rostock : The body is present in the Lord's Supper immediately after the consecration and before the distribution (A. D. 1568-69). Similiar superstitions spring up elsewhere (hair of the beard upon which a little of the wine has hung is plucked out ; stones upon which it falls are crushed and the powder gathered up and preserved ; the upsetting of the cup is regarded as a serious offense). See HEPPE, Gesch. des Prot. ii. 385 ff.

stroyed free-will, but depraved it[1] (p. 49). Nor does grace
move this will in a mechanical or natural way. "The conversion of man differs from a violent and natural movement (of an
object). And the will acts in its own way in conversion, and is
not a statue or a log in conversion" (p. 73). Strigel means,
therefore, that even in conversion man's peculiar "mode of
action" must be preserved, *i. e.*, that no inward transformation
can be real except the will has also given its assent. But he
combined with this mode of action also features of a material
freedom of will. He conceives of the natural man as only bound,
wounded, and hindered by sin, and hence teaches a material co-
operation of the will in conversion. Although it be but weakly,
yet the will of man co-operates ; its attitude toward grace is not
simply passive, but only "more passive than active" (p. 232). At
this point, Flacius parts company with him. A co-operation of
the will is acknowledged also by the latter, but only as beginning
after the actual moment of conversion. This was with him the
only question : " I ask whether you say that the will co-operates
before the bestowal of faith, or after faith has been received ?
Whether you say, that it co-operates by its natural powers, or in
so far as (the power) to will well has been granted to it by the
renewal of the Holy Spirit ?" (p. 43, 71, 100, 178, 233). But
to this clear-cut question Strigel did not give a precise answer.[2]

(*c*) According to Flacius, the sinner is completely dead to
good impulses. His attitude in the (momentary) act of conversion is "merely passive ;" yea, before, in, and after conversion, his attitude is purely one of resistance (ib., p. 131).[3]
Thus he asserts, that " man is converted (while) willing and re-
sisting (*volentem, repugnantem*);" and that he " is converted,
not only when his natural free will co-operates, but even when it
raves and howls" (p. 131 and thesis 4). " God alone converts
man—he does not exclude the will, but every efficacy or operation of it " (p. 118). As Flacius, reversing Strigel's method,
starts with the material bondage of the will, he loses sight of its

---

[1] Strigel is here evidently thinking of the formal freedom of the will.

[2] What he had in view is evident from the following illustration : " A child
cannot seek nourishment from its mother unless the mother gives it to him.
She must even turn his mouth in the proper direction. But the child must itself draw the milk from the mother's breast" (p. 131 f.). The fundamental
mistake of Strigel was that, while he had a proper sense of the personal character of conversion, he failed to give proper expression to his conviction, because the natural, formal freedom of choice was transformed under his hand
into a material and ethical freedom. He was, accordingly, unable to ascribe
the ground and beginning of conversion absolutely to God.

[3] Cf. Amsdorf: " God deals with willing and knowing men just in the
same way as with all other created things, a stone or a log, through his own
sole willing and decreeing (*velle et dicere*)." See Schlüsselburg, v. 547.

formal freedom.   Conversion thus becomes, in the end, a transformation of man's nature.   From this point Flacius went a
step further, and maintained that sin is not an attribute (*acci-
dentia*), but of the essential substance of man.   He was guided
by the Aristotelian definition of an attribute : "That which is
present or wanting without destruction of the subject."   According to this, original sin, regarded as an attribute, would appear
to be only an accidental trait.   But in the view of Flacius, the
essential nature of man has been itself transformed by sin.
Although Flacius may have used the term, substance (*substanz*),
rather in the sense of formal nature (*essentia formalis*), or substantial form (*forma substantialis*), there yet remained the idea
of a transformation of man's nature by sin.   A "horrible
metamorphosis" has taken place ; the image of God has been
replaced by the "true and living image of the devil."   Man's
nature has been distorted into a diabolic nature, and every point
of attachment for divine influences has been lost.   For the
advocacy of these ideas Flacius sacrificed his position and the
fortunes of his life (see esp. Theil. ii. of the Clavis, p. 651 ff.,
and " De essentia justitiae originalis et injustitiae," 1568).
(*d*) The Lutherans persisted in their external and mechanical
conception of conversion, and the Philippists also maintained
their position.   To the latter, the conceptions of the purely
passive attitude of man in conversion, his resistance to it, and
the illustrations of the animating of a stone or log, appeared
overdrawn and enthusiastic (see the Endl. Bericht, 1570).
They were anxious, on the other hand, to retain in some way
the personal and psychological element in the process of conversion.   But it is of the greatest significance that they clearly
and plainly deny "any kind of ability or a free will for their
own conversion " in the unregenerate.   Man can, they held, do
nothing whatever toward his own conversion (Endl. Bericht,
form Ii, 1 b ; 4 b ; 4 a).   This acknowledgment opened the
way for a possible understanding with the theologians of the
former group.   The controversy therefore effected a positive
clearing of the atmosphere.

7. THE OSIANDRIAN CONTROVERSY.   (*a*) In A. D. 1850 and
the following years attention was drawn to a new theory of justification taught by ANDREAS OSIANDER (Disput. de justificatione,
1550 ; Von dem einigen Mitler Jhesu Christo vnd Rechtfertigung des Glaubens, 1551 ; Widerlegung der vngegrundten vn
dienstlichen Antwort Phil. Melanthonis, 1552).   "They teach
(doctrines) colder than ice, that we are accounted righteous
only on account of the remission of sins, and not also on account
of the righteousness of the Christ dwelling in us by faith.   God

24

is not indeed so unjust as to regard him as righteous in whom there is really nothing of true righteousness '' (De justif. thes., 73 f.). This citation reveals his aim. Justification as connected solely with imputation is to his mind an irreligious conception. Justification is more than a mere declaring the sinner to be righteous. But the talented man now placed these ideas in a wider setting. To understand him, we must briefly reproduce his entire scheme of thought. Man was created in the image of God. This image of God is in the Son, and in the Son, furthermore, as from eternity appointed to become incarnate. Accordingly, the appointed goal of human nature can be realized only by the indwelling of God in it. This was actualized in the case of Adam, as in him the Son of God already dwelt before the fall.[1] Through this indwelling he became righteous. Through sin this '' original righteousness '' was lost. The renewal of the race is now effected by Christ's entering it in the incarnation. But Christ is brought to the individual soul through the word. He is himself the '' inner word '' (according to Jn. i.); but the latter enters the human soul in and through ''the outer word.'' The words of Jesus and his apostles are thus the vehicle through which the Logos takes up his abode within us (Von d. Mitler, C. 1). It is, therefore, through this indwelling that man becomes righteous. Righteousness is '' no work, no act, no endurance; '' '' but it is the character (die Art) which makes him who receives and possesses it righteous and moves him to act and endure aright'' (ib. H. 4). It is the piety (Frommbkeit) which makes the man absolutely a new man. Thus the righteousness of man is a condition, but a condition which is and will be effected by God himself. This righteousness is God himself. As the humanity of Christ became righteous through its union with God as the essential righteousness, so we also become righteous by virtue of such a union with Christ (H. 3 b).

But this union depends upon Christ's mediatorial work as its prerequisite. The latter has two aspects: redemptio and justificatio. Redemption embraces two things. The sinner is under obligation to bear the eternal penalty of his sin, or the wrath of God, and also to fulfill the law. By his innocent sufferings, Christ endured the wrath of God and obtained for us the forgiveness of sins. And since we, even after regeneration, are unable to fulfill the law perfectly, he, in order that the law might not further accuse us, ''fulfilled it purely and perfectly for us and for our benefit, in order that it might

---

[1] See already Methodius, supra, Vol. I., p. 174.

not be imputed to us, nor we be accursed because we do not in this life perfectly fulfill the law" (ib. A. 3 b; 4 a). By both of these aspects of redemption[1] our objective salvation is effected. Everyone who belongs to the church of Christ is by it—without regard to his subjective attitude—objectively saved.[2] But this reconciliation, or forgiveness of sins, is not yet by any means our righteousness. The relation of justification to redemption is to be conceived of as that of a consequent : "That righteousness is granted because sin has been before forgiven" (Widerleg. J. 4 a). We are righteous only in so far as we become alive; but we become alive, or righteous, only through the indwelling of Christ. Justification is therefore not to be conceived forensically, but as a making-righteous (B. 2 a). *Justificare* is "from an ungodly to make a righteous man, *i. e.*, to recall the dead to life" (De justif., thes. 3). This indwelling of the divine nature of Christ, with which at the same time the Triune God dwells in us, is our righteousness before God. Still more precisely, " his divine nature is our righteousness" (Widerleg. L. 2 a ; Von d. Mitler, B. 1 b). It is therefore perfectly clear, that justification is the renewal of man wrought by the presence of Christ, or at least that it embraces this as its chief element. If the Scriptures make righteousness dependent upon faith, faith is thus mentioned by them because its content is Christ (J. 1 b), *i. e.*, " Jesus Christ, true God and man, who dwells in our hearts by faith " (J. 2 b). In this connection, Osiander acknowledges, after all, a certain imputation. When we are united with Christ by faith, we are "overwhelmed and filled" with divine righteousness. And although sin indeed still clings to us, yet it is only as an impure drop compared with a whole pure ocean, and, on account of Christ's righteousness which is within us, God will not regard

---

[1] *I. e.*, the *passive* and the *active obedience* of Christ, cf. Luther supra, p. 268. This discrimination became, as a result of the present controversy, a permanent feature of the accepted doctrine of the church. See, *e. g.*, Flacius, Von d. Gerechtigk. D 2 : " The essential righteousness of God . . . demands two kinds of righteousness : the first is, that we make full satisfaction for the transgression and sin which we have committed ; the other, that we thereafter be also perfectly obedient to his law in heart and works." Cf. THOMASIUS, Das Bek. d. Luth. Kirche v. d. Versönung, 1857, p. 56 ff. Osiander also gave a peculiar coloring to this double obedience of Christ by representing the active obedience as filling out the deficiencies in the incipient righteousness. The original idea associated by Luther with the two terms was, that by the sufferings of Christ the penalties of the law were nullified, and by his active fulfilling of the law the whole economy of law (which as the "law of nature" held sway over all men) was abrogated for us. See citations, supra, p. 271 f.

[2] But, despite this, man remains under the wrath of God until repentance and justification take place (Von d. Mitler, B. 4 a ; 2 b).

it (X. 4 b). "When he dwells in us by faith, he brings with
him into us his righteousness, which is his divine nature, and this
is then also *imputed* to us, as though it were our own " (Q. 3 a).

The theory of Osiander is thus, briefly stated, as follows :
Christ through his sufferings appeased the wrath of God, and
through his fulfillment of the law made satisfaction for our continuing disobedience. We are thereby objectively redeemed.
Salvation becomes ours subjectively in this way : In the preached
word the Logos enters us, and he, embraced by faith, begets in
us a new life.   Thus is our righteousness really begun, and yet it
is righteousness only because Christ's abiding presence in us
maintains it and leads God to regard our beginning of righteousness in the light of his (Christ's) perfection. This theory is evidently not Roman Catholic ; for it neither takes any account of
merit upon our part, nor does it really base justification upon our
new life, the ground of the latter being, on the contrary, the power
of Christ.[1] Penetrating to the heart of Osiander's contention,
it cannot be denied that he was endeavoring to reproduce the
early Protestant doctrine of justification, and in this he had
a right to make appeal to Luther. Like the latter, he intoned
with unwearying energy the indwelling of Christ within us, and,
like him, he saw the believer's righteousness and goodness in
faith because of its content, *i. e.*, Christ (supra, p. 260). And
yet, if we compare with him the entire Luther, we will observe
a distinct difference. Osiander was distinctively a scholar—
dominated by thoughts, and not by experience—and he wrote
also under the stimulus of a visible opposition. This made him
one-sided. He was not able by his train of connected ideas to
combine, as did Luther, the legality and the consolation of the
imputed righteousness. The accent is differently placed by the
two men. According to Luther, the Christ for us is our consolation and is the effectual power of the Christ in us ; while
according to Osiander, the former is but the logical prerequisite
for the latter. The practical result of the forgiveness of sins is
for Luther above all else faith ; for Osiander, the power of doing
the good. But we should not on this account minimize the service which Osiander rendered by advocating ideas embraced in
original Lutheranism as against Melanchthonianism.[2]

[1] The connection between *redemptio* and *justificatio*, the objective and subjective aspects of the work of salvation, remains for Osiander thoroughly beclouded. His most serious fault is his placing of the forgiveness of sins in the
background. In this, he reminds us somewhat of Duns.

[2] A broad systematic instinct permeates the discussions of Osiander. He
had a connected general theory of Christianity, such as no other among
the theologians succeeding Luther possessed until Calvin appeared. Among
the men of second rank in the Reformation period, he was perhaps the

Cf. MÖLLER, A. Os., 1870. THOMASIUS, ii. ed. 2, 437 ff. FRANK, Theol. d. CF. ii. 5 ff. RITSCHL, Rechtf. u. Vers. i., ed. 2, 235 ff. LOOFS, DG. 423 ff.[1]

(*b*) Both Philippists and Lutherans at once arose with one accord against the theory of Osiander. There was no appreciation of the relative (historical) justification of his contention.[2] His charge, that under the doctrinal formulas sufficient emphasis was not laid upon man's renewal, was indignantly resented (Mel. C. R. vii. 895). The chief objections to his theory were the following. He depreciated, it was said, the forgiveness of sins, by separating it from justification, and laid the emphasis, not upon the revealed gracious disposition of God toward us, but upon the "gift" (*donum*) of grace (Mel. C. R. vii. 899. Menius, Von d. Gerechtigk., E. 4 a). He thus reverses the proper order, regarding renewal as the ground instead of the result of justification. But this, it was further said, was connected with his second chief error, namely, that he tears asunder redemption and justification. The obedience of Christ, by virtue of which he both made atonement for our sins and fulfilled the law in our stead, is at the same time our righteousness and our redemption (see esp. the Censur of the theologians of Electoral Saxony, B. 4 b, C. 2 b, and Flacius, Von d. Gerechtigk. wider Os., Magdeb., 1552, D. 4 a). "In such a way that this obedience of the Mediator, Jesus Christ, at the same time delivers and justifies the poor sinner and reconciles God who has been angry" (Menius, l. c., E. 2. Flac., l. c., D. 3 a). As we lay hold upon this righteousness of Christ in faith, it becomes ours, and the objective certainty of this righteousness secures us the comfort of the assurance of salvation. Osiander, on the contrary, bases our righteousness and salvation upon our own state, or condition, and thus the assurance of salvation is stolen from "poor distressed consciences" (Lauterwald, Fünf. Schlussprüche wider Os., 1552, A. 3 b. C. R. viii. 583. Flacius, Verlegung Os., J. 3 a). These objections were certainly well

greatest. Viewed historically, his attempt constitutes the contemporaneous counterpoise to the doctrine of justification taught by the later Melanchthon. Both men gave one-sided interpretations of ideas of Luther's ; the latter, through undue emphasis, upon the imputed, the former by exalting out of proper proportion the effective, righteousness of faith. But it must, after all, be accounted a blessing, that the Melanchthonian and not the Osiandrian scheme met the approval of the church.

[1] My estimate of Osiander agrees, so far as I can see—up to a certain point—with that of LOOFS.

[2] Brenz opposed an express condemnation of Osiander at Worms in 1557 (see G. WOLF, Gesch. d. deutsch. Protestanten, 1555-9, 1888, p. 334, 339, 363). Calvin also most vigorously combated his views (Institut. iii. 11. 5 ff.; cf. ii. 12. 5 f.; i. 15. 3).

taken.   Osiander's method of presenting the doctrines involved was in fact liable to the serious peril of making the redemption wrought by the historical Christ but a comparatively unimportant precursor of the effective agency of the Logos, and of confusedly mingling our righteousness and that of Christ.   But was not the Melanchthonian doctrine also liable to the perilous misconception, that man may by simply giving intellectual assent to the theory of satisfaction become sure of his salvation ?

(*c*) In opposition to Osiander, FRANZ STANCAR, appealing to the Lombard, for whom he entertained an exceedingly warm regard, maintained :[1] "Christ is (our) righteousness only according to his human nature" (sent. iii. dist. 19. 7).   Since it was the mission of the Mediator to reconcile men to God and to die for them, his works, because mediatorial, were human (*e. g.*, SCHLÜSSELBURG, ix. 244).   And the human voluntary acts of the Mediator cannot be attributed to the immutable God (ib. 277).   He thus moved in the direction of Nestorianism.

8. The Christological conflicts belong to a later period.   (*a*) The Heidelberg theologians assailed the Lutheran Christology (see esp. Gründl. Bericht, v. h. Abendm., 1566) by denying the *ubiquitas* and the *communicatio idiomatum* (Thomasius, ii., ed. 3, 603), and the Würtembergers, especially BRENZ (De personali unione duarum naturum, 1561 ; De divina majestate domini nostr. Ies. Chr., 1562), appeared in its defense.   According to Brenz, the entire fullness of the divine attributes was at the moment of the incarnation infused into the human nature of Christ.   And Christ, even during his life on earth, actually exercised these divine attributes, although secretly.   Whilst he lay dead in the tomb, he was filling and ruling heaven and earth ; whilst he was, at the time of the death of Lazarus, outwardly far from Bethany, he was according to his divine nature present at his death-bed.[2]   Cf. THOMASIUS, Christologie, ii., ed. 2, 384 ff. H. SCHULTZ, Gottheit Christi, p. 216 ff.

(*b*) A similar conflict of views was developed in Saxony. The Crypto-Calvinists, P. Eber, G. Major, Krell) also rejected the *communicatio idiomatum* (Von der Person vnd Menschwerdung vnseres HEerrn J. Christi, der waren christl. Kirchen Grundfest, 1571).   The "great and high gifts and glories"

---

[1] Thus already Augustine (Vol. I., pp. 260, 361 n.) as well as Thomas and the other Scholastics.

[2] Brenz based his theory upon ideas developed by Luther in the controversy upon the Lord's Supper.   The interests of Christology are for him entirely wrapped up in the *communicatio idiomatum* ; but, measured by the historical career of Christ, his theory, framed entirely in conformity with the ubiquity idea, proves insufficient.

which the humanity of Christ received are "not eternal, infinite attributes of the divine nature" (l. c., 23, 25). Each of the two natures retains its own peculiar attributes and energies unmingled with those of the other nature. Against this, MARTIN CHEMNITZ directs his treatise, *De duabus naturis in Christo*, 1571.[1] If we compare the ideas here presented with those of Brenz, we are favorably impressed with his strict adherence to the scriptural terms,[2] his familiarity with the historical development of doctrine and his dogmatic carefulness; but he lacks the broad, pacific temper which impresses the reader so favorably in the works of Brenz. He holds that the human nature of Christ receives infused gifts, qualities, and habitus (*dona, qualititates, habitus*, p. 253 ff., 267, 40) from the divine nature. It receives these in the fullest measure possible to a finite nature,[3] and its susceptibility is thereby increased, so that it is enabled by virtue of the hypostatic union to receive the essentially divine attributes (c. 20 f.). This leads to a real manifestation of divine attributes in the human nature. The human nature is permeated by the divine as iron by fire (c. 23, 6). An interpenetration (περιχώρησις) takes place. But—and this is a significant thought —Chemnitz very frequently conceives of this relationship as an exertion of the energy of the divine will in the human nature and its natural powers. The divine will with its energy constitutes the divine nature in Christ; the human nature is the appropriate Organ for the actualizing of its *operationes*. "He wished to assume as an organ our nature, taken up into the communion of his divine energies (*operationes*), particularly in the work of the Messiah," p. 323. The human nature is the intelligent and self-determining Organ through which Christ accomplishes his redeeming work. There is a co-operation, since the powers of the human nature have an *organon co-operans* in the divine nature, and *vice versa* (p. 224, 363, 261). The will of the Logos guides the human will, and the latter willingly accepts the leadership. The human will in Christ desires, craves, wills, and approves what Christ performs in his offices by his divine power (p. 224). "For this soul (*anima*) of Christ willed those things which the divine will of the Logos willed that it should will" (p. 473). As, according to this, the divine nature of Christ consists, in the last analysis, in the omnipotent Loving-will which is revealed in the works of Jesus; the whole character of the

---

[1] The citations are from the Leipzig edition of 1578.

[2] P. 328: "For concerning God we should neither think nor speak otherwise than as he has in the very word (employed) revealed himself in the Scriptures."

[3] He sees a parallel in the indwelling and operating of God in the believer.

life and sufferings of Jesus must be traced to the will of the
Logos (p. 39, 72, 227, 46). With this connection of ideas the
Ubiquity appears in a new light. It is now the power of the
God-man to determine to be bodily present where he will (multivolipresence): "That the Son of God is by virtue of the hypostatic union able to be present with his assumed nature wherever, whenever, and in whatsoever way he will, *i. e.*, wherever
he has in a positive word taught and promised that he desires to
be present with it" (p. 517, 477, 479, 480, 496). Upon this
basis, Chemnitz secures more room for the human development of
Jesus and for discriminating between the states of humility and
exaltation. The divine nature refrains from exercising its energy
upon the human nature (*paullisper retrahens et retinens*), although
the latter has from the moment of the conception really possessed
and had at command the fullness of the divine nature.[1] Thus the
sufferings and death of Christ became possible, and we can thus
understand also that the divine nature should, during the state
of humiliation, deliberately refrain to a certain extent from the
exercise and revelation of its full glory, in order to again bring
into action the fullness of its divine glory in the state of exaltation. But as Jesus, from the commencement of his human existence, really possessed the whole compass of the divine attributes, or the divine nature itself, this refraining was also a concealing. The human nature therefore possessed the fullness of the
divine nature (*plenitudo divinitatis*), but " did not always
exercise and apply it " (p. 57). This is the meaning of the
term *exinanition :* " He concealed and withdrew and made
quiescent the employment and display of his divine glory and
power in the flesh and through the flesh " (p. 353). Chemnitz
further declares : " He, as it were, restrained and withdrew
the rays of the indwelling fullness of the divine nature, not
only in order that they might not shine forth from him, but
that they might not always be fully and perfectly cast even
upon the nature assumed, . . . but slowly and gradually,"
making a growth possible (p. 553). As the exercise of the
divine glory was thus restricted in the state of humiliation, so in
his state of exaltation should the plenary and manifest possession and employment of his majesty be reässumed (p. 58, 295,

---

[1] Chemnitz was, therefore, by no means a Kenotist in the modern sense of
the term. Every form of alteration in the divine nature in the sense of diminution or accretion is excluded (p. 163, 250, 252). On the other hand, all
the attributes of the divine nature, as *essentialia*, are inseparable from the divine
essentia, or nature (p. 253 ff., 267, 14, 23, 279 f., 328). Christ, therefore,
as God, retained the full possession of these attributes and placed a voluntary
limitation only upon their employment and manifestation.

346). These ideas are all combined in the exposition of the *communicatio idiomatum*. Chemnitz discriminates three forms of the latter, a classification which had an important influence in the shaping of Lutheran dogmatics: (1) Each of the two natures imparts its attributes to the One person (p. 161 f.). (2) The action of the two natures is always a combined action ; the person effects salvation "according to both natures. The Son of God did not wish to operate in one nature alone, but in both, with both, and through both " (p. 162). (3) The human nature, since it cannot of itself perform all the works necessary to our salvation, is illuminated in every part by the divine light, and is the Bearer and Organ of the operations of the Logos (p. 163 f.).[1] Inasmuch as this mode of presenting the subject does not deal merely with quiescent "substances," but sets forth the two natures of Christ as actively engaged (in the work of redemption), it proved successful in preserving some important elements in Luther's conceptions of Christology.[2] Cf. THOMASIUS, Christol. ii., ed. 2, 383 ff. H. SCHULTZ, Gotth. Christi, 223 ff.

But the Würtemberg theologians also gradually learned to think more specifically than formerly of the state of humiliation. Christ as a child " did not know, did not see, did not hear, did not do all things, although the power of God, of which he became partaker through the personal union, is infinite and uncircumscribed." His condition while his body lay in the sepulchre is to be compared with that of a sleeping person. As the union of body and soul continues during sleep, although the sleeper does not see, hear, nor do anything, so the soul of Christ was also in the state of death without detriment to its union with the divine nature (Würtemberg Theologen, Bekenntn. v. d. Majestät des Menschen Christi, 1585, p. 37 ff. Cf. THOMASIUS, Christol. ii., ed. 2, 365 ff.).[3]

---

[1] The later dogmatics discriminated the *genus idiomaticum, majestaticum*, and *apotelesmaticum*, see SCHMID, Dogmatik d. luth. Kirche, ed. 7, p. 226 ff.; English Transl., Hay and Jacobs, ed. 3, p. 312 ff.

[2] But the concentration of the divine and human life under the category of the *will* is, after all, less energetic than might have been expected. Contrast with Luther, supra, p. 253.

[3] Mention may be here made of the controversy upon the *Descensus ad inferos*, started by JOHANN AEPINUS (from A. D. 1549). In his view, 1 Pet. 3. 18 refers, not to a preaching after the descent of the soul of Christ into Hades, but to a proclamation made by Christ in his divine nature before the Incarnation. The Descensus, as a part of the obedience rendered by Christ, must be considered as the final act of his humiliation. The soul of Christ descended into Hades while his body lay in the grave ; but, although the obedience thus rendered by Christ certainly vanquished hell, this was not a manifestation of the power of the Risen Saviour. Cf. FRANK, Theol. d. C. F. iii. 398 ff., 434 ff.

9. A CONTROVERSY UPON PREDESTINATION arose in Strassburg, A. D. 1561, between HIERONIMUS ZANCHI and JOHANN
MARBACH, HESSHUSEN having already in 1560 assailed the Calvinistic view of that doctrine.   The controversy was precipitated
by the request of the Lutheran, Marbach, that his Calvinistic
colleague should base the certainty of election not *a priori* upon
the eternal counsel of God, but upon the will of God as revealed
in the word.   It was not until later that Marbach attacked the
doctrine, that God grants faith but once to the elect and
that they, by virtue of the " gift of perseverance," cannot lose
it (LÖSCHER, Hist. motuum, iii. 30).   The way was opened for a
settlement of the conflict by the adoption of a formula of compromise in 1563 (vid. Löscher, ii. 286 ff.).   According to this,
everyone who believes on Christ obtains grace.   The promises
are universal, and everyone may therefore lay claim to them.
Why the divine call does not work faith in all, or why God does
grant faith to all, is a mystery.   Into this mystery we should not
seek to pry, but confine our attention to the gracious will of
God as revealed in Christ.   These explanations lay along the line
of the Lutheran development.   Cf. SCHWEIZER, Die prot. Centraldogmen, i. 418 ff.

§ 78. *The Formula of Concord.*

LITERATURE.   PLANCK, Gesch. des protest. Lehrbegriffs, vol. vi.   FRANK-
SEEBERG, PRE. x., ed. 3, 732 ff.   FRANK, Die Theolg. der C. F., 4 parts,
1858 ff.   THOMASIUS, Das Bek. d. ev. luth. Kirche in der Consequenz s.
Princips., 1848, and DG. ii., ed 2, 425 ff.   HEPPE, Gesch. d. deutsch. Prot.,
vol. iii., 1857 ; Die Entstehung u. Fortbildung d. Luthertums u. die kirchl.
Bek.-schriften desselben, 1548, 1576, 1863.   G. WOLF, Zur Gesch. d.
deutschen Protestanten, 1555-59, 1888.   K. MÜLLER, Die Symbole des
Luthertums in Preuss. Jarbb., vol. 63, 129 ff.   MÖLLER-KAWERAU, KG. iii.,
265 ff.

1. The pernicious principle, that religious differences pro-
hibit even political combination, gave a double importance to
the embittered controversies above reviewed.   When the Gnesio-
Lutherans at the Religious Colloquy at Worms, in 1557, denied
to the Philippists the right to claim adherence to the Augsburg
Confession, thus excluding them also from the benefits of the
Religious Peace secured at Augsburg in 1555, the Protestant
princes felt themselves compelled to place all possible restraint
upon the theological conflicts which were dominating all other
interests.   The passion displayed and the worship of formulas
reminded of the worst periods of the dogmatic struggles upon
Byzantine territory.   As then, the attempt was made to restore
peace either by prohibiting contention, or by constructing

formulas upon which all could agree. The movement originated indeed among the theologians, but its direction and the fixation of definite ideas as legally-authorized dogmas was, as heretofore, taken in hand by the princes, and political considerations also influenced the course of thought. The first attempt to restore peace was made in the Frankfort Recess of 1558 (C. R. ix. 489 ff.). The princes, "as a Christian, pious civil government, to which has been solemnly committed and commanded the protection and secure establishment of divinely-revealed truth,"[1] here affirm that they desire always to support the "pure true doctrine" as contained in the Scriptures "and also in the three chief symbols and likewise in the Augsburg Confession, together with its Apology" (494). It is then asserted in detail: that righteousness consists in "the forgiveness of sins and imputed righteousness" (495); that new obedience and good works are indeed necessary for the begetting of faith, but that no one should place his trust in them (498); that Christ "is true, living, substantial, and present" in the Lord's Supper, or that "the bread is communion (*die Gemeinschaft*) with the body of Christ" (499 f.).[2] Non-essential (*mittelmässige*) ceremonies are to be conducted in so far as possible in harmony with the word of God, and local differences in their celebration are to be tolerated without quarreling (501). In cases of "conflicting opinions," the counsel of the learned, "gently and kindly" given, as will readily be done by the consistories and superintendents, should be followed. No "writing nor booklet in religious matters" should be printed "which has not first been examined by the constituted authorities and found in accord with the true confession of our faith" (502). This document—which is instructive as showing the spirit of the incipient secular ecclesiasticism—accomplished nothing. The strict Lutherans published in response to it in 1559 the *Weimar Confutation*, which vigorously condemned the Philippists. The conflict in regard to the *Invariata* and *Variata* editions of the Augsburg Confession[3] first appeared at the Imperial Diet of Naumburg, in 1561, leading at that time to no results. It was the controver-

---

[1] P. 492. This is the conception of the "Christian government" (p. 495), when just upon the verge of transformation into the secular "ecclesiastical government."

[2] Here, as in what precedes, the Melanchthonian basis is traceable, cf. C. R. ix. 407, 409 f.

[3] It was the edition of 1531 which was subscribed. Of the editions of 1540 and 1542 it is said, that they "reproduce the above-named Confession in a somewhat more becoming and detailed form; also, explained and enlarged upon the basis of the Holy Scriptures." It is the "Amended (*verbesserte*) Confession," *i. e.*, an exposition and development of the Invariata.

sies upon the Lord's Supper (p. 366) which now proved the
chief obstacle in the way of conciliatory movements. The
authority of Luther was here arrayed too distinctly against
Melanchthon. So long as the Philippists would not agree to
reject the Melanchthonian view of the Lord's Supper, there
could be no thought of reconciliation. On the other hand,
some progress was made toward a comparative unity of doctrine
in the separate territorial churches by the introduction of Bodies
of Doctrine (*corpora doctrinae*). The first of these, the so-
called "Corpus Philippicum," or "Misnicum," was a private
undertaking of the book-dealer, Vögelein, in Leipzig, who
in 1560, shortly after the death of Melanchthon, edited a
collection of the latter's doctrinal writings, which contained, in
addition to the three ancient symbols, the Augsburg Confession, the Apology, the Confessio Saxonica, the Loci
(ed. 1556), the Examen ordinandorum, and the Respon-
siones ad impios articul. Bavaric. inquisitionis. This collection
was not only introduced into Electoral Saxony, but was
received with favor in other regions (*e. g.*, in Hesse and Pomerania). There at once appeared in opposition to it a number of
strictly Lutheran *Corpora doctrinae.* There were commonly
found in these—besides the three ancient symbols, the Augsburg
Confession and the Apology—only writings of Luther, such as
the two catechisms, the Smalcald Articles, various smaller publications, and extracts from controversial works.[1]

2. A fixed doctrine was thus secured for the separate territorial churches. The plan of uniting the various churches by a
common confession seemed now more feasible. The efforts to
promote concord which JACOB ANDREAE had been making since
A. D. 1569 (see JOHANNSEN in Ztschr. f. hist. Theol. 1853, 344 ff.)
were at first fruitless. But the times were constantly becoming
more auspicious. A new generation had succeeded the earlier
leaders of the Gnesio-Lutherans, less deeply involved in the old
doctrinal controversies, and hence able to pass calmer judgment
upon their merits. In the general apprehension of evangelical
doctrine, as well as upon many separate points, the Melanchthonian views prevailed. But the only reformatory authority
was Luther, as Melanchthon had himself maintained. Wherever they openly differed, the views of Luther were accepted.
The specific Lutheranism of this circle really consisted, there-

---

[1] *E. g.*, the city of Brunswick, 1563; Prussia, 1567; Brunswick-Wolfen-
büttel, 1569; also the so-called *Corpus Julium*, 1576; the dukedom of
Saxony, 1570; Brandenburg, 1572; Lüneburg, 1576. Vid. the first collection
of the documents in the Book of Concord of 1580, in the *Corpus* of Brunswick-
Wolfenbüttel, which was also composed by Chemnitz and Andreae.

fore, only of the doctrine of the Lord's Supper, in connection with the *communicatio idiomatum*, and in the rejection of Synergism.[1] On the other hand, the specific Philippism was dying out. There were no conspicuous leaders to carry forward the work of Melanchthon. The great Reformer had two souls, one of which was orthodox Lutheran and the other Humanistic. The heirs of his Humanism had since A. D. 1574 (cf. p. 367) been branded as Crypto-Calvinists and regarded with suspicion, and they were also the supporters of the positions in which Melanchthon differed from Luther. Some of them—influenced in part by the adoption of the Formula of Concord—went over to Calvinism.[2] The peculiar characteristics which marked German Calvinism in many particulars may be at least partly accounted for by this commingling of Humanistic-Melanchthonian and of Calvinistic elements.[3] Other followers of Melanchthon, drifting away from the peculiar teachings of their master, became Lutherans from conviction (*e. g.*, Chemnitz, Selnecker, Chytraeus). They were at heart in harmony with the new group of Lutherans, although always characterized by the dogmatic caution of their great teacher (cf. Chemnitz, supra, p. 375). It was not accidental that two such men as Chemnitz, an original Melanchthonian, and the Würtemburger Andreae, who came from a church which had attested its Lutheranism especially by its fidelity upon the doctrine of the Lord's Supper (Brenz, supra, p. 366), were found to lead in the interest of concord. The consensus aimed at was, in its essential aspects, here already actualized—a Melanchthonian Lutheranism.[4]

The movement for concord must, in view of the circumstances, address itself to a two-fold task. It must (1) Construct a Body of Doctrine which should find acceptance with all Lutherans,

---

[1] This course of historic events explains the fact that the general estimate of Lutheranism has been more and more restricted to these two points.

[2] Cf., *e. g.*, the biographies of Widebram, Pezel, Hyperius, Fink, Ursinus, and the younger Cruciger.

[3] This furnishes HEPPE and others the point of attachment for their construction of history, in which a great general reformatory movement, embracing Melanchthonianism, a humanistic undercurrent, and Calvinistic elements, is represented as crushed out by the domineering spirit of the Gnesio-Lutherans.

[4] It furnishes an instructive illustration of the confusion which existed in regard to the divergences between the teachings of Luther and Melanchthon—apart from their views of the Lord's Supper—that at the colloquy at ALTENBURG in 1569, the Lutherans charged the Melanchthonians with holding "that we become righteous before God alike by *imputatio* and by *inchoatio, i. e.*, from imputed righteousness and obedience begun" (HEPPE, Gesch. des Prot. ii. 217). They were here thinking of the Interim (vid. supra, p. 364). They thus seized in an entirely superficial way upon Melanchthon's formula of good works, although this very error might have been charged upon Luther instead, at least with an appearance of justice (supra, p. 260).

and (2) Formulate its consensus with due regard to the controversies of the preceding decennium ; for only thus could there
be any hope of finally disposing of them (see Pref. Form. Conc.).
The former of these requirements was met by including in the
Book of Concord a collection of the normative documents (the
three ancient symbols, the Augsburg Confession, the Apology,
the Smalcald Articles, and Luther's Catechisms); the latter, by
the second portion of the work, viz.: the Formula of Concord.
The Formula of Concord thus at once assumed a position among
the regulative symbols of Lutheranism. It would lead us too far
from our purpose to attempt in this connection a history of the
genesis of this important composition.[1] It was published officially
at Dresden, June 25, 1580. Fifty-one princes, counts, and barons,
thirty-five cities, and more than eight thousand theologians had subscribed to it. The book was not accepted by Brunswick-Wolfen-
büttel (because of hostility to Chemnitz), Schleswig-Holstein,
Hesse, Pomerania, Anhalt, Pfalz-Zweibrücken, Nassau, Ben-
theim, Tecklenburg, Solms, Magdeburg, Nordhausen, Bremen,
Dantzic, Frankfort, Worms, Strassburg, Spires, Nuremberg,
Weissenburg, Windsheim.[2]

In forming our estimate of the Formula of Concord, it must
be borne in mind that it is based upon the fundamental symbols
of the Lutheran Church ; that the problems with which it deals
were dividing the church in that age ; that it actually gave expression to a consensus already inaugurated ; and that it consequently succeeded in gradually restoring the peace of the church.
The detailed theological definitions of the pure doctrine which
it presented were in keeping with the spirit that had prevailed in
the church it represented for about a century and a half.[3] We

---

[1] The process of its development is regulated by the following documents :
Six controversial sermons of Andreae (in HEPPE, iii., suppl. 3 ff.); the Tübingen Book, or Schwäbian Concord, 1574 (Ztschr. f. hist. Theol. 36. 234 ff.); the
Schwäbian Saxon Concord (in HEPPE, suppl. 75 ff.); the Maulbronn Formula,
1576 (Jarbb. f. deutsche Theol. 11. 640 ff.); the Torgau Book, 1576 ; the
Bergen Book, 1577 (see HEPPE, Der Text d. Bergischen C. F. verglichen
mit dem Text der Schwäb. Conc., der Schwäb. sächs. Conc. u. des Torgauer
Buches, 1857). The original plan of having the work adopted by a great assembly of the churches—such as was often spoken of—was afterward abandoned.
Such an assembly, modeled after those of the ancient church, had been desired by the Jena theologians as early as 1560 (HEPPE, i., suppl. 124). The
Formula of Concord is composed of the *Epitome* and the *Solida declaratio.*
The latter is the Bergen Book ; the former a summary of the Torgau Book,
prepared by Andreae and revised at Bergen.

[2] Silesia took no part in the proceedings. Strassburg accepted the Formula
in 1597. Pomerania in 1593 added to an edition of the Corpus Philippicum,
enlarged by a volume of Luther's writings, some parts of the Formula of
Concord.

[3] I cannot agree with the opinion of KAWERAU (Möller, KG. iii.), p. 268,

can, therefore, as little ignore the historical necessity of the enter-
prise, as we can fail to be impressed with the tactful and energetic literary labor which it reveals. The Formula of Concord
did indeed make final the breach between the Lutheran-Melanch-
thonian and the Calvinistic-Melanchthonian types in the evangelical church of Germany ; but this breach was, under the existing
circumstances, unavoidable. No reproach can be cast upon a
confession for giving expression to a condition of affairs already
existing.

We must note the leading doctrinal statements of the Formula.
3. Articles I. and II. are devoted to Original Sin and Free
Will. (*a*) The Formula opposes Flacius' theory of original sin
and every view which does not acknowledge that man is "utterly
corrupted and dead toward good" (p. 589. 7). There yet remains, indeed, in the natural man a certain knowledge of God and
the capacity of "civil righteousness" (589. 9). This makes him
capable of experiencing conversion (593. 22). (*b*) Accordingly,
God does not deal with man as with a log or a stone (603. 61).
He does not coërce man (602 f.), although the latter does not
possess the "power of applying himself to grace" (590, 594).
In this respect, it may be said that "not even a spark of spiritual
strength remains" (589. 7), and "no more than a stone, log,
or lump of clay;" even "in this particular he is worse than a
block, because he is rebellious and hostile to the divine will"
(578. 23 ; 591 ff.; 599. 46). (*c*) The only cause of conversion is therefore the Holy Spirit, who through the word lays
hold upon the heart and works faith, "new spiritual emotions,
regeneration. and renovation, and new obedience." Man is
"merely passive" in conversion (530. 22). But this dare not
be so represented as when "a seal is impressed upon wax," but
in such a way that, in the very moment of the beginning of the
divine operation within us ("until the Holy Spirit has first
. . . begun in us . . . his work of regeneration"), the will,

---

that the Formula of Concord abandons Luther's conception of faith. He appeals in its support to the passage : "The gospel is properly the doctrine
which teaches . . . what that most miserable sinner ought to believe in order
that he may obtain the forgiveness of sins before God" (Müller, p. 637. 20).
This sentence is certainly unfortunately framed, but the context shows clearly
what is meant: "For whatever consoles fearful minds, whatever offers the
favor and grace of God to transgressors of the law, this is, properly and correctly speaking, the gospel, *i. e.*, the most joyful announcement that the Lord
God does not wish to punish our sins, but for Christ's sake to forgive them.
Wherefore penitent sinners ought to believe, that is, they should place their
entire confidence in Christ alone, *i. e.*, because he was offered up on account of
our sins," etc. (ib. § 21 f.). We are here told what evangelical faith is. The
"rightlv-believing" are those "who have true and living faith in Christ" (p.
534. 39). Similarly also Luther (supra, p. 225, n. 1).

impelled by God, engages according to its own nature in active
Synergy ('' we are able, and ought, to coöperate '' (604. 65).
Hence it is said : The man who is of himself absolutely unfree
for the doing of good is by the Spirit of God made free
(*liberatum arbitrium*, 604. 67), and, in the moment of the
effectual touch of the Spirit, the will is able to co-operate
actively in the work of renewal.

4. Article III. treats of Justification.   (*a*) It is asserted, in
opposition to Osiander and Stancar, that our righteousness
depends exclusively upon neither the divine nor the human
nature of Christ, but : '' in his whole person, who, as both God
and man, is alone in his entire and most perfect obedience
our righteousness '' (622. 55 ; 629).   The personally rendered obedience is thus the point of view under which the
work of Christ is regarded.   This obedience was manifested
'' in doing and suffering '' (612. 14, 15).   It was a '' most perfect obedience, by which he fulfilled the law for us.''   It constitutes the merit of Christ, which God imputes to us for righteousness (618. 30).   That man now receives grace, is based
upon the fact that Christ by his double obedience has first nullified both the penalties and the demands of the law (supra, p.
371, n. 1).   (*b*) Justification consists in this imputation of the
righteousness (*i. e.*, the obedience) of Christ (611. 4; 612. 15;
613. 17).   The result of this imputation is forgiveness of sins,
reconciliation with God, adoption, and the inheritance of
eternal life (615. 25 ; 613. 16).   But this justification is apprehended by faith, not because the latter is the beginning of
a new life, but because it is the receptive organ for the appropriation of the merit of Christ (612. 13 ; 616. 31).   The
genesis of faith is expressly traced to the operation of the Holy
Spirit in the gospel (619. 41).   (*c*) Faith and Justification are
therefore the central acts.   They must be preceded by '' true
and not simulated contrition,'' for only thus can faith exist
(614 f., 23, 26).[1]   The Holy Spirit now works faith.   '' And
this apprehends the grace of God in Christ, by which the person
is justified.''   But the believer is also '' renewed and sanctified
by the Holy Spirit, which renewal and sanctification are then
followed by good works.''   But this '' inaugurated righteous-

---

[1] 615. 36: '' Contrition precedes, and justifying faith exists in those who
truly, not fictitiously, exercise repentance.''   The last term here has a
narrower signification (= *contrition*, penitence) than in the earlier confessions,
cf. also the remark, p. 634. 7 ff.   This may be explained by the fact that the
original parallel with the sacrament of penance was gradually fading from
memory and in its stead such passages as Mk. 1. 15 regulated the usage of the
term.

ness of the new obedience'' dare never be taken into consideration as influencing justification itself, since no one can stand before God upon the ground of this yet ''incomplete and impure'' righteousness. Justification has to do only with the '' righteousness of the obedience, sufferings, and death of Christ, which is imputed to faith'' (617. 32 ; cf. 620. 44 ff.). By means of this exposition, the Melanchthonian construction of justification secured definite ascendancy.[1]

5. Article IV. discusses Good Works. (*a*) There was here a general agreement upon the following points : That, according to the will of God, believers should perform good works ; that good works are not such as are self-chosen, but such as are commanded by God ; that works are pleasing to God in so far as the person of the one performing them is acceptable to him ; that faith is the ''mother and original source of good works'' (625 f.). (*b*) It was pointed out how dangerous and liable to misunderstanding was the position assumed by Amsdorf (supra, p. 364). Against Major it was argued (supra, p. 364), that works dare in no wise be introduced into the ''article of justification and salvation,'' as otherwise '' assailed and distressed consciences will be robbed of the consolation of the gospel '' (629. 23). The thesis of Major concerning the necessity of works to salvation is therefore untenable (632. 37). (*c*) The doctrine, positively stated, is that faith brings with it good works, as the determination to persevere in evil-doing is inconceivable as cherished along with faith (627. 15);[2] and that these works are voluntarily performed (628. 18).

6. Articles V. and VI. treat of the Law and the Gospel. (*a*) The law is the '' divine doctrine, in which is revealed the most just and immutable will of God, as to what manner of person man ought to be,'' together with the threatening of temporal and eternal penalties (636. 17). The gospel, in the ''proper understanding'' of it, is the preaching of the grace of God (634. 6 ; 637. 21). The law teaches us to recognize our sin and the wrath of God. But, in order that man may not fall into despair, the preaching of the gospel must follow (635. 9 f.).[3]

---

[1] Yet the presentation of the Formula is to be preferred for lucidity and well-considered statement to that of Melanchthon. A number of problems were allowed to remain unsolved, *e. g.*, the genesis of contrition, the relation of the operations of the Holy Spirit in the begetting of faith and works, etc.

[2] Many erroneously hold a dead faith, or a certain empty persuasion, which is without repentance and good works, in place of true faith.

[3] It is therefore not only the office of the Holy Spirit to administer comfort, but he also, as a ''strange work,'' administers rebuke (635. 11). This is analogous to Christ's taking the law into his own hands and interpreting it spiritually (ib. 10).

This works faith, and through it righteousness (637 f.). (*b*) If the law is thus necessary at the beginning of the Christian life, it is none the less so during its progress : First, because sin and infirmity still cling to the regenerate, and they therefore still require "instruction and admonition, warning and threatening" (641 f.); secondly, in order "that they do not fall into a holiness and worship of their own," and may be preserved from imagining that their " work and life are entirely pure and perfect " (644. 20 f.). Yet it must ever be borne in mind that the Christian "fulfills the will of God, in so far as he is regenerate, from a free and joyous spirit " (643. 17).

7. Article VII. discusses the Lord's Supper. (*a*) The view of Zwingli is rejected (646. 4), as well as that of Calvin, the latter of which acknowledges indeed in words a " presence of the body of Christ," but means by this only a "spiritual presence " and that of the divine nature (647. 5 f.). Upon the basis of the words of institution, the bodily presence of Christ in the Lord's Supper is taught (646 ff., 656 f., cf. supra, p. 14 f.)—in harmony with the Augsburg Confession, the Apology, the Wittenberg Concord, the Smalcald Articles (by which "all evasions and loopholes are stopped up" against the sacramentarianizing interpretations of the Wittenberg Concord), and the catechisms. Thus it is said : " that in the Lord's Supper the body and blood of Christ are truly and substantially present, and that they are together with the bread and wine truly distributed and taken" (539). From this follows the " oral manducation," which does not mean the Capernaitic eating of the body of Christ, but which takes place, although " with the mouth " (*ore*), yet in a spiritual way (*modus spiritualus*) (543. 661). The reception by the unworthy (*manducatio indignorum*) also follows as a logical conclusion (666. 89). (*b*) It is therefore to be confessed, that "under the bread, with the bread, in the bread is present and offered the body of Christ " (654. 35). Between the substance of the bread and the substance of the body of Christ there is a union, which may be compared to the union of the two natures in Christ. Yet this union is not a *unio personalis*, but a *unio sacramentalis* (654. 36 f.). The possibility of this union is based upon the Ubiquity, which is defined in the sense of Chemnitz (supra, p. 376): "that, namely, even according to that assumed nature and with it, he can be present, and is indeed present, wherever he wishes to be " (692. 78). (*c*) This furnishes also the point of view from which may be understood the effect of the reception of the Supper. The Formula, with a fine tact, brings out the leading ideas of Luther. The Lord's Supper testifies that Christ desires to be continuously operative in believers according to his human

nature (622. 79). It is a seal, assuring us that the blessings which Christ obtained for us in his body are through it present for us (cf. supra, p. 287, 329). "And the pious, indeed, receive the body and blood of Christ as an infallible pledge and assurance that their sins are surely forgiven them, and that Christ dwells in them and wishes to be efficacious in them (661. 63 ; 655. 44). Thus the forgiveness of sins is recognized as the substantial result of participation in the Lord's Supper (661. 63).[1] (*d*) "Christians who are weak in faith, timid, and distressed, who are terrified at heart on account of the magnitudé and multitude of their sins and think they are in this their great uncleanness not worthy of this noble treasure and the benefits of Christ . . . these are the truly *worthy* guests, for whom this sacrament was principally instituted and appointed" (662. 69). (*e*) But it is only as a *transaction* that the Lord's Supper is a sacrament : the mere consecration makes no sacrament, if distribution and reception do not follow (665. 83 f.). But where this transaction occurs, there Christ is himself present as the real transacting personage (663. 75). These definitions, which follow essentially in the line of Luther's views, form one of the chief dogmatic contributions of the Formula.

8. Christology is presented in Article VIII. (*a*) The Formulas of Chalcedon furnish the point of departure. *The communicatio idiomatum*[2] is based upon the personal unity constituted by the combination of the two natures (676. 11). The entire glory of God has entered into the human nature and manifests this glory in and through it, "whenever and however it seems good to itself." But a full and continuous revelation of the divine glory occurs only after the laying aside of the "form of a servant," in heaven (688 f., 679). The God-man, as it were, concealed the glory dwelling in him : "he held it secretly, . . . employed it as often as seemed good to him" (680. 26). These ideas may be traced to Chemnitz (supra, p. 376). (*b*) The union of the two natures and their attributes is, here also, presented under the view-point of coöperation (689. 66 ; 685. 51 f.). But in this combined operation, the relations of the two natures are not strictly mutual, since the divine nature can be subject to no addition nor diminution (684. 49). (*c*) As to the Ubiquity of Christ, in addition to the *Multivolipresence* mentioned in paragraph 7, he is said to be "present in all created things" (547. 16 ; cf. 682 ff., 667 ff.). The presentation of this topic, regarded as a whole,

[1] The Formula is silent—and certainly rightly so—in regard to Luther's occasional references to effects of the Lord's Supper upon the body (p. 329).

[2] It presupposes that human nature is capable of receiving the divine, 685. 52 f.; 549. 14.

leaves the impression of incompleteness. It is hampered by the differences of opinion existing between Brenz and Chemnitz. The ideas of Luther are really presented in a connected way only in the discussion of the Lord's Supper. The influence of Chemnitz, on the other hand, is everywhere felt.

9. In regard to the Descent into Hell, it is said in Article IX. " that the entire person and man descended after the burial into hell, vanquished the devil, and destroyed the power of hell " (696). Yet we should lay aside "lofty and precise thoughts " as to the manner in which this occurred.

10. Article X., discussing *Adiaphora*, asserts that the church has the authority at any time to change ceremonies and church customs (698. 9), but that when the church is in the state of confession (*in statu confessionis*), it must not yield to its opponents even in such matters.

11. The topic of Article XI. is Predestination. (*a*) As contrasted with foreknowledge (*prescientia*), which relates to both the good and the evil, predestination is the ordaining to salvation (705. 5). Prescience has no causative character, but the cause (*Ursache*) of the salvation of the elect is the divine election (554. 36). But prescience includes the fact, that God has " set bound and measure " to those whose wickedness he has foreseen (705. 6). It is, of course, to be understood that God, before the beginning of the world, foresaw who of the called should believe and persevere in faith, and when his call should reach each individual and nation, and when it should be withdrawn from them (716. 54 ff.; 708. 23). (*b*) But the Christian should confine his attention to the gracious revealed will of God and avoid all speculation in this field (717 f.; 719. 70; 715. 52 ff.; 706. 9 ff.; 707. 13 f.). He should further remember that the " promise of the gospel " is really "universal," *i. e.*, it " pertains to all men " (709. 28); that the call (*vocatio*) is therefore always sincere (710. 29 ; 257. 18); and that the Holy Spirit is always operative in the word as heard (712. 39). It is not the divine foreknowledge, but the human will, which is to blame if the word does not attain its end (713. 41). The divine will aims at the salvation of all, and does not desire that any should perish (555. 12 ; 722. 83 f.). (*c*) There is, therefore, an " eternal predestination " (717. 65). It is the active will of God, that all men who believe on Christ shall be saved through the gospel. This will is based upon the merit of Christ, not upon our works (720. 75 ; 723. 88). Upon the ground of this eternal will, we may be certain of our salvation ; for it rests in the hands of God (724. 90), and is based " upon his eternal purpose, which cannot fail nor be overthrown " (714. 45). There

is thus "completely and fully given to God his glory," since salvation is traced alone to his gracious will (556. 15 ; 723. 87).

Of these propositions, it must likewise be said, that they do not furnish a conclusion in all respects satisfactory. Yet their logical consistency is not so obscure as is often thought. God, by virtue of his foreknowledge, knows everything which shall ever happen. This foreknowledge enables him to set measure and bound to that which is to happen. We must distinguish from this the gracious will of God to save through Christ all who shall believe. If this aim be not achieved, the fault lies with man. This view can, indeed, scarcely be designated predestination in the strict sense of the term.[1]

12. Article XII. speaks " of Other Factions and Sects," and recounts the "erroneous articles" of the Anabaptists, the Schwenkfeldians, and the "new Antitrinitarians." Here again, the breach, now put upon record, had long been complete.

13. Such are the doctrinal articles of the Formula of Concord. They record the conception entertained of Lutheran doctrine in the second generation of the Reformation period, or the form of Lutheranism which became the basis for the development of Lutheran theology. Historical investigation can only record, that the Formula accomplished the purpose which it had in view. It presented the fixed results of doctrinal development, and exhibited in connected form the ideas of Luther and Melanchthon which were influential in that generation. But, when compared with the entire scope of Luther's religious and theological ideas, the decision must be, that the Formula of Concord was not in a position to rescue from neglect and recoin all the valuable truth—the whole historical material—which Luther had given to the church. The contribution which Luther brought to the church still furnishes material for earnest study. Evangelical theology must continue to seek, and seeking shall yet find, in

---

[1] 708. 23 : " And God, indeed, by this his counsel, purpose, and ordination (*i. e.*, that all who believe on Christ shall be saved, vid. ¿ 18), not only procured the salvation of his own in general, but also mercifully foresaw, all and each, the persons of the elect who should be saved through Christ, elected them to salvation, and decreed that . . . he wished through his grace . . . to make them partakers of eternal salvation . . . to strengthen and preserve them." Even this passage does not lead to strict predestination ; for, in the context in which it is found, it can scarcely mean more than the following : God, by virtue of his prescience, knows in advance what particular result will be accomplished by his gracious will, which is in itself considered universal in its application. And, just as his prescience in general guides him in the ordering and directing of all things (vid. supra), so also in this particular instance, since God takes a particular interest in the guidance and protection of those whom he foresees as believers. The connection of this article with the Strassburg Concord should not be overlooked (supra, p. 378).

the marvelous intuitions of the Reformer's ideas view-points, inspiration, energy, and a renewal of her strength.

CHAPTER II.

COMPLETION OF DOCTRINAL CONSTRUCTION IN THE REFORMED CHURCH.

§ 79. *The Theology of Calvin and its Influence Upon the History of Doctrines.*

SOURCES. CALVIN, Opp. ed. Baum, Cunitz, Reuss (= Corp. Ref. xxix. ff.). We shall have occasion to refer especially to vols. xxix. and xxx. (Institutio religionis christianae), vol. xxxiii. (the catechism), vol. xxxvi. (theol. discussions), vol. xxxviii. (ordonnances écclesiastiques). Upon the life of Calvin, see HENRY, 3 vols., 1835 ff. E. STÄHELIN, 2 vols., 1863. KAMPSCHULTE, J. Calvin, seine Kirche u. sein Staat in Genf., vol. i., 1869. A. LANG, De Bekehrung Joh. Calv., 1897 (Studien z. Gesch. d. Theol. u. Kirche, ed. Bonwetsch u. Seeberg, ii. 1). Upon his theology, vid. KÖSTLIN, Calv. Institutio, in Stud. u. Krit., 1868, 7 ff., 410 ff. RITSCHL, Rechtf. u. Vers. i., ed. 2, 203, 227 ff. SEEBERG (Thomasius, DG. ii., ed. 2), p. 638 ff. LOOFS, DG., ed. 3, 427 ff. A. LANG, Die ältesten theol. Arbeiten Calv., in Neue Jarbb. f. deutsche Theol. ii. 273 ff. SCHWEITZER, Centraldogmen, i. 150 ff. MULLER, De Godsleer von Calvijn, 1881. SCHEIBE, Calv. Praedest.-lehre, 1897. USTERI, Calv. Sakraments u. Tauflehre, Stud. u. Krit., 1884, 417 ff. SEEBERG, Begriff d. Kirche, i. 119 ff. LOBSTEIN, Die Ethik Calvins, 1877. DILTHEY, in Archiv. f. Gesch. d. Philos. vi. 528 ff. ELSTER, Calv. als Staatsmann, Gesetzgeber u. Nationalökonom, in Jarbb. für Nationalökonom, vol. 31. 163 ff.

1. As Zwingli's political plans were frustrated by his death, so the direct influence of his theology also, within a comparatively short time, ceased to be felt. Even men who stood so near to him as BULLINGER accepted his doctrinal views only in their general outline, and proceeded to "deepen" and develop them (see PESTALOZZI, H. Bull., 1858, and cf. USTERI, in Stud. u. Krit., 1883, p. 730 ff.). In the circles in Southwestern Germany in which Zwingli's influence had been particularly felt arose a new theological type, which, with a close adherence to the principles of Luther, combined a certain leaning toward ideas of Zwingli. The most important and active representative of this group was the great compromise theologian, MARTIN BUCER († 1551). Its characteristic features were the following: "The fundamental ideas of the Reformation upon sin, grace, justification, and sanctification were reproduced in harmony with

Luther and Melanchthon. The relation to Luther is incompara-
bly more intimate and evident than was Zwingli's.[1] The assurance
of salvation was commonly based upon predestination, or the " gift
of perseverance." In the doctrine of the sacraments, and especially of the Lord's Supper, the attempt was made to find a median ground between the views of Luther and Zwingli. The
men of this group very earnestly insisted upon referring everything to the Scriptures in a somewhat legalistic way, the statements of the latter being regarded as fixed formulas of doctrine
and of ecclesiastical life. With this tendency is closely associated
the marked biblical character of the theology in question, as well
as the effort by the fuller application of biblical ideas to carry
out the principles of the Reformation more completely than
had been done upon more strictly Lutheran territory. Standing upon the historic ground of the earlier ideas of reform,
and inspired by Erasmian ideals, it was sought to realize the
practical ideas of reform by a strict discipline and by benevolent operations and careful church organization, in so far as this
appeared possible and desirable within the scope of the evangelical reformation. The church was regarded as the " kingdom of
Christ," in which there exists a new covenant (*foedus*) with
God. Living under the sovereignty of God, it is proper for us
to minister to his glory. As, on the one hand, the entire Christian life became, in the light of this conception, one of active
service, so, too, it was thought that the glory of God demands
that he alone—and not our works nor any agency other than
divine—be recognized as effecting the salvation and life of the
church.[2] Hence their advocacy of predestination. Not, indeed, in the form of a connected theological system, but as a
practically influential combination of opinions and sentiments,
this tendency secured adherents and became a recognized power
in the church.

It may be studied most readily in the writings of Bucer. His
last publication treats of the Kingdom of Christ, *De regno
Christi* (vid. in Scripta Anglicana, Basil, 1577, p. 3-173).
This kingdom is an *administratio populi* (p. 3). "The kingdom
of our Servitor, Jesus Christ, is an administration and procuring

---

[1] This is plainly seen in Bucer's first publications. The *Summary* of his
sermons of 1523 presents in its positive explanations an excellent outline of
the fundamental religious conceptions of Luther.

[2] In Bucer, as in Zwingli (supra, p. 312), the thought of the glory of God
constantly recurs. How practically pervasive was this idea is indicated, *e. g.*,
in the subscription appended by the citizens of Strassburg to a petition, A. D.
1527, for the complete abolition of the mass : " The obedient citizens of your
Excellencies, who desire the advancement of the glory of God and of the kingdom of Christ " (in BAUM, Capito u. Butzer, p. 393).

of the eternal salvation of the elect of God, by which he himself, our Lord and the King of heaven, by his doctrine and discipline administered through special ministers appointed for that purpose, . . . gathers his elect to himself and incorporates them in himself and his church, and in it so governs them that, daily purged more fully from their sins, they may live well and blessedly'' (p. 31). The elect allow themselves to be guided and governed by the ''ministry regularly constituted (p. 34). The ministry teach, confining themselves strictly to the Holy Scriptures (p. 36).[1] The first marks of the true church are scripturalness of doctrine and of the administration of the sacraments ; the third is discipline (p. 40 ff.), to which is added care for the poor (p. 50). The second Book contains a fully detailed plan for the introduction of the Kingdom into England.[2] In the Introduction to the exposition of the Epistle to the Romans is found a brief statement of Bucer's Soteriology.[3] He here also presents at length his view of predestination (vid. excurs., p. 358 ff.). This is, in the proper sense, an election to salvation. The practical importance of the doctrine lies in its making known to us '' this certain and immovable will of God concerning our salvation, which no creature is able to prevent '' (p. 358 a, 360 b). If salvation is based upon the eternal counsel of God, we may then be sure of it. Predestination leads to the measures for attaining its end, i. e., vocation, justification, and glorification. He to whom the call is given may, therefore, be sure of his election (p. 359 b). In a wider sense, predestination in general is traced to the divine pre-determination (praefinitio); in which sense we may also speak of a '' predestination of the wicked.'' They, too, have an appointed place in the divine plan of the world. God knows in advance for what purpose he will use them : '' He then ordained and destined them to these ends, ad ea '' (p. 358 b). '' God foresaw and destined even these to this lot before he created them. For he does all things by predeterminate and infallible counsel '' (p. 359 a). Predestination is thus utilized in a purely practical way as a means

[1] Cf. in the Einleitung zur Enarratio ep. ad Roman. (Argentorat. 1536), p. 19 a : '' To this republic the Scriptures are instead of law, for they set forth and appoint the will of its head concerning all the duties of life.''

[2] See also the interesting suggestions for the advancement of farming, industry, and commerce in England, p. 136-140.

[3] *Justificare = absolvere.* We are assured of this pardon of sins, secured through Christ, by the Holy Spirit, who begets faith in us, but at the same time subdues evil lust and calls into being a new will (vid. Enar. in ep. ad Rom., p. 11 ff.). Faith is a ''*persuasio* (= πίστις, p. 22 a) of the mercy of God toward us,'' p. 14 b, or an *assensus*, not only with the intellect, but also with the will, p. 15 f. See also briefly in the Epitome doctr. eccles. Argentorat., in Scripta anglicana, p. 173 ff.

in establishing the certainty of salvation. Zwingli's speculative method of theorizing on the subject is foreign to Bucer, nor does he follow Luther's deductions as to the enslavement of the will. As to his doctrine of the Lord's Supper, vid. supra, p. 331, n. 1.[1]

These excerpts from Bucer may serve to illustrate the above-noted characteristics. The theological type which they represent—which may be briefly styled Bucerism—is the contemporaneous pendant of Melanchthonian Lutheranism. The ideas of Luther were by Bucer, as by Melanchthon, recast in the forms demanded by his practical aims. The parallel may readily be carried out in detail. In neither of these men, with the tendencies which they represented, was the process developed without omissions and displacements in the Lutheran complex of ideas.[2] But, while it was the fortune of Melanchthon to construct formulas which should dominate the thought of two centuries, Bucerism became but the stepping-stone to Calvinism. Bucer's mediating theology was almost everywhere merged in Calvinism. This did not involve any violence to the former, but was but the transition from a lower to a higher form. Calvin, like Bucer, drew his first inspiration from Luther. Luther's ideas moulded him in a general way as a theologian, and also in his views of particular doctrines.[3] Yet he was a Lutheran only in the same sense as Bucer. Or, we may say, the impulses which made Calvin a theologian and churchman proceed, not only from the influence of Luther, but also from that conception of religion and of the church and her duty which prevailed at Strassburg and which pervades the writings of Bucer. Not only his ethical apprehension of the work of reformation, but his views upon a number of important doctrines—as of the sacraments, particularly the Lord's Supper, of predestination, and of faith—point distinctly to this source. Calvin starts therefore, not with Zwingli, but with Luther,[4] and promotes that conception of the work of the Refor-

---

[1] For the biography of Bucer, see BAUM, Capito u. Butzer, 1860. A worthy presentation of his theology has recently been published by A. LANG. Vid. Das Evangelienkommentar M. Butzers, u. die Grundzüge seiner Theologie (Bonwetsch-Seeberg, Studien zur Gesch. der Theol. u. der Kirche, ii. 2), 1900.

[2] In the doctrine of the Lord's Supper, Melanchthon and his school draw from Bucer.

[3] See LANG, Bekehrung Calvins, p. 47 ff., and the same author's collection of utterances of Calvin concerning Luther in Deutsch-Evang. Blätter, 1896, 322 ff.

[4] Zwingli's significance for the History of Doctrines really consists therefore only in the fact, that he by his energetic opposition prevented the complete dominance of the Lutheran doctrine of the Lord's Supper. The statement of DILTHEY (Archiv. vi., 529, 531), that Calvin drew his inspiration from Zwingli's "freely breathing religious animation" and from his spiritual wealth (Seelenfülle), is historically untenable.

mation which originated—not indeed without Zwinglian influences —in Southwestern Germany, particularly at Strassburg. These historical facts explain the divergence of view from that of the Wittenbergers upon methods of practical reform (supra, p. 391), and also the phenomenon, that a Calvinistic church should arise upon German soil, and, as is acknowledged, win the allegiance of a number of Melanchthonian Lutherans.[1] As the Calvinistic type became the dominant one in the Reformed church, it falls to the province of the History of Doctrines to present an outline of his teachings. As to their historical relations, the above must for the present suffice.

2. It is of the first importance, for a proper appreciation of Calvin, to remember that he is a man of the second generation of this great period. He received his ideas and program of action by tradition in an essentially complete form. It was his task, in the church as in theology, to complete and organize— and for this his special talents also fitted him. Calvin was not a genius like Luther, nor did he possess the happy balance of endowment which distinguished Zwingli. Neither was he a scholar unskilled in the ways of the world, like Melanchthon. He possessed the wonderful talent of comprehending any given body of religious ideas in its most delicate refinements and giving appropriate expression to the results of his investigations. This made him the greatest exegete of the Reformation period, and enabled him to accomplish a remarkable work in organizing the dogmatic materials within reach. As a dogmatician, he furnished no new ideas, but he with most delicate sense of perception arranged the dogmatic ideas at hand in accordance with their essential character and their historical development. If we compare Melanchthon and Calvin, for example, in their views upon the appropriation of salvation, we shall observe that the former constructs tenable formulas, while the latter traces the inner relations of spiritual experience. His was a keen and delicate, but not a creative mind.[2] With these intellectual gifts was combined the will of a nature born for organizing—the tenacious, imperial spirit and govermental skill of the ancient Roman. But this was held in check and guided by the obedience which dedicates the life to the glory of God, without regard to the demands of the world.[3] Thus Calvin was just the man to represent most

[1] At this point must begin the study of the interesting question of the genesis of the Reformed Church in Germany.

[2] We may compare Melanchthon and Calvin as dogmaticians, separately and in their mutual relationship, with the Lombard and Thomas Aquinas.

[3] Cf. C. R. xliii. 738 : " I am not ignorant of what is pleasing or offensive to the world, but nothing is of more concern to me than to follow the rule prescribed by the Master."

worthily and effectively the second type of reformatory character which sprung from Luther's prolific principles. That its peculiar characteristics were due in measure to the influence of earlier ideals of reform, has been already observed (p. 391).

3. Our study of the theology of Calvin must be confined to the points bearing particularly upon the history of doctrinal development.[1] Beginning with the source of Christian truth, we find this to be the Holy Scriptures, and they alone. "For the Scriptures are a school of the Holy Spirit, in which, as nothing necessary or useful to know is omitted, so nothing is taught except what it is profitable to know" (iii. 21. 3).[2] God has deposited in them the "oracle" of his truth, and, since they come from heaven, they are endowed with full authority (*plena autoritas*) among men (i. 7. 1). "Belief (*fides*) of the doctrine is not established until we have been indubitably persuaded that *God is its author*" (ib. 4). God first revealed the law, "then followed the prophets, through whom God published, as it were, new oracles." By divine command, the prophets recorded the latter, all of which served for the explanation of the law. "With these came at the same time the histories, which are themselves also productions from the pens of the prophets, but composed under the dictation of the Holy Spirit" (*dictante spiritu sancto*, iv. 8. 6). Then followed the New Testament (ib. 8). Of the authors of these writings, it is said : "They were infallible and authentic amanuenses of the Holy Spirit, and therefore their writings are to be held to be oracles of God" (ib. 9). The truthfulness of these scriptural oracles is therefore established from the fact, that they, together with the historical narratives, were dictated and inspired by the Spirit of God (cf. i. 18. 3).[3] This conviction as to the origin of the Scriptures is confirmed by the testimony of the Holy Spirit, which is effectually given through them, and through the divine majesty which characterizes them (i. 7. 4). Through this unique testimony we become certain of the character of the word (i. 8. 1 ; 9. 3). Thus Calvin establishes the authority of the Scriptures partly upon their divine dictation, and partly upon the testimony of the Holy Spirit working through them. His-

[1] We depend, in so doing, chiefly upon the last revision of the *Institutio religionis Christianae*, A. D. 1559. We shall occasionally quote, for the purpose of comparison, from the first edition, A. D. 1536, and from other doctrinal writings of Calvin.

[2] These and similar references indicate books, chapters, and paragraphs of the last edition of the *Institutio*.

[3] HEPPE'S remark in referring to Calvin (Die Dogmatik d. ev.-ref. Kirche, 1861, p. 16 f.): "He is not speaking of any real inspiration in the recording," is not well founded.

torically considered, he thereby combines the later medieval conception of inspiration (supra, p. 192) with the theory of Luther. Calvin is therefore the author of the so-called inspiration theory of the older dogmaticians.[1] Of the ancient symbols and decrees of the councils, Calvin says, that they formulated Biblical truth more exactly in opposition to the heretics (i. 13. 3 f.): "For they contain nothing but pure and native interpretation of the Scriptures" (iv. 9. 8). He set a high value upon pure doctrine for the church [2] (ii. 2. 7), but acknowledged also that no one should forsake his church for the sake of "any little differences of opinion" (iv. 1. 12).

4. In the doctrine concerning God, the Reformation conception of the Divine Being as omnipotent Will is the controlling thought. The divine omnipotence is not to be represented as alternating between action and non-action, but as in "continual action." It is manifested in the divine providence which rules all things (i. 16. 3). Calvin meets the charge of Stoic fatalism by pointing out that the latter rests upon the inviolability of the natural order of cause and effect, while Christian faith, on the contrary, refers all events to the determination of the divine will : "We acknowledge God as the arbiter and director of all things, who, according to his wisdom, decreed from the most remote eternity what he would do, and now by his power performs what he has decreed " (ib. 8). Accordingly, the totality of all events, as well the course of nature as all that men endure or do, is referred back to the eternal counsel of God. In other words, everything that happens, happens as it does because God so wills.

[1] It is just this combination which constitutes the theory in question : Because there proceeds from the Scriptures an influence of the Holy Spirit which attests their contents to the heart as truth, their origin must be traced to the Holy Spirit. This combination, in itself considered, is open to no objection. But, since the inspiration is conceived of as a dictation of the entire historical material, the proof of it from religious experience cannot be sustained, because this experience can by no means attest all the separate words of Scripture. We need not here refer to the objections raised against the theory by historical criticism. Calvin writes : "I know how some obscure men clamor in their little corners to show the keenness of their talents in assailing the truth of God. For they inquire, Who will make us very sure that these things which are read under the names of Moses and the prophets were written by them ? For they even dare to raise the question whether there ever was any Moses ? But if anyone should raise a doubt as to whether there ever was any Plato or Aristotle or Cicero, who would not say that he deserved to be thrashed with cuffs or lashes ? " (i. 8. 9).

[2] This is attested by the sworn confession of faith, based on his catechism, to be required of the citizens of Geneva (C. R. xxxiii. 355-362). This contains in a nutshell a system of dogmatics in a plain and practical form. No attempt is made to present the doctrines of the Trinity or Christology in a scholarly way.

What transpires in the world serves the interest of man, of the church, and of salvation (ib. 6 ; i. 17. 1); but its final purpose is the revelation of the glory and honor of God (i. 16. 1ff.): "That our salvation was a matter of concern to God in such a way that, not forgetful of himself, he kept his glory primarily in view, and therefore created the whole world to this end, that it might be the theatre of his glory" (C. R. xxxvi. 294). The purpose of God therefore extends beyond the salvation of the human race. It follows from the above that even the actions of the wicked must be referred to the divine will. Calvin rejects as frivolous the explanation of these as due to divine *permissio* (i. 18. 2). It is to be said, on the contrary, that the will of God "not only exerts its power in the elect, who are controlled by the Holy Spirit, but also compels the reprobate to obedience" (ib.). The application of these principles in the sphere of the religious life leads to the theory of a double election (vid. sub), namely, that the divine will leads the elect to the goal by causing duly appointed means to work upon them in a determinative way. The elect, accordingly, do not die until they have been regenerated and sanctified (iv. 16. 18). We have thus here, as in Thomas or Zwingli, a religious determinism carried out to its logical conclusions. The cosmic system has been established by God as a complex of means inwardly adapted to the realization of the end in view. Thus regarded, the adoption of the particular means employed may be maintained as being a rational necessity. Or, where there is an election, the redemption through Christ, the church, and her means of grace are involved in it as necessary means for its realization. This explains the energy of the adherents of these views in prosecuting the work of the church, with her means of grace and her morality ; for these are the means requisite to the carrying out of the divine purpose, which can only thus be realized. But now, as in Luther's treatise upon the Enslaved Will, this logical structure is apparently buttressed, but really broken down, by the introduction of the Scotist idea of the irresponsibility of the divine will. The reason for the introduction of this idea is, as in Luther, easily discovered. By the association of the divine will with a system of earthly means, its absolute freedom and its exalted majesty appear to be endangered. Hence the inner necessity of these means is called in question, and their employment looked upon as a fixed rule indeed, but their selection regarded as accidental, and the original possibility of the adoption of other means or of the abolition of all means asserted : "which means he certainly employs in the calling of many, upon whom he bestows a true knowledge of himself by the illumination of the

Spirit in an internal way without the intervention of preaching''
(iv. 16. 19; 1. 5 in.).   Even of Christ's work it must accordingly be said : "not except by the good pleasure of God could
it merit anything'' (ii. 17. 1).[1]   The aim of Calvin is clear
from such passages as iii. 23. 2 : "For so truly is the will of God
the highest rule of right, that whatever he wills is, just because
he wills it, to be accounted right.   Therefore when it is asked,
why the Lord did thus, the response must be, Because he wished
to do so.''   God is not, indeed, to be considered lawless (*exlex*),
for his will is the "law of all laws;'' but all seeking for the
ground of any divine appointment is forbidden.   Its ground lies
simply in the will of God, as otherwise we would have to acknowledge something superior to the divine will (ib., cf. § 5, C.
R. xxxvi. 115).   Hence, the election of some men and rejection of others must be traced simply to the unrestrained will of
God[2] (iii. 22. 1).   But just at this point this second line of
thought falls into the first.   The will of God is alone the ground
of all events.   As the ultimate end of all things is fixed by this
Will, so also the means by which that end is to be attained ; but
a rational necessity for the latter cannot from our point of view
be proved or maintained.   This conclusion confirms our view of
the relation existing between the two lines of thought,[3] a point
to which we shall recur (¶ 7 e).

5. The Sin of Adam consisted in disobedience (ii. 1. 4).   His
sinful character was handed down to his posterity: "From a
corrupt root have sprung corrupt branches.''   But no good end
can be served by brooding over specific possibilities.   It
is the divine appointment, that the sin of Adam should
become the sin of his posterity : "The cause of the con-
tagion lies neither in the substance of the flesh, nor in that of
the soul ; but because it has been thus ordained by God, that
man should hold or lose at the same time both for himself and
for his posterity whatever gifts God had at first conferred upon

---

[1] This passage taken alone is not sufficient to appear in evidence, as we
must grant to SCHEIBE (Calv. Präd.-lehre, p. 110 f.), for it merely asserts
that Christ was "foreordained to the end that he might appease the wrath of
God by his sacrifice.''   But it must be studied in the light of Calvin's general
apprehension of the subject (vid. ii. 12. 1) and the parallels in Luther's
writings have weight in deciding upon its proper interpretation (vid. supra,
p. 271).

[2] Calvin rejects in this connection the "profane'' idea of "absolute
power.''   But what have we in the above-cited passage, iv. 16. 19, but an
application of this idea that goes even beyond the position of Duns ?

[3] This doctrinal conception of God is inferior to that of Luther in animation and consistent force, if for no other reason, because Calvin assumes a
two-fold source of our knowledge of God, *i. e.*, in the course of nature and
in Christ (i. 2. 1 ; v. 1 f.).

him " (ii. 1. 7).[1] Original sin is defined as " the hereditary
depravity and corruption of our nature . . . which first makes
us subject to the wrath of God, then also produces in us works
which the Scriptures call works of the flesh " (ib. 8). Thus the
entire man is depraved : " From the crown of the head to the
sole of the foot, not a spark of good can be found " (iii. 14. 1).
The natural freedom of the will yet remains, but not as though
it had an equally free choice of good and evil, but because it
commits evil by free-will and not from coërcion " (ii. 2. 7).
There still remain the natural talents, which are requisite for
the prosecution of political affairs, science, and art, although
they have also become depraved (ii. 2. 12. ff.).[2]

6. The consideration of this our natural condition, combined
with the stress of the law (ii. 7. 2 f., 6 ff.), awakens in man the
sense of helplessness (ii. 2. 11). Grace alone saves us, through
Christ. The purpose of God is the " first cause " of our salvation.
He appoints his only-begotten Son to be a " fountain of grace "
(ii. 17. 1). Since now it was to be the mission of Christ, both
to convince men of the gracious disposition of God toward them,
making them his children, and to render satisfaction to the
Father in our stead, it was necessary that the Son of God should
become man, since for both the purposes indicated both divine
and human nature would be required in him (ii. 12. 1-3 ; iii.
11. 9). Yet we cannot speak here of an " absolute necessity,"
but only of the divine decree by which this was made the
method of our salvation (ii. 12. 1).[3] With this general premise, Calvin presents the mediatorial work of Christ under the
three aspects of the prophetic, royal, and high-priestly offices
(ii. 15). According to Hebr. 1. 1, Christ is the last and perfect revelation of God (ii. 15. 1, 2). Endowed by God with
eternal power, he exercises spiritual and eternal dominion over
the church. " Such is the character of his government, that he

[1] Even here we can trace the influence of the Scotist element in Calvin's
conception of God ; but he rejects as insufficient the Scotist definition of original sin, and frames his positive statement of the subject upon Augustinian
lines.

[2] But conscience remains to man as the organ of innate natural law : " It is
affirmed that the law of God, which we call the moral law, is nothing else
than the testimony of the natural law and the inner sense (*conscientiae*) of it
which has been inscribed by God upon the hearts of men" (iv. 20. 16. Cf.
Luther, supra, p. 247, 243, n. 2). Similarly (ii. 8. 1), where its operation is thus described : " it sets before us the discernment between good and
evil, and thus accuses us when we depart from duty."

[3] Calvin warns against " vain speculations," as to whether Christ would
have become man if there had been no need of redemption, since the Scriptures present the incarnation as subordinate to the purpose, "that he should,
as a victim, make satisfaction to the Father for us " (ii. 12. 4).

may share with us whatever he has received from the Father "
(ib. 4). As priest, finally, he procures for us the grace of God
by making atonement for us through his sacrifice and appeasing
the wrath of the Father (ii. 12. 3 ; 15. 6, *ad placandam iram
dei*). " He poured out his sacred blood as the price of redemption, by which was extinguished the wrath (*furor*) of God
burning against us, and our iniquities also were purged " (C. R.
xxxiii. 339). But this result was achieved by the obedience
covering his entire earthly life (according to Rom. 5. 19). The
latter was manifested both in his sufferings and death, and
(according to Phil. 2. 7) in " the other part of obedience which
he rendered in this life " (ii. 16. 5). In the course of this
obedience, he became an atoning sacrifice (*victima satisfactoria*),
the condemnation merited by our sins being visited upon him
(ib. 6. 5).[1] The enduring of the wrath of God included also
the struggle with eternal death and condemnation : " Whence it
was necessary for him to wrestle, as it were, hand to hand with
the powers of hell and with the horror of eternal death"
(ib. 10). Not alone his body was the price of our deliverance,
" but there was another greater and more excellent price, that
he endured in his soul the dire agonies of condemned and lost
man " (ib.). Discrimination is made between the effects of the
death and of the resurrection of Christ. By the former, " sin
is abolished and death destroyed," while by the latter " righteousness is restored (*reparata*) and life established " (ib. 13).
The ascended Lord ministers in heaven as our *advocatus et
intercessor*, attracting the eye of the Father from our sins upon
his righteousness. He also sanctifies us from heaven by his
Spirit (ib. 16).

If we disregard the three-fold division of the work of Christ,
which, in Calvin's discussions as elsewhere, does not prove
helpful in elucidating the subject, we may trace a clear line of
thought. The human race was, as sinful, subject to the wrath
and curse of God. The God-man endured this wrath and curse
in obedience to the divine will, without perishing beneath the
burden. He thereby secured the forgiveness of sins and abolition of all penalties, as well as the positive bestowal of grace
upon man, which he now, as the Ascended Lord, administers
through the Spirit. This leaves only the question of the existence
of wrath and love together in God. It is, says Calvin, a pedagogical mode of speech, when the Scriptures represent God as the

---

[1] The dominant idea in this connection is that of *satisfaction*. It is only
incidentally that he introduces, in ii. 17, the idea of *merit*, without at all
designing thereby to change the general conception of the subject. Cf.
RITSCHL, Rechtf. u. Vers. ii., ed. 2, 228.

enemy of the sinner (ii. 16. 2). It is however fully justified; for as God is righteousness, he cannot love sin. As sinners, we rest under his wrath. Yet even thus we are still his creatures, and his love therefore goes out toward us, so that his love became the motive (Eph. i. 4) for the mission of Christ (ii. 16. 3, 4).[1] Love is accordingly the fundamental attitude of God toward the elect of the race. On account of sin, wrath is also awakened, but this is dissipated by the work of Christ which was planned and executed by love (ii. 17. 2). It might here easily have occurred to Calvin to make this work of Christ also the principle of the effectual renewal of the race, but he does not broach this idea.[2] On the contrary, it was clearly his conception, that " God, to whom we were odious on account of sin, was reconciled by the death of his Son, so that he is propitious toward us " (ii. 17. 3). Thus the objective reconciliation of God is the ground of the effectual bestowal of grace. This type of doctrine forms an average presentation of the ideas upon the atonement in the Reformation period.[3]

7. From the work of Christ, Calvin turns to the Application of Redemption to the individual soul. As he describes the course of man's renewal and, in this connection, develops the idea of justification, he not only brings into play his great systematic talent, but reveals especially his profound appreciation of the original aims of Luther. Christ is the Head of the human race. What he by his sufferings and works secured from the Father becomes ours by virtue of fellowship with him (iii. 1. 1). This occurs, however, through the imparting of his Holy Spirit to us: " by the grace and virtue of his Spirit we are made members of him, so that he holds us in union with himself (*sub se*), and we in turn possess him " (ib. 3). (*a*) The essential thing which the Spirit works in us is Faith (ib. 4). By faith we apprehend Christ and his kingdom (iii. 2. 1, 6): " Faith itself is a certain infallible and secure *possession* of those things which have been promised us by God " (ib. 41 ; cf. iii. 3. 1). It is not " a certain assent to the evangelical history," but the apprehending of God revealed in Christ (ib. 1); not the regarding as true that

---

[1] Calvin here follows Augustine. See in Joh. tract., 110. 6.

[2] Cf. the rejection of the idea, that Christ's righteousness is given to us only as an example for imitation, ii. 1. 6.

[3] The theological difficulties connected with this conception are not overcome by Calvin. This will be the more evident, if we remember that here too the idea of the irresponsibility of the divine action appears as a disturbing feature, and if we have in mind the complications inevitably attending the conception of a predestination according to which the work of Christ is available only for the elect.

which the church instructs us to believe,[1] but the recognition of
the fact that God is through Christ gracious to us (ib. 2),
together with the repose of the heart in this assurance (7). We
believe, not only with the understanding, but from the bottom of
our hearts (36). Faith is a "knowledge of the divine will
toward us," united with a firm conviction of the truth of revelation. "But the foundation of this (knowledge) is a presumed
conviction concerning the truth of God" (*praesumta de veritate
dei persuasio*) (6. 14, 15). Thus is derived the definition of
faith: "We may say that it is a firm and certain knowledge
(*cognitio*) of the divine benevolence toward us, which, the truth
of the free promise in Christ having been established, is through
the Holy Spirit revealed to our minds and sealed to our hearts"
(7). Faith is the firm conviction of the grace of God, together
with the sense of repose and security begotten of such conviction. "In short, no one is truly a believer unless, assured
by firm conviction that God is to him a propitious and benevolent Father, he promises to himself all things from the divine
goodness" (16).[2] Upon the ground of this, "it is a firm and
solid confidence (*fiducia*) of the heart, by which we *securely
acquiesce* in the mercy of God promised to us through the
gospel" (C. R. xxxiii. 333 f.). Since this faith is the appropriation of Christ, it not only assures to man the forgiveness of
sins, but also constitutes the beginning of a new life in him.
"Christ cannot be known except in connection with the sanctification of his Spirit. It follows, that faith can by no means be
separated from pious affection" (iii. 2. 8). Thus by faith we are
united to Christ and become partakers of all his gifts and
blessings (ib. 35). It follows, that faith essentially lays hold of
the promises of God; but it also "obediently accepts his commandments" (29). It is noticeable, further, that Calvin lays
more stress than Luther upon the intellectual element of faith.

(*b*) Faith leads to Repentance (iii. 3. 1), *i. e.*, with faith a
new moral condition is inaugurated (ib. 2).[3] But repentance is
conversion and regeneration extending through the whole life of
the believer. "Thus repentance might be defined to be the

---

[1] This excludes *implicit faith* in the Catholic sense. Yet Calvin acknowledges a kind of implicit faith, in that there may be, as in the case of the disciples, some belief before full enlightenment, though of course only as a *fidei
praeparatio*, or *initium*. See l. c., § 4 f.

[2] The term *persuasio* (conviction) is characteristic of Calvin's expositions of
faith—and was so from the beginning—see C. R. xxix. 56; xxxiii. 334. It
appears to have been derived from Bucer (supra, p. 392 n. 3).

[3] We are therefore not to insert a "space of time" between faith and
repentance. Nor is repentance to be confused with the *timor initialis* which
often precedes the reception of grace, II. 3. 2.

true conversion of our life to God, proceeding from a sincere and serious fear of God, and consisting in the mortification of our flesh and of the old man, and in vivification by the Spirit " (iii. 3. 5). "I interpret repentance therefore with one word . . . regeneration, whose scope is nothing else than that the image of God . . . be re-formed in us" (ib. 9). Repentance is therefore the state of regeneration, and one of its essential elements is faith. Without faith, there can be no repentance (ib. 5). This repentance consists in mortification, or anguish of soul, in view of recognized sin, together with the crucifying of the old man, and vivification, or the "effort to live holily and piously" (ib. 3. 8). Both are results flowing from fellowship with Christ (9). Both penitence and the new moral striving in repentance are wrought through Christ and the blessings of his kingdom (19). The antecedent fear (*timor initialis*) which frequently precedes this state is not to be included under repentance (2). These statements lead us in the path which Luther followed during the controversy upon confession and absolution (supra, p. 238 f.).[1] There is no thought in this connection of the influence of the law.[2] But the Christian possesses this new life only in a constant conflict of self-preservation (ib. 10.). The goal toward which he strives is the actual manifestation of the filial character bestowed upon him (iii. 8. 1). As an external means to the attainment of his goal, the law is mentioned (ii. 7. 12 f.; iii. 19. 2), as also the example of Christ. "He adds, that Christ has been set before us as an example, whose image we should express in our lives" (iii. 8. 3). But the goal of "evangelical perfection" Christians cannot attain in this life; yet it is their duty to strive earnestly to advance upon the road which leads toward it (ib. 5) and, in this way, in obedience to the divine will, to promote the glory of God (iii. 7. 1, 2).[3]

(*c*) Now only does Calvin treat of Justification. This arrangement of topics does not, however, by any means imply that justification is to be understood, as in the Roman Catholic system, as

---

[1] Differently conceived in the first edition of the *Institutio*, where Calvin limits repentance to "mortification of the flesh," denying, however, that the latter can exist without faith (xxx. 149).

[2] In Calvin's doctrine of the law, we are taught that the law fills the sinner with a sense of his unrighteousness, in order that he may feel his need of grace (iii. 7. 6, 8). Since this influence of the law is exerted upon such as yet lack faith (ib. 11. 12), there is always in Calvin's mind a stage of conscious condemnation under the law as an experience preparatory to evangelical repentance—a stage which finds a parallel in the Catholic attrition (cf. supra, p. 251 n.).

[3] In this connection, Calvin treats of evangelical asceticism, iii. 3. 16; iii. 8, cf. iv. 12. 15. See also his critique of Stoic ethics, iii. 8. 9.

a result of effectual grace.   The meaning is, that the fellowship
with Christ which we secure in faith brings to us a *double grace*.
First, on account of his innocence we are reconciled to God ;
and, secondly, "that, sanctified by his Spirit, we may practice
innocence and purity of life" (iii. 11. 1).   In thus understanding justification as intimately connected with the new life springing from faith, Calvin falls back into the original channel of
early Reformation thought.   Justification and sanctification cannot be separated *de facto :* "for, since God really renews for the
practice of righteousness those whom he graciously regards as
righteous, he combines that gift of regeneration with this gracious acceptance."   But it does not follow from this that the two
conceptions dare be confounded, as was done by Osiander (ib.
6 ; cf. iii. 11. 10 ; 16. 1).   Justification is God's regarding of
the sinner for Christ's sake as righteous.   "He is justified by
faith who, shut out from the righteousness of works, apprehends
by faith the righteousness of Christ, clothed in which he appears
in the sight of God, not as a sinner, but as righteous."   It is the
"acceptance by which God regards us, having been received into
his grace as righteous."   It consists, accordingly, in the "remission of sins" and in the "imputation of the righteousness of
Christ" (ib. 2).   The consciousness of righteousness does not,
therefore, at all rest upon the beginnings of the new life or its
works (3. 2), but solely upon the gracious imputation of the
obedience of Christ.   "What else is it to locate our righteousness in the obedience of Christ, than to assert that we are for his
sake alone accounted righteous, because the obedience of Christ
is said to be accepted for us as though it were our own?" (23).
Although it is thus perfectly clear that the assurance of salvation depends solely upon divine grace, yet it dare not be forgotten that
this assurance can never arise nor be preserved unless there is first
a living fellowship with Christ.   "We may distinguish between
them, yet Christ contains them both (justification and sanctification) in himself.   Dost thou desire therefore to attain righteousness in Christ ?   It is necessary for thee first to possess Christ.
But thou canst not possess (him) unless thou becomest a partaker of
his sanctification, because he cannot be rent asunder and made of
no effect. . . .   It is hence clear how it is true that we are not justified without works, nor yet by works, since in the fellowship (*par-
ticipatio*) of Christ, by which we are justified, is contained sanctification no less than justification" (iii. 16. 1 ; xxxiii. 335).   As
thus with faith the new life is effected in man by the Spirit, there
is at the same time implanted in him an active, ethical principle,
as the organ with which, despite all the imperfections and defects
of the incipient new life, to apprehend the pardoning grace of

God. Believers attain assurance and confidence in God not through the "gift of regeneration—which, as it is always mutilated in this flesh, so also contains in itself mutiform material to awake doubt"—but, "because they are implanted in the body of Christ, they are freely accounted righteous. For, so far as justification is concerned, faith is a merely passive thing, contributing nothing to our conciliating of the grace of God, but receiving from Christ what is lacking in us " (iii. 13. 5 ; cf. 11. 11 ; 14. 9 ff.). This way of regarding the matter is said to give the glory to God, as well as to actually assure rest and peace to us (iii. 13. 1 ff.).[1] It is just as evidently in harmony with the profoundest impulses of the teaching of the Reformation as it surpasses the formulas of the later Melanchthonian doctrine.

(d) For a proper understanding of the evangelical doctrine of justification, it is further necessary to note the significance of Christian liberty, which, for Calvin, implies three things : (1) That from our conception of justification we exclude all thought of legal righteousness (iii. 19.2). (2) That we obey God, not under the pressure of the law, but willingly (ib. 4 ; cf. ii. 7. 14). (3) That we do not allow the religious life to be bound or determined by any external things or *adiaphora* whatsoever (ib. 7); although the law teaches us to recognize really good works (ii. 8. 5).

(e) Calvin concludes this presentation of the order of salvation[2] with a discussion of Election. The place thus assigned in itself reveals the practical interest which he felt in this doctrine. Man can be certain of his salvation only if the latter is founded upon the eternal will of God ; and this certainty is but increased by the fact, " that he does not choose all for the hope of salvation, but gives to some what he denies to others " (iii. 21. 1). But with this is combined another thought, arising from the conception of the divine nature. According to the doctrine of Determinism, all things that occur must be understood as caused by the divine determination. But the call to salvation fails entirely to reach some, and with others it is ineffectual. In both cases, the cause must be located in the divine will (ib. 1 init.). This explains the importance attached by Calvin to the doctrine of predestination. He defines the term as follows: " We call the eternal decree of God by which he has determined with him-

---

[1] The *efficient* cause of salvation is, therefore, the mercy of God ; the *material* cause, Christ with his obedience ; the *formal* or *instrumental* cause, faith, iii. 14. 17.

[2] Prayer is treated of (iii. 20), between Liberty and Election, as the principal exercise of faith " and as the daily means for the reception of divine blessings.

self what he wishes to have come to pass concerning every man, predestination. For not all are created under the same condition (*condicio*), but to some eternal life is foreordained, and to some eternal damnation. Therefore, accordingly as anyone has been formed for one or the other end, we say that he has been predestinated to life or to death " (ib. 5). When, therefore, God wins for himself particular men by calling, justification, and sanctification, this achievement accomplished in time is an expression of his eternal will. But it is just as truly an expression of his will, when this does not occur in the case of others, but in its place a devoting to destruction (*exitio devovere*) (ib. 7). But it is impossible to refer the election and not the reprobation to a positive act of the divine will (iii. 23. 1 ; ib. 8 : " Why do we say ' permit ' unless because he wills?"), which is evident enough in view of the determinism of the system. Just as God has chosen some, he has also rejected all those whom he has seen fit (C. R. xxxvi. 109). On the other hand, the Scotist element in the conception of God (supra, p. 397) here asserts itself, since the only reason which can be assigned for the election of some and the reprobation of others is the purely arbitrary will of God (ib. 2. 5). But if God thus foreordains the final destiny, together with the means which bring it about, then must the first occasion for this evil destiny of man have also been foreordained by him, *i. e.:* " God not only foresaw the fall of the first man and the ruin of his posterity in him, but appointed it by his own will." In general, it is his special prerogative " to rule and govern all things by his hand" (ib. 7). His will is " the necessity of things." He willed that Adam should fall, and that all the misery of sin should descend upon his posterity. Why he so wills we know not. This does not, however, in Calvin's view, exclude the opinion that man of himself found occasion for the fall, and by it became guilty : " Therefore man fell, the providence of God so ordaining ; but he fell by his own fault " (8 ; cf. xxxvi. 110). All attempts to cast reproach upon God in view of this double election must fail, because no one has authority to coërce the divine will, and because no wrong is done to sinners by their reprobation. The justice of God is made manifest in them, as his mercy in the elect (11 f.).

Calvin's theory of predestination goes beyond that of Bucer in that it lays special stress upon the double predestination. His view embraces chiefly the following points : (1) The idea that everything which occurs on earth is a direct result of divine causality. Hence the divine call with its results is but the carrying out of predestination (iii. 24. 1, 10). Only the elect attain to real faith (iii. 2. 11); and they alone receive the gift of perseverance and gain the assurance of salvation (iii. 24. 6).[1] In this way the sole sovereignty of God and his glory and honor are displayed in all earthly events (vid. citations in SCHEIBE, C's Praedestinationslehre, p. 115 ff.). (2) Thus our salvation, being based upon the eternal will of God, is absolutely assured.   (3) Predestination embraces a double election : that in some men only the divine justice, while in others his mercy also is made manifest, has no other ground than the will of God.   At this point we observe a Scotist influence moulding the thought.[2]

If we now seek to estimate the significance of this doctrine in the Calvinistic theology, it is not correct either to see in it his "central dogma" (SCHWEIZER, Centraldogmen, i. 57), or to pronounce it an "appendage" attached to the doctrine out of regard for the authority of Paul (RITSCHL, Jarbb. f. deutsche Theol., 1868, 108).   It is not the former, as the doctrines of redemption and justification are not deduced from it ;[3] nor the latter, as exegetical considerations have but a subordinate place in this connection.   It is, however, true that this doctrine has for Calvin an entirely different significance than for Luther.   For both it is a subsidiary conception.   Calvin bases upon it the certainty of salvation ; Luther, the sinner's lack of liberty.[4] But this conception found in Calvin an important point of attachment in his idea of God as the Almighty Lord, who works all things, and to whose glory all things minister.   The God of Luther is the Almighty Loving-will revealed in Christ.   As Calvin's thought was not controlled by Luther's vivid sense of Christ, so, in his conception of God, sovereignty and omnipotence assumed the place of prominence rather than love.   It was to him not an intolerable thought, that God, for the display of his justice, never felt any love whatsoever for a portion of the human race.   From this, it may be readily understood that predestination should have con-

---

[1] At this point is seen the injustice of the charge brought against Calvin, that this doctrine leads to moral indifference ; for God is represented as working effectually in the predestinated to the end of the sanctification, so that predestination is the most powerful stimulus to the new life, iii. 23. 12.

[2] This is the case when Calvin appeals only to the divine *will* as such (iii. 23. 2); but he also at times pointed to the inscrutability of the divine purposes to the human intelligence (*e. g.*, iii. 21. 1 ; C. R. xxxvi. 10).   This is evidently another thought.   In the former case, the course of events, being determined by the will of God, is without cause and incomprehensible : here, being divine, it is inscrutable by the finite reason.   In the one instance, Calvin may be said to be Scotist in conception ; in the other, Thomistic or Augustinian.

[3] Let it be observed, *e. g.*, that predestination is not in itself justification, but the latter becomes a reality only in those who believe.

[4] Luther used predestination chiefly as an argument against the Pelagian doctrine of sin ; Calvin, against the Pelagian doctrine of grace.

tinually grown in importance for him, and that the theologians who attached themselves to him should have made it the first principle of their theology.[1] Compare SCHEIBE, C's Praedestinationslehre, p. 117 f.

8. The doctrine of the Church logically follows the discussion of the redemption wrought by Christ and its attainment through the Holy Spirit. (*a*) The Church is the totality of all the predestinated (iv. 1. 2, 7 : "it comprehends, not only the sanctified who dwell upon earth, but all the elect who have existed from the beginning of the world"), as well as also the totality of all those who have been led by the Holy Spirit to fellowship with Christ (ib. 3 fin., 7). This coördination of the elect and the sanctified may be understood when we remember that election is realized in the individual through sanctification. The elect have now a desire to influence one another. In this way the church becomes also a communion : "in order that they may mutually distribute among themselves whatever blessings God confers upon them" (ib. 3). This takes place through external means, *i. e.*, word and sacrament, which human weakness requires and which God has therefore bestowed upon the church (ib. 1) : "God inspires faith in us, but by the agency (*organo*) of his gospel." In harmony with this, the development of the believer is secured only "by the tuition of the church" (5). Thus the entire empirical activity of the church is brought into the relation of a means to the work of salvation implied in predestination. (*b*) The church, as the totality of the *elect*, is invisible and an object of faith. But, inasmuch as the elect are found in an empirical communion, which has its marks in the profession of faith in God and the true doctrine, in a common participation in baptism, the Lord's Supper, and works of love, as well as in the maintenance of the office of the ministry, we are to acknowledge also a visible church, which includes hypocrites among its members. We are to believe in the former ; of the latter, it is said : "we are commanded to respect it, and to cultivate its communion " (7). Since this attitude toward the visible church is required on account of its recognized aim, the title "church" in the creed may also be applied with some reservation (*aliquatenus*) to the visible church (3 init.). Further, we may always from the presence of word and sacrament infer the presence of an actual church, as the former can never remain fruitless (ib. 9, 10). Severance from the (visible) church is, therefore, also a denial of God and Christ (10). This view of the

---

[1] This point requires further elucidation through historical research; Ritschl's investigations are here not satisfactory.

church approaches that of Luther, as the attempt is here also made to deduce from the presence of the means of grace the assurance that the true church is likewise present. But there remains the difference, that for Luther grace is always effectually present with the means of grace, whereas Calvin—influenced by his conception of God—regards the external means of grace as, after all, merely symbols of a possibly accompanying divine influence (ib. 6; iv. 14. 8; 16. 19). Since there is, accordingly, such a thing as a proclamation of the word without an accompanying influence of the Holy Spirit, the motto: "Where the word, there the church," has not the profound basis for Calvin which it finds in the teaching of Luther.

(*c*) But Calvin always antagonized with the greatest energy the conclusion which sectarian leaders might easily deduce from his premises, that the external organization of the church is of small importance. He emphasized the necessity of ecclesiastical forms and ordinances more strongly than Melanchthon himself. The administration of the means of grace and the preservation of pure doctrine necessitated the divine appointment of definite ecclesiastical offices. "For this reason it has seemed good that the spiritual government, such as our Saviour has indicated and appointed by his word, should be reduced to good form. . . . First, there are four orders, or kinds of offices, which our Saviour has appointed for the government of his church : namely, pastors ; then teachers ; after that, elders ; fourthly, deacons" (xxxviii. a. 92 f.; cf. 15 ff.). Christ has, therefore, instituted "a ministry of men . . . as it were a vicarious work" (iv. 3. 1); "he has shown the human ministry which God employs for the governing of the church to be the chief nerve by which believers are held together in one body" (iv. 3. 2). It is not an ideal plan of organization, resulting with historical necessity from the nature of the tasks assigned, which here confronts us, but a divine commandment, *i. e.*, a precept of the old divinely-ordained ecclesiastical law. It must be remembered, further, that these officers have not only the duty of preaching, teaching, and the care of the poor ; but, above all, the duty of exercising Christian discipline. "Just as the saving doctrine of Christ is the soul of the church, so this discipline stands for its strength (*pro nervis*)." Discipline restrains the opponents of Christian doctrine ; it is the goad for the indolent and the rod for the erring (iv. 12. 1). The consistorium, composed of spiritual and lay-elders, or the "assembly of the elders," exercises the disciplinary power, which includes that of excommunication (ib. 2). Upon the particulars of this authority it is not the province of the History of Doctrines to enter.

But it is important to recognize clearly the fact, that Calvin believed in a divinely-appointed form of church government. Cf. Sohm, Kirchenrecht, i. 648 ff. Cornelius, in Abhandl. d. bayr. Akad. der Wiss. Hist. Cl., vol. xx., 1893, 251 ff.

(*d*) Since the church has, in this way, a form of government given by God himself and therefore immutable, the sphere of her independence of the state is a wider one than upon the territory of the Saxon reformation. But even in Geneva the idea of Calvin was but imperfectly carried out,[1] since the state retained in its hand as well the regulation of the ecclesiastical judicatory as the confirmation of the election of clergymen ; and further-more, the extension of moral discipline required an enlarged co-operation of the state in the sphere of religion and morals. Calvin, therefore, found it possible to carry out his ideas of re-form only by regarding the civil authority as the agency for the exercise of Christian discipline, or by ascribing to the state the duty, in its service of God, of putting into execution the ideals of the church even by worldly means.[2] "And it is the duty of the chief magistrates to consider whom they serve in their office, and not to permit any harm to the ministers and vicars of God. But their whole care should properly lie in this, that they may preserve the public form of religion unpolluted, that they may mould the life of the people by the best laws, and that they may secure the prosperity and tranquillity of their realms both publicly and privately" (C. R. xxxiii. 354 ; cf. iv. 20. 3, 2). The state is therefore under obligation to punish every uprising against the recognized religion, and to be solicitous for the observance of the commandments, not only of the second table of the decalogue, but of the first table as well. This is attested not only by the history of the Israelites, but even by the view of heathen nations, which makes the guarding of piety the first duty of the state (iv. 20. 3, 9). Of course, in so doing the state dare make no change in the divine law (ib. 3). In reality, it will therefore only be required to carry out what is prescribed by the incumbents of the spiritual offices. From this point of view we can understand the personal attitude assumed by Calvin in Geneva, as well as the drastic rigor of the government and its administration under his leadership. Since every sin is an act

---

[1] "The consistent application of Calvin's ideas of church government first became possible in those Reformed churches which were compelled to develop their polity in opposition to the authority of the State." Sohm, KR. i. 655 f.; cf. Weber, Geschichtl. Darstellung d. Calvinism. im Verhältnis zum Staat, 1836.

[2] It must here be borne in mind that Calvin most strenuously discriminated *in principle* between the "spiritual kingdom of Christ" and the "civil government."

of rebellion against the divine majesty, it is also to be visited with the severest civil penalties (cf. ELSTER, Jarbb. f. National-ökon., vol. 31, p. 182 ff., 207 ff.).[1] Hence, Calvin's reformation was conducted after the manner of the theocracy. God is the Lord, whose worship the church desires and the state compels. But, inasmuch as this attitude of the civil government toward the church in the end coincides with the ecclesiastical office endued with divine authority, the coincidence of Calvin's ideal of the church with the conceptions of the Middle Ages is yet far more evident than in the case of Zwingli.[2] And in this parallel we are confirmed by observing the narrow spirit, hostile to all natural enjoyment and social pleasure, which marked the civil administration of Calvin (vid., *e. g.*, the laws concerning luxury in Gaberel, hist. de l'église de Genève, i., 1858, p. 339 ff.). It is manifest, therefore, that the enlarging of the reformatory aims of Luther was accomplished only by re-adopting the ideals of the Middle Ages.

9. We are led to consider, finally, the doctrine of the Sacraments. Calvin defines a sacrament as an " external symbol by which the Lord seals to our consciences the promises of his benevolence toward us, and we, in turn, . . . testify our piety toward him " (iv. 14. 1). The sacrament itself is thus a symbolic confirmation of the grace announced in the words of institution (ib. 4). But it is more—a sure pledge of his grace (7). It confirms to us what the word has taught us (8). But the sacrament in itself is just as little accompanied by the Spirit of God as is the word. The Spirit follows the word and sacrament, and only where this inner teacher (*interior magister*) inwardly opens, moves, and enlightens the heart, do they bring grace to man (ib. 8-12 ; cf. Consens. Tigur. 16). Hence, for the unbelieving, they are merely signs without content (15). Here again the idea of predestination asserts itself—only the predestinated receive anything through the sacrament. In them God works immediately, just as all things are only means

[1] C. R. xli. 76 : " The great and enormous corruptions which I see everywhere constrain me to beseech you to have solicitude that men may be kept in strict and honest discipline. Above all, the honor of God is maintained in punishing the crimes of which men have not been accustomed to take much account. I say it, since larcenies, fightings, and extortions will sometimes be severely punished, because men are injured. Yet they will suffer lewdness, adultery, drunkenness, and blasphemy of the name of God, either as lawful things or as of very little importance. Now we see, on the contrary, in what esteem God holds them. He declares how precious his name is to him. It is not possible then that he should allow such wrongs to be unpunished."

[2] Although, of course, even in Calvin's view this office has no authority to do more than maintain and execute the commandments of the Bible. But this does not essentially transcend the limits of the theory of the Middle Ages.

through which his agency is exerted.   Not to them, but to God
alone, belongs the glory (12).

(*b*) Baptism is "like some sealed diploma " and testifies to
us the forgiveness of sins (iv. 15. 1).   The recollection of his
baptism serves the believer therefore as a standing testimonial,
that God will forgive us our sins (3).   It thus takes the place of
the Romish sacrament of repentance (4).   Baptism, further,
introduces us into fellowship with Christ, with his death and
resurrection, for our *mortification* and *vivification* (5).   Through
it we become partakers of all the blessings of Christ (6).   As in
his general view of the sacraments, so also here in his doctrine
of baptism, which is in thorough harmony with the former,
Calvin goes further than Zwingli.   While the latter regarded
the sacraments as purely symbolical, there was, in the view of
Calvin, a real divine energy connected with the administration of these symbols.[1]   But this energy is not involved in the
mere external ceremony, but accompanies it—only, however, in
the case of the predestinated.   This view thus becomes in form
analogous to the Scotist theory of the sacraments (see p. 127),[2]
except that with Calvin the accompanying divine energy is
limited to the elect.

(*c*) We find that in Calvin also, as so frequently in other cases,
the doctrine of the Lord's Supper oversteps to a certain extent
the limits of the general definition of the sacraments.   In this
sacrament we receive the body of Christ, "in order that, as we
see ourselves made parta¹ ers of it, we may assuredly believe that
the virtue of his vivifying death shall become efficacious in us."
It is, as it were, a reminder of the covenant established through
the blood of Christ (iv. 17. 1).   As bread and wine become
one with us and nourish our bodily life, so the Lord's Supper
effects a real spiritual fellowship with Christ, which nourishes our
soul (ib. 3. 5).   As we receive the body of Christ, we experience
the continuous efficacy of his sacrifice, and his blood as a "perpetual drink."   There is, therefore, here a real presence of
Christ, even a presence of his corporeal nature (*Leiblichkeit*):

---

[1] An evidence of this is seen in Calvin's idea, that, in the case of children,
regeneration is effected in an initial way by baptism without the word : " We
confess that the word of the Lord is the one and only seed of regeneration ;
but we deny that it is to be inferred from this that infants cannot be regenerated by the power of God, which is to him as easy and plain as it is to us incomprehensible and wonderful " (iv. 16. 18).   Why should not God, since
he can awaken faith even without the word, bestow also upon children "some
share of his grace," or a certain knowledge of God, " the full abundance of
which they are soon after to enjoy ? " (ib. 19).   Cf. Luther, supra, p. 285, n. 2.

[2] As Duns denies that God binds his power to the sacraments (p. 127), so
Calvin says : " No power is by us located in created things " (iv. 14. 12).

" I declare that in the mystery of the Supper through the symbols of bread and wine *Christ is truly offered to us,* even as to his body and blood " (11). It is not sufficient to speak merely of a spiritual fellowship with Christ, since he has designated his flesh and his blood as veritable food (7). Christ, coming from heaven, has infused into his flesh his life-giving energy, " in order that thence the communication of life might extend to us " (8). From his flesh, life flows into us as from a gushing fountain (9). But the body of Christ is now far removed from us in space : how then can his flesh come to us and serve us as food ? This occurs through the " secret power of the Holy Spirit : therefore what our mind does not comprehend, faith accepts, *i. e.,* that the Spirit truly unites things which are separated in localities." We must, therefore, believe that where the visible symbols are offered to us, " the body itself is also certainly given to us " (10 ; cf. C. R. xxxvii. 72). The reception of the body takes place therefore by means of faith (5, 11, 32).

Accordingly, Calvin teaches a real presence of Christ,[1] which is mediated through the symbols of the bread and wine—he even speaks of a presence and energy of the body of Christ. But it is, according to 1 Cor. x. 16, a κοινωνία of the body of Christ : " but a communication is something different from the body itself " (22). We do not receive the body of Christ, " but all the blessings which Christ has offered to us in his body " (C. R. xxix. 123). If we would understand this view, as contrasted with that of Luther, we must bear three things in mind : (1) That the " substance " of the sacrament is " Christ, with his death and resurrection." (2) That the " prodigious ubiquity " is unconditionally excluded. If we do not wish to volatilize the body of Christ into a phantasm, we must firmly maintain his circumscribed local existence in heaven (12, 26, 29, 30). (3) That, in strict consistency with the above, the presence of the body of Christ is to be represented as a presence mediated by the Spirit to faith, yet in such a way that " the flesh itself of Christ does not enter into us " (10, 32). Calvin's view is, therefore, clear. Christ is present in the Supper as he who in his body and through it has accomplished our salvation : his power (*potentia*) and efficacy (*virtus*) as Redeemer is present. " He is always present with his own, breathing into them his life ; he lives in them, sustains them, confirms them, quickens them, keeps them safe, *not otherwise than* if he were present in body : finally, indeed, he feeds them with his very body, the commu-

---

[1] He expressly guards himself against the misunderstanding : " As though, when I say that Christ is received by faith, I should wish to be understood as meaning only by the mind and the imagination " (ib. 11).

nion of which he infuses into them by the power of his Spirit. In this way the body and blood of Christ are offered to us in the sacrament '' (18). The difference between this doctrine and that of Luther is manifest. However emphatically Calvin maintains the earlier position of Luther, that the significance of the body of Christ consists in the presence, as a pledge to us, of him who has suffered for us (supra, p. 287 f.), yet the difference is always equally manifest—Calvin having in mind the spiritual influence, and Luther the real bodily presence. When the question is raised, whether Calvin's doctrine of the Lord's Supper is nearer to that of Luther or to that of Zwingli, the decision is usually, under confessional bias, given in favor of the latter opinion.[1] But when it is remembered that, in contrast with Zwingli's purely subjective commemorative view, Calvin maintains both a special '' presence of the living Christ '' (Apol., vid. supra, p. 342) and the religious influences exerted by it, quite in the spirit of Luther,[2] the conclusion may, nevertheless, be reached, with due account of the differences above noted, that in his religious conception of the sacrament Calvin stands nearer to Luther than to Zwingli.[3] Calvin himself pronounced Zwingli's theory of the sacraments profane (C. R. xxxix. 438). The words of institution are, according to Calvin, to be understood as a metonomy, somewhat as circumcision is called a covenant ; the Rock, Christ ; the Old Testament sacrifices, atonements. But '' it does not only represent, as a bare and empty token, but also truly offers '' (ib. 21). Such is Calvin's doctrine of the Lord's Supper. It affords additional evidence of his dependence upon Luther in his apprehension of religious truth.

10. The significance of Calvin for the History of Doctrines lies in the fact, that his view of Christianity and the church expresses in classical completeness the conception of the Reformation which prevailed in Switzerland and Southwestern Germany. To the wide acceptance which this type of doctrine gradually

---

[1] SCHWEIZER, Glaubenslehre d. ev.-ref. Kirche, ii. 656. HAGENBACH, DG., ed. 6, 556. THOMASIUS, DG. ii., ed. 2, 550, 554 f.

[2] The sacrament not only brings the fullness of the gifts of Christ and fills us with the assurance of eternal life, ''but it even makes us secure in regard to the immortality of our flesh '' (ib. 32); it also lays upon us the duty of brotherly love (44).

[3] This also throws light upon the relation of Bucer's theory and the later teaching of Melanchthon to Luther. For Luther's mild judgment of Calvin and his doctrine of the Lord's Supper, vid. STÄHELIN, C. Leben, i. 226 f. Luther firmly maintained his own position to the last, notwithstanding the well-known utterance said to have been made to Melanchthon. See KÖSTLIN, Luther, ii., ed. 4, 627 f., and Stud. u. Krit., 1875, 373 ff., as also DIESTELMANN, Die letzte Unterredung Luther's mit Mel. üb. d. Abendmalsstreit, and especially HAUSSLEITER, Neue kirchl. Ztschr., 1898, 831 ff.

attained, we can here merely refer in passing.[1]   The close connection between Calvin's conception of the central ideas of Christianity and Luther's underlying thoughts need not be further
emphasized.   We must not allow the confessional conflict of the
following century to obscure for us the important fact, that the
two types of Reformation doctrine which gained ascendancy in
Protestantism, *i. e.*, the type of Luther and Melanchthon and
that of Bucer and Calvin, are in essential accord in their understanding of faith and works, of justification and atonement, of
repentance and sanctification, in their recognition of the dogmas
of the ancient church, as well as in their rejection of the Roman
Catholic Pelagianism and hierarchism.   At the same time, the
differences must not be overlooked.   But it is not correct, so
far as I am able to judge, to attribute these differences to a
religious conception begotten upon the territory of the church as
remoulded by the Reformation.   Rather are they sufficiently
explained—when studied from the purely historical point of
view—as the preservation and propagation, upon the territory of
the so-called Reformed Church, of ideals and doctrines of the
pre-reformation period.   This is true, for example, (1) of the
aim and scope of the assumed task of practical reform, which included a reformation of the moral life, to be enforced with
stringency and finding its justification in positive biblical ordinances, and also a thorough revision and revolution of the
ecclesiastical system.   (2) In this undertaking, the ecclesiastical
offices ordained of God come into prominence; a covenant
must be formed between the civil authority and the church,
which involves a subordination of the former to the ordinances
of the latter.   (3) The prevalent ideal of a practical life frequently betrays a relationship with the medieval renunciation of
the world and of the natural impulses.   (4) The Scriptures, as the
source of authority for the conduct of the reformation sought,
are verbally inspired ; both ideas being, as we have seen (supra,
p. 169 172, 192, ff.), embraced in the theory of the later
Middle Ages.   (5) The conception of the sacraments is related
to the ideas of Erasmas, and reminds us of the Scotist-Nominalist
theory.   (6) The difference in the doctrine of the Lord's
Supper rests chiefly upon the adherence to the Augustinian and

---

[1] The influence of Calvin as a theologian upon his church exceeds that
exerted by Melanchthon, and even by Luther, in a similar respect upon their
followers ; for it may be said, that *his theology has become the accepted doctrine of the Reformed Church.*   Nearly all the later confessions reproduce his
formulas, and we may hence pass them by with slight notice.   Calvin did not
leave behind him questionable coins, as did Melanchthon ; nor, on the other
hand, like Luther, uncoined gold.

Scholastic idea of the corporeal nature of Christ as transported to a heavenly place. (7) Even the determinism, which is a natural outcome of the conception of God, is no new discovery, but is the common factor in a number of reformatory movements appearing in the Western church since the days of Augustine. We need but briefly point to the Thomistic and Scotist elements which appear concurrently.

It is precisely in this conception of the nature of God—more in the practical, unwritten conception than in the theoretical formulas—that we find the basis of the peculiar character of the Reformed view, and at this point accordingly begins the divergence from the Lutheran view.   God is, to pious minds in the Reformed church, the Lord who rules omnipotently.[1]   The development of the universe is the product of his sovereign will ; its goal his honor or glory.   But the sovereignty of God is displayed above all through the " Law," which controls all life and all its ramifications.   All that is and is done in the world, everything personal and natural, must subserve this end. Obedience is the whole content of life.   Natural inclinations are bent and crushed beneath the pressure of the " law ;" the state and society at large are agencies for its enforcement.   There is something "unmodern " in this magniloquent portrayal of the energy of obedience and the fanaticism of submission.   We always, when we allow the system as a whole to make appeal to us, receive an impression of a piety in keeping with that of Augustine and the Middle Ages.   This impression is often confirmed in a startling way by the history of the Reformed Church.   This history rests upon a foundation-wall of holy zeal, and a cloud of strong-willed witnesses overshadows it.   But the gospel, as it appears in Paul and John, we find in clearer and brighter form in Luther than in Calvin.   The God of Calvin is the omnipotent Will, ruling throughout the world ; the God of Luther is the omnipotent energy of Love manifest in Christ.   In the one case, we have acts of compulsion even in the heart, subjection, law, service ; in the other, inward conquest by the power of love, free self-surrender, filial love without compulsion.   The one does not necessarily exclude the other ; but the tone and emphasis give rise to the differences which undeniably exist. From the practical energy of the Reformed ideals—with which praxis has not always been able to keep pace—the Lutheran church may learn a valuable lesson.   But when, in any age of

[1] *E. g.*, Heidelb. Cat., Niemeyer, p. 398 : What dost thou understand by the providence of God ?   The almighty and ever-present power of God, by which he still upholds and also governs heaven and earth, together with all created things, as with his hand.

evangelical Christianity, faith grows dim, and love grows cold, and it seems as though the gospel were no longer sufficient to satisfy the advanced spirit of the "modern" world, then will deliverance be found, not in the views of Calvin, but in return to the gospel and the faith of Luther.[1] Evangelical Christianity has yet much to learn from her Luther.

§ 80. *The Triumph of Calvin's Doctrine of the Lord's Supper.*

LITERATURE. NIEMEYER, Collect. confessionum in ecclesiis reformatis, 1840. HUNDESHAGEN, Conflikte des Zwinglianismus, Luthertums u. Calvinismus in d. bern. Landeskirche, 1842. PESTALOZZI, Bullinger, 1858, p. 229 ff., 373 ff. STÄHELIN, Calvin, ii. 91 ff.

1. Luther's severe condemnation of Zwingli in his "Kurz. Bekenntnis vom h. Sakr.," 1545, induced Bullinger to revive the Zwinglian doctrine of the Lord's Supper in the baldest form ("Warhaftes Bekenntnis der Diener der Kirche zu Zurich"). At about the same time, a series of conflicts arose in the church at Berne in consequence of the demand of the Council that all pastors should accept the Zurich doctrine of the Lord's Supper. Calvin took a hand in the controversy, as he had a large number of adherents in the territory of Berne. Under his influence, the CONSENSUS TIGURINUS appeared in A. D. 1549, setting forth the doctrine as agreed upon between Bullinger and Calvin.[2]

2. The Consensus, while bringing the doctrine in outward form nearer to the position held by Zwingli, is in substance Calvinistic. The sacraments are signs of recognition and commemoration (art. 7). Yet these signs are not empty, but accompanied by God with special exertions of his energy. With the sacramental signs the believer also really receives Christ with all spiritual gifts (9). More precisely speaking, this is true only in the case of the elect (16, 17). A bodily presence of Christ is to be rejected (21, 24). The words of institution are to be understood figuratively (*figurate*, 22).

3. The Reformed Confessions did not here depart from the

---

[1] I cannot therefore agree with K. MÜLLER (Symbolik, 540), who regards it as "certain" that in the evangelical church of the future "the spirit of the general Evangelical Reformed Church will be in the ascendancy," since Luther's contributions to the church "were substantially already adopted in the sixteenth century." Müller has moreover acknowledged that in a certain sense the Reformed Church stands nearer to Roman Catholicism than does the Lutheran (p. 387 A.).

[2] This document is pronounced by E. Stähelin (Calv. ii. 121): "the solemn act by which the Zwinglian and Calvinistic reformations were joined in everlasting wedlock as the one great Reformed church.

27

teachings of Calvin. The sacraments are efficacious signs (*efficacia signa*) of grace (39, art. 35). Accordingly, with the reception of the bread and wine, there is an impartation of grace, not only in that we are thereby enabled to realize the sacrifice of Christ upon the cross, but also : " that he himself feeds and refreshes my soul to eternal life with his crucified body and shed blood as certainly as I receive . . . the bread from the hand of the administrator" (Heidelb. Cat., Niemeyer, p. 409). Believers "through the Holy Spirit receive also the flesh and blood of the Lord, and are by these nourished (*pascuntur*) unto eternal life" (Conf. Helv. poster. a. 21). The body and blood of Christ are thus really received, but by the soul in faith, their presence being secured by an operation of the Holy Spirit. When, *e. g.*, the Gallican Confession (a. 36) teaches : "nourishes and vivifies us with the substance (*substantia*) of his body and blood," this is at once (a. 37) explained to mean that the body and blood are food and drink of the soul, as the bread and wine of the body (cf. Westminster Conf. c. 29. 7 ; 39 a. 28. Conf. Belg., Scot. i., Niemeyer, p. 386, 352). This is the Calvinistic doctrine.

§ 81. *Fundamental Evangelical Principles in the Later Confessions of the Reformed Church.*

SOURCES. Cf. NIEMEYER, l. c. K. MÜLLER, Symbolik, 1896, p. 415 ff., 445 ff.

1. The later Reformed Confessions all distinctly display the controlling influence of the spirit of Calvin (cf. Conf. Gallicana, 1559. Conf. Czengerina, 1557. Conf. Belgica, 1566. The 39 Articles, 1562. Conf. Scoticana prior, 1560. Conf. Helvetica posterior, 1566. Heidelberg Catech., 1563. Westminster Conf., 1646. Declaratio Thoruniensis, 1645). Of these various confessions, the Heidelberg Catechism, the Westminster Confession, and the Later Helvetic Confession attained the greatest authority.

2. The fundamental evangelical ideas find clear expression in these writings. For the sake of the satisfaction and obedience of Christ, God forgives the sins of those who believe on Christ and regards them as righteous : " God, without any merit of mine, out of pure grace, bestows upon and imputes to me the perfect satisfaction, righteousness, and holiness of Christ, as though I had never committed any sin and had myself rendered all the obedience which Christ has rendered for me, if I only accept such benefit with a believing heart" (Heidelb. Cat., p. 405 f.;

cf. Helv. 15, 16.   West. Conf. 8. 5 ; 11. 1, 3).[1]   God works faith through the Holy Spirit in the elect " by means of the preaching of the gospel and the prayer of the believer " (Helv. post. 16.   Westm. Conf. 14. 1).   Faith is "not only a sure knowledge by means of which I regard as true everything which God has revealed to us in his word, but also a heartfelt confidence " (Heid. Cat. 396).   It is an assured acknowledgment of the divine truth " presented (*proposita*) in the Scriptures and the Apostles' Creed " (Helv. 16).   Since faith accepts the contents of the Scriptures as true "on account of the authority of God himself speaking therein," it embraces obedience to the commandments, as well as the acceptance of the promises and repose in Christ (Westm. Conf. 14. 2).   These, too, are Calvinistic ideas, which deviate from the view of Luther.   Faith is not only acceptance of Christ, but also the obedient subjection to God and the reception of the doctrines revealed by him.[2]   The emphasis laid upon penitential discipline is also to be traced to Calvin (Heid. Cat. 412.   Westm. Conf. 15).   The Helvetic Confession defines repentance as follows : "a change of mind in man the sinner, incited by the word of the gospel and the Holy Spirit, and accepted by true faith."   It is " conversion " to God and to all good, and " aversion " from the devil and evil (a. 14. Heid. Cat. 413 f.).

3. The recognition of the spiritual nature of the church is epitomized in the formula :   The church is the fellowship of the predestinated (*e. g.*, Westm. Conf. 25. 1.   Heid. Cat. 404). This definition stands by the side of a strong emphasizing of the visible church, with its offices, and discipline, and the obligation to submit to the latter and diligently use the means of grace

[1] Upon Original Sin and the Enslaved Will, vid. Helv. 8.   Gal. 10, 11. Scot. 3.   Heid. Cat. 393.   Belg. 15, 39, art. 9, 10.   Westm. Conf. c. 6 and 9.

[2] We in this connection naturally recall the strong emphasis upon the inspiration of the Scriptures and the enumeration of the books of the canon in the Reformed confessions, *e. g.*, Helv. 1 : "We believe, therefore, that from these Scriptures are to be sought true wisdom and piety ; also, the reformation and government of churches, and the institution of all the duties of piety." The West. Conf., 1. 1 and 2, after enumerating the canonical books, says : " Which have all been given by divine inspiration as the rule of faith and life." In 4 : " The authority of the Holy Scriptures . . . depends . . . alone upon their author, God."   In 5 : " A full persuasion and certitude, as well of their infallible truth, as of their divine authority, is not otherwise begotten than by an internal operation of the Holy Spirit, testifying through the word and with the word in our hearts."   Thus the Small Catechism of the Puritans, in Niem., p. 98 : " There are two things which the Scriptures teach first of all : what man should believe concerning God, and what duty God demands of man."   Gal. 2-5.   Belg. 3-7 ; 39 art. 6 (8 : the three symbols, the Nicene, Athanasian, and what is commonly called the Apostles', are to be entirely received and believed).

(*e. g.*, Heid. 407. Helv. 1. 17, 18. Westm. Conf. 25. 2 f.). It is precisely the predestinarian determinism and the representation of God as the Lord who does all things that are done, which afford the explanation of the strictness and severity of Reformed church life. All that is done by the church and its members is but the carrying out of the divine Will. Through *vocatio* and *justificatio* predestination is realized (Westm. 10. 1 ; 11. 1).[1] Thus God alone works, and all human action serves his ends. These ideas find utterance in the term, "the divine glory" (cf. supra, pp. 312, 391, 416, and Müller, Symbolik, p. 445 ff.). We are thus brought to the doctrine of predestination.

§ 82. *Triumph of the Doctrine of Predestination.*

LITERATURE. SCHWEIZER, Centraldogmen, 2 vols., 1854-6. SEEBERG-THOMAS., ed. 2, 660 ff. LINSENMANN, A. Pighius u. sein theol. Standpunkt, in Tüb. Quartalschr., 1866, 571 ff. Upon Bolsec, vid. C. R. xxxvi. 145 ff.

1. In harmony with his fundamental religious temper, and in opposition to foolish opposers, Calvin developed the doctrine of predestination with constantly increasing clearness and distinctness. ALBERT PIGHIUS had in A. D. 1542 made a vigorous assault upon this doctrine in his publication, *De libero arbitrio et divina gratia*, ll. 10. To this Calvin replied in his *De libero arbitrio* (C. R. xxxiv. 233 ff.). He here develops the ideas grown familiar to us : that God alone works salvation, but to a certain extent includes his working in the church's means of grace (252 ff.); that the sinner himself is to blame (256 f.); that the doctrine of predestination is not equivalent to Stoic fatalism (257). If Pighius had employed against the doctrine the common arguments, that it leaves no room for morality and human responsibility, nor for merits, etc., JEROME BOLSEC, who came to Geneva in A. D. 1551, endeavored to find the source of faith in grace alone, but with the exclusion of election. God, he held, works faith through efficacious grace (*gratia efficax*). That it is not always produced, is to be attributed to *rebellio* in man, and not to the decree of God (C. R. xxxvi. 217, 213). But he taught also "that man has not been entirely deprived of free-will . . . but his will remains, wounded and corrupt" (ib. 218). Though Bolsec by no means questioned salvation by grace, he strongly opposed the idea of a pretemporal election (vid. also l. c., p. 179 f.).

[1] Vid. esp. 3, 6 : "But, just as God has destined the elect to glory, so he has foreordained all the means by which they shall attain it. Wherefore the elect, after they had fallen in Adam, have been redeemed by Christ, are by the Holy Spirit efficaciously called to faith in Christ, justified, sanctified, and by his power kept through faith unto salvation."

An appeal issued from Geneva to the other Swiss theologians awakened but a lukewarm response, instead of the clear and incisive testimony in favor of the double predestination which the Genevans expected (cf. SCHWEIZER, i. 218 ff.). The CONSENSUS GENEVENIS, *De aeterna dei praedestinatione*, in which Calvin, in A. D. 1552, again presented his view (C. R. xxxvi. 249 ff., in Niemeyer, Coll. conf., 218 ff.), was hence officially accepted only in the Genevan church.

2. The doctrine is treated in the most of the Reformed confessions in a very moderate way.   God elects some in Christ and leaves others to perdition (Belg. 16 ; Gal. 12). The Heid. Cat.. passes over the subject of predestination entirely (but see 404 : the elect church, *ausserwelte gemein*). The Helv. recognizes it, indeed, but warns : " Nevertheless we should hope well for all, nor is anyone to be rashly counted among the reprobates," and also : " It is to be considered as beyond doubt, if thou believest and art in Christ, that thou art elect " (a. 10 ; cf. SCHWEIZER, i. 290 f.).[1]   The definitions of the Westm. Conf. are more positive ; but even there the doctrine of predestination serves only to enforce the certainty of salvation, since it is the basis underlying the entire soteriological activity of God (3. 8, 6, also 1 : " Neither is liberty, or the contingency of second causes, taken away, but rather more firmly established "). But, in contrast with this moderation, in the theology of the leaders of the second generation (Beza, Peter Martyr, Musculus, Zanchi) the doctrine of predestination is advocated in its most extreme supralapsarian form. This emphasis upon predestination became but the more pronounced in the course of the development, and thus this doctrine, *i. e.*, of the divine decrees, gradually became the starting-point of Reformed dogmatics.

3. The growing prominence of this doctrine is reflected in the decrees of the Synod of Dort, A. D. 1618-9, which was devoted to its consideration (cf. Acta synodi Dortrechti habitae Lugd. Bat., 1620, Niemeyer, 690 ff. GRAF, Beiträge zur Kenntnis d. Synode v. D., 1825. SCHWEIZER, ii. 141 ff.). The occasion for the holding of this Synod was the Arminian controversy. JACOB ARMINIUS, from A. D. 1603 professor at Leyden, was brought, in consequence of his freer views upon the subject, into conflict with his colleague, FRANCIS GOMARUS, who held to the strict doctrine of predestination. His death occurring A. D. 1609, JAMES UYTENBOGAART and SIMON EPISCOPIUS became the

---

[1] In the *Confessio Sigismundi* (A. D. 1614), salvation is indeed traced to the pretemporal election, but it is, on the other hand, denied " that he (God) does not desire to have all saved " (Niemeyer, p. 650).

leading champions of the modified position. In A. D. 1610,
the Arminian leaders, branded as heretics by their opponents,
united in a protest, the REMONSTRANTIA (Schaff., The Creeds
of Christendom, iii. 545 ff.), whose positions are the following :
God determined, before the foundation of the world, to save
through Christ those of the fallen human race who should believe
on him. Man does not by the power of his free will attain
saving faith, but he is born and renewed to such faith by Christ
through his Holy Spirit. As the beginning, so also the progress
and completion of good in man, is dependent upon grace, but
grace does not work irresistibly. Those who have received the
Spirit and faith are able, through the assistance of grace, to
struggle against all temptations and come off victorious. The
question, whether the regenerated can fall from grace, is left
undecided.

The Remonstrants were at once confronted by the Contra-
remonstrants. The agitation increased, and it was decided to
settle the dispute by a synod, to which nearly all the Reformed
national churches were invited. It was held at Dort, lasting
from November 13, 1618, till May 9, 1619. Delegates were
present from the Palatinate, Hesse, Nassau, East Friesland,
Bremen, Emden, England, Scotland, Geneva, and German
Switzerland. It was a council which has no parallel in the history of Protestantism. In view of the overwhelming majority of
the Contra-remonstrants, the result could not be doubtful,[1] and
it is not surprising that the Remonstrants were from the first
placed in the position of defendants. The canons of the synod
cast a strong light upon the significance of the doctrine of predestination for the later Reformed church. We reproduce the
leading thoughts : The fact that only some of the race of sinful
men come to faith must be attributed to the eternal counsel of
God. God elected a definite number of men in Christ to
salvation, whilst in his justice leaving the others to perdition.
But the election is realized in the mission of Christ, the effectual
call, the bestowal of faith, justification, sanctification, and glorification (c. 1. 6, 7). Hence man is assured of his election by
its infallible fruits. Faith, the fear of God, sorrow for sin,
hunger and thirst after righteousness, constitute thus the basis of
our recognition of predestination ; or, the latter is the real basis
of the entire new life (1. 12). The activity of God in the interest of human salvation is therefore regarded as, in its entire
scope, nothing more than the actualizing of predestination.

[1] The assembly decided for the infralapsarian view of the doctrine, only
Gomarus still adhering to the supralapsarian formula.

Consequently, the sacrifice of Christ, or the satisfaction rendered by him, which is in itself considered of infinite value and abundantly sufficient for the salvation of all men, effects only the salvation of the elect (2. 3, 8). Hence, God accompanies the calling through the word with illumination through the Holy Spirit and the agency of regenerating grace: "He infuses new qualities into the will and makes it from dead, living; from evil, good; from unwilling, willing" (3. 10, 11).[1] This regeneration is a creative act of God, like the recalling of the dead to life. It is not accomplished by means of moral persuasion, and it does not impart to man the mere possibility of conversion; but it is a wonderful work of divine agency: "In order that all those in whose hearts God operates in this wonderful way may *certainly*, *infallibly* and *efficaciously be regenerated* and *actually believe*" (3. 12). In the case of the elect, therefore, the call certainly produces regeneration; but, on the other hand, it is also held that "as many as are called through the gospel are seriously (*serio*) called," so that it is to be ascribed only to their unwillingness if they are not converted (3. 8, 9). As this latter position is evidently out of accord with the former, so, if strictly interpreted, it carries us entirely beyond the bounds of the determinism which otherwise pervades the document.[2]

The certainty of the salvation of the elect is secured finally by the Perseverance of the Saints. Although the elect may fall into grave sins, and thereby lose for a time the consciousness of grace (5. 1-5), yet God so preserves his Holy Spirit in them that they can never fall entirely out of the state of grace nor commit the sin against the Holy Ghost (5. 7). The unchangeableness of the divine decree excludes the possibility that they should entirely fall away or be lost (5. 8).

4. In this document, the later Reformed view attained adequate expression.[3] Predestination was exalted to the position of a dogma, and its opponents defeated. But the decrees of Dort

[1] It is necessary merely to contrast with this the prudent remarks of the Formula of Concord (supra, p. 383) in order to understand the benefit of the Philippistic ideas.

[2] For, according to the leading principles here maintained, the call is an effectual expression of the divine will only in the case of the elect. Upon these it *must* have its effect; upon others it cannot have any inward efficacy at all. The idea expressed above is hence a concession, similar to the other one already noted, *i. e.*, that the death of Christ was sufficient to effect the salvation of all men, although it is intended to actually benefit only some.

[3] The decrees of Dort were officially recognized by the Netherlands; but they were received largely also in Switzerland, France, and the Palatinate, as well as by the Puritans.

—as also the Westminster Confession (supra, p. 419)—indicate a displacement of the original order of thought in the sphere of soteriology. Predestination was once a support for the assurance of salvation ; now it has itself been made the fundamental conception. The course was once from below upward, *i. e.*, from justification to predestination ; now it is from above downward, *i. e.*, from predestination to justification.[1] This transformation indicates something different from a victory for the theoretical idea of Calvin ; for the *Institutio* did not observe the order followed in the later statements of the doctrine, and, on the other hand, the Confession of Dort did not fully reproduce the rigor of the Calvinistic ideas. It was rather that practical conception of God which marks the writings of Calvin—God, the all-working Lord, who rules all things for his own glory—which was here victorious. This practical point of view must be kept in view in order to understand the later form and relationship of the doctrine of predestination.

But the definitions of Dort are also, in another direction, of the greatest historical significance, since they mark the breach between ecclesiastical Calvinism and its humanistically-inclined followers. Among the adherents and forerunners of the Reformation in the spirit of Zwingli and Calvin were not infrequently found representatives of the Erasmian ideals of reform. Practical ethical reforms, a large-hearted undogmatic Christianity, and scholarly tastes were often combined in these circles. It was among them especially that the Arminians found recruits. Their opposition by no means signified merely dissent from a single doctrine, but it was rather a protest against the enlargement of the sphere of dogma and against the limitation of exegetical freedom by dogmatic formulas. This is proved by the further history of Arminianism. As against this tendency, the Synod of Dort marks the victory of strict orthodoxy within the Reformed church.

5. This may be seen, as well as the important place occupied by the doctrine of predestination in the theological thought of the age, in the discussions called forth by the modifications of this doctrine, in themselves of no great moment, suggested by MOSES AMYRALDUS in Saumur (vid. Traité de la predestination et de ses principes, 1634 ; cf. SCHWEIZER, ii. 280 ff.). He maintains firmly the Reformed doctrine of predestination, that God has elected some to salvation, but has purposed to leave others to perdition. He, however, modified this position at two

---

[1] The original view may be expressed in the formula : Because there is justification, there is predestination ; the later view reverses this : Because there is predestination, there is justification.

points in a way which was out of harmony with the prevalent view. In the first place, he held, upon the ground that the will always follows the intellect, that the irresistible working of God upon the will of man is effected through the illumination of the intellect.[1] The process of conversion, he claimed, was thus made psychologically more intelligible.[2] Secondly, he introduced the idea of the so-called *hypothetical universalism* of grace. In order to throw some light upon the rejection of the reprobate —acknowledging, as he did, the absolute inscrutability of the grounds upon which the divine election is based—he conceives that there is in nature and history, independent of the gospel message, a certain dim revelation of the grace of God. Both forms of revelation have been made possible, however, only because satisfaction has been rendered to the divine justice by the sacrifice of Christ. But neither this general revelation, nor the preaching of the gospel in itself, can bring salvation to the sinner. This depends upon the divine election. Yet since, upon this theory, a certain announcement of the grace of God has in some way reached all men, the destruction of such multitudes is more easily accounted for, since all have been guilty of rejecting either the general or the special offer of grace.

Whether Amyraldus succeeded in establishing his positions, may well be doubted. But he was certainly justified in defending his position as within the bounds of orthodoxy. A French national synod, at Alencon, in A. D. 1637, certified to this, and simply advised him to avoid such unusual and startling forms of expression. Another synod in A. D. 1645 (vid. Aymon, Tous les synodes nationaux des églises reformées de France, 1710, vol. ii. 571 ff., 663), pronounced the same judgment. But the Swiss theologians were also greatly disturbed by the teachings of Amyraldus. They feared that they might thus become "the sport of the exultant Papists, Luthoromanites, and Arminians, to whose doctrines the windows were thus opened," and they felt themselves under obligation to construct a new symbol in the interest of orthodoxy. Thus originated, after many conferences and conflicts, the FORMULA CONSENSUS HELVETICA, composed by Heidegger, and adopted as a symbol, A. D. 1675 (Niemeyer, p. 729 ff.). This document rejects the view of Amyraldus (c. 6), teaches the strictest particularism in the election (4), and maintains with emphasis, that Christ died only for the elect and recon-

---

[1] Just as sin began in the intellect and passed thence into the will. Amyraldus in this follows JOHN CAMERO in Montauban († A. D. 1625); vid. SCHWEIZER, ii. 235 ff.

[2] Cf., on the other hand, the severe formulas of Dort upon the transformation of the will, supra, p. 423.

ciled them alone to God (13).　Only the elect come through the *external call*, which is serious and sincere (*seria et sincera*), to faith.　"But that, by the will of God, in the call thus universally announced, only the elect are led to faith, but the reprobate are hardened—this proceeds from the discriminating grace of God alone" (19).　The theory of predestination in its strict form is thus formally proclaimed as the doctrine of the church.[1]

In view of the above, we cannot avoid the conclusion that the theology of Calvin has become, in its essential points, the doctrine of the Reformed church.　What has been said in Section 79, 10 is, therefore, here equally applicable.

---

[1] It is here also, in view of the controversy of L. Capella with Buxtorf, declared, that the Hebrew text of the Old Testament " is inspired (θεόπνευστος) both as to the consonants and as to the very vowels or points, or as to the force and power of the points, and both as to the subject-matter and as to the words " (2).

PART III.

COMPLETION OF DOCTRINAL CONSTRUCTION IN THE ROMAN
CATHOLIC CHURCH.

§ 83. *Establishment of Medieval Theology as the Doctrine of
the Church by the Council of Trent.*

SOURCES. Canones et decreta Conc. Trid., ed. RICHTER ET SCHULTE,
1853. Doctrinal formulas also in STREITWOLF ET KLENER, Libri symbol.
eccl. Rom. i., and in DENZINGER'S Enchiridion, in Mirbt, Quellen z. Gesch.
d. Papstt., 124 ff. A. THEINER, Acta genuina conc. Trid., 2 vols., 1874.
LE PLAT,, Monum. ad histor. conc. Trid., 7 vols., 1781 ff. V. DÖLLINGER,
Ungedruckte Berichte u. Tagebb. z. Gesch. d. Conc. v. Tr., 1872. Con-
cilium Tridentinum, diariorum, epistularum tractatuum nova collectio, vol. i., ed.
Merkle, Freiburg, vol. i., 1901 ff. This work when completed will include the
protocols and a comprehensive collection of all other original documents bear-
ing upon the work of the Council ; vid. SEEBERG, in Theol. Litt.-bl., 1903, 6 ff.
PAOLI SARPI, Istoria del conc. Trid., 1619, Germ. translation by Rambach,
6 vols., 1761 ff. SFORZA PALLAVICINI, Istoria del conc. di Trid., 1656,
Latin translation, Antwerp, 1673, cf. RANKE, WW., vol. 39, append.,
p. 25 ff. SALIG, Vollst. Hist. d. trid. Conc., 3 parts, 1741 ff. MENDHAM,
Memoirs of the Counc. of Trent, 1834. RANKE, vol. 37, 129 ff. MAUREN-
BRECHER, in Hist. Taschenbuch, 1886, 147 ff.; 1888, 305 ff. MÖLLER-
KAWERAU, KG. iii. 215 ff. Upon the doctrines, vid. CHEMNITZ, Exam.
conc. Trid., 1566. SEEBERG, Beitr. z. Entstehungsgesch. d. Lehrdekrete v.
Tr., in Ztschr. f. k. Wiss., 1889, p. 546 ff., 604 ff., 643 ff., and in THOMASIUS
ii., ed. 2, 688 ff.

1. The Reformation made astonishing progress during its first
decades. The intellectual activity of the closing Middle Ages
had prepared the way before it both positively and negatively.
The old church was incapable of damming the current. This
can be plainly seen in the course of the early antagonists of the
new movement. In the general consternation, the Catholic theo
logians accepted the challenge of their opponents,[1] defended
with half-heartedness the worst outgrowths of medieval Chris-

[1] *E. g.*, the defense of indulgences by Tetzel and Eck. DIETENBERGER'S
publication, "Der leye, ob der gelaub allein selig mache." BERTHOLD of
Chiemsee, Tewtsche Theologey (ed. Reithmeyer, 1852). SCHATZGEIER'S
works (1543). A review of the positions maintained in this pre-Trentine
theology is given by LÄMMER, Die vortrid. kath. Theologie, 1858. Our
space forbids a fuller delineation, but a further study of this literature—from
a wider historical point of view than LÄMMER (Schul- und Ordens-Theo-
logie)—would yield valuable results.

tianity assailed by the latter, fell back upon the "authority" of the church, and relied for protection and victory in the great intellectual conflict upon politics and measures of external force. It was, indeed, a difficult task to defend the ancient positions at large. The theologians were soon divided into a number of hostile groups. In every important point of doctrine, the differences of the ancient schools of theology came to light. The Thomistic, and the Scotist, or Nominalist, views were still zealously advocated. The confusion was increased by the fact that the age looked with misconception and contempt upon the technicalities and methods of theology. Finally, it must not be overlooked that in their own camp, the champions of Roman Catholicism were compelled to hear clamorous demands for reform (Spain, Italy, the Oratorium, the Theatines, etc.). And yet all these tendencies—advocates of reform and strict adherents of the curia, mystics and dogmaticians of every class—constituted from one point of view, *i. e.*, their common opposition to Protestantism, a compact unity. The will was present, and a way was found. We can understand therefore how it came to pass that the internal differences were reconciled, and that, in the compromise, the ruder and coarser ideas and tendencies held the ascendant.

It is not our task to trace the reforms in the ecclesiastical life which were forced upon the Romish church by the Reformation. We are concerned only for the theological development. The Thomistic theology again assumed the lead in this post-reformation age. There had at an earlier period been a disposition to regard it as the specifically ecclesiastical doctrine. It now became a necessary equipment of the church. It was free from the foreign skepticism and critical temper of Duns Scotus, and it was simpler—a compacted system. Authority and dogma were here securely fixed and rationally established, and curialism found here a valiant champion. This theology was the destruction of the ideals and the faith which prevailed in the thirteenth century, at the time of the church's greatest power. We are not surprised that appeal should be constantly made to this earlier period. But in every attempted repristination of the former doctrines, the original accurate adaptation to actual circumstances has vanished, and the ideas are in consequence eviscerated and vulgarized. The system of Thomas, once a lofty conception of ecclesiastical idealism, was forced into the narrow limits of ecclesiastical positivism as fixed by Duns. There was no use in this age for the keen criticism of the Nominalists, their impertinent skepticism, and their remorseless dialectics— and they became a thing of the past. But there was need now of *implicit faith* and subjection to formulas—and these were retained.   That which was great and imposing in Thomas and Duns must be eliminated from them, and the dregs—their formulas—remain.

2. But if medieval theology had been shattered by its contact with the spirit and the religious needs of the modern man, then no victory could be permanent which should fail to take due account of this spirit.   Here the Jesuits found their field (cf. GOTHEIN, Ignat. v. Loyola u. die Gegenreformation, 1895). They required obedience and subjection to the church as strictly as had ever been done in the Middle Ages ; but they were shrewd enough to adapt the form of this requirement to the spirit and temper of the modern man.   The old theology was adopted, but it was adorned with the embellishments of modern humanistic learning.   The authors wrote in elegant style, and exegetical and historical studies were pursued with diligence. But it was in the Sacrament of Repentance that the force of the movement was most distinctly felt.   It was here that the Jesuit praxis gained its greatest triumph—it constructed the modern Roman Catholic sacrament of repentance.   The penitential discipline, which in the closing period of the Middle Ages had been so often utterly neglected (vid. DÖLLINGER and REUSCH, Gesch. d. Moralstreitigkeiten in d. röm.-kath. K., 1889, i., p. 20 n.), was revived and enlarged (ib. i. 19 ff., 61 ff. GOTHEIN, l. c., p. 324 ff.).   It became again, with its attrition and probabilism, its intentionalism, and mental reservations, the dominant force in the church, forming the historical counterpart to justification by faith and the new life of faith among Protestants.   And it was at this point that the worst elements in the theology of Duns and the Nominalists poured in a great flood upon the church, viz.: the minimizing of sin and the fondling of the sinner ; the dialectic trifling with the intentions, the will, and the sensuous impulses ; the juggling with the authorities (cf. LUTHARDT, Gesch. d. chr. Ethik, ii. 120 ff.).   But it was just in this way that the chasm between the church and the world was spanned.   In the confessional was learned the art of living in the world, continuing to cherish the spirit of the world, and yet being sure of salvation.   This was the "*dévotion aisée*," the compact of the church with the world.   Dogmas no longer formed the theme of the pulpit—that remained dangerous ground—but preachers discoursed eloquently upon the beauty of virtue and the repulsiveness of vice.   Thus the minds of men were diverted from the burning questions of the day.[1]   But a

---

[1] Cf. GOTHEIN, p. 319 ff., who very correctly says : "The preaching of the

compromise was effected also in the sphere of dogma. A new definition of faith was framed. Even the old faith of assent seemed to require too much—and it had no really practical object. It was therefore replaced by the faith of silent obedience. It is sufficient that one do not publicly oppose the formula of the church. Thus the dogma appeared to be saved, and faith made possible to everyone. In this way, the freest modern spirits could submit to the rule of the church. Everyone now became churchly again. As the art of the confessor met the wants of the great masses, so the change in the ascetic method was carried out in a way to suit the modern man. The age of merely sensuous discipline was past, as was that of simple obedience to authority. Ignatius accordingly attached little importance to outward asceticism. In its place came the inwardly transforming meditations of spiritual exercises (*exercitia spiritualia*). Ascetic exercises in the outward form were but means to an end (cf. GOTHEIN, p. 227 ff., 240, 416 ff.). In accordance with this, the aim of obedience is to be seen, not only in the outward subjection which it manifests, but in the regulation of the life according to one's own convictions.[1] And even though this aim should in separate instances not be attained, yet it would still have a suggestive influence upon the inward disposition. The deed thus prompted was done from obedience; but it was done by the man himself, and was done to further the glory of God.[2]

Such are some of the ideas which stirred Roman Catholicism after the Reformation. First of all, the return to Thomas, the ancient dogma and curialism, together with the rejection of all critical and skeptical elements in theology. In the sphere of dogma and ecclesiastical politics, Thomism appeared to gain a

Jesuits, dealing with things near and comprehensible, was well calculated to wean the Catholic masses from their anxiety about the dogmas; it was for them a soothing potion'' (p. 321). This method has become characteristic of the preaching of the Roman Catholic church.

[1] Upon this obedience, vid. DÖLLINGER AND REUSCH, Moralstreitigkeiten i. 623 ff. GOTHEIN (p. 332) finds a contradiction between the emphasizing of the will and the will-less obedience. This is scarcely justified, since the obedience is supposed to be rendered with delight and devotion (vid. ib. 455) as a voluntary personal act. On the contrary, it is just in this refined adaptation of all requirements to the temper and spirit of the modern man that the power of the Jesuits lies.

[2] Ignatius, too, speaks frequently of the relation of obedience to the '' glory of God'' (vid. GOTHEIN, p. 334, 426, 452, 455). If we would find upon the so widely different territory of Protestantism a parallel to this remarkable man, we must look for it not in Luther, despite the inner struggles which constitute a feature of similarity—but in Calvin, the fellow-student of Loyola at Paris.·

decisive victory.   But as its energy was lost under the pressure
of the positivism of Duns, so in the sphere of practical Christianity, the emasculating of the conceptions of sin and grace and
the refinement of the dialectics that excuses all things and makes
all things possible—for which Duns was also responsible—gained
ascendancy in the church.   Much was borrowed from the two
great leaders of medieval theology, but no way was found to
make use of that which was best in either.   The legacy which
they had left was deftly woven into the texture of the practical
church politics of the Jesuits.   In a word, it was Jesuitism—the
history of its spread being the history of the counter-reformation—which accomplished the great task of making the traditions of the Roman Catholic Middle Ages acceptable to the
Spirit of the modern age.   In this consists its historic significance, and in this way it became the counterpart of the Reformation.

3. The COUNCIL OF TRENT (A. D. 1545-63) discharged the
difficult task of marking out a median course between the conflicting views of scholastic theology, which was then proclaimed
as the official doctrine of the church.   Only with great difficulty
was the result attained.   The contradictory principles of the
opposing schools came into prominence in the discussion of
nearly every question.   It was possible to preserve an outward
unity only by the employment of the most studied diplomatic
arts.   The points of controversy were either avoided altogether
or carefully veiled.   Thus, to the student familiar with the history of the formation of the doctrinal definitions of the council,
the latter but too often appear as the deliberate productions of
church politics and diplomatic refinements.   The decrees do not
present to us a vigorous and joyous confession of sincere faith,
but formulas of compromise artfully welded together, bent to
this side or that with great labor and pains, and then finally filed
into proper dimensions.

4. Turning now to the doctrinal decrees of the Council of
Trent, we must first observe their attitude toward the Scriptures
and Tradition (session 4).   We note at the outset the complete
co-ordination of the two.   The council receives the Holy Scriptures and the traditions of the church "with equal feeling of
reverence" (*pari pietatis affectu*).   The former have God for
their author ; the latter have been " dictated by Christ or by
the Holy Spirit."   The opposition to this co-ordination of tradition with Scripture was in vain.   The council distinctly recognized the ecclesiastical traditions, being inspired as truly as
the Scriptures, as of equal dignity.   It carefully avoided, however, any designation of the particular traditions to which this

principle was to be applied.   " We receive those which we wish, but reject altogether those which displease us " (acta, i. 71 b) —these naïve words of a bishop betray the general attitude. The Vulgate is, with appeal to tradition, established as the authentic translation.   The apocryphal books of the Old Testament are also acknowledged.   The attempt to co-ordinate Scripture and tradition here, as always, results in the actual subordination of the former to the latter.   But it might now be rightly claimed that the church had gone half-way in the right direction.[1]

5. The 5th session established the doctrine of Original Sin. Here, too, the contrary principles of the opposing schools were manifest, the one party wishing to locate original sin in concupiscence, while the other regarded it as merely the lack of righteousness.   The subject was at once complicated by the question as to the relation of the Virgin Mary to original sin (acta, i. 145 f.).   The doctrine finally adopted is, in brief, as follows : (a) The first man, through his own fault, lost the righteousness and holiness into which he had been inducted (constitutus)[2] in paradise, and thereby fell under the wrath of God and the power of the devil.   There was, in consequence, a deterioration of the whole man.   " The whole Adam was by that offense of transgression changed for the worse according to body and soul."   Yet this is true only in the sense : " Although freewill had by no means been extinguished in them, yet it was weakened in its power and perverted " (ses. 6, c. 1).   (b) The sin and guilt of Adam passed over upon the whole human race. (c) Since the sin of Adam passed over upon his descendants " by propagation, not by imitation," human means are not able to release from it.   (d) Even children can be purified from their inherited condition only by the regeneration of baptism. (e) Not only is original sin forgiven by imputation through baptism, but the latter actually renews the sinner.   There remains in him, however, concupiscence (concupiscentia) or the tinder of

---

[1] Cf. the Profess. fid. Trid.: " I most firmly acknowledge and embrace the apostolic and ecclesiastical traditions and other observances and appointments, of the same church.   Also the Holy Scripture, according to that sense which the holy mother, the church, has held and holds, whose (part) I acknowledge it to be to judge concerning the true sense and interpretation of the Holy Scriptures, nor will I ever accept and interpret them except in accordance with the unanimous consensus of the 'Fathers.'"   In these declarations the Scriptures are not only assigned a place second to tradition, but they are also bound and gagged.   At the same time all attempts to attain a profounder religious or scientific knowledge of the Scriptures were excluded.

[2] Instead of constitutus, the original draft of the decree had creatus (acta, i. 130 b).   The words occurring in the original draft : " no part of the soul remaining uninjured," were also stricken out.   The first-mentioned change was required by the doctrine of the donum superadditum (supra, p. 115).

evil (*fomes*). Concupiscence is, indeed, sometimes spoken of by the apostle as sin, but this must not, according to the doctrine of the church, be understood in the sense "that it is in the regenerate truly and really sin, but because it comes from sin and inclines to sin." (*f*) These definitions do not apply in the case of the Virgin Mary.

6. The 6th session undertook to treat of Justification. Upon this topic much time and labor were expended. Sarpi relates that at least a hundred sessions were devoted to it, and that the second president of the council, Cervino, made emendations of the decree daily in order to meet all demands and make it acceptable to all parties. This may be readily understood. On the one hand, the opposition of the Protestants made a precise definition necessary ; on the other hand—and in this, as Cervino pointed out, lay the difficulty—the scholastic tradition afforded no material,[1] as in it justification was treated only, and that but briefly, as an element in the sacrament of repentance. The specific doctrine of justification, as it was now framed, was forced from the Roman Catholic church by the pressure of Protestantism. It was modeled upon the pattern found in Thomas. The doctrine was at the council divided originally into three sections: (1) How one may attain justification ; what part God has to do in it, and what part man ; what is the significance of faith in relation to it. (2) How one may preserve the justification attained. (3) How one may again secure justification when it has been lost. The first was the decisive section. Agreement was, indeed, soon reached upon certain definite fundamental points, *i. e.*, (1) That the call comes through the law and the gospel, to the preaching of which man gives assent through faith. (2) That grace is a new disposition of the soul, which is attested by good works. (3) Accordingly, there are everywhere traces of a certain synergism, and faith is the condition of justification, because the latter presupposes the acceptance of the teachings of the church. But within the lines of these fundamental Roman Catholic ideas, which all held in common, there were not lacking marked differences. The Thomistic tradition made the forgiveness of sins dependent upon the previous effectual equipment with grace (supra, pp. 121, 201); the Scotist view, on the contrary, placed forgiveness first, to be followed by the infusion of grace (supra, pp. 161, 201). Under the influence of the Protestant, or Pauline, doctrine of justification, the latter way of viewing the subject had come to have a significance which by no

---

[1] Note also the obscurity in the decree upon justification (c. 1), according to which all men are "servants of sin, although free-will had by no means been extinguished in them, yet it was weakened in its power and perverted."

means attached to it when understood in the sense of its greatest medieval advocate.[1] Both points of view were advocated at the council. The one party maintained : "The imputation of Christ effects in us that sins are not imputed, yet it does not justify ; but, after the remission of sins, God justifies us ; and justification is not remission of sins, because remission occurs before justification " (acta i. 176 a); the other party held that " God first infuses grace, then remits sins " (ib. 180 b). Finally, we meet in some of the fathers of the council a certain sympathy for the evangelical view.[2] Another difference appears in the fact, that one party (e. g., acta i. 179 b, 176 b, 180 a) would ascribe a meritorious character, disposing to the reception of grace, to works done under the general influence of the grace of the call (gratia vocationis),[3] whereas others would attach importance only to the works wrought through grace (ib. 181 a ; cf. Sarpi, ii. 366 ff.). There were divergent opinions also as to the measure of the divine influence and of human liberty in the bestowal and reception of grace.

As to the second section in the statement of the doctrine, the use of the sacrament, prayer, and good works were mentioned as the means by which justification once secured was to be retained. He who is in a state of grace can secure for himself by worthiness (de condigno) eternal life (acta i. 195). The restoration of the state of justification, when lost—treated of in the third section of the doctrinal statement—is accomplished through the sacrament of repentance, just as that condition was in the first instance attained through baptism. There is, however, this difference in the two transactions, that if, in the latter case, the lapsed one has not lost his faith, there is no necessity for the re-

---

[1] We are reminded here of PIGHIUS and GROPPER, both of whom represent the imputed righteousness of Christ as preceding the infused righteousness and place the emphasis, for the practical religious consciousness, upon the former. Cf. LINSENMANN, Tüb. Quart.-schr., 1866, 641 ff. BRIEGER, in Ersch. and Gruber's Encycl., sect. i.,.vol. 92, p. 135. DITTRICH, Gasp. Contarini, p. 660 ff. If I am not mistaken, this view, which was advocated also by Seripando at Trent (SEEBERG, Ztschr. f. kirchl. Wiss., 1889, 671 ff.), points back to the Scotist scheme. I have proved the Thomistic and unevangelical character of Cardinal Contarini's theory of justification, l. c., 657 ff.; cf. 676 f. In this KAWERAU agrees with me (MÖLLER, KG. iii. 129).

[2] Here may be mentioned JUL. CONTARINI (nephew of the well-known cardinal), THOMAS SANFELICE, Bishop of Cava, and the Augustinian Genera. SERIPANDO. We must be on our guard, however, against the error of pro nouncing the opinions of these men—without large reservation—as " evangel˜ ical." Vid. SEEBERG, l. c., 652 ff.; also the Archbishop BANDINI of Siena (Pallavicini, viii. 4. 7).

[3] Upon this term, vid. supra, p. 122.

establishment of this (ib. 188 b).[1] Furthermore, the lapsed
one must himself satisfy the temporal penalties of sin by works
of penance, since the sacrament of repentance releases him only
from the eternal penalties ; whereas by baptism both the temporal and the eternal penalties are removed.

The first draft of the decree was rejected (i. 203 ff.). While
a new formula was being prepared, a number of questions arose
for discussion, upon which no agreement could be reached : for
example, whether the inherent "righteousness" imparted to man
is sufficient, through the works which it produces, to merit eternal
life, or whether there is needed in addition the imputation of grace
for the completing of the human works. Very many prelates
maintained the former view, e. g., i. 258 b : "The justified
man, if he shall have retained his inherent righteousness and
done good works, is able with this to appear before the tribunal
of God without any other imputation of righteousness." Similarly, in regard to the assurance of salvation, some held it to be
unattainable without a special revelation, while others maintained
that one may, by virtue of his reception of the sacraments and
fulfillment of the commandments, be sure of his salvation. The
former is a Thomistic, the latter a Scotist theory (supra, pp. 121,
202). The discussions upon Justification by Faith are especially instructive. Both the *fide* and the *sine operibus* gave rise
to difficulties. There were not wanting some who desired to
strike out the last words from the decree (1. 340 f.); and they
were finally suppressed. Faith was conceived as a completed faith
(*fides formata*), or as another designation of the Christian religion (*religio christiana*), or as an inclination (*dispositio*) toward
justification. Cf. my studies in Ztschr. f. k. Wiss., 1889, 649-700.

We now turn our attention upon the finally accepted Decree.
We note traces of the original three-fold division of the material,
both in the positive statement of the decree and in the canons
condemning the contrary teachings (cap. 1-9, 10-13, 14-16, and
can.   1-22,   23-26,   27-33).   (*a*) Of justification, it is said :
"That it is a translation from that state in which man is born a
son of the first Adam into the state of grace" (c. 4).   The
order of salvation begins, in the case of adults, with prevenient
grace (*gratia praeveniens*), *i. e.*, with the call and the awakening (*excitans*) and assisting (*adjuvans*) grace which accompanies
it.   Man himself now, by consenting to the work of God and
working with him (*eidem gratiae libere assentiendo et co-operando*)
prepares himself for justification (c. 5).   There is thus, on the

[1] At this point the utterly unevangelical conception of faith, which pervades
the whole discussion, is clearly revealed.

one hand, a recognition of a coöperation preceding justification, and an acknowledgment that the works preceding justification are not altogether sinful (can. 7); while, on the other hand, the call comes before any merit exists (*nullis eorum existentibus meritis*). With this both the Thomists and the advocates of the *meritum de congruo* could be satisfied. The preparation for justification produced by this general influence of grace embraces, first of all, faith : "Receiving faith by hearing, they of free-will draw near to God, believing those things to be true which have been divinely revealed and promised," above all, that God out of grace will justify the sinner in Christ.[1] From fear of the divine justice, they rise in faith to the contemplation of the mercy of God: "believing that God will for Christ's sake be propitious." Now begins love to Christ as being the source of righteousness, "and afterward they are impelled against sins by a certain hatred and detestation," and this is followed by the resolution to lead a new life (c. 6). Thus faith, the beginnings of love to God and abhorence of sin, and the resolution to obey the commandments of God—are all wrought by the word before the actual infusion of grace.

(*b*) Upon this inclination (*dispositio*), or preparation, now follows justification itself : "which is not the bare remission of sins, but also sanctification and renewal of the inner man through the voluntary reception of grace and of gifts, whence the man from unrighteous becomes righteous" (c. 7). The opinion is expressly condemned : "that men are justified by the bare imputation of the righteousness of Christ, or by the bare remission of sins, the grace and love being excluded which are shed abroad in their hearts by the Holy Spirit and abide in them ; or, that the grace by which we are justified is only the favor of God " (can. 11). Justification consists in the renewal of the inner man, which occurs through baptism. By this, faith, hope, and love are imparted to man at the same time as the forgiveness of sins. This impartation is granted in such measure as seems good to the Holy Spirit, and "according to the peculiar inclination and coöperation of each individual" (c. 7).[2] The decree differs from Paul so widely as to understand by the term, "by faith " (*per fidem*), only that faith is "the basis and root of all justification," and by the term "freely" (*gratis*), that the faith and works

---

[1] Even here the expression is not clear: "Christ died for the sins of the whole world, for all ; but only they receive the benefit of his death to whom the merit of his passion is communicated " (*communicatur*, c. 2, 3).

[2] Here again all is designedly left in uncertainty. It is not clear whether the infusion precedes forgiveness or follows it. Similarly, the free imparting of grace is at once corrected by this "coöperation."

preceding justification do not merit grace.   As to the term, "without works" (*sine operibus*), nothing is said (c. 8).   Just as artfully is the question as to the assurance of salvation evaded, while at the same time a thrust is made "against the empty confidence of the heretics."   Certainly sins are forgiven through grace, but if any man boasts of the certainty of this forgiveness, or trusts in it alone, his sins are not forgiven !   It is not desirable that all who are justified should be sure of their justification. We dare not, of course, have any doubts as to the efficacy of Christ and the sacraments ; but everyone "may" have some fear as to "his grace" in view of his own weakness (c. 9).[1] This basal section of the document is a combination of two lines of thought : (1) The word is accompanied by a general preparatory influence of grace, which, in a psychological way, begets faith and a striving after the good.   (2) The power to pursue the good—faith, hope, and love—is infused into man by the sacrament of baptism.   He here receives justification as an impartation of grace, together with the forgiveness of sins.   Although the former of these ideas appears to approximate the Protestant position, yet the difference is very evident, since the influence here accorded to the word does not embrace the gracious acceptance of the individual, and since the emphasis in the discussion is laid, not upon the word and faith, but upon the sacrament and the inherent grace.[2]

(c) The gift of justification is preserved by obeying the commandments and by good works.   By this means there is effected also an increase of the justification : "Through the keeping of the commandments of God and of the church, faith coöperating by good works, they grow in that righteousness itself received through the grace of Christ, and are *more justified*" (c. 10). Justification, as a creative act of God, is, indeed, a momentary act (vid. Thomas, supra, p. 121); but, since it also establishes a moral condition, an advance in it is yet possible, as is indicated by the above citation.   Man ought to and can obey the divine commandments, since God gave them to him for that purpose. If the justified man, in seeking to render this obedience, fall into venial sin, he does not on that account cease to be righteous, or justified (c. 11).   No one dare be secure in view of his supposed predestination (c. 12 ; can. 15, 16).   The fundamental spirit of

---

[1] This chapter is a laboriously-constructed composition.   The decision of points at issue is avoided, but it inclines more toward the Thomists, since the opposition of the Protestant position—which is horribly caricatured— drove its authors in that direction.

[2] How the process is realized in the case of those baptized in infancy is not explained.

the Christian life is fear, which can never do enough to satisfy itself in the works of the prescribed devotion in the Roman Catholic church: "With fear and trembling let them work out their salvation in labors, in vigils, in alms, in prayers and oblations, in fasting and chastity ; for they ought to fear, knowing that they have been regenerated to the hope of glory and not yet to glory" (c. 13). To one reading these declarations in a central position in the formal statement of the church's doctrine, it must appear as though there had never been an Augustine in the Western church. The decree, in its practical aspects, moves in the circuit of Cyprian's ideal of piety, with its legal observances and its servile fear (Vol. I., p. 194 ff., 308). The moral life is dominated by this idea of *merit*. Whoever doubts this, falls under the anathema (can. 26). It is insisted, indeed, that these *merita*, being wrought in the members by the power of Christ, the Head of the church, and being a product of the *inherent righteousness*, are gifts of God (c. 16). But "the good works of a justified man" are also "merits of the justified himself" and, as such, merit eternal life (can. 32). It is evident enough—the old positions must be preserved unchanged !

(*d*) But the grace of justification may be lost, not only through unbelief, but by any mortal sin (c. 15). Those who have mortally sinned may again be justified (*rursus justificari poterunt*), *i. e.*, by the sacrament of repentance, and not, as some fancy, by faith alone ('can. 29). But to secure this, there is need, not only for *contrition*, but also for *confession*, at least in pledge and to be made at the appropriate time, together with *absolution* and the works of *satisfaction*. The eternal penalties, as well as the guilt, are removed by absolution, but for the canceling of the temporal penalties (*poena temporalis*) there must be works of satisfaction (c. 14). The practical experience of justification can be realized, accordingly, only within the limits of the sacrament of repentance.

This is doctrinally but a reproduction of the average scholastic views (cf. Chemnitz, Examen conc. Trid., i. 369). But the reception of this teaching is now the necessary antecedent of justification ; "which (*t. e.*, the Roman Catholic doctrine of justification) unless anyone shall faithfully and firmly accept he cannot be justified " (c. 16 fin.). In the apprehension of the Christian life here set forth, it is no longer a matter of the adoption of theological views, but of the acceptance of the fixed doctrines of the church, which are absolutely necessary to salvation.

7. The 7th session was devoted to the doctrine of the Sacraments. The scholastic conflict was here also at once renewed—

the one party maintaining that the sacraments include in themselves grace, the other regarding them as signs, which God, in view of his covenant, accompanies with his own energy (vid. supra, p. 126 f.). This question was not solved, nor was that of the " indelible character." [1] There was essential agreement in the general doctrine of the sacraments, and as the discussion of the differences might have led to the revival of profounder points of opposition between Thomists and Scotists,[2] it was decided to frame no decree upon the subject, but merely to condemn the teaching of the adversaries by appropriate canons. It is possible, however, to gather from the discussions the positive views which found general acceptance. They were essentially as follows : The seven sacraments were instituted by Christ (can. 1).   They are necessary to salvation, since without them the *gratia justificationis* cannot be secured (4).   They do not merely serve for the nourishment of faith (5), nor are they only external signs and badges of discipleship ; but they contain grace (6).[3] They work *ex opere operato*, and they—and not only faith—bring grace (8). Three of them impress a *character* upon the soul, " that is, a certain spiritual and indelible mark (signum)" (9).

8. In regard to Baptism also, the council contented itself with the framing of canons. The baptism of heretics is valid, provided it is administered " with the intention of doing what the church does " (4). Baptism does not release from the obligation to obey the law of Christ and all the commandments of the church (7, 8). Sins committed after baptism are "not forgiven simply by the remembrance and the faith of the baptism," *i. e.*, are not venial (10). Finally, the Anabaptists are condemned (12-14).

9. In the discussion of Confirmation, anathemas are pronounced upon the views : that it is not a true sacrament ; that it " was formerly nothing more than instruction " (1); that it may be administered by a " simple priest," and not only by a bishop (3).

10. It was not until the 13th session, that dogmatic utterances were again attempted. The doctrine of the Lord's Supper was now the topic of discussion. (*a*) Here again we meet the conflicting scholastic principles (SARPI, iii. 240 ff.). The positive

---

[1] This theory never recovered from the shattering criticisms of Duns (vid. supra, p. 128).

[2] Cf. PALLAVICINI, ix. 7. 1, and SARPI, ii. 597 ff.

[3] *Continere gratiam*—is the ancient formula (vid. supra, p. 126). Here Zwingli is rejected, but at the same time the way is paved for the Scotist theory.

dogma is as follows : Under the form (*species*) of the elements, Christ, the God-man, is really and substantially (*realiter et substantialiter*) present. He is, indeed, seated at the right hand of God "according to the natural mode of existing," which does not, however, exclude a "way of existing" (*existendi ratio*) which we cannot indeed express, but which we can recognize as possible, in accordance with which Christ, "sacramentally present in many other places, may be in his substance (*sua substantia*) present with us" (c. 1). By means of the consecration, there is a "conversion (*conversio*) of the entire substance of the bread into the substance of the body of Christ" (c. 4). The entire Christ (*totus et integer Christus*) is present under the form of the bread and in every portion of it (c. 3). Whereas in all other sacraments the sanctifying power (*vis sanctificandi*) enters only in the moment of the administration, in the eucharist the body of Christ is present already before the reception of the elements by the communicant, since the Lord called his body bread before the disciples had received it (c. 3). These views naturally led to the defense of "the worship of adoration (*latriae cultus*) which is due to the true God," for the host, and to the advocacy of the festival of Corpus Christi (c. 5). The blessing of the sacrament consists in the forgiveness of venial sins and in preservation from mortal sins. The sacrament is, further, a pledge of future blessedness and glory, and a symbol of the unity of Christ's body (c. 2).

The following, among other positions, are condemned : That the substance of the bread remains the same after consecration (can. 2); that Christ is present in the celebration, while it is being received (*in usu, dum sumitur*), but not before nor after (4); that the forgiveness of sins is the chief, or even the only, fruit of the eucharist (5); the rejection of self-communion by the priest (10); the characterizing of faith as a "sufficient preparation" for the reception of the sacrament (11).[1]

(*b*) It was not until the 21st session (A. D. 1562), that action was taken upon the demand for the granting of the cup to the laity, although this had been often urged upon the attention of the council. It was then decided, that the institution of the Supper does not require that all believers must receive it in both forms (c. 1.), and that the church has authority to introduce changes "in the administration (*dispensatione*) of the sacraments, their substance being preserved." This was done when it, "led by weighty and just reasons," ex-

[1] In the original draft of the canons, the demand of the cup for the laity is also anathematized (8. 10 ; act. i. 520 b). But political considerations led to the postponement of a decision upon this point (act. i. 503 a, 521 b, 528 b).

cluded the laity from the cup (c. 2). And there is the less occasion for objection to this upon internal grounds, since the entire Christ is present under each of the two forms, and hence no one is robbed of a blessing by the withdrawal of the cup (c. 3). Those are accordingly condemned who doubt that the church for just reasons withdrew the cup from the laity (can. 2). Finally, consideration of the question, whether the church must always exclude the laity from the cup, or whether " under any conditions" it might grant the cup to a particular nation or kingdom, was postponed. It was afterward decided that the matter should " be referred to our most holy lord " (*ad sanctissimum dominum nostrum*, act. ii. 96 ff.). No decision was given.

(*c*) In this connection we naturally consider the Mass, which was the subject treated at the 22d session. Christ, the Melchizedekian High-priest, in order that his sacrifice might not be obliterated, instituted in the Lord's Supper a sacrifice to be repeated by his disciples, " by which that bloody (one) once offered on the cross should be represented " (*repraesentaretur*). The repetition of the sacrifice is commanded by the words: " This do in remembrance of me " (c. 1). Whoever questions this exegesis, is anathematized (can. 2).[1] The same Christ who offered himself up upon the cross is here in the mass sacrificed in an unbloody way. The anathema is pronounced upon everyone who questions the reality of this sacrifice (can. 1). By this offering God is reconciled, and grants grace and the gift of repentance, and forgives even great sins (*peccata etiam ingentia*).[2] This sacrifice avails also for the dead. Its efficacy is due to the fact that it is in content identical with the sacrifice upon the cross, " only the method of offering being different" (c. 2). The entire Romish praxis in connection with the mass is thus dogmatically stated: Masses " in honor and memory of the saints " and private masses (*missae privatae*) (c. 36); the mixing of water with the wine (c. 7); the canon of the mass (c. 4); the cere-

---

[1] This theory involves a complete confusion of thought. The sacrifice of the mass is said to be merely a copy, or representation, of the offering upon the cross ; but yet it is to preserve the priesthood of Christ in the world and to repeat the sacrifice made upon the cross. We may easily understand what difficulties this must have occasioned in the debates. If the Lord's Supper— already in the first celebration—is the sacrifice of Christ, for what purpose then the subsequent death upon the cross? (*e. g.*, act. ii. 78 b, 82 b, 81 a, 83. DÖLLINGER, Berichte u. Tagebücher, ii. 81).

[2] Here, too, the decree is full of contradictions. According to this passage (c. 2), the mass, as a sacrifice of Christ, blots out all sins—even mortal ; but in c. 1 it is said : " the virtue of this is applied for the remission of those sins which are daily committed by us." In view of these diffiulties, we can understand the origin of the theory mentioned *supra*, p. 203, n. 1 ; cf. p. 335.

monies and garments; the alternation of the "lowered and elevated voice" (c. 5). Anathemas are pronounced upon all variations from these positions (c. 5-9). There was thus again adopted a feature of the popular Christianity of the Middle Ages, with all its murkiness and fallacies. The work of Christ was committed to the hands of the church, *i. e.*, the priests,[1] which was in perfect keeping with the entire tendency of the medieval doctrine of the sacraments.

11. The 14th session treats exhaustively of the Sacrament of Repentance. This is said to have been instituted by Christ (Jn. 20. 22 f.) for the forgiveness of the sins of those who have lost the grace of their baptism (c. 1, 2). Its essence consists in the priestly absolution (cf. supra, p. 136, 140 n.). It embraces *contrition, confession,* and *satisfaction.* It works reconciliation with God, which is at times followed in the case of the pious by peace of conscience and the comfort of the Holy Spirit[2] (c. 3). The opinion that repentance consists in "terrors of conscience" and faith is condemned (ib.). The decree then treats of Contrition (c. 4). This embraces sorrow for past sins and the determination to sin no more. It obligates itself to the right reception of the sacrament, "with confidence in the divine mercy and with a vow to perform the things remaining." Even when the contrition, being combined with love, is perfect, it does not itself work reconciliation, but does so only by virtue of the "vow of the sacrament" connected with it.[3] "Imperfect contrition," which is called attrition, not only does not make man a hypocrite, but is a gift of the Holy Spirit, by the help of which the sinner "prepares for himself a way to righteousness." It is not indeed able *per se* to lead the sinner to justification, but

[1] Observe also the crass conception of the effect of the sacrifice of Christ which was perpetuated by the sacrifice of the mass (vid. already Gregory, supra, p. 24). It would be a profitable exercise to trace historically the mutual influences of the theory of satisfaction and the doctrine of the sacrifice of the mass. The ecclesiastical sacrifice was not seldom the counterpart of the sacrifice of Christ.

[2] The language is instructive: "Reconciliation with God, which sometimes (*interdum*), in pious men and those receiving this sacrament devoutly, peace of conscience and serenity, with great consolation of spirit, are accustomed to follow." The *opus operatum* is of itself sufficient, and its "objective" result, the peace of repentance, is an accessory which sometimes in the case of the "pious" follows! Luther's comment was, that this "objective" result was not sufficient, but that a way should be sought by which the "*interdum*" might become the rule. The 5th canon pays its respects to this proposed search by condemning the view, that a man will by simply recounting his sins become a hypocrite.

[3] This requirement, in itself considered, removes a difficulty of the medieval system, but it is no more consistent with the connection in which it is found than was the position of Thomas. Vid. supra, p. 136.

it "disposes" him toward the sacrament. This is essentially the popular medieval doctrine. But it is now further asserted with emphasis, that no impartation of grace is granted " without a good motive of the recipients," and that the Ninevites advanced from the imperfect penitence of one beneficially alarmed (*utiliter concussus*) to " repentance full of terrors." Thus contrition again appears to be necessary, but it will be observed upon careful examination that even this presentation of the matter does not indicate any real advance upon the popular medieval view, as the latter also required a transformation of the attrition into contrition—by means, it is true, of the sacrament (vid. supra, p. 137, 175).[1]

Upon contrition follows Confession, in which all mortal sins which can be remembered—and that not only in general (*in genere*), but in particular (*in specie*)—must be confessed, together with a detailing of all the circumstances which may be essential to a correct judgment of the offense. Only thus can the priest form a correct opinion and find the appropriate penalty (c. 5). The priest has not merely the " ministry . . . of declaring that sins are forgiven; but after the manner of a judicial act, in which sentence is pronounced by him as by a judge " (c. 6). Sins of particular gravity are " reserved " for the decision of the higher authorities (bishop, pope) (c. 7).

Works of Satisfaction are designed, first of all, as a pedagogic measure, to restrain the sinner from future sins : " As by a kind of rein, these satisfactorial penalties make penitents more cautious and vigilant in the future." In the second place, they make the sinner like Christ, " since in making satisfaction we suffer for our sins." This determines, thirdly, their atoning, satisfactorial character, in which connection, however, emphasis is laid upon the fact, that it is only from the satisfaction rendered by Christ that " all our sufficiency comes." Of the design of satisfaction, it is said : " It is not only for the guarding of the new life and a medicine for infirmity, but also for a punishment and castigation of past sins " (c. 8). Finally, it is observed, that

---

[1] But the matter is not clear. The original draft of the decretal said of attrition : " but it suffices for the constitution of this sacrament" (act. i. 584 a). These words were indeed afterward stricken out, but the other statements in regard to attrition were allowed to stand (vid. PALLAVICINI, x. 12. 25, 26). But DÖLLINGER-REUSCH, Moralstreitigkeiten, i. 72, go too far in their attempt to acquit the Tridentine Confession of the charge of attritionism. Here, too, there was doubtless a deliberate avoidance of clear definition. The Constitution designates Pius VI. as the " Promoter of the faith " (*auctor fidei*) and describes the " fear of Gehenna " as a *donum supernaturale* and as a " way (*modus*) inspired by God, preparing for the love of righteousness" (DENZINGER, Enchirid. n. 1388).

there is a satisfactorial significance, not only in the penalties imposed by the priest, but also in the patient endurance of the
temporal chastisements which are appointed by God (c. 9).
But as to the relation of the latter penalties to the former—a
point often assailed by the later criticism (vid. supra, p. 210)—
nothing is said.

The canons condemn the Protestant doctrine, *e. g.*, that baptism contains the sacrament of repentance (2); that repentance
consists of only penitence (*terrores*) and faith (4); that contrition alone leads to hypocrisy (5); that the sacramental confession and the extension of its scope to cover "all and separate
mortal sins, which can be held in memory by due and diligent
premeditation, even those which are secret"—are not "of
divine right" (6, 7); that the priestly absolution is not a
"judicial act" (9); that Matt. 16. 19 and Jn. 20. 23 give to
all Christians the authority to pronounce absolution (10); that
bishops do not have the "right of reserving cases to themselves"
(11); that satisfaction is nothing more than faith in forgiveness
(12); that satisfactions are merely human traditions (14); that
it is a "fiction," that, after the removal of the eternal penalties,
temporal penalties often remain to be discharged (15).[1]

Indulgences were considered at the 25th session (Dec. 4,
1563). The impatient haste with which all business was trans-
acted toward the close of the council did not admit of a
thorough discussion of this subject (act. ii. 676 b. Sarpi, vi.
368 f.). But in order not to pass over the topic entirely, a
sketch was prepared in the last night (act. ii. 680 a). Since
Christ, it is held, gave indulgences to the church, this "practice very salutary for the people" is to be retained. Those who
pronounce indulgences useless, or challenge the right of the
church to grant them, are condemned. But in the granting of
them moderation should be exercised, in accordance with the
ancient and approved custom of the church, in order not to
weaken ecclesiastical discipline. The abuses which have attached themselves to the system of indulgences and have given
to the heretics an occasion for blasphemy against "this noble
name of indulgences," are to be corrected—especially "all unworthy (*pravos*) gains in return for the securing of these,
whence has come the greatest cause of abuses among the Christian populace, are to be entirely abolished."[2] Furthermore, the
bishops are to take notice of the abuses and make report of them
to Rome. The pope would then see to it, "that thus the favor

---

[1] As to public repentance, vid. sess. 24, De reformat. c. 8.
[2] Here, too, in the last minute it may be said, there was an alteration which

(*munus*) of the holy indulgences may be sacredly and without corruption dispensed to all believers.'' Even here, it will be observed, there was no surrender of any part of the traditional dogmatic position.[1]

Purgatory was also here discussed (ses. 25). The decretal drawn up in great haste (vid. ses. 6, can. 30) affirms that help may be given to souls in purgatory by the intercession of the saints and the sacrifice of the mass. This doctrine is to be preached without entering into discussion of the difficult questions connected with it. Masses, prayers, alms, and '' other pious works'' should be ''piously and devoutly'' rendered in behalf of the dead.

12. Extreme Unction (ses. 14) is said to remove the remains of sin in the dying and to lighten and confirm the heart (c. 2)—again, it will be observed, a reäffirmation of traditional doctrine.

13. The sacrament of Ordination, it is affirmed (ses. 23), was instituted in connection with the New Testament sacrifice. It was, therefore, instituted by Christ, who thereby committed to the apostles and their followers the ''power of offering and administering his body and blood both for the remitting and for the retaining of sins'' (c. 1). In view of the sacredness of the matter, it was appropriate that there should be in the church '' more and diverse orders of ministers.''` The Scriptures attest the priesthood and the diaconate, and the other ranks have been appointed from time to time since the early days of the church (c. 2). But since, according to the Scriptures, apostolic tradition, and the harmonious consensus of the Fathers, grace is conferred in ordination by words and outward signs, it is without doubt to be counted among the sacraments of the church (c. 3). Whoever denies this, or that the '' character '' is impressed by ordination, falls under the anathema (can. 4). The universal priesthood of believers is directly rejected. Not all have the same spiritual power (*spiritualis potestas*). Priests are discriminated from the laity not only by a '' temporary power.'' All these opinions are refuted by Eph. 4. 11 and 1 Cor. 12. 28 ff. The hierarchical government of the church is of divine appointment (*divina ordinatione*) (can. 6). Bishops are superior to presbyters (*presbyteris superiores*); to them are reserved confirmation and ordi-

---

was not in the interest of lucidity. '' Nevertheless, in this there were then stricken out certain words, which expressly forbade that certain large sums be impo-ed for the securing of indulgences '' (act. ii. 680 b); vid. PALLAVICINI, xxiv. 8. 1.

[1] Cf. the condemnation of the theses of the Synod of Pistoja in the Constitution, '' Auctorem fidei '' (1794), where the doctrine, that indulgences effect the forgiveness of temporal penalty, is presupposed (DENZINGER, Enchirid. n. 1403).

nation "and many other things." Ordination thus confers the spiritual office. The approval of the civil government, its call and authority, are not required in the sense "that without this ordination would be invalid."[1] On the other hand, all who are called and inducted into office only by the people or the civil authority are, like those who arrogate a spiritual office to themselves, "thieves and robbers" (Jn. 10. 1) (c. 4).[2]

14. The discussion of Marriage (ses. 24) is in very general terms, treating of its nature and the grace which Christ has won for it. As by the latter, Christian marriage is made superior to that of earlier times, it must now be reckoned among the sacraments. The canons discuss a number of canonical questions, forbid marriage to clerics and monks (can. 9), and condemn the view, that "it is not better nor more blessed to remain in virginity, or celibacy, than to be joined in marriage" (can. 10). Thus the medieval ideal of life is transported into modern times, which, aside from the practical ecclesiastical situation of the period, constitutes the historical significance of these canons.

15. Although the defenders of the old church placed the definition of the church at the centre of discussion—and rightly so —it was yet deemed prudent at Trent to refrain from a full discussion of this topic.[3] The debates occasioned by the presentation of the section upon ordination reveal the grounds for this caution. The highest officials desired a recognition of the papal system; but a great number of the bishops were thoroughly episcopal in their ideas. The original draft of the decretal upon ordination gave quite open expression to papalistic premises, the hierarchical organism being described as standing "under one supreme hierarch, the vicar of Christ on earth;" or (according to the second draft) the bishops standing under the pope being said to be "called to participation in care (*in partem sollicitudinis*), but not to plenitude of power" (*in plenitudinem potestatis*) (act. ii. 152 a, 155 b, with can. 7, 156 a). It was but logically consistent, when in the subsequent proceedings it was maintained, that all ecclesiastical authority belongs primarily to the pope, who can appoint and endow bishops at his will—he the sun, they the rays. The pope is, accordingly, the "vicar of Christ" in an absolute sense (*e. g.*, act. ii. 158 b, 175 a, 168 a: "Bishops are, therefore, not directly from Christ, but from the pontifex").

---

[1] Observe the prudent selection of language which would permit in praxis many interpretations. The entire conception is only a deduction from the sacramental character of ordination.

[2] The 8th canon also deserves mention : "If anyone shall say that bishops appointed by the authority of the Roman pontiff are not legitimate and true bishops, but a Roman figment, let him be anathema." Cf. act. ii. 155 f.

[3] Eck's Loci, *e. g.*, begin with a section, *De ecclesia*.

In opposition to this it was, however, maintained by many, that the pope is only " the chief vicar (*summus vicarius*) of Christ " (act. ii. 157 a, 165 a, 170 a, 193 b, et pas.). The apostles received their power, not from Peter, but from Christ.   Not Peter, but Christ, selected the substitute for Judas.   Thus the bishops also receive the " power for ruling and for governing the church of Christ " directly from Christ, and not from the pope (ib. ii. 188 f.).   Primacy is ascribed to the pope only for the sake of earthly order : " Therefore the bishops have (their) power originally from God, but from the pope as a second cause " (ii. 165). The episcopal power (*potestas*) comes from Christ ; the specific earthly territory within which it is to be exercised is assigned by the pope (ii. 168 f., 191 b, 192 f., etc.).   Hence the constantly-recurring controversy as to the introductory clause of the decretals, *i. e.*, whether to the word *synodus* should be added the words *universalem ecclesiam repræsentans*.   Under these circumstances, it was certainly the most practical course to follow the counsel of those who advised an avoidance of this point of the controversy. The final draft of the decretal presents, therefore, in an almost unrecognizable form the original curialistic conception.

This clashing of views is historically intelligible ; but it appeared impossible in the situation then existing to find any way of harmonizing the antagonistic parties.   Both agreed in acknowledging a double tradition.   To the bishops belongs, by virtue of the apostolic succession, a peculiar power over the church, and—the popes, as the successors of Peter, are the rulers of the church.   The episcopal party reasoned : If the bishops have apostolic power by *divine right*, then the papal primacy must have reference only to the external economy of the church. But no one ventured to draw the further inference, that the papacy must then exist only *by human right* (cf. supra, p. 167 f.), since the primacy of Peter was also instituted by God.   Here lies the fault of the system.   At this point the logic of the Curialists is brought to bear, the actual conditions in the church constituting an argument in their favor.   If the papal primacy exits *jure divino*, then the pope is the lord of the church ; to him belongs all power in the church ; and the bishops are only called by him to a share in his practical oversight (*in partem sollicitudinis*).   They possess the apostolic succession only in the form—illustrated in the apostolic age—of dependence upon Peter.   But, in this case, can the power of the bishops be described as of divine right?[1]   Does it not fall merely under

[1] Cf. the definition of the " divine right " oy the Jesuit Salmeron : " That is of divine right which God himself does directly through himself " (LE PLAT, Monument. v. 524).

the category of canon law, or *jus humanum?* This neither party could or would acknowledge. There was at this point a very patent failure of logical consistency. The apostolic succession bound the hands of the Curialists, while Peter stood in the path of the Episcopalists; and neither of these obstacles could be cast aside.

That which the council could not do was accomplished at a later day by the CATECHISMUS ROMANUS. The doctrine of the church is here treated on the basis of Thomas (cf. supra, p. 144 f.). The church is the assembly of believers (*congregatio fidelium*, i. c. 10). Pious and wicked live in it side by side, possessing in common "the profession of faith and the communion of the sacraments." The pious are united to one another "by the spirit of grace and the bond of love" (ib. quaest. 6). But in this fellowship there must prevail obedience to that rank which is not only entrusted with the proclamation of the gospel, but is also judge and physician for the sinful (c. 7, q. 2, 28). But all this power is concentrated in the pope. · "For there is indeed one ruler and governor of it (the church), the invisible Christ; but also that visible (one) who occupies the Roman chair as the legitimate successor of Peter, the chief of the apostles" (c. 10, q. 10; cf. 7, q. 24). Christ, who rules the church, "appointed a man as vicar and minister of his power; for, since the visible church needs a visible head, therefore our Saviour established Peter as the head and pastor of the whole race of believers" (c. 10, q. 11). The papalistic theory here finds a positive recognition which it could not have secured at the council.

The PROFESSIO FIDEI TRIDENTINA contains, as a component part of the Catholic faith—"outside of which no one can be saved"—the assertion : "I promise and swear true obedience to the Roman pontiff, successor of the blessed Peter, the chief of the apostles, and the vicar of Jesus Christ."

16. The council preserved intact the Christianity of the Middle Ages. Nothing of importance in it was overlooked. Even the worship of saints and the veneration of images and relics are commended (ses. 25). Medieval theology was exalted to the position of ecclesiastical dogma. In this lies the chief significance of the Confession of Trent. We cannot but regard with amazement the great work which was here accomplished. Out of the innumerable array of contradictory formulas and theories, a reduction was made which, in a most masterly way, presents the fundamental principles of the Scholastic theology. True, many things are passed over or concealed, and others are expressed ambiguously ; but, viewed as a whole, the result was a self-

consistent system of doctrine such as the Roman Catholic church had not hitherto possessed.   By this means the medieval theology was made independent of the shifting favor or disfavor of the schools.   The Tridentine Confession rescued the Scholastic theology from the Scholastics, by placing it upon an elevation beyond their reach.   But, comprehensive as was this doctrinal scheme in general, in particular points it was just as noticeably capable of indefinite expansion and modification.   Many variant tendencies and shades of opinion might be gathered beneath it, and interpret their views into its language.   In fact, Thomists and Scotists, Augustinian mystics and Jesuits immersed in practical politics, did just this, and did it without rebuke.   It is only the gospel, as understood by Protestantism, to which there is no bridge from the Tridentine theology.   In this direction only its declarations are clear, sharp, unyielding, and enclosed in a hedge of innumerable anathemas.   The supremacy of tradition, the sacramental infusion of grace, faith as an assent or subjection to formulas, the hierarchy as the almoner of supernatural powers and gate-keeper of the celestial world, the ascetic ideal of life—upon these points there is no wavering and no uncertain sound.   It is here, therefore, that the ways part.   The anathemas of the Tridentine canons branded as heresy the Protestant teaching in its entire compass, as the decretals elevated the Roman Catholic theories to the position of dogmas.   This constitutes the two-fold significance of the Council of Trent.

§ 84. *Revival of the Augustinian Doctrine of Grace and Its Ecclesiastical Rejection.*

LITERATURE.   LINSENMANN, Mich. Bajus, 1867.   MÖLLER-SEEBERG, PRE. ii., ed. 3, 363 ff.   SAINTE-BEUVE, Port-Royal, ed. 3, 6 vols., Paris, 1867. REUCHLIN, Gesch. v. Port-Royal, 2 vols., 1839-44.   SCHNEEMANN, Entstehung u. Entwicklg. d. thomist.-molinist. Controverse, 2 parts, 1879-80. SCHRÖCKH, KG. seit der Reformat. iv. 310 ff.   HENKE, Neuere KG., ii. 98 ff.   RANKE, Französ. Gesch., vols. iii. and iv.   SCHILL, Die Constitution Unigenitus, 1876.   REUSCH, Index der verbotenen Büeher, ii. 457 ff., 539 ff., 552 ff., 724 ff.   THOMASIUS-SEEBERG, DG. ii., ed. 2, 717 ff.   HARNACK, DG. iii., ed. 3, 647 ff.

1. The Augustinian doctrine of grace found recognition at Trent in but a mutilated form.   More emphasis was laid upon it in the Romish Catechism, as the latter was influenced by Thomas.   But the ethics and dogmatics of the Jesuits soon banished this doctrine entirely from the regnant theology. There were not lacking, indeed, some theologians of Augustinian tendencies to oppose this growing Pelagianism.   They

29

asserted themselves in Belgium and France, being influenced also
by humanistic predilections.   Their distinguishing characteristic was merely the advocacy of the Augustinian doctrine, their
orthodoxy being unassailable in all other points.   More important, therefore, than their views is the papal condemnation which
was visited upon them, as this falls with all its force upon
Augustine himself.   They were accordingly in the right who, in
A. D. 1563, laid before the pope the complaint : " Under a
mask, they condemn the doctrine of Augustine," or : " O
grief ! Augustine is condemned under the name of the Jansenists " (REUSCH, Index ii. 469).   We must trace the course
of the controversies induced by Baius, Jansen, and Quesnel.

2. MICHAEL BAIUS (De Bay, A. D. 1513-89), a professor in
Louvain, advocated the Augustinian doctrine of grace.   Original
righteousness, as the subjection of the sensuous nature to the spirit
united with God, is not to be designated as an added endowment
(*donum superadditum*).   If man was created good by God, then
concupiscence, as the rebellion of the flesh against the spiritual
nature, is really sin.   Man is utterly depraved by sin : " free-
will without the assistance of God avails for nothing except for
sin."   As the entire man, so also the entire race has become
subject to sin.   The justification of the sinner takes place through
the transformation of his will by God : " Our evil will is transformed into a good (will)."   This new will man now employs
in good works : " Righteousness is properly obedience to the
law." [1]   But since this righteousness wrought in man upon earth
by grace can never be flawless, God here grants as supplementary
the forgiveness of sins.   " Justification is nothing else than a
certain continuous progression both in the practice of virtues and
in the remission of sins."   This whole structure of thought is
thoroughly Catholic. [2]   Nevertheless, the 79 theses of Baius were
condemned by Pope Pius V. in the bull, *Ex omnibus afflictioni-*
bus.   Thus genuinely Augustinian ideas were rejected, *e. g. :*
That the will without grace can only sin ; that even the con-

[1] This is a definition strongly emphasized by Bajus, *e. g.*, in his theses condemned by the pope, n. 42 : " Righteousness, by which the man is justified
by faith, consists formally in obedience to the commandments ;" 69 : " The
justification of the wicked man occurs formally through obedience to the law,
but not through a secret communication and inspiration of grace which causes
those who are justified to fulfill the law through it."

[2] The independent role here attributed to the forgiveness of sins—which is
not, as in Thomas, the recognition of an act of making righteousness already
accomplished—reminds us of PIGHIUS and GROPPER (supra, p. 434, n. 1).   Let
it not be overlooked, however, that forgiveness removes only the guilt
(*reatus*) of sin, whereas grace in the proper sense atones for or transforms the
act itself.

cupiscence that is contrary to the will is sin ; that the sinner is moved and animated by God alone, and not by the ministrations of the priest ; that merits are bestowed upon men gratuitously.[1] Bajus recalled his assertions.

3. The controversy associated with the name of the Jesuit, LUDWIG MOLINA († A. D. 1600), ran its course without producing any permanent result. In his work, *Liberi arbitrii cum gratiae donis, div. praescientia, providentia, praedestinatione et reprobatione concordia* (A. D. 1588), an acute attempt is made to reconcile Pelagianism, Semipelagianism, and Augustinianism. Man is even in his sinful state free to perform, not only natural, but also surpernatural works, the coöperation of grace being presupposed. Grace elevates and stimulates the soul, making it capable of supernatural works ; but the real act of decision is not wrought in the will by grace, but is made by the will itself, the will being, however, in union with grace. Thus, as the free decision of the will and the capacitating of the soul for the supernatural (grace) in their coöperation mark the beginning of the state of acceptance with God (*Heilsstand*),[2] so both combined in simultaneous combination (*concursu simultaneo*) produce the supernatural acts. They work together like two men who tug a vessel with one rope. Now the thoroughgoing coöperation thus attained becomes a mere illusion if all the free acts of created beings are really recognized, as among the Thomists, as willed

[1] A few of the important theses (vid. the Bull in DENZINGER, Enchiridion, 881 ff.) are as follows : 20. " No sin is by its nature venial, but every venial sin merits eternal punishment." 25. "All works of unbelievers are sins, and the virtues of the philosophers are vices." 27. " Free-will without the assistance of the grace of God avails only for sin." 28. " It is a Pelagian error to say that free-will avails for the avoiding of sin." 35. " Everything which the sinner, or servant of sin, does is sin." 51. " Concupiscence, or the law of the members and its depraved desires, which men now willingly feel, is a real disobedience of the law." 73. " No one except Christ is without original sin ; hence the blessed virgin is mortal on account of sin contracted from Adam, and all her afflictions in this life, just as those also of other righteous persons, were avengings of actual or original sin." 58. " The penitent sinner is not vivified by the ministration of the absolving priest, but by God alone, who, suggesting and inspiring (his) repentance, vivifies and resuscitates him ; but by the ministration of the priest guilt alone is removed." 8. " In those redeemed by the grace of Christ, no good merit can be found which is not conferred gratuitously upon the unworthy." 77. " Temporal satisfactions do not avail to expiate *de condigno* temporal punishment remaining after sin has been pardoned." 10. " The remitting of the temporal punishment, which often remains after sin has been pardoned, and the resurrection of the body, are properly to be ascribed to nothing but the merits of Christ."

[2] Molina gains a place for *prevenient grace* by maintaining that, in the first act (*actus primus*), before the advent of the second act (*actus secundus*) of the will, *i. e.*, in the habituality of the will while not as yet realized in acts, grace alone acts. The coöperation is posited only of the *actus secundi*.

by God himself of his own original motion. At this point, Molina's theory of a "median knowledge" (*scientia media*) is introduced. God, he maintains, foresees what his free creatures under any given circumstances will do or not do. The *scientia media* is, therefore, a knowledge of the contingent future. By means of it God beholds the entire future, and he orders the course of the world in accordance with the knowledge thus in his possession. In contrast with the theory of a causal connection of events strictly determined by divine decree, there is here retained a place for human freedom. Upon the metaphysical questions which are thus left unanswered, it is not needful for us to enter. The aim of Molina is clear. Grace and human freedom are to be combined with one another in a peaceful union. The ancient problems are to be thus solved in a very simple way. Predestination and reprobation may be readily accounted for by the *scientia media*, by virtue of which God foresaw which men would coöperate with grace, and which of them would not do so. But this foreseen free activity of man is to be regarded only as a means, and not as a cause, of predestination, as the latter idea would be Semipelagian.

It is true, a critical eye will readily discover that the combination thus assumed is only apparent, and that the Augustinian-Thomistic conception of grace is here torn out by the roots. It is not the all-working power of the divine will which effects salvation ; but the hands of God and man work together as coördinate factors. Synergism in its boldest form is the confessed first principle of this theology. But the opposition to it inaugurated by the Dominicans was crippled by the championship of the Jesuits, who adopted this theory of grace as the official doctrine of their order. The popes did not dare to give decision against the powerful order, and hence the whole matter was buried in the sessions of the commission of the *congregatio de auxiliis gratiae* without the promised papal declaration. As a result, the Jesuits were allowed to propagate their doctrine without opposition from the church. Cf. SCHNEEMANN, l. c. MORGOTT, in Kirchenlex. viii., ed. 2, 1737 ff., and iii., ed. 2, 897 ff.

4. The most powerful reaction against the lax and Pelagianizing moral principles of the Jesuits came from circles which centred about the abbey Port Royal, situated not far from Paris. The medieval form of piety was indeed preserved in these circles, but they drew their inspiration from Augustinian Mysticism, and in this they believed themselves to possess the means of rescuing all serious-minded persons from the nets of the Jesuits. Hence it was that this party could find its program in a work which professed to be, and really was, nothing else than a revived Augustine. This was

the publication of the Bishop of Ypres, CORNELIUS JANSENIUS
(† A. D. 1638): *Augustinus seu doctrina Augustini de humanae
naturae sanitate, aegritudine, medicina adv. Pelagianos et Massi-
lienses*. It was published in A. D. 1640, Jansen having completed
it shortly before his death.   As Bradwardina had done at an
earlier day, Jansen holds up as a mirror before his age, sunken in
Pelagianism, the genuine teachings of Augustine.   This is done
with historic fidelity, and not, as was the case with the English
theologian, in order to establish a deterministic system.   Original sin, he taught, has filled the entire human race with lust and
ignorance.   The sinner is now free in the domain of sin.   Justification by grace is by no means to be identified with the forgiveness of sins, as is done by the Protestants.   Christ brings the
"medicinal aid of the Saviour."   Irresistible grace, and this
alone, works the good in men : it "makes them will" (*facit ut
velint*).   Grace consists essentially in the inspiration of good
concupiscence, or love.   Grace aims at love as its goal, and love
is crowned with the forgiveness of sins.   These ideas are mar-
shaled within the lines of the Augustinian doctrine of predestination.

The Augustinian character of Jansen's teaching cannot be
called in question.   He in reality simply reproduced Augustine.
Yet this book precipitated a bitter conflict, which convulsed all
France for more than a century.   Upon the suggestion of the
Jesuits, Pope Urban VIII. in A. D. 1642 in the bull, *In Eminenti*, called attention to the condemnation of the doctrine of
Bajus, of which it declares the teaching of Jansen to be a revival.
This was the signal for the strife.   Protests were uttered
against the moral principles of the Jesuits, the secularized Christianity of the age, and the smothering of liberty by the church.
The contestants strove with flaming words and glittering irony,
not only for dogmatic formulas, but for the genuine Christian
religion—for the rights of the inner life and personal conviction
(*e. g.*, ANTON ARNAULD, BLAISE PASCAL).   Nevertheless, they
thought it still possible to remain good Catholics, and no attempt
was made to assail the infallibility of papal deliverances.   Outwardly less untrammeled, and with a fuller inward apprehension
of the truth, than the representatives of the great reformatory
movement upon the same territory in the fifteenth century, the
Jansenists were at one with their predecessors in the idealism
which thought it possible to mend and make available for practical purposes the old garment by sewing upon it the great patch of
a reform conducted upon the ancient ecclesiastical and national
basis.   When this attempt at the restoration of the church without tearing down any part of her structure collapsed, Jansenism

fell with it ; not, indeed, without contributing its share to induce the great calamity which overwhelmed its adversary in the Revolution.

But the doctrine of Augustine never again gained the ascendency. Five theses selected from Jansen's book by the Sorbonne were condemned by Innocent X. in the bull, *Cum occasione* (A. D. 1663). They were as follows : 1. "Some commandments of God are impossible to righteous men willing and striving according to the present powers which they have : there is lacking also to these the grace by which they would be made possible." 2. "Resistance is never offered to inward grace in the state of fallen nature." 3. "For meriting or demeriting in the state of fallen nature, there is not required in man freedom from necessity, but freedom from coërcion suffices." 4. "The Semipelagians admitted the necessity of prevenient inward grace for single acts, even for the beginning of faith, and they were heretics because they maintained that this grace was of such a nature that the human will was able either to resist it or to conform to it." 5. "It is Semipelagian to say that Christ died, or shed his blood, for all men whatsoever."[1]

Inasmuch as the Jansenists did not wish to call in question the papal authority, they attempted to extricate themselves from their embarrassing position by discriminating between the "question of fact" and "the question of right," maintaining that, as a matter of fact, Jansen had not advocated the theses which the pope thus—and rightly—condemned. The compromising position of the Jansenists soon brought them into further difficulty, as Pope Alexander VII. plainly declared, that the five theses had been condemned "in the sense intended by the same Cornelius Jansen" (Constitut. *Ad sanct. Petri sedem*, A. D. 1665)! The five theses remained therefore under condemnation, and even the "obsequious silence" observed by Clement IX. (A. D. 1668) was declared insufficient by Clement XI. (1705). Port Royal was destroyed, A. D. 1710. The particulars must be referred to Church History.

5. Yet once again the embers of the strife were rekindled. The occasion was the publication by the Oratorian, PASCHASIUS QUESNEL († A. D. 1719), of his Meditations upon the New Testament (*Le nouveau test. en français avec des réflexions*

---

[1] These theses, although torn from their context and therefore difficult to fully comprehend, no doubt reproduce the doctrine of Jansen. The first thesis means to maintain, that for each separate good work there is necessary a reception of efficacious grace (*gracia efficax*). It must be borne in mind also that beneath them all lies as a premise the predestinarian *gratia irresistibilis*. Cf. HENKE, ii. 103 f. REUCHLIN, Port-Roy. i. 761, 778 f.

morales sur chaque verset).   At the instigation of the Jesuits,
the notorious constitution, *Unigenitus*, condemned no fewer
than 101 theses of this biblical commentary.   With terrific
directness, not only the Augustinian theology, but the entire
structure of Augustinian Christianity was here condemned.   It
is heretical to teach : that the natural man is only sinful ; that
faith is a gift of God ; that grace is given only through faith ;
that faith is the first grace, and the first grace is the forgiveness
of sins ; that grace is needed for all good works ; that grace
works in us what God has commanded.[1]   But, in reality, this
condemnation strikes at a higher authority than Augustine.   It
is directed, in the last instance, against Paul, who had occasioned the Council of Trent so many laborious hours (cf. supra,
p. 436); for Quesnel was influenced not only by Augustine, but
also by Paul (*e. g.*, thesis 26).   Intense excitement was awakened (the Appellants *versus* the Acceptants), but it subsided
without result when compelled to face the firm alliance of the
papal infallibility (to which the Appellants could at best submit

---

[1] We cite a few of the most important theses : 38. " The sinner is not free,
except toward evil, without the grace of the Redeemer." 62. " He who
does not abstain from evil except from fear of punishment, commits it in his
heart, and is already guilty before God." 48. " What else can we be than
darkness, than error, than sin—without the light of faith, without Christ, and
without his love ? " 39. " The will which grace has not anticipated (prae-
venit) has no light (lamp) except for erring," etc. 29. " Outside of the
church no grace is granted." 73. " What is the church, except the assembly
of the sons of God, abiding in his bosom ? " 74. " The church, or the
entire body, has Christ the incarnate Word as its head, but all the saints as its
members." 76. " Nothing is broader than the church of God, since all the
elect and righteous of all ages compose it." 79. " It is useful and necessary
for every age, every place, and every class of persons to study and know the
spirit, piety, and mysteries of the Holy Scriptures." 80. " The reading of
the Holy Scriptures is for all." 82. " The Lord's day ought to be sanctified
by Christians by readings of piety and, above all, of the Holy Scriptures."
85. " To forbid to Christians the reading of the Holy Scriptures, especially
of the gospel, is to forbid to the children of light the use of the lamp, and to
make them suffer a kind of excommunication." 69. " Faith, the practice,
increase and reward of faith—all is a gift of the pure generosity of God."
26. " No graces are given except through faith." 27. " Faith is the first
grace and the fountain of all others." 28. " The first grace which God grants
to the sinner is the remission of sins." 51. " Faith justifies when it works,
but it does not work except through love." 2. " The grace of Jesus Christ,
the efficacious source of every kind of good, is necessary for every good work ;
without it, not only is nothing done, but neither can anything be done."
3. " In vain, O Lord, dost thou command, unless thou thyself dost also give
what thou commandest." 11. " Grace is nothing else than the will of the
omnipotent God, commanding and effecting what it commands." Are not
these almost literally Augustinian propositions ? And how remarkable is the
condemnation of the 29th thesis ! To the naturalistic Pelagianism of this bull,
even Cyprian appears dangerous !

only against the protest of their consciences) with the influence of the court and the Jesuit interpretation of the gospel. Benedict XIV. finally decided, that the Constitution, *Unigenitus*, must be regarded as legally valid, but that no one was to be persecuted who did not publicly assail it (A. D. 1756). We note here the intrusion of that worst of all the externalizations of faith effected by the Jesuits, viz.: the theory that assent to dogma is not necessary, but silent submission is sufficient. Within the whole range of the History of Doctrines, there is no official document which so richly merits condemnation as scandalous as does this. And yet it has not only been confirmed by a great number of popes, but accepted by several French councils and "by the entire Catholic world" (vid. DENZINGER, ante n. 1216). It marks the definite expulsion of Augustinian piety from the official Roman Catholic church.

6. Here may be mentioned the dogmatization of the doctrine of the Immaculate Conception of the Virgin by Pius IX. in the Constitution, *Ineffabilis deus* (8. dec., 1854). In proportion as the strict logical consistency of the Augustinian doctrine of sin and grace was impaired, did it become possible to give to the doctrine of tne immaculate conception dogmatic authority, especially as the masses of the populace had long regarded Mary as miraculously endowed and holy. The pope now proclaimed:

"We declare, pronounce, and define, that the doctrine which holds that the most blessed Virgin Mary was in the first moment of her conception, by the peculiar grace and privilege of the omnipotent God, in view of the merits of Christ Jesus the Saviour of the human race, preserved immune from all pollution of original sin, has been revealed by God, and is therefore to be firmly and constantly believed by all the faithful," etc. Thus, here too, a doctrine of the Scotist and Jesuistic theology triumphed.

§ 85. *Completion of the Romish Dogma of the Church. The Vatican Council.*

SOURCES. PLANCK, Neueste Religionsgesch., vol. i. 2, 1787 ff. V. MÜNCH, Vollst. Sammlg. aller älteren u. neueren Konkordate, 2 vols., 1830 f.; ib., Gesch. des Emser Kongresses u. seiner Punktate, 1840. NIPPOLD, Handb. d. neuesten KG., ed. 3, vols. i. and ii. MEIER, Zur Gesch. d. röm.-deutschen Frage, 2 vols., 1871-3; ib., Febronius, ed. 2, 1885. H. SCHMID, Gesch. d. Kath. Kirche Deutschlands, 1874. HENKE, Neuere KG., vol. iii. NIELSEN, Gesch. d. Papstt. im 19 Jarh. i., ed. 2, 1880; ib., Aus dem inneren Leben d. kath. Kirche im 19 Jarh. i., 1882. FRIEDBERG, Sammlg. von Aktenstücken zum Vat. Conc., 1872. Die Constitutiones d. Conc., also in DENZINGER, Enchirid. n., 1630 ff., and MIRBT, Quellen, p. 255 ff. FRIEDRICH, Gesch. d. Vat. Conc., 3 vols., 1877, 1883, 1889. QUIRINUS, Röm.

Briefe v. Conc., 1870. ACTON, Zur Gesch. d. Vat. Conc., 1871. FROMMANN, Gesch. u. Krit. d. Vat. Conc., 1872. JANUS, Der Papst u. d. Conc., 1871.

1. The ancient struggle between the curial and the episcopal systems was, as we have seen, not brought to a conclusion at the Council of Trent. The episcopal view subsequently asserted itself with great energy in both France and Germany. The inconsistencies, which had always been involved in this view (vid. supra, p. 446), were even now not eliminated. Despite the resort to rationalistic and illuministic principles in support of it, the advocates of the episcopacy did not yet venture to draw the final conclusions to which their theory logically pointed. In the nineteenth century, it was definitely vanquished.

In France, under Louis XIV., the *Declaration du clergé de France* had plainly asserted the liberties of the Gallican church. It contains the following propositions: 1. " The power of Peter and his successors extends only to spiritual, but not to secular and temporal things, so that in matters of the latter kind princes are in no way subject to the spiritual government." 2. The "full power (*plena potestas*) of spiritual things" inheres in the popes in such a way that at the same time the decrees of tne Council of Constance, "upon the authority of the general councils," recognized by the popes and the entire church, also remain in force. 3. The papal power is, therefore, to be circumscribed : "The rules, customs, and institutions adopted by the Gallican kingdom and church are also valid." 4. "In questions of faith also, the chief parts belong to the supreme pontiff, and his decrees pertain to all churches and every church ; nevertheless, his decision is not irreversible (*irreformabile*) unless the consensus of the church shall have been added to it " (in MIRBT, 209 f.).

These articles were at various times condemned at the instigation of Rome. Louis XIV. did not dare to maintain them without modifications. It was Napoleon I. who, in A. D. 1810, made them a part of the civil law. But since he, without regard to the French episcopate, in the Concordat of A. D. 1801, combined with the pope in regulating the affairs of the French church, he in reality brought the latter again under the dominion of the pope. The despot used the pope for the furtherance of his own plans ("if there had not been a pope, we would have had to invent one "), but he incidentally increased the latter's power.

2. In Germany, the suffragan, NICHOLAS OF HONTHEIM, in Treves, impressively advocated the episcopalistic theory in his work published under the pseudonym, FEBRONIUS, *De statu ecclesiae et legitima potestate Romani pontificis*, . . . *Bullioni, 1763."* All the apostles, he maintained, were on an equality, and all were entrusted with the same power of the keys. The

bishops have their authority directly from Christ. The papal primacy dare not claim to exceed that of Peter himself. The papacy is designed only to serve for the promotion of church order. It is not the pope, but the general council, which represents the church. The pope is subordinate to the whole council, and is merely on a parity with its separate members. These principles, it was held, must be carried out with all energy.

Occasion was given for the practical application of these ideas by the controversy in regard to the nunciatures. A part of the episcopal functions had been unlawfully assigned to the papal nuncios.[1] When the Elector of Bavaria now applied for a nuncio, the archbishops of Cologne, Mayence, Treves, and Salzburg attempted to break the curial system. Their representatives prepared at Ems the so-called "Punctation of Ems" (vid. VON MÜNCH, Emser Kongr., 103 ff.). In this it is acknowledged that the pope is "the chief-overseer and primate of the whole church— the central point of her unity, and endowed by God with the jursidiction requisite to this end." But, on the other hand, the bishops are the immediate successors of the apostles, and hold directly from Christ the power to bind and loose and te make laws, as well as to grant dispensations from the latter (*e. g.*, in regard to hindrances to marriage). Romish bulls and breviaries are therefore valid only in so far as they are acknowledged by the bishops. By these principles, the ground is torn from beneath the nunciatures.

But Bavaria persevered in her request, and the pope in his claims. The attempt to exalt the episcopacy based upon divine right above the primacy based only upon human appointment was met by Rome with the exaltation of faith in the divine right of the papacy : "And that this is the power of primacy, which he holds by divine right in order that he may outrank other bishops, not only in the degree of honor, but also in the fullness of supreme power." The theory, that Christ gave to all the apostles equal authority, and that all bishops have the same claim as the pope to participation in the government of the church, is rejected as folly (vid. the brief, *Super soliditate*, 1786, in Denzinger, n. 1363).[2] The old title of Peter as the rock did good service also in this modern age.

3. It must be noticed, finally, that at the Synod of Pistoja (A. D. 1786), under the leadership of Recci, a reform program

[1] Vid. MEIER, Die Propaganda, ihre Provinzen und ihr Recht, ii. 180 ff. The Nunciatures are the incorporated claims of the curial system, in which the latter, against law and order, seeks to encroach upon the episcopal jurisdiction.

[2] The brief condemns the book of *Eybel*, "Was ist der Papst?" 1782. Cf. Kirchenlex. iv., ed. 2, 1152 f.

was prepared, which also included a recognition of episcopal principles. But the constitution, *Auctorem fidei* (A. D. 1794), condemned, in connection with the whole program, particularly the theses : " That the Roman pontifex is the ministerial head ; " " that the bishop has received from Christ all necessary rights for the good government of his diocese ; " " that the rights of the bishop, received from Jesus Christ for the governing of the church, can neither be altered nor impeded " (Denzinger, n. 1366, 1369, 1371). The French Revolution at this point distracted the growing interest in these plans, associated as they were with the general movement of the Illumination.

4. On the other hand, the conditions prevailing in the age of the Restoration were as favorable as possible for the papacy. Talented advocates arose for its defense, who skillfully directed the thought of the age, impressed, as it now was, with its need of authority, toward Christianity, identifying Christianity at the same time indissolubly with the papacy. The kingdom of the devil must be destroyed and the old order of things restored. Two citations may serve to exhibit the spirit in which this program was carried out : " If it were permitted to establish degrees of importance among the things of divine institution, I would place the hierarchy before the dogma, so much is it indispensable to the maintenance of the faith " (de Maistre). " The company of the devil cannot but recoil before the company of Jesus " (Bonald). With the open and sinister reactionary ecclesiastical tendencies was combined a romantic enthusiasm for the rock of Peter, which had defied the storms of the Reformation and the floods of the Illumination, and a deep interest in the political reaction. It was imagined that these drifts of sentiment might now be encouraged without danger, since the Illumination had ensured absolute security against all Romish attempts.   This was a sad mistake. At scarcely any period since the great days of the Middle Ages has the Curia ever displayed such a susceptibility to the whole course of events, such a ready adaptation in tactics and in speech, such zeal in well-considered action—as in the past century. The results are clearly manifest. The concordats, for which Napoleon had set the example, and which were from A. D. 1816 concluded with many states, subjected the church to the pope as her lord.   Their significance consisted less in that which they contained than in the fact that they were concluded, and that, too, with the pope directly, without any recognition of the bishops. The course of action deliberately chosen by the curia with a view to the achievement of the end in view was acquiesced in by the states and nations.   No more is henceforth to be heard of the episcopalistic ideas of reform which

agitated so many minds before the Revolution.   Curialism has triumphed.

5. The VATICAN COUNCIL (1869-70) really did no more than give dogmatic form to the conquest thus long before achieved. There was at the outset laid before the council an outline of the faith (*Schema de fide*).   This was approved April 24th, 1870 (vid. MIRBT, Papsturkunden, p. 255 ff.   Denzinger, n. 1630 ff.). This summary contains nothing new.   In opposition to Rationalism and Naturalism, the pope declares with the assent of the bishops,[1] "relying upon the word of God written and handed down," what is the true doctrine.   First of all, God—" an entirely simple and unchangeable spiritual subsistence "—is acknowledged as the Creator and Ruler of the world (ses. 3, c. 1).   Secondly, it is taught, that God has revealed himself.   This revelation "is contained in written books and traditions without writing." The latter come from Christ or the apostles ; the former embrace the books approved at the Council of Trent, which are to be found in the Vulgata.   These books are canonical, not because they contain the revelation without error, " but for this reason, that, written by inspiration of the Holy Spirit, they have God as their author, and, as such, they have been handed down to the church."   The church establishes the meaning of the Scriptures : " That is to be considered as the true sense of the Sacred Scriptures, which the holy Mother, the church, whose office it is to judge concerning the true sense and interpretation of the Holy Scriptures, has held and holds " (c. 2).[2]   To this revelation we are to render obedience in faith : " We are under obligation to render obedience of intellect and will in faith." Faith consists in this : " that we, the grace of God inspiring and assisting, believe the things revealed by him to be true."   This "assensus " pertains to all things " which are contained in the written or handed-down word of God, and which are by the church, either by solemn decision or in her ordinary and universal ministrations, pronounced worthy to be believed as divinely revealed " (c. 3).

6. But these were merely incidental matters.   More and more plainly the real object had in view by the curia and a considerable number of the members of the council was revealed.   The

---

[1] Ses. 3, c. 1 : "The bishops of the whole world, assembled to this ecumenical synod by our authority in the Holy Spirit, sitting and judging with us"—these words, as indeed the very superscription of the " Constitution : " " Bishop Pius, servant of the servants of God, the holy council approving," assume as granted the curial conception.

[2] Vid. this view of inspiration and the interpretation of Scripture also in the apostolic circular letter of Leo XIII. (A. D. 1894), in MIRBT, Quellen, p. 280.

pope was, in a formal address, requested to present a paper upon the Infallible Authority of the Pope. A smaller party made some opposition, expressing themselves no opinion upon the subject, but pronouncing the definition of the new dogma as inopportune and ill-timed. The pope "felt" his infallibility.[1] An appendix upon the infallibility was added to the outline previously presented to the delegates (in FRIEDBERG, Akten-stücke, p. 572). What difference did it make, that the public opinion of Europe arose in amazement against the new dogma : that the anti-infallibilists assailed the document before them with well-grounded arguments; that they besought the pope to withdraw or modify the passages in question in the new paper laid before the Council on May 10th? The pope held to his opinion. The Infallibilists produced a mass of arguments—some of them most astonishing—for their theory.[2] Many of its opponents left the city. On July 18th, the vote was taken, of the 535 bishops present only two voting "Non placet."

The constitution, *Pastor aeternus*, defines the new dogma. In order that there might be one episcopate, and that the multitude of believers might by it be held together in harmony, Christ placed Peter above the other apostles : "In him he established both a perpetual source of unity and a visible foundation upon whose stability should be constructed the eternal temple" (Pref.). The "primacy of jurisdiction over the universal church of Christ" was imparted by Christ directly and immediately to Peter and to Peter alone. It conflicts with the teachings of the Scriptures to say that "this same primacy was conferred, not immediately and directly upon the blessed Peter himself, but upon the church, and through it upon him as a minister of this church" (c. 1). This power has passed from Peter upon his successors : "Whence whoever succeeds in this chair of Peter, he, according to the institution of Christ himself, obtains the primacy over the universal church" (c. 2). According to this doctrine, which is demanded by the Scriptures and tradition, the pope—as the Florentine decretal has taught—is to be recognized. as the successor of the prince of the Apostles, "the

---

[1] Cf. his declarations : "As for infallibility, being the priest Mastai, I always believed it ; now, being the pope Mastai, I feel it ;" and with this, his pendant to the well-known saying of Louis XIV.: "The tradition I am" (Quirinus, p. 107, 555).

[2] Among the "proofs" were the passages, Lk. 22. 32 ; Iren. iii. 3 ; the title, Vicar of Christ ; the fact that Peter was crucified with his head downward, his head thus bearing the burden of his body ; that Peter himself in Sicily claimed for himself infallibility ; and that Mary, being asked, declared that Christ had indeed granted this plenary authority to Peter. Vid. QUIRINUS, p. 412 ff.

true vicar of Christ and head of the whole church and father and teacher (*pater et doctor*) of all Christians." To him belongs the actual "power of jurisdiction" (*potestas jurisdictionis*). This power is "ordinary" and "immediate," and extends to every single believer, *i. e.*, the pope exercises such power, not only in special cases as a last resort, but he can employ it at all times and under all circumstances. It is a "truly episcopal" power, inasmuch as the pope is authorized to perform all episcopal functions in all places. Every individual is therefore bound to render direct obedience to the ordinances of the pope in all things affecting faith and life, or the discipline and government of the church: "This is the doctrine of Catholic truth, from which no one can deviate without forfeiting faith and salvation." The pope is the supreme judge of believers (the faithful). It is an error to desire to appeal from his decision to a council as a higher authority (c. 3). The popes have always been acknowledged as the supreme authority in matters of faith. A "charism of never-failing truth and faith" has been bestowed upon Peter and his followers, in order that the church may remain free from error and the pure doctrine be preserved in power. Since in our time many oppose this authority, the new dogma is, for the glory of God and the salvation of the nations, formulated as follows:

"Therefore we . . . the holy council approving, teach and declare to be divinely revealed the dogma : That the Roman pontiff, when he speaks from the chair (*ex cathedra*), that is, when he, exercising the office of pastor and teacher of all Christians by virtue of his supreme apostolic authority, defines the doctrine concerning faith or morals (*fide vel moribus*) which is to be held by the universal church, he acts, through the divine assistance promised to the blessed Peter himself, with that infallibility by which the divine Redeemer wished his church to be instructed in the defining of doctrine concerning faith and morals ; and therefore the definitions of such Roman pontiff are *of themselves, but not by virtue of the consent of the church*,[1] beyond revision (*irreformabiles*). If anyone (which may God prevent) shall presume to contradict this our definition, let him be anathema" (c. 4).

7. The excitement caused by the Vatican Council subsided within a remarkably short period. A small party of pious Idealists protested vigorously, but few listened to them. There was no opportunity for a popular demonstration upon the part of Old Cath-

---

[1] The words: "*non autem ex consensu ecclesiae,*" which in as crass a form as possible express the personal infallibility, were not placed before the council until July 15th (FRIEDRICH, Documenta ad illustr. conc. Vat. ii. 318).

olicism. The unexampled rapidity with which the aims of the council were secured may be understood when we remember that the whole world had long since become accustomed to think of the pope as the legitimate lord of the Roman Catholic church, and that the very ancient claims of the popes to be the bearers of divine truth had ever since the days of the Counter-reformation been constantly gaining a firmer foothold in Catholic circles. That which in the days of the reform-councils would have appeared inconceivable could become a reality in the Nineteenth Century—the acknowledgment of the infallibility of the pope as over against and superior to that of the council. The Vatican Council caused but little excitement in the church because it produced nothing new. But there was also another reason. The influence of Jesuitical teaching had long since dissipated the interest of the Catholic masses in doctrine as such. Their attitude toward the dogmas of the church was very largely the same as toward the Scriptures—they have them as though they had them not. Obedient submission to the formulas, *i. e.*, refraining from criticism of them, is sufficient. Or, the dogmas might be used for an ascetic disparagement of the "reason." But the real sources of religious life do not, for the Roman Catholic masses, lie in the realm of doctrine. Sacraments and good works, relics and scapularies, the sacrifice of the mass and all kinds of holy water, the mother of God with her appearances and her adoration, the worship of the heart of Jesus and that of the Virgin,[1] etc.—bring grace and regulate the intercourse of the soul with God. The most of these customs could not well stand the test of dogmatic authorization. But there was no need of this as long as the dogma and the church but left room for them. It must not be forgotten that it was only at the Council of Trent —and then only under the pressure of the opposition of the Protestant church and its Augustana—that Roman Catholicism secured any consistent system of ecclesiastical doctrine. It is, therefore, not difficult to understand that, now that the strain of the conflict has been moderated by time, the church should gradually sink back into the medieval forms, although a somewhat different shading may be given by the influence of Jesuit skill upon the character and temper of the modern church life. In the Oriental churches, dogma has become a mystery and a relic (supra, Vol. I., p. 306); the mystagogy of worship is to produce life. In the West, it has become chiefly a means for discipline and an incentive to obedience; but—at least in the present age—it ap-

[1] Vid. esp. REUSCH, Die deutschen Bischöfe u. der Aberglaube, 1879. For Italy material is furnished in TREDE, Das Heidentum in der kath.-Kirche, 1889 ff.

pears to represent as little vital influence in the church as in the Middle Ages. And yet the Roman Catholic church has of late again—not without some effort—urged the study of Thomas and prescribed it as a panacea.. Truly it is possible to adorn the graves of the prophets without catching their spirit! But no one can deny that, even in Catholic theology, the spirit of serious labor and earnest effort has not died out. Are there still lurking here the elements which are yet to infuse into Roman Catholicism the "principle of progress" (Schell)? Shall scientific culture—as Thomas understood it—or shall the ecclesiasticism of the Ultramontanes assume the spiritual leadership in the further doctrinal development of Roman Catholism?

Be that as it may, the Protestant student of the History of Doctrines cannot turn from the subject without calling attention to the different conception of Dogma which prevails in his own church as contrasted with the positions which the churches of the East and of Rome have finally assigned to their dogmatic utterances. It was the church of the "pure doctrine" which made Dogma again a vital and powerful factor in history. Luther put new life into the ancient dogma. It had become a toy of theology ; he made it a sword of the Spirit. The ideas embodied in divine revelation, not mysticism nor magic, are to give birth and guidance to the church of the gospel. "Doctrine" and "dogma" have their source in the ideas grasped by faith. The evangelical church as such cannot sink into "undogmatic Christianity"— there is always in the individual soul an eternal "undogmatic" life—without losing its very life. But while the church clings steadfastly to her doctrine, she does it, and must ever do it, in the spirit of Luther. This will mean : (1) That the dogma which she proclaims, and which regulates her preaching, must be the *evangelical doctrine of salvation.* Her doctrines must find their source in the redemption which is in Christ, and their goal must be faith in Christ. They must be from faith and for faith. The significance of this may be most clearly seen in the teachings of Luther himself, above all in the manifest relation of his interpretation of the Creed to the Creed itself. (2) That the evangelical church must always continue to labor upon her dogmatic statements, always ready—not only in principle and in word —to prove and improve them upon the basis of the divine revelation given in the Scriptures. From this it follows, (3) That the evangelical church highly values a free theology, in the assured conviction that such a theology has a vital function to perform in the church of the pure doctrine. The immense accumulations of dogmatic tradition will otherwise rest heavily upon her, as upon the Romish and the Oriental churches. She cannot pass around this mountain by any arts of interpretation or of silence, but must surmount it. It is true, life itself will here silently and unobserved accomplish much. The course of the ages alters the accentuation placed upon various parts of the traditional doctrinal structure. Some members of the organism become rudimentary and others attain fuller development. But all of this will not suffice. If evangelical theology is not to become merely an episode of the " History of Religion," if it is to remain an ecclesiastical science—and who will seriously doubt that it shall so remain ?—then must it in the future, as in the past, recognize its calling to study the treasures of tradition with all the means which God has given to man, with all the watchfulness and keen criticism which the importance of the subject demands (biblical and historical theology), and, upon the basis of this earnest and conscientious study, seek the forms and formulas which the age may require for a proper comprehension of the gospel (systematic theology). The " ancient truth " remains ; the method of presenting it will change, as it has constantly changed in the past. From this may be readily understood the entirely different attitude which the Protestant—Luther himself being an illustrious example—assumes toward the dogma of the church from that which the Roman Catholic must hold. Even the thought of a " new dogma " has for him—however fully he may realize the immense historical difficulties which such a proposition would have to face, since all the forms of the church's life are attached to the ancient dogma[1]—nothing repulsive in principle, so long and in so far as this should be a true expression of the divine revelation in the Scriptures.

But against one stupendous error must the spirit of the Protestant world be ever scrupulously upon its guard, viz.: the delusion so readily embraced by the ecclesiastical politician, that sufficient honor has been accorded to the dogma of the church when it is publicly confessed and silence maintained as to the points in which it contradicts the convictions personally held. We may in our day hear voices openly raised in defense even of the ancient delusion of " implicit faith." The principles above stated protest with united voice against this thoroughly unevangelical position, and the protest is abundantly confirmed by the History of Doctrines.[2] What we Protestants need is a living and life-

[1] Cf., e. g., LASSON, Zur Theorie des Dogmas, 1897, p. 18 ff., 100 f., 112, 120.

[2] The demand might at this point be made, that the History of Doctrines

producing, an intelligible and convincing system of doctrine (dogma)—not a relic of the past nor a manual of ascetic practices (supra, 463, 430).   Such a system of doctrine the evangelical church possesses in the ancient symbols and the Confession of the Reformation.   To comprehend and give proper expression to the religious depth and the wealth of practical suggestion of these inherited treasures, with unhesitating return, if need be, to the ideas of the original sources of evangelical truth —the *ritornar al segno*—is the task of the Protestant theology of the present, and, in a measure also, of the History of Doctrines.

should trace the development of Christian teaching down to the present time (cf. the works of BAUR and HAGENBACH upon the subject, and KRÜGER : Was heisst and zu welchem Zweck studirt man DG. ? 1895).   But, although the possibility of thus extending the scope of the History of Doctrines must be granted, yet we must maintain also the scientific propriety of the presentation of the publicly acknowledged and binding statements of the church's official doctrine.   It is a historical fact, to be recognized by the historian—whether or not it be in accord with his own preferences—that the church of the present knows and acknowledges such a public doctrine (*doctrine publica*).   Our position is confirmed by the consideration, that in any such " History of Modern Theology" there would be lacking the organic principle of the proper History of Doctrines, viz.: the relation of the views therein delineated to the Dogma of the future ; for who shall to-day venture to say which of the negations and affirmations, which of the buttressing arguments and destructive criticisms, which of the omissions and supplements registered in the progressive history of theology, shall lead to the completer Dogma of the future ?   The history of theology may be represented as the history of the varying experiences of Dogma ; but to attempt to treat it as "Prolegomena to any and every future" dogma is a most indefinite and uncertain task.   The writing of a history of modern theology—when one considers the state of the investigations which must necessarily precede such delineation—is in itself an undertaking sufficiently great, without the complication of keeping ever in mind the relation of the theological views of the present to the yet unknown official statements of the future.

Finally, even a history of the Union (cf. LOOFS, DG. 462 f.) does not, in my opinion, strictly speaking, lie within the province of the History of Doctrines ; for the Union, as known to history, did not effect any transformation or reconstruction of the dogmas of the church.   The original aim to accomplish something of this character spent its force in a comparatively short time.   Cf. the decree of the Cabinet, February 28, 1834 : " The Union indicates and effects no surrender of the previous confession of faith, nor is the authority which has been hitherto enjoyed by the confessional writings of the two evangelical confessions destroyed by it.   Adherence to it is merely an exhibition of the spirit of moderation and mildness," etc.   The details of the movement lie within the sphere of Symbolics.

INDEX.

A.

Abelard, estimate of, 56, 57 f., 62, 64, 96, 98, 100 n., 185; opposition to, 60; on reason, faith, tradition, Scriptures, 58; Trinity, 58 f.; sacraments, 59, 7⁻, 79; knowledge, 60; person of Christ, 64, 155; atonement, 70, 110; love, 71; Lord's Supper, 77 n.; repentance, 81 f.; contrition, forgiveness, 81; confession, 81, 92 n.; purgatory, 81; satisfaction, 82; communion of saints, 144.

Ability, human. In Gregory, 21 f.; Semi-Augustinians, 32 f.; Thomas, 118 f.; Bonaventura, 120; Biel, 138; Duns, 159; Bradwardina, 207; Luther, 243 f., 256; Zwingli, 313; Augsburg Confession, 335; Melanchthon, 349; Synergistic controversy, 367 f.; Formula of Concord, 383; Calvin, 399; Arminius, 421; Remonstrants, 422; Amyraldus, 425; Council of Trent, 433 f.; Quesnel, 455 n.

Absolution. In Gregory, 24; Early Middle Ages, 44; Hugo, 82, 92; Pullus, 83; Lombard, 83, 92; Gratian, 92; Council of Treves, 92 n.; Thomas, Duns, 137 f.; Bonaventura, 137 f., 142 n.; Durand, 142 n.; John of Paltz, 176; Wessel, 210; Luther, 234, 240; Augsburg Confession, 342; Council of Trent, 438, 442, 444.

Acceptants. In Unigenitus controversy, 455.

Adiaphora, 388.

Adiaphoristic controversy, 364.

Adoptionist controversy, 27 f.

Advent, Second, 344.

Aegidius of Colonna, works of, 187; on sin and grace, 187; immaculate conception, 188 n.

Aepinus. On descent into hell, 377.

Agobard, works of, 27; on Scriptures, 101 n.

Agricola. On law and gospel, 251, 366.

Alanus ab Insulis. On attrition, contrition, 136 f.; preaching, 92 n.

Albert, The Great. Works of, 96, 98; philosophy of, 99, 105; influence of, 99; on original state, 114; infused grace, 115; sacraments, 128; confirmation, 130; Lord's Supper, 134; extreme unction, 140; marriage, 143.

Albert of Padua, philosophy of, 187.

Alberus, Zwingli's letter to, 319.

Alcuin, works of, 27, 29; on Adoptionism, 28; Lord's Supper, 35.

Alexander III. On Nihilianism, 65; and Jansenists, 454.

Alexander of Hales, estimate of, 98 f.; on person and work of Christ, 110 f.; original state, synteresis, 114; original sin, 116; indelible character, 128; sacraments, 125 f., 126 n.; Lord's Supper, 131 f., 133; repentance, 135 f.; attrition, contrition, 136 f.

Alger. On Lord's Supper, 76 f.

Alloeosis. In Zwingli, 321; Luther, 324.

Almsgiving, 91, 92.

Amolo, works of, 30; on predestination, 32.

Amsdorf. In Majoristic controversy, 364 f.; in Synergistic controversy, 367 f.; on conversion, 367 f.

Amyraldus. On predestination, 424 f.; revelation, human ability, conversion, 425.

Anabaptists, opposition to, in Luther, 292; Zwingli, 316; Augsburg Confession, 339; Formula of Concord, 389; Council of Trent, 439.

Andreae, Jacob, sermons of, 382 n.; on concord, 380.

Angels. In Gregory, 17, 25.

Anselm, estimate of, 56, 58, 64, 98; legalism of, 69; on immaculate conception, 34; universals, 56; faith, person of Christ, 57; atonement, 66 ff., 200; sin, 67, 110; satisfaction, 67 f., 267, n. 2; forgiveness, 68; God, 69; devil, 67, 70; example of Christ, sacraments, 72.

Antinomian controversy, 365.

Apocalypse, 300.

Apocrypha. In Luther, 300; Council of Trent, 432.

Apology of Augsburg Confession, as standard, 332; on justification, 338; repentance, 342; sacraments, 343.

Appellants. In Unigenitus controversy, 455.

Arabic Philosophy, 96.

Aristotle, study of, 55, 96 f.; influence of, 98; philosophy of, 95; Luther on, 224 n.; Melanchthon on, 348, n. 3; on attributes, 369.

Arminian controversy, 421 f., 424.

Arminius. On predestination, 421 f.

Arnauld, Anton, vs. Jesuits, 453.

Arno, philosophy of, 60; on real presence, 66.

Asceticism. In Mystics, 179 f.; Savonarola, 190 n.; Luther, 276 n.;

Augsburg Confession, 339; Calvin, 403, n. 3, 441; Reformed church, 415, 420; Jesuits, 430; Council of Trent, 438, 449.

Assurance. In Gregory, 23; Thomas, 121; Biel, Duns, 202; Formula of Concord, 388; Calvin, 404, 407; Synod of Dort, 422, 435; Council of Trent, 435, 437.

Atonement. In Gregory, 19 ff.; Anselm, 66 ff., 200; Abelard, 70 f., 110, 267, n. 2; Bernard, 72, 111 n.; Honorius, Hugo, Pullus, 73; Alexander, Bonaventira, 110; Thomas, 111 f.; Duns, 156; Wickliffe, 198; Later Middle Ages, 198; Luther, 261, 266 ff.; Melanchthon, 359; Zwingli, 310; Calvin, 400; Synod of Dort, 423; Council of Trent, 442, n. 1; Later Reformed Confessions, 418.

Attribute, definition of, 369.

Attrition. In Alanus, Alexander, William of Paris, 136 f.; Biel, 138, 199, 201 f.; Duns, 160; John of Paltz, 175 f.; Luther, 222, 237; Council of Trent, 442.

Augsburg, Religious Peace of, 332, 333, 378.

Augsburg Confession, estimate of, 332, 344, 466; genesis of, 334; aim of, 335; and Zwingli, 334; on sin, human ability, nature and work of Christ, 335; faith, 336 ff., 342; justification, 336 ff., 343; regeneration, 337 f.; merit, 337; marriage, monasticism, Christian life, 339; good works, 339, 343; church, 340; bishops, 341, 344; ministry, human ordinances, civil power, 341; baptism, 341; Lord's Supper, 341, 351; repentance, contrition, absolution, 342; confession, 342, 344; law and gospel, 342; power of keys, 341, 343;

sacraments, 341 f.; worship of Mary and saints, mass, meats, vows, hierarchy, second advent, 344.

Augsburg Confession, Variata. On Lord's Supper, 351 ; justification, 360.

Augustine, influence of, 15, 16, 52, 97 f., 189 ; on church, 85 ; Trinity, 306 n.

Augustinianism, revival of, 449 f., and Jansenists, 453 f.

Aureolus, works of, 187 ; on work of Christ, 187, 198.

Averroes, philosophy of, 187.

Avicenna, philosophy of, 105.

B.

Bacon, Roger, philosophy of, 105.

Baconthorp, John of, philosophy of, 187 ; on work of Christ, 198.

Bajus, Michael, theses of, 450, 451 n.; on original state, grace, free-will, sin, justification, good works, 450.

Bandini, Archbishop, evangelical views of, 434, n. 2.

Baptism. In Gregory, 22 ; Lombard, 74, 80, 83, 130 ; thirteenth century, 129 f.; Eugene IV., 130 ; Thomas, Bonaventura, Duns, 130 ; Luther, 283 f.; Zwingli, 316 ; Augsburg Confession, 341 ; Reformed Confessions, 345 ; Calvin, 412 ; Council of Trent, 432, 434, 436, 439, 444 ; benefits of, 22, 80, 129 f., 283, 345, 412, 432, 434 ; of infants, 22, 130, 284, 285, 315, 316, 341, 412 ; by heretics, 439.

Basel, confession of, 344 f.; council at, 166.

Beatus. In Adoptionist controversy, 28.

Bec, school at, 55, 98.

Begards, 95.

Benedict of Aniane, works of, 27.

Benedict XI. On papacy, 165.

Benedict XIV. On Unigenitus, 456.

Berenger, works of, 74, 76; philosophy of, 55 ; on Lord's Supper, 75 f.

Bergen Book, 382 n.

Bernard, influence of, 88, 96 ; on papacy, 52 ; imitation of Christ, 53, 54, 72 ; good works, 53 ; work of Christ, 72, 110 ; sacraments, 79 ; heresy, 92, n. 3 ; person of Christ, 155.

Berthold of Ratisbon. On sacraments, 93.

Beza. On predestination, 421.

Biel, Gabriel, works of, 186 ; Nominalism of, 186 ; Luther on, 224 ; on sacraments, 127, 187, 200 ; church and state, 128 ; Lord's Supper, 132 n., 134 f., 204 ; repentance, 134 f., 138, 201 ; contrition, 136 f., 201 ; attrition, 138, 199, 201 f.; purgatory, 139 ; indulgences, 139, 176 ; Scriptures, 192 f.; faith, 195 f.; original state, sin, free-will, 197 ; work of Christ, predestination, 198 ; merit, 199, 202 ; grace, 201 f.; social problems, 202 n.

Bishops, authority of. In Early Middle Ages, 41 ; scholastic age, 50, 86 f.; Hugo, 86 ; Innocent III., 87 ; Thomas, Bonaventura, Duns, 141 f., 145 f.; Marsilius, Occam, 167 ; Augsburg Confession, 341, 344 ; Leipzig Interim, 364 ; Council of Trent, 439, 443, 444, 445, 446 f., 449 ; Gallican church, 457 ; Bavaria, 458 ; synod at Pistoja, 459 (see Hierarchy).

Blaurer. On Lord's Supper, 331, n. 2.

Blessedness, 148.

Boëtius, philosophy of, 56.

Bohemian Brethren. On Lord's Supper, 288.

Bolsec. On grace, divine call, predestination, 420.

Bonaventura, works of, 100; mysticism of, 89 f., 100; influence of, 98; philosophy of, 100; on Scriptures, 101; communicatio idiomatum, 110; person and work of Christ, 110; original state, 115; original sin, 116; infused grace, 115, 119; free-will, 120; justification, 120 f., 201; human merit, 122; monastic life, 124; sacraments, 125 f.; indelible character, 128; baptism, 130; repentance, 134 f.; absolution, 137 f., 142 n.; purgatory, 139; extreme unction, 140; ordination, 141; marriage, 143; communion of saints, 144.

Boniface VIII. On hierarchy, 88, 165; pope, 88, 97, 165.

Bradwardina, Thomas of. On person of Christ, 110; predestination, 189, 207.

Brenz and Osiander, 373, n. 2; on Lord's Supper, 320; person of Christ, 374.

Brethren of Poor Life, 88 f.

Brotherhoods, 173.

Bruno. On communion of saints, 144.

Bucer and Melanchthon, 393, n. 2, 350; and Luther, 393; and Calvin, 393; and Reformed Confessions, 344; on kingdom of Christ, 391; church, divine call, faith, 392; justification, 392, n. 3; predestination, 392 f.; free-will, 393.

Bull, unam sanctam, 88, 165; porro subesse, 97; exultate deo, 125; pastor aeternus, 166, 461; ex omnibus afflictionibus, 450, 451 n.; in eminenti, 453; cum occasione, 454; ad sancti Petri sedem, 454;

unigenitus, 455, 456; ineffabilis deus, 456; auctorem fidei, 459.

Bullinger and Zwingli, 390; and Luther, 417.

Buridan, philosophy of, 186.

C.

Cajetan, commentaries of, 187.

Call, the divine. In Henry, 122; Luther, 244; Formula of Concord, 388; Bucer, 392; Calvin, 405 f.; Bolsec, 420; Later Reformed Confessions, 420; Synod of Dort, 423; Consensus Helveticus, 425; Council of Trent, 433, 435.

Calvin, works of, 390, 395 nn.; and Bucer, 393; and Luther, 393, 394, 401, 414 f., 416; and Loyola, 430, n. 2; and Melanchthon, 394; and Osiander, 373, n. 2; and Zwingli, 393, n. 4, 394, 412, 414; estimate of, 394, 407, 415 n.; on Lord's Supper, 366, 386, 412 f., 417; Scriptures, 395, 396 n.; ancient symbols, 396; God, 396 f., 407; Trinity, 396, n. 2; will of God, 396 ff.; glory of God, 397; predestination, 397, 405 ff., 420; original sin, 398; conscience, 399 n.; free-will, 397, 399; grace, 399; person and work of Christ, 399; wrath of God, 400; Holy Spirit, 395, 401, 411; faith, 401 f., 405; renewal, sanctification, 402, 404; repentance, 402 f.; contrition, 403; regeneration, justification, 403 f.; law, 403; asceticism, 403, n. 3, 411; Christian life, 403, 405; communion with Christ, good works, 404; prayer, 405 n.; divine call, 405 f.; assurance, 405, 407; fall, 406; church, 408; ministry, discipline, 409; church and state, 410; ideas

of reform, 411 ; sacraments, 411 ff. ;
baptism, 412 ; ubiquity, 413.

Calvinism. In Germany, 381, 394 ;
and Synod of Dort, 424.

Calvinists, energy of, 397, 407, n. 1,
416.

Camero. On will, 425 n.

Canterbury, Council of, 93.

Capito. On Lord's Supper, 319.

Capocci, philosophy of, 187.

Capreolus, works of, 186 ; on work
of Christ, 198.

Carlstadt. On Lord's Supper, 288,
322.

Catechismus Romanus. On church
and papacy, 448 ; on Augustinianism, 449.

Cathari, 94.

Celibacy, 173 ; of priesthood, 142.

Ceremonies. In Frankfort Recess,
379 ; Formula of Concord, 388 ;
Romish, at Leipzig Interim, 364.

Character, indelible. In Alexander,
Eugene IV., Innocent III., 128 ;
Lombard, Bonaventura, Duns, 130 ;
Trent, 439, 445.

Charlemagne, works of, 29 ; on
papacy, 40.

Chemnitz, works of, 375 ; estimate
of, 375, 381 ; on person of Christ,
375 f. ; Lord's Supper, 377 f. ;
communicatio idiomatum, 375 ff. ;
ubiquity, multivolipresence, 376,
388 ; exinanition, 376 ; states of
Christ, 376, 387.

Chiersy, Council at, 32, 33.

Children, unbaptized, 22, 117, 245.

Christ, as head of race, 401 ; as example, 19, 21, 53, 68, 70, 71, 73,
90, 91, 112, 158, 198, 200, 270,
310, 311 f., 401, n. 2, 403 ; as
teacher, 53, 71, 72.

Christ, body of, in Lord's Supper.
In Later Middle Ages, 203 ff. ;
Luther, 286 ff., 322 f. ; Zwingli,

318 ff. ; Augsburg Confession, 341,
351 ; Eucharistic controversy,
366 f. ; Consensus Tigurinus, 417.

Christ, indwelling of, 53, 230 f., 270,
370 f.

Christ, intercession of. In Gregory,
19 f. ; Thomas, 113 ; Luther, 269 ;
Melanchthon, 359 ; Calvin, 400.

Christ, merit of. In Gregory, 20 ;
Abelard, 71 ; Anselm, 72 ; Lombard, 73 f. ; Alexander, Bonaventura, 110, 111 ; Thomas, 113 ;
Duns, 154 f., 156 f., 199 ; Later
Middle Ages, 198 ff. ; Melanchthon, 359 ; Formula of Concord,
384.

Christ, active and passive obedience
of. In Luther, 371 n. ; Osiander,
371 n. ; Menius, Flacius, 373 ;
Calvin, 400.

Christ, offices of, 399.

Christ, omnipresence of, 66 (see
Ubiquity).

Christ, person of. In Gregory, 18,
19 ; Synod of Toledo, 28, n. 1 ;
Roland, Omnebene, Lombard, 65,
74 ; Anselm, 57, 66 f. ; Gerhoh,
66 ; thirteenth century, 109 ; Alexander, Bonaventura, 110 ; Thomas,
110 f. ; Duns, 154 f. ; Bernard,
155 ; Luther, 229 f., 235, 253,
266, n. 3, 298, 304 f., 323, 324 n. ;
Zwingli, 321, 323 ; Augsburg
Confession 335 ; Heidelberg theology, 374 ; Brenz, Krell, Eber,
Major, 374 ; Chemnitz, 375 ;
Formula of Concord, 387 ; Calvin,
399.

Christ, states of, 325 n., 376 f., 377 f.

Christ, sufferings of. In Gregory, 19 ;
Bernard, 53 ; Anselm, 69 ;
Thomas, 112 f. ; Duns, 156 f. ;
Luther, 266 f. (see Atonement,
Work of Christ).

Christ, work of. In Gregory, 19 ff. ;

Gottschalk, 31 ; Anselm, 66 f.;
Bonaventura, 72 f.; St. Florian,
Honorius, Hugo, Pullus, 73 ;
Lombard, 73 f., 91 ; Alexander,
Bonaventura, 110 ; Thomas,111 f.;
Duns, 154 f.; Mystics, 179 ; Later
Middle Ages, 198 ff.; Aureolus,
187, 198; Biel, 198 ; Capreolus,
Baconthorp, Durand, 198 ; Luther,
230, 261, 266 ff.; Zwingli, 309 f.;
Melanchthon, 359; Augsburg
Confession, 335 ; Osiander, 370 ;
Eber, Stancar, 374 ; Formula of
Concord, 384 ; Calvin, 399;
Synod of Dort, 423 ; Council of
Trent, 436.

Christian Life, in Middle Ages, 16 ;
Gregory, 24, 26 ; Later Middle
Ages, 178 f., 202 ; Luther, 256,
273, 275, 296; Zwingli, 312 ;
Augsburg Confession, 339 ; Osian-
der, 370; Formula of Concord,
386 ; Calvin, 403, 405 ; Reformed
Theology, 415 ; Jesuits, 430 ;
Council of Trent, 438.

Chronicles, Luther on, 300.

Church, The. In Gregory, 25 ; Au-
gustine, Hugo, Pullus, John of
Salisbury, Alanus, 85 f.; Gregory
VII., 50, 85, 86 ; Waldenses, 94 ;
Thomas, 144 f.; Duns, 144 f., 149 ;
Occam, 192 f.; Huss, 211, 290;
Wickliffe, Wesel, Wessel, 211 ;
Luther, 226, 235, 289 f., 291 ff.;
Bucer, 392 ; Zwingli, 315 ; Augsburg Confession, 340 ; Melanchthon, 340, 351, 354 f., 362 ; Calvin, 408 ; Later Reformed Confessions, 419 ; Council of Trent, 446 ;
Catechismus Romanus, 448 ; Quesnel, 455 n.; Vatican Council, 460 ;
as kingdom of heaven, 25 ; as communion of saints, 25, 85, 144, 212,
291, 292, 315, 340, 455 n.; as assembly of the called, 354 ; as assembly of the predestinated, 211,
290, 408, 419 ; necessary to salvation, 26, 293, 362, 408 ; unworthy
members of, 294, 354 ; authority
of, 18, 149, 163, 170, 192 f., 211,
226, 235, 289 ; infallibility of, 50,
149, 192 ; rulers and subjects
in, 26, 86, 145, 211 f.; secularization of, 52, 97 ; visible and invisible, 235, 291 f., 293 f., 315, 317,
340, 345, 355, 408, 419 ; marks
of the true, 294, 340, 341, 352,
354, 355, 357, 408 ; and secular
learning, 353, 362, 363.

Church and State. In Gregory, 28 ;
scholastic age, 50 f.; John of Salisbury, 86 ; Innocent III., 87 f.;
Louis of Bavaria, 165 ; Marsilius,
Occam, 167, 170 ; Savonarola, 190
n., 318 ; Zwingli, 317 f.; Reformation era, 332 f.; Frankfort Recess,
379 ; Calvin, 410 ; Reformed theology, 415 ; Augsburg Confession,
341 ; Council of Trent, 446 ; Gallican Church, 457.

Chytraeus, Lutheranism of, 381.

Civil Life, 273 f.

Classics, study of the, 213.

Clement XI. and Jansenists, 454.

Clermont, council at, 45.

Clergy, orders of the, 141 ; and laity,
170.

Cluny, reformatory ideas at, 49.

Colet. On faith, justification, grace,
215, 216 n.

Comester, on Lord's Supper, 77.

Communicatio idiomatum. In
Thomas, Bonaventura, 110 ; Occam, 192 ; Luther, 323 ; Cureus,
366 ; Brenz, Heidelberg theologians, 374 ; Chemnitz, 375 ff.;
Gnesio-Lutherans, 381.

Communion with Christ. In Luther,
231 ; Calvin, 404 (see Mysticism,

Imitation of Christ) ; of saints, 144 f., 212, 235, 286 f., 291 ff., 408.

Communism, 182 f.

Conception, carnal, 21 f.; immaculate, 81, 91 n., 155, 188 n., 456.

Concomitance. In sacraments, 127 ; in Lord's Supper, 132.

Concord, attempts to secure, 380 ; Formula of, genesis of, 378 f., 382 ; estimate of, 382, 389 ; on original sin, free-will, conversion, 383 ; faith, 383 n., 384, 385 ; synergism, justification, forgiveness, work and merit of Christ, 384 ; Holy Spirit, 383 f., 385 nn.; contrition, 384, n. 1 ; renewal, 384, 423 n.; good works, 384 f.; Christian life ; Lord's Supper, 386; person of Christ, 387 ; predestination, word, divine call, assurance, descent into hell, adiaphora, 388 ; Book of, 382 ; the Schwabian, 382 n.; the Schwabian-Saxon, 382 n.; the Wittenberg, 321, 386.

Concordat of, A. D. 1801, 457.

Concupiscence (see Sin, original).

Confession. In Gregory, 24 ; Early Middle Ages, 43 f.; Abelard, 81, 92 n.; Hugo, 82, 92 ; Pullus, 83 ; Lombard, 83, 92 ; Gratian, 92 ; Innocent III., 93 ; Alexander, Albert, 130; Thomas, William of Paris, 137 ; Eugene IV., 140 ; Durand, 140 n.; Luther, 234, 240 ; Zwingli, 316 n.; Augsburg Confession, 342, 344 ; Council of Trent, 438, 442.

Confession, private, 93, 174, 234, 240, 358 n.

Confirmation. In Hugo, Roland, 81 ; Later Middle Ages, 130 ; Eugene IV., 131 ; Council of Trent, 439.

Congregation, rights of the, 294, 333, 334.

Conscience, 171 n., 243 n., 399 n.

Consensus Genevensis, 421 ; Helvetica, 425 ; Tigurinus, 417.

Conservatism. In Middle Ages, 15 f.

Consistorium, 409.

Constance, Council at, 166.

Constantine, Donation of, 40, 213.

Constantinople, councils at, 18, 29.

Contarini, Cardinal, on justification, 434, n. 1.

Contarini, Julian, evangelical views of, 434, n. 2.

Contemplation of Christ, 53, 54, 72, 124, 179 f.

Contingency, 150.

Contra-remonstrants. On predestination, 422.

Contrition, Gregory, 24 ; Early Middle Ages, 43 ; Abelard, Epitome, Roland, 81; Gratian, 92 ; Alexander, Thomas, Alanus, William of Paris, 136 f.; Biel, 136 f., 201 ; Luther, 222, 234, 237 ff.; Augsburg Confession, 342 ; Melanchthon, 358, 361 ; Formula of Concord, 384, 385, n. 1 ; Calvin, 403 ; Council of Trent, 438, 442, 444.

Conversion. In Melanchthon, 349 ; Synergistic controversy, 367 ff.; Ambrose, Strigel, Flacius, 367 f.; Formula of Concord, 383 ; Later Reformed Confessions, 419 ; Amyraldus, 425.

Co-operation. In divine nature, 375, 387 ; between God and man (see Synergism).

Corpora doctrinae, 380.

Corpus Christi, 134.

Corpus Philippicum, 380.

Council, at Nice (A. D. 325), 18 ; (A. D. 787), 29 ; Constantinople (A. D. 553), 18 ; (A. D. 754), 29 ; Ratisbon (A. D. 794), 29 ; Frankfort (A. D. 794), 29 ; Aachen (A. D. 799), 29 ; (A. D. 809), 30 ;

(A. D. 836), 84 ; Rome (A. D. 799), 29 ; (A. D. 1050, 1059, 1079), 76 ; Toledo (A. D. 444), 30 ; (A. D. 633, 638, 675), 28 ; Gentilly (A. D. 767), 30 ; Mayence (A. D. 848), 31 ; Chiersy (A. D. 849), 32 ; (A. D. 853), 33 ; Valence (A. D. 853), 33 ; Toucy (A. D. 860), 33 ; Chalon (A. D. 813), 42 ; Tribur, (A. D. 895), 45 ; Clermont (A. D. 1095), 45 ; Soissons (A. D. 1121), 61 ; Sens (A. D. 1141), 61 ; Fourth Lateran (A. D. 1215), 78, 93, 95, 108 ; Piacenza (A. D. 1095), 78 ; Treves (A. D. 1227), 92, 93 ; Narbonne (A. D. 1227), 93 ; Lauterberg (A. D. 1236), 93 ; Toulouse (A. D. 1229), 93 ; London (A. D. 1237), 125 ; Constance (A. D. 1414-17), 92, n. 3, 166, 290 ; Second Lyons (A. D. 1274), 146 ; Florence (A. D. 1439), 125 ; Third Lateran (A. D. 1179), 125 ; Pisa (A. D. 1409), 166 ; Basel (A. D. 1431-47), 166 ; Trent (A. D. 1545-63), 431 ; Vatican (A. D. 1869-70), 460.

Councils, authority of, 166, 289, 290 f., 293, 303, 457 ; the four primary, 18.

Counsels, evangelical, 124, 274.

Counter-reformation, 428 ff.

Creationism, 22, 117.

Creed, Apostles'. In Thomas, Bonaventura, 102 ; Later Middle Ages, 174 ; Luther, 303 f.

Creed, Nicene, 102 n.

Crisis, at close of Middle Ages, 173, 181, 213, 216, 221.

Criticism, biblical, 300 f. ; of dogmas, 192 ff.

Cross, sign of, 79.

Crusades, 45.

Crypto-Calvinism, 367, 381.

Cup, withholding of, 132, 440.

Cureus. In Eucharistic controversy, 366.

D.

D'Ailli, philosophy of, 186 ; on Scriptures, 192 f. ; Lord's Supper, 204.

Dead, masses for the, 25, 441, 445.

Decalogue, 174.

Decretals, papal, 50, n. 2, 52, 290 ; Pseudo-Isidorean, 41.

Descent into hell, 135, 377 n., 388.

Devil, claim of, on man, 67,70 ; conquest of, 68, 74 ; outwitting of, 21, 74, 267, n. 2.

Devils, faith in, 17, 173, 246 n.

Dialectics. In Middle Ages, 60, 96.

Dionysius, Areopagita. On God, 107.

Discipline, church. In Calvin, 409 ; Later Reformed Confessions, 419.

Doctrine, the pure, 295, 330, 351 ff., 396 ; and the Lutheran Church, 358, 379 ; Protestant construction of, 347 ff.

Doctrines, gradation in, 356.

Dogma. In ancient church, 332 ; in Middle Ages, 15, 17, 55, 332 ; in Reformation era, 333 f., 347 ff. ; Luther, 302 ff. ; modern Roman Catholic church, 46 ; Protestant and Roman Catholic churches, 464 f. ; provisional, 347.

Donation of Constantine, 40, 213.

Donum superadditum. In Gregory, 21, n. 1. ; Henry, Thomas, Bonaventura, 115 ; Duns, 153 ; Biel, 197 ; Council of Trent, 432 n. ; Bajus, 450.

Dort, Synod of, estimate of, 422 ; influence of, 423, n. 3 ; and Calvinism, 424 ; on Arminianism, predestination, 421 ff. ; faith, grace, election, 422 ; will, 423, 425 n. ; work of Christ, divine call, regeneration, perseverance, 423 ; justification, God, 424 ; assurance, 422, 435.

Duns Scotus, works of, 147 ; estimate of, 97, 106, 146, 162 f.; influence of, 428 f., 431 ; philosophy of, 98, 147 ; on sacraments, 127 f., 161 ; indelible character, 128 ; baptism, 130 ; Lord's Supper, 131 f., 133, 150 ; confession, absolution, 137 f.; satisfaction, indulgences, purgatory, 139 ; extreme unction, 140 ; ordination, 141 ; marriage, 142 ; communion of saints, 144 ; church, 144 f., 149 ; will, 148 f.; blessedness, 148 ; faith, 150, 160 ; God, 150 f., 163 f.; predestination, 151, 156, 164 ; original state, 153 ; original sin, 153, 154 n., 163 ; person of Christ, 154 f.; work of Christ, 156 f.; merit of Christ, 154 f., 156 f., 199 ; immaculate conception, 155 ; grace, 158 ; attrition, justification, forgiveness, 160 f.

Durand, philosophy of, 186 ; on Lord's Supper, 76 f., 203 ; public repentance, 93 ; confession, 140, 142 n.; work of Christ, 198 ; grace, 201 f.

E.

Eber. On person of Christ, 374.

Ecclesiastes, Luther on, 300.

Eck, theses of, 334.

Eckhart, works of, 178 ; on imitation of Christ, 178 f.

Ecstasy, 180 f.

Eisenach, synod at, 365.

Elipandus, works of, 27 ; in Adoptionist controversy, 27.

Episcopacy (see Bishops) *vs.* papacy, 457.

Episcopus. On predestination, 421.

Epitome, The, 382 n.; on repentance, 81.

Eremites, Augustinian, 187.

Esther, Luther on, 300.

Etherius. In Adoptionist controversy, 27.

Eucharistic controversy, 366.

Eugene IV. On sacraments, 125 ; indelible character, 128 ; baptism, 130 ; confirmation, 131 ; repentance, extreme unction, 140 ; ordination, 142 ; marriage, 143.

Ex opere operante, 129.

Ex opere operato, 128, 343, 439.

Excommunication, 168, 210, 211, 409.

Exorcism, 130 n.

Eybel, work of, 458, n. 2.

F.

Faber Stapulensis. On Lord's Supper, 205 n.

Faith. In Gregory, 17, 22 ; Early Middle Ages, 15, 46, n. 3 ; Radbertus, 37 ; Anselm, 57 ; Abelard, 58 ; Innocent IV., 90 ; Thomas, 103, 120 f.; Lombard, 123 n.; Duns, 150 ; Biel, Occam, 195 f.; Erasmus, 215 n.; Colet, 216 n.; Innocent III., 196 ; Luther, 223, 225, 232 ff., 240, 241, 252 ff., 275 f., 296, 297 f , 302, 328 ; Calvin, 401 f., 405 ; Zwingli, 310 f., 313 ; Augsburg Confession, 336 ff., 342 ; Reformed Confessions, 344 ; Melanchthon, 356, 360 f.; Osiander, 371 f.; Formula of Concord, 383 n., 384, 385 ; Bucer, 392 ; Later Reformed Confessions, 419 ; Remonstrants, Synod of Dort, 422 ; Jesuits, 430 : Council of Trent, 433, 435, 436, 437, 440, 449 ; Quesnel, 455 n.; Unigenitus, 455 ; Vatican Council, 460 ; as trust, 215 n., 233, 235, 254, 310, 356, 361, 365, 401, 419 ; as conviction,

402, 419; as disposition toward grace, 435 f.; implicit and explicit, 90, 103, 104, 150, 170, 195 f., 255, 402, 429; infused, 103, 150, 195, 254; acquired, 232 f., 254; and love, 103, 121, 209, 436; and sacraments, 80, 282, 328; and Lord's Supper, 413.

Fall, The. In Gregory, 21; Anselm, 116; Duns, 153; Biel, Occam, 197; Luther, 242; Zwingli, 309; Osiander, 370; Calvin, 398, 406; Council of Trent, 432.

Fasting, 92.

Faustus. On grace, 23.

Fear, province of, 26, 136, 138, 249, 438 (see Law).

Felix of Urgellis. On Adoptionism, 27.

Filioque, 30.

Flacius. In Adiaphoristic and Majoristic controversies, 364; in Synergistic controversy, 367 f.; in Osiandrian controversy, 373.

Florence, council at, 125.

Florian, St., work of, 59; on work of Christ, 73; Lord's Supper, 77; sacraments, 79.

Florus, works of, 30; on predestination, 32.

Foreknowledge (see Prescience).

Forgiveness of Sins. In Gregory, 24; Radbertus, 37; Early Middle Ages, 46; Anselm, 68; Abelard, 81; Lombard, 83; Gratian, 92; Thomas, 112 f., 121; Duns, 160 f.; Luther, 260 f., 283, 284, 372; Melanchthon, 356, 358, 360; Osiander, 372; Formula of Concord, 384; Council of Trent, 433, 437; Bajus, 450, n. 2; Jansen, 453; Quesnel, 455 n.

Francis of Assisi, estimate of, 89, 96; mysticism of, 89; order of, 90; on Virgin Mary, 91 n.

Franciscans, 95.

Frankfort Recess, 379.

Fredeland, consecration of host, 367 n.

Free-will. In Gregory, 20 f.; Rabanus, 31 f.; Hincmar, 32; Councils of Chiersy and Valence, 33; Thomas, 118 f.; Bonaventura, 120; Biel, 138, 197; Duns, 148; Occam, 197; Bradwardina, 208; Wickliffe, 208; Luther, 243 f.; Zwingli, 313 f.; Melanchthon, 349; Leipzig Interim, 364 n.; Synergistic controversy, Strigel, 367 f.; Flacius, 367 f., 383; Formula of Concord, 383; Bucer, 393; Calvin, 397, 399; Bolsec, 420; Remonstrants, 422; Synod of Dort, 423, 425 n.; Council of Trent, 433 f.; Bajus, 450, 451 n.; Molina, 451 f.; Jansen, 454 f.; Quesnel, 455 n.

G.

Gallican Church, struggles of, 457.

Gelasius. On Lord's Supper, 34.

Gendulph, Sentences of, 63.

Genesis, Luther on, 300.

Gentilly, council at, 30.

Gerbert. On Lord's Supper, 39.

Gerhard of Sienna, philosophy of, 187.

Gerhoh, philosophy of, 60; on person of Christ, 66.

Germanic church, 15 f.

Germanic legal system, 69.

Germanus of Paris. On Lord's Supper, 77.

Gerson. Reformatory ideas of, 188; on communion of saints, 144.

Glory, the divine, 397, 420.

Gnesio-Lutheranism, 380, 381, n. 3.

Goch, Pupper of, and Augustinianism, 190 ; on grace, 208 f.; Scriptures, evangelical liberty, 209.

God, conception of. In Gregory, 18 ; Germanic, 29 n.; in Anselm, 69, 107 ; Thomas, 100, 107 ; Augustine, Dionysius, 107 ; Duns, 150, 163 f.; Luther, 253, 265, 298, 407, 416 ; Zwingli, 314 ; Calvin, 396 f., 407 ; Reformed theology, 416 ; Synod of Dort, 424 ; Vatican Council, 460 ; existence of, 56 ; as love, 107, 151, 164, 253, 265, 401, 407,. 416 ; relation to the world, 107 ; wrath of, 229 n., 245, 249, 358, 370 f., 400 ; glory of, 397, 420.

Gnosticism, 94.

Goddam, philosophy of, 186.

Gomanus. On predestination,. 421, 422 n.

Gospel, The, 228, 246, 248 f., 250 251, 311, 342, 358, 366, 385.

Gospels, the Synoptic, Luther .on, 300.

Gottschalk, works of, 30 ; condemned, 32 ; on predestination, Trinity, work of Christ, 31.

Grace. In Gregory, 22 f.; Faustus, 23; Council of Chiersy, 33 ; Thomas, 115, 128 ; Lombard, 118 ; Biel, John of Paltz, Durand, 201 f.; Bonaventura, 115, 119 ; Duns, 158 ; Goch, 208 f.; Wesel, Wessel, 209 ; Colet, 216, n. 1 ; Luther, 231 f., 263 ff., 297 ; Zwingli, 314 ; Melanchthon, 360 ; Southwestern Germany, 390 ; Calvin, 399 ; Bolsec, 420 ; Remonstrants, Synod of Dort, 422 ; Council of Trent, 433, 435, 439, 449 ; Bajus, 450 ; Molina, 451 f.; Jansen, 453 ; Quesnel, 455 n.; Unigenitus, 455 ; *creata* and *increata*, 118, 158, 208, 232 n., 264 ; *gratum faciens*, 115, 119, 122, 127, 128, 129, 338 ; *gratia*

data, 122, 128, 209 ; infused, 78, 80, 115, 119, 120, 123, 137 f., 153, 160 f., 190, 201 f., 208 f., 216 n., 232, 239, n. 2, 240, 263, 265, n. 1, 297, 433, 449 ; operating and co-operating, 119 ; irresistible, 23, 422, 453, 454 (see free-will); prevenient, 22, 32, 208, 435, 454 ; in sacraments, 80, 85, 126 ; in ordination, 84 ; means of, 293, 336, 409.

Gratian, and Lombard, 62 f.; on contrition, confession, absolution, forgiveness, 92.

Greek Church. In Middle Ages, 16.

Gregory the Great, works of, 17, 25 ; estimate of, 17, 26 ; theology of, 15, 16 ; and Augustine, 26, 32 ; Melanchthon on, 26 n.; on Trinity, 17 ; angels, 17, 25 ; God, 18 ; homousia, 18 ; Holy Spirit, 18, 20 n., 30 ; incarnation, 19 n.; person of Christ, 18 f.; work and intercession of Christ, 19 ff.; Scriptures, 18, 19 ; church, ancient symbols, 18 ; example of Christ, 19, 21 ; saints and martyrs, 20 ; original state, 21 n.; demons, 17 ; devil, 21 ; faith, 17, 22 ; free-will, 21, 22 ; sin, 21 f.; fall, guilt, 21 ; vices, 21 n.; carnal conception, 21 f.; Creationism and Traducianism, 22 ; unbaptized children, 22 ; grace, 22 f.; justification, predestination, co-operation, merit, 23 ; baptism, 22 ; repentance, contrition, confession, absolution, satisfaction, good works, forgiveness, 24 ; Lord's Supper, mass, purgatory, 24 f.; church, 18, 25 ; Christian life, 24, 26.

Gregory VII., estimate of, 96 ; on church, papacy, 50, 85, 86 ; state, 51, 85, 86 ; Lord's Supper, 75.

Gregory of Rimini, philosophy of,

188 ; on immaculate conception, 188 n.; Luther on, 242.

Gropper, imputed righteousness, 434 n.

Grosseteste, philosophy of, 98; theology of, 164 n.

Guibert. On preaching, 92 ; Lord's Supper, 39.

Guilt, 21, 81, 117.

Guitmund. On Lord's Supper, 76 f.

H.

Habitus, 103, 131 f., 150, 158 f., 195 (see Faith, Grace).

Hadrian. On Adoptionism, 29.

Haimo. On Lord's Supper, 39.

Hardenberg. In Eucharistic controversy, 366.

Heathen, salvation of. In Zwingli, 315.

Hebrews, Epistle to the, Luther on, 300.

Heidelberg Catechism. On Lord's Supper, 418 ; predestination, 421.

Heidelberg theologians. On person of Christ, ubiquity, 374.

Helvetic Confession, estimate of, 344 ; on predestination, 421.

Henry of Ghent, works of, 106 ; philosophy of, 98, 106 ; on universals, 106; will, 106 ; original state, 115; divine call, 122 ; indulgences, purgatory, 139.

·Heretics and sacraments, 50, 51, 142 ; and baptism, 439 ; and ordination, 142.

Hervaeus Natalis, philosophy of, 186.

Hierarchy. In Early Middle Ages, 40 f., 50, 87 f., 96 ; Nicholas, 40 ; Donation of Constantine, 40 f.; Pseudo-Isidorian decretals, 41 ; Boniface VIII., 88, 165 ; Waldenses, 94 ; Later Middle Ages, 165 ff.; Marsilius, Occam, 167 ff.; Wesel, 211 ; Augsburg Confession,

344 ; Luther, 290, 294 ; Council of Trent, 445, 449.

Hincmar, works of, 30 ; on Trinity, 31 ; predestination, 32.

Hildebert. On Lord's Supper, 77.

History of Doctrines, method of, 55 ; scope of, 466.

Holkot, philosophy of, 186.

Holy Spirit. In Gregory, 18, 30 ; Luther, 248 n., 256, 263, 280 f., 305 ; Zwingli, 311 ; Melanchthon, 360 ; Majoristic controversy, 365 ; Formula of Concord, ·383 f., 385 nn.; Calvin, 395, 401, 411 ; procession of, 18, 30 ; intercession of, 20, n. 2 ; work of, 385.

Homousia, 303 ; of Christ, 18 (see Christ, Person of); of the Holy Spirit, 18, 30.

Honius. On Lord's Supper, 288, 319.

Honorius. On systematic theology, 61 ; work of Christ, 73 ; Lord's Supper, 77 ; public repentance, 93.

Host, desecrated, 77 n., 132 ; adoration of, 440.

Hugo of Langres. On Lord's Supper, 76, 77.

Hugo of St. Victor, estimate of, 64 ; and Lombard, 62 ; on systematic theology, 61 ; sacraments, 19, 80, 61 ; work of Christ, 73 ; confirmation, 81 ; repentance, confession, absolution, satisfaction, 82, 92 ; extreme unction, ordination, 84 ; church, 85 f.; state, 86.

Humanism, 213 ff.

Huss, influence of, 185, 289 n.; on church, 211, 290.

Hussites. On Lord's Supper, 206 f.

I.

Images, worship of, 29, 94, 448 ; adoration vs. veneration of, 29.

Imitation, of Christ. In Bernard, 54, 72 ; Francis, Ludolf, 89 ; Tauler,

Eckhart, 178 f.; Wickliffe, 184;
Erasmus, 215; Luther, 270;
Zwingli, 312; of parents' sins, 21,
n. 1.

Impanation, 75.

Impulses, natural. In Luther, 273;
Reformed theology, 415.

Indulgences. In Middle Ages, 92;
Biel, 139, 176; Alexander,
Thomas, Duns, Henry of Ghent,
139; Later Middle Ages, 165,
173; John of Paltz, 176; Wickliffe, Wesel, Wessel, 210; Luther,
234, 236, 241; Zwingli, 316 n.;
Council of Trent, 444; for money,
177.

Indwelling, of God, 231, 270, 370 f.;
of Christ, 53, 230 f., 270, 370 f.

Infallibility, of church, 50, 149, 192;
of pope, 169, 170, 461, 462 f.;
decree of, 462 f.

Innocent III., estimate of, 96; on
papacy, church and state, 87;
private confession, 93; indelible
character, 128; faith, 196.

Innocent IV. On faith, 90.

Ino. On communion of saints, 144 n.

Intention. In sacraments, 125; in
baptism, 439.

Intercession, of Christ, 19, 113, 269,
359, 400; of saints and martyrs,
20, n. 2, 309; of the church, 20,
n. 2; of the Holy Spirit, 20, n. 2.

Interim, Leipzig, estimate of, 355 n.;
and Melanchthon, 363, 364; on
justification, bishops, Romish ceremonies, 364; free-will, 364 n.;
righteousness, 381, n. 4.

Interpretation, allegorical, 15, 19.

Isidore, works of, 16; on predestination, 30.

J.

James, Epistle of, Luther on, 300.

Janduno, philosophy of, 187.

Jansen, work of, 453; theses of,
454; and Augustinianism, 453;
and Bradwardina, 453; on original
sin, will, justification, forgiveness,
love, predestination, 453; irresistible grace, 453, 454.

Jansenists, estimate of, 453 f.

Jesuits, estimate of, 429 f.; condemnation of, 453; on repentance,
429; faith, asceticism, preaching,
Christian life, 430; grace, 449.

Joachim of Floris, apocalyptic visions
of, 95, 183; on Trinity, 108.

John, Gospel of, Luther on, 299.

John of Damascus, influence on Lombard, 63.

John of Paltz, works of, 179, n. 3,
201, 175 f.; theology of, 188; on
attrition, 175 f.; absolution, indulgences, 176; grace, 201 f.; justification, 201.

John of Paris. On Lord's Supper,
203 n.

John of Ruusbroec, works of, 178.

John of Salisbury, philosophy of, 60;
on church, 85 f.

Joslenus. On communion of saints,
144.

Jubilee indulgences, 176.

Jude, Epistle of, Luther on, 300.

Justification. In Gregory, 23; Scholastics, 120 ff.; Bonaventura, 120
f., 201; Thomas, 120 f.; Lombard, 123 n.; Middle Ages, 175;
Duns, 160; John of Paltz, 201;
Wessel, 209; Colet, 216 n.;
Luther, 233, 235, 260 f.; Zwingli,
307, 310; Augsburg Confession,
336 ff.; Apology, 338; Early Reformed Confessions, 344; Melanchthon, 351, 356, 358, 360 f.,
362, 372, n. 2; Leipzig Interim,
364; Majoristic controversy, 365;
Osiandrian controversy, 369 f.,
373; Formula of Concord, 384;

Southwestern Germany, 390; Bucer, 392, n. 3; Calvin, 403 f.; Later Reformed Confessions, 420; Synod of Dort, 424; Council of Trent, 433 ff., 435, 436, 437; Contarini, 434, n. 1; Bajus, 450; Jansen, 453; Quesnel, 455 n.; progressive, 437.

K.

Kempis, Thomas à, works of, 178; mysticism of, 178 f.
Kenotism, 376 n.
Keys, power of the. In Gregory, 26, 51; Hugo, 86; Thomas, 145; Marsilius, Occam, 168; Luther, 293; Augsburg Confession, 341, 343; Council of Trent, 444.
Klebitz, in Eucharistic controversy, 366.
Krell. On person of Christ, 374.
Kilwardby, philosophy of, 98.
Kingdom of Christ, 266, 277, 292, 340, 391, 410, n. 2.
Kings, Books of the, Luther on, 300.
Knowledge, median, 451 f.; original, 115; theory of, in Boëtius, 56; Thomas, 104 f.; Albert, Anselm, 105; Abelard, 60; Duns, 148; Occam and his school, 186 f., 190 f.; Henry of Ghent, 106.

L.

Lanfranc, works of, 74; on reason, 55; Lord's Supper, 76 f.
Lauterwald, Osiandrian controversy, 373.
Law, The. In Luther, 239, 246 ff.; Zwingli, 311; Melanchthon, 358; Augsburg Confession, 337; Osiander, 370 f.; Calvin, 403; Reformed theology, 416; preaching of the, 248 f., 250.

Law and Gospel. In Luther, 228, 246, 248 f., 250; Agricola, 251, 366; Augsburg Confession, 342; Zwingli, 311; Formula of Concord, 385; Antinomian controversy, 365.
Law, natural, 52, 55, 171 f., 183, 184 n., 246 f., 309, 399.
Legalism. In Middle Ages, 46; Anselm, 69.
Leipzig Disputation, 225, 289 f., 291, 298.
Leo I. In filioque controversy, 30.
Leo III. On Adoptionism, 29; filioque controversy, 30.
Leo X. On councils, 166; bull of, 166.
Leo XIII. On inspiration of Scriptures, 460, n. 2.
Liberty, evangelical. In Later Middle Ages, 182 f.; Goch, 209; Luther, 275.
Life, civil, 273 f.; eternal, 359; the new, 231, 256 f., 337, 360.
Lombard, Peter, estimate of, 62, 64, 185; system of, 63; and Abelard, 59; Luther on, 224; on person of Christ, 65, 74; work of Christ, 73 f., 91; sacraments, 63, 80; Lord's Supper, 78; repentance, 74, 80, 83, 92; confession, absolution, satisfaction, 83, 92; forgiveness, purgatory, 83 f.; extreme unction, ordination, 84; Trinity, 108; original sin, 116; grace, 118; faith, justification, 123 n.; baptism, 130; marriage, 143.
Lord's Supper. In Middle Ages, 16, 34; Gregory, 24 f.; Gelasius, 34; Carlovingian period, 34; Alcuin, 35; Radbertus, 35, 37, 76; Rabanus, 37, 39; Ratramnus, 38; Guibert, Haimo, 39; Gregory VII., 75; Durand, 76, 203; Berenger, 75 f.; Lanfranc, Hugo of Langres,

Alger, Guitmund, 76 f.; Comester, Hildebert, St. Florian, Roland, Honorius, Omnebene, 77; Abelard, 77 n.; Pullus, Lombard, Rupert, 78; Duns, Alexander, 131 f., 133; Biel, 132, 134 f., 204; Thomas, 133; Occam, 133, 202, 327; Albert, 134 n.; Eugene IV., 134; John of Paris, 203 n.; Thomas of Strassburg, Wesel, Wessel, D'Ailli, 204; Faber, 205 n.; Wickliffe, 206; Erasmus, 215 n.; Luther, 235, 286 ff., 322 ff.; Bohemian Brethren, 288; Brenz, 320, 366; Zwingli, 318 ff.; Honius, 288, 319; Oecolampadius, 319, 322; Bucer, 319, 331; Capito, 319; Carlstadt, 288, 322; Pirckheimer, 320; Blaurer, Schnepf, 331 n.; Schwabach Articles, 330; Augsburg Confession, 341; Variata, 351; Reformed Confession, 345; Chemnitz, 377; Melanchthon, 350, 366, 380; Calvin, 366, 386, 412 f., 417; Hesshusen, 366; Eucharistic controversy, 366; Westphalia, 366; Saliger, Cerveus, 367 n.; Frankfort Recess, 379; Gnesio-Lutherans, 381; Formula of Concord, 386; Southwestern Germany, 391; Reformed theology, 415; Bullinger, 417; Consensus Tigurinus, 417; Heidelberg Catechism, Helvetic Confession, 418; Council of Trent, 439 f.; as bond of unity, 331f.; as food for the soul, 134, 345, 418; as a memorial, 134, 319, 322, 345, 412; as a pledge of fidelity, 322; as a sacrifice, 134, 441, et passim (see Mass); as a symbol, 36, 38, 39, 75, 126, 206, 286 f., 318, 320, 340; matter and form in, 135; elements in, 289, 440; *in usu*, 386, 440; spiritual

reception of, 36, 207, 328, 330; worthy and unworthy reception of, 77, 329 n., 366, 386; miracles accompanying, 35, 76; and immortality of the body, 36, 329, 387, 414, n. 2; and the unbelieving, 36, 38, 206 n., 328 n., 331, 386; benefits of, 25, 36, 37, 38, 78, 133, 134, 287 f., 327 f., 329, 345, 386 f., 440, 441, 442 (see Christ, Body of).

Loyola, estimate of, 429, 430 n.; and Calvin, 430, n. 2.

Louis XIV. and papacy, 457.

Louis of Bavaria, and papacy, 165; on papacy, 165, 167 f., 174.

Ludolf of Saxony, mysticism of, 89.

Lullus. On logical demonstration, 105.

Lupus, Seratus, works of, 30; on predestination, 32.

Luther, works of, 221, 225 n., 226 nn., 227; theses of, 236; scholastic training of, 223; estimate of, 221 f., 225 f., 296 f., 348, 389, 417; and Bucer, 393; and Calvin, 393, 394, 401, 414 f., 416; and Melanchthon, 349, 352, 363, 381, n. 3; and Osiander, 372, 373 n.; and Southern Germany, 320; and Southwestern Germany, 391; and Zwingli, 303, 308 n., 319 f., 323 n.; on Aristotle, Lombard, Thomas, Biel, 224; on attrition, 222, 237; contrition, 222, 234, 237 ff.; repentance, 224, 234, 235, 241, 251 n., 272, 358; confession, 240; absolution, 234, 240; satisfaction, 234, 241, 265 f.; indulgences, 234, 236, 241, 267, n. 2, 268 n.; law, 239, 246 ff.; law and gospel, 228, 246, 248 f., 250; Scriptures, 226, 228, 290 f., 298 f., 301 f.; Apocrypha, 300; criticism of Scriptures, 300; Word, 234,

31

279 f., 299 f., 322 ; Books of the
Bible, 300; reason, 224, 243,
247, 299 n.; personal experience,
224, 225, 228 f., 230, 233, 235,
256 f., 281 n., 296, 298, 301,
304; human merit, 229, 264;
synteresis, 229, n. 2; sin, 229,
242 f., 297, 309 ; free-will, 243 f.;
will of man, 256, 243 f., 255, n.
4; fall, 212; conscience, 243 n.;
conception of God, 253, 265, 298,
407, 416 ; will of God, 244 ; Trinity, 303, 305 f.; wrath of God,
229 n., 245, 249 ; predestination,
244, 407 ; person of Christ, 229 f.,
235, 253, 266, n. 3, 298, 304 f.,
323, 324 n.; work of Christ, 230,
261, 266 ff.; intercession of Christ,
269 ; indwelling of Christ, 231,
270 ; Holy Spirit, 248 n., 256,
263, 280 f., 305 ; grace, 231 ff.,
263 ff., 297 ; love of God, 245,
253, 265, 407, 416 ; justification,
233, 235, 260 f.; forgiveness,
260 f., 283, 284, 372 ; faith, 223,
225, 232 ff., 240, 241, 252 ff.,
275 f., 296, 297 f., 302, 328;
regeneration, 283 f.; sanctification,
new life, 256 f., 284, 231, 337,
360 ; Christian life, 256 f., 273,
275 f., 296 ; imitation of Christ,
270 ; good works, 234, 240, 247,
258, 264, 274, 277, 364 ; love to
fellow-man, 238 f., 275 f., 248 ;
devil, 267, n. 2 ; devils, 246 n.;
communion of saints, 235, 286 f.,
291 ff.; Virgin Mary, 235 ; Sabbath, 246, 247 n.; sacraments,
235, 279, 282 ; baptism, 283 f.,
285 ; Lord's Supper, 235, 286 ff.,
322 ff.; alloeosis, 324 ; right hand
of God, 325 ; ubiquity, 288, 320
n., 323 f.; kingdom of God, 277 ;
church, 226, 235, 289, 291 ff.;
keys, 293 ; hierarchy, 290, 294 ;

Romish Church, 295, 289 ; creed,
303 f.; "chief article," 297 n.;
preaching, 281, 293 ; councils,
291, 303 ; tradition, 291, 302 ff.;
mass, 235, 289 ; monasticism,
274 ; asceticism, 276 n.; civil life,
273 f.; natural impulses, 273;
social problems, 278 ; the state,
274, 290.
Lutheranism, and Calvinism, 415 ;
and Catholicism, 417, n. 1 ; Melanchthonian, 381, 383.
Lychetus, philosophy of, 186.
Lyons, second council at, 146.

M.

Major. In Majoristic controversy,
364 ; on person of Christ, 374 ;
good works, 364, 385.
Majoristic controversy, 364 f.
Manducation, oral, 327, 350, 386.
Marbach. On predestination, 378.
Marburg colloquy, 330.
Marriage. In Lombard, 80, 143 ;
scholasticism, 85, 125 ; Bonaven-
tura, 143 ; Council of Trent, 446.
Marriage of priests. In Thomas,
Duns, 147 ; Albert, Eugene IV.,
143 ; Augsburg Confession, 339 ;
Council of Trent, 446.
Marsilius of Inghen, philosophy of,
186.
Marsilius of Padua. On hierarchy,
167.
Martyr. On predestination, 421.
Mass, The. In Gregory, 24 f.;
Luther, 235, 289 ; Zwingli, 309;
Marburg colloquy, 330 ; Augsburg
Confession, 344 ; Council of Trent,
441, 445 ; modern Roman Cath-
olic church, 463.
Massa perditionis, 33.
Maulbronn, Formula of, 382 f.
Mayence, council at, 31.

Meats, distinction of, 344.

Melanchthon, works of, 348, 351 ff.; estimate of, 348, 363 ; and Protestant doctrine, 348 ; and ancient symbols, 352 ; and Bucer, 350, 393, n. 2 ; and Calvin, 394 ; and hyper-orthodoxy, 356 ; and Interim, 355 n., 363, 364 ; and Luther, 349, 352, 363, 381, n. 3 ; and Majoristic controversy, 365 ; and Oecolampadius, 350 ; and Osiander, 372 n., 373 ; and Zwingli, 350 ; on Luther, 352 ; fundamental ideas of, 351 ; on church, 340, 351, 354 f., 362 ; Scriptures, 348, 351 f.; ancient symbols, 348, 352 ; speculation, 348 ; reason, science, 353 ; Aristotle, 348, n. 3 ; free-will, sin, predestination, conversion, 349 ; Lord's Supper, 350, 366, 380 ; repentance, 351, 358, 361 ; experience, 353 ; justification, 351, 356, 358, 360 f., 362, 372, n. 2 ; pure doctrine, 352 f., 354 ff.; Romish Church, 355 ; ministry, 355 n.; law, wrath of God, 358 ; contrition, 358, 361; faith, 356, 360 f.; regeneration, 360 ; merit, 361 ; gospel, 358 ; work, merit and intercession of Christ, fruits of redemption, eternal life, 359 ; grace, Holy Spirit, 360 ; new life, 360 ; good works, 361, 364.

Mendicants, 146.

Menius. In Majoristic controversy, 364 ; in Osiandrian controversy, 373.

Merit, human. In Gregory, 23; Albert, 116; Thomas, 116, 121 f., 124, 136; Bonaventura, 116, 121 f., 124; Duns, 158; Occam, 192; Biel, 199, 202; Luther, 229, 264; Zwingli, 313; Augsburg Confession, 337; Melanchthon, 361;

Council of Trent, 434, 438; of fitness and worthiness, 112, 115, 123, 138, 160, 199, 202, 229, 337, 434, 436.

Migetius. On Trinity, 27.

Ministry, The. In Luther, 293 f., Zwingli, 316 n.; Augsburg Confession, 341; Melanchthon, 355 n.; Calvin, 409; Council of Trent, 445.

Miracles, 35, 76, 91.

Molina, work of, 450; on grace and free-will, 451 f.; median divine knowledge, 452.

Monastic life, 124, 274.

Monastic vows, 344.

Monastic works, 339.

Money, abuse of, in the church, 165, n. 1, 177, 203.

Moralism. In Middle Ages, 91.

Multivolipresence, 376, 386, 387, 388.

Musculus. On predestination, 421.

Mysticism. In Bernard, 52 f., 88 ; Bonaventura, 88 n., 89 f., 100 ; Hugo, Richard, 88 n., 89 f.; Francis, Ludolf, 89 ; Scholastics, 124 ; German, 178 ff., 280.

N.

Napoleon I. In Gallican church, 457; on pope, 457.

Narbonne, council at, 43.

Naumburg, diet at, 379.

Nestorianism. In thirteenth century, 66.

Netter vs. Wickliffe, 189.

Nice, councils at, 29, 290.

Nicholas of Clemanges. On greed of papacy, 166 n.

Nicholas of Hontheim, work of, 457; on episcopacy, 457; papacy, 458.

Nicholas I. On papacy, 40, 41 n.

Nihilianism, 65.

Niphus, philosophy of, 187.
Nominalism, 56, 186, 188, 190 ff.,
    428, 429.
Nunciatures, papal, 458.

O.

Obedience. In Jesuitism, 430.
Obedience of Christ, 371, 373, 400.
Objective vs. subjective, 191.
Obstacle, in sacraments, 129.
Occam, estimate of, 185 f., 191 ; on
    communion of saints, 144 ; Scrip-
    tures, 162, 172, 192 f.; hierarchy,
    167 ; natural law, 183 ; Nominal-
    ism, 190 ff.; Trinity, communicatio
    idiomatum, 192; transubstantiation,
    church, 192 f.; faith, 195 f.; sin,
    free-will, 197.
Oecolampadius.   On Lord's Supper,
    319, 322.
Offices in church, Calvin, 409.
Omnebene, work of, 59 ; on person
    of Christ, 65 ; Lord's Supper, 77 ;
    sacraments, 79.
Omnipresence of Christ's body, 66,
    77, 288 (see Ubiquity).
Opus operatum, 46.
Ordinances, human, 341.
Ordination.   In Gregory, 51 ; Hugo,
    Roland, Lombard, 84 ; Scholastic-
    ism, 125 ; Thomas, Bonaventura,
    Duns, 141 ; Eugene IV., 142;
    Council of Trent, 445.
Osiander, works of, 369 ; estimate of,
    372; and Brenz, 373, n. 2 ; and
    Calvin, 373, n. 2 ; and Melanch-
    thon, 372 n.; and Luther, 372,
    373 n.; on justification, 369 ff.,
    373 ; person and work of Christ,
    370 f.; inner word, faith, right-
    eousness, obedience of Christ,
    371 n.; forgiveness, 372 f.; re-
    newal, Christian life, 370, 373 ;
    symbolic subscription, 352 n.

Osiandrian controversy, 366 ff.
Otto, Anton. Antinomianism of, 366.
Otto of Freising. On papacy, 146.
Otto the Great. On papacy, 40.

P.

Palude, Petrus de, philosophy of,
    186.
Pantheism, 95.
Papacy, greed of, 166 n.
Pascal vs. Jesuits, 453.
Paternoster, 92.
Paul of Venice, philosophy of, 187.
Paulinus, works of, 27.
Peckham, philosophy of, 98.
Penance, forms of, 45 ; redemption
    of, 44 f.
Penitence, compulsory, 24 n.
Penitential books, 42.
Perfection, Christian.   In Francis,
    Ludolf, 89 f.; Thomas, 124 ; Bona-
    ventura, 89 f., 124; Luther, 275 f.;
    Augsburg Confession, 339 ; Cal-
    vin, 403.
Perseverance, 378, 391, 406, 423.
Peter, Epistles of, Luther on, 300 ;
    primacy of, 168.
Pfeffinger.   On Synergism, 367.
Philippism, 381.
Philosophy of Aristotle, 95 ; Arabian.
    95.
Piacenza, council at, 78.
Pictaviensis, Petrus, works of, 64.
Pighius.   On predestination, 420,
    righteousness, 434 n.
Pilgrimages, 173.
Pirckheimer.   On Lord's Suppei
    320.
Pisa, council at, 166.
Pistoja, synod at, 445, n. 1, 458.
Pius IX.   On immaculate concep-
    tion, 456 ; Vatican Council, 460.
Poach.   On law and gospel, 365.
Polygamy, 142, n. 3.

Pope, authority of. In Nicholas I.,
Donation of Constantine, 40;
Humbert, Gregory VII., 50 f.;
Hugo, Pullus, 86; Innocent III.,
87; Boniface VIII., 88, 97, 165;
Thomas, 102, 145 f.; 2d Council
of Lyons, 146, 165 f., 167 f.;
Wickliffe, 211; Luther, 225 f.,
289 f., 298 n.; Council of Trent,
440, 446 f., 448; Catechismus
Romanus, 448; Louis XIV., 457;
Gallican church, Nicholas of Hontheim, 457; Punctation of Ems,
458 f.; modern church, 459; Vatican Council, 461.

Porphyry, philosophy of, 56 n.

Port Royal, abbey at, 452, 454.

Poverty, Book of Spiritual, 178.

Prayer, 405 n., 419.

Preaching. In Middle Ages, 91 f.;
Guibert, 92; Later Middle Ages,
174; Luther, 281, 293; Jesuits,
430.

Predestination. In Gregory, 23;
Florus, 30 f.; Isidore, 30; Gottschalk, 31; Rabanus, 31, 32;
Council of Mayence, 31; Councils
of Chiersy and Valence, 32, 33;
Prudentius, Remigius, Ratramnus,
Lupus, Hincmar, Amolo, Scotus,
32; Council of Toucy, 33; Duns,
151 f, 156, 164; Biel, 198;
Bradwardina, 207; Wickliffe, 208;
Luther, 244, 407; Zwingli, 313 f.,
315; Melanchthon, 349; Calvin,
397, 405 ff., 420; Zanchi, 378,
421; Marbach, Hesshusen, 378;
Formula of Concord, 388; Southwestern Germany, 391; Bucer,
392 f.; Reformed theology, 416,
421; Later Reformed Confessions,
419, 421; Pighius, Bolsec, 420;
Gomarus, 421, 422 n.; Beza,
Martyr, Musculus, 421; Synod of
Dort, 421 ff.; Arminius, Uyten-

bogaart, Episcopius, 421; Remonstrants and Contra-remonstrants, 422; Consensus Helvetica,
425; Amyraldus, 424 f.; Jansen,
453 f.; Helvetic Confession, Heidelberg Catechism, Westminster
Confession, 421.

Presence, mode of, in Lord's Supper,
133, 204, 326, 329, 440; sacramental, 350, 440; Real (see
Christ, Body of).

Prescience. In Gottschalk, 31;
Council of Valence, 33; Formula
of Concord, 388 f.; Bucer, 392.

Prophecies, Luther on, 300.

Prosper of Reggeo, Eremite, 187.

Prudentius, works of, 30; on predestination, 32.

Pullus. On work of Christ, 73;
transubstantiation, 78; sacraments,
79; confirmation, 81; confession,
absolution, purgatory, 83; church,
85 f.; state, 86.

Punctation of Ems, 458.

Purgatory. In Gregory, 24 f.; Early
Middle Ages, 44; Abelard, Ro-
land, 81; Lombard, Pullus, 83 f.;
Waldenses, 94; Alexander, Bona-
ventura, Biel, Henry, Duns, 139;
Luther, 241; Zwingli, 316 n. •

Purification. In Mysticism, 179 f.

Q.

Quesnel, work of, 454; theses of,
455 n.; on Scriptures, church, will,
faith, forgiveness, justification,
grace, 455 n.

R.

Rabanus, Maurus, works of, 16, 30;
on predestination, 31, 32; Lord's
Supper, 37, 39.

Radbertus, works of, 16, 34; on Virgin

Mary, 34 ; faith, 37 ; Lord's Supper, 35, 37, 76.

Rationalism. In Abelard, 58 ; Frederick II., 91 ; thirteenth century, 60.

Ratramnus, works of, 30, 34 ; on predestination, 32 ; Virgin Mary, 34 ; Lord's Supper, 38.

Realism. In William of Champeaux, 60 ; William of Auverne, Alexander, 98 ; Duns, 147 ; Later Middle Ages, 186 f.

Reason. In Scotus, 15 ; Abelard, 58 ; Anselm, 57, 68 ; Berenger, Lanfranc, 55 ; Thomas, Bonaventura, 104 ; Luther, 224, 243, 247, 299 n.; Pullus, 62 ; Melanchthon, 353.

Recarred, Confession of, 30.

Redemption. In Hugo, 61 ; Mystics, 119 ; benefits of, in Lombard, 14 ; Thomas, 113 ; Duns, 106 f.; Melanchthon, 359 ; Osiander, 370 (see Christ, Work of).

Reformation, attempted, 49 f.; need of, 188 f.; forerunners of, 190.

Reformation, The, 217, 222, 225 n., 308 f., 411, 415.

Reformed Church, asceticism in, 415, 420.

Reformed Confessions, Earlier, 344 f.; Later, 345 f., 418 f.

Reformed Theology, pre-reformation ideals of, 415; and Roman Catholicism, 417, n. 1; and Calvin, 426; on sacraments, 415, 418; predestination, 416, 421, 422.

Regeneration. In Luther, 283 f.; Augsburg Confession, 337 f.; Melanchthon, 360; Calvin, 403 f.; Synod of Dort, 423 (see Renewal).

Relics, worship of, 91, 94, 173.

Religion, natural, 353.

Remigius, works of, 30; on predestination, 32.

Remonstrants. On predestination, 422.

Renaissance, The, 27.

Renewal. In Luther, 231, 256 f., 284, 337 f., 260; Majoristic controversy, 365; Osiander, 370 ff.; Formula of Concord, 384, 423 n.; Calvin, 402 f., 404.

Repentance. In Middle Ages, 16, 41 to 47; Durand, 92; Waldenses, 94; Biel, 134 f., 138, 201; Later Middle Ages, 175 ff.; Mystics, 179; John of Paltz, 201; Luther, 251 n., 272, 358; Augsburg Confession, Apology, 342; Melanchthon, 351, 358, 361; Later Reformed Confessions, 419; public vs. private, 42, 93.

Repentance, sacrament of. In Gregory, 24, 47; Abelard, 81 f.; Epitome, Roland, 81; Hugo, 82, 92; Pullus, 83; Lombard, 83, 92; Thomas, Alexander, Bonaventura, Biel, 134 ff.; Eugene IV., 140; John of Paltz, 174 n., 175 f., 201 n.; Wickliffe, Wesel, Wessel, 210; Luther, 222, 224, 234 ff., 241; Calvin, 402 f.; Jesuits, 429; Council of Trent, 434, 438, 442, 444.

Revelation of grace, in Amyraldus, 425.

Reward, 23, 91 (see Merit).

Richard of Middleton, philosophy of, 98; on will, 106.

Richard of St. Victor. On Trinity, 108; communion of saints, 144.

Rickel, philosophy of, 187.

Righteousness, actual, 259 f., 338, 370 f., 381, n. 4, 384, 438; imputed, 260 f., 337 f., 359, 370 f., 379, 381, n. 4, 384, 404, 418, 43 f., et passim ; original, 114, 153, 370.

Right Hand of God, 325, 413, 440.

Roland, work of, 59; on person of

Christ, 65 ; Lord's Supper, 77; sacraments, 79; repentance, contrition, confirmation, ordination, purgatory, 81.

Roman Catholic Church before the Reformation, 146 ; reformation within, 428 ; modern condition of, 463 f.; Luther on, 289, 294 ; Melanchthon on, 355.

Roman Catholic Theology, sources for, 427 ; estimate of, 427 f., 430, 431 ; Thomistic character of, 428 ; influence of Duns upon, 428, 431 ; and Paul, 455 ; and opposing schools, 428, 431, 432, 433, 438, 439.

Romans, Epistles to, Luther on, 301.

Rome, councils at, 29, 76.

Roscellin, philosophy of, 56 ; on Trinity, 56.

Rupert. On Lord's Supper, 78 n.

S.

Sabbath. In Erasmus, 215 n.; Luther, 246, 247 n.; Zwingli, 311, n. 1.

Sacraments. In Abelard, 59, 72, 79 ; Hugo, 61, 79, 80; Lombard, 63, 80; Anselm, 72; Bernard, Roland, Pullus, Omnebene, St. Florian, 79; Berthold, 93 ; Later Middle Ages, 98, 124 f.; Eugene IV., 125 ; Thomas, Bonaventura, 125 f.; Alexander, 125, 126 n.; Duns, 127 f., 161 ; Albert, 128 ; Biel, 187, 200 ; Luther, 235, 279, 282 ; Zwingli, 316 ; Augsburg Confession, 341 f.; Apology, 343 ; Calvin, 411 ff.; Reformed theology, 415, 418 ; Consensus Tigurinus, 417 ; Reformed Confessions, 345 ; Council of Trent, 438 f.; definition of, 79, 80, 93, 125, 411 ; number of, 37 n., 63, 79, 80, 93, 125, 135,

282, 316, 439 ; place of, in dogmatic system, 59 ; validity of, 94 ; matter and form of, 126 ; intention in, 125 ; as symbols, 126, 127 f., 282, 316, 411, 417, 439 ; as pledges, 411 ; and word, 78, 123 n., 285 f., 411 ; administered by heretics, 50, 51, 142 ; benefits of, 80, 93, 127, 345.

Saints, communion of, 144 f., 212, 235, 286 f., 291 ff., 408.

Saints, intercession of. In Early Middle Ages, 44, 91 ; Waldenses, 94 ; Thomas, 124 ; Later Middle Ages, 173 ; Augsburg Confession, 344 ; Council of Trent, 445.

Saliger. On Lord's Supper, 367 n.

Salmeron. On divine right, 447 n.

Salvation, causes of, 405, n. 1 ; of souls, 94, 225.

Sanctification, in Apology, 338 ; Luther, Melanchthon, 360 ; Southwestern Germany, 390; Calvin, 402, 404 (see Life, New).

Sanfelice, evangelical views of, 434, n. 2.

Satisfaction. In Early Middle Ages, 43, 47 ; Anselm, 67 f.; Roland, 81 ; Abelard, Hugo, 82 ; Lombard, 83, 92 ; council at Aachen, 84 ; Thomas, Duns, 139 ; Eugene IV., 140 ; Wessel, 210 ; Luther, 234, 241, 265 f., 267, n. 2, 268, n. 1 ; Council of Trent, 435, 438, 443, 444 ; Bajus, 451 n.

Savonarola. On asceticism, church and state, 198 n.; politics, 318.

Scepticism, Abelard, 58 ; thirteenth century, 60 ; Frederick II., 91.

Scholasticism, estimate of, 54 ff., 57, 105, 146, 196, 214 ; in Luther, 223 ; Luther on, 224.

Schnepf. On Lord's Supper, 331 n.

Schwabach Articles, 330,

Schwabian Concord, 382 n.

Schwenkfeldians, 389.

Scotus Erigena, works of, 30; on predestination, 32.

Scriptures, authority of. In Gregory, 18; Abelard, 58; Thomas, 100; Bonaventura, 101; Duns, 149; Occam, 169, 172, 192; Wickliffe, 184; D'Ailli, Biel, 192 f.; Goch, 209; Erasmus, 215 n.; Luther, 226, 228, 290 f., 298 f., 301 f.; Zwingli, 308, 309 n.; Reformed Confessions, 344; Melanchthon, 348, 351 f.; Southwestern Germany, 391; Calvin, 395, 396 n.; Later Reformed Confessions, 419 n.; Council of Trent, 431; Bajus, 450, 451 n.; Jansen, 453; Quesnel, 455 n.

Scriptures, criticism of, 301, 301 n.

Scriptures, inspiration of. In Gregory, 18; Abelard, 58; Thomas, 101; Agobard, 101 n.; Occam, Biel, 192; Erasmus, 301 f.; Luther, Calvin, 395; Reformed theology, 415, 419 n.; Consensus Helvetica, 426; Council of Trent, 431; Vatican Council, 460; Leo XIII., 460 n.

Scriptures, interpretation of, 15, 19.

Scriptures, reading of. In Gregory, 19, 455 n.

Secular learning and religion, 353, 362, 363.

Secular life, 273 f.

Self-communion, 440.

Selnecker, Lutheranism of, 381.

Semi-Augustinianism, 32.

Semi-Pelagianism, 16, 63.

Sens, council at, 61.

Seripando, evangelical views of, 434, n. 2.

Seuse, works of, 178.

Sigismund, confession of, 421 n.

Silent Submission, to doctrine, 456, 463, 465.

Simon Baringundus, Eremite, 187.

Simony, 50.

Sin. In Gregory, 21 f.; Anselm, 67, 110; Luther, 229, 242 f.; Augsburg Confession, 335; Zwingli, 309, 317; Biel, Occam, 197; as disease, defect, 22, 117, 309; venial vs. mortal, 43 f., 92, 135 et passim; propagation of, 117; results of, 117, 118.

Sin, original. In Gregory, 21; Anselm, Lombard, Alexander, Bonaventura, Thomas, 116 f.; Duns, 153, 154, 163; Biel, Occam, 197; Luther, 229, 242 f., 297; Melanchthon, 349 n.; Zwingli, 309, 317; Augsburg Confession, 335; Earlier Reformed Confessions, 345 n.; Formula of Concord, 383; Southwestern Germany, 390: Calvin, 398; Later Reformed Confessions, 419; Council of Trent, 432; Bajus, 451 n.; Jansen, 453.

Sins, actual, 154, 242; enumeration of, 443.

Social Problems, 182, 202 n., 278, 292 n. 2.

Soissons, council at, 61.

Solida Declaratio, 382 n.

Southwestern Germany, theology in, 390 ff., 414.

Spires, diet at, 333.

Stancar. On Osiandrian controversy, 374.

State, The. In Gregory VII., 51, 85, 86; Pullus, Hugo, Innocent III., 86 f.; Boniface VIII., 88; Louis of Bavaria, 165; Marsilius, Occam, 167, 170; Luther, 274, 290; Zwingli, 317 f.; Augsburg Confession, 341; Calvin, 410.

State, original. In Gregory, 21 n.; Alexander, Bonaventura, Albert, Thomas, 114 f.; Henry, 115;

Duns, 153 ; Biel, 197 ; Council of Trent, 432 n.; Bajus, 450.

States of Christ, 325 n., 376 f., 387.

Stephen of Paris, philosophy of, 98.

Strigel. In Synergistic controversy, 367 f.

Stuttgart, synod at, 366.

Subjective vs. objective, 191.

Sufferings of Christ. In Gregory, 19, 53 ; Anselm, 69 ; Thomas, 112 f.; Duns, 156 f.; Luther, 266 f. (see Atonement, Work of Christ).

Supererogation, works of, 23, 124, 139.

Superstition, 49.

Symbols, estimate of, 466 ; the ancient, in Gregory, 18 ; Thomas, Bonaventura, Anselm, Alexander, Richard, Durand, 102 ; Duns, 149 ; Luther, 303 ; Zwingli, 317 ; Melanchthon, 348, 352 ; Calvin, 396 ; later Reformed theology, 419 n.

Synergism, controversy upon, 267 ff.; in Formula of Concord, 384; Council of Trent, 433, 435 f.; Molina, 451 f.

Syngramma, 320.

Synod, at Alençon, 425 ; Dort, 421 ; Eisenach, 365 ; France, 425 ; Pistoja, 445 n. 1, 458 ; Stuttgart, 366 ; Torgau, 367 (see Council).

T.

Tauler, works of, 178 ; on word and sacraments, 128 ; imitation of Christ, 178 f.

Tetrapolitan Confession, 344 f.

Theodulf. On filioque, 30.

Theology, Systematic. In Abelard, 59 ; Honorius, Hugo, 61 ; John of Damascus, Lombard, 63 ; Middle Ages, 96, 189, 214 ; Albert, Thomas, 99 ; Gerson, 189 ; Me-

lanchthon, 348, 362, 363 ; nature of, 104 n., 149, 150 n.; German, 178.

Thomas of Aquino, estimate of, 96, 97, 98, 99, 100, 146, 185, 224 ; method of, 99 ; on God, 100, 107; revelation, 100 f.; Scriptures, 101 ; faith, 103, 121 ; will, 103; universals, 104 ; Trinity, 100, 109 ; communicatio idiomatum, 110 ; person of Christ, 110 f.; work of Christ, 111 f.; intercession of Christ, 113 ; fruits of redemption, 113 ; synteresis, 114 ; original state, 114 f.; infused grace, 115, 119 ; original sin, 116 ; forgiveness, 112 f., 121 ; free-will, 119 f.; justification, 120 f.; faith, 103, 120 ; guilt, 117 ; grace, 115, 118 ; good works, 116, 121 ; human merit, 116, 121 f., 124 ; merit of Christ, 113 ; monastic life, 124 ; sacraments, 125 f.; indelible character, 128 ; baptism, 130 ; Lord's Supper, 133 ; repentance, 134 f.; contrition, 136 f.; confession, absolution, 137 f.; indulgences, satisfaction, 139 ; extreme unction, 140; ordination, 141 ; marriage, 142 ; church, 144 f.; pope, 102, 145 f.; blessedness, 148.

Thomas of Bradwardina. On person of Christ, 110 ; predestination, 189, 207.

Thomas of Strassburg, philosophy of, 187 ; on immaculate conception, 188 n.; Lord's Supper, 204.

Thomas sel Vio (see Cajetan).

Tilmann. On Eucharistic controversy, 366.

Timann. On Eucharistic controversy 366.

Torgau, synod at, 367.

Torgau Book, 382 n.

Toucy, council at, 33.

Toulouse, council at, 93.

Tours, council at, 76; school at, 55, 98.

Tradition. In Middle Ages, 17; Abelard, 58; Luther, 291, 302 ff.; Council of Trent, 431 f., 449; Vatican Council, 460; Protestant Church, 464 f.

Traducianism, 22.

Transubstantiation. In Radbertus, 35; Rabanus, 37; Haimo, 39; Berenger, 76; Comester, Hildebert, Roland, St. Florian, Omnebene, Honorius, Hugo, 77; Germanus, Stephen, William of Thiersy, 77 n.; Pullus, Lombard, Fourth Lateran Council, 78; Later Middle Ages, 127, 205; Thomas, Alexander, Duns, 131 f., 150; Occam, 192 f.; Wickliffe, Hussites, 206; Luther, 235, 286 n., 287; Zwingli, 318; Augsburg Confession, Apology, 342; Council of Trent, 440.

Treasure, of the church, 139, 236, 241.

Trent, Council of, estimate of, 431, 448, 463; history of, 431 ff.; and scholasticism, 55; and modern theology, 448; on Scriptures, 431; tradition, 431, 449; Apocrypha, 432; original state, 432 n.; sin, fall, Virgin Mary, 432; baptism, 432, 434, 436, 439, 444; concupiscence, donum superadditum, 432; divine call, 433, 435; faith, 433, 435, 436, 437, 440, 449; grace, 433, 435, 439, 449; justification, 433 ff.; 435, 436, 437; imputed and infused righteousness, 434; merit, 434, 438; free-will, 434; repentance, 434, 438, 442, 444; satisfaction, 435, 438, 443, 444; assurance, 435, 437; good works, 434, 435, 437, 443; love to God, 436; work of Christ, 436,

442, n. 1; forgiveness, 433, 437; asceticism, 438, 449; Christian life, 438; contrition, 438, 442, 444; confession, absolution, 438, 442, 443, 444; sacraments, 438 f.; Lord's Supper, 439 f.; mass, 441, 445; hierarchy, 443, 444, 446 f., 445, 449; indulgences, 444; purgatory, extreme unction, ordination, priesthood, 445; marriage, church, 446; pope 446 f., 448, 449; and Augustinianism, 450.

Treves, council at, 92, 93.

Tribur, council at, 45.

Trinity. In Gregory, 17; Migetius, 27; Gottschalk, Hincmar, 31; Roscellin, 56; Abelard, 58 f.; Thomas, 100, 109; Richard, Lombard, Joachim, Fourth Lateran Council, 108; Occam, 192; Luther, 303, 305 f.; Augustine, 306 n.; Calvin, 396, n. 2.

Tübingen Book, 382.

U.

Ubiquity, of body of Christ. In Alger, 77; Occam, 204; Luther, 288, 320, n. 2, 322 ff.; Melanchthon, 350; Cureus, 366; synod at Torgau, 367; Heidelberg theologians, 374; Chemnitz, 376, 388; Formula of Concord, 386 f.; Calvin, 413.

Unbelief, 243.

Unction, extreme, 84, 140, 445.

Unification with God, 180 f., 328.

Union, mystical, 328.

Union, sacramental, of elements and body of Christ, 326 f., 386.

Union, the Protestant, relation to dogmas, 466 n.

Universals, 56, 60, 104 f., 147, 190 f.

Urban of Bologna, philosophy of, 187.

Urban VIII. and Jansenism, 453.

Uytenbogaart. On predestination, 421.

V.

Valence, council at, 33.

Valla, Lorenzo. On spurious documents, 213.

Vatican Council, 456 ff.; sources on, estimate of, 463; and scholasticism, 55; on God, Scriptures, tradition, church, faith, 460; infallibility of pope, 461.

Vercelli, council at, 76.

Vices, the principal, 21 n.

Vincent of Lerius. On tradition, 304.

Virgin Mary, immaculate conception of, 18, 19 n., 155, 456, 188 n.; intercession of, 44, 91, 173; parturition of, 33 f.; worship of, 235, 344; and original sin, 432, 451 n.; in modern Roman Catholic church, 463.

Vorillon, philosophy of, 186.

Vows, monastic, 344.

Vulgate, 432, 460.

W.

Waldenses. On repentance, church, saints, images, purgatory, 94; good works, 95.

Walther of St. Victor, philosophy of, 60.

Weimar Confutation, 379.

Wesel, relation to Augustine, 190; on Lord's Supper, 204; grace, 209; repentance, absolution, indulgences, 210; church, 211.

Wessel, relation to Augustine, 190; on Lord's Supper, 204; grace, justification, 209; repentance, indulgences, satisfaction, excommunication, 210; church, 211 f.; communion of saints, 212.

Westminster Confession. On predestination, 421.

Wickliffe, works of, 183; influence of, 183 n., 189 n.; on "evangeli-

cal law," Scriptures, imitation of Christ, 184; work of Christ, 198; Lord's Supper, 206; predestination, 108; repentance, indulgences, 210; church, pope, excommunication, 211.

Will, of God. In Richard, 106; Duns, 151, 156, 163; Luther, 244; Zwingli, 313; Calvin, 396 ff.; 405 ff.; Reformed theology, 416; secret and revealed, 244.

Will, of man. In Middle Ages, 97; Thomas, 103; Henry, Richard, 106; Duns, 148, 159, 163; Biel, Occam, 197; Luther, 243 f., 255, n. 4, 256; Synergistic controversy, 367 f.; Formula of Concord, 383; Camero, 425; Jansen, 453 f.; Quesnel, 455 n.

William of Auverne. On sacraments, 98.

William of Champeaux, philosophy of, 60.

William of Paris. On attrition, contrition, 136 f.

William of St. Thierry. On Lord's Supper, 77 n.

Wittenberg, disputation at, 349.

Wittenberg Concord, 386.

Word, The. In Gregory, 23; Tauler, 178; Luther, 234, 279 f., 299 f., 322; Formula of Concord, 388; Calvin, 409; Osiander, 370 f.; significance of, 123; outer and inner, 23, 279 f., 280 f., 370 f.; and sacraments, 78, 123 n., 285 f., 411.

Words of Institution. In sacraments, 126; in Lord's Supper, 131, 132, 135, 322, 328, 414.

Worms, colloquy at, 378.

Works, good. In Gregory, 24; Early Middle Ages, 43; Bernard, 53; Waldenses, 95; Thomas and followers, 116, 121; Luther, 234,

240, 247, 258, 264, 274, 277, 364;
Zwingli, 311 ; Augsburg Confession, 339, 343 ; Reformed Confessions, 345 ; Melanchthon, 361,
364 ; Major, Amsdorf, Menius,
364, 385 ; Flacius, 364 ; Antinomian controversy, Poach, 365 ;
Otto, Agricola, 366 ; Frankfort
Recess, 379 ; Formula of Concord,
384 f.; Calvin, 404 ; Council of
Trent, 434, 435, 437, 443 ; Bajus,
450 ; Unigenitus, 455.

Worship of Christ, 65, 66; of images,
29, 94, 448; of relics, 91, 94, 173;
of saints, 94, 344; of Virgin Mary,
235, 344.

Würtemberg theologians. On person
of Christ, 374 ; state of humiliation, 377.

Z.

Zanchi. On predestination, 378, 421.
Zwingli, works of, 306, 319 f.; estimate of, 307, 317, 390, 393, n. 4;
reformatory ideas of, 308, 318 ;
and Augsburg Confession, and Bullinger, 390 ; and Calvin, 393, n. 4,
394, 412, 414 ; and Erasmus, 307,
317, 318 ; and Luther, 303, 308 n.,
319 f.; and Reformed Confessions,
345 ; and Savonarola, 318 ; on
Scriptures, 308, 309 n.; justification, 307, 310; sin, 309, 317;
mass, work of Christ, 309 f.; person of Christ, 317, 321, 323;
faith, 310 f., 313; Holy Spirit,
311 ; experience, good works, law
and gospel, 311 ; Sabbath, 311 n. 1 ;
Christian life, imitation of Christ,
312 ; divine will, human merit,
313; predestination, 313 f., 315;
God, grace, 314; church, salvation
of heathen, 315 ; sacraments, baptism, 316 ; confession, indulgences,
purgatory, priesthood, 316 n.; ancient symbols, 317 ; church and
state, 317 f.; Lord's Supper,
318 ff.; alloeosis, 321.